Mac OS 9

D1227875

The Complete Reference

Mac OS 9

Gene Steinberg

Osborne/**McGraw-Hill**

Berkeley   New York   St. Louis   San Francisco
Auckland   Bogotá   Hamburg   London   Madrid
Mexico City   Milan   Montreal   New Delhi   Panama City
Paris   São Paulo   Singapore   Sydney
Tokyo   Toronto

Osborne/McGraw-Hill
2600 Tenth Street
Berkeley, California 94710
U.S.A.

For information on translations or book distributors outside the U.S.A., or to arrange bulk purchase discounts for sales promotions, premiums, or fund-raisers, please contact Osborne/**McGraw-Hill** at the above address.

Mac OS 9: The Complete Reference

1234567890 VFM VFM 019876543210

ISBN 0-07-212506-3

Publisher:	Brandon A. Nordin
Associate Publisher and Editor-in-Chief:	Scott Rogers
Acquisitions Editor:	Jane Brownlow
Project Editors:	Carolyn Welch and Lee Ann Pickrell
Acquisitions Coordinator:	Tara Davis
Technical Editors:	Pieter Paulson and Lisa Lee
Copy Editor:	Marcia Baker
Proofreader:	Susie Elkind
Indexer:	Valerie Robbins
Computer Designers:	Lucie Erickson and Elizabeth Jang
Illustrators:	Michael Mueller and Beth Young
Series Design:	Mickey Galicia
Cover Design:	William Voss

This book was composed with Corel VENTURA ™ Publisher.

Dedication

To my family, who made it possible for me
to realize the impossible dream.

About the Lead Author

GENE STEINBERG first used a Mac in 1984 and never looked back. He is the author of 18 books on computers and the Internet, including *Upgrading & Troubleshooting Your Mac* for Osborne/McGraw-Hill and runs a comprehensive Mac support Web site, The Mac Night Owl (http://www.macnightowl.com). He's also a Contributing Writer for "MacHome," and a regularly featured guest on Craig Crossman's "Computer America" radio show. His weekly column for *The Arizona Republic*/azcentral.com, "Mac Reality Check," reaches many thousands of readers worldwide.

About the Contributing Author

Pieter Paulson has been working with Apple computers since the days of the Apple II and has been using a Macintosh since 1984. Currently, Pieter works as a network engineer specializing in the design and implementation of high capacity, high performance LAN and WAN networks along with designing and implementing Windows and Macintosh integration solutions for mixed environments.

About the Technical Reviewers

Lisa Lee has helped develop many hardware and software products for Silicon Valley–based companies for over ten years. She was the technical editor for *Teach Yourself Mac OS 8.5 in 24 Hours, Complete Idiot's Guide to Mac OS 8.5, Using Mac OS 8.5, Teach Yourself the iMac in 10 Minutes,* and *Mac OS in a Nutshell.* Lisa has also written about Macintosh computers, Linux, WebTV, and Palm devices.

Pieter Paulson has been working with Apple computers since the days of the Apple II. Currently, Pieter works as a network engineer specializing in LAN and WAN network design and implementation. He also designs and implements integrated Windows and Macintosh solutions for mixed environments.

Contents At A Glance

Contents

Acknowledgments

So all I had to do was write an encyclopedia about the Mac and Mac OS 9. I sputtered, I gasped and said (with hardly a moment's thought), sure, I can do that. It seemed an impossible task, but somehow I managed to get it done with a little help from my friends.

First on the list is my long-time friend and coauthor, Pieter Paulson, who ably assisted the project by developing initial drafts of ten of the most complex chapters covering networking, Mac and Windows connectivity, and other complex issues, and thus helped me accomplish a miracle.

And, as usual, my friend and agent, Lew Grimes, was always there with his sage advice and counsel on a variety of issues related to this book.

I should also like to thank the miracle workers at Apple Computer for developing what will be the last major upgrade consisting of traditional Mac operating system technology, Mac OS 9. I am especially grateful for the kind assistance of Apple's corporate communications team, including Rhona Hamilton, Matt Hutchison, Keri Walker, and Nathalie Welch.

I want to give special praise to the folks at one of Apple's premier retailers, Computer Town, and especially to Richard Bolinski at their Phoenix, AZ store for his assistance in providing information and extensive hands-on encounters with some of Apple's newest products, including the iBook and the AirPort.

Osborne/McGraw-Hill's highly skilled editing team was, as usual, on hand to deliver the final product you have in your hands. They consisted of Jane Brownlow, Tara Davis, Carolyn Welch, and Marcia Baker. I want to give still another thank you to Pieter Paulson and also to Lisa Lee for their careful, exacting technical editing.

Certainly, I could never have done any of this were it not for my little family, my brilliant son (and sometimes coauthor), Grayson, and my beautiful wife and business partner, Barbara, for tolerating the long hours I spent glued to my computer keyboard to finish this book on schedule.

Introduction

1984 seemed so long ago and far away. At the time, we wondered whether George Orwell's science fiction novel and its frightening vision of Big Brother watching over all we do every minute of the day, would somehow come to pass. Although government and business intrude in our lives more and more, the level hasn't quite reached what the novel suggested.

But another development from 1984 has, indeed, made a significant impact on our lives, a little personal computer called the Apple Macintosh and the Mac operating system.

Although the Macintosh doesn't dominate the computing world, its presence is felt everywhere. The distinctive graphical user interface of the Mac remains the hallmark of a modern computer operating system. From the Finder to the desktop to the trash icon, the Mac's unique look has been featured in publications, movies, and TV programs around the world.

Through the years, amid victories and some notable defeats, Apple Computer has managed to upgrade and refine its operating system. Fifteen years later, Mac OS 9 represents the total of all the lessons Apple has learned. Mac OS is the final great example of the classic technology (before the new Aqua user interface of Mac OS X takes over), still showing elements of the original ideas that bore fruit at the beginning of its lifecycle.

Is Mac OS 9 for You?

Maybe you already have a Mac OS 9 or the upgrade box awaits you at your office. Or, perhaps you only bought this book to learn more about the Mac OS 9 before you take the plunge.

Obviously, I'm prejudiced. All my Macs run Mac OS 9 and, certainly, I wrote this book from the standpoint of someone who likes the Mac OS 9 and wants to show others how to get the most value from it.

Here's my blanket response: If your Mac meets the basic system requirements (Power PC CPU, 32MB of RAM minimum, and about 200MB free storage space), the answer is most likely yes. As with any major system upgrade (and, even though Mac OS 9 doesn't look altogether different from its predecessor, Mac OS 8.6, it has vast changes under the surface), you can realistically expect to perform a few upgrades of some of your programs. You get a basic idea of what those upgrades are and where to find them throughout this book.

But, if your software is pretty current, you'll find the migration path is definitely worth the effort in terms of performance and stability. Apple has learned its lessons well and has worked hard to provide the highest possible level of stability using its traditional operating system technology.

Let's Look at the Menu

Because this book carries the label "The Compete Reference," I don't necessarily expect you to read it from cover to cover in a single sitting or in several sittings. Instead, refer to the specific chapters that offer the information you need about Mac OS 9, from setup to configuration, and about the ways you can get the most value from your Mac computing experience.

This book is organized in four parts to make finding the information you want easier.

Part One, "Introducing Mac OS 9," first describes the new features of Mac OS 9. You go through all the steps of installation (whether a one-click install or a clean install), and then you learn how to configure your new system software for the best possible performance. You learn the secrets of efficient networking, how to use Apple's magnificent Sherlock 2 program to search your Mac, your network, or the Internet, and you also discover how to configure your computer for multiple users.

In Part Two, "Installing and Configuring Mac Hardware," you get to put Mac OS 9 to some use. You learn how to set up a complete Mac system from the basic computer to the various accessories you want. You receive tips, tricks, and troubleshooting hints about installing such devices as extra hard drives, digital cameras, scanners, and even a high-quality speaker system, so you can enjoy audio CDs, games, and movie trailers with the highest quality sound.

From there, Part Three, "Using the Software," introduces you to a number of important software categories, covering word processors, graphic software, desktop publishing software, financial management programs, desktop video editing programs, games, utilities, and much more. You also learn how to address conflicts quickly before they get out of hand.

You probably also use your Mac to explore the Internet. In Part Four, "The Road to the Internet," you learn about browsers, e-mail software, FTP software, instant messaging software, and you explore the new broadband technologies, such as cable modems and DSL, which promise to deliver Internet content to your Mac at previously unheard of speeds.

How This Book Is Assembled

To make getting the information you want easier, each chapter consists of the following basic elements:

- Plenty of background information, so you know why something works and, more importantly, why things sometimes go wrong.

- Step-by-step descriptions of installation and troubleshooting processes.

- Tips, tricks, and guidelines to help you handle routine installations and complex setups with ease and to diagnose both common and obscure problems.

This Has Been a Glorious Learning Experience

I started using Macs very early on, not long after they were introduced in 1984. I saw each evolution of the Mac operating system. Some of those revisions represented great leaps forward, such as the migration from System 6 to System 7, and then to Mac OS 8 and, finally, to Mac OS 9.

Through the years, I watched Apple lose money, make money, and then I witnessed its great rebirth and the introduction of the iMac, the iBook, the Power Macintosh G4, and the promise of even greater things to come.

I hope you find *Mac OS 9: The Complete Reference* is a valuable learning tool to help you master Mac OS 9 and get the greatest value from your Mac computing experience. Please don't hesitate to write to me if you have any questions or comments about the book.

Gene Steinberg
Scottsdale, Arizona
E-mail: gene@macnightowl.com
http://www.macnightowl.com
http://www.rockoids.com

Part I

Introducing Mac OS 9

Chapter 1

Mac OS 9:
What's New, What's Different?

Every time Apple produces a new system upgrade, it comes with both a flourish and a huge marketing effort. A tremendous amount of anticipation also occurs because users want to know what has changed in the new system version and how it will affect their Mac computing experience.

On the surface, Mac OS 9 doesn't seem altogether different from the various Mac OS 8 versions (as you see in the pictures that appear later in this chapter). But as you continue to use Mac OS 9, you find a wealth of changes in the way you use the software and the way you configure it.

Apple counts over 50 changes. This chapter focuses on the most significant ones. If you worked with older Mac system versions, you should find this information useful. If you're new to the Mac, you should get a greater insight into what older system versions did and how Mac OS 9 impacts you.

What You Need for Mac OS 9

Here's Apple's official recommendation. Some possible exceptions are listed later.

To install Mac OS 9, you need a Mac OS-based Apple computer with a PowerPC microprocessor. You also need a minimum of 32MB built-in memory (RAM) with virtual memory set to a minimum of 40MB.

> **NOTE**   *The minimum rating is enough to get you up and running with Mac OS 9, but don't expect to run more than a single application or a professional graphics program, such as Adobe Photoshop, with that amount. A more realistic minimum is 64MB RAM, with 96MB to 128MB for the best performance.*

In addition, to need a minimum of 194MB free disk space.

All right, that's the official recommendation.

What about those Mac OS clones?

Apple doesn't support installing Mac OS versions 8.5 or later on such products. On the other hand, if the clone manufacturer's hardware was engineered to properly conform to Apple's guidelines, the installation should work in most cases, though I cannot recommend it either.

My suggestion is to proceed with extreme caution in doing such an installation. Have a recent backup of your files and be sure to follow the guidelines for a clean installation in Chapter 2. This way, if the installation doesn't "take" properly, you can revert to your Previous System Folder and get up and running without undue delay.

For the rest of this chapter, I assume you can run Mac OS 9 and introduce you to the new features, as well as the changes from previous versions of the Mac OS.

Introducing Mac OS 9

Dubbed "your Internet copilot," Mac OS 9 extends Internet support to greater heights, with support for Internet-based file sharing, expanded searching, and more. In addition, Apple has made a huge number of under-the-hood changes that are designed to ensure improved performance and stability across-the-board.

In addition, Mac OS 9 paves the way toward the next-generation version of the Mac operating system, Mac OS X. A number of the changes aren't visible, but they are, nonetheless, significant. These include expanding the maximum number of fonts and files you can handle, and the new CarbonLib, which allows applications compiled to support Mac OS X also to run with older Mac OS versions.

The New Features—In Brief

In this section, many of the most useful new features of Mac OS 9 are covered. The chapters where you can locate more information on the topic are also listed.

Because this is a book for Mac users, and not Mac programmers, extensive space isn't devoted to under-the-hood programming architecture. You experience many of those features indirectly, however, as you find your Mac experience becomes more reliable, with fewer and fewer unexpected system freezes and crashes.

NOTE   *I'm serious about improved stability for Mac OS 9; I'm not simply repeating a claim from Apple's marketing team. I run lots of heavy-duty programs on my Macs and I have definitely seen much more reliable behavior while writing this book.*

■ **Automatic Updating**   Apple Computer releases updates and bug fixes on a fairly regular basis. You no longer have to spend time searching Apple's Web site or your favorite Mac publication for information about them. The Software Update control panel (shown in Figure 1-1), part of the regular Mac OS 9 installation, can be set to check Apple's support site periodically to locate updates. Once retrieved, they are installed automatically as part of the process. Chapter 10 covers the subject in more detail.

FIGURE 1-1   The Software Update control panel scours Apple's Web site for the latest updates to Mac OS 9

■ **Multiple Users**   In the past, Apple Computer had a multiple user-based security program, At Ease, which enabled you to create simplified environments for less-experienced users. Building on that technology, Apple's Multiple Users feature creates a separate user experience for up to 40 users on each Mac. These begin with simple things, such as access to files and folders, and extend to the desktop patterns you create and the printers and networks with which you work. The technology can be easily managed by a network administrator. You learn how to harness this new feature in Chapter 6.

■ **Voiceprint Verification**   In addition to typing a password in the old-fashioned way, you can also log in to your Mac using your own speaking voice (see Figure 1-2). When you use this feature, Mac OS 9 analyzes four digitized samples of your voice to make sure it's really you and not an imitation. Once you create this voiceprint, you can either use it or a typed-in password to log in to your Mac (use the latter as a precaution in case you have a cold or sore throat, and your voice isn't recognized). Chapter 6 has more information on the subject.

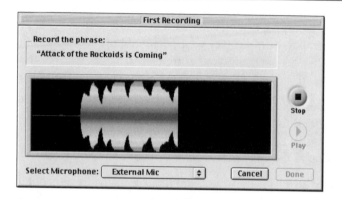

FIGURE 1-2   Let your speaking voice be your password to log in to your Mac

■ **Internet File Sharing**   File sharing is no longer limited to your own network. You can also share files across the Internet, in much the same fashion (as long as you have some sort of Internet access). Files can be accessed from FTP servers and regular Internet sites, as well. Read Chapter 8 for more information on Apple's new network features.

■ **Fewer disk directory problems**   Apple has made changes to the File Manager that prevents overwriting disk directory data by applications. The net result is you encounter fewer problems of hard drive corruption and fewer problems with hard drives. This is especially true if your Mac crashes and you have to force a restart. In addition, Apple's Disk First Aid is improved to work more efficiently to handle drive-related problems. Chapter 14 covers this subject.

■ **File Encryption**   Using a new menu command in the Finder's File menu, you can password-protect any selected file. When you decrypt the file, it is automatically launched for you. The file encryption is 56-bit, which offers adequate protection against password "crackers" for most users. Chapter 6 contains more information about this.

NOTE   *If you need more robust encryption, you still should consider using a dedicated security program.*

■ **Keychain**   This feature was part of Mac OS 7.1.1 (also known as System 7 Pro), but was discontinued in later operating system versions. Keychain enables you to create a single repository for all your various user IDs and passwords, which can be used with programs that support the feature. You then password-protect your personal keychain so it cannot be accessed by another person using your computer. Chapter 6 covers this subject in more detail.

■ **Palm Desktop 2.5**   If you're using one of 3Com's or Handspring's popular desktop organizer computers, you should be pleased to find a program that enables you to HotSync with your Palm Pilot. The installer shows up in the CD Extras folder on the Mac OS 9 CD.

■ **CarbonLib**   This may not seem like a hot new feature, but it should prove valuable because it enables programmers to develop software for Mac OS X, and yet allows the programs to work with earlier operating systems (without the special features of the new operating system). Mac OS X is going to be an industrial-strength operating system that can offer improved reliability, preemptive multitasking, and protected memory. Mac OS X is based on the NeXT technology that Apple acquired when it bought out Steve Jobs's company and paved the way for Jobs's return to Apple.

■ **FontSync**   If you have a large font library or you need make sure your documents can open and print properly from computer to computer, this feature enables you to create a way to keep tabs on all those fonts. The subject of handling fonts is covered in Chapter 22.

■ **Support for Velocity Engine**   The Velocity Engine feature of the G4 CPUs provides much faster performance for programs optimized to support the feature. At the system level, Apple extends multimedia performance by offering Velocity Engine support with QuickTime.

NOTE   *The basic concept of Velocity Engine is similar to the MMX feature of recent Intel Pentium CPUs. With support from application developers, basic graphics routines are accelerated, thus speeding performance tremendously (up to several times, in some cases).*

What's Changed in Mac OS 9

As stated at the beginning of this chapter, some of the most significant changes for Mac OS 9 are couched in the arcane language of programmers and they don't impact what you see on the screen. You see other changes from previous Mac OS versions that you directly experience, however.

Here's a list of the changes that can impact you in some big way:

- **File Exchange**   This is Apple's control panel that helps you easily exchange files with Windows-based computers. The Mac OS 9 version fixes bugs and adds support for PC-formatted 120MB Imation SuperDisks. The subject of exchanging files with users of other computing platforms is dealt with in Chapter 28.

- **GameSprockets**   This is a set of system extensions that enables programmers of games to access a common set of routines for input devices, Internet gaming, and sounds. By making these system extensions part of the standard installation, developing games to work with the Mac is easier and you needn't install lots of extra software. The Mac OS 9 version reduces the number of files needed for these features and improves gaming performance. You learn more about some of the most popular games you can run on Mac OS 9 in Chapter 26.

- **Network Assistant**   The Apple Network Assistant is a program that enables systems administrators to manage Macs by remote control. This program enables you to control Mac workstations from a centralized location and to perform such actions as setting up computer labs and software updates.

- **New alert boxes**   The feature Apple uses to display system alerts such as a notice about a printing problem, the Notification Manager, has been revised in a more friendly fashion. The alert appears in a floating window that doesn't interrupt the work you're doing on a Mac, and it can be quickly dismissed by clicking a close box. System crash messages, however, are unchanged.

- **ColorSync 3.0**   The updated version of Apple's ColorSync allows for additional custom settings and the capability to use AppleScript to automatic color matching of display, input, and output devices. You learn how to calibrate your Mac's display in minutes with ColorSync in Chapter 21.

- **Maximum number of fonts increased**   From System 7 on through Mac OS 8.6, you could only install a maximum of 128 bitmap and TrueType font files in the Fonts folder (PostScript printer or outline fonts are not counted in this number). This has been increased to a maximum of 512 fonts. If you want to keep your font menus uncluttered, however, consider a font management utility, such as Adobe Type Manager Deluxe, Alsoft's MasterJuggler Pro, DiamondSoft's Font Reserve, and Extensis Suitcase 8. Chapter 22 has more on this subject.

What's Changed in Mac OS 9

Because of the increase in the number of files allowed in Mac OS 9 and other changes, some of the font management programs need updates. Please check with the publisher for information.

- **Maximum number of open files increased**   All through the various versions of Mac System 7 and Mac OS 8, you could have up to 348 files open at a time. This may seem like a lot, until you consider that when the Mac operating system loads, over 100 files are opened. In addition, many larger graphic programs, such as Adobe InDesign, Adobe Photoshop, Microsoft Word, and QuarkXPress, each open dozens of files when they're running. Add to this what the operating system requires, plus the fonts you are using, and you see how you can reach the limit quickly. With Mac OS 9, the limit increases to 8,169 files. As explained in the previous note, however, this change creates potential problems with programs that directly accessed the original operating system feature (*File Control Block* or *FCB*). Chapter 31 has a long list of programs that might conflict with Mac OS 9 and the solutions to these issues.

- **Sherlock 2**   The new version of Apple's natural-language Internet search utility integrates all functions in a single interface that's similar to QuickTime Player (see Figure 1-3), a look that's controversial, but nonetheless striking.

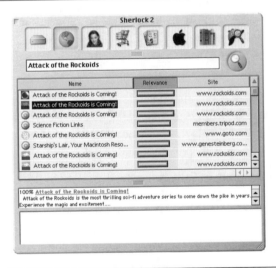

FIGURE 1-3   Sherlock 2 offers improved Internet search capabilities

The Internet search tools are divided into channels, which sport a different set of search sources. Chief among these is the Shopping feature, which searches the items you want, and then produces a list that includes prices, so you can do your comparisons before you place an order. Additional options for file and content searching also exist. You learn more about the advanced features of Sherlock 2 in Chapter 7.

■ **AppleScript**   An improved version of AppleScript now enables you to automate repetitive tasks over TCP, so you can, in effect, operate another Mac on a local network or the Internet by remote control. If you want to get started with AppleScript, check out Chapter 9.

■ **Network Browser**   The new version of the program that enables you to network with other Macs on a local or Internet-based network has been expanded to include connections to FTP sites. Chapter 8 covers the subject of local and Internet networking.

■ **File Sharing**   An updated version of the File Sharing control panel contains an IP option that enables you to use TCP/IP to share files. In addition, the Users & Groups control panel has been integrated into the File Sharing control panel as a separate tab. This simplifies the setup process. You learn more about sharing files with other Macs in Chapter 27.

■ **Enhanced USB device support**   A new USB Device Extension supports many USB products without the need to install separate software. This includes the Imation SuperDisk and other removable devices (including Iomega's Zip drives). This eases the plug-and-play aspect of USB. You literally don't have to consider installing software for a USB device unless it fails to function (in which case you see an onscreen message to that effect) or the manufacturer brings out a newer version to address bugs or performance issues. Chapters 15, 16, 17, and 31 cover USB-related issues in more detail.

■ **Improved PlainTalk technology**   Apple's speech recognition software, PlainTalk, was fun to use to test the potentials of the technology, but wasn't always accurate or reliable. It has been improved to allow for scripted dialogs with users and expanded features, including the capability to launch programs in the favorites and recent folders, plus an improved set of speakable actions.

■ **AppleWorks Update**   The 5.0.4 update provides added compatibility with Mac OS 9 for users of Apple's popular integrated program suite.

What's Changed in Mac OS 9

■ **Support for files over 2GB**   The Mac OS 9 Finder enables you to copy individual files over 2GB in size (this was the previous limitation). The capability to create files this large must also be supported by specific programs. This feature is of special value to those who edit video productions on Macs. You learn more about desktop video production with your Mac and Mac OS 9 in Chapter 24.

■ **Monitors & Sound control panels separated**   This is a throwback to earlier operating systems. In large part, both the Monitors and Sounds control panels have the same options as the previous versions. The Sounds control panel has a somewhat different look and feel (see Figure 1-4).

■ **Mouse control panel**   A new look, displaying the rounded mouse that first appeared with the iMac. It's also scriptable via AppleScript.

■ **Upgraded OpenGL**   OpenGL is an industry-standard technology for display of 3D graphics. Its most immediate use is, of course, games and animation software, which are being developed for the Mac in greater numbers since OpenGL became part of the Mac OS. The new version offers better performance (that is, as long as you have a Mac with an ATI graphics controller or another graphics card that supports these features).

NOTE   *At press time, Formac delivered OpenGL support for its ProFormance line of graphic cards. In addition 3dfx Interactive was preparing to ship Mac versions of its popular Voodoo line of 2D/3D graphic cards, also with full support for OpenGL.*

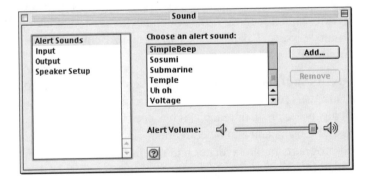

FIGURE 1-4   Apple has given its Sounds control panel a different look, but the same choices

What Doesn't Work

As with any new Mac operating system release, some programs break or are no longer supported. As explained earlier in this chapter, programs that used so-called unsupported ways of accessing Apple's File Manager stop working because of the change in the maximum number of open files supported. If you have such a program, you encounter a –119 system error and, perhaps, a message that the program needs an update.

Also, some older Apple software no longer works with Mac OS 9. These include the following:

■ **Apple Telecom**   This program included support for some Apple internal modems, mostly those coming in Performa models and the late, but not lamented, GeoPort. If you still have one of these modems, try a third-party fax program, such as FaxSTF. If you need an Apple Telecom driver to recognize your internal model, you are probably better off removing it and buying something new (none of these older modems, for example, support 56K speeds). Getting the most from your online access is covered in Chapter 32.

■ **QuickDraw GX**   This feature was supposed to herald a new era of improved support for fonts, graphics, and printing. Some of the printing features are now part of the regular LaserWriter driver (including desktop printing icons and the capability to switch among some, but not all, printers via the Print dialog box). The rest of QuickDraw GX proved difficult to implement efficiently and few productivity applications supported the feature. In fact, I can only count two—LightningDraw (a drawing program in the spirit of Adobe Illustrator) and Ready,Set,Go GX (a desktop publishing program). GX is now history.

■ **Color StyleWriter 4000 and HP DeskJet 600 Printers**   The Color StyleWriter 4000 series was basically a relabeled HP printer. HP has released Mac OS 9 compatible updates for most of its printers, including the DeskJet 600, which works with the Apple-branded version of the product. You can find them at HP's Web site at http://www.hp.com.

■ **LaserWriter 8f printer driver**   This printer driver worked with a small number of printers that supported integrated faxing. This is no longer supported, but because so many low-cost fax modems and separate fax machines are now available, it's probably not a serious loss (unless you spent a large sum for the fax module option for one of these printers).

The Look of Mac OS 9

When you first install Mac OS 9, you see a look that may seem familiar, yet unfamiliar, depending on the version of the Mac OS you previously ran.

In the next few pages, the basic features of the Mac OS 9 Finder are covered. You can find a lot more detail on these and other Mac OS capabilities throughout this book.

- **The Mac OS 9 desktop**   When you first install Mac OS 9, you are greeted with the Mac OS Setup Assistant (Chapter 3 covers this subject) and the standard Mac desktop pattern (see Figure 1-5). If you ran a version of the Mac OS prior to 8.5, the most significant change is the use of names, not only icons, in the application menu at the right side of the menu bar.

- **File menu**   The standard Mac commands are here (see Figure 1-6), with two significant differences. The first is the Encrypt command, which enables you to protect a file. The second (especially for users of Mac OS versions prior to 8.5) is Search Internet. This feature harnesses the power

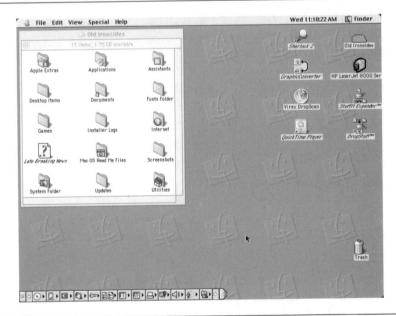

FIGURE 1-5   A typical Mac OS 9 desktop with one of Apple's standard backdrops

FIGURE 1-6   Notice the Encrypt and Search Internet commands in Mac OS 9's File menu

of Sherlock 2 to find the information you want on the Web without learning complex or arcane search commands.

NOTE   *All the items that begin with the cloverleaf icon are keyboard shortcuts you can use to access these various commands.*

■ **Edit menu**   No surprises (see Figure 1-7). Most of your basic Finder preferences are configured by the Preferences command.

FIGURE 1-7   Do your basic editing functions with the Edit menu

- **View menu**   Use this menu to specify how your desktop and Finder window items are displayed (see Figure 1-8). The View Options command enables you to set various preferences, so you can fine-tune the look of your Mac.

- **Special menu**   The standard Mac OS commands are here (see Figure 1-9), ranging from Empty Trash to Shut Down. But a new one, Logout, only appears if you have set up Mac OS 9's Multiple Users feature. Once you Logout, you are basically closing down your Mac environment, allowing another user to log in. Chapter 6 covers this subject in detail.

- **Help menu**   Beginning with Mac OS 8, Apple replaced the help icon with a Help menu (see Figure 1-10). Although copied from the Windows platform, the meaning of this menu is more obvious to the notice user or to one migrating from that "other" platform.

FIGURE 1-8   Choose your Finder display options here

FIGURE 1-9   The last command is only there when you're set up for Multiple Users

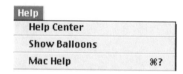

FIGURE 1-10   Choose your Help options from here

Summing Up

In this chapter, I touched on only the surface of the changes that come with Mac OS 9. In Chapter 2, you learn how to set up your Mac to run Mac OS 9 and how to install it easily, safely, and with as little fuss and bother as possible.

Summing Up

Chapter 2

Safe Installation Techniques

No doubt you're champing at the bit to install Mac OS 9. You've read about all the great new features that can make your Mac more productive and more reliable than ever.

So, now you want to begin.

In this chapter, I cover two methods of installing Mac OS 9. The first is the standard Apple way, the one-button variety. The other method is recommended, particularly if you're upgrading from a much older system version or you've had performance problems with your Mac.

Once you learn about the installation methods, I cover all the choices Apple gives you to customize the installation, so your system software is set up precisely the way you want.

The One Button Way to Install Mac OS 9

Apple has designed its system installations to be as simple as possible and, hopefully, reasonably painless experiences. This is the reason for the one-button installation. You accept every default, have a cup of coffee, and Mac OS 9 is installed, just awaiting your restart to be running on your Mac.

I don't want to pour cold water onto this method. Apple tests its system software upgrades quite thoroughly and, for many of you, this is the way to go. The software Apple recommends for your Mac will be placed on your hard drive, and all outdated Apple system components are replaced with the Mac OS 9 versions. None of your non-Apple files, Internet, or application preferences will be changed.

All it takes is a few brief setups after restart (explained in Chapter 3) and you should be ready to use your new system software.

This sort of installation process is still more complicated than the way it was done with the first Macintosh. Back then, the System Folder would only fill a single floppy disk. Today, it would take perhaps a few hundred floppies to contain all the files of a typical Mac OS installation. Thank heavens all Macs that can run Mac OS 9 come with a CD or DVD drive!

Two Roads to Mac OS 9

Before you install Mac OS 9, you should make a choice. Which one you take depends on your particular setup and your experience with your previous system installation. Naturally, it would be nice if you could do it the easy way.

■ **Easy install**   Just click the Start button after a few brief setups, and the Mac OS installer goes to work to update or replace the Apple system software it finds on your destination drive. After a short period, you restart and you're ready to run Mac OS Setup Assistant to finish. But, if your Mac has had a lot of system problems, such as regular crashes, or if you are upgrading from a much older system version (maybe even one of those from the System 7 family), this road may be littered with many bumps.

■ **Clean install**   Even the term is intimidating: clean. Does "clean" mean you have to replace all the files on your Mac's hard drive and reinstall everything? This would take hours. You have spent many hours lovingly customizing every aspect of your Mac user experience, from desktop patterns to the way your programs look and feel when you work with them. Do you have to change all that? No, not at all. A clean system installation simply puts a brand new Mac OS 9 System Folder on your hard drive. The original System Folder is deactivated, renamed Previous System Folder. Absolutely nothing is removed. (This is covered in-depth a little later in the chapter.)

NOTE *If you already have a Previous System Folder present from an older system installation, I recommend you remove it before you do a new clean installation.*

What's Right for You

It's your decision. If you opt for a clean installation, you must go through the process of removing stuff you need from that Previous System Folder and placing it in the new Mac OS 9 System Folder before you can trash the old one. The process can take a little time and some attention to the details. I explain a simpler way, using Casady & Greene's brilliantly designed program, Conflict Catcher, later in this chapter.

But, if you have a recent version of the Mac OS installed and you haven't had a lot of problems with it, taking the easy way isn't a bad idea. For most folks, it works fine. But you want to be aware of the alternative in case Mac OS 9 begins to misbehave and you experience slow performance or frequent crashes.

NOTE *Performance problems are not always the result of a bad system installation. These problems may only be the result of using programs that aren't compatible with the new system version. I cover troubleshooting in more detail in Chapter 31.*

The One Button Way to Install Mac OS 9

The Easy Way to Install Mac OS 9

All right. You decided you don't want to bother with a clean system installation.
The standard Mac OS 9 installation will be fine for you.

Let's get ready:

1. Get your Mac OS 9 CD and place it in your CD drive.

2. Restart your Mac. As soon as you hear the startup chord, hold down the
   C key. This little step makes your Mac start from the CD. Release the key
   once you see the Happy Mac icon on your Mac's display. On a Mac with a
   high-speed CD or a DVD, you might hear a faint, or not so faint, whir from
   that drive if the Mac is booting from it. If your Mac won't start from the CD,
   go to the Startup Disk Control Panel and select the CD as your Startup Disk.
   You can change it back after the system installation is finished (Apple has
   also included the Startup Disk Control Panel as part of the CD).

NOTE   *If you have a recent Mac, such as the second generation iMac, iBook,
or Power Mac G4, follow this procedure instead: Hold down the OPTION
key when you start. You see a list of startup volumes within a few seconds.
Pick the CD icon, and then click the right arrow to continue the startup
directly from the CD.*

3. When the startup process is complete, the Mac OS 9 CD icon should be
   at the top right of your Mac's desktop. If another disk icon is shown there,
   you need to restart and repeat the previous step. Otherwise, locate and
   double-click the Mac OS Install icon. This will produce the installation
   screen shown in Figure 2-1. To proceed, click Continue.

4. If you want to install Mac OS 9 on a drive other than the one listed, pick
   the Destination Disk from the pop-up menu (see Figure 2-2).

5. Once you select a disk for installation, click Select to continue.

6. Apple's Mac OS Read Me file, labeled Important Information, comes next
   (see Figure 2-3). You should spend a few moments reading it, just to see
   if some of the information affects your Mac or software. When you finish
   reading this information, you can opt to save it or print it for later review.
   Now click Continue to move on to the next step in the installation setup
   process.

FIGURE 2-1   Get ready to install Mac OS 9

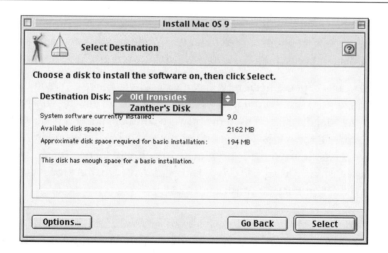

FIGURE 2-2   This option is only needed if you want to change the disk on which Mac OS 9 is installed

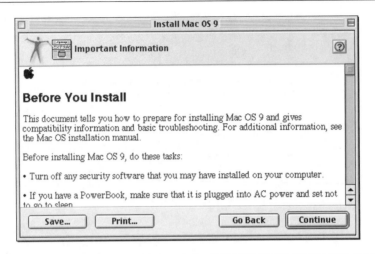

FIGURE 2-3 This document has important information you should read before you install Mac OS 9

NOTE *If you find something in the Important Information file that prevents you from doing your system installation right away (such as discovering a possible software conflict), choose Quit from the File menu to end the process. You can always go back to it later. Nothing is changed on your Mac unless the actual installation is done.*

7. The next screen contains Apple's Software License Agreement. As you might expect, you must agree to its terms before you can continue to the main installation screen (see Figure 2-4)—you don't have a choice.

8. Once you accept the license (you can't say No to move on), you can commence the installation now or make some more choices. By pressing Start, the standard list of system software components will be installed. I describe all the options at the end of this chapter. The installer displays a progress bar showing the approximate time it will take to finish. Depending on how fast your Mac, CD drive, and hard drive are, the process can take from 5 to 25 minutes to finish.

NOTE *Your destination drive will be checked by Disk First Aid at the beginning of the installation process. Any problems that can be repaired will be fixed. If a directory problem is encountered that cannot be repaired, the installer will notify you. Should that happen, you'll probably want to check Chapter 14 for other methods to address the problem.*

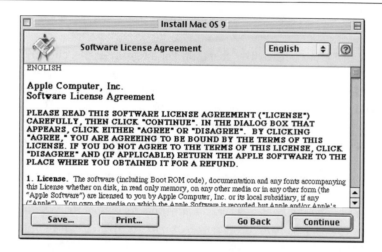

FIGURE 2-4 You must agree to Apple's software license before you can continue

9. If you want to review or change the components that are installed as part of Mac OS 9, click Customize (see Figure 2-5).

10. You may add or remove portions of the installation by checking or unchecking the listed items.

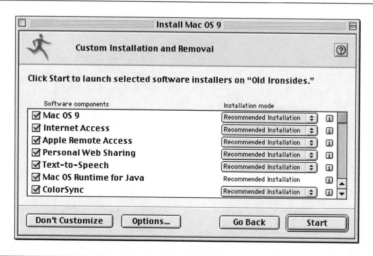

FIGURE 2-5 Each check box represents an additional software component that is part of the Mac OS 9 installation

NOTE *I'll cover all the Mac OS 9 options at the end of this chapter.*

11. If your Mac has a hard drive that didn't come from Apple, click the Options button (see Figure 2-6). Once you see that dialog box, I recommend you uncheck the box with the Update Apple Hard Disk Drivers label. Otherwise, you see a dialog box indicating Then uncheck the box labeled Update Apple Hard Disk Drivers. When you leave this checked, the Apple installer puts up a message warning you it was unable to update the drive. Click OK to continue.

CAUTION *Unchecking this option is extremely important for still another reason. On rare occasions, the Mac OS installer has been suspected of actually trying to update the drivers on a non-Apple formatted drive with potentially disastrous consequences, such as loss of data. While I have not personally encountered this sort of situation (on my part of that of a friend or business contact), exercising some extra care is never a bad idea.*

CAUTION *Apple's ongoing changes to the Mac OS might affect compatibility of non-Apple disk formatting programs. You may want to check with the publisher to be sure the version you have works with Mac OS 9.*

12. At the completion of your system installation, click Quit to leave the installer.

13. Go to the Finder's Special menu and select Restart. Or, press the power key on the keyboard and click the Restart button (or just type *R*).

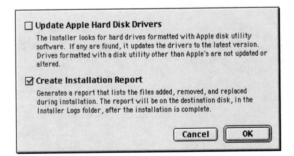

FIGURE 2-6 Uncheck the Update Apple Hard Disk Drivers option if you install on a non-Apple hard drive

NOTE
If you changed the Startup Disk Control Panel settings to boot from the CD, you want to open the Control Panel from the Apple menu and change it back to the disk on which you installed Mac OS 9.

After your Mac has restarted, the Mac OS Setup Assistant will be launched. I guide you through all the steps you need to follow in using that Assistant and the Internet Setup Assistant in the next chapter.

Installing Mac OS 9 on Mac OS Clones

Although Apple Computer has often been urged to license other manufacturers to make Macs, they actually tried it only once, a period in which Apple was suffering great financial losses. They licensed several companies, new and old, to build Mac OS licensed computers.

Such manufacturers included APS Technologies (a manufacturer of Mac peripherals), MacTell, Motorola, Umax, and an upstart company called Power Computing. Apple hoped that these clones would help extend the Mac to new markets.

The hope and the reality were at odds. For the most part, sales of these computers cannibalized sales of genuine Apple products. Power Computing, for example, went with a vengeance after Apple's core market of content creators with cheaper computers, using faster CPUs. By putting Mac OS components into low-cost boxes that were based on PC clone case designs, they could undercut Apple's prices. In addition, they didn't have to buy huge stocks of faster PowerPC microprocessors, so they could get speedier computers to market first.

NOTE
It has also been suggested that Power Computing also sold their computers at a loss to build market share rapidly, but this was never officially confirmed while the company was in existence.

When Steve Jobs returned to Apple, he looked at the numbers and decided to pull the plug. Apple was hemorrhaging from increasing financial losses and rapidly sliding market share. Jobs claimed later that Apple was also losing money on every clone computer sold, because the contract didn't give them enough in the way of license fees to cover their costs to maintain the project.

Despite the departure of clones, there are still hundreds of thousands of them out there, still working. The question is, can you install new Mac OS versions on them?

The One Button Way to Install Mac OS 9

Officially, Apple will only support these models for the last systems certified to work with them, which is Mac OS 8.1. Apple no longer tests these units for compatibility as part of their operating system development programs, so you are at your own risk if you install a newer operating system, since the products are long out of warranty (and some clone makers, such as MacTell and Power Computing are history).

In practice, since the clone computers were based on Apple designed logic boards, they should function essentially the same as a similar Apple model. For example, the APS and Motorola compatibles used the same logic board design as Power Macintosh 4400. Power Computing and Umax built models similar in design to such products the Power Macintosh 7200 and 9500.

In addition, many users have upgraded to newer Mac OS versions without a problem.

If you choose to attempt to install Mac OS 9 on a clone, the best thing to do is follow my instructions later in this chapter for doing a clean installation. That way, if the installation doesn't deliver satisfactory performance, you can quickly revert to your previous operating system version.

Clean Installation Techniques

If you have the time and patience, I recommend you do a clean installation of Mac OS 9. Contrary to what some expect, clean installations don't mean you must erase your hard drive or reinstall all your software.

A clean installation, simply stated, builds a brand new System Folder, but leaves the old one intact, only it's renamed "Previous System Folder." Also it's *deblessed,* which means it's no longer active.

By building a new System Folder, you don't carry over any damaged or incompatible files from the old System Folder. You can, therefore, get as stable an upgrade as possible. However, if you need any of the items in the Previous System Folder, such as preference files for your programs and Internet connections, or perhaps third-party system enhancements, be prepared to spend a little time sorting through everything.

My personal recommendation is that you consider getting a program that not only manages the items in your System Folder, but also guides you through the clean installation process. The program is Casady & Greene's Conflict Catcher, which you might call an Extensions Manager on steroids.

You learn more about Conflict Catcher later in this chapter.

Clean Installations from A to Z

If you don't need anything from your original System Folder, you can skip the first part of these instructions. Otherwise, you want to follow the process to the letter to be assured of as seamless a system upgrade as possible.

1. Take your Mac OS 9 CD and place it in your CD drive.

2. If you intend to merge your Previous System Folder with your new System Folder, you want to make an Apple System Profiler first of what you have. Just click the Apple menu and launch Apple System Profiler (see Figure 2-7).

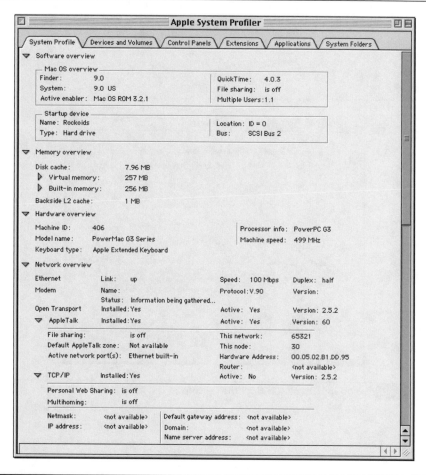

| FIGURE 2-7 | This program can make a comprehensive report on your Mac hardware and software setup3. |

Clean Installation Techniques

If your Mac doesn't have a copy of Apple System Profiler installed, you can simply do a custom install of Mac OS 9 to restore it (it is offered among the Apple Menu Items). Check the final section of this chapter for more information.

3. Click the File menu and choose New, which brings you a set of report options (shown in Figure 2-8).

4. You are going to make a report listing the contents of your System Folder, so uncheck everything but the items at the right of the screen. Once you're done, click OK to set the profile creation process in motion (see Figure 2-9).

5. Within a short time, the report will be finished. Once it's ready, click the File menu and choose Print to create a copy of the report.

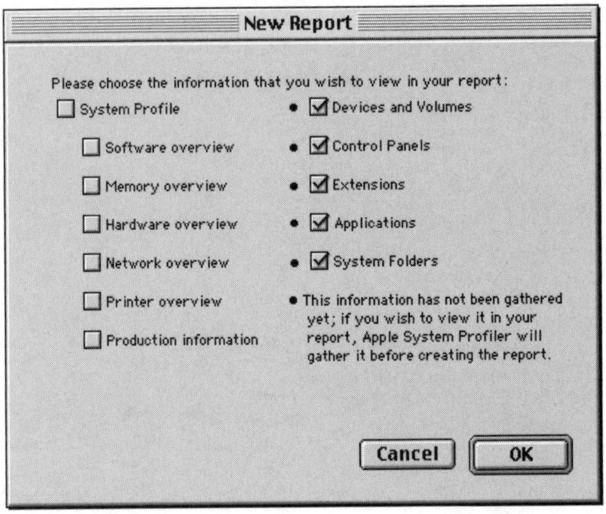

FIGURE 2-8   You only need to select the options at the right

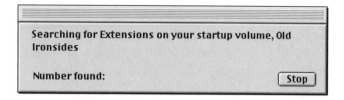

Searching for Extensions on your startup volume, Old Ironsides

Number found: [Stop]

FIGURE 2-9   Your Mac's System Folder is being checked by Apple System Profiler

CAUTION   *You can easily save the profile as a document if you don't have a printer, but having a hard copy at hand to examine makes the process noticeably easier.*

6. Assuming your Mac OS 9 CD is in its drive, restart your Mac. Immediately hold down the C key to make your Mac start from the CD. Once you see the Happy Mac icon on your Mac's display, release the key. If your Mac cannot start from the CD, open the Startup Disk Control Panel and select the CD as your Startup Disk. Just remember to switch it back to your regular startup disk when your Mac OS 9 installation is done (Apple also has thoughtfully included the Startup Disk Control Panel as part of the CD).

NOTE   *If you have a newer Mac, such as the second generation iMac, iBook, or Power Mac G4, do this instead: Hold down the OPTION key when you start. Then you see a display of available startup volumes. Click the CD icon, and then click the right arrow to continue the startup directly from the CD.*

7. Once the startup process is over, the icon for the Mac OS 9 CD should show up at the top-right corner of your Mac's desktop. Should another disk (your regular startup disk) icon appear there, restart and repeat the previous step. If everything is all right, locate and double-click the Mac OS Install icon, which is in the middle of the CD's directory. This opens the installation screen you see in Figure 2-10. To proceed, click Continue.

Clean Installation Techniques

<!-- figure caption -->**FIGURE 2-10**   Your clean installation begins with this screen

8. Should your Mac have more than one drive attached, be sure to pick
the Destination Disk from the pop-up menu (see Figure 2-11) if it's not
already displayed.

FIGURE 2-11   Pick the disk for your Mac OS 9 installation

FIGURE 2-12   Choose the Perform Clean Installation option here

9. When you have selected the destination disk, click the Options button. Now click the Options button. This brings up the screen shown in Figure 2-12.

10. Click the Perform Clean Installation check box to select that option, and then click the OK button.

11. Apple's Mac OS Read Me file, labeled Important Information, comes next (see Figure 2-13). You should spend a few moments reading it, just to see if some of the information affects your Mac or software. When you finish reading this information, you can save or print it for later review. Now click Continue to move on to the next step in the installation setup process.

Clean Installation Techniques

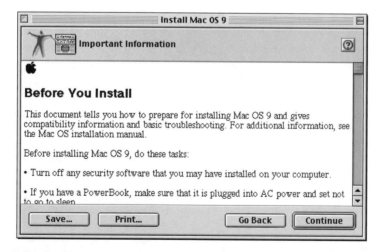

FIGURE 2-13   Check this document for important information you need to know before you install Mac OS 9

NOTE   *If the Important Information document contains information that may prevent you from installing Mac OS 9 right now (such as a software conflict you need to fix), choose Quit from the File menu to end the process without changing anything on your Mac's drive. You can always go back to it later once you have addressed the problem.*

12. The screen displays Apple's Software License Agreement. You must agree to its terms before you can continue to the main installation screen (see Figure 2-14).

13. When you click the Start button, the standard list of system software components Apple recommends for your Mac are installed. (Other options are described at the end of this chapter.) The installer displays a progress bar showing the approximate time it will take to finish. Depending on how fast your Mac, CD, or DVD drive and hard drive are, the process takes from 5 to 25 minutes to finish.

NOTE   *Apple uses Disk First Aid to check your drive at the start of the installation process (though you don't see it displayed). Any directory problems discovered will be fixed. If an unrepairable disk problem is found, the installer will notify you about it. If that happens, you should stop the installation and check Chapter 14 for other methods to address the situation.*

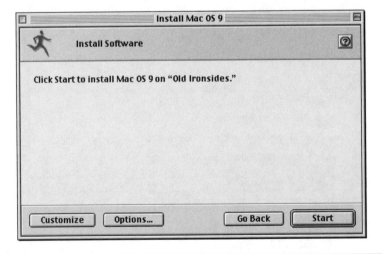

FIGURE 2-14   To begin installing Mac OS 9, click the Start button

FIGURE 2-15   Each check box represents an additional software component that is part of the Mac OS 9 installation

14. Click Customize if you want to check or change the components installed as part of Mac OS 9 (see Figure 2-15).

15. Check or uncheck items to add or remove them from the installation process.

16. If your Mac's hard drive didn't come from Apple, click the Options button (see Figure 2-16). Once you see that dialog box, uncheck the box with the Update Apple Hard Disk Drivers label. If you don't uncheck this item, the Apple installer puts up a message warning you it was unable to update the drive. Once you make this setting, click OK to continue.

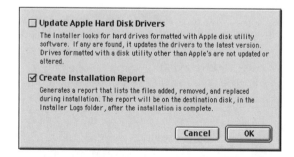

FIGURE 2-16   Uncheck the Update Apple Hard Disk Drivers option if you install on a non-Apple hard drive

CAUTION   *I'll emphasize this point. While it's unlikely that Apple's installer will attempt to update a non-Apple drive, better to be safe than sorry. There have been scattered reports of trouble from the process, although nobody I've encountered has ever reported such a situation.*

NOTE   *You may also want to contact the publisher of your disk formatting software to be sure it's compatible with Mac OS 9.*

17. When the system installation is done, click Quit to leave the installer.

18. Go to Special menu and select Restart.

NOTE   *If you changed the Startup Disk Control Panel settings to boot from the CD, don't restart. First open the Startup Disk Control Panel (check the Apple menu) and switch it back to the hard drive on which you installed Mac OS 9.*

Once your Mac has restarted and you're running Mac OS 9, you see the Mac OS Setup Assistant. You learn how to use this in the next chapter.

How to Merge System Folders

Once you finish a clean system installation, you're left with two System Folders. One is called System Folder, the other is called Previous System Folder. The second one is your former System Folder, which has been made inactive as part of the installation.

NOTE   *As mentioned previously, if you already have a Previous System Folder from a prior clean installation, the best thing to do is delete it before continuing.*

You have two choices here. You can reinstall all your third-party System Folder utilities and redo your critical application and Internet settings. If you don't have too many extra programs to install or settings to make, there is no problem in doing this. In fact, this may be the most stable way to go, especially if your original System Folder caused you grief.

More than likely, though, you'll prefer to move only the non-Apple items (including preference files) from the Previous System Folder to your new Mac OS 9 System Folder. This is a daunting process, requiring some attention to detail. But

you can usually do it in 30 to 45 minutes. You want to check everything carefully
before you move files.

Here are the steps to follow to merge the System Folders:

1. Find the Apple System Profiler report you printed before you started the
   clean install.

2. Open the Previous System Folder and new System Folder directories, and
   place them side-by-side, so you can easily compare them.

3. To make comparing the two folders easy, open the Finder's View menu
   and select as List (see Figure 2-17). Change the view setting for each folder
   you want to compare to speed the merging process.

4. First look for any folders in the Previous System folder that are not in your
   new System Folder. Press the SHIFT key, and then select each of them.

5. Now press the OPTION key and drag all those folders to your new System
   Folder. A plus sign (+) is displayed on the mouse cursor during this action.

NOTE   *When you press* OPTION *while dragging a file to another location, it makes
a duplicate and leaves the original alone. This way, you can go back to
your original "Previous System Folder" if problems occur with the new
installation once it's merged.*

How to Merge System Folders

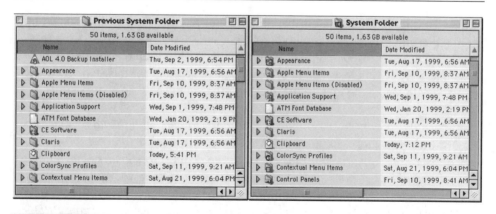

FIGURE 2-17   The Previous System Folder sits at the left, the new System Folder at
the right

6. Double-click the System file icon on your Previous System Folder to open it if you want to transfer any custom system sounds to the new System Folder.

7. Press OPTION and drag the sounds to the System file in the new System Folder. The copying process can be slow, so be patient if it seems to drag.

8. The Apple Menu Items folder is next on the agenda. Compare the contents from both System Folders and OPTION-drag the nonduplicated files to the new System Folder.

9. So far, the process has been fairly simple. Now it gets more difficult. Look at your Apple System Profiler report and see which items in your Previous System Folder are from Apple and which are not.

10. Now, select and OPTION-drag all the non-Apple files from the Previous System Folder to the same folder within the new System Folder. But leave the Fonts and Preferences folders alone for now. I'll get to them shortly.

11. Now the Fonts folders. Select all the fonts from the one in the Previous System Folder, and then OPTION-drag the fonts to the new System Folder.

NOTE   *Not to worry. You cannot replace duplicate fonts in the new Fonts folder. The Finder will simply declare them in use. Just OK each message to complete the process.*

12. The Preferences folder is next on the agenda. Select and OPTION-drag the nonduplicated files to the new Preferences folder.

13. To carry over your Internet access preferences, you must replace some of the files in your new System Folder. Select and OPTION-drag Apple's Internet Preferences, Modem Preferences, and the TCP/IP Preferences files to the new System Folder. Omit the Remote Access folder for this step. Then OK the dialog box to replace the matching files in the new System Folder.

NOTE   *You also want to select and OPTION-copy folders with the name America Online, Eudora, Explorer, or Netscape, or any other Internet software you use. This process transfers program settings, bookmarks, downloads, e-mail and various system files you need to continue your Internet access seamlessly. In addition, you want to copy custom modem profiles, if any, from the Modems folder inside the Extensions folder, and custom PPD printer files from the Printer Descriptions folder. You may also want to use Sherlock 2 (available from the Apple menu) to help you locate the files if they aren't easy to access.*

14. Now open the Remote Access folder.

15. Select and OPTION-drag the Remote Access Connections file (which contains the username, password, and dialing options used for your ISP) from this folder to the Remote Access folder in your New System Folder.

> NOTE   *You cannot just replace the entire folder because it will be labeled as "in use" by the Finder. This is because another file in that folder, Remote Access Log, is always active (you needn't bring it over).*

16. Once you've done the basics, it's time to recheck the two System Folders to be sure you have transferred all the files you want to move. Don't be alarmed if you missed a few files here and there. You can take care of them now.

17. When you finish, choose Restart from the Special menu.

18. The restart process should be successful. If it is, take a few moments to recheck basic Finder functions, such as opening folders and, perhaps, launching an application or document. You also want to confirm that your Internet access still functions. If any problems occur, go to the next section of this book.

> CAUTION   *A good idea is not to delete the Previous System Folder until you're certain everything is working correctly. If it is, go ahead and remove that folder. If a problem exists, read on.*

Clean System Installation Problems and Solutions

Normally, a clean system installation fixes problems; it doesn't introduce them. But sometimes the new installation goes badly. If this happens to you, go through this section and try some of the remedial steps. The first thing to try, though, is simply to go back to your Previous System Folder.

If you still wish to try a clean system installation, you also want to consider doing one that's much more complete. For example, in addition to reinstalling Mac OS 9, you also want to reinstall all of your programs, or at least the ones you know install System Folder components. But, this is a last resort and an option you probably won't have to consider.

Clean System Installation Problems and Solutions

Apple's newest computers come with a System Restore disk, which puts everything back the way it was when the computer shipped. You can even erase the hard drive as part of the process (but don't do that unless you have backups for your document and preference files).

Here's how to go back to your Previous System Folder:

1. If your Mac crashed, restart. If the Mac won't restart from the startup drive, use the Mac OS 9 CD as the startup disk, holding down the C or OPTION key, as described in the previous section.

2. Once you restart, locate your new Mac OS 9 System Folder on your startup drive and remove the System file.

3. Then click the folder's title and rename this folder "Obsolete System Folder."

4. Return to the Previous System Folder, click the folder's title, and change it back to System Folder.

5. Now, open and close the System Folder. That's it! This action will bless the System Folder (no handkerchiefs necessary), which makes it active again.

6. Now restart your Mac. At this point, you should have restarted normally and now you're ready to go to the next step.

7. Locate the Obsolete System Folder and trash it. Then empty the trash.

8. Your choice now is to stick with your original System Folder and postpone the Mac OS 9 upgrade to another day or to consider trying the clean installation again to return to Mac OS 9. Review the steps described in the previous section, but don't merge the two System Folders. Set up and verify that your Mac is running properly.

9. Once you have made sure your Mac works smoothly, the next step is to reinstall all your non-Apple System Folder programs. Then reinstall any of your other programs that put things in the System Folder (this may mean all your software because few programs out there don't have something, at least a single item, in the System Folder).

NOTE

Don't worry about current versions of Microsoft Office or Microsoft's Internet programs. They have a self-repair routine that automatically reinstalls any missing System Folder item. So you can go ahead and leave these programs alone (except for some Mac OS 9 updates Microsoft produced for its Office suite, which must be reinstalled manually).

10. After the installation process is done, restart your Mac, and try your programs. You also have to redo program and Internet preferences as part of this process.

If the steps previously described don't help you resolve your problem, here are some more options to consider:

■ **Examine your hard drive for directory problems** Disk First Aid should be sufficient to locate any problem of significance, but giving a third-party disk repair program a try also wouldn't hurt. You may choose Alsoft's DiskWarrior, MicroMat's TechTool Pro, or Symantec's Norton Utilities for the task. Chapter 14 covers the subject in more detail.

■ **Backup and reformat your drive** The task seems far more daunting than anything else described, but sometimes starting from scratch works when all else fails. Make sure your backup is current first. Depending on the size of your hard drive and the amount of files you have to restore, be prepared to give up the better part of a long morning or afternoon for this process. That long lunch or visit to the golf course may look most inviting at this point.

NOTE

You find more information about backups in Chapter 29.

■ **Let your dealer check your Mac** This is something you may want to consider before reformatting the drive. If every possible step you've tried fails to get your Mac running in a stable fashion, contact your dealer and have your Mac looked over to see if it has a hardware problem. If the unit is still under warranty, don't think twice about doing this. Desktop Macs are eligible for free onsite service under warranty.

Clean System Installation Problems and Solutions

Conflict Catcher's Clean System Installation Process

When Jeffrey Robbin was developing his fabulous Conflict Catcher 8, a number of his loyal beta testers (including your hard-working author) suggested he devise a clean-installation merge feature. Robbin was, to be truthful, a little skeptical about having enough time to do it properly, but he answered the call.

As you see from the previous sections, doing a clean system installation is not an easy task. You must pay careful attention to every step of the process to do it properly. Or, just reinstall everything and be prepared to wait a long time to get back to work, running Mac OS 9.

Conflict Catcher's Clean-System Install Merge helps make the process much more painless. The next few pages describe how the process works.

1. Make sure Conflict Catcher has been installed on your original System Folder.

2. Perform a clean Mac OS 9 installation, as described in the previous section "Clean System Installs from A to Z."

3. After restarting with your new System Folder, also install Conflict Catcher on the new System Folder.

4. As soon as your Mac restarts after installation of Conflict Catcher, hold down the SPACEBAR. This brings up the Conflict Catcher window (see Figure 2-18).

5. Go to the program's Special menu and select **Clean-System Install Merge.**

6. A dialog box, as pictured in Figure 2-19, requests you confirm you have restarted with your new System Folder. To continue, click Yes.

7. When the next dialog box appears, select your present System Folder and the Previous System folder from the list.

8. Once selected, you return to a previous dialog box where the name Previous System Folder appears.

9. Now the process begins in earnest. Click Compare Folders. Conflict Catcher will check for damaged system items, and then search out the differences between your Mac OS 9 System Folder and the Previous System Folder. Once the search process is over, you see a screen listing all the nonduplicated items.

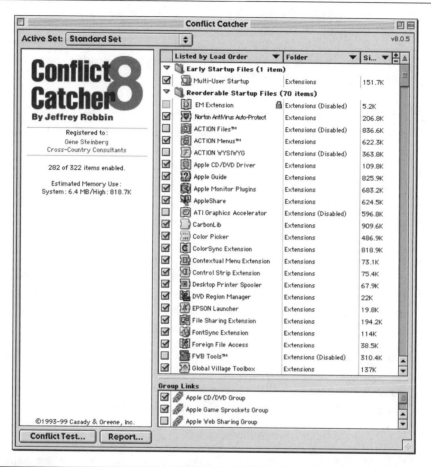

| FIGURE 2-18 | Conflict Catcher offers a number of system management capabilities |

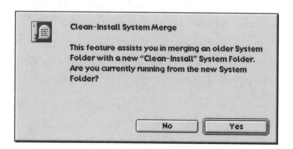

| FIGURE 2-19 | The Clean-System Install Merge procedure begins |

Clean System Installation
Problems and Solutions

If Conflict Catcher reports finding a damaged file, go ahead and let the program repair it. Conflict Catcher can usually fix minor damage, but serious file corruption cannot be fixed. If a file cannot be fixed, consider reinstalling that file from the original installer, if it needs to be transferred to your Mac OS 9 System Folder.

10. Once the list is presented to you, check it and (this can be confusing) select the check boxes for the items you don't want copied to your new Mac OS 9 System Folder.

Conflict Catcher has a huge reference file it can examine to display information about many System Folder components. You want to use this feature if you're unsure for what a particular file is used.

11. Before merging System Folders, click the Options button in Conflict Catcher's list. This brings up a dialog boxes of choices, the main one being if you prefer to copy files or move them. In the first case, duplicates will be made of the files you are merging. I suggest you choose this option, in case you need to go back to using your Previous System Folder.

12. Another option simplifies preference settings for your new System Folder. The feature is called Merge System File Resources. It takes your Owner Name, Computer Name, Password, printer selection, and custom system sound and transfers them as part of the merging process.

13. Now you are ready. When the next screen appears, click Merge Systems.

14. Over the next few minutes, your System Folder items will be merged. Once the process is over, you return to the main Conflict Catcher screen. Take a few moments to recheck the merge process before you confirm them. If everything is all right, click Continue Startup to resume the startup process with the newly modified System Folder.

If Conflict Catcher has added a file that must load before Conflict Catcher, you'll go through a second restart before you're finished.

CAUTION   *To be sure your Internet access continues without problems, make sure all your Internet-related preference files are transferred during the Clean-System Install Merge process. These include Internet Preferences, Modem Preferences, Remote Access folder, and TCP/IP Preferences, plus the folders that contain files from America Online, Eudora, Explorer, Netscape, or any other Internet programs you use.*

A Look at Installation Options

As part of the standard installation of Mac OS 9, Apple selects a set of basic software components. You can change these selections if you prefer, so only what you want is included as part of the installation process. Just click Customize when you reach the final installation screen to bring up the choices (see Figure 2-20).

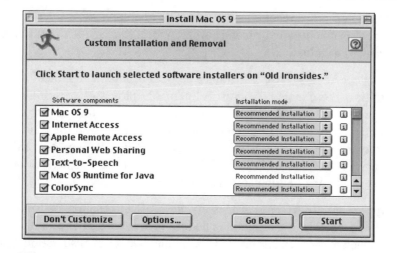

FIGURE 2-20   Select your Mac OS 9 extras from this screen

A Look at Installation Options

Three options are offered with each installation:

- **Recommended Installation** These are the components Apple recommends for your Mac.

- **Customized Installation** If you need to restore an item that was deleted by mistake or is damaged, pick this option and click the check box next to the items you want to install.

- **Customized Removal** You can select the items you want to remove from this list.

The following lists the various Mac OS 9 options offered:

CAUTION *While you can customize many parts of your core Mac OS 9 installation, this part of the installation is best left alone because it's easy to omit something you truly need. It might not be labeled in the most informative fashion.*

- **Mac OS 9** The recommended Mac OS 9 components needed for your Mac. What is installed can vary from model to model. It's part of the standard installation.

- **Internet Access** Apple installs a core set of Internet applications and utilities. These include Microsoft Internet Explorer, Microsoft Outlook Express, Netscape Communicator, and a handful of Internet enhancement utilities, such as StuffIt Expander to extract compressed files and Apple's Internet Access software to help you select and sign up with an ISP. This is part of the standard installation and I recommend it, unless you prefer to stay with the Internet software you have.

- **Apple Remote Access** This software is used to enable you to make a PPP connection to the Internet and also to access another Mac via a dial-up connection for file sharing. This is another necessary installation, unless you are using a cable modem or DSL to access the Internet.

- **Personal Web Sharing** You can set your Mac up as a personal Web server, so you can share files with others on the Web. This option has some tradeoffs, such as the need to password-protect your Web files if you wish to restrict access and the need to keep your Mac running whenever someone is likely to need the files you have. You may want to omit this installation.

■ **Text-to-Speech**   This software uses Apple's speech software to activate talking alert messages and to allow selected text to be read back to you. The feature is also needed for some games, so I recommend you leave it on, even if you find the talking alerts annoying.

■ **Mac OS Runtime for Java**   Java is a cross-platform language supported by many Web sites. Small Java applications, or *applets,* load when a site needs to display a special feature (such as one with animation, sound, or ticker tape-type announcements). I recommend you install this component, part of the standard installation, to ensure a complete Web experience.

■ **ColorSync**   This technology enables you to calibrate your Mac's display and also to match up the color you see (more or less) with that of a scanner or printer. This one is a standard installation and recommended highly.

■ **English Speech Recognition**   An optional installation. This is the latest version of a program Apple used to call PlainTalk. It lets your Mac respond to spoken commands. The capabilities of Apple's Speech Recognition software are somewhat limited, so don't expect a Star Trek-like capability to have a dialogue with your Mac. This is an acquired taste, at best, and surely worth trying if you have the time. In a noisy office, though, it's definitely a no-no.

■ **Language Kits**   If you intend to use your Mac overseas or in a multilingual environment, you want to check out these options.

NOTE   *Installing a Language Kit doesn't guarantee that all of your programs will work properly with an alternate language selection, especially if a non-Roman alphabet is involved. You'll also want to check a program's documentation as to what foreign language options are supported.*

■ **Network Assistant Client**   If your Mac is part of a network in which the system is managed with Apple's Network Assistant Management software, you want to install this item. It enables the network administrator to control your Mac setup direct from the unit used as a server.

The Add/Remove Installation

If you're already running Mac OS 9 and you need to reinstall the system software or just one or more components, you'll be presented with this option when you launch the Mac OS 9 installer and select your destination disk (see Figure 2-21).

A Look at Installation Options

FIGURE 2-21   This screen only appears when Mac OS 9 has been previously installed

You have two choices to consider:

■ **Reinstall**   This option simply reinstalls Mac OS 9, but you can still customize the installation to include additional components.

■ **Add/Remove**   This option enables you to delete a system component you don't want to use or to add one that is needed or was mistakenly deleted. When you select this option, you go right to the same screen that appears when you click Customize, only none of the options are checked (see Figure 2-22). From this screen, select the items you want to install or uninstall.

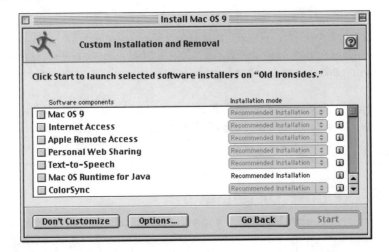

FIGURE 2-22   Select the items you want to install or remove from this screen

Remove Mac OS 9 items with caution. Deleting the wrong thing is easy, which may impact your Mac's capability to perform a certain function, such as printing a document or accessing the Internet.

Summing Up

In this chapter, you learned about the various roads to a successful installation of Mac OS 9. Once your new system is running, you are ready for the next step, configuring Apple's Mac OS Setup Assistant, which is the topic of the next chapter.

Summing Up

Chapter 3

Setting Up User Preferences

Once you install Mac OS 9, you're ready to set it up to your needs. Fortunately, the process of configuring your Mac and Mac OS 9 is quick and painless.

The process begins with the Mac OS Setup Assistant, which is described in this chapter. You're taken through every step of the process, to make sure your Mac is configured to meet your exact needs. If you want to select a new *Internet service provider* (*ISP*), you'll also be guided through the Internet Setup Assistant.

NOTE   *As a result of Apple's agreement with EarthLink, it is Apple's default ISP. If no EarthLink access is in your city, however, you can choose a different ISP. In addition, you can easily add the settings for your present ISP in the Internet Setup Assistant, as I explain later in this chapter.*

If you already have an account with an ISP, I show you how to transfer the settings as painlessly as possible.

Mac OS Setup Assistant

The Mac OS Setup Assistant is a tool provided with Mac OS 9 that enables you to step through a basic set of system and network settings. In this section, you get an in-depth look at the Mac OS Setup Assistant and how you can use it to set up your Mac to suit your needs. At each setting, I describe all the options you can set and exactly what each option does. The Mac OS Setup Assistant is launched automatically after you reboot from installing Mac OS 9, but you can also launch it manually.

NOTE   *If Mac OS Setup Assistant didn't launch when your Mac started, it is located in the Assistant's folder on your startup drive. Open the folder, and double-click the Mac OS Setup Assistant icon.*

Once Mac OS Setup Assistant starts, you are presented with the Introduction dialog box that discusses the setup of your Mac. After you finish reviewing the information in the dialog box, click the button shaped like a right arrow located in the lower right-hand corner to start the setup process.

1. The first thing the Setup Assistant asks is what are your regional preferences. These preferences dictate in what format the number, date, time, keyboard layout, and text are displayed. Mac OS 9 supports five different sets of formats based upon where they are from around

the world. The five different formats Mac OS currently makes available (shown in Figure 3-1) for you are Australian, Brazilian Portuguese, British, Spanish, and U.S. standard. Select the one that best suits your needs from the list, usually U.S., and then click the right arrow button to proceed to the next step of the setup process.

> **NOTE** *If you do not have time to configure your Mac now, you may quit Mac OS Setup Assistant and run it later. The settings primarily affect your basic networking and printer setups, plus owner, date, and time information.*

2. Next, the Setup Assistant asks you to enter your name and the company or organization to which you belong. Enter the name you want the Setup Assistant to use when setting up your Mac. This is frequently either your full name or the user name you use on your network. In later stages of the setup process, you see your name is used in the naming of the shared files folder that is created later in the setup process. If your Mac is only for personal use, you can leave the company name or organization blank, if you want. Otherwise, you should fill in the company or institution that owns the Mac you are configuring. Once you finish entering your name and organization name, click the right arrow button to move on to the next step of the setup.

Mac OS Setup Assistant

Regional Preferences

Your system software has default settings for keyboard layout, time, date, text, and number formats. This assistant adjusts those settings based on the specific language version you are using.

Which set of formats do you prefer to use?

Australian
Brazilian Portuguese
British
Spanish
U.S.

Choose a language, then click the right arrow to continue.

◁ 2 ▷

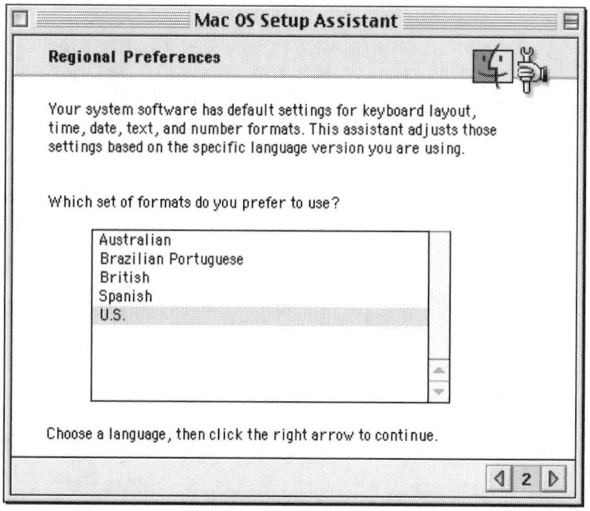

FIGURE 3-1   Choose the character and number formats you want to use

NOTE   *The information you enter on this setup screen also appears in the File Sharing Control Panel (which is described in more detail in Chapter 27).*

3. Now you are asked to set the clock on your Mac. Looking at this part of the Setup Assistant, as you see in Figure 3-2, you need to set the time and date. The first question you need to answer when setting the time on your Mac is whether you observe daylight saving time at the present time. If you are setting up your Mac during daylight saving time, then click the Yes radio button.

4. Moving down the dialog box, check the time that's displayed and see if it is accurate. If the time is off, then click the two numbers that indicate the hour. Next, either type in the current time using the number keys or click the up and down arrows located at the end of the time field to increase or decrease the number. Repeat this for the minutes and then to set A.M. or P.M. Next, look at the date field to see if the time is accurate.

5. If the date is off, then you need to correct it. To change the date, click the numbers for the month, and then click the up or down arrows located at the end of the date field to change it. Or, you can simply select the number you need to change, and then type in the number using the keyboard. Once you

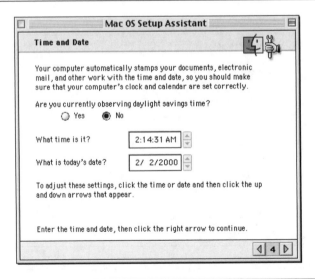

FIGURE 3-2   Set the date and time on your Mac

have set the date and time correctly, click the right arrow to proceed to the next phase of the setup.

NOTE   *Depending on the regional preferences you chose, the date and time formats will be different from those displayed in the previous figures. All the figures pictured in this chapter are based on U.S. regional preferences. In addition, once you set your date and time information, you can use the Date & Time Control Panel to synchronize your Mac's clock. See Chapter 3 for more information on this subject.*

6. In the next phase of the setup process, the Setup Assistant asks where you are located so it can determine time zone differences if the need arises. Looking at the list of cities in Figure 3-3, locate the city you are in or to which you live the closest. If you can't find a city close to you, select a city in the same time zone. To select the city closest to you, simply scroll down the alphabetically organized list of cities, and then click its name to select it. Once you select the proper city, click the right arrow button to proceed.

7. Now, the Setup Assistant asks if you want to use the Simple Finder preferences when using your Mac. The Simple Finder Preferences mode causes the Finder, the program that controls the way you work with your Mac, to display a simpler menu bar, with fewer commands.

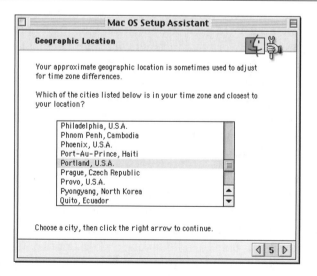

FIGURE 3-3   Select the city where you are located

NOTE   *Using simple Finder preferences greatly limits the number of functions and settings available to you when using the Finder. For example, instead of having 17 options under the File menu, covering everything from Get Info to Make Alias, the File menu using Simple Finder Preferences only has the six most essential options. Although the Simple Finder Preferences may make using your Mac a bit easier, you sacrifice access to many useful functions. This is a good reason not to use this option.*

8. If you are interested in trying the Simple Finder Preferences, select the Yes radio button in this dialog box to turn on this option. Later, if you decide you want to use the options normally available in the Finder, you can switch back by turning off the Simple Finder Preferences. To do this, click the application menu located in the upper-right corner of the screen, and then select Finder from the list of currently running applications.

9. Next, click the Edit menu and scroll down to select Preferences.

10. Looking at the Preferences dialog box, uncheck the check box for Simple Finder Preferences, and then click the close box to save the changed preferences.

11. Once you decide which Finder preferences to use, click the right arrow to proceed to the next portion of the setup.

12. The Setup Assistant now informs you that you are now going to set up your network connections. Today, most Macs are members of a network (except for consumer Macs with a personal, USB-based printer). This could be a small network that links you and an Ethernet or LocalTalk based printer, or it could be a large network that connects your Mac to many different computers and printers. Unlike previous versions of the Mac OS, which required you to have a network connection to share files and programs, users of Mac OS 9 can now share them over the Internet. As such, you want to pay close attention to the settings you choose. Click the right arrow to proceed to the first network setup dialog box.

13. In the network dialog box you see in Figure 3-4, the Setup Assistant asks you to name your computer. The name you give your computer must be unique on the AppleTalk zone where your Mac is located. If your Mac is one of many, then you should be careful when choosing the name for your Mac. Make sure its name is both unique and descriptive. If the name for your Mac is not unique, when you try to move to the next portion of the setup, you will be warned your Mac's name is not unique and you need to

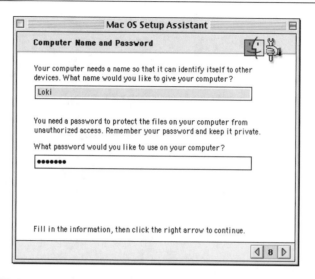

FIGURE 3-4   Name your Mac and set your personal password

change it. You will then be sent back to this portion of the setup to change your Mac's name.

> **NOTE** *If you are an individual user or on a small network, of course, the process of selecting a unique name is greatly simplified. Choose whatever suits you; use your imagination, if you like.*

14. Once you select the name for your Mac, you are asked to enter your password. This is the password assigned to the user account created for you during the installation process. Because this is the password you use when you access this Mac over the network, make certain the password is a good, secure one. A good password is one not easily guessed or broken by a computer program that keeps trying different words in the dictionary until it hits on your password. After you name your Mac and select the password you want to use, click the right arrow to proceed to the next setup dialog box.

15. The Setup Assistant now asks if you want to share files with the other users on your network by setting up a shared folder (see Figure 3-5). If you want to set up a shared folder now, all you need to do is click the Yes radio button.

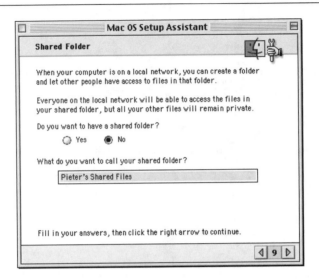

FIGURE 3-5   Configure the name of your shared folder

16. Next, you want to select the name of the folder you are sharing. By default, this is the name you entered at the beginning of the setup process, along with the phrase Shared Files. Because I entered Pieter as my user name in the beginning of the setup procedure, the default name for my shared folder would be Pieter's Shared Files. If the default name is fine, then click the right arrow to proceed; otherwise, select the default share name and type in the name you want. Once you enter the name you want, click the right arrow to move on to the next phase of the setup.

NOTE   *You do not, of course, have to designate a shared folder. This is strictly a choice you might consider if your Mac is on a network where you wish to use a shared folder as a sort of "drop box" in which to send and receive files; otherwise you can pass this option by without a problem. I'll go over the subject of sharing files in more detail in Chapter 27.*

17. After setting up your shared folder, Setup Assistant walks you through setting up your printer. If your printer is connected to you by a network connection, then you want to click the radio button labeled Network Connection, as seen in Figure 3-6. Otherwise, click the radio button labeled Direct Connection to signify that the printer is connected directly

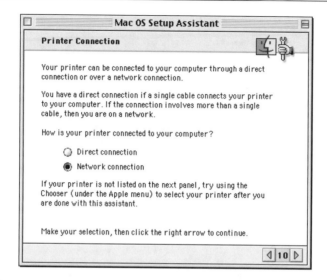

FIGURE 3-6   Choose the type of printer connection you are using

to your Mac. Once you select the type of printer connection you will use, click the right arrow to select your default printer.

NOTE *If you are running the Setup Assistant right after installing Mac OS 9 for the first time, and you are using a non-Apple printer that is directly connected to your Mac, you may be unable to set up your printer correctly because it won't be visible in the Assistant dialog box. The reason for this is that most non-Apple printers require special software to be installed on your Mac to be recognized and work properly. Don't be concerned about this, though. You can go right to the Chooser and select your printer after its driver software is installed. The newest HP inkjet printers, for example, guide you through the printer selection process right after restart, once you install the software.*

18. Because we chose a network-based printer in the previous part of the setup process, the Setup Assistant now displays a list of all the available network-based printers on your local AppleTalk network. If your network has more than a single zone, only the ones on your zone are displaced. When you look at the dialog box (as seen in Figure 3-7), select the printer you want to use and then click the right arrow button to choose the selected

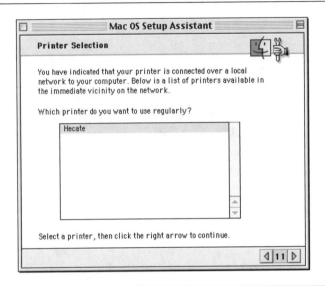

FIGURE 3-7   Select the printer you want to use normally

printer as the default printer used by your applications (you can change it later). Next, click the right arrow to proceed to the final part of the Setup Assistant.

19. Finally, the Setup Assistant asks if all the settings you have just set up are the way you want them and if you would like to save your settings. If all settings are set the way you want them, click the Go Ahead button to have the Setup Assistant save your Mac's configuration. You can always click the back or previous arrow to review each setup, in sequence, to confirm the settings. Once all the settings are saved, you are asked if you want to continue and configure your connection to the Internet, or if you want to quit now and start using your Mac. Clicking the Continue button launches the Internet Setup Assistant, which then walks you through the steps needed to connect your Mac to the Internet.

CAUTION   *If you want to change any settings, you still have to navigate to the end of the Setup Assistant's screen and click the Go Ahead button to save your settings. Also, if you stop the initial setup process at any time before the Go Ahead button is accessed, you need to redo the setups when you launch the Setup Assistant again.*

How to Select a Secure Password

To make a password secure, a good idea is to use random uppercase and lowercase letters, with at least one number and at least one use of punctuation or a special character. A bad password would be something like "apple" because not only can it be easily guessed, but it also does not contain any numbers or special characters. You should also avoid other easily guessed letter and number combinations, such as a child's name or birth date.

A good password would be something like "1lUvMac$" because it is easily remembered, but contains uppercase and lowercase letters, as well as a number and a special character to make it difficult to break.

Using good passwords is especially important when working on the Internet because many people will try to break your password and access your Mac without your permission.

Internet Setup Assistant

The *Internet Setup Assistant (ISA)* is designed to help you select an ISP if you don't already have one, or to walk you through the various steps you must perform to connect to your ISP.

You can start the ISA either by clicking the Continue button located in the last part of the Mac OS Setup Assistant or by double-clicking the ISA icon located in the Assistants folder on your startup drive.

NOTE *If you are an AOL member or want to join AOL, don't use ISA. Instead, check your Mac's drive to see if a copy of AOL is already present. You can launch that program and follow the instructions to transfer your account information. Otherwise, you can use one of those ubiquitous AOL CDs to set up an account and take advantage of one of their latest limited trial offers.*

Here's a description of the full Internet setup process:

1. After it's launched, the ISA asks if you want to set up your Mac so it can connect to the Internet. If you want to proceed with configuring your Mac so it can connect to the Internet, then click the OK button to start going through the various configuration settings.

Internet Setup Assistant

2. The next question the ISA asks is if you already have a connection to the Internet through an ISP or your network. If you do not have a connection to the Internet and want to set up one, then click the No button to have the ISA help you set up a connection. After clicking the No button, the ISA starts up the ISP Referral Assistant, which then begins walking you through the necessary steps to get hooked up with an ISP.

Setting up a New ISP Account Using the ISP Referral Assistant

If you do not already have an account with an ISP, you can use the ISP Referral Assistant to set you up. The following section takes you through the basic steps.

> NOTE   *Since Apple's preferred ISP is EarthLink, they will get first priority in this setup process, unless, of course, EarthLink doesn't have dial up access in your city.*

1. The first dialog box you see when using the ISP Referral Assistant describes the steps you must go through to select and set up a new account with an ISP. Once you finish reading the information, click the right arrow button located in the lower-hand corner of the dialog box to move on to the next step.

2. Now, look at the dialog box in Figure 3-8. Click the pop-up menu labeled Modem to select the modem you want to use to connect to the Internet.

3. Once you select your modem, click the pop-up menu labeled Port and select the port your modem is using, normally the modem port. For new Macs with an internal modem, these settings are generally set up by default.

> NOTE   *If the model number of your modem is not present, try selecting one by the same manufacturer and see if that works. If the manufacturer of your modem is not listed, try using one of the Hayes modems and see if they work. You may also want to contact the modem's manufacturer to see if it has an Open Transport/PPP-Remote Access script file for you to use.*

4. Next, you need to tell the ISP Referral Assistant if you use a Touch-Tone telephone or if you use an older, rotary dial telephone. Click the radio button that describes the type of telephone you have.

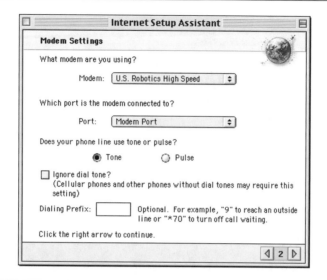

FIGURE 3-8   Set up the modem you want to use with your Mac

5. Finally, you need to let the ISP Referral Assistant know if your modem should be set to ignore a dial tone and what number it should dial, if any, to reach an outside line. Once you set up your modem, click the right arrow to continue the ISP setup process.

NOTE   *If you are using a cell phone or you are located in a country other than the U.S. or Canada, then you want to have your modem ignore a dial tone. Likewise, if you are dialing from a hotel or some other private telephone exchange, you want to have the modem dial the number needed to reach an outside line before it dials the Apple ISP Referral server.*

6. Next, you are presented with a disclaimer from Apple. This disclaimer warns you that the ISP listed by the server is only as accurate as the information provided when the system was designed and that Apple is not responsible for how well the ISP works. Once you read the disclaimer thoroughly, click the right arrow to move on to the next step in the ISP Referral Assistant.

7. Now you are asked to select the country where you are located, as seen in Figure 3-9. If you are not located in the U.S. or Canada, then click the pop-up menu and select the appropriate country.

FIGURE 3-9   Enter your area code and telephone number prefix to help select an ISP

8. Next, enter your local area code and the three-number prefix for your telephone number. Once you enter in your information, click the Register button to have the ISP Referral Assistant dial the ISP Referral server and download a list of the ISPs in your area.

Once you click Register, the ISP Referral Assistant dials the ISP Referral Server and downloads a list of ISPs located in your area. You can then select a service from the list and follow the instructions on setting up your new Internet account.

NOTE   *The setup procedures vary from one ISP to another, so I won't detail them here. You will see a detailed information screen on what you have to do to establish an account.*

Setting Up an Existing ISP Account Using ISA

If you already have an account with an ISP, then you want to click the Yes button when the ISA asks you if you already have an ISP.

Once you click Yes, the ISA starts the *Internet Editor Assistant* (*IEA*), which then walks you through configuring all the settings you need to have set to connect to your ISP.

Here's how to make those settings:

1. The first screen the IEA displays to you is a list of all the different information you need to know when using the IEA to set up your Internet configuration.

2. The IEA now asks you the name you want to assign to this connection, as shown in Figure 3-10. This name can be whatever you want because the name is only used to identify the connection when you are using the Configuration Manager control panel.

3. After you enter the name of the configuration, you need to specify if you will be connecting to the ISP by either a network connection, as you would if you have a cable modem or DSL connection, or by dialing with a modem. Select the radio button that describes the type of network connection you are using, and then click the right arrow to move to the next screen. The following few sections only apply if you are using a modem to dial your ISP. Those of you who connect to your ISP by a network can skip over the next three sections that refer to modem configuration.

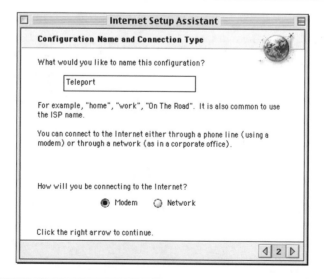

FIGURE 3-10   Name the connection, and then select your connection type

Internet Setup Assistant

4. Now the IEA asks you for information about the type of modem you plan to use to dial your ISP. Click the pop-up menu labeled Modem (see Figure 3-11) and then select the modem you are using from the list.

5. Next, click the pop-up menu labeled Port and choose the port to which your modem is connected. Depending on the model Mac you have, the port may be listed as Internal Modem, Modem Port, or Modem/Printer Port.

6. Now you need to tell the IEA if you are using a Touch-Tone telephone or if you have one of the older rotary dial phones. Click the radio button that describes the kind of phone you are using.

7. Next, you need to let the IEA know if your modem should ignore the dial tone and if it should dial a number to reach an outside line before dialing your ISP. You should set your modem to ignore a dial tone if you are using a cell phone or are located in a country other than the U.S. or Canada. Once you finish setting up your modem, click the right arrow to proceed.

8. After you set up your modem, the IEA then asks you to enter the telephone number it should dial to connect to your ISP (see Figure 3-12), along with the user name and password you use to connect to your ISP. Once you have entered all three pieces of information, click the right arrow to go to the next configuration screen.

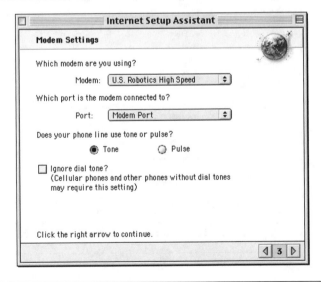

FIGURE 3-11   Set up the modem you will use to connect to your ISP

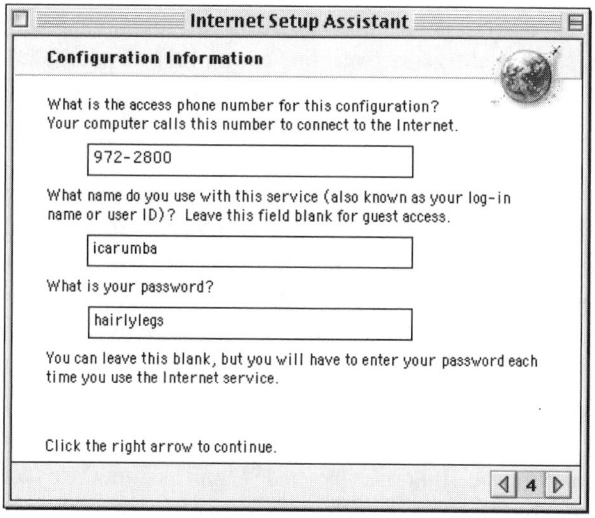

FIGURE 3-12   Configure the telephone number and user name/password used
for your ISP

9. Once you finish setting up your ISP information, you are asked if your ISP
requires you to run a PPP connection script when you connect to set up
various options. Most ISPs do not require you to run a PPP connection
script. If yours does, click the Yes radio button.

10. Next, click the right arrow button to proceed to the screen where you can
select the PPP script you need to run. If this script is not already on your
Mac, you need to get a copy from your ISP, along with instructions on how
to install it on your Mac.

11. If you are not required to run a PPP connection script, click the No radio
button, and then click the right arrow to proceed.

12. At this point, IEA asks if you use a fixed *Internet Protocol* (*IP*) address
with your ISP. Normally, your ISP assigns you a IP address dynamically
every time you connect to them. This allows your ISP to reuse its limited
number of IP addresses, instead of giving each user his or her own IP
address, and then refusing new users once the pool of IP addresses is
exhausted. Some users, however, especially those with a cable modem
or a DSL connection, have a fixed IP address assigned to their Mac.
If you do use a fixed IP address, click the Yes button, and then click the
right arrow to set up the IP address you plan to use.

Internet Setup Assistant

13. Now, the IEA asks you to enter the IP address your ISP assigned to
you. The IP address is composed of four numbers, each ranging from
0 to 255, separated by a period. For example, one possible IP address is
192.168.100.10. After you enter the proper IP address, click the right
arrow to proceed to the next setup screen.

> **NOTE**   *Because each ISP has its own settings, the settings aren't shown here. If
> you don't have any of this information at hand, check the documentation
> that came with your ISP's setup kit, if there is one. Otherwise, you need to
> call your ISP's technical support people to get this information. And, by
> the way, don't accept claims that they cannot configure their service to
> run on a Mac. If the ISP doesn't require special software, this should
> present no difficulty at all.*

14. After you enter the IP address your ISP has assigned to you and clicked the
right arrow, the IEA asks you for the subnet mask used with this address
and the address of the router, also known as the *default gateway,* that is
associated with the IP address. In the dialog box, as shown in Figure 3-13,
enter the subnet mask associated with the IP address your ISP has given
you. Normally, this subnet mask looks something like 255.255.255.0.

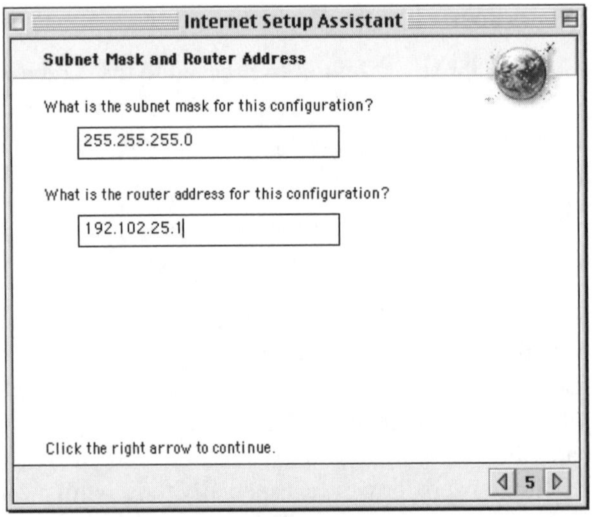

	Internet Setup Assistant	
	Subnet Mask and Router Address	

What is the subnet mask for this configuration?

    255.255.255.0

What is the router address for this configuration?

    192.102.25.1|

Click the right arrow to continue.

◁ 5 ▷

FIGURE 3-13   Set up your subnet mask and router's IP address

15. Next, you need to enter the IP address of the router, or default gateway, that connects the portion of the Internet your Mac is located on to the rest of the Internet. Once you enter both of these numbers, click the right arrow to move on to the next step in the configuration.

16. IEA now asks you to enter the IP addresses of the Domain Name Servers (DNS servers) you plan to use to match the names of servers on the Internet with their IP addresses. Without a DNS server, your Mac is unable to match the name, such as www.apple.com, with the server's IP address that you must use to connect to it over the Internet. In the dialog box you see in Figure 3-14, enter the IP addresses of the DNS servers provided by your ISP. While some ISPs provide this information automatically, many do not, and you must set them here.

NOTE   *You can enter the IP addresses for up to ten DNS servers, each one on its own line. Once you enter all the DNS servers you want, enter the name of the domain by which your ISP is known. While this is optional, it makes locating servers, like your mail server, at your ISP a bit faster. Once you finish configuring your DNS servers and domain name, click the right arrow to move to the next step.*

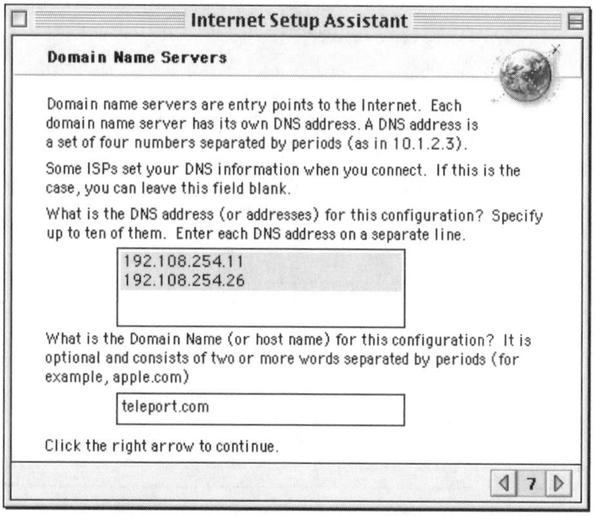

Internet Setup Assistant

Internet Setup Assistant

Domain Name Servers

Domain name servers are entry points to the Internet. Each domain name server has its own DNS address. A DNS address is a set of four numbers separated by periods (as in 10.1.2.3).

Some ISPs set your DNS information when you connect. If this is the case, you can leave this field blank.

What is the DNS address (or addresses) for this configuration? Specify up to ten of them. Enter each DNS address on a separate line.

    192.108.254.11
    192.108.254.26

What is the Domain Name (or host name) for this configuration? It is optional and consists of two or more words separated by periods (for example, apple.com)

    teleport.com

Click the right arrow to continue.

◁ 7 ▷

FIGURE 3-14   Enter your DNS server addresses and domain name

17. The next information you are asked to provide is your e-mail address and the password you use to log in to the mail server. Figure 3-15 displays an example. This information is strictly optional and you needn't enter it if you choose not to do so. If you do enter this information, however, e-mail programs, such as Outlook Express 5.0, can configure themselves using it. Enter your e-mail address in the space provided at the top of the dialog box, and then type your password in the space provided below your e-mail address. Once you enter these two pieces of information, click the right arrow to proceed to the next portion of the IEA.

18. IEA now asks you about the actual e-mail account assigned to you by your ISP and the mail server where you mail is stored. Your e-mail account is different from your e-mail address: it contains the full name of your mail server instead of only the domain name of your ISP. For example, your e-mail address might be jdoe@teleport.com, while your e-mail account is jdoe@mail.teleport.com.

19. Next, you want to enter the name of the mail server that receives your e-mail from the Internet. After setting your e-mail account and mail server information, click the right arrow to set up your newsgroups server.

FIGURE 3-15   Type your e-mail address and password in this dialog box

20. The next item IEA asks you to configure is the server you plan to use to read Internet newsgroups. These newsgroups contain messages from all over the world, covering nearly every topic under the sun. In this portion of the Internet setup, you are asked to enter the name of the server that contains the newsgroups at your ISP. In the space provided, type the name of the newsgroups' server to which you plan to connect at your ISP. Once you type in the name of your newsgroups, click the right arrow to proceed to the next step in your Internet configuration.

NOTE *Some ISPs, such as EarthLink, also require you to enter your user name and password to gain access to their newsgroup servers. This is being done to prevent the servers from being bombarded with junk e-mail and other unsavory messages.*

21. As a final step, IEA asks if your Mac connects to the Internet through a proxy server or a firewall. If your Mac does connect to the Internet through a proxy server or a firewall, click the Yes radio button. Next, click the right arrow to go to the dialog box where you can set up your Mac to access the Internet through the proxy server or the firewall. If you do not use a proxy server or a firewall, click the No radio button, and then click the right arrow to go to the final setup dialog box.

22. As shown in Figure 3-16, enter the IP address of the proxy server or firewall you plan to use, along with the port number the firewall is set up to use. Once you do this, click the check boxes for the different network protocols you will send through the proxy server or firewall.

NOTE *IEA enables you to specify different proxy servers or firewalls for http—Web browsers—Gopher, an older version of the World Wide Web, and FTP. All other network traffic to and from the Internet is directed through the proxy. Once you set up your proxy server or firewall settings, click the right arrow to go to the final step of the setup process.*

CAUTION *Setting up a connection to the Internet through a proxy server or firewall is not a trivial task. If you don't have all this information at hand, contact the people in your company or organization responsible for the set up and maintenance of your network's Internet connection.*

Internet Setup Assistant

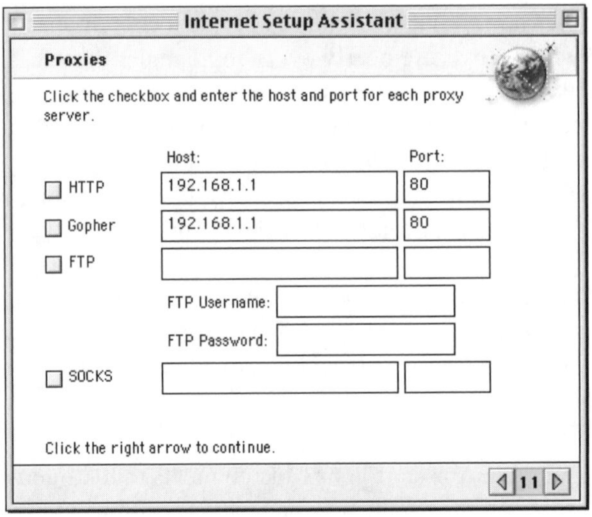

FIGURE 3-16   Enter your proxy-related information on this screen

23. Finally, IEA asks if you want to save all the settings you made during the
setup procedure. If you want to save all the settings you entered, click the
button labeled Go Ahead. For those of you using a modem to connect to
your ISP, the check box labeled Connect when finished is available for you
to select. If you select this option, your Mac dials your ISP and connects
you to the Internet upon quitting the IEA.

Simplified System Setups

Unlike the PC world where you can set up a PC to boot from a file server and
download all the user settings from a central server, Mac users are not so lucky.
Some modern Macs, like the iMac, the Blue & White G3s, and the new G4, can
boot from a Mac OS X and download the system preferences. While this is
a workable solution, it still leaves much to be desired.

Now with Mac OS 9, Apple has given you the ability to store multiple user
configurations on the same Mac. Using the keychain and the options you can set
up in the Multiple Users Control Panel, you can store such critical information
as a user name and passwords, as well as other settings that are specific to them.
While you cannot customize all the settings for each user, as you can on the PC

using Windows NT or Windows 2000, the capabilities provided by Mac OS 9 are a major step in this direction. This subject is covered in more detail in Chapter 6.

Summing Up

Setting up Mac OS 9 using the Setup Assistant and the Internet Setup Assistant makes configuring your Mac's user and network settings easy. Using the Mac OS Setup Assistant, you can set all the most critical settings on your Mac in only a few minutes, enabling you to get up and running. Likewise, using the Internet Setup Assistant, you can arrange to find a local Internet service provider to enable you to connect to the Internet or, if you already have an Internet connection, configure your Mac to use it.

By walking you through each step of the setup process, the Setup Assistant and the Internet Setup Assistant make the task of configuring your Mac to suit your needs a bit simpler and they make an already easy-to-use computer that much easier.

The subject of system setups is covered in more detail in Chapter 4. You learn how to set Finder preferences and how to adjust various Control Panel settings, such as synchronizing your Mac's menu bar clock, adjusting mouse-tracking speed, and activating the Launcher at every startup.

Summing Up

Chapter 4

Exploring the Mac OS 9 Finder

When you run your Mac, one application is working all the time, even when you aren't running a single program. That application is the Finder.

The *Finder* is the interface you use when working on your Mac to perform the daily tasks of moving files, starting applications, and anything else you do outside an application. Like the rest of the Mac OS, the Finder has evolved from its rather primitive beginnings to the version we see in Mac OS 9. The present-day Mac Finder bears little resemblance to the Finder that first appeared in Mac OS 1.0 back in 1984. The Finder now has many additional features and much greater functionality than the previous versions.

Configuring the Mac OS 9 Finder

Configuring the Mac OS 9 Finder to suit your specific needs is an easy task. To start setting up the Finder the way you want, click the Edit menu, and then select Preferences from the list of options. The Preferences dialog box displays a number of options that control the look of Finder actions and display. You start by selecting one of the three tabs, each of which is covered in the following sections.

The General Tab

Looking at the General Preferences dialog box you see in Figure 4-1, you can chose from three basic options to customize the way the Finder behaves. The first option in the dialog box enables you to use the Simple Finder option. The second option you can modify enables you to enable or disable Spring-loaded folders and then to set the way they behave. In the third option, you can set the way files and folders are spaced in a folder or on the desktop.

The first option you want to look at is the Simple Finder option. Clicking the check box for Simple Finder causes the Finder to reduce the number of functions drastically that are made available to the user. All but the most critical functions from the Simple Finder are removed.

For example, in the File menu of the Mac OS 9 Finder, you can select from 16 different commands (see Figure 4-2). Under Simple Finder, however, only five options are available to you in the File menu (see Figure 4-3). Simple Finder reduces the commands available to the user to only those that are absolutely necessary for opening, closing, and manipulating files and folders. While Simple Finder does make the Finder easier to use for a novice user, by limiting the commands available, it tends to make the process more difficult for an experienced user.

Now you want to look at the next option, the Spring-loaded feature present in Mac OS 9. *Spring-loaded folders* enable you to drag a file or folder on top of a

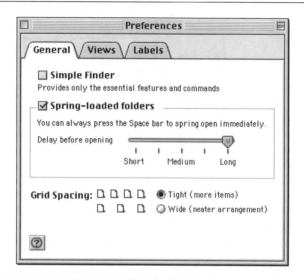

FIGURE 4-1   You can set the general Finder options from this dialog box

FIGURE 4-2   The Finder's File menu is in its normal configuration

FIGURE 4-3   The Finder's File menu is now in Simple Finder mode

folder and, when you hold the mouse cursor above it, the folder pops open, revealing all the items stored within it (including nested folders). This enables you to drag a file on top of a folder and have it pop open enabling you to place the file in a folder located on a lower level.

You can use the slider bar under the Spring-loaded feature to set the amount of time you need to hold the file or folder on top of the folder before it will spring open. If you want your folders to spring open fairly quickly, then move the slider to the left. Otherwise, move the slider so it resides in the middle. If you want a long delay before the folder opens, drag it all the way to the right. To turn this feature off, uncheck the check box labeled Spring-loaded folders.

The last option you can configure in this portion of the Finder Preferences is Grid Spacing. Grid Spacing works when you look at files and folders in the Icon and Button views. If you like a denser view, where your icons are grouped closely together, then click the radio button labeled Tight (this is the default setting). If you prefer a looser look for your files, you can click the radio button labeled Wide. This causes the icons in your folders and on the desktop to be spaced more widely apart than they would if you chose the Tight option. While this option may not seem all that important to you, it can make a real difference in the way you look at files when you use the Icon and Button view in the Finder.

The Views Preferences

Once you finish setting the Finder preferences in the General Preferences dialog box, click the tab labeled Views to switch over to the Views Preferences. Check the various options you can adjust to customize the way your Mac presents your files. Looking over the options available, you can configure the way the Finder displays the three different file views available to you: icons, buttons, and list.

TIP   *Another way to open the Views Preferences dialog box is to click the Views menu, and then select View Options from the list of commands. This brings up a modified version of the Views Preferences for the view setting you are currently using. For example, if you have a window that displays all its files in List mode, then you see all the preferences you can set for the List view. Unfortunately, unlike using the Views Preferences portion of the Finder Preferences dialog box, you cannot switch between the Preference dialog boxes for the different views.*

In the Views dialog box, click the pop-up menu labeled Standard View Options for: and then select the view you want. To begin, click the pop-up menu and select the options for the Icon view. The dialog box shown in Figure 4-4 displays two different options you can change. The first option you can set is the arrangement of the icons located in a folder or on your desktop. If you want your icons to stay where you put them, then you want to click the button labeled None. This tells the Mac OS not to move the icon around unless you explicitly tell it to do so by using a Clean Up or Arrange by command in the Finder.

If you want your icons to be neatly arranged when you place them in a folder or on the desktop, then you can choose to have the icons snapped to a grid so they are nicely arranged in your folder. Or, you can click the button labeled Keep

FIGURE 4-4   The Finder's icon arrangement is set from this dialog box

arranged, and then select what criteria you want to use when arranging the files. You can arrange your files and folders by their name, the date they were created or modified, their size, the kind of file, or by the label you attached to them.

Next, you have the chance to select the size of the icon you will see when using the Icon view. You can select between two sizes: The larger icon is the default value for the icon view; the smaller icon enables you to pack more icons on the screen.

To change the way you see things in the Button view, click the "Standard View Options" pop-up menu and then select Buttons from the list of options. The dialog box that you see in Figure 4-5 displays the options that you can configure to customize the way that the Finder displays files and folders in the Button view. From this dialog box, you can choose the way the buttons are arranged in your folders and on your desktop as well as the size of the button that is displayed.

The first option in this dialog box gives you three button arrangement choices. The first option is to leave the buttons as you place them in the folder or on your desktop. This radio button, labeled None, says the Finder should not move the buttons from where you place them in a folder or on the desktop unless you use the Clean Up or Arrange commands to reorganize them. This is the default value for the Finder when you first install Mac OS 9.

FIGURE 4-5   Set up the view options for the Button view in this Preferences dialog box

The second and third options have the Finder rearranging the buttons as you place them in a folder or on your desktop. The second radio button, labeled Always snap to grid, moves the button so it is perfectly aligned with an invisible grid the Finder uses to keep things nice and neat. The third radio button, labeled Keep arranged, enables you to have the Finder arrange the buttons by their name, the date they were created or modified, their size, the type of file they represent, or by the label you have assigned to the button.

Next, you can choose between using a full-sized button to represent the files and folders in the Finder or you can use a smaller button. Look at the two button sizes represented in the dialog box, and then click the radio button connected to the size of the button you want to see. The default value for the button view is the large button.

> NOTE   *You'll observe that the Button view provides the same effect as the buttons on the Launcher, or when using the Panel's user setting established with Mac OS 9's Multiple Users feature (see Chapter 6 for more information).*

The last view you can set options for is the List view. Click the pop-up menu labeled Standard View Options for: and select List from the options available. The dialog box displayed in Figure 4-6 shows various options you can use to customize

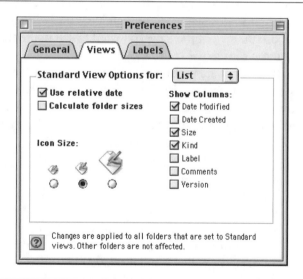

FIGURE 4-6   You can set the various List view options from this dialog box

the List view. This dialog box enables you to decide how you want to calculate file dates, and if you want to calculate the size of the folders in the folder and the size of the icons to be displayed in the list. You can also set the columns and contents shown in the List view for each file.

The first option you should look at is Use relative date. This option tells the Finder to display the date a file was created or modified in a relative format, rather than a strict calendar date. What this means is that dates are displayed in relation to the current date. For example, instead of displaying today's date, the Finder says the file was created or modified Today or Yesterday. Older files display the standard calendar date.

The second option you want to look at is the option to Calculate folder sizes. This option tells the Finder to calculate the size of all the files and folders contained by the folder that is located in the folder at which you are looking. If you have a large number of folders and files located under the folder you are looking at, then this option can become a serious drain on your Mac's performance. This is because the Finder must go through all those files and folders to calculate the space they consume. Normally, this option is left off to improve the Finder's speed. But, if you are working on folders where you need to know how much space each one consumes, then this option is quite useful, at least while you are doing this sort of work. After you finish, you can turn off this option.

Next, in the dialog box are the settings that enable you to set the size of the icons in the List view. You can choose between a small icon, a slightly larger icon, and a full-sized icon. Choose the size of the icon you want to see in the List view by clicking the radio button next to the icon size you want.

Finally, look at the right-hand portion of this dialog box and see the columns you can display in the List view. The Finder is capable of displaying up to eight columns, including the name of the file. By choosing the check boxes in the Preferences dialog box, you can display columns that have information regarding a file or folder creation date, modification date, file size, and the type of file. You can also add columns to the display that provide information regarding the label you applied to the file, along with any comments, and an application and version number.

The default settings for the Finder have the date modified, the size of the file, and what kind of file is being displayed when you open a window set to the List view. A key thing to remember when setting up the columns to be displayed in the List view is that too much information is as bad as too little. In other words, setting the preferences so all the columns are displayed can make you spend extra time scrolling right and left in a window to retrieve information you want to see because of the space taken up by information you don't want.

> TIP
>
> *Another way to organize an open Finder list window is to click, drag, and then drop columns to a new position. This enables you, for example, to place the Size column ahead of the Date Modified column. The width of columns can also be changed by clicking at the edge of a column title, and then dragging back and forth to resize it. The changes, however, apply strictly to that window, and not to others.*

The Labels Preferences

One of the nicer features in the Finder for those of us who are organizationally challenged is the capability to label files and folders with different colors. You can configure the colors of the labels and the names associated with each label. To see the current settings for the different labels, click the Labels tab in the Preferences dialog box. After you click the Labels tab, you see a list of all seven labels, along with their colors and the text descriptions associated with them.

The dialog box that appears in Figure 4-7 shows the color and text tied to each of the seven labels available to you in the Finder. From this dialog box, you can change both the color and the text you associate with a given label. To change a label color, click the colored button for the label that you want to change. Then,

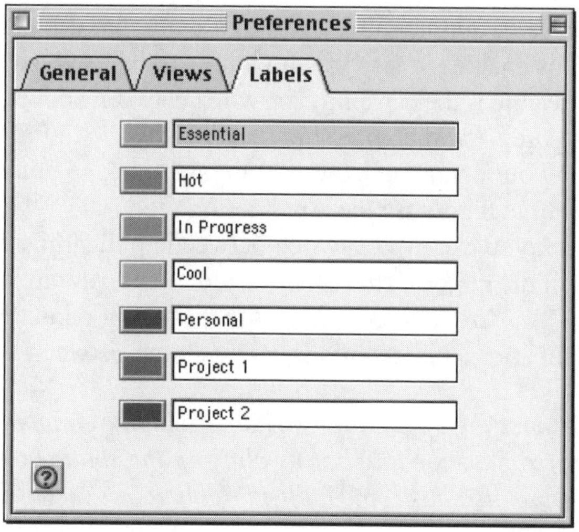

FIGURE 4-7   You can configure Finder Labels from this dialog box

from the color picker displayed, choose the color you want to use with this label. Once you select the proper color, click OK to choose the color and have it applied to the Label. Changing the text tied to a label is also simple. Highlight the text in the text box located to the right of the colored button, and then type in the text you want to use with the label. Once you finish configuring the colors and text used with each label, click the close box to save the Finder Preferences.

> TIP   *You can also perform Finder searches by label using Mac OS 9's Sherlock 2 search tool. You learn more about Sherlock 2 in Chapter 7.*

Finder Hints

The Mac OS 9 Finder has many different features you can use to make your life easier and yourself more productive. From using the control key to bring up the Finder's Contextual menu, to the simple act of double-clicking the title bar of a window to collapse it, you can use many simple tricks to make use of the Finder easier. Some of these tricks are quite simple, others are a bit more complex, but all of them are easy to use and remember.

One of the most useful tricks to use when you have a cluttered desktop is collapsing your open Windows so only the title bar remains. Like the old Windows Shade program, you can set an option in the Options Tab of the Appearance control panel that enables you to double-click a window's title bar or collapse box and have it collapse. This enables you to free up more space on your desktop.

Another useful feature is the capability to switch between applications by holding down the Command key and then pressing the Tab key. With this shortcut, you can switch between your open applications, one at a time, so you can change applications without having to use the Application menu.

Still another trick you can use to switch between applications is to click the Application menu in the upper-right corner of the menu bar and then drag it down onto your desktop. You are then presented with a floating menu (see Figure 4-8) listing all your applications and enabling you to switch between them easily.

> TIP   *You can dismiss the application switcher window simply by clicking the close box or reduce the title bar by clicking the shade box at the right of the title. Apple also has some built-in application switcher shortcuts in its Help menu. Go to the Finder, choose Mac Help from the Help menu, and search for "application switcher." You might be surprised at how many ways the switcher window can be changed.*

FIGURE 4-8   Mac OS 9's application switcher

Perhaps the most useful option you can use in the Mac OS 9 Finder is Contextual menus. By holding down the Control key and then clicking the mouse on a file, folder, volume, or open space in a window, or on the desktop, you bring up a menu that contains all the available commands (see Figure 4-9). You can use this menu to perform all the functions you would normally have to use for either the Finder's menu bar or the keyboard shortcut; additional items are added when you install some system utilities. Because you only see those commands that are available for the item on which you have clicked, you needn't worry about trying a command that is unavailable for this type of item.

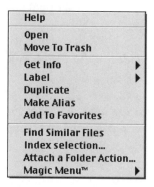

FIGURE 4-9   The Contextual menu you see depends on the item you Control-click

Finder Hints

TIP *Windows users should find the feature reminiscent of the right-mouse menu. Apple isn't against copying a feature when it makes sense, and this one is most useful.*

CAUTION *Not all applications support Contextual menus. A fast way to check is to Control-click a window displaying an open document and to see whether one appears.*

Keyboard Shortcuts in the Finder

Unlike Windows or UNIX, which rely on you to use the keyboard when entering many commands, the Mac relies on you to use the mouse and the various menus provided by the Finder to control your Mac. While many Mac functions are controlled by your mouse, you can access many of the commands and controls available in the Finder by using the keyboard. These keyboard shortcuts enable you to perform certain functions without having to select the command from the menu under which it is located.

As you may suspect, the Finder's File menu has both the largest number of commands from which you can choose, along with the greatest number of keyboard shortcuts. Each of these shortcuts is a two- or three-key combination that begins with the Command key located on either side of the spacebar (with an apple and/or cloverleaf icon on it) along with one or more characters. For example, to close a window, hold down the Command key, and then press the *W* key. This tells the Finder you want to close the current window, just as if you had selected the Close Window command from the File menu.

The following is a list of the keyboard shortcuts you can use to replace commands in the Finder's menu:

NOTE *Finder keyboard shortcuts are disabled if you use the Simple Finder option.*

TIP *The following shortcuts are also available via Apple's Contextual menus feature; the choices you see depend on the items on which you Control-click.*

■ **Command-N (New Folder)**   This command causes the Finder to create a new folder in the window you currently have selected or, if you have no windows selected, the new folder is created on the desktop. By default, the new folder is called "untitled folder"; click the title to change it. If a folder is already named "untitled folder," then the next folder being created is called "untitled folder 1."

■ **Command-O (Open)**   This command enables you to open the highlighted volume, folder, or file. Using the shortcut for the Open command is effectively the same as double-clicking the icon of the file, folder, or volume you want to open.

■ **Command-P (Print)**   This command opens a selected document file by the application that created it or by an application that is the default application for that file type. The file is then printed. Once the document has been sent to the printer, the application that opened the file quits and you are returned to the Finder.

■ **Command-Delete (Move to Trash)**   This command moves a currently selected file or folder to the trash. COMMAND-DELETE is useful when you are working with a large number of files. Missing the trash when you are dragging-and-dropping a large number of files into it can lead to an unnecessary mess on your desktop.

■ **Command-W (Close Window)**   The active (frontmost) window is closed, the same as if you had clicked the window's close button. The Close Window command is a great way to close windows quickly without having to move your mouse all over the screen, clicking each window's close box.

TIP   *A quick way to close all the currently open windows in the Finder is to hold down the Option key, located next to the Command key, and then press the W key. This causes all the windows currently open in the Finder to close.*

■ **Command-I (Get Info)**   This command displays the General Information dialog box for the file, folder, or volume you currently have selected. If you are looking at the information on a folder or volume, then you can click the pop-up menu labeled Show and then select Sharing. If File Sharing is turned on, then you are presented with the current sharing settings for this folder or volume. If File Sharing is not currently active, you are asked if you want to open the File Sharing control panel and start it.

NOTE   *If you use the Get Info command on an application, you are presented with a third option, Memory, which enables you to set the amount of program memory dedicated to that application.*

Keyboard Shortcuts in the Finder

■ **Command-D (Duplicate)** This command creates a copy of the currently selected item. For example, if you were to click the Assistants folder to select it, and then press COMMAND-D to make a copy, you would see a new folder named Assistants copy.

■ **Command-M (Make Alias)** This command creates an alias to the file currently selected. Aliases are a useful feature in the Mac OS. They enable you to place a pointer to a useful program or file in a variety of places on your Mac without having to duplicate the file. For example, you might find it useful to keep an alias to StuffIt Deluxe on your desktop so you can easily decode or unstuff files you download from the Internet. This way, you can simply drop the files you want to unstuff on the alias and have StuffIt launch, instead of having to dig through all your folders looking for the actual StuffIt program.

■ **Command-Y (Put Away)** This command automatically ejects and dismounts the currently selected volume; it's the equivalent of dragging a disk icon to the trash. For example, if you want to drag a Zip disk to the trash, all you need to do is click the Zip disk's icon and then press COMMAND-Y. The Finder then puts away the Zip disk by dragging it into the trash.

■ **Command-F (Sherlock 2/Find)** This keystroke activates Sherlock 2, Mac OS 9's powerful search utility. Sherlock 2 can locate files on your Mac's drive, a shared volume, or the content of a file, and it can perform Internet searches. This shortcut takes you directly to the program's file search window. Enter the name of the file for which you want to search, click the magnifying glass icon, or press RETURN. Sherlock 2 does the rest. For more information on harnessing the extraordinary capabilities of Sherlock 2, please read Chapter 7.

■ **Command-H (Search Internet)** Use this command to bring up Sherlock 2's Internet search feature. As you did when searching your local Mac, enter text you want to find, and then click the magnifying glass icon or press RETURN to start the search. Chapter 7 covers Sherlock 2 in more detail.

■ **Command-R (Show Original)** This command is used when you select an alias. It brings up the original file, folder, or volume. For example, if you have an alias of *StuffIt Expander,* a file expansion program from Aladdin Systems that comes with Mac OS 9, on your desktop, click its icon and type COMMAND-R. You then see the folder that contains the original program, and the icon itself is highlighted. This is a useful command when you need to make a change to the original application.

- **Command-Z (Undo/Redo)**   This command reverses the last action you took. You only get one Undo with the Finder, although some programs, such as Microsoft Word 98, NisusWriter, Adobe Photoshop, and Adobe InDesign, offer additional undos and redos.

- **Command-X (Cut)**   This command removes the currently selected text and places it in the clipboard, a repository for items removed or copied. You can then paste the text back in or discard it by copying another item into the clipboard.

- **Command-C (Copy)**   You can use this command to make a copy of the selected text and place it in the clipboard. You can then paste the text back in somewhere else or discard it by copying a new item of text into the clipboard.

- **Command-V (Paste)**   Use this command to place or paste copies of the text into the selected text area.

- **Command A (Select A)**   This command selects all items in the current window or desktop. You can then perform group or batch operations on them all, such as applying a label, copying, moving, or dragging them to the trash.

- **Command E (Eject)**   Under Mac OS 9, this is the equivalent of the Put Away command, COMMAND-Y.

- **Command-? (Help)**   Pressing these keys brings up the Mac OS 9 help program. The help system present in Mac OS 9 is a major improvement over the help systems in previous versions of the Mac OS. Using the help system is extremely easy, with a good search system to find the topics you want, plus the capability to print fully formatted help text.

TIP   *If your Mac has an extended style keyboard, you can also access the Help menu by pressing the HELP key.*

- **esc (Escape)**   This key, located in the upper left-hand corner of the keyboard, is used to cancel operations and dialog boxes. For example, if you are looking at a dialog box that has a cancel button, you can press the ESC key to cancel the dialog box.

Once you get used to using these keyboard shortcuts, you will wonder how you ever got along without them. By concentrating more on the task at hand and less on repeatedly going to the menu bar to select the commands you want, you can significantly increase your productivity when using your Mac.

Keyboard Shortcuts in the Finder

Simple Control Panel Setups

While the Finder is the primary interface you want to configure, several Control Panels can be configured to suit your needs better. In the next section, you learn about the basic options you can set with these Control Panels and how they impact the way your Mac works.

> **NOTE** *This list doesn't cover all the Control Panels on your Mac. For example, Apple includes two Control Panels, CloseView and EasyAccess, to provide easier mouse and keyboard navigation for disabled users. You can find coverage of iBook and PowerBook Control Panels in Chapter 12 and Chapter 13, and the Appearance Control Panel in Chapter 25.*

Each of these Control Panels can be easily accessed via the Control Panels submenu in the Apple menu.

Apple Menu Options

Apple Menu Options is the control panel that turns folders located in the Apple menu into submenus you can browse. The Apple Menu Options dialog box you see in Figure 4-10 can be switched on and off. In addition, you can indicate how

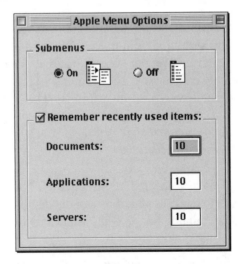

FIGURE 4-10   Apple Menu Options enables you to configure the number of recently used files, applications, and servers

many recently used files, applications, and server hookups you want to display. As you open and close documents and applications, they appear in one of these submenus for fast access. Once the number of items exceeds what you specify, the older items are automatically deleted.

TIP   *To get the best possible performance from Apple Menu Options, a good idea is to limit the number of servers listed to the actual number of Macs you intend to share on your network.*

Date and Time

The Date and Time Control Panel controls the way time and dates are handled by your Mac. In addition to the menu bar clock, this information is also needed to time stamp files, folders, and your e-mail. This Control Panel, as shown in Figure 4-11, is used to set a number of data and time parameters on your Mac, along with the format the Mac uses when displaying them. Here are the choices available through this Control Panel:

■ **Current Date**   This option enables you to change the date displayed on your newly created or saved documents or updated programs. Just click the

FIGURE 4-11   The Date and Time Control Panel can be set to synchronize your Mac's clock automatically via the Internet

month, day, or year, and enter the change or use the scrolling arrows to change a selected item.

- ■ **Date Formats**   Use this to change the standard month, date, or year format to your preference or to conform to a non-U.S.A. style.

- ■ **Current Time**   Use this option to change the time displayed on your Mac's menu bar or in your newly saved documents or updated programs. To change the time, click the hours, minutes, seconds, or the A.M./P.M. display, and enter or use the scrolling items to change the item.

- ■ **Time Zone**   Click **Set Time Zone** to change the city used as the basis for your time zone. If your city isn't shown, select a nearby city in the same zone. Check Set Daylight-Saving Time Automatically to compensate for the twice-yearly change. You can uncheck this for the few U.S. locales (such as Arizona and Indiana) that do not observe daylight saving time.

- ■ **Use a Network Time Server**   This is one of the most useful Mac OS 9 features. It allows your Mac to log onto the Internet or a networked server, and it synchronizes your Mac's clock to that setting. When you click the **Server Options** button, you have a choice of having the settings changed automatically or at specified intervals.

- ■ **Menu Bar Clock**   Click the appropriate radio button to switch the clock on or off (it still calculates the correct time, regardless of whether the menu bar clock appears). The **Clock Options** button enables you to change the font used to display the time, as well as whether the display includes day and seconds. You can also set the Menu Bar Clock to chime at regular intervals, using the sound you select.

Energy Saver

The *Energy Saver Control Panel* enables you to set the time your Mac will wait when it's idle before it shuts down or goes into sleep mode, provided your Mac is capable of sleeping. This applies to nearly all Macs except the first-generation Power Mac models.

Figure 4-12 displays a slider bar that sets the idle time interval for sleeping or shut down. Energy Saver also enables you to set a schedule your Mac can use to start up and shut down automatically.

You can also set separate intervals for display and hard disk sleep modes by clicking the **Show Details** button, which adds an expanded view.

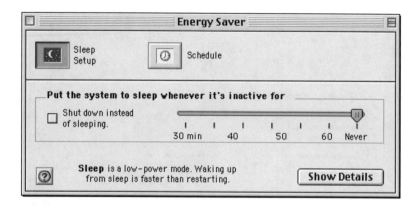

FIGURE 4-12 Energy Saver enables you to have your Mac shut down when it's not in use

Simple Control Panel Setups

NOTE *When you use an Apple iBook or PowerBook, you see two Energy Saver options, available via a pop-up menu, just above the slider settings. One is AC Adapter and the other is Battery. Apple's laptop computers are covered in more detail in Chapters 12 and 13.*

General Controls

General Controls directs a variety of Finder-related functions. This Control Panel sets the way desktop backdrop appears upon startup, how fast the cursor blinks, where an application should look for files, and if you should be warned when your Mac is started up after a crash. The dialog box displayed in Figure 4-13 shows the available options.

General Controls includes the following options:

- **Desktop** This option displays whether the desktop items are displayed when you are using another application.

- **Launcher** This option displays Apple's Launcher application and document-launching utility, which displays these items with single-click buttons.

- **Shut-Down Warning** If your Mac wasn't shut down properly, or you had to force a restart, Apple's Disk First Aid checks your startup drive after restart and attempts to repair any drive directory problems it finds.

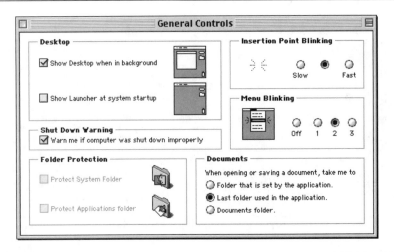

FIGURE 4-13   General Controls handles all the options that are not dealt with elsewhere

CAUTION   *Since the disk scan is limited to your startup volume, you'll want to run Disk First Aid manually on other mounted volumes (if available) to check for possible directory damage after a forced restart.*

- **Folder Protection**   This option is no longer available because Apple's Multiple User feature offers additional choices to protect various items on your Mac's drive.

- **Insertion Point Blinking**   This option sets the speed at which the insertion point blinks in a text box.

- **Menu Blinking**   When you choose a menu command, this setting adjusts the rate at which it blinks.

- **Documents**   You can decide where the Finder will take you when you use the Open or Save dialog box. You can use the folder set by a program, the last folder used by the application, or your Documents folder.

Keyboard

Mac OS 9's Keyboard Control Panel (see Figure 4-14) performs several functions. First, it enables you to choose keyboard layouts for different languages. You can also set key repeat and delay rates, so if you press and hold any key, the same keystroke is repeated until you release the key.

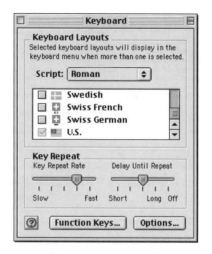

FIGURE 4-14   Set keyboard layout and repeat functions here

And second, if your Mac supports the feature (many models released before 1998 do not), you can create special shortcuts for your Mac's Function Keys. Here's how it's done:

1. Click the Function Keys button at the bottom of the Keyboard Control Panel window, which brings Hot Function Keys screen (see Figure 4-15).

2. Click a button that represents the function key you want to modify.

3. An Open dialog box appears next. Here, locate and select an application or document you want to assign to that keystroke.

4. Click the Assign key to dismiss the Open dialog box and to add the shortcut.

TIP   *You can also drag-and-drop an item to a box to assign it a shortcut key.*

5. If you are working with one of the few programs that use the function keys, click the Function Key Settings check box at the bottom of the screen. This setting requires you to press the OPTION key at the same time you press a shortcut key to activate the function.

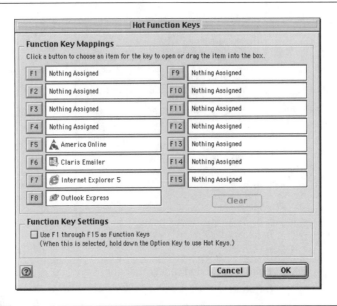

FIGURE 4-15 Click a button, which then assigns a program or document to the Hot
Function Keys

6. When you finish adding shortcuts, click OK to store the shortcut settings,
   and then dismiss the Keyboard Control Panel. From here on, when you
   press the function key (along with the OPTION key, if necessary), it opens
   whatever item it has been assigned.

*The Keyboard Control Panel knows whether your Mac's keyboard has 12
or 15 function keys. If you plan to switch from a larger, extended keyboard
to the smaller Apple USB keyboard, you might want to think twice about
adding the additional shortcuts.*

Memory

As its name implies, the Memory Control Panel (see Figure 4-16) enables you to
determine how both virtual memory and your Mac's disk cache are handled.

Here are the settings you can make:

■ **Disk Cache**   Apple's disk cache sets aside a part of your Mac's built-in
memory to store recently accessed data from the hard drive. This can result
in faster Finder performance. This also allows applications to launch faster

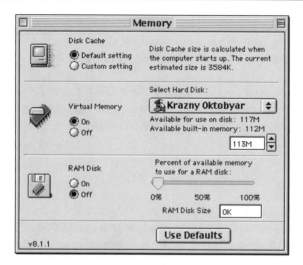

| FIGURE 4-16 | Memory enables you to set up your Mac's memory options |

the second, and subsequent times, you open them. The first radio button, Default setting, establishes a disk cache of 32K per MB of installed RAM. This automatically increases when you add RAM to your Mac. Click Custom setting to change the Default setting.

■ **Virtual Memory**   Virtual memory sets aside a part of your hard drive to simulate RAM. Because RAM is much faster than a hard drive, this can result in somewhat slower performance if you set it too high. But Mac OS 9 has a pretty efficient virtual memory feature. If you set the virtual memory feature to the standard 1MB above your built-in RAM (such as 65MB, total, for a Mac with 64MB of RAM), it should provide the maximum benefit. Another advantage of virtual memory: Applications that are in PowerPC code, which represents nearly all the programs you are apt to use, run with a smaller memory footprint when virtual memory is on.

NOTE   *If your Mac has less than 64MB of RAM, virtual memory is set at that level automatically because of the requirements of Mac OS 9.*

■ **RAM Disk**   The RAM Disk sets aside a portion of RAM to simulate an ultra-fast hard drive. You can use a RAM disk if your Mac has plenty of RAM and you want to maximize performance from an Internet cache or a frequently used program. But remember, whatever setting you make to the RAM Disk is subtracted from the built-in memory available to your Mac. This adjustment is made with the slider after activating the RAM Disk or by entering the size manually in the text field.

CAUTION   *While it's normal for the contents of the RAM disk to be saved to your hard drive when you shut down, if your Mac crashes, you can lose the contents of your RAM disk. My personal recommendation is that you leave this feature off.*

Mouse

The Mouse control panel, shown in Figure 4-17, enables you to set how fast your mouse moves on the screen, as well as how fast you need to double-click the mouse button for the Mac to open a file (or to perform any other action that would normally be done by double-clicking).

NOTE   *If you have an iBook or a PowerBook, you can use the Trackpad Control Panel to set tracking and double-click speeds (unless you also installed a regular mouse, joystick, or trackball). In addition, some third-party input devices, from companies such as Kensington and Microsoft, use their own software to set tracking and double-click values.*

FIGURE 4-17   Mouse enables you to decide how fast your mouse runs

Monitors

The Monitors Control Panel tells your Mac what type of video display you want to use. In the dialog box you see in Figure 4-18, you can set the screen resolution the Mac is to use, along with the color depth. To set the proper screen resolution and refresh rate for your monitor, select it from the list of recommended resolutions presented in the dialog box. If the resolution you want is not present, click the menu labeled Show, and then select All to see all the possible resolutions your Mac can support. Likewise, to set the color depth, simply choose the number of colors you want from the list of those available.

Numbers

The Numbers control panel, shown in Figure 4-19, enables you to set the numeric format that your Mac uses when displaying numbers. You can set the regional format in which numbers are to be displayed, or you can change the character used as the thousands separator and the character used as the decimal point. You can also set the symbol used to denote your national currency.

Sound

The Sound Control Panel (see Figure 4-20) enables you to select and add system alert sounds and other sound-related options under Mac OS 9.

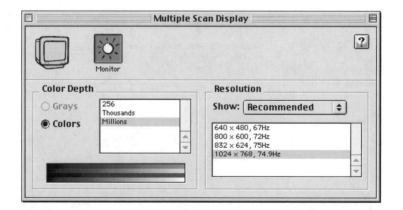

FIGURE 4-18   Monitors enables you decide what resolution your screen displays

Simple Control Panel Setups

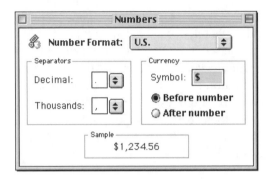

FIGURE 4-19 Numbers enables you to set how your Mac displays numeric values

NOTE *If you are upgrading from earlier versions of the Mac OS, note the Sound Control Panel used to be combined with the Monitor's Control Panel, available by a clickable icon.*

Here are the sound choices available under Mac OS 9. Click the item at the left of Figure 4-20 to select the setup screen:

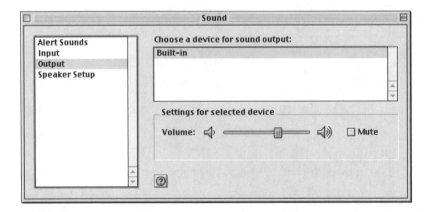

FIGURE 4-20 Choose Alert Sounds and other parameters from the Sound Control Panel

■ **Alert Sounds**   Choose a sound from a scrolling list for announcing alerts on your Mac. You can also use a Mac's mike or audio input (such as a CD) to record a custom alert sound.

■ **Input**   Use this settings panel to pick your Mac's input options, such as a mike or CD.

■ **Output**   Use this settings panel to adjust the volume of the input source.

■ **Speaker Setup**   Depending on the capabilities of the speaker system that comes with your Mac, you can use this setting to balance the stereo output or to select custom surround options, such as SRS surround sound.

Text

Another Control Panel that has its greatest value outside the U.S., *the Text Control Panel,* shown in Figure 4-21, enables you to set the script used when displaying text, as well as the way the text behaves. This does not set the font you use; it sets the character set you will use.

Summing Up

In this chapter, you discovered some of the flexibility of the Mac OS Finder. In the next chapter, you learn more about desktop management and how to use the various flavors of Open and Save dialog boxes.

FIGURE 4-21   Text enables you to set how your Mac displays text

Chapter 5

Secrets of Desktop Management

Once you finish installing Mac OS 9 and configuring the Finder and the rest of the operating system the way you like, it's time to start using it.

In this chapter, you learn about using the Finder to move your files, as well as all the tricks to make using your Mac OS 9 that much easier. You discover the differences between the various views you can use to set up the way you view the files located in your folders and on the desktop. You also learn some of the more interesting features of the Mac OS 9 Finder, such as the Contextual menus, customizing the Apple menu, and the simple Finder option. Finally, you find out some neat ways to organize your Mac's desktop.

Appearance Control Panel

Starting with Mac OS 8, Apple introduced users to a new desktop enhancement tool called the Appearance Control Panel. The features were greatly expanded beginning with Mac OS 8.5.

The *Appearance Control Panel* enables you to pick or create a theme for your Mac by changing the colors and pictures used for background display, the color of progress bars, the colors of highlighted text, and the fonts used by the Finder. The Appearance Control Panel can also change the way your scroll bars behave and if your window rolls up (collapses) when you double-click on it. You can even download new themes that dramatically change the way the Finder looks to you.

To open the Appearance Control Panel, click the Apple menu and scroll down to the Control Panels. Then, from the submenu that appears off to the right of the Apple menu, select Appearance from the list of Control Panels.

As shown in Figure 5-1, the Appearance Control Panel has six tabs you can click to control different parts of the Mac OS 9 interface. The tab you see first is the one you looked at last. If you're opening the Appearance Control Panel for the first time, you should be looking at the tab labeled Themes. Otherwise, click that tab.

Mac OS 9 comes with a variety of predesigned themes that provide a good range of desktop makeover motifs. Each of these themes contains a specific combination of background colors and patterns, highlight colors, and variations used for progress bars and controls. In addition to the colors and patterns used, you can choose the fonts that will be used when displaying text items, like a filename or a folder name,

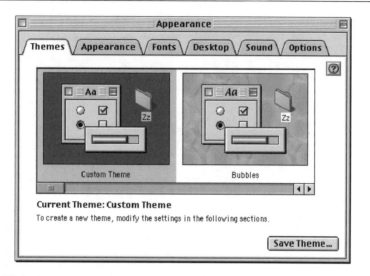

FIGURE 5-1	Choose a Theme to use for your Mac

and the sounds associated with specific Finder actions. To create a new theme using the Appearance Control Panel, follow these steps:

1. Open the Appearance Control Panel and click the Appearance tab, as shown in Figure 5-2. Click the Appearance menu to select the Appearance you want. Mac OS 9 ships with only the Apple Platinum Appearance module. Other Appearance modules are available for downloading from a variety of sites around the Internet.

2. Next, choose the color for highlighted text (your hard-working author prefers azul or lavender). You should choose a color that is light enough so you can read any text you have highlighted. Using a dark color or one with a high opacity can make reading highlighted text impossible.

3. Once you choose the highlight color, you want to select the Variation color. This is the color to be used when highlighting controls and for such items as progress bars.

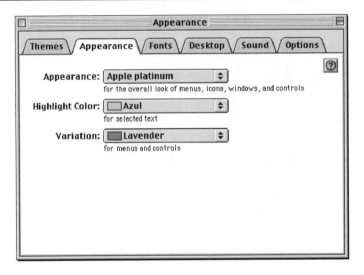

FIGURE 5-2   Choose the Colors you want to use for your windows and highlights

4. Now, click the Fonts tab, shown in Figure 5-3, to select the fonts you plan to use with the Theme you are creating. To set the font to be used for all your menus and headings, click the Large System Font menu and select your preferred font from the list. This should be a readable font because it will be the one you see whenever you look at a menu or heading.

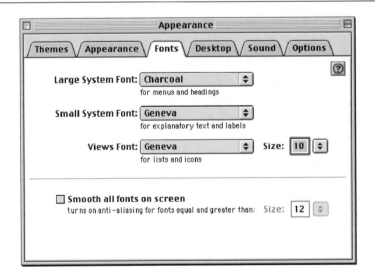

FIGURE 5-3   Choose the Fonts you want to use when looking at text in the Finder

NOTE *Not all fonts are suitable for menu and heading display, so don't expect to see more than a handful. You may find additional system fonts on the Web or AOL's software libraries.*

5. Once you have set the Large System Font, you want to choose the fonts used for explanatory text labels, as well as the font used to display the names in lists and icons. To set the font to be used for explanatory text and labels, click the Small System Font menu and select the font you want.

6. Next, click the menu labeled Views Font and select the font you want for file and folder names when looking at them in the Finder. Again, when choosing the fonts you plan to use in this view, you need to look for easy-to-read fonts, or you might spend your time squinting to read a file name or label. If you find a font that seems suitable, go ahead and try it. The font changes as soon as you select it, and you can easily switch to something else if it doesn't suit your needs.

7. After you choose the colors and fonts you want to use with this Theme, then it's time to select the background you want to use. Click the Desktop tab to bring up the Desktop dialog box, as seen in Figure 5-4. The dialog box enables you to choose between using one of the predefined desktops in the list located on the right or to using a picture for your desktop.

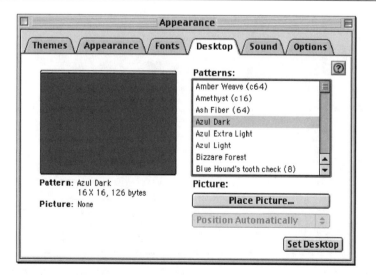

FIGURE 5-4   Select the picture or the pattern you want to use as your Desktop in your Theme

Appearance Control Panel

8. To use one of the predefined desktops that come with Mac OS 9, simply scroll through the list of available desktop designs, and then click one that looks promising. Once you click a desktop, you see a preview of what it looks like on the left-hand side of the dialog box.

9. After you select the desktop you want, simply click Set Desktop, and then proceed to the next step of creating a new Theme.

10. If you decide a picture would make the perfect desktop for your Mac, then you want to click the Place Picture button. Clicking the Place Picture button brings up the Open File dialog box you see in Figure 5-5. Use the Open File dialog box to navigate through the various folders on your Mac to locate the picture you want to use as your Desktop.

11. Once you locate the picture you want to use, click to highlight it, and then click the Preview button to see what it will look like. When you are satisfied with the picture, click the OK button. Now you are returned to the Desktop dialog box.

12. You can set how the picture is placed on the Desktop by clicking the Position Automatically menu and selecting from the options available to you. Using this menu, you can place the picture automatically, tile on screen, center on screen, scale to fit screen, and fill screen.

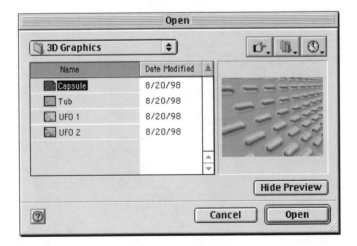

FIGURE 5-5   Set a Picture to use on the Desktop in your new Theme

NOTE

Tile on screen *means the picture will be duplicated and placed like tiles on the screen until it fills the screen.* Center on screen, *as the name implies, simply centers the picture on the screen.* Scale to fit screen *allows the Mac OS to scale the picture so it fits the screen without losing its proportions.* Fit to screen, *as the name suggests, simply stretches the picture, without regard to the original proportions, so it fits the screen.*

13. Once you set the picture and how it should be displayed, click Set Desktop, and then go on to the next step of building your theme.

14. Now, click the Sound tab to see the sounds bound to this theme. With the Sound dialog box on the screen, as shown in Figure 5-6, click the Sound Track pop-up menu to see which Sound Sets are available. Mac OS 9 ships with only the Platinum Sounds soundtrack; however, more Sound Sets are available on the Internet. Use Sherlock 2 (as described in Chapter 7) to locate them.

NOTE

Because the third-party themes are not officially endorsed by Apple, the best I can suggest is you use them with caution. If they work, fine. They are installed in the Appearance folder, inside the System Folder (in the Desktop Pictures, Sound Sets, or Themes folders). If they don't perform as you want, just remove them.

Appearance Control Panel

| FIGURE 5-6 | Choose the soundtrack you want for your Mac OS Theme |

15. When you click the Sound Track menu, you can choose between None and Platinum Sounds. Once you select a sound track like Platinum Sounds, four check boxes become available to you. These check boxes determine when your Mac should play sounds. You can choose to have sounds play when you are clicking menus or selecting items from them. Likewise, you can have your Mac sound off when you move or resize windows, click or move controls, or use the Finder to manage the files on your Mac.

NOTE   *If your Mac is located in an office environment, you may find that the sounds made when you perform these actions can disturb others, so consider reducing the volume level in the Sound Control Panel or think twice about attaching sounds to your actions.*

16. Next, look at the two options you can set to change the way your windows look and behave. Click the Options tab to display the dialog box you see in Figure 5-7.

17. The first option you can set in this dialog box is called Smart Scrolling and changes how the scroll bar is displayed and where the scrolling arrows are

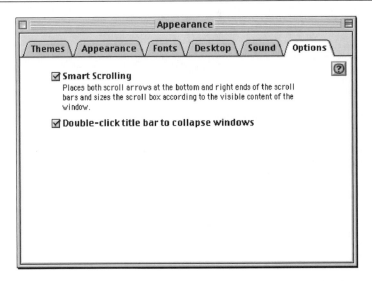

FIGURE 5-7   Set up the Smart Scrolling and Collapsible title bar options

located. Using Smart Scrolling, the scroll bar is made inversely proportional to the distance it must scroll. This means the scroll bar will be large when you only have to scroll a short distance and small when you need to scroll a long way. Smart Scrolling also moves both of the scroll arrows to the lower-right corner of the window. This makes scrolling a bit easier because you no longer must go to either the top or the bottom of the window to scroll up or down.

18. The second option you can select in this dialog box is called Double-click title bar to collapse window. Selecting this option enables you to collapse or roll up a window simply by double-clicking the window's title bar. For users with lots of open folders, this feature can be useful because it enables you to collapse unused windows without closing them.

NOTE   *The collapse window feature is a descendant of the Window Shade utility, which used to be shipped with the Mac OS. This feature began as a separate shareware program.*

19. Once you have set up the theme the way you want it, click the Themes tab once again, and then click the Save Theme button. Now name your theme and click the Save button to store it. Once you save your Theme, simply close the Appearance Control Panel.

Simple Finder

As you read in the previous chapter, one of the options you can use is called Simple Finder. Simple Finder dramatically simplifies the operation of the Finder by removing many of the functions normally available. While this makes using the Finder easier, it has the side effect of severely limiting what you can do.

To turn on the Simple Finder, follow these steps:

1. Click the Edit menu and scroll down to Preferences.

2. When the Preferences dialog box appears, click the General tab.

3. Then click the check box labeled Simple Finder.

4. Once you select Simple Finder from the Preferences dialog box, click the close box to save your changes.

Appearance Control Panel

To see the changes Simple Finder made, click the File menu and look at the options available to you. The menu you see in Figure 5-8 shows a reduced command set. With the regular Finder setup, you would have 17 commands available to you. Simple Finder limits you to only the six most basic commands and removes all the keyboard shortcuts available when you run the Finder in normal mode.

Next, look at the other menus in the Finder. Notice how the Edit menu, shown in Figure 5-9, the View menu (see Figure 5-10), and the Special menu (see Figure 5-11) are all much shorter and no longer have keyboard shortcuts associated with some of the items. All three of these menus, like the File menu, have been reduced to the bare minimums you need to use your Mac. While Simple Finder makes it easier to get used to a new Mac or Mac OS 9, the loss of the extra commands and keyboard shortcuts may become inconvenient when you begin to need those missing Finder functions.

FIGURE 5-8   The File menu under Simple Finder is much shorter

FIGURE 5-9   The Edit menu is also shorter when using Simple Finder

FIGURE 5-10   Simple Finder reduces the View menu to three commands

| FIGURE 5-11 | The Special menu also gets the Simple Finder treatment |

Contextual Menus

Contextual menus are one of the cooler features available in Mac OS 9. As you learned in the previous chapter, Contextual menus appear when you hold down the Control key and click a file or the desktop. The key point about Contextual menus is they change depending on what you are clicking. As such, clicking an alias, while holding down the Control key, brings up a menu that shows all the commands you can use when working with an alias, as you see in Figure 5-12. Likewise, clicking the Desktop while holding down the Control key brings up a menu containing all the commands you can use in the Finder to manipulate the Desktop.

NOTE   *Many programs add their own custom Contextual menus. For example, Figure 12 shows extra menu options added by Casady & Greene's Grammarian and Aladdin's Magic Menu. Depending on the extra software you have installed on your Mac, you might see other menu commands related to those programs.*

Contextual Menus

| FIGURE 5-12 | Clicking an alias brings up this Centextual menu |

NOTE *Contextual menus are similar in form and function to the right-mouse menus available under Microsoft Windows.*

Check the menu shown in Figure 5-13. When you click a file icon while holding down the Control key, you see a menu containing all the Finder commands you can use with that file. In addition to the Finder commands you can use with the item you clicked, any other utility residing in Finder's menu bar is included in the list of available commands.

When you CONTROL-click a folder, you see a menu similar to the one shown in Figure 5-14. Notice how the commands available to you have changed to reflect that you are clicking a folder, rather than a file or an alias to a file. When you look at the two menus, notice how the Encrypt command is only available when you click a File and not when you click a folder.

Likewise, CONTROL-clicking the Desktop brings up the menu you see in Figure 5-15. Notice how only the Finder commands that are applicable to how the Desktop looks and is arranged are displayed. Along the same lines, clicking text, either selected or unselected, while holding down the Control key brings up menus that reflect the commands available to you when you are working with the text, as shown in Figures 5-16 and 5-17.

FIGURE 5-13   Clicking a file shows a menu with different options related to the file

FIGURE 5-14   Folders show a different set of commands in the Contextual menu

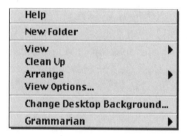

FIGURE 5-15   Clicking the Desktop provides you with all the commands that relate to Finder actions

FIGURE 5-16   Clicking selected text shows one set of commands

Contextual Menus

FIGURE 5-17   Clicking unselected text shows a somewhat different set of available commands

> TIP   *Most new Mac programs also support Contextual menus in one form or another. The quickest way to find out if they work is to click a document window and see what pops up.*

List View Versus Icon and Button View

When using the Finder, you can display files in one of three modes: List view, Button view, and Icon view. As the names suggest, List view displays all your files in a list, while Button and Icon view display your files as a group of buttons or icons spread out on either your desktop or in a window. These view options have their strengths and weaknesses. The following sections discuss these views to show how they benefit your Mac OS 9 experience and where they are located.

List View

As its name implies, using *List view* causes the Finder to display all the files and folders in a window as a list. The Finder normally displays the files and folders in a window with a small icon, as shown in Figure 5-18, followed by the file's name and other information you have told it to display. Normally, this extra information includes the date the file was modified, the size of the file, and the kind of file it is. In addition to this basic information, you can use the Finder preferences to add or subtract the amount and types of information the Finder displays when looking at your files and folders in the List view.

List view is ideal for folders with many files and folders in it. List view makes locating and organizing the files much easier than it would be if you used Icon or Button view. To change a folder from Icon or Button view to List view, all you need to do is click the folder to select it. Once you select the folder you want set to List view, click the View menu, and then select as List from the list of options. All the files and folders are now displayed as members of a list and sorted by name.

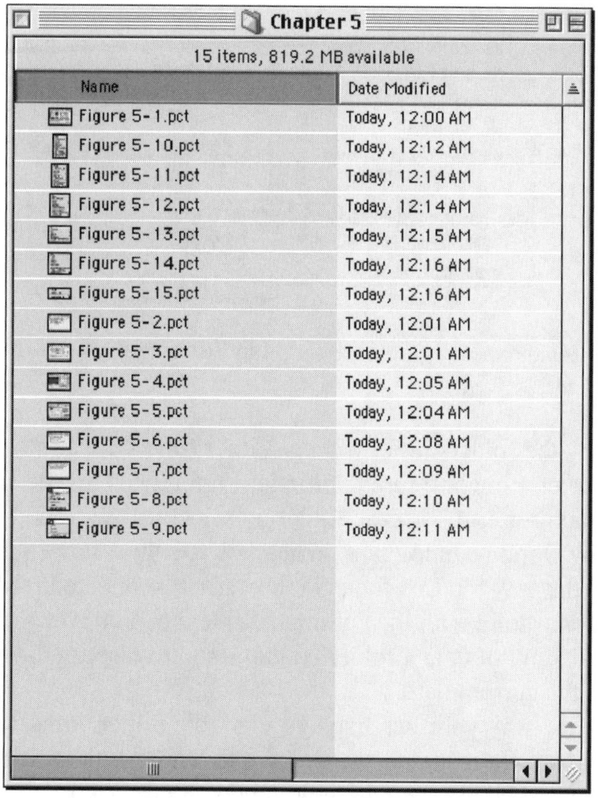

	Chapter 5	
15 items, 819.2 MB available		
Name	**Date Modified**	
Figure 5-1.pct	Today, 12:00 AM	
Figure 5-10.pct	Today, 12:12 AM	
Figure 5-11.pct	Today, 12:14 AM	
Figure 5-12.pct	Today, 12:14 AM	
Figure 5-13.pct	Today, 12:15 AM	
Figure 5-14.pct	Today, 12:16 AM	
Figure 5-15.pct	Today, 12:16 AM	
Figure 5-2.pct	Today, 12:01 AM	
Figure 5-3.pct	Today, 12:01 AM	
Figure 5-4.pct	Today, 12:05 AM	
Figure 5-5.pct	Today, 12:04 AM	
Figure 5-6.pct	Today, 12:08 AM	
Figure 5-7.pct	Today, 12:09 AM	
Figure 5-8.pct	Today, 12:10 AM	
Figure 5-9.pct	Today, 12:11 AM	

FIGURE 5-18   List view helps you organize folders with lots of files

Once you set the folder to display its contents in List view, it is time to start redesigning the List to suit your specific needs. Click the View menu, and then scroll down to the Sort List submenu, as shown in Figure 5-19. Now select the way you want to sort your files. The way you can sort your list of files and folders depends on the columns you have set up in the View Options dialog box. To reverse the order by which your files and folders are sorted, click the grayish triangle located at the top of the scroll bar on the right-hand side of the dialog box.

List View Versus Icon and Button View

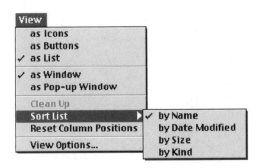

FIGURE 5-19   Change the way files are sorted in List view

To set the way the folders look, you can either follow the procedures described in Chapter 4 to configure the Finder Preferences for the List view or you can customize them for each specific folder by selecting the folder, and then opening the View Options dialog box. When you use the View Options dialog box, you can set the way the List looks in the currently selected folder by changing the size of the icons along with the columns displayed. You can also set the Finder to calculate the amount of data a folder contains and to display the file dates in terms relative to the current date.

To configure the way your list displays, click the folder you set to List view, and then click the View menu and scroll down to View Options. You can also open the View Options dialog box by holding down the Control key, and then clicking the window to bring up the Contextual menu for the window or desktop. With the Contextual menu open, select View Options from the list of available options. From the View Options dialog box you see in Figure 5-20, you can set the List to look just the way you want. To set up the List view as you want it, follow these steps:

1. To see the size of each of the folders in your list, click the check box for Calculate Folder Size. This option forces the Finder to go through the contents of the folders and to add up the amount of disk space each folder consumes.

NOTE   *The downside to the Calculate Folder Size feature is it can take up a great deal of processing time and, as such, it can make your Mac seem a lot more sluggish.*

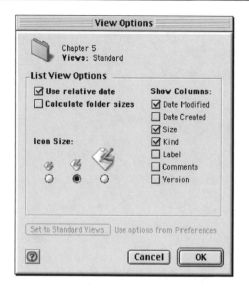

FIGURE 5-20   The View Options dialog box enables you to customize the look of the List view

List View Versus Icon and Button View

2. The next option you want to look at is Use relative date. This option causes the Finder to display all dates so they are relative to the present date. For example, if a file was modified on January 5th, and the date on your Mac shows January 6th, then the Finder indicates the file was modified yesterday.

3. Once you set the two options available in the List view, then you want to choose the size of the icon to be displayed in the List view. You can choose between a small icon, the medium-sized icon, which is the default, and a much larger icon. The choice of icon size helps determine the size of the font and the spacing of the files in the List view. As you can see in Figure 5-21, the choice of icon size can make a dramatic difference in the appearance of the list.

4. Next, you want to look over the various columns of information available from which you can choose. When you check the list of columns, you see you can display seven different columns of information. By default, the Finder displays the date the file was modified, the size of the file, and the kind of file. The other columns you can display include the date the file was created, the label applied to the file, any comments attached to the file, and the version of an application.

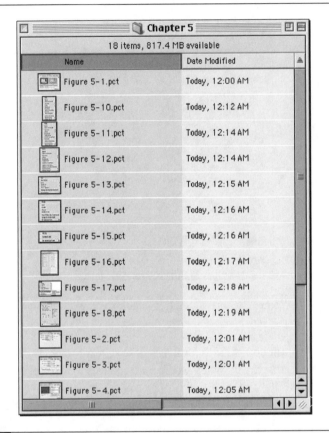

FIGURE 5-21   Changing the size of the icon can make a dramatic change in the
                List view

5. Finally, if you decide you do not like the way the list is set up and you
   want to return the list back to the standard settings you have configured in
   the Finder preferences dialog box, click the Set to Standard Views button.

After you finish setting up the List view for this folder as you want it to appear,
click the OK button to close the dialog box or click Cancel to discard the changes
you made and to dismiss the dialog box.

Icon View

The other view you might use is Icon view, which is the Mac OS 9 default setting.
As the name implies, *Icon view* displays your files and folders as icons on either

the desktop or in a window. As previously discussed, Icon view is an excellent
choice for folders that don't contain a large number of files and folders. In the Icon
view, you can arrange your icons in a variety of ways, as well as setting the size of
the icons and the way they behave when you move them around. When you look at
a window that's set to use Icon view, as shown in Figure 5-22, you can see how all
your files and folders are displayed.

Like the List view, you can arrange the files and folders that are in your
window or on the desktop by selecting the window or desktop and then clicking
the View menu. Then select Arrange and choose the option by which you want to
arrange the files and folders. Or, you can CONTROL-click the window or desktop
to bring up the Contextual menu. Then select Arrange from the menu and choose
how you want the files and folders to be arranged. In the Icon view, files and
folders can be arranged by the name of the file, when the file was modified,
when it was created, its size, the kind of file it is, or the label you have attached
to the file.

To customize the way your files and folders look in Icon view, you can choose
to customize the way all your windows and your desktop look by choosing to
change the Finder preferences for the Icon view, as discussed in Chapter 4. You
can also change the way the files and folders look in a specific window by clicking
the View menu, and then selecting the View Options option.

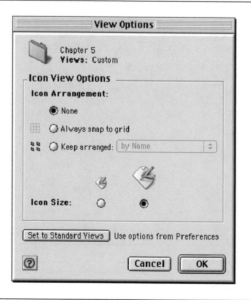

FIGURE 5-22   The Icon view enables you to see items as icons

List View Versus Icon and
Button View

To change the way your files and folders look and behave in a specific window or on the desktop, click the window or desktop to select it, and then click the View menu and scroll down to select View Options.

TIP   *Another method of opening the View options dialog box is to* CONTROL-*click the window or the desktop to bring up the Contextual menu for the window or desktop. Once the Contextual menu is open, select View Options from the list of available commands.*

The dialog box you see in Figure 5-23 displays several options you can select to customize the way your files and folders are displayed.

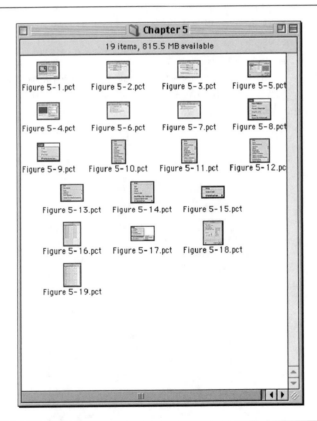

FIGURE 5-23   The View Options dialog box enables you to customize the look of the Icon view

To customize the way your desktop or window looks, follow these simple steps:

1. When you look at the dialog box, the first thing you want set is how the files and folders are arranged as they are placed in the window or on the desktop. The first option you can choose is None. This option tells the Finder not to move the icon from where you place it.

2. The second option you can choose is called Always snap to grid and, like its name, it causes the Finder to move files and folders around so they are aligned to an invisible grid.

3. The third option is called Keep Arranged. This option enables you to have the Finder rearrange files and folders in the window or on the desktop based on the criteria you select.

4. Once you click Keep Arranged, a pop-up menu appears to the right of the radio button.

5. When you click a pop-up menu, you can choose among sorting the files and folders by name, date modified, date created, size, kind, and label.

6. Next, you want to choose the size of the icons you want the Finder to use when displaying your files and folders. You can choose between a small icon, the size usually seen with the list view, or the more common larger icon.

7. Finally, if you have changed some of the settings from the default value, you can click the Set to Standard View button to change all the Icon view settings back to the default values you set in the Icon View portion of the Finder Preferences.

Once you finish setting the Icon view for this window or the desktop, click the OK button to apply your settings. If you want to go back to your previous setup, click Cancel.

Button View

The window shown in Figure 5-24 displays the Finder's Button view. As the name implies, *Button view* causes all your files and folders to become buttons you can click once to open or execute (the same as the buttons in Apple's Launcher). While this feature makes it simple to set up windows with a few files and folders that can be accessed via a single click of a button, it does not lend itself to the management of a large number of files and folders. The primary reason is that you can only select files and folders by clicking their text label or by clicking the desktop or window, and then dragging the mouse to highlight one or more buttons.

Manipulating the way files and folders look in Button view is similar to the way you set the preferences for files and folders in the Icon view. Following the instructions you read in Chapter 4, you can set up the global preferences for Button view in the Button view portion of the Finder preferences.

To set the preferences for Button view in a specific window or on the desktop, click the window you want to modify, and then click the View menu and select View Options.

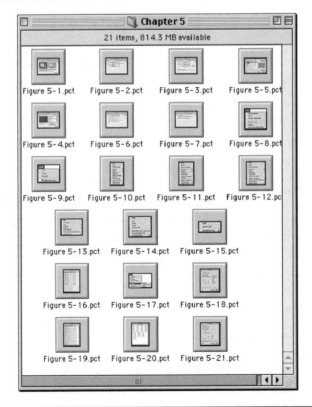

FIGURE 5-24   The Button view enables you to display your items as buttons

List View Versus Icon and Button View

> NOTE
>
> *Another trick you can use to open the View Options dialog box is to* CONTROL-*click the window you want to modify, and then select View Options from the menu.*

When you look at the dialog box shown in Figure 5-25, you can see the options available to you when customizing your files and folders in Button view. To set up Button view the way you want, follow these simple steps:

1. With the dialog box displayed, the first thing you want set is how the files and folders are arranged as they are placed in the window or on the desktop. The first radio button you can select is None. This option tells the Finder not to move the button from where you place it in the window.

2. The second radio button you can choose is called Always snap to grid and like its name, it causes the Finder to move files and folders around so they are aligned to an invisible grid in the window.

3. The third radio button is labeled Keep Arranged and enables you to have the Finder rearrange files and folders in the window or on the desktop based on the option you select.

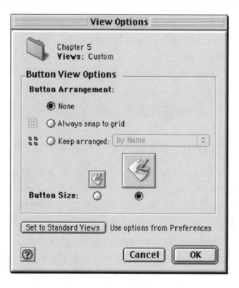

FIGURE 5-25   The View Options dialog box enables you to customize the look of the Button view

4. Once you click Keep Arranged, a pop-up menu appears to the right of the radio button. Clicking the pop-up menu, you can choose to arrange the buttons by name, date modified, date created, size, kind, and label.

5. Next, you want to select the size of the button you want the Finder to use when displaying your files and folders. You can choose between a small button, the size usually seen with the List view, or the more common larger button.

6. Finally, if you have changed some of the options from their default values, you can click the Set to Standard View button to change all the Button view settings back to the default values you set in the Button view portion of the Finder Preferences.

Once you have set the Button view options for this window or the desktop, click the OK button to apply your settings. If you decide you don't want to keep the changes you have made, you can click Cancel to throw away all the changes and return to the previous setup.

Desktop Features

A variety of built-in desktop enhancements are available to you in Mac OS 9 to make your life a bit easier. One of the coolest features in Mac OS 9 is the Applications Switcher, which enables you to switch easily among all the programs you are running on your Mac, either by clicking the application listed in the menu or using the keyboard to switch among them. Some of the other options discussed in this section are how to use the Pop-up window feature to manage your open windows and how to use the option key to change the way your Finder functions behave.

Application Switcher

The Application menu is located in the far right-hand corner of the menu bar and displays the currently running application. Clicking the Application menu, you see a list of all the applications active on your Mac and whether they are currently hidden. The menu you see in Figure 5-26 displays the applications active on your Mac (this illustration shows the programs the author was using at the time this figure was produced). Notice the icon for Microsoft Word is lighter than the other icons. This indicates Microsoft Word is hidden from view and can only be seen when using the Application menu or by using the keyboard shortcut to switch applications.

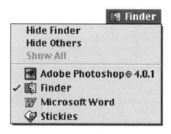

FIGURE 5-26   The Application Switcher menu displays your opened applications

To move among the open applications, click the Application menu, and then scroll down to the application to which you want to switch. If you want to hide the application you are currently running, and then switch to the other application, hold down the Option key when selecting the application to which you want to switch. Another way of hiding the current application and switching to the next application in the application list is to select the Hide application name. To hide all the other applications currently running on your Mac, click the Application menu, and then select Hide Others from the list of options. To reverse the procedure and show all the applications currently running, click the Application menu, and then select the Show All command.

You can also use your Mac's keyboard to switch between your open applications. By default, the keyboard shortcut is COMMAND-tab. This shortcut works fine for most purposes, but it also conflicts with a popular shortcut in Adobe Illustrator, so you may want to change it if you use that program.

Here's how to modify Application Switcher settings:

1. To change the keyboard shortcut in the Finder, you need to open the Mac Help dialog box either by selecting Help Center from the Finder's Help menu or pressing the Help key on your keyboard while in the Finder.

2. Now type in Application Switcher and click the Search button. Once the Help search has completed, you see a list of subjects that matched your search criteria. From the list of responses, click the one labeled Switching between open programs.

3. Looking at the dialog box you see in Figure 5-27, scroll down to the section labeled Help me modify the keyboard shortcuts, and click it.

4. You now see a dialog box asking if you want to enable the shortcut. Click the Yes button to proceed.

Desktop Features

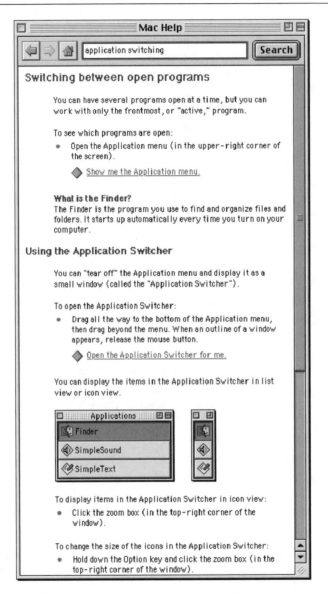

FIGURE 5-27 From the Apple Help dialog box, you can make a number of changes to the Application Switcher

5. Now you are asked if you want to change the current keyboard shortcut from Command-Tab to another shortcut. If you do want to change the keyboard shortcut, click the Yes button and proceed to the next dialog box.

> **CAUTION** *Before you change a keyboard shortcut, you might want to check the documentation for your favorite programs to see if any conflicts occur. No way exists to predict which shortcuts may apply to which program without this information (or some experimentation).*

6. Next, you are asked to choose the modifier key you need to hold down when switching applications. You can choose among using the Command, Option, and Control key. Click the button representing the key you want to use to move to the next dialog box.

7. Finally, you are asked to choose the character you want to use for the keyboard shortcut. The character must be a standard alpha-numeric key or you can use /t to indicate the Tab key. Press the key you want to use or enter /t, and then press the OK button to set the new keyboard shortcut.

> **TIP** *As you scroll through the help screen, you find some built-in AppleScript options that enable you to customize the application switch in several ways. You might want to experiment with the options to see which you prefer.*

Once you set the shortcut, you can start using it to move through your open applications.

> **TIP** *If you want to switch to the application listed previously in the application list, hold down the SHIFT key while using the keyboard shortcut.*

If you always want to see a list of the running applications on your Mac, simply click the Application menu, and then drag down so the menu detaches and appears as a small floating window on your desktop, as shown in Figure 5-28. From this menu, you can click the individual entries for each application to switch among them. To hide the application you are currently using, simply hold down the OPTION key when you click the application to which you want to switch.

> **TIP** *The Option key shortcut to hide other programs also works if you hold down the key when picking another program from the Application menu.*

Desktop Features

FIGURE 5-28   The floating Applications window shows which applications are running

Rearranging this window is also a simple procedure you can do to make it fit the way you work. Click the zoom box located second-to-the-right in the window's title bar. This causes the window to shrink, so it displays only the application's icons, as in Figure 5-29. To change the size of the icons displayed, hold down the OPTION key, and then click the zoom box. This causes the icons to switch between the large and small icon sizes.

To change the window so it displays all the applications in a horizontal rather than a vertical list, hold down the OPTION and the SHIFT keys when clicking the zoom box. This causes the window to list all the applications in a horizontal list, as you can see in Figure 5-30. Once the window is in the horizontal mode, you can change it to display all icons or change the size of the icons using the same commands described previously.

FIGURE 5-29   Changing the size of the icons makes a big change to the window

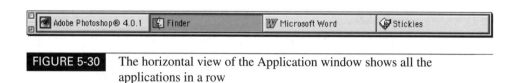

| **FIGURE 5-30** | The horizontal view of the Application window shows all the applications in a row |

If you decide all the changes you made to the Application Switcher are not working, then you can restore them to their default values by performing these steps:

1. Click your Mac's desktop.

2. Choose Help from the File menu and select Mac Help.

3. Enter Application Switcher as your search request.

4. When you see the search results, click "Switching between open programs," and then scroll to the option labeled "Restore the default display settings for the Application Switcher for me." Within seconds, the Application window is restored to its standard configuration.

Pop-up Windows

Another cool feature of Mac OS 9 is its capability to turn a folder you have open on the desktop into a Pop-up window you can minimize and expand simply by clicking its tab. To turn a window into a Pop-up folder, simply select the window you want to turn into a Pop-up folder, and then select the "as Pop-up window" command under the View menu.

Another way to turn a window into a Pop-up menu is to use press COMMAND-SHIFT-W to close the selected window and turn it into a Pop-up window. Once you select the "as Pop-up window" command, notice your window has moved and changed in appearance, as shown in Figure 5-31. Clicking the window's tab causes the window to hide and the tab to be displayed at the bottom of the desktop. Clicking the window's tab at the bottom of the desktop causes the window to be restored to its original position. To convert your window back into a normal window from a Pop-up menu, simply click the window and drag it to another location.

Desktop Features

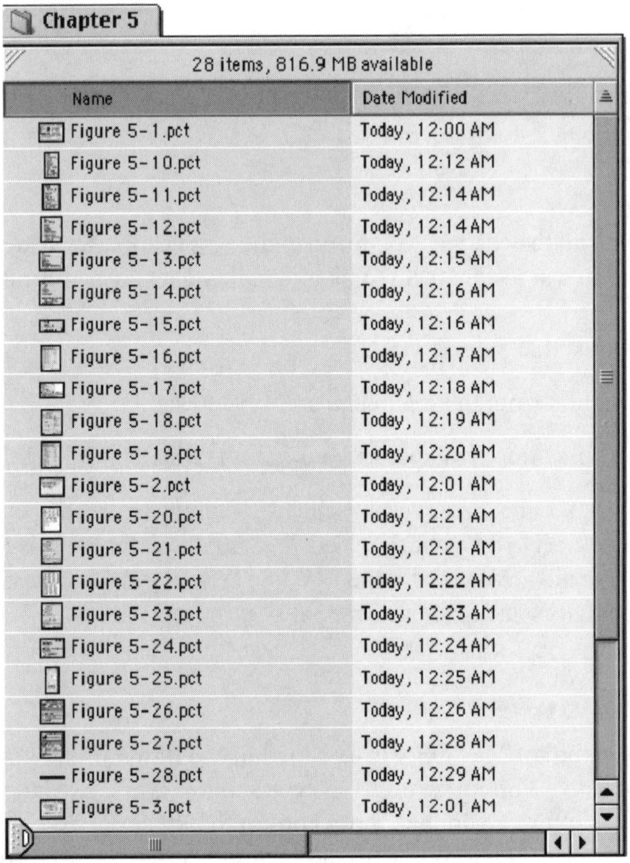

FIGURE 5-31   Pop-Up windows are another way of looking at a window

Using the Option Key

The Option key is one of the great unsung heroes of the Finder. You can use the *Option key* to change the way many commands function in ways to make your life easier. The Option key changes the behavior and the scope of certain commands. In this section, you learn the way the Option key affects the various Finder commands you use to maintain your system and desktop.

The Option key can change the way the Finder behaves in the following ways:

- Pressing the OPTION key while clicking a window's close box or using the COMMAND-W command causes all the open windows in the Finder to close.

- Clicking the collapse box of a window while pressing the OPTION key causes all the windows in the Finder to collapse.

- Using the COMMAND-SHIFT-W keyboard shortcut while pressing OPTION causes all the windows open in the Finder to close and turn into Pop-up windows.

- Pressing the OPTION key while clicking the Expand Folder arrow in a List view causes all the folders beneath the one you are expanding to be expanded.

- Likewise, when you hold down the OPTION key, while clicking the Collapse Folder arrow in a List view, this causes all the folders beneath the one you are collapsing to be collapsed.

- Dragging-and-dropping a file or folder while pressing the OPTION key causes the file or folder to be copied to the new location. The original file stays put.

Using the Option key to change the way these common commands behave enables you to perform certain functions more efficiently and should make your Mac experience more enjoyable. Try a few Option shortcuts for yourself to see the results they deliver.

Organizing Your Desktop

The desktop on your Mac, much like your desk at work or at home, is a place you can set up to suit the way you work. Unfortunately, the way the Mac works is not always suited to the way you might want it to work. Organizing your desktop is one way you can configure your Mac for optimum efficiency.

When you look at the desktop, you see the list of volumes starting at the upper right-hand corner of the screen and going down the right side of the desktop. Down in the lower left-hand corner, you see the Control Strip tab or, if it is expanded, across the bottom of the desktop. Aside from these two items, you have a big blank space to use and customize.

As you learned earlier in this chapter, you can change the color and pattern used for the desktop or even replace the desktop with a picture using the Appearance Control Panel. Once you set the way the desktop looks, you might want to make other changes to your desktop by adding aliases to commonly used files and applications. Along the bottom or left-hand side of the desktop, you may want to add aliases to the most commonly used applications or files. This enables you to access your applications and files easily, without having to dig through your various volumes and folders to find them.

Another great way to customize your desktop is to add files and folders to the Apple menu so they are easily available from the Finder and all your other applications. To add files and folders to the Apple menu, follow these steps:

1. Open the System folder, and then double-click the Apple Menu Items folder to open it.

2. Open the volume or folder that contains the file, folder, or application you want to add to the Apple.

3. Locate the file folder or application you want to add to the Apple menu, and then click to select it.

4. Once you select it, click the File menu and scroll down to the Make Alias command.

5. After you make the alias, click it and drag it into the Apple Menu Items folder.

NOTE   *While you needn't use aliases for the files, folders, and applications you want to add to the Apple menu, doing so makes your work easier. Using aliases means you don't end up having to place huge applications, such as Microsoft Office, in the System folder (and this would be impractical, since these programs require dozens of support files to run) so you can launch Microsoft Word from the Apple menu.*

Once you move all the aliases to the files, folders, and applications you want to add to the Apple menu, close the Apple Menu Items folder, and then close the System Folder, along with all the other folders you don't want to leave open. Within seconds the System Folder appears in the Apple menu.

If you are using Apple Menu options to expand folders, then you can access all the contents of the folders you have added to the Apple menu simply by clicking the menu, and then scrolling through the submenus displayed. This way, you can keep a folder of commonly used files or template files in the Apple menu so they are always available to you, regardless of which application you are in currently.

Another useful tool is the Stickies utility you find in the Apple menu. *Stickies* enable you to leave little colored notes on your desktop reminding you of things you need to do, much like the Post-it™ notes that litter your real desk.

Using Stickies is simple; simply click the Apple menu and select Stickies. Then type in your text and save the stickie, see Figure 5-32. To create a new note, simply click the File menu and select New Note or press COMMAND-N.

TIP

When you quit Stickies the first time, you see a message asking if you want to open the program at startup. If you accept the option, an alias to Stickies shows up in the Startup Items folder inside the System Folder, and your desktop is once again adorned with all your Stickies the next time you start your Mac.

Organizing Your Desktop

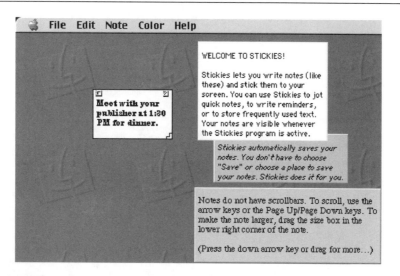

FIGURE 5-32 Stickies are little notes you can leave on your desktop

Summing Up

In this chapter, you learned some of the ways you can modify the way the Finder and your Mac's desktop look and function. Using Contextual menus, you can bypass the standard menus to execute commands directly in the window in which you are working, without having to move your mouse up to the menu bar. You also learned how you can set all the different ways to look at your files and folders that appear in List view, Icon view, and Button view. You learned how you can use the Option key to change the way certain commands behave in the Finder. And, you learned ways to organize your desktop and the Apple menu to suit the way you work best.

In the next chapter, you learn how to set up your Mac for multiple users.

Chapter 6

Customizing Your Mac
Environment for Multiple Users

Perhaps the most interesting new feature in Mac OS 9 is the greatly expanded capability to enable separate users to share the same Mac. This enables you to provide a custom environment for each person who plans to work on your computer.

The Simple Finder feature provides a reduced set of commands for the user. Multiple Users provides a much greater degree of customization of the experience of an individual user.

In previous versions of the Mac OS, if you wanted to share your Mac with others, you were sharing everything on your Mac, including all your files and applications, unless you purchased a dedicated security program. You also gave those using your Mac access to all the applications you may have stored passwords in, such as your e-mail, AOL, or your PPP connection.

All this changes under Mac OS 9 with the addition of Multiple Users support. *Multiple Users* is similar to the At Ease software Apple has offered for several years, but it's standard for any Mac that can run Mac OS 9. In addition, it provides a greater array of user customization and security options. If you're used to At Ease, you are apt to find similarities, however.

In this chapter, you learn how to set up users on your Mac using the new Multiple Users Control Panel and all the options you can set to enable or limit each user's access. You also learn about one of the cool features in Mac OS 9, setting up a voiceprint password. Once the process for setting up a user and setting his or her password has been discussed, you learn about the Keychain Access feature and how to use the keychain to store all your users' passwords in a secure place.

Setting Up a New User in Multiple Users

The *Multiple Users Control Panel* is a new feature in Mac OS 9 that enables multiple users to share the same Mac without having full access to all the available applications and resources. The Multiple Users Control Panel accomplishes this by enabling you to create user profiles, so anyone who logs on to your Mac is only granted access to those programs and resources to which you have given him access.

This section covers all the steps you need to follow to set up a new user on your Mac and how you can limit her access to the various programs and resources to what you want her to have.

Before you set up a new user on your Mac, you should consider a few things. The first thing you need to decide is what kind of user you want to create on your Mac. Is this someone you want to be able to run all the applications and access all the resources available to your Mac? Or, do you want to create a user who has only limited access?

NOTE   *If the setups are being made by a system administrator, rather than an individual who is using a specific Mac, you should consult with that administrator about setting specific user levels.*

If you have decided to limit this user's access to your Mac, you need to determine which applications and resources you want to grant to this user and how you want the user to see these resources. To begin setting up a new user on your Mac, follow these steps:

1. Click the Apple menu and scroll down to Control Panels.

2. Move your mouse to the right and select the Multiple Users Control Panel to open it.

3. The Multiple Users Control Panel you see in Figure 6-1 lists the users currently configured and indicates if the Multiple User Accounts option is turned on already. If Multiple User Accounts is not already turned on, do so now. Once turned on, this option enables users to log in and log out of your Mac. If you do not turn on this option, the various users you create will be unable to log in and log out, thus opening up your Mac to anyone who wants to use it.

4. Once you turn on Multiple User Access, you need to click the New User button to create a new user on your Mac.

5. In the New User dialog box, shown in Figure 6-2, enter the name of the user you are creating. Type the name of the User in the space provided, and then press the Tab key to move down to the Password area where you need to type your password.

CAUTION   *Always use strong passwords when setting up a user's written password. Using a strong password means your passwords should contain a combination of uppercase and lowercase letters, numbers, and special characters. For example, while the password Mac might seem nice and easy to remember, it is not a secure password because it is too easy to guess. The password mAc1nt$h is a much harder password for a hacker to decipher. While strong passwords are more difficult to think up and remember, they provide you with a significantly greater amount of protection.*

6. Now you want to select the type of user you are creating.

Setting Up a New User in Multiple Users

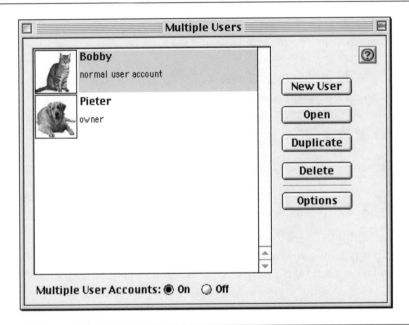

FIGURE 6-1   This Control Panel displays the names of the users who can access your Mac

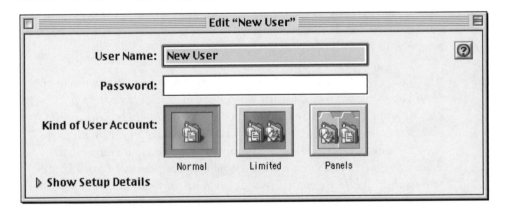

FIGURE 6-2   Type the name and password for your new user

User Profiles Defined

You can create three types of users: Normal users, Limited users, and Panels users.

Normal users are the most powerful users on your Mac, aside from you, the owner. *Normal users* can access all the available applications and resources. The only things Normal users cannot do, unless you want to give them access, is to have the ability to manage user accounts and to look at the contents of other users' personal folders.

Limited and *Panels users* have only as much access to your Mac as you want them to have. When you create a Limited or Panel user, you must decide which applications users can run and what resources on your Mac they can access.

The main difference between a Limited User and Panels is that a Panels user can see all the available applications in one window or panel as a series of buttons and all her available documents in another panel, also as a series of buttons. Once you choose the type of user you are creating, click the appropriate button.

NOTE
The Panel user feature provides a user interface similar to Apple's original At Ease software, where the available features for a particular user were available as single-click buttons for ease of use.

Next, you want to look at the Setup Details for the user you are creating. To do this, click the small triangle in the lower left-hand corner labeled Show Setup Details. When you click the triangle, you see four different tabs, User Info, Applications, Privileges, and Alternate Password. Each one contains a variety of options you can set for this user. For Normal users, the Applications and Privileges tabs are grayed out because Normal users have access to all the applications and resources on your Mac.

The User Info options screen, shown in Figure 6-3, enables you to set the picture used for your user by scrolling through the different pictures in the User Picture section of the dialog box. To scroll through the different pictures, click the up and down arrows located just to the right of the picture. If you cannot find a picture you like, you can copy a picture and paste it into the space provided.

NOTE
The only problem with choosing your own photo is this: If the image is too large, the photo will not fit into the space provided. To get around this, simply select the portion of the picture you want to use and copy it into the picture space.

Setting Up a New User in Multiple Users

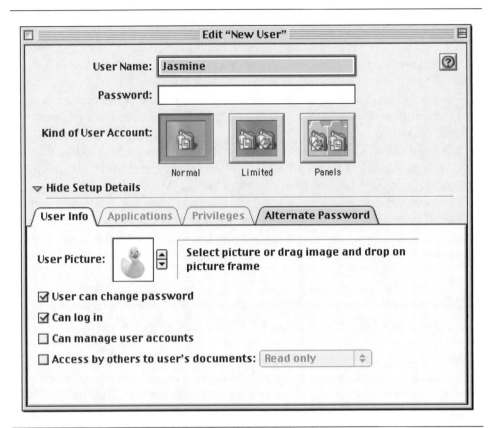

FIGURE 6-3   Set the User Options for your new user

Now look at the options you can set for this user. You can enable a user to change her password and to log in to your Mac. These two options are set by default. While all users need the ability to log in to your Mac to use it, you may not want to let users change their own passwords. The reason for this is to ensure that they only use strong passwords that cannot be easily guessed or broken by crackers. On the other hand, not letting your users change their own passwords forces you to do it for them, a task you may not want to do.

Once you make your choices about login and password options, look at the other two options, which enable the user to manage user accounts and to look into and possibly modify the files stored in other users' personal folders.

> NOTE *Only Normal users have the option of managing user accounts on your Mac. All three types of users can be granted access to the files stored in other users' private folders. You can grant the following to each user you have given the ability to look into other users' private folders: Read access, write access, or, if you are extremely trusting, read and write access. As the names imply, granting users read rights allows them to look at all the files and folders in each user's private folders. Likewise, write access allows the user to write files to all the other users' private folders. Read and Write access lets the user both read all the files in a user's private folder and place new items in that folder.*

If you are setting up a Limited or Panels user, you want to click the tab labeled Applications. The dialog box you see in Figure 6-4 displays a list of all the applications currently available on your Mac. Click the check boxes next to each application to which you want this user to have access.

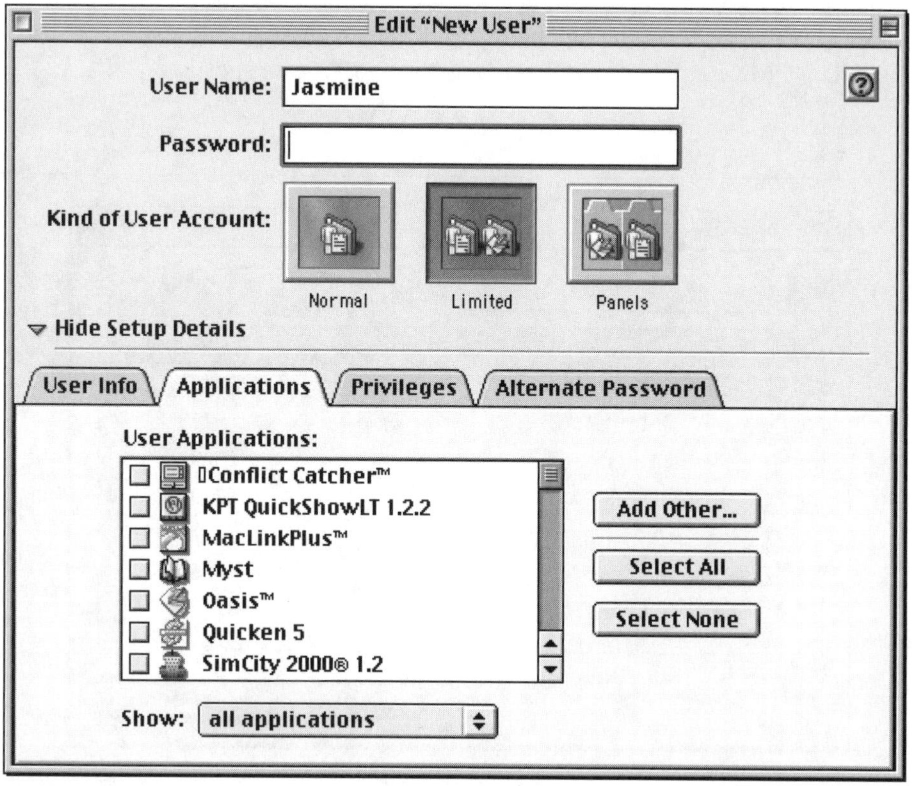

FIGURE 6-4   Select the Applications your Limited or Panels users can run

To change the list of applications, click the pop-up menu located beneath the list of applications. From this pop-up menu, you can choose to show all applications, all applications except AppleScripts, or only those items you selected.

If you find an application you want to restrict is unlisted, you can click the Add Other button to bring up the Open File dialog box you see in Figure 6-5. Using the Open File dialog box, navigate to the application you want to add to the list, and then click the Open button to add it to the list.

NOTE *To select all the applications in the list, click the Select All button. To clear all the applications you selected, click the Select None button to clear out all your selections.*

For Limited and Panels users, click the Privileges tab to specify which resources you are granting to this user. Under the Privileges tab you see in Figure 6-6, click the check box labeled CD/DVD-ROMS to give this user access to the CD/DVD-ROM drive in your Mac. By clicking the radio buttons just beneath the check box for CD/DVD-ROM access, you can allow this user to access all your CD/DVD-ROMs or you can limit this user to accessing only those CD/DVD-ROMs you have specified in a list we will create shortly.

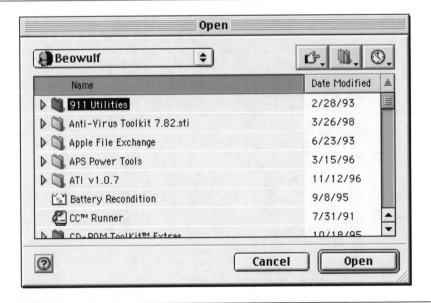

FIGURE 6-5   Add applications not in the list through the Add Other open file dialog box

NOTE

You would consider limiting access to a CD to prevent users from installing software they are not authorized to use or simply to prevent them from using a game or audio CD when there's work to be done.

Further down in the dialog box, you can click the check box that allows the user access to other removable media, such as floppy drives, Zip disks, and any other drive whose disk can be removed.

At the bottom of the dialog box, you can click the check box labeled User can print. If you want to let the user print, you can also let the user choose between any printer on the network or only the one you specify.

NOTE

You might limit printing to prevent printed copies being made of secure company documents a user might be working on or simply to conserve resources.

| FIGURE 6-6 | Determine which resource your Limited and Panels users can access |

Once you set all the removable media options, you want to determine to what other system resources you want this user to have access. The right-hand side of the dialog box shows four check boxes that enable you to limit which resources on your Mac this user can access. The first check box allows the user to access the globally shared folders located on your Mac. The second check box allows the user to access the Chooser and the Network Browser to select printers and log in to folders and volumes available on the network. The third dialog box allows the user to access the various Control Panels installed on your Mac. While this option is off by default, you may want to grant it to some users, so they can customize the settings on your Mac. The last check box enables you to permit or deny the user to access the Apple Menu items aside from the Chooser, Network Browser, and Control Panels.

Finally, when setting up any type of user, click the Alternate Password tab to see the options available to you. The dialog box you see in Figure 6-7 enables you to set another password that users can use to log in with if they forget their primary password. As discussed earlier, if you have the Speech Control Panel installed, then you can also set your Mac to use voiceprint authentication as the user's alternate password. This particular Multiple Users feature is described in the next section.

If you want users to be able to change their alternate password, then you need to click the check box labeled Allow this user to change his or her voiceprint.

Once you finish setting all the options you want to use with this user, click the close box to save the user's alternate password and return to the main Multiple Users Control Panel. If you have not created a voiceprint, then a dialog box pops up asking if you want to create a voiceprint right now or if you want to do it later. If you want to wait, click the Skip It button. If you want to create a voiceprint password, click the Create Now button.

Setting Global User Access

Now that you have completed adding your new user, you are ready to start managing your users and to set your Multiple User global options.

All you must do to set up these options is to follow these steps:

1. The Multiple Users Control Panel you see in Figure 6-8 displays five buttons you can click to manage the various users configured on your Mac. The first button in the list, New User, enables you to go through the process of creating a new user, which we just covered.

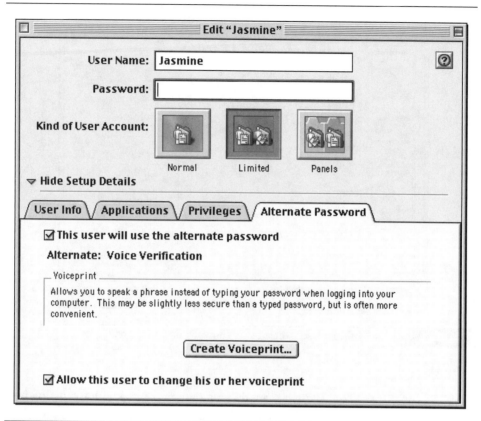

FIGURE 6-7   Set up the Alternate Password for your new user

2. The second button in the list is Open. The Open button enables you to open the user you have currently selected and change his settings if you like.

3. The third button in the list, Duplicate, enables you to create a new user by making a copy of the currently selected user profile, and then opening it so you can change the new user's name and password. To save the new user you just created by duplicating another user, click the close box.

4. The fourth button in the dialog box is Delete and enables you to remove the currently selected user from the list of users that you have created on your Mac. Once you click the "Delete" button, you will be presented with a dialog box that asks you if you really want to delete this user (see Figure 6-9). Click "Don't Delete" to stop the deletion process and return to the Multiple Users Control Panel, or click "Delete" to get rid of the user.

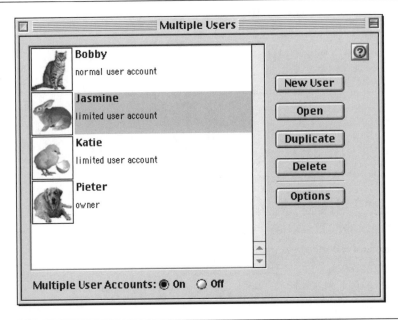

FIGURE 6-8   The Multiple Users dialog box shows your newly created user

5. If you clicked the Delete button, then you are presented with the dialog box you see in Figure 6-10. This dialog box asks if you want to cancel the Delete process or if you want to keep or delete the private folder created for the user you are deleting. If you want to keep the deleted user's private folder, press the Keep button. Otherwise, click the Delete button to eliminate the user's personal folder, along with the user.

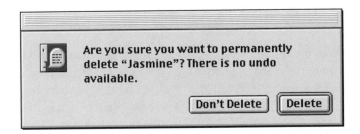

FIGURE 6-9   Clicking Delete brings up this confirmation dialog box

FIGURE 6-10 Multiple Users asks if you want to delete the user's files along with the user profile

6. The fifth button in the dialog box is Options. Clicking this button brings up the Multiple Users Options dialog box you see in Figure 6-11. From this dialog box, you can set all the global options that can be applied to the users you have configured on your Mac. The next steps describe these setup options.

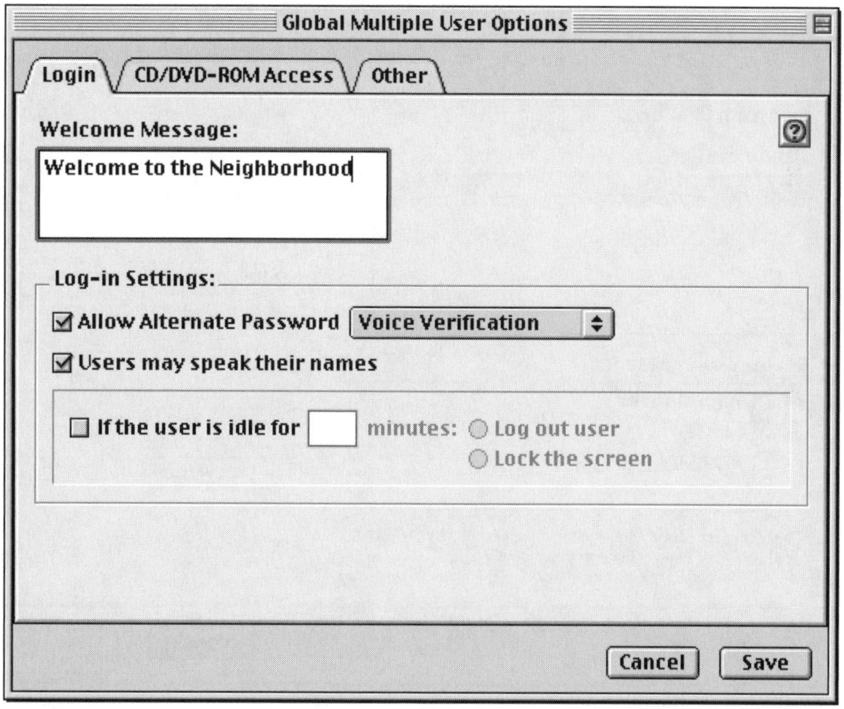

Setting Up a New User in
Multiple Users

Global Multiple User Options

Login | CD/DVD-ROM Access | Other

Welcome Message:

Welcome to the Neighborhood

Log-in Settings:

☑ Allow Alternate Password [Voice Verification ⬍]
☑ Users may speak their names

☐ If the user is idle for [ ] minutes: ○ Log out user
○ Lock the screen

[Cancel] [Save]

FIGURE 6-11   Clicking the Options button brings up Multiple Users Options dialog box

7. The Login tab has a variety of options you can configure. In the upper left-hand corner of the dialog box, you can enter the message to greet everyone who logs in to your Mac. Type the message you want or leave the space blank.

8. Next, you can enable the alternate password option for all your users and, if you want, allow users to speak their names instead of selecting their names from the list of configured users when they log in. You can also set the Login tab so your Mac logs out the current user or locks the screen if the user has been idle for a set period of time.

9. When you click CD-DVD-ROM Access tab, you see the dialog box shown in Figure 6-12. In this dialog box, you add all the CD/DVD-ROMs you want to let your users use. To add a new CD/DVD-ROM to the list of CD/DVD-ROMs your Limited and Panel users can access, put the CD/DVD-ROM into your Mac so it is mounted. The name of the disk is then displayed in the menu labeled Inserted.

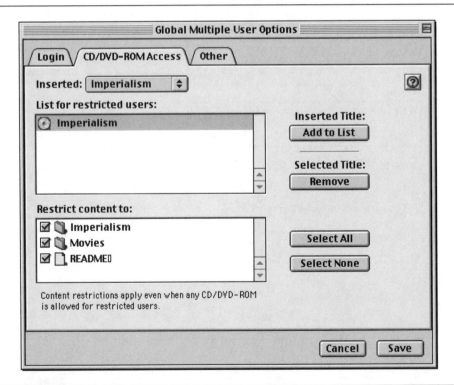

FIGURE 6-12   The CD/DVD-ROM tab shows the list of approved CD/DVDs your users can access

10. Then click the Add to list button to add this disk to the list of CD/DVD-ROMs your users can access. The window labeled Restrict content to at the bottom of the dialog box shows you all the files and folders on the disk. If you want to allow the users access to only part of this disk, uncheck the files and folders you do not want the users to access.

11. Repeat this procedure until all the CD/DVD-ROMs you want to add to the approved use list are added.

12. Now, click the Other tab to set the miscellaneous Multiple User options (see Figure 6-13). In this dialog box, you can set it so Multiple users can allow a guest to log in to your Mac.

13. To allow guests have access to your Mac, click the check box labeled "Allow a Guest User Account."

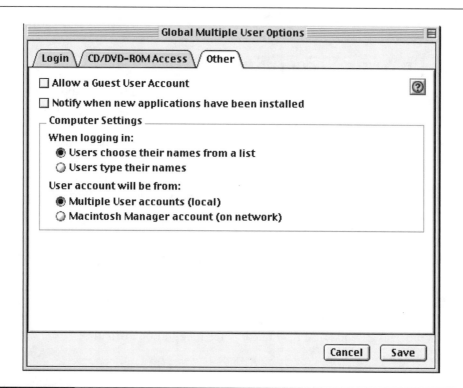

Setting Up a New User in Multiple Users

FIGURE 6-13   The Other tab sets the miscellaneous Multiple Users options

14. Next, you want to decide if you should be notified when a new application is installed. The purpose of this check box is to make sure you add access to new applications to the Limited and Panels users you want.

15. Now you need to set up the way users log in to your Mac. The first option you can set is how users tell your Mac who they are. You can either let users choose their name from a list of users when they log in or you can force users to type in their user names.

16. Next, you can set your Mac to draw the names in the user's list from either the Multiple Users Control Panel on your Mac or from a Mac Manager account located on the network.

 Normally, letting guests log in to your Mac is not a good idea because you have no control over who is logging in.

17. Once you specify all the options you want to use in the Multiple Users Control Panel, click the Save button to save all your changes or click Cancel to discard all your changes.

Setting Up Your Voiceprint

A unique feature of Apple's Multiple Users Control Panel is the capability to speak, rather than type, your password. The process is by no means perfect, but it provides an interesting alternative to the usual setup routine.

Here are some things to think about before you decide whether to use a voiceprint:

- **It doesn't always work.**   If you don't speak each word clearly, your Mac may not recognize your voice.

- **Changes in your voice hurt the process.**   If you have a cold or sore throat, the Mac won't be able to identify you when it compares your voice to the stored setup files.

- **Noisy environments hurt.**   If your Mac is in a busy office with lots of ambient noise, you need to keep the mike close to your mouth. Even then, the background noise may make voice recognition difficult.

NOTE *While some Macs come with microphones, others do not. The first generation iBooks didn't even come with a sound input jack, so you have to buy a USB mike adapter to plug a mike into these models.*

Once you consider the limitations, you'll find setting up a voiceprint is an easy process, but it does require quiet and some concentration. You can create a voiceprint for a user either when you create the user's account on your Mac or later when you have more time. To create a voiceprint for your user, follow these steps:

1. Click the Apple menu and scroll down to the Control Panels. Then select Multiple Users from the submenu.

2. In the Multiple Users Control Panel, select the user for whom you want to create a voiceprint and then click the Open button to bring up the Edit dialog box for the selected user. Click the triangle in the lower left-hand corner of the dialog box to display the user's setup details.

3. Now, click the Alternate Password tab and when there, click the Create Voiceprint button.

4. You are now presented with a dialog box (see Figure 6-14) asking if the default password phrase you plan to use is acceptable.

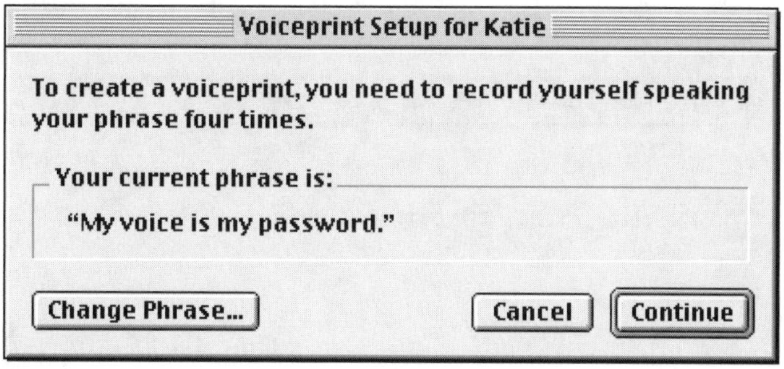

Setting Up Your Voiceprint

Voiceprint Setup for Katie

To create a voiceprint, you need to record yourself speaking your phrase four times.

Your current phrase is:

"My voice is my password."

[Change Phrase...]   [Cancel] [Continue]

FIGURE 6-14   See if the default password phrase is to your liking

5. If you want to change the password, Click the Change Phrase button and then type in a new phrase (see Figure 6-15), and click the OK button. Remember, if you do decide to change your password, make it long enough to be unique to the way you speak and not something that's too hard to pronounce evenly.

NOTE *If you want, you can check a check box when setting your new password phrase so the phrase is not displayed when asking you to speak your password phrase to log in.*

6. Once you settle on your password phrase, click Continue to record your voice. Now you see the dialog box in Figure 6-16. To record your voice properly, the Mac needs to record your voice four times while speaking the password phrase you have selected. This allows the Mac to have a variety of samples, so it can more closely match your voice.

7. To record the first voiceprint, click the Record First button.

8. Now click the record button located on the right-hand side of the dialog box, as you see in Figure 6-17.

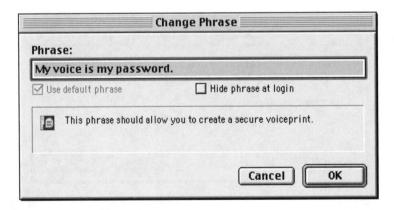

FIGURE 6-15   Choose a password phrase that suits your needs

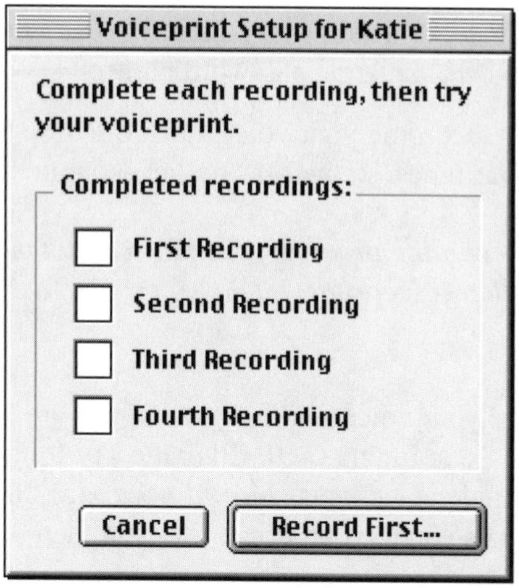

Voiceprint Setup for Katie

Complete each recording, then try
your voiceprint.

Completed recordings:

☐ First Recording

☐ Second Recording

☐ Third Recording

☐ Fourth Recording

[Cancel]   [Record First...]

FIGURE 6-16   You must record your voiceprint four times

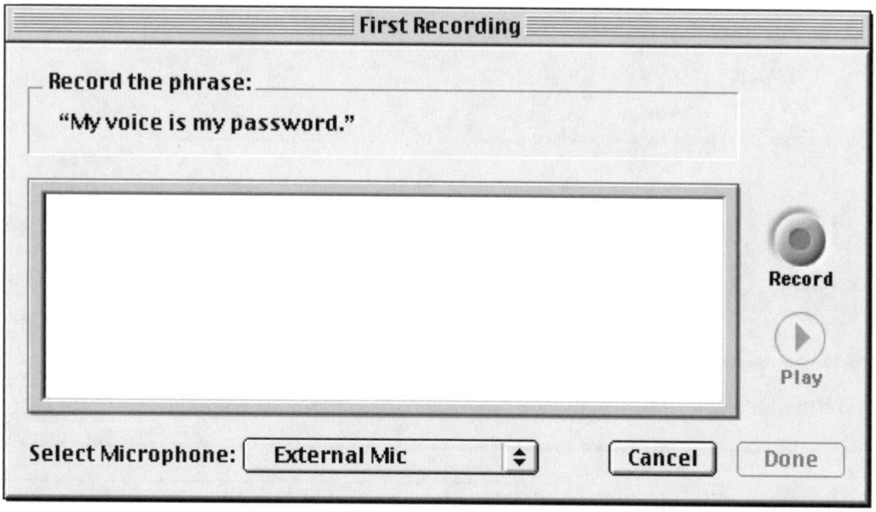

First Recording

Record the phrase:

"My voice is my password."

Record

▶
Play

Select Microphone: [External Mic ◆]   [Cancel]   [Done]

FIGURE 6-17   Click the Record button to start recording your voiceprint

Setting Up Your Voiceprint

9. Speak the password phrase clearly so the Mac can properly record it. When you look at the Record window (see Figure 6-18), you can see how your Mac "hears" you speaking the password phrase.

10. Once you finish recording your voice, click the Stop button. Repeat this procedure all four times, so the Mac has an accurate record of your voice.

NOTE   *If, during the recording process, your Mac cannot match your voice to any of the other voiceprints, it tells you so and asks you to repeat the recording.*

11. After you record your voiceprint four times, you are presented with the dialog box you see in Figure 6-19. Click the Try It button to see if you can get the Mac to understand your voice. If your Mac does understand your voice and matches you to your voiceprint, you then see the dialog box in Figure 6-20.

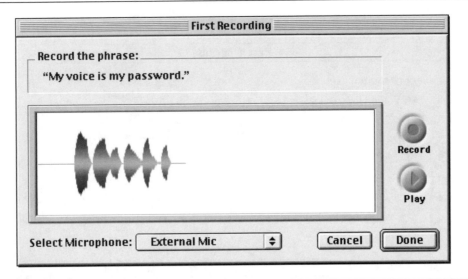

FIGURE 6-18   See the way your Mac hears you speak the password phrase

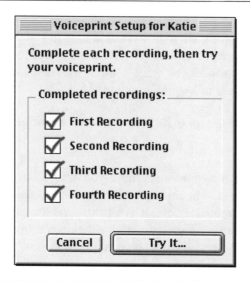

FIGURE 6-19   After you have completed setting your voiceprint you will want to try using it

After you have your voiceprint configured on the Mac, you can use it to log in. If you find using the voiceprint is not suited to your particular Mac setup, you can easily use a written password as an alternate or dispense with voice verification altogether.

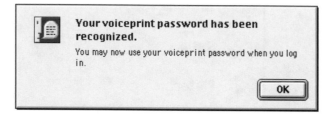

FIGURE 6-20   Once Mac can match your voiceprint, you are ready to use it

Logging In

Once you finish configuring all your users, it is time to restart your Mac and the log in to your Mac. Once you restart your Mac, it displays the dialog box you see in Figure 6-21. Select the user you want to log in as, and then click the Log in button to start the process of logging into your Mac.

> **TIP** *Another way to log off is simply to choose Logout from the Finder's Special menu.*

Now you are asked for your voiceprint if you have set it as your alternate password (see Figure 6-22). Speak your password and, if the Mac understands it properly, you will be granted access. If you cannot get the Mac to understand you after repeated tries, you are presented with the dialog box you see in Figure 6-23, asking you to type in your password. Once you type in your password, click OK to log in.

FIGURE 6-21 Select a user to log in

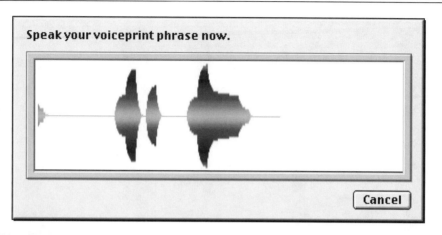

Speak your voiceprint phrase now.

Cancel

FIGURE 6-22   Watch your Mac listen as you speak your password

For Normal and Limited users, logging into your Mac reveals a look familiar to anyone who has used a Mac before. The only difference is that all the Finder preferences are set to their default values, enabling users to customize their Finder settings to exactly the way they want, without fear of impacting any other user on the Mac.

Panels users, on the other hand, see a different display than Mac users are used to seeing. Figure 6-24 shows this view, the Panel user's view. The screen is divided in to three distinct panes: the first pane, labeled Items, contains all the applications you can run; the second pane with the User's name, contains all the user's files; and a third pane contains the files and folders available on the currently inserted CD/DVD-ROM.

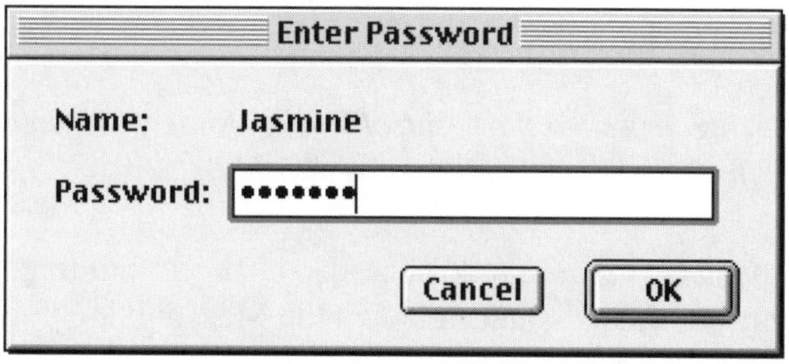

Enter Password

Name: Jasmine

Password: •••••••

Cancel   OK

FIGURE 6-23   If your Mac has a tin ear, type your password

Setting Up Your Voiceprint

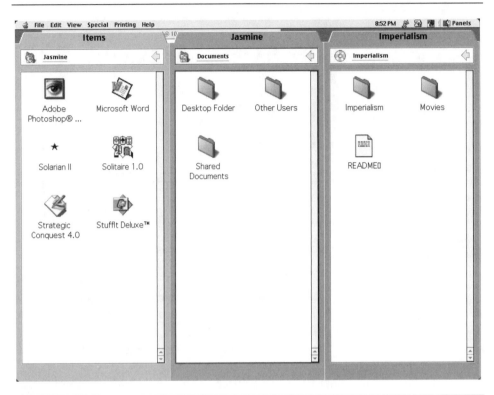

FIGURE 6-24 Panel users see an alternate view of the Mac environment

Even the menus you can see have been changed to reflect your more limited access. The Apple menu (see Figure 6-25) no longer lists Control Panels. Likewise, looking at the View menu, you can now only choose between Icon view and List view. Button view is no longer an option.

NOTE *By not having access to the Control Panels folder, the user is prevented from making system level changes to that Mac.*

The Special menu (see Figure 6-26) has also changed, limiting you to manipulating the users' folder, shutting down the Mac, and logging out.

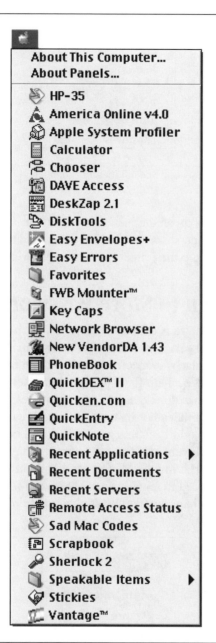

FIGURE 6-25   Although a number of extra items are added to this user's Apple menu, Control Panels are absent

FIGURE 6-26   Notice how your Special menu is changed

Finally, a new addition is on the menu bar in the Panels view, a menu called Printing. The Printing menu shows you which printer is currently selected and enables you to start and stop the printer queue on your Mac (see Figure 6-27).

Using the Keychain to Store Passwords

Mac OS 9's Keychain feature is a tool that enables you to manage many of your passwords for a variety of services, from your Internet mail account to the file servers to which you regularly connect. While Keychain is a new feature in Mac OS 9, the concept of the Keychain first appeared in System 7 Pro many years ago. Like many things Apple has done over the years, however, the Keychain in that old system version was far ahead of its time and never really caught on. Now in Mac OS 9, Apple has brought back this great utility and improved it significantly.

The idea behind the Keychain is that you currently have many different passwords to remember. Having the Mac remember them for you would be simpler. Then you only need to remember the password for your Mac. As such, whenever you tell a Keychain-compatible application to remember a password, it

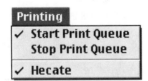

FIGURE 6-27   The Printer menu is a new addition to the menu bar

adds that password to your Keychain. When you want to use the application or to connect to a file server whose password you have saved in the Keychain, all you need to do is enter your password to unlock your Keychain. Once unlocked, the Keychain then takes care of filling in all your passwords when necessary.

To create a new Keychain for yourself or another user, follow these steps:

1. Click the Apple menu and scroll down to Control Panels. Then select Keychain Access from the submenu.

2. Click the Keychain Access File menu and then select New Keychain. If no Keychains are on your Mac, you are presented with a dialog box and asked to click the Create button to create one.

3. Enter the name of the Keychain and the password. Then confirm the password by entering it again to confirm you have entered it correctly.

NOTE
You should follow the previous suggestions about setting up a global password for your Keychain. Select a random collection of numbers and letters (and remember to put them in a safe place, in case you forget the password).

4. Once you create a new Keychain, the empty Keychain file is displayed to you (see Figure 6-28). When you start saving passwords in your Keychain, it stores information about each of the passwords you have stored, including the name of the service the password is for, the kind of password it is, and the date the password was added to the Keychain.

FIGURE 6-28   This window displays all the passwords you have stored in the Keychain

Using the Keychain to Store Passwords

5. If you want to delete one of the passwords in your Keychain, click the offending password name, and then click the Remove button. You are then asked to confirm your deletion of this password. Click OK if you want to eliminate this password or click Cancel to keep it.

6. To get additional information about any one password in your Keychain, click the name of the password and then click the Get Info button. You are then presented with the dialog box you see in Figure 6-29.

7. If you want to see the actual password stored in the Keychain, click the Show Password button. Then you are asked to enter your Keychain password to verify it is you, type in your password, and click OK to display the password or click Cancel to abort the action.

8. If you want to open the connection the password you are looking at is bound to, click the Go There button to open the connection.

9. Once you finish with the Keychain Access Control Panel, click the close box to close the Control Panel and save any changes.

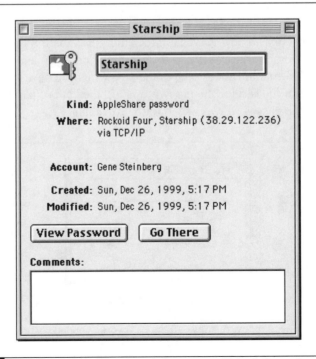

FIGURE 6-29   Getting Info on a password shows you all the information the Keychain contains for this password

Once created, you can copy your Keychain file to another computer you regularly use so you do not have to retype all your passwords. Because the Keychain file is portable between various Macs running Mac OS 9, moving between the various Macs at your site or even in your own home becomes a much simpler task.

Summing Up

In this chapter, you learned the power of Apple's new Multiple Users capability that is built into Mac OS 9. You learned how you can create new users and set them up so they only have limited access to the files and resources available on your Mac. You also learned how to use Apple's Voiceprint feature to let your voice gain access to your Mac.

Finally, you learned about the Keychain feature in Mac OS 9 that simplifies your password management by centralizing all your passwords for Keychain-enabled applications in one file, greatly reducing the number of passwords you must remember.

In the next chapter, you learn about Apple's multifaceted search tool, Sherlock 2. You learn how to find files on your Mac, the text inside those files, and how to broaden your search to cover the entire Internet.

Summing Up

Chapter 7

How to Find Information with Sherlock 2

M ac OS 9 has been labeled "your Internet co-pilot" by Apple. And it's not just an advertising claim. Internet integration extends to many areas of your Mac OS 9 experience, particularly with file sharing.

In this chapter, the focus is on how searching enters the picture.

Finding files and information both on your Mac and the Internet has never been simpler than when using Mac OS 9. The Sherlock 2 application that comes with Mac OS 9 enables you to search your Mac's drives to find files or folders containing the information for which you are looking. Sherlock 2 isn't confined to searching for something on your Mac, though. You can also use Sherlock 2 to search the entire Internet. And this doesn't only include a list of Web sites for you to check. Sherlock 2 can even help you find things to buy on the Internet by enabling you to search various auction sites and online merchants.

Sherlock 2's other main advantage over the normal Internet search engine is that you can make your search request in plain English. You needn't learn special search language, add additional symbols, or speak in Boolean language to refine the search as you do with some of the Internet search engines.

In this chapter, you learn all about using Sherlock 2 to find information located on your Mac and on the Internet. Starting with the basic features of Sherlock 2, you learn how to locate the files on your Mac that contain the information for which you are looking. Next you see how easy it is to tap the power of Sherlock 2 to hunt down files, people, and lots of other information from sources all across the Internet. Then you learn about Sherlock 2's e-commerce feature, which enables you to track auction prices and regular sales prices so you can get the best price (at least, if the online merchant has delivered a Sherlock 2 search module to you).

How to Find Files Using Sherlock 2

Like the previous incarnation of Sherlock found in Mac OS 8.5 and 8.6, Sherlock 2 is an extremely fast and powerful search engine, capable of finding all the files and folders on your Mac that match the criteria you are using. Sherlock 2 can locate files based on their file or folder name, the contents of a file, or, if it's an application larger than 1MB, whether it was modified today or yesterday, or if has been deleted.

Consider all the drudgery you'd have to go through to look for files or folders manually on your Mac whenever you need to look up something, plus the further aggravation of picking the right Internet site from among millions.

Here's how to use Sherlock 2:

1. Click the Finder's File menu and then select Find from the list of
available commands or type COMMAND-F to bring up Sherlock 2. You
can also launch Sherlock 2 by clicking the Apple menu and selecting it
from the list. Once Sherlock 2 is open (see Figure 7-1), follow these few
steps to search for the files and folders you are trying to find
on your Mac.

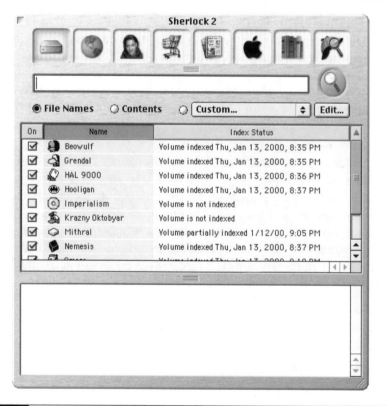

FIGURE 7-1   Sherlock 2 is Mac OS 9's powerful file search utility

2. To find files and folders by their name using the Finder, click the radio button labeled "File Names," and then enter the name of the file or folder you want to find.

NOTE *If you don't know the full name of the file or folder you are looking for, enter a fragment of the file name in the text box located directly above the radio buttons. For example, if you are looking for a file or folder named The Bears of Jellystone, you could have Sherlock 2 search for either Jelly or Jellystone and expect to find the files fairly easily. Choosing Bears might also work, but that could result in a much larger number of found files, depending on the number of files with Bear in their name. The key thing to remember is that you should use unique words or fragments of words.*

3. To find files using the contents of the file, click the Contents radio button and then enter the text you want to find. Make sure you enter text unique enough so the number of files Sherlock 2 finds is not excessive.

CAUTION *You cannot search the contents of a file until your drive is indexed. For more information on how Sherlock 2 finds files by their content, look at the next section in this chapter.*

4. If you cannot remember what the file or folder's name is, or if you cannot remember what might be in the file to search on, then you should search for the file using one of the other options. Click the radio button labeled Custom, and then click the pop-up menu to select the type of search you want to use. Under the custom menu, you can search only for application files, files greater than one megabyte, files modified today, and files modified the day before. You can even choose to have Sherlock 2 delete all the files that meet the search criteria you want to use.

5. To refine your search further, click the custom radio button and then click the Edit button to bring up the dialog box you see in Figure 7-2.

Sherlock 2 Search Criteria

To add additional criteria to the file and folder search you will perform, click the check boxes for each option you want to add to your search.

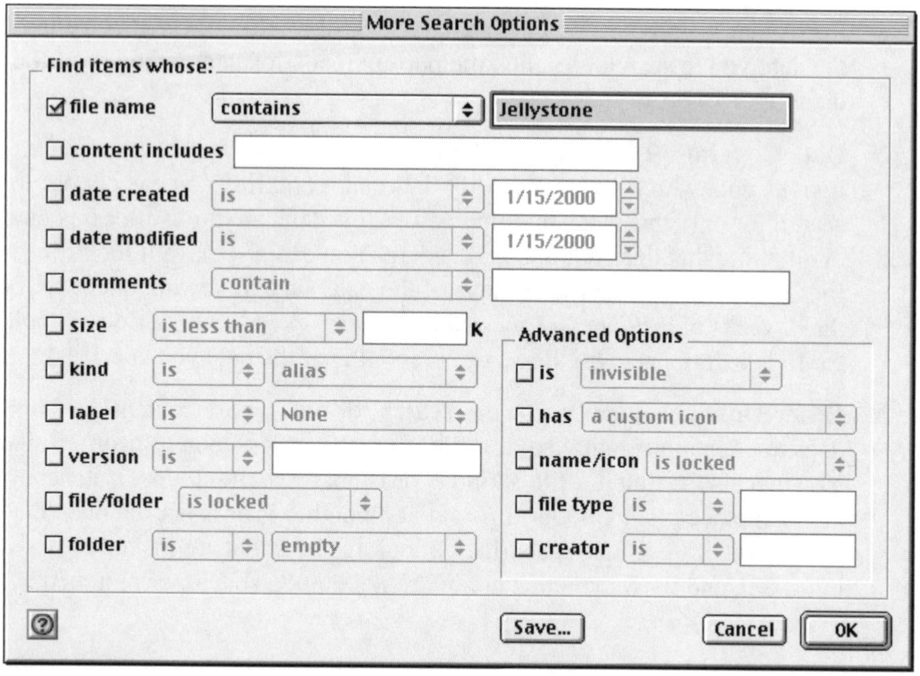

```
┌─────────────────────────────────────────────────────────────────────┐
│ ═══════════════════════ More Search Options ═══════════════════════  │
│ ┌─ Find items whose: ─────────────────────────────────────────────┐ │
│ │ ☑ file name      [ contains              ⬍ ] [ Jellystone      ] │ │
│ │ ☐ content includes [                                          ]  │ │
│ │ ☐ date created   [ is                    ⬍ ] [ 1/15/2000   ⬍ ] │ │
│ │ ☐ date modified  [ is                    ⬍ ] [ 1/15/2000   ⬍ ] │ │
│ │ ☐ comments       [ contain               ⬍ ] [                ] │ │
│ │ ☐ size  [ is less than    ⬍ ] [     ] K  ┌─ Advanced Options ──┐ │ │
│ │ ☐ kind  [ is  ⬍ ] [ alias      ⬍ ]   ☐ is  [ invisible    ⬍ ] │ │
│ │ ☐ label [ is  ⬍ ] [ None       ⬍ ]   ☐ has [ a custom icon ⬍ ] │ │
│ │ ☐ version [ is ⬍ ] [           ]     ☐ name/icon [ is locked ⬍ ] │ │
│ │ ☐ file/folder [ is locked   ⬍ ]      ☐ file type [ is ⬍ ] [   ] │ │
│ │ ☐ folder [ is ⬍ ] [ empty     ⬍ ]    ☐ creator [ is ⬍ ] [    ] │ │
│ │ ⊘                          [ Save… ]    [ Cancel ]  [  OK  ]      │ │
│ └─────────────────────────────────────────────────────────────────┘ │
└─────────────────────────────────────────────────────────────────────┘
```

FIGURE 7-2   Clicking the Edit button displays all the available search options

Here are the available options and what they do:

- **Name**   First click the name check box, enter the text you want to use, and then click the pop-up menu located to the left of the text box.

TIP   *You can quickly move through fields in a search options window simply by pressing the* TAB *key. You can return to a previous selection by the* SHIFT-TAB *keys.*

- **Name Criteria**   The pop-up menu under name enables you to search for a name containing the text you entered, starts with the text, ends with the text, is exactly equal to the text, is not equal to the text, or does not contain the text at all.

How to Find Files
Using Sherlock 2

■ **Dates**   Selecting one of the two date check boxes enables you to search for files based on the date they were created or modified. Once you enter the date you to search for, click the pop-up menu located to the left of the date field.

■ **Date Criteria**   The menu you see in Figure 7-3 displays the various options with which you can modify the search criteria. You can choose to search for only this date, anything before this date, anything after this date, or anything that does not match this date. You can also have it look for files within one, two, or three days of the date, or if you want, one, two, or three weeks of the date you specified. You can even have Sherlock 2 look for files within one, two, three, or six months of the date you specified.

■ **Other Options**   Finally, you can search for files whose content does or does not contain certain text, if a file is greater or less than a specified size. You can also search if a file's kind is or is not a specified type, if its label is or is not a certain kind, or if its version number is or is not the one you enter. You can even have Sherlock 2 look for files that are locked or unlocked, and for folders that are or are not empty, shared, or mounted.

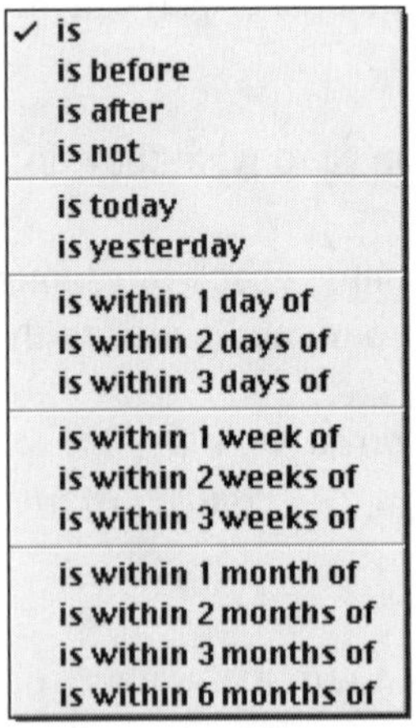

```
✓ is
  is before
  is after
  is not

  is today
  is yesterday

  is within 1 day of
  is within 2 days of
  is within 3 days of

  is within 1 week of
  is within 2 weeks of
  is within 3 weeks of

  is within 1 month of
  is within 2 months of
  is within 3 months of
  is within 6 months of
```

FIGURE 7-3   Sherlock 2 offers a wide variety of search modifiers when searching by Date

NOTE

A file's kind includes the information you see in the Kind column when you view a file with the Finder's List option. A Microsoft Word document, such as the one used for the manuscript of this book, may be listed as a Microsoft Word 97-98 document.

■ **Other Search Options**   For the serious searcher, you can also search for files that are visible or invisible, use a custom or a standard icon, as well as one whose name or icon is locked or unlocked. The Advanced Options also enable you to search for files whose file types and creator types either match or do not match the values you entered.

NOTE

The Mac OS Finder stores a database of file types and creator information. This is not something you would normally be expected to know. Some shareware programs, however, such as FileTypeChanger v 4.0 (available via VersionTracker.com or AOL), enable you to view and change file types. Changing a file type isn't a normal practice (unless you want to make one document open in a different program), but having this information might help you refine your searches.

To continue your search, follow these steps:

1. Once you enter all your search criteria, click the OK button to return to the primary Sherlock 2 dialog box.

TIP

You can also click the Save button to save the search options you have created for later use. Saving your preferences causes them to be added to the pop-up menu located next to the Edit button. If you want to throw away all the changes you have made, click the Cancel button.

2. Next, you need to select all the volumes on your Mac you want Sherlock 2 to search. Normally, all your fixed volumes are selected and all your removable media drives, like CD/DVD-ROMs, are not selected as part of the search criteria.

3. If you want to select all the volumes when none are currently selected, click the Edit menu and then select the command Turn All On, or press COMMAND-T.

4. To deselect all the volumes when one or more volumes are selected, click the Edit menu and then select Turn All Off from the menu press COMMAND-T again.

5. After you select all the volumes you want search, click the magnifying glass or press the return key to start the search process.

6. Once Sherlock 2 has finished searching your Mac, it displays all the files and folders it found that match the search criteria you selected. The list box in the upper portion of the Sherlock 2 dialog box (see Figure 7-4) displays all the files and folders Sherlock 2 located on your Mac.

FIGURE 7-4 Sherlock 2 found two files on your Macintosh that meet your description

TIP

You can also modify your search to include some of the words of a file selected in Sherlock 2's window. CONTROL-CLICK *the file's name to bring up Mac OS 9's handy Contextual menu and choose Find Similar Files. You can only perform this custom search if the files on your drive have been indexed (see the next section for more information).*

7. To open one of the files and folders located by Sherlock 2, double-click it. Or, you can simply click the file or folder found by Sherlock 2 to see where it is located. You can open any of the folders displayed in the lower window, which shows the path to the folder or file Sherlock 2 found by double-clicking them.

NOTE

Sherlock 2 can be configured the same as any Finder window. You can drag the edges of columns to resize them or click a column label to change the sort criteria.

Searching for Files by Content Using Sherlock 2

As you learned in the previous section, Sherlock 2 is capable of locating files on your Mac based on the content of the files. Using Sherlock 2 to search for files by content is a two-step process. First, you have to activate the Sherlock 2 feature that indexes all the files on your Mac. Once you index the files on your Mac, then you can use Sherlock 2 to start searching through all your files by their content.

The first part of the process is to index all of the volumes on your Mac that you wish to search. To begin the process of indexing the various hard drives on your Mac, follow these few steps:

1. Open Sherlock 2 by pressing COMMAND-F while in the Finder or by clicking the Apple menu, and then selecting Sherlock 2 from the list of items. Another way to open Sherlock 2 is to click the Finder's file menu and then select Find from the list of available options.

2. When Sherlock 2 has been launched, click the Find menu and then scroll down to the Index Volumes command. You can also open the dialog box by pressing COMMAND-L.

3. Look at the dialog box shown in Figure 7-5, and select the volumes you want Sherlock 2 to index. After you select all the volumes you want to index, click the Schedule button.

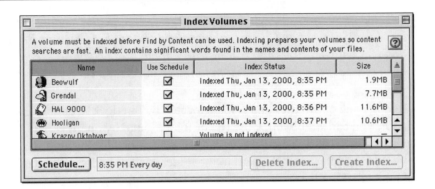

FIGURE 7-5   Select the volumes whose files you want to index

> **NOTE**   *Which volumes you want to index is completely up to you. Because the process can take a while, you may want to concentrate only on those containing items for which the text must be searched. Any mounted volume, including a removable drive, CD, or networked volume, can be indexed.*

4. If you want the index to scan on a schedule, click on the check box labeled Schedule for each of the volumes you want to index. If you want to index a volume right away, highlight the volume you want to index, and then click the Create Index button.

> **NOTE**   *By indexing the files, Sherlock 2 crawls through all the documents located on the hard drive, so it can read them and then index their content. Once this index is complete, Sherlock 2 can search for files on your Mac based on the data contained in the index.*

5. In the schedule dialog box (see Figure 7-6), you can set the time, along with the days of the week, you want Sherlock 2 to scan your hard drives. Set the time of day when you want Sherlock 2 to scan all the files.

6. Now set the days of the week you want to have scanned by clicking the various check boxes.

7. Once you set up the schedule you want, click OK to go back to the Sherlock 2 index dialog box.

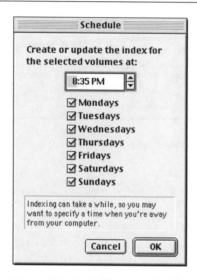

FIGURE 7-6   Set the times and dates Sherlock 2 should index your volumes

CAUTION   *Make sure to have your Mac on when the index is scheduled to be created or updated. Don't forget to disable the automatic sleep function in the Energy Saver Control Panel. While you have the Control Panel open, click the Schedule button to make sure the Mac is not scheduled to shut down before the indexing is scheduled to occur.*

8. If you want to index a volume right away, highlight the volume you want to index, and then click the Create Index button. You are then shown the dialog box displayed in Figure 7-7. Because creating an index can take a long time, Sherlock 2 asks if you want to have the new index created during the next scheduled time or if you want to create it now. If you decide you do not want to create the index now, click the Cancel button.

NOTE   *A long time can be an understatement. A drive of several gigabytes with thousands of text files can take several hours to index. But the update process moves much faster because only the files that have changed or have been added are scanned.*

9. Once you click the Create button, your Mac begins scanning the hard drive you selected to build its index. The progress bar (see Figure 7-8)

You can create an index now or have it scheduled for later

shows you which files are being indexed and how long the index will take to complete.

NOTE
Because accessing and copying files can take different amounts of time, the time displayed in the progress bar is approximate. The time can vary up and down the scale as the indexing process continues.

10. After the Mac finishes scanning your hard drive and recording the Index, you are returned to the main Sherlock 2 Index Volumes dialog box.

TIP
You can also index a selected file or folder. CONTROL-CLICK the file's name, and then select Index selection from the Contextual menu.

NOTE
Sherlock 2 creates a separate index for each hard drive you specify.

11. Once you create some indexes, you can then delete them by highlighting the hard drive whose index you want to delete, and then click the Delete button. When you click the Delete button, Sherlock 2 asks if you really want to delete the Index (see Figure 7-9). Click OK if you want to delete the index for the selected hard drive or click the Cancel button to abort the delete.

NOTE
It's not that we expect you to delete your index immediately after you make it. If you don't need to search for the content of files on a specific drive volume and you want to save a little hard drive space, however, you should delete it.

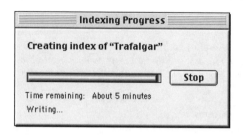

FIGURE 7-8   Sherlock 2 shows you the progress of your indexes' creation

12. Once you finish building all the indexes, click the close box to close the Index Volumes dialog box and return to the main Sherlock 2 dialog box.

You can simply start searching right here and now, without doing anything more. But, you can also refine your content searches to guide the way Sherlock 2 behaves on your Mac. From Sherlock 2's Preferences dialog box, you can set the way Sherlock 2 works over the Internet, as well as how it behaves when indexing and what languages it supports.

To configure Sherlock 2's preferences, follow these steps:

1. Open Sherlock 2 as described in the previous section.

2. Click the Edit menu and select Preferences.

3. When the Preferences dialog box, shown in Figure 7-10, is displayed, click the pop-up menu labeled Maximum number of connections and choose the number of HTTP connections to Web servers, connections Sherlock 2 will open while it is searching the Internet.

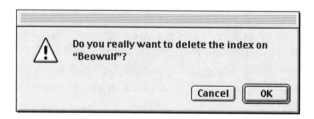

FIGURE 7-9   Click OK if you really want to delete the Index for this volume

Searching for Files by Content Using Sherlock 2

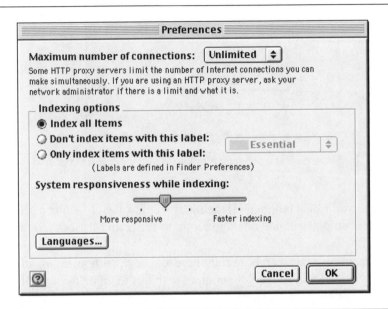

FIGURE 7-10   The Sherlock 2 Preferences dialog box enables you to configure
your Search

NOTE   *Normally, the number of connections are set to Unlimited, allowing
Sherlock 2 to create as many HTTP connections as necessary to the
various search engines being queried on the Internet. Some networks
and ISPs, however, limit the number of connections you can open at once.
Sherlock 2 enables you to specify the number of connections, starting with
four, which is the number usually opened by a Web browser like Internet
Explorer, all the way up to ten. If you are uncertain how many HTTP
connections to open, you might as well select Unlimited. If, however,
a limit is set by your ISP or your network, select the appropriate value
from those available in the pop-up menu.*

4. Next, look down at the various indexing options. The first option you
   want to set is the files and folders indexed by Sherlock 2. Using the three
   radio buttons in the dialog box, you can choose to index all the files, index
   files not labeled with a specific label, or index only those labeled with a
   specific label.

5. Once you tell Sherlock 2 what files to index, you want to tell it how much
   time to spend indexing the files. More specifically, you can set Sherlock 2

to spend more time indexing, thus making your Mac less responsive if you are working on it while the indexes are being created.

NOTE   *If you want your Mac to be more lively while indexing, you can set it to be more responsive, but slower at creating the indexes. To set the speed of Index creation, click the Slider, and then move it to the setting you want to use.*

6. Finally, click the Languages button and bring up the Languages dialog box (see Figure 7-11). Review the Languages dialog box to make sure you selected all the languages that contain words your Mac should index. Once you select the languages used for searching, click OK to save your changes or click Cancel to discard them.

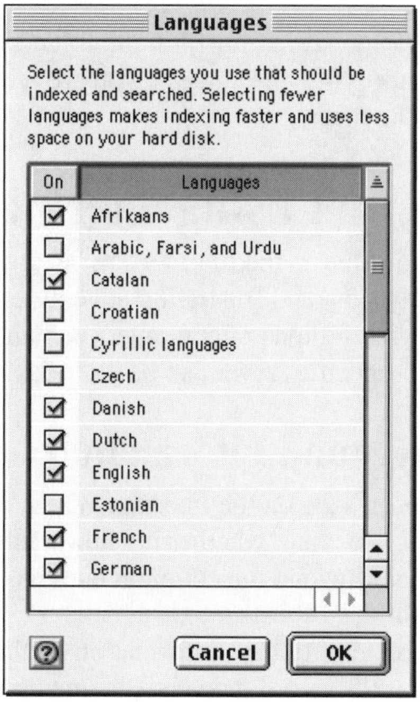

Languages

Select the languages you use that should be indexed and searched. Selecting fewer languages makes indexing faster and uses less space on your hard disk.

On	Languages
☑	Afrikaans
☐	Arabic, Farsi, and Urdu
☑	Catalan
☐	Croatian
☐	Cyrillic languages
☐	Czech
☑	Danish
☑	Dutch
☑	English
☐	Estonian
☑	French
☑	German

[Cancel] [OK]

FIGURE 7-11   The Languages dialog box enables you to set the languages for which words will be indexed

CAUTION

Every bit of additional criteria you set for Sherlock 2 brings a further slowdown in performance. You should only set language options you actually need, if any.

7. Once you finish configuring Sherlock 2, click the OK button to save your changes, or click the Cancel button to discard your changes and return to the main Sherlock 2 dialog box.

The settings described here may take a few moments to complete (and you might want to consider some of them carefully). They will go a long way toward refining your searches for items on your Mac.

NOTE

Mac OS 9 also enables you to create a summary of a selected text file. Once the drive has been indexed, simply click the file's name on the Finder desktop. Then pick Summarize File to Clipboard from Mac OS 9's handy Contextual menu. The summary can then be pasted into any open word processing or desktop publishing (or even e-mail) document.

Now that you know how to search for files and folders on your Mac and to configure Sherlock 2 to meet your exact needs, you are ready to start using Sherlock 2 to search the Internet.

Searching the Internet Using Sherlock 2

Looking for information or files on the Internet can be, at best, time consuming and, at worst, an extremely slow and frustrating adventure. Because the Internet is a huge network filled with millions of computers containing trillions of files, finding a specific file on a specific server can be a serious challenge.

First, Some Background Information

Literally millions of Web sites are on the Internet. Where do you go to locate the ones that have the content you want, whether it's news, information, or simply current prices on a new car? Beyond the common names of sites you've read about, where do you go for the answers?

To help solve the problem of finding information on the Internet, some inventive college students at Stanford University came up with a clever idea. They had a computer start scanning all the Web sites it could find on the Internet, and then indexing all the files it found.

This new Internet search engine was called Yahoo! It began simply as a project to help these students locate the information they wanted on the Internet, but they soon realized its commercial possibilities.

Yahoo! quickly grew from humble beginnings to become the huge Internet portal it is today, one that has garnered respect around the world (and, as a consequence, delivered a healthy profit for those who bought its rapidly rising stock early on). Today, Yahoo! provides lots more than just a search engine. It's also an online community, with e-mail, instant messaging, and many other features designed to keep visitors coming back again and again, even after your search requests are answered.

People were quick to embrace the idea and produce their own Internet search engines. Today, several large search engines exist, in addition to Yahoo!, such as AltaVista, Excite, HotBot, Google, and others, each one with its own custom index of the Internet. Because each search engine works slightly differently, each one contains different Internet-based information. While some overlap occurs in the files each search engine has indexed, many files will have been found by one search engine and not seen by the others.

Each of these sites has, like Yahoo!, gone beyond the basics and provides a broad range of services that also help attract advertisers, their primary source of revenue.

Because looking for some pieces of information on the Internet requires you to use a variety of different search engines, you can often spend hours searching through all the results returned before you find the information you want. In addition, each search engine usually interprets the search criteria you enter differently, so the same search criteria you used with one search may return different results. As such, conducting accurate information searches on the Internet is neither an easy nor a quick proposition.

How to Use Sherlock for Internet Searches

Beginning with Mac OS 8.6, Apple decided to extend its "Think Different" philosophy to Internet searches, coming up with Sherlock.

Sherlock was a revolution. Rather than making your search request using arcane language and inserting such so-called Boolean operators as AND or NOT, Sherlock 2 takes your plain English requests. Then it translates the requests and communicates with many different Internet search engines, using

Searching the Internet Using Sherlock 2

add-on modules that are easily installed into your Mac's System Folder (Sherlock already includes a useful collection).

Sherlock then takes the information returned by the Internet search engines and sorts it, looking for results that match your search criteria the best. As such, Sherlock makes searching the Internet for information almost as simple as finding a file on your Mac.

Sherlock 2 builds on the already impressive Sherlock technology to improve on the way it talks to the various search engines on the Internet, as well as including a variety of preset search configurations you can use (called channels). You also have the ability to create your own channels, customized with the search modules you want.

Sherlock 2 also has improved search technology, allowing it to sift through the different results that are returned to better provide you with the most likely choice.

To use Sherlock 2 to locate information on the Internet, follow these steps:

1. Open Sherlock for Internet searches by either clicking the File menu in the Finder and then scrolling down and selecting Search Internet from the menu, or by pressing COMMAND-H.

2. The Sherlock 2 Internet window you see in Figure 7-12 shows the text box where you type your search criteria. Below the text box is the list of search modules Sherlock 2 uses for its searching.

3. Once you enter your search criteria, scroll through the list of sites Sherlock 2 will search. Look over the sites Sherlock 2 has been set to search, and add or remove sites you want by clicking the check box next to each site.

NOTE *You can also choose one of the many predefined Sherlock 2 channels to use when searching or you can create your own.*

NOTE *While the predefined search channels may work for a wide variety of subjects, inevitably, for certain subjects, you might want to create your own custom search Channel. For more information on creating your own custom search Channel, refer to the section on "Creating Channels and Adding Plug-ins to Sherlock 2" later in this chapter.*

FIGURE 7-12 Sherlock 2 enables you to search the Internet from your Mac

4. Once you enter the search criteria you want to use and choose the search Channel you want to use, start the search by clicking the Start button, the round button with a picture of a magnifying glass in it, or press RETURN to start the search.

5. Sherlock 2 now goes out to the Internet and contacts all the servers you have told it to contact. It then waits until all the different servers have responded or Sherlock 2 has decided they will not respond because they are not functioning. As Sherlock 2 receives the responses it expects to get, it sorts through the results and displays the ones that are most likely what you want.

6. When you see the list of results displayed by Sherlock 2 (see Figure 7-13), double-click the one you want to see. Or click once on the item, and you'll see more information about the site in the bottom pane of Sherlock 2, after which one more click on the link in the bottom pane will be enough to get you to the site. Either way, your Mac then launches your default browser, usually either Internet Explorer or Netscape Navigator, and then opens the site you found using Sherlock 2.

FIGURE 7-13   Look over the Web pages Sherlock 2 found for you

Introducing Channels

Channels are a new concept in Sherlock 2. *Channels* are designed to enable you to create a special group of sites you will search based on what you seek. For example, if you want to search for a person on the Internet, click the Channel menu, and then select the channel labeled People. Once you select People, notice a different list of sites to search in the window, located directly below the search criteria. These sites are devoted to searching for people.

You can also click the various channel icons shown above the search criteria text box.

The channels that come with Sherlock 2 are Internet, People, Apple, Shopping, News, and Reference. As the names imply, each one is optimized to search for a specific type of information. If you are looking for something on the Internet, an article on a game, perhaps, then you want to use the Internet channel. Likewise, if you were trying to hunt down information regarding a patch for your brand new G4 Mac, then you want to select the Apple channel before clicking the search button.

What makes the Channels concept so powerful is that they enable you to create focused search groups that greatly improve your chance of locating the information you are searching for on the Internet.

Getting a list of sites that match your search request is only part of what Sherlock 2 can do. In the next section, you learn how to search for merchandise offerings on the Internet and some popular online auction houses.

Using Sherlock 2 to Find Bargains on the Web

One of the really cool features of Sherlock 2 is its capability to search sites like Amazon and eBay to find books, records, movies, and many other things for you to purchase. You can also use Sherlock 2 to monitor an auction on eBay for which you've placed your bid. This is extremely useful when you need to keep a close eye on an auction you want to win (you must watch the current price the item is selling for carefully, along with the amount of time left). This way, you can prepare your winning bid and swoop in immediately before the auction closes.

To use Sherlock 2 to monitor an auction site for items you want or to search for that special book or piece of music you want, do the following:

1. Bring up Sherlock 2 in the Internet search mode either by selecting Internet Search from the Finder's File menu or by pressing COMMAND-H.

2. Now that Sherlock 2 is up, click the icon that looks like a shopping cart.

3. Once you switch to the Shopping Channel (see Figure 7-14), look over the sites on which Sherlock 2 is planning to search. By default, the Shopping Channel is designed to search the various Amazon book, music, video, and auction sites, as well as Barnes and Noble, and, of course, eBay.

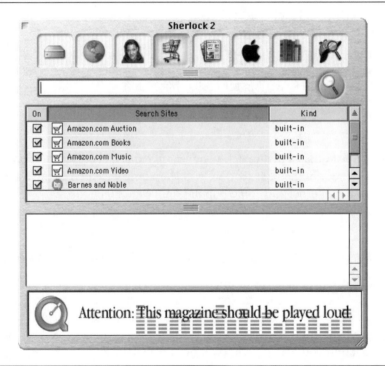

FIGURE 7-14   See the Web sites Sherlock 2 searches when in the Shopping Channel

4. Once you choose the sites you want Sherlock 2 to search, enter the search criteria you want Sherlock 2 to use when looking for things on the Internet. For example, let's see if some bargains are out there by searching for PowerMac G4.

5. Next, click the start button, the one with the magnifying glass to the right of where you typed your search criteria, or press RETURN to start Sherlock 2 scanning.

6. When you look at the results Sherlock 2 returned in Figure 7-15, you can see a variety of responses look promising. To check out one of the offerings that seem attractive, all you need to do is double-click on the title of the item Sherlock 2 found. Your Mac then launches your favorite Web browser and takes you right to the site Sherlock 2 found.

FIGURE 7-15   See what Sherlock 2 found when looking to buy a PowerMac G4

Using Sherlock 2 to Find Bargains on the Web

Now that you can use Sherlock 2 to find things to buy on the Internet, it's time to start looking at how you can expand your Sherlock 2 searches by adding additional plug-ins and creating custom Channels to use when you search the Internet.

Creating Channels and Adding Plug-ins to Sherlock 2

Sherlock 2 was designed from the start as an extensible search engine, allowing you to add additional sites for it to search by simply dragging a new plug-in file into it (or to the closed System Folder icon). Likewise, creating a new custom search Channel simply involved copying and pasting the various search sites you want to have in your new Channel. In fact, moving search sites around in Sherlock 2 is almost identical to the way you move files and folders around in the Mac OS 9 Finder.

When you create a custom search Channel, you provide a search environment that meets your specific requirements. You can add only the search tools that provide the information you want, nothing more, nothing less.

Creating a new search Channel is an extremely simple task you can complete in only a few minutes. Once you create it, though, you will probably spend months adding sites to and removing sites from your Channel.

Because the Internet never seems to stay in one place for any length of time, you will probably add new site plug-ins and remove those that are out-of-date or whose sites did not prove to be exactly what you need in this Channel. To create a custom search Channel, follow these few steps:

1. Open Sherlock 2 either by pressing COMMAND-H while in the Finder or by clicking the File menu, and then selecting Search Internet from the list of options. Or, you can click the Apple Menu, and then scroll down and select the entry for Sherlock 2.

2. Once Sherlock 2 is open, click the Channels menu and select New Channel from the list. Once you do this, Sherlock 2 brings up the New Channel dialog box (see Figure 7-16) and asks you to enter the name of the Channel, the type of channel it is, the icon you want to use, and your description of the Channel.

3. Click the pop-up menu for the Channel type where you can select a Channel optimized for searching, one optimized for finding people, one optimized for online shopping, and one designed to retrieve news.

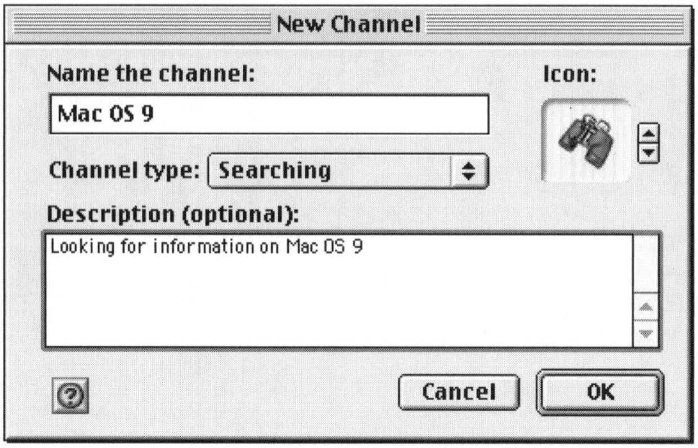

FIGURE 7-16   Set up the name and other specifics for your new Channel

4. Now enter the name of the Channel you created, and then click the pop-up menu to select the type of Channel you want this to be.

5. Once you select the type of Channel you want, scroll through the list of icons to choose one for this Channel.

6. Then enter any comments you want to make to give a better description of the kind of Channel you created.

7. Click OK to save your Channel or click Cancel to throw away this new Channel.

NOTE   *If you do not see an icon you like, you can copy a new one in by simply dragging a small picture into the new Channel window.*

Now you are looking at an empty search channel, which you just created (see Figure 7-17).

If you don't see the icon for your new Channel, you should resize the Sherlock 2 dialog box so it is a bit larger. Once you resize the dialog box, click the window size mark (it looks like three parallel lines), and then drag it down to show your Channel's icon.

To add sites to search into your new Channel, you can either download new plug-ins from the Internet, and then drag them into the Channel, or you can go to a channel that has the sites you want to search and copy them.

Creating Channels and Adding
Plug-ins to Sherlock 2

Your Channel looks a bit empty when you first create it

Adding Sherlock 2 Plug-ins

You can easily add new plug-ins to your Channel or to Sherlock 2 by copying search
sites from one Channel to another. Follow these simple instructions:

1. Open Sherlock 2 using the various methods that were previously discussed.

2. To install a new site plug-in in Sherlock 2, use your Web browser to go
   to a site that contains a nice collection of Sherlock 2 plug-ins. Or, go to

a site that has the specific plug-in you are looking for, and then simply download it. One of the best collections of Sherlock 2 plug-ins is the site Apple maintains at http://www.apple.com/sherlock/plugins.html. Other sites, like the one at Corel that houses their clip-art library search plug-in (see Figure 7-18), offer only their plug-in for Sherlock 2.

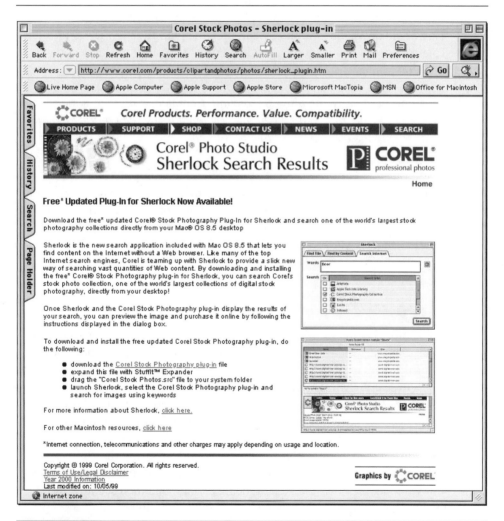

Creating Channels and Adding Plug-ins to Sherlock 2

FIGURE 7-18   Corel offers you a Sherlock 2 plug-in to search their clip-art library

3. Once you download the Sherlock 2 plug-in and decompress it, all you must do is drag the plug-in into the Channel in which you want to use it.

TIP   *If you want to use this plug-in in multiple Channels, hold down the Option key while dragging it into each Channel. Then you only copy the plug-in into the Channel; you do not actually move it.*

4. To copy site plug-ins between Channels, all you need to do is go to the Channel that has the plug-in you want to use and click it to highlight it. Now, hold down the Option key and drag the plug-in onto the icon for the Channel where you want to add this plug-in. The plug-in is then copied into that Channel.

TIP   *If you want to move the plug-in from one Channel to another, simply drag the plug-in from the existing Channel (without using the Option key) and drop it onto the one where you want it to go.*

After you finish moving or copying all the Sherlock 2 plug-ins so they are located in the Channels you want, look at the task of Channel maintenance. Using the Edit Channel command in the Channel menu, you can edit the various settings you set up when you first set up the selected Channel. Likewise, using the Delete Channel button enables you to remove the Channel you currently selected from Sherlock 2.

Summing Up

Sherlock 2 is probably the most advanced search utility currently in existence on any personal computer today. It provides you with an immense amount of power to search for files on your Mac, either by their name or by their contents, as well as enabling you to search the Internet. Sherlock 2's Internet search tools are a major advance from the ones present in the original Sherlock and, with the addition of search Channels, they have made searching for information on the Internet a much simpler proposal.

The Internet is, at its core, a vast computer network covering the entire globe. In the next chapter, you learn how networking works with Mac OS 9. Beginning with your own Mac, see how it talks to a local network, and then see how these skills are extended to include networking your Mac via the Internet.

Chapter 8

Secrets of Local and Internet Networking

From the very first Mac, the lowly 128, through the latest Power Mac G4, all Macs have been designed with networking in mind.

Mac networking had its humble start with the original LocalTalk networks capable of transferring 140Kbits/sec. Networking was impressive then, but as with other computer standards, it has become faster and easier to use with each generation of Mac.

Today's Macs, including the iBook and iMac, are all equipped with 100Mbps Ethernet connections allowing for file transfers over 1,000 times faster than the original LocalTalk.

As the performance of the network hardware that is built into the Mac has grown, so has the capability of the Mac to communicate with other computers over the network. In this chapter, you learn how to configure your Mac to talk with the other computers and network devices located on your *local area network* (*LAN*). Then, you learn how to harness Mac OS 9's powerful Internet integration tools, so you can connect to other Macs across the Internet, and how you can protect your files by setting security. You also learn about the highly sophisticated technology that underlies the Internet and how your Mac can work with it.

How to Network Your Mac

As previously mentioned, the Mac was designed from the beginning to network with other computers and printers. While the networking capabilities in the original Mac 128 are a far cry from those available in the latest models, the basic concepts remain the same.

Unlike the PC, where networking was discovered late in life and then grafted into the operating system, the Mac OS was designed from the ground up with networking in mind. As such, networking components are deeply integrated into the Mac OS, making the connection of your Mac to the network quick and easy.

When you start out to connect your Mac to the network, you need to find out a few things. The first and most important piece of information you need to discover is what type of network you will be connecting to and what network protocols will be used on the network. Next, you want to learn how shared volumes and printers are set up on your network so you can connect to them. Finally, you want to get the information you need to connect your Mac to the Internet.

Originally, Macs were only able to communicate using LocalTalk, an older network technology Apple Computer developed in 1984. As time passed, Macs began to use the much faster Ethernet to talk to other computers and network devices on the network. Today, LocalTalk is all but extinct in most Mac networks, as recent generations of Macs (beginning with the hot-selling iMac) do not even support LocalTalk networking. Current Macs come equipped with 100Mbit Ethernet, enabling you to move files and information over the network quickly.

As previously mentioned, when you start the process of connecting your Mac to the LAN, you need to learn how your network works. Most networks are currently either Ethernet or Fast Ethernet over twisted-pair wire (similar to telephone wire), however, some older LocalTalk networks still exist. For Ethernet or Fast Ethernet networks, you need to learn if the network supports both the older Ethernet and the newer Fast Ethernet, or if it supports only one of the two.

While many networks support both types of Ethernet, some do not. Because only the newer Macs support Fast Ethernet, you need to get a Fast Ethernet adapter for any other Mac if you want to connect to a Fast Ethernet only network. When you're connecting your Mac to a Fast Ethernet network, you also want to determine what version of Fast Ethernet your network uses. Most networks use the 100BaseTX network standard. Some, however, use a different standard called 100BaseVG. If your network is based upon 100BaseVG, then you need to get a special adapter for your Mac.

> **NOTE** *If you are uncertain which network typology is used in your installation, contact your network administrator or the system installer for the information.*

Once you determine the type of network that is being used, then you need to determine what protocol(s) are supported. The four major protocols commonly used on LANs are AppleTalk, TCP/IP, IPX/SPX, and NetBEUI.

Here are brief descriptions of these network protocols:

- **AppleTalk**   As the name implies, AppleTalk is the native network protocol used by Macs and many other network devices designed to work with Macs.

- **TCP/IP**   This network protocol runs the Internet, along with a large number of private networks.

- **PX/SPX**   This network protocol is primarily used on Novell NetWare networks.

How to Network Your Mac

A Brief Look at Fast Ethernet Networks

The two different types of 100Mbit Ethernet for twisted-pair networks, 100BaseTX and 100BaseVG, were developed during the 1980s and 1990s. These two standards were developed by competing groups of companies, one led by Intel and the other led by Hewlett-Packard.

100BaseTX was developed by the team led by Intel and focused on providing 100Mbit performance using modern, high-quality network cabling, also known as Category 5 and the newer Category 5+. While this is a fine solution for modern buildings, not all buildings are equipped with up-to-date cabling. This was the view the team led by Hewlett-Packard took when it developed the 100BaseVG standard. 100BaseVG is capable of delivering 100Mbit performance over older, lower-quality cabling, also known as Category 3 and Category 4 cabling.

Since the development of these two standards many years ago, the 100BaseTX standard has become the dominant standard. As the dominant standard, 100BaseTX adapters and network components are cheaper and far more readily available than 100BaseVG adapters and equipment. In fact, the latest generations of Macintosh, starting with the iMac, all come equipped with 100BaseTX adapters. While 100BaseVG networks do exist, they are a small minority of the 100Mbit networks installed. When installing a 100BaseTX network, remember to make sure you use high-quality components so network errors from shoddy cables or low-quality network plugs don't happen.

NOTE *For more information on Novell's products, check the publisher's Web site at http://www.novell.com.*

■ **NetBEUI**   This protocol, also known as NetBIOS Extended User Interface, is the network protocol used by Windows-based computers to communicate. The subject of networking with Windows users is covered in Chapter 28.

Right out of the box, Mac OS 9 is able to communicate using both AppleTalk and TCP/IP. This chapter is devoted primarily to these two protocols.

NOTE *If you need to use one of the other network protocols in your installation, check with your dealer for utilities that allow your Mac to communicate using IPX/SPX as part of a Novell network, or for those using NetBEUI to communicate directly with computers on a Windows-based network.*

Configuring AppleTalk

If you plan to use AppleTalk on your network, then you need to know if any zone(s) are present on the part of the network where you will be connecting and which one you should set your Mac to use.

About AppleTalk Zones

On most home AppleTalk networks and some small business AppleTalk networks, you won't ever see a zone. Zones are used almost exclusively on larger AppleTalk networks, so you can divide the Macs into smaller logical workgroups. You may, for example, set up one zone for your accounting department and another for your graphic arts department. Or, you can set up one for the equipment on one floor and another on a different floor.

Back when AppleTalk phase II was introduced, Apple created the idea of zones as a way of linking many different AppleTalk networks together. By creating zones, Apple was able to extend the size of an AppleTalk network from 254 Macs or other AppleTalk devices to whatever you want it to be. Apple did this by dividing the network into zones, so the maximum number was never exceeded.

Because most home and small business Macintosh networks don't have anywhere near 254 Macintoshes, more than one zone is not needed, except perhaps, for organizational purposes.

If you have a lot of Macs and other networked devices in your company, or they are spread out around your company, then you should consider setting up a zone.

You can set up a zone on your network in two simple ways. If you have Windows NT or Windows 2000 Server on your network and you have Mac support enabled, then you can use the server to create (or *seed* as the process is known) your AppleTalk zones. You learn more about networking with Windows-based computers in Chapter 28.

The second common way of creating an AppleTalk zone is to have the routers that direct the traffic on your network create the zone. All routers capable of handling AppleTalk traffic can seed your network with AppleTalk zones. For more information on how to set up AppleTalk zones with your network router, look at the documentation provided by your router's manufacturer.

How to Network Your Mac

To set your Mac to use the proper AppleTalk zone, do the following:

1. Click the Apple menu and scroll down to Control Panels. Then select the AppleTalk Control Panel from the submenu.

2. With the AppleTalk Control Panel displayed, as shown in Figure 8-1, click the pop-up menu labeled Connect via and select the connection standard you are using to connect to the network. For this example, we select Ethernet built-in.

3. Next, click the pop-up menu labeled Current zone and select the zone you want your Mac to use.

NOTE *Your Mac automatically selects the default AppleTalk zone. If the AppleTalk zone is not the zone you want your Mac to use, click the pop-up menu and change it.*

4. Finally, click the close dialog box to save your changes and exit the AppleTalk Control Panel.

NOTE *As previously explained, zones are the exception rather than the rule on a typical Mac network. The AppleTalk Control Panel will, most likely, only be used to pick your network connection. For newer Macs, without LocalTalk available, Ethernet is selected by default. Otherwise, LocalTalk is the standard setup.*

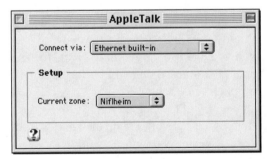

FIGURE 8-1   The AppleTalk Control Panel enables you to set the network interface and AppleTalk zone

Wireless Networking and the Mac

With the introduction of the iBook, Apple's consumer laptop, wireless networking was given a big boost on the Mac. Apple's AirPort network technology supports IEEE 802.11, a worldwide standard for wireless networking.

NOTE   *Support for a worldwide standard means non-Apple networking products that adhere to the standard can be used in an AirPort network. This also allows Macs that do not support AirPort cards to be part of such a network.*

AirPort technology lets Macs network in a home, office, or outside, up to a distance of 150 feet. Apple implements AirPort technology with two products. One is the AirPort Card, a PC card-sized module you install in an Apple computer that supports the technology, such as the iBook, slot-loading iMac, and Power Macintosh G4.

This card allows one AirPort-equipped Mac to communicate with another.

The other component in the wireless system is the AirPort Base Station. This is a central connection point that enables up to ten users to share a single modem connection (using a built-in 56K modem) and to plug directly into a traditional wired Ethernet network.

Maximum networking speed is rated at 11 megabits per second, slightly faster than 10BaseT Ethernet. You learn more about setting up and configuring an AirPort wireless network system in Chapter 12.

Advanced AppleTalk Configuration

If you want more control over AppleTalk networking on your Mac, then you want to go into the advanced user mode. To configure your AppleTalk networking in the advanced mode, do the following:

1. Go to the Apple menu, choose the Control Panels submenu, and then open the AppleTalk Control Panel.

2. Once you see the AppleTalk Control Panel, click the Edit menu and select User Mode, or press COMMAND-U.

3. With the User Mode dialog box open, as shown in Figure 8-2, click the Advanced radio button and then click OK.

4. The AppleTalk dialog box now changes to display all the AppleTalk settings (see Figure 8-3). The Connect via and the Current zone pop-up

How to Network Your Mac

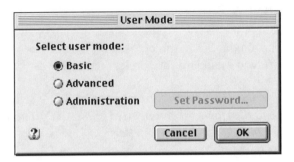

FIGURE 8-2   The User Mode dialog box enables you to choose the mode from which you look at the AppleTalk Control Panel

menus are shown in the dialog box, along with information on your AppleTalk Node, Network number, and the Network range available on your network. Looking at the middle of the dialog box, you see a check box labeled AppleTalk address user defined. Clicking this button makes the Node and Network numbers user configurable.

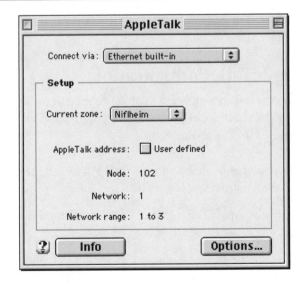

FIGURE 8-3   The Advanced user mode shows you much more AppleTalk information

CAUTION *The option to configure Node and Network numbers is dangerous. AppleTalk was designed to issue AppleTalk addresses automatically. As such, unless all your Macs have their AppleTalk addresses set manually, two Macs could end up with the same AppleTalk address.*

Finally, you can go into Administration mode and set up the AppleTalk Control Panel so only you, or someone who has your password, can change the network interface your Mac uses, the AppleTalk zone this Mac uses, and the AppleTalk address. To enter Administration mode and lock down your AppleTalk network settings, take these steps:

1. Open the AppleTalk control Panel and then open the User Mode dialog box by selecting User Mode from the Edit menu or press COMMAND-U.

2. With the User Mode dialog box displayed, click the radio button labeled Administration and then click the Set Password button, which is now active.

3. Looking at the Administration Password dialog box (see Figure 8-4), enter the password you want to use for the AppleTalk Control Panel.

4. Once you enter the password, type it again in the second text box to confirm it.

5. After you enter your password a second time, click the OK button to close this dialog box and return to the User Mode dialog box.

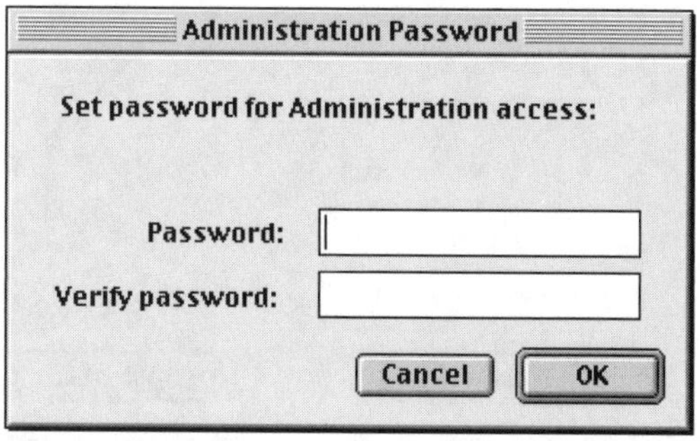

FIGURE 8-4 Set a password for the AppleTalk Control Panel's Administration mode

NOTE
If the two passwords do not match, then you are asked to reenter them until they do match.

6. After you return to the User Mode dialog box, click the OK button to return to the main AppleTalk Control Panel dialog box.

7. The AppleTalk Control Panel dialog box has now changed to display three small boxes, each with the image of an unlocked lock in them (see Figure 8-5). The check boxes are located next to the interface you connect to the network, the AppleTalk zone you are using, and the AppleTalk address. Click the check box located to the right of the item you want to lock. Notice that the icon in the check box has changed from an open to a closed lock.

8. After you lock all the options you want to secure, click the close box to close the AppleTalk Control Panel and save your changes.

In both the Advanced and the Administration user modes, two buttons, labeled Info and Options, are located at the bottom of the AppleTalk Control Panel dialog box. The Info button brings up the AppleTalk Info dialog box you see in Figure 8-6.

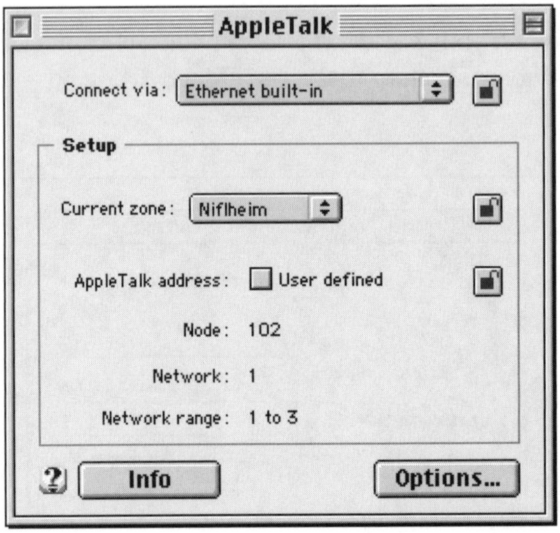

FIGURE 8-5   The Administration user mode enables you to lock certain AppleTalk settings

You can also get to the AppleTalk Info dialog box by clicking the File menu in the AppleTalk Control Panel and then selecting Get Info, or by holding down the Command key and pressing the I key from all three user modes.

This dialog box displays a variety of information about your AppleTalk network connection. This information includes the AppleTalk address of your Mac, the hardware address of the Ethernet interface on your Mac (also known as its MAC address), and the AppleTalk address of the router located on your network.

In the bottom half of the AppleTalk Info dialog box, you can see the versions of Open Transport, AppleTalk, and the AppleTalk driver. Clicking the Options button brings up the AppleTalk Options dialog box where you can make AppleTalk either Active or Inactive on your Mac.

You can also use the AppleTalk Control Panel to save your network configuration and even export it to a file, so you can transfer it to another Mac. Here's how this is done:

1. To open the Configurations dialog box from any of the different user modes, click the File menu in the AppleTalk Control Panel, and then select

AppleTalk Info

Addresses:

This Macintosh: 1.102
Hardware address: 08 00 07 EF 44 C1
Router: 1.164

Versions:

Open Transport: 2.5.2
AppleTalk: 2.5.2
AppleTalk driver: 61.0

OK

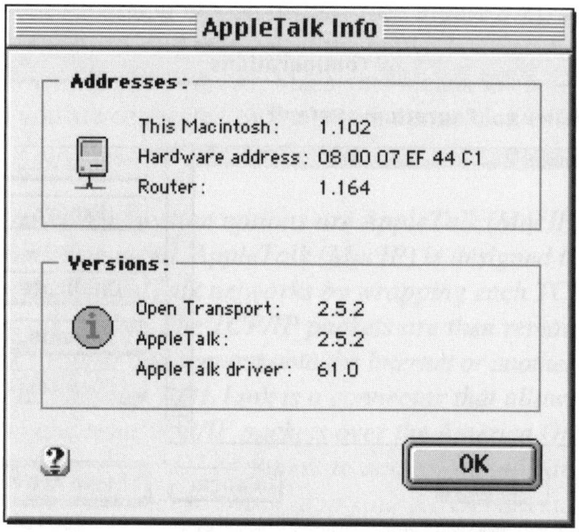

FIGURE 8-6 Get Info shows you all your AppleTalk addresses and the software versions

How to Network Your Mac

Configurations from the list options. Or, press COMMAND-K to open the Configurations dialog box.

2. With the Configurations dialog box displayed (see Figure 8-7), you can import a network connection from a file or export the currently selected network configuration. You can also duplicate the currently selected configuration, rename the selected configuration, and, if you have more than one configuration, you can click an inactive network configuration and delete it.

3. Once you create all the network configurations you want, highlight the configuration you want to use and then click the Make Active button.

4. After you make a configuration active, click the Done button to exit the Configurations dialog box and return to the AppleTalk Control Panel, or click the Cancel button to throw away any changes you have made.

Once you finish configuring AppleTalk the way you want it to work, you should move on to configuring TCP/IP so your Mac can communicate with computers that do not communicate using AppleTalk.

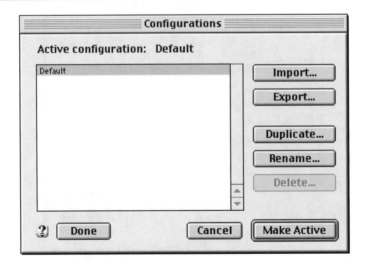

FIGURE 8-7 The Configurations dialog box enables you to import and export AppleTalk configurations

Configuring TCP/IP

Transmission Control Protocol/Internet Protocol (TCP/IP) is the network protocol that runs the Internet. Developed during the 1970s by researchers working on the ARPANET, the predecessor to the Internet, TCP/IP was designed to provide reliable communications between computers on a *wide area network (WAN)*.

As time went by, and the ARPANET began to transform itself into the Internet we know today, TCP/IP became the protocol used to connect all the different computers together.

On the Mac, support for TCP/IP was originally provided by the MacTCP Control Panel. With the development of Apple's Open Transport network technology, however, MacTCP went by the wayside and was replaced by the newer TCP/IP Control Panel you see today.

In Mac OS 9, Apple has gone to great lengths to support many of the options available on TCP/IP networks, as well as making it as fast and reliable as possible. As such, configuring and using TCP/IP on the Mac is a simple procedure. To get started configuring TCP/IP for your Mac, follow these steps:

1. Click the Apple Menu and scroll down to Control Panels. Then select TCP/IP from the submenu.

2. With the TCP/IP dialog box on display (see Figure 8-8), click the menu labeled Connect via, and then select the network connection you are using. For the owners of most modern Macs, this means selecting either Ethernet built-in if you are connected by a network connection or PPP if you are connecting via a modem.

NOTE *Other common connection options are AppleTalk (MacIP) and AOL Link or AOL Link Enhanced. AppleTalk (MacIP) is designed to allow TCP/IP to be sent over LocalTalk networks by wrapping each TCP/IP packet in an AppleTalk packet. The TCP/IP packets are then removed from their AppleTalk wrapper and sent out onto the Internet or another type of network by a MacIP gateway. AOL Link is a connector that allows your Mac to connect to and send TCP/IP packets over the America Online network. AOL Link is used by AOL members to access the built-in Web browser or to run other Internet software atop your AOL connection.*

3. After you select your connection type, select the configuration method you want to use. Click the pop-up menu labeled Configure, and then select how

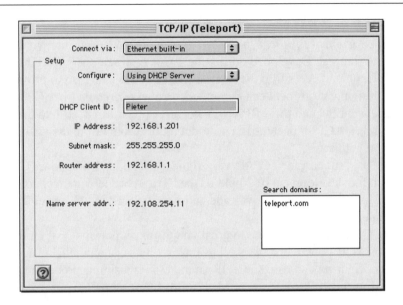

FIGURE 8-8 The TCP/IP Control Panel enables you to configure all your TCP/IP network settings

you want to configure TCP/IP on your Mac. Looking at the options available on the pop-up menu, you can select between manually adjusting all your TCP/IP settings, using a BootP server to configure TCP/IP, using a DHCP server to configure TCP/IP, or using a RARP server to configure TCP/IP.

Choosing TCP/IP Options

Dynamic Host Configuration Protocol (*DHCP*) is a system that automatically assigns an IP address and various other TCP/IP configuration settings to any computer on the network that requests one.

Bootstrap protocol (*BootP*) is another network service designed to assign TCP/IP addresses and other configuration information to a computer requesting an address. BootP has largely been replaced by the newer DHCP protocol on many networks. The sole exception to this is UNIX or Mac OS X Server-based networks that have diskless clients that need to download an operating system to boot.

Reverse Address Resolution Protocol (*RARP*) is the oldest and least used of the automatic configuration systems. RARP servers listen to a request from a computer for an IP address, and then match the Ethernet address of the requesting computer with an IP address assigned to it. Of course, if the computer is new and the RARP server has not been updated to know about the Ethernet address of your new computer, RARP fails to give it an IP address.

Choosing which configuration method you use depends on how your network is set up. For many small Mac-oriented networks, you would choose to set all of your TCP/IP settings manually. For many slightly larger networks, DHCP is used to distribute TCP/IP configuration information. While you can still find BootP and RARP on some networks, they are nowhere near as common as DHCP.

To set up TCP/IP in the manual mode, you need to know the IP address assigned to your Mac, the subnet mask you need to use with this IP address, the IP address of the router for your subnet, and the IP address of the name server you will use.

NOTE *If you are setting up TCP/IP to access an ISP, the IP information is supplied to you by the service directly, sometimes in an instruction book and sometimes, as part of a software installation. Because so many variations exist to this theme, no individual setting is covered.*

Once you have all this information, then you are ready to proceed.

1. With the TCP/IP Control Panel open (see Figure 8-9), enter your IP address in the space provided. Your IP address consists of four numbers, each one ranging from 0 to 255 and separated by a ".".

2. Next, click the area provided for the Subnet mask and then enter the subnet mask that goes with your IP address.

NOTE *A subnet mask normally looks something like 255.255.xxx.xxx, where the xxx is a number between 0 and 255.*

3. Now you want to enter the IP address of the router or gateway you plan to use when communicating to computers on another network. This IP address should be substantially similar to the one assigned to your Mac. For example, if your IP address is 192.168.1.120 and your subnet mask is 255.255.255.0, then your Router address should be 192.168.1.x, where x is a number between 0 and 255.

4. Then you are asked to enter the address(es) for the name servers with which your Mac will communicate to resolve the server names you type in with that server's IP address. Enter all the IP addresses for the name servers you plan to use.

How to Network Your Mac

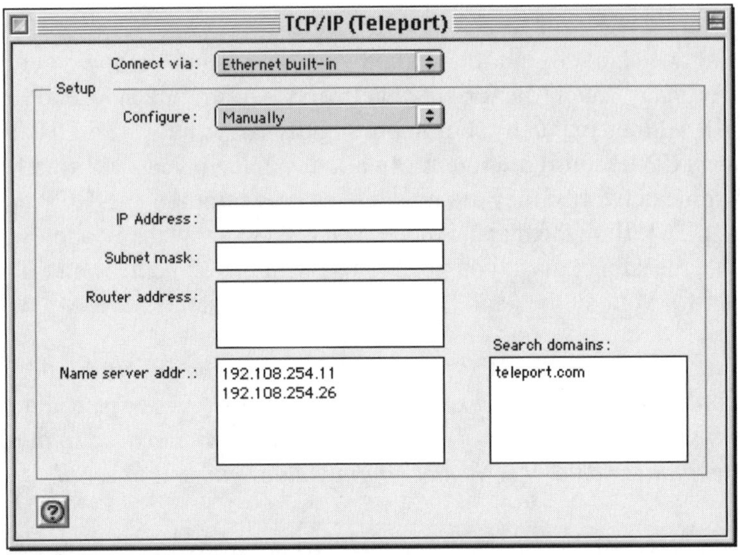

FIGURE 8-9   Manually configure the TCP/IP Control Panel by entering the IP address and other settings

CAUTION   *If you don't have the name servers configured, then your Mac will be unable to resolve the proper service name. For example, the server name www.apple.com is resolved with the IP address 17.254.0.91. Your Mac would then use that IP address to contact the Web servers that host www.apple.com.*

5. Next, you want to enter the search domains your Mac will use when trying to resolve some names. For example, if you set the search domain to earthlink.net, when you try to connect to the server www, your Mac will append .earthlink.net to the name and direct you to www.earthlink.net. If you enter in multiple search domains, your Mac will start with the first one and, if there are no matches, it will move to the next one on the list until it finds a match or runs out of search domains.

6. Finally, after you enter all your configuration information into the TCP/IP Control Panel, click the close box and then accept the Save option to store all your configuration changes.

DHCP Configuration Procedures

Because DHCP is capable of distributing information about your network along with the IP address to your Mac, most of your Mac's TCP/IP configuration is handled automatically. Depending upon the way your network's DHCP server is configured, however, you may not get all the network configuration information you need.

Specifically, you need to know if your network's DHCP server sends out configuration information detailing the IP address of the router (also known as the *default gateway*) and the IP address(es) of the name servers or *domain name service (DNS)* servers.

If the DHCP server does provide this information when distributing your Mac's IP address, then all you need to fill in are the search domains your Mac will use when trying to resolve names.

Look at the TCP/IP Control Panel, shown in Figure 8-10. You can see two items you can configure: the DHCP Client ID and the Search Domains. The DHCP Client ID is a completely optional field because it is not used by most DHCP servers and can be set to whatever value you want. The Search Domains, on the other hand, control the way some names are resolved, so you must

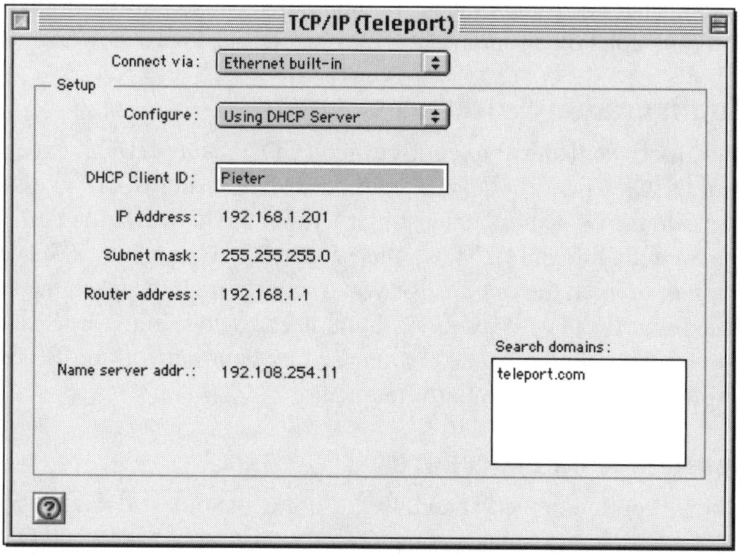

How to Network Your Mac

```
┌─────────────────────── TCP/IP (Teleport) ───────────────────────┐
│                                                                  │
│          Connect via:  │ Ethernet built-in        ▼ │            │
│   ┌─ Setup ───────────────────────────────────────────────────┐ │
│   │        Configure:  │ Using DHCP Server         ▼ │          │ │
│   │                                                            │ │
│   │    DHCP Client ID:  │ Pieter                            │  │ │
│   │       IP Address:   192.168.1.201                          │ │
│   │      Subnet mask:   255.255.255.0                          │ │
│   │    Router address:  192.168.1.1                            │ │
│   │                                        Search domains:     │ │
│   │  Name server addr.: 192.108.254.11     ┌─────────────────┐ │ │
│   │                                        │ teleport.com    │ │ │
│   │                                        │                 │ │ │
│   │                                        └─────────────────┘ │ │
│   └────────────────────────────────────────────────────────────┘ │
│  ⓦ                                                               │
└──────────────────────────────────────────────────────────────────┘
```

FIGURE 8-10   Using DHCP to configure your TCP/IP connection makes networking much simpler

make sure they are configured properly. In the search domain field, enter the domain name or names of the network or your ISP.

Sharing an Internet Connection

Several products use DHCP to enable you to share a dial-up Internet connection across a network. One of these products, the *MacSense Palm Router Elite,* has two ports for a regular or ISDN modem. It also incorporates an 8-port 10BaseT hub, so it can serve double duty. If you already have an Ethernet hub (perhaps 100BaseTX), you can simply uplink this device to your existing network.

Administration of the system is done via your Web browser. According to the company, up to 252 users can share the Internet connections, though performance is apt to suffer terribly if more than a handful attempt to do so at once.

The product costs $260 at computer retailers. You can get more information on the company's product line, which includes regular Ethernet hubs, at http://www.macsensetech.com.

Another way to share an Internet connection is IPNetRouter, a shareware program from Sustainable Softworks. The program implements its features directly in software. Once configured, you launch the application, and then it dials up your ISP, running your Mac as a DHCP server.

Once connection is achieved, other Macs can network with your Mac, which is the server, and share the same Internet hookup. You can get information on this product and download the program directly from http://www.sustworks.com.

BootP Configuration Procedures

Configuring BootP is identical to configuring TCP/IP using DHCP, except you don't have a DHCP Client ID field. If your network is using BootP to distribute the IP address to the computers requesting them on the network, then all you need to set is the Search Domain(s). Thus, once you select Using BootP Server as the configuration option, all the options for you to configure, other than the Search Domain (see Figure 8-11), disappear. All you need to do is enter the Search Domains, normally only the domain name used by your network or ISP. For a user of EarthLink this would be Earthlink.net.

RARP Configuration Procedures

RARP is the last option in the list and, because it is the oldest IP address distribution system, it lacks many of the features present in BootP and DHCP.

Once you select Using RARP Server from the Configuration pop-up menu, you see the TCP/IP dialog box shown in Figure 8-12. Because the RARP server only sends back an IP address, you must manually configure the rest of the TCP/IP settings.

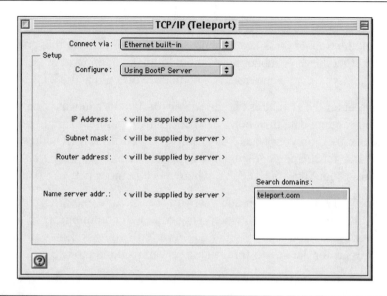

FIGURE 8-11   Using BootP to configure your TCP/IP connection makes everything much simpler

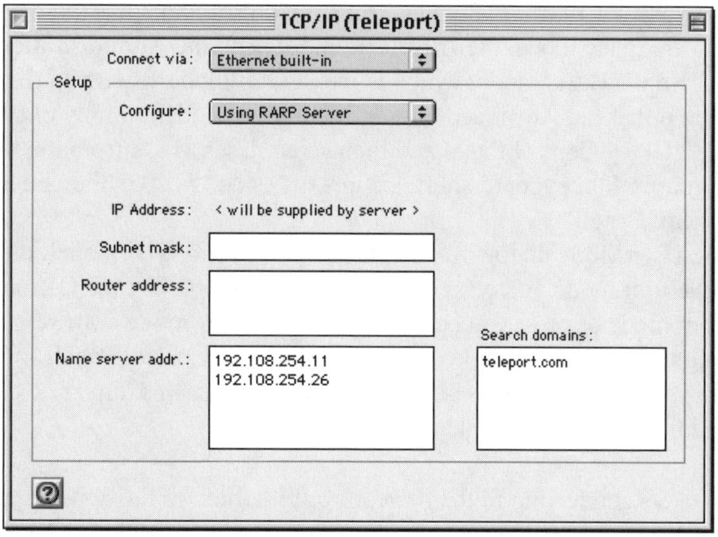

FIGURE 8-12   RARP only sets the IP address, leaving you to configure the rest of the TCP/IP settings

How to Network Your Mac

To configure the various other TCP/IP settings, follow these steps:

1. Click the Subnet mask section and enter the subnet mask that goes with your IP address. A subnet mask should look something like 255.255.xxx.xxx, where xxx is a number between 0 and 255.

2. Next, enter the IP address of the router (or default gateway) you plan to use when sending data to another network. This IP address should be similar to the one used on your Mac. For example, if your Mac's IP address is 192.168.1.120 and your subnet mask is 255.255.255.0, then your Router address should be 192.168.1.x, where x is a number between 0 and 255.

3. Once you enter the router address, you are asked to enter the address(es) for the name servers with which your Mac will communicate to resolve the server names you type in with that server's IP address. Enter all the IP addresses for the one-to-three name servers you plan to use.

4. Finally, you need to enter the search domains your Mac will use when trying to resolve some names. After you have made all your configuration changes, click the close box to save all your configuration changes.

Advanced TCP/IP Configuration

Like the AppleTalk Control Panel, the TCP/IP Control Panel has three different user modes: the Basic mode, the Advanced mode, and the Administration mode. To switch from the Basic mode, which is the default mode when you first Install Mac OS 9, to either the Advanced or Administration modes, simply click the Edit menu in the TCP/IP Control Panel and then select User Mode from the list of options. If you prefer keyboard shortcuts, press COMMAND-U while you are in the TCP/IP Control Panel.

With the User Mode dialog box displayed (see Figure 8-13), click the radio button for the user mode you want to switch to, and then click the OK button to switch to that mode or press Cancel to return to the user mode you are in already.

Selecting the Advanced mode changes the TCP/IP Control Panel, so it looks like the one you see in Figure 8-14. When you look over this dialog box, you can see a few additions from the basic user mode.

1. For users connecting to the network by Ethernet, in the upper right-hand corner, next to the Connect via pop-up menu, is a check box labeled Use 802.3. Selecting this check box tells the Mac to use the 802.3 or Ethernet II

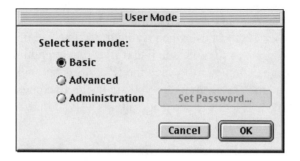

FIGURE 8-13   The User Mode dialog box enables you to set the view you use in the
TCP/IP Control Panel

network type when communicating via TCP/IP. While common on many
Novell-based networks, 802.3-based Ethernet networks are a variation on
the original Ethernet standard in use on the majority of computer networks.
Unless you are certain your network is using 802.3 Ethernet, do not select
this check box.

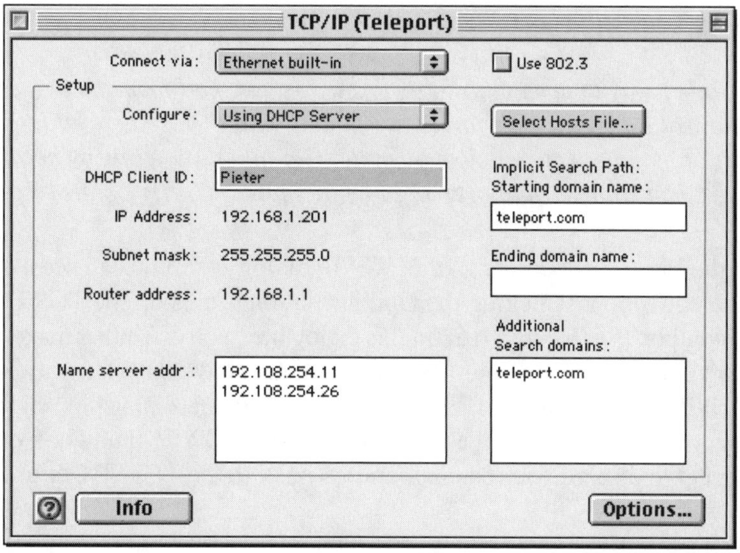

FIGURE 8-14   The Advanced user mode shows some new options in the TCP/IP
Control Panel

2. Another addition is the Select Hosts File button located to the right of the Configuration pop-up menu. Clicking this button enables you to choose a hosts file your Mac can use when trying to resolve a computer's name to its IP address. *Hosts files* are small text files that contain the IP address and the name of the computer to which the IP address belongs. When trying to resolve the name of the computer you are trying to connect to, your Mac reads that file and looks to see if it contains a IP address associated with the name it is seeking.

3. To the right of the IP address is a field allowing you to enter the Implicit Search Path Starting domain name, and then, in a space below, the Ending domain name. If you have only one name entered in your Search domain, then enter that value in the Starting domain name field. Otherwise, enter the first domain you want to search in the Starting domain name field and the last domain you want to search in the Ending domain name field.

4. In the bottom-left corner of the TCP/IP dialog box, you can see a button labeled Info. Clicking the Info button brings up the TCP/IP Get Info dialog box you see in Figure 8-15. In this dialog box, you can see the IP address of your Mac, its hardware or Ethernet address, and the router address. In the bottom part of the Get Info dialog box, you can see the versions of Open Transport and TCP/IP you are using.

TIP *Another way to open this dialog box is to click the File menu in the TCP/IP Control Panel from all three user modes, and then select Get Info from the list of options. You can also open the Get Info dialog box by holding down the Command key and pressing I while in the TCP/IP Control Panel.*

5. In the lower right corner of the TCP/IP dialog box, you can see a button labeled Options. Clicking the Options button brings up the TCP/IP Options dialog box (see Figure 8-16). In this dialog box, you can either make TCP/IP Active or Inactive on your Mac. You can also have the Mac only load TCP/IP when it is needed. When you finish with this dialog box, click the OK button to save your changes and return to the TCP/IP dialog box or click Cancel to discard your changes and go back to the TCP/IP Control Panel.

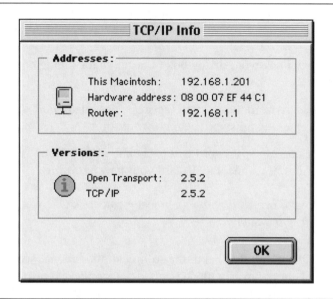

FIGURE 8-15   The TCP/IP Get Info dialog box shows you the TCP/IP addresses and the software versions

NOTE   *While the option to load TCP/IP when needed can save a bit of memory, it has been known to cause some problems with applications that need TCP/IP. It is the default setting, and you may as well leave it alone. But if you experience problems with a TCP/IP-aware application, you may want to uncheck this option and see if performance improves.*

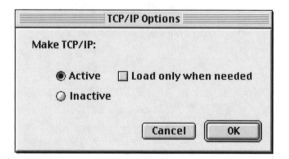

FIGURE 8-16   TCP/IP Options enables you to turn TCP/IP on or off

How to Network Your Mac

If you click the Administration button in the User Mode dialog box, you can set the Administration password. To set the Administration password, follow these steps:

1. Click the Set password dialog box to bring up the dialog box you see in Figure 8-17.

2. To set the password, type it into the space provided in the dialog box, press Tab, and enter the password again to confirm it.

3. After you enter the password twice, click the OK button to save your new password or click Cancel to discard your new password.

NOTE   *If the two passwords do not match when you click OK, you are asked to retype them and then press OK.*

With the TCP/IP Control Panel in the Administration mode (see Figure 8-18), you can see small check boxes with an open lock icon located next to all the user-configurable options. For a Mac that gets most of its configuration data from a DHCP server, the locks appear next to the Connect via and Configure pop-up menus, as well as the Use 802.3 check box and DHCP client ID. Check boxes are also located next to the addresses for the name servers, the starting and ending domain names, and the Search domains.

If the TCP/IP settings are manually set on your Mac, you also see check boxes enabling you to lock down the IP address, Subnet mask, and the Router IP address.

Administration Password

Set password for Administration access:

Password:

Verify password:

Cancel   OK

FIGURE 8-17   Set the TCP/IP Control Panel Administration Password

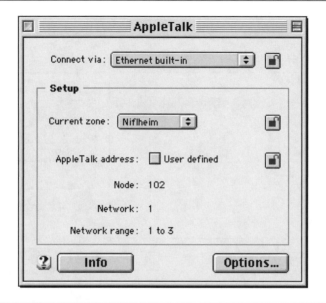

FIGURE 8-18   The TCP/IP Administration mode enables you to secure specific
TCP/IP settings

To lock the options you do not want other users to change, click the appropriate
check boxes so their icons turn into closed locks. After you finish, click the close
box to close the TCP/IP Control Panel.

Another option located under the File menu in the TCP/IP Control Panel is
Configurations. To open the Configurations dialog box, click the File menu in the
TCP/IP Control Panel and then select Configurations from the menu. Or, press
COMMAND-K.

Like the Configurations dialog box you saw in the AppleTalk Control Panel,
the Configurations dialog box (see Figure 8-19) enables you to import a TCP/IP
configuration from a file or to export the currently selected TCP/IP configuration.
You can duplicate the selected TCP/IP configuration, rename the current selection,
and, if there is more than one TCP/IP configuration, you can click a network
configuration other than the active one, and then click the Delete button to delete it.

Once you set up all the TCP/IP configurations you need, select the
configuration you want to make active and click the Make Active button. After
you make a configuration active, click the Done button to exit the Configurations
dialog box and return to the TCP/IP Control Panel, or click the Cancel button to
throw away the changes you made.

How to Network Your Mac

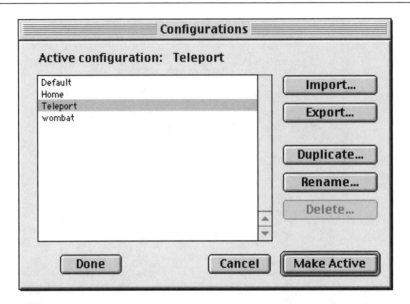

The Configurations dialog box enables you to import and export your TCP/IP settings

Using Mac File Sharing on the Internet

One of the new features on Mac OS 9 is the capability to access and share files with another Mac over the Internet. Unlike previous operating system versions, which limited File Sharing to only those Macs located on the same network, the Mac OS 9 version has extended those capabilities to cover the Internet.

As you learn in Chapter 27, sharing files with other Macs is a quick and easy procedure, even when the Mac you are sharing with is half a world away on the Internet. As with most procedures involving the Internet, however, you need to make sure your Mac is protected by setting the permission levels on your shared files, so only those you want to access those files can do so.

Connecting to a Mac File Share Using the Chooser

Connecting to a Mac located on the Internet is as quick and simple as connecting to a Mac on your own network. Even the basic setup is nearly the same.

> **NOTE**
> *For the other Mac to be available for Internet file sharing, the user of the other Mac must open the File Sharing Control Panel, and then click the check box labeled Enable File Sharing clients to connect over TCP/IP. The correct IP number for that Mac will be listed in the Control Panel. Once this is done, File Sharing must be enabled and the Mac must be logged into an ISP to make the Internet connection. In some cases, it may take the actual ISP connection to reveal the IP number.*

Follow these steps to access a networked Mac on the Internet:

1. Click the Apple menu and select Chooser from the list.

2. With the Chooser on display (see Figure 8-20), click the AppleShare icon and then click the Server IP Address button.

3. Looking at the dialog box you see in Figure 8-21, enter the IP address of the Mac to which you want to connect, and then press OK. You must get

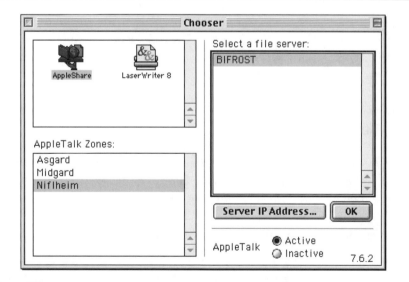

FIGURE 8-20   In the Chooser, click AppleShare to connect to a Mac server

FIGURE 8-21   Enter the IP address of the Mac you want to connect to over the Internet

this number from the user of the Mac you want to share. If your Mac is not yet connected to the Internet, your ISP will be dialed out in the normal fashion.

NOTE   *IP addresses that belong to one of these three ranges, 10.x.x.x, 172.16.x.x-172.32.x.x, and 192-168.x.x, are considered private addresses and are not accessible over the Internet. This means if you are trying to connect to a Mac that uses an IP address from one of these three private IP address ranges, you cannot do so because the Internet prevents you from opening a connection.*

4. Next, you are asked to enter the user name and password needed to access the shared Mac.

NOTE   *If the other Mac has been configured to allow Guest log-ins via the Users & Groups panel in the File Sharing Control Panel, you can click the Guest radio button and connect to the Mac as a guest.*

5. Then click OK to complete the log on procedure.

6. Once you connect to the Mac, you see a list of the shared volumes that are available to you, the same as you do when accessing a networked computer on a local network. Highlight the volumes you want to access.

7. Click OK to mount them on your desktop.

Connecting to a Mac Shared Volume Using the Network Browser

Another method for connecting to a Mac over the Internet is to use the Network Browser.

To use the Network Browser to connect to a shared volume located on a Mac on the Internet, do the following steps:

1. Click the Apple Menu and then select Network Browser from the list of items. If you are not yet logged on to the Internet, you will be connected to your ISP.

2. With Network Browser on display (see Figure 8-22), click the leftmost icon at the top of the dialog box (the one that looks like a hand pointing at something). You then bring up a pop-up menu with two entries: Network and Connect to Server. Select Connect to Server from the list.

3. Once you select Connect to Server, you are presented with a request for the IP address of the server to which you want to connect (see Figure 8-23). After you enter the IP address of the server to which you want to connect, click OK to try to connect or click Cancel to abort the operation.

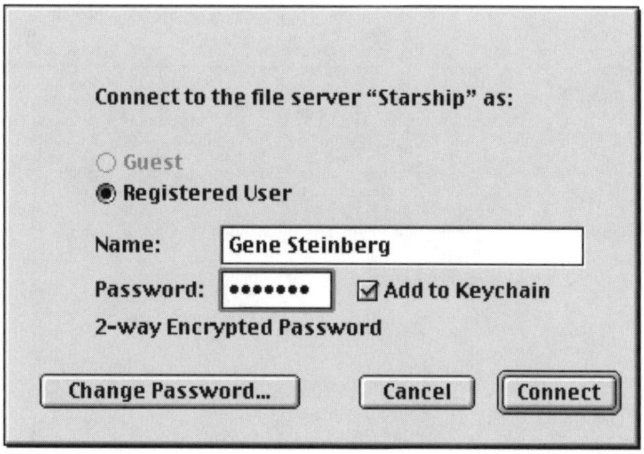

Connect to the file server "Starship" as:

○ Guest
● Registered User

Name: Gene Steinberg
Password: ●●●●●● ☑ Add to Keychain
2-way Encrypted Password

Change Password...   Cancel   Connect

FIGURE 8-22   Enter your name and password to log in to the Mac file share

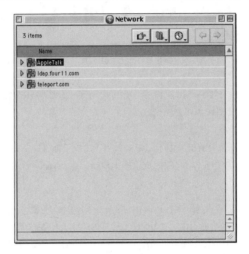

FIGURE 8-23   The Network Browser displays all the resources available on the remote Mac

4. If your Mac can connect to the server whose IP address you specified, then you are presented with the log in dialog box.

5. Next, you see a list of the networked volumes available on the Mac to which you have connected (see Figure 8-24). To access any of the

FIGURE 8-24   These volumes on the author's hard drive are acessed via Internet File Sharing

resources you see, simply double-click them. The networked volumes mount on your Mac's desktop, the same as if you accessed them directly from your local network.

6. After you finish with the Network Browser, click the check box to dismiss it.

To eliminate any volumes you have mounted from a Mac located either on your LAN or over the Internet, simply select the volume you want to delete and drag them to the Trash. Or, type COMMAND-Y to put them away.

Protecting Your Mac while Networking on the Internet

While sharing files over the Internet is a great idea, it does potentially expose your Mac to millions of unknown users. Remember security when you share files over the Internet. Because you are exposing your files to such a huge audience, you must be prepared either to limit the access you provide to people connecting over the Internet or to accept the chance that someone could read and/or abuse your files.

This section covers setting file permissions. You should also check out chapter 27 for a more in-depth discussion of the subject.

If you are concerned about protecting the files you are sharing on your Mac, then make sure all the files and folders you share are set to read-only for both you and all the users you grant access. Another good suggestion is to disable Guest access on your Mac, which limits access to your Mac to only those users you know.

You may also want to consider creating a separate *shared volume* or *folder*, which means to create a file share set to write-only for you and the users you have configured on your Mac. This enables other users to drop off files on your Mac without worrying about others reading the files being left for you.

NOTE   *Setting the share permissions on the files and folders you are sharing does not change the way you can access the files when you're working on the Mac. These permission settings only affect you when you try to access them from another Mac over a network or by the Internet.*

Once you complete both these steps, you can be sure your files are reasonably well protected. Of course, your files are only as well protected as the password you use to secure your account. A weak password, such as the name of a family member or a pet, is a security hole that's easy for a hacker to guess.

Strong passwords include mixed uppercase and lowercase letters along with numbers and punctuation marks. For example, a weak password would be

Using Mac File Sharing on the Internet

something like macsrcool, where a much stronger password would be something like Mac$Rc00l.

As mentioned before, the key point to remember is less is more. While this sounds like an oxymoron, it is a key element when setting up security on your Mac. Less access to users on the network means you have more security for your files, and this means you can feel comfortable in sharing important files with other users.

An Overview of Internet Networking

The Internet had its humble beginnings over 30 years ago via ARPANET, which started as a research project for the Department of Defense's *Advanced Research Projects Agency* (*ARPA*).

At that time, the entire system consisted of two mainframe computers connected by a dedicated circuit. Over the years, the system expanded incredibly, to the tune of hundreds of millions of computers connected to the Internet as we know it today.

Yet, through all this, the core purpose of the Internet has remained the same: sharing information and resources.

As the ARPANET evolved from a few computers tied together by a few slow network connections to many computers connected by faster network links, a company called BBN in Boston developed the first network router to allow one computer to talk to multiple computers over many different network links.

While this is a far cry from the big Cisco routers that run most of the Internet today, these routers were a breakthrough because they allowed computers to use multiple network connections to reach the same destination. This meant that you could cut one connection and still be able to reach the destination through another path. The capability to support multiple paths to the same destination is a critical element in the success of the Internet because it ensures that the Internet is capable of still functioning, even when major portions of its backbone have failed.

Another key element to the success of the Internet was the development of TCP/IP by Vincent Cerf and others at BBN. TCP/IP allowed network traffic to flow between the various computers on the ARPANET by being capable of handling out-of-order packets. This meant receiving the last part of a file before the first part has arrived, as well as being able to regulate the speed at which the files are received by the destination computer.

TCP/IP also supported the capability to detect bad packets and to request their retransmission. This ensured that communications between the two computers were reliable and that the files made it through intact.

The final element that really made the Internet what it is today was the development of the World Wide Web by Tim Berniers Lee at the CERN laboratory in Switzerland. Started as a way to share knowledge between scientists, the Web has grown into a huge industry. From alphabet soup to yachts, there's not much you cannot find information about or even buy on the Web. With the development of the Web, an easy-to-use and highly graphic way to browse the Internet finally existed, just the catalyst needed to cause its growth to explode.

While the Internet you know today is a far cry from the early ARPANET, most of the key elements developed for that research project are still with us today. From the routers that were developed at BBN to TCP/IP, all these technologies are still in use today and, while highly evolved, they still share many of the same features as the first units.

Summing Up

Setting up AppleTalk and TCP/IP networking on your Mac enables you to connect to other Macs, as well as the other computers and devices connected to both your LAN and to the Internet. In this chapter, you read about the settings and options available to you in both the AppleTalk and the TCP/IP Control Panels. In both of these Control Panels, you learned how to configure your network settings so your Mac can connect to the other computers and resources on your network. You also discovered Mac OS 9's Internet file-sharing techniques and how to set up your shared volumes so your Macs are protected from hackers and others who you do not want to access your computer.

In Chapter 9, you learn about one of the unsung heroes of the Mac OS, a program that comes free with a Mac OS installation, yet isn't used nearly as much as it should be: AppleScript.

Summing Up

Chapter 9

Introduction to AppleScript

Do you ever wish your Mac could take on more of the routine, repetitive tasks you do over and over again? You place files in a folder, copy to a networked drive for backup, open and save a graphic file to change the format. This can get tiresome. Despite the incredible computing power of a Mac, you do a lot of work manually, clicking here, clicking there, to accomplish specific tasks.

Wouldn't it be nice if the Mac could take on some of those tasks for you, simply by clicking a mouse or running a little application?

Well, it can. A convenient way to automate repetitive tasks is by using a program called AppleScript, which is included with the standard installation of Mac OS 9. *AppleScript* uses a plain English language you can understand to write documents called *scripts,* which perform a set of tasks automatically, once activated.

In this chapter, you learn about the scripts Apple includes with Mac OS 9. And you learn how to get started using this powerful Mac automation tool, so you can easily harness its extraordinary power.

Using Apple's Standard Scripts

Once you have Mac OS 9, AppleScript is all set up and ready to go for your use without any additional installation. You don't even have to write your own scripts to get started. Apple has thoughtfully provided a number of scripts you can use for basic tasks. To begin, locate the AppleScript folder inside the Apple Extras folder on your Mac's drive.

TIP   *In addition to the scripts included as part of your Mac OS 9 installation, you find additional choices on the system CD. Open the CD Extras folder and look for a folder labeled AppleScripts. Before using the scripts, check the ReadMe file on what the scripts do and how they're to be used.*

First let's look at the Automated Tasks folder, which offers five "prerecorded" scripts. These scripts run simply by dragging an item on the script file document or selecting the item, and then activating the script. If the script doesn't act on an item, double-clicking makes it run, the same as any normal application.

NOTE *Apple used to provide a direct link to these Automated Tasks in the Apple Menu but, for some reason, it stopped doing so beginning with Mac OS 8.5 (as they say, go figure). That doesn't stop you, however, from using one of the following scripts to put an alias to this and other AppleScript folders in the Apple Menu, so you can access them quickly.*

■ **Share a Folder**   This script creates a folder called Shared Folder at the top level of your startup disk, assuming one with that name isn't already there, of course. File sharing is then turned on and a guest is then allowed to access the folder's contents (assuming guest access has been previously granted under the File Sharing Control Panel).

■ **Share a Folder (No Guest)**   The functions of this script are nearly the same as the previous one, except for one thing. To open the folder, anyone connecting to your Mac must log in using the correct user name and a password.

■ **Start File Sharing**   This script does what the title implies—it turns on file sharing.

■ **Stop File Sharing**   Again, the title says it all. Once file sharing is on, this script deactivates it.

■ **Add Alias to Apple Menu**   You can use this script to put the AppleScript folders in your Apple Menu—or any other item, for that matter. Just drag an item onto this script (or select and launch the script). In a few seconds, the alias to that item (without the *alias* name, thank heavens), appears in the Apple menu. This script is a real time-saver and one of my favorites.

The next group of scripts are found in the More Automated Tasks folder in the AppleScript folder.

■ **Alert When Folder Changes**   This script enables you to know when a certain file has been put in a folder. You can either drag a folder onto this script or launch it and select the folder from the Open dialog box.

■ **Hide/Show Folder Sizes**   This script enables you to show or hide the size of a certain folder whenever it is open on your desktop.

Using Apple's Standard Scripts

■ **Synchronize Folders**   This script makes sure you have the absolute latest copies of the same files in two different folders. It's a useful companion for backups. The subject of backups is covered in more detail in Chapter 29.

Folder Actions

One of AppleScript's key features is something called *Folder Actions*. Whenever you attach a Folder Action to a certain folder, it can do any number of things, including opening or closing the folder, changing its size, or even adding or taking out files from the folder. The possibilities are numerous. You can even create your own Folder Actions once you learn your AppleScript skills. Here are the Folder Actions Apple has provided for you to get started with this useful feature.

■ **add-duplicate to folders**   This script is useful for automatically backing up your most critical files. Whenever you place a certain file, folder, or disk icon in a folder with this script attached to it, a copy automatically is placed in another folder of your choice (even if that folder is located on another drive on a networked computer).

■ **add-new item alert**   This script presents a warning on your desktop every time you put a new item in a scripted folder. If you use a shared folder as a drop box, to receive items from other users on your network, you should find this script useful.

■ **add-reject added items**   This script keeps additional items from being put in the scripted folder. This is a way to control the contents of a folder (aside from limiting access via Mac OS 9's Multiple Users feature, of course).

■ **add-set view prefs to match**   When you use this script, it synchronizes the view preferences of the scripted folder with that of any new folder you add to it.

■ **close-close sub-folders**   This script automatically closes any open windows in a scripted folder.

■ **mount/unmount server aliases**   This script automates your network access and consists of two parts. When you open a scripted folder containing an alias for a server, you are asked if you want to mount that server onto your desktop if this hasn't been done already. When you close the scripted folder, it asks if you want to unmount the server if you haven't already done that.

- **move-align open subfolders**   This script is useful if you don't have a lot of desktop space to spare. Whenever you move or resize the window of a scripted folder, it automatically aligns the windows of any open subfolders to reduce desktop clutter.

- **open-open items labeled**   From the Preferences in the Edit menu, you can choose to label an important folder a certain way to identify it more easily. Whenever you open the scripted folder, any items in that folder are automatically opened.

- **open-show comments in dialog box**   This script automatically shows any text comments in the information dialog box of a scripted folder.

- **remove-retrieve items**   You can use this script to return files to the folder from which you took them away.

Making Your Own Folder Action

Making a Folder Action script using Apple's prebuilt scripts is easy. Here are the steps you should follow to add a Folder Action to a specific folder:

1. Choose the folder to which you want to attach a Folder Action and click once to select it.

2. CONTROL-click the folder, which brings up a contextual menu.

3. From the menu, select Choose a Folder Action. An Open dialog box appears.

4. Make your way to the System Folder in the Open dialog box and open the Scripts folder.

5. Locate and open the Folder Action Scripts folder.

6. Choose one of the Folder Action scripts and click Open. In a moment or so, a tiny script icon appears on the icon of that folder. This indicates the script has been applied to the selected folder.

Removing a Folder Action

When you finish using that script, here's how to remove the action:

1. Choose the folder from which you want to remove a Folder Action and click once to select it.

2. CONTROL-click the folder, which brings up a contextual menu.

3. From the menu, select Remove a Folder Action, and then choose whichever script you want removed from that folder in the dialog box. After you do this, the little script icon no longer appears on the folder, and the Folder action is removed.

AppleScript Extras

Besides the basic scripts provided in the AppleScript folder, there is also a folder called AppleScript Extras, in which you can find a number of additional scripts, as well as some third-party applications to help you manage and run AppleScripts.

- **OSA Menu**   This third-party system extension is designed to show a list of all your scripts, including ones you are currently using in an open program. It places a script scroll icon on the upper right of the menu bar. If you select one of the scripts in the list, it automatically runs the chosen item.

NOTE   *If you find OSA Menu interesting after you've tried it, you might want to look into a more feature-rich version at the author's Web site, http://www.lazerware.com.*

- **iDo Script Scheduler**   A third-party application made by Sophisticated Circuits, Inc., Script Scheduler enables you to run AppleScripts automatically whenever you want. It can be used to perform such tasks as automatically checking your e-mail at specified times and backing up your critical files when you aren't working with your Mac. The program can also be used to create several different kinds of events that occur repeatedly. For each of the events, a certain AppleScript can be run and you can specify what tasks you want your Mac to perform when that script is active.

More Sample Scripts Folder

In this folder, you find additional scripts that can be used with the OSA menu. These scripts are divided into four different categories with scripts that are appropriate to those categories: Universal Scripts, Finder Scripts, Script Editor Scripts, and More Folder Actions Scripts.

Follow these instructions to install one or more of these scripts:

1. Open the System Folder, look for the Scripts folder, and then open it.

2. Place one or more of the scripts from one or more of the folders into the Scripts folder.

Once you do this, you can access these scripts directly from the OSA menu.

About the Additional Scripts

The following offers a brief explanation of the AppleScripts found in the More Sample Scripts folder, divided by category.

Universal Scripts

This handy selection of scripts can be used in any active program.

- **Open Folder**   This script enables you to choose a folder to open from a dialog box that appears when you run it.

- **Unmount/Eject All Disks**   This script unmounts or ejects any other active disks on your desktop, including other hard drives and removable drives (not including your startup drive).

Finder Scripts

These scripts apply actions to Finder functions.

- **Add Prefix/Suffix to Files, Add Prefix/Suffix to Folders**   This script could be especially useful if you need to send a file or folder to someone using the PC platform and you have to make them compatible with that person's computer. It adds a prefix to the beginning (or a suffix to the end) of the name of a chosen file or folder. It's also useful if you want to apply a specific label to files or folders to make them easier to identify, such as attaching the name of a specific client or purpose to the item.

- **Change Case of All Names**   This script automatically transforms the case of the name of every file in a selected folder.

- **Info for Selected Items**   Whenever you run this script, it displays the information dialog boxes for the files or folders you choose.

- **Replace Text in Item Names**   Using this script enables you to change the text you selected in a file or a folder's name. When you need to change the names of a large number of files, perhaps to reflect a change in job description or number, this is a terrific way to automate the task.

Using Apple's Standard Scripts

■ **Size of Finder Selection**   This script tells you the total size of all selected files or folders. It's a superior substitute to the calculate folder sizes option in your Finder Views preferences. Instead of enduring endless waits for each folder size to be calculated, you only wait for the folder you selected for the action.

■ **Trim File Names**   You can use this script to delete text from the beginning or end of the name of a file. This is a fast way to remove the ever-present alias name from an alias file.

Script Editor Scripts

The scripts in this folder are considered *subroutines,* which can be edited and used as part of your own custom scripts (so you needn't reinvent the wheel as you begin to learn your scripting skills). For starters, you can copy text to the clipboard, and then apply the script to make them perform the labeled task. The titles describe precisely what they do, so the following explanations are minimal.

■ **ASCII Sort**   This one sorts items by ASCII code number (as opposed to alphabetically or numerically).

■ **Change Case of Text**   A batch text editing component used to convert uppercase letters to lowercase or vice versa.

■ **Convert Number to Text**   Precisely what the name implies, this script is used for mathematical or scientific notations.

■ **Date Slug**   This script automatically inserts the current date in the text to which the script applies, using whatever date format is used in the text.

■ **FilePath-Extract File Name**   This script picks out the file's name from the path or location of the file.

■ **FilePath-Parent Fldr Name**   This script digs up the name of the folder containing a specific file.

■ **FilePath-Parent Fldr Path**   This script digs up the path of a folder containing a specific file (so you know in which folder that folder is placed).

■ **Name Item**   You can use this script to name or rename an item quickly.

■ **Read File**   This script extracts the contents of a text file.

- **Return High/Low From List**   This script provides the highest or lowest number from a list of numbers (even if they are out of sequence).

- **Round-Convert-Truncate**   This script is used to simplify numbers, rounding them off to between zero and three decimal places. So if you have the number 20,000.008882, you can round it off to 20,000.009.

- **Time Slug**   You can use this script to insert the exact time in your text.

- **Write to File**   This script is designed to create a text file from text .

More Folder Action Scripts

To use the scripts in this folder, they must be placed individually into the Scripts folder of the System Folder.

- **add-add to activity log**   This script creates a log file with information about whichever files you placed in the folder to which this script was attached.

- **add-match parent label**   Using this script enables you to change the label of any file or folder in the scripted folder so it has the same label as that folder.

- **summarize added text files**   This script examines every text document you put in a scripted folder and summarizes what it contains in three sentences. This Folder Action can be edited to change a number of its specifications, including how many sentences are in the summary.

How to Use AppleScript with Your Programs

A great number of Mac programs, including (and this is a brief list) Adobe InDesign, Extensis Fetch, FileMaker Pro, Microsoft Word 98, QuarkXPress, Casady & Greene's SoundJam, and Aladdin's StuffIt Deluxe currently support AppleScript. This enables you to create your own scripts to automate repeating tasks.

Some programs, such as Outlook Express 5 and AppleWorks, even come with their own scripts to get you started, accessible right from a scripts menu. A partial list of all the programs that support AppleScript can be found at Apple's Web site at this address: http://www.apple.com/applescript.

Three different levels of support are available for AppleScript. Apple's site rates programs on the basis of the type of support offered.

How to Use AppleScript with Your Programs

■ **Scriptable**   This type of support is probably the most simplistic. It enables you to use scripts in a certain program.

■ **Recordable**   This is one level higher than Scriptable support. This type of support enables you to record a special script simply by opening Apple's Script Editor program, and then performing the actions within the program. Once the action is performed, you can save the completed script. If a program doesn't support this feature, however, and you want to create a custom script for it, you need to type the information manually for the script, using Apple's scripting lingo.

■ **Attachable**   With this type of support, you can attach scripts to various menus in the menu bar or to other elements of a program. Whenever you click or activate that part of the program, the script runs.

Scripts and Outlook Express

Microsoft's free e-mail program for the Mac supports the capability to record and edit scripts. Some scripts are already included with the program by Microsoft's programmers. You find the scripts in the Script Menu Items folder in the Outlook Express folder. They are accessible from a menu in the program itself with a little script icon. The following describes the scripts:

■ **Insert Explorer Address**   This script automatically puts the URL of a Web site in Internet Explorer into an e-mail message.

■ **Insert Text File**   This script automatically places a text file into an e-mail message.

■ **Save Selection**   This script saves selected text into a separate document.

■ **Color**   This script is found in a separate folder of the Script Menu Items Folder. It changes the color of the names of messages to blue, black, green, or red. A Use Default Color script also changes the color back to its original shade.

AppleWorks

Apple's own productivity suite supports AppleScript, so you can easily automate certain tasks. Apple includes four scripts in the program. The scripts themselves can only be used; they cannot be edited in any way. As in Outlook Express, the scripts can be quickly accessed by the script icon in the menu bar.

> **NOTE**   *As this book was written, AppleWorks 6, a major upgrade to this productivity suite, had not yet been released. It may indeed offer additional AppleScript features that you'll want to examine more closely.*

- **Convert Documents**   This script converts a file created in another program, such as earlier versions of AppleWorks itself (called ClarisWorks), Microsoft Word or format—including text, PICT, and GIF—to the appropriate AppleWorks 5 format.

- **Mail Merge**   This script can be used to import selected data from FileMaker Pro. After the data has been imported from FileMaker, it is placed in database document in AppleWorks, and then put into a word processing, text frame, or spreadsheet document.

- **Print documents**   This script can be used to print one or more documents automatically that were made in AppleWorks. If you want to print one or more documents that weren't created in AppleWorks, you must first convert them to AppleWorks format.

- **Remote Slide Show**   With this script, you can take control of a slide show being run on a different computer, so you needn't be right in front of that computer at the time. To do this, however, the two computers must first be connected over the same network. The subject of networking is covered in Chapter 8.

A Fast Tutorial on AppleScript Programming

The AppleScript Web site gives you a full online tutorial in basic scripting techniques. This brief explanation tells how to create a simple script in AppleScript's Script Editor.

> **NOTE**   *The scripting technique shown here works with Finder actions and any program that is recordable (the program's documentation or the list at the AppleScript Web site discusses this).*

1. First, open the AppleScript Folder in the Apple Extras Folder. The Script Editor is there.

2. Double-click the application.

3. Once the program has been launched, click the record button. Now perform whatever function you want to be automated. For example, you can open a certain folder and move a file in that folder somewhere else on your desktop, or you can move that folder to another folder or even to another disk (as in the script shown in Figure 9.1)

4. Once you perform the action, go back to Script Editor, and click the Stop button. Text explaining what you did appears in the lower box in the Script Editor window, written in perfect AppleScript language. This surely is a useful way to learn some of the basics of scripting.

5. In the Description window at the top part of the Script Editor window, type a brief description of what the script does when it's activated. After you do this, double-check the script to make sure it works correctly.

6. To double-check the script, click the Run button just above the text containing the script itself.

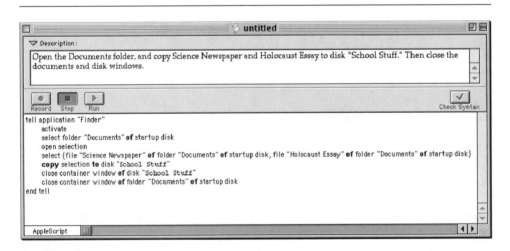

FIGURE 9-1 You can use AppleScript to automate a number of different tasks to make your computing experience much easier

7. If the script doesn't seem to function, click the Check Syntax button in the Script Editor window to examine the language to make sure the commands are all correct.

8. After you are certain everything in your script works as it should, save your script by choosing Save As or Save As Run-Only from the File menu.

NOTE

In this situation, I recommend you choose Run-Only. This enables you to use the script, but you cannot edit the script once it has been saved. On the other hand, choosing Save As enables you to both use and edit the script.

9. After selecting your save options (as shown in Figure 9–2), put your script in a place where it is most convenient for you to access it.

10. Give your script a name and choose classic applet from the pop-up menu.

11. Finally, click Save. Your first script is now available for your use. The script bears the standard AppleScript icon, the same as the ones Apple provides or those that ship with some of your favorite programs.

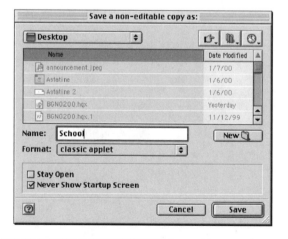

FIGURE 9-2   When you save your script, this dialog box shows up

A Fast Tutorial on AppleScript Programming

Summing Up

In the end, AppleScript isn't so daunting after all. In this chapter, you learned about the scripts Apple includes with your system software, as well as how to use AppleScript in various programs. You were also introduced to the process of creating a script.

Armed with these basics, you are now ready to go on and build your scripting skills. While the language may appear to be English with an unusual dialect, it is consistent and you can easily progress from modifying your scripts to building your own from scratch.

In the next chapter, you learn how to install and remove software correctly, as well as how to deal with any potential problems that may occur when installing the latest applications on your Mac.

Chapter 10

Installing New Software

New consumer model Macs, such as the iBook and iMac, come with plenty of software already installed. And it's possible for you to compute happily for years with these programs without buying upgrades or anything totally new.

But thousands of programs are actually available for Macs and, chances are, at some point during the life span of your Mac, you may want to add more programs to your computer.

What you add may be a word processing program or an office suite, such as AppleWorks or Microsoft Office. Perhaps you're interested in installing the latest games, desktop publishing, graphic design, or financial software.

Installing new software ought to be simple. You find some sort of installer icon, double-click it, and wait a few minutes. But not all installations are seamless and you ought to consider a few things before you click that installer to run it.

In this chapter, I cover the basics of installation and then some of the things you need to think about to prevent problems.

Then, soon enough, you'll have your hard drive bursting with new software.

A Quick Look at Bundled Software

Wouldn't it be nice if you could buy a brand new Mac and never have to worry about the software? Apple took a move in that direction when it first came out with consumer-oriented Macs some years back with a line called Performa.

The poor-selling Performa with its confusing model naming structure is now history, but the basic concept remains: Provide a new Mac with enough software to meet the needs of most users, so you don't have to add anything extra when you bring it home to surf the Internet, write a letter, make a financial report, or just play a game.

The enormously successful iBook and iMac lines fulfill this concept very well, thank you. They begin with AppleWorks, a pretty good office suite with word processing, database, spreadsheet, and draw and paint capabilities. To that mix Apple adds enough Internet software to get you connected to browse the Web and to write e-mail. You'll also find a few games, an encyclopedia, and, with the iMac at least, financial management software (Intuit's Quicken).

There are downsides to all this free stuff. For one thing, you aren't always assured of getting the latest versions of a program, because the agreements Apple made with software publishers (other than its own product, AppleWorks) may cover just one version. A case in point is Quicken 98, which was still being included on new iMacs as of the time this book went to press, even though Intuit had previously introduced an updated version, Quicken 2000.

Another example: Apple offers Smith-Micro's FaxSTF for its built-in modems, but the version you get is a "lite" featured one. If you want to take advantage of some extra features, such as drag and drop faxing and multiple address book support, you have to upgrade to the retail version, FaxSTF Pro.

You may also be shortchanged on documentation. With the retail product you buy at your favorite computer dealer, there will usually be some sort of printed manual (though it's true more and more publishers are putting the most extensive documentation in help menus or with electronic documentation, usually in Adobe Acrobat format).

In addition, bundled software offers change frequently, as Apple negotiates new agreements with publishers and sets aside others. You do not have a choice as to which software is provided with that bundle; you have to accept what's in the box.

But even with these limitations, it doesn't mean the bundled software isn't good or isn't useful. The best thing to do is consider it a useful starting point, a way to get your Mac up and running and productive as quickly as possible.

And with thousands of Mac software titles out there, you can easily move beyond the basics of bundled software when the need arises.

How to Avoid Installation Pitfalls

Although the installation process may seem fairly straightforward, things don't always run seamlessly. Before you actually install a program, especially one that seems to have a lot of complicated elements to it, you may want to consider a few things that may cause trouble for you later:

- **Make sure you have enough RAM**   Some programs, such as Adobe Photoshop, and most games gobble up RAM like crazy. Make sure your computer is outfitted with enough RAM to run the program. Remember, Mac OS 9 needs 40MB total memory (including 32MB RAM; the rest coming via activating virtual memory to make the total) at a bare minimum for itself and one or two simple programs. You need to allow for whatever a program requires; the box should list minimum requirements. In addition, you need to add several megabytes of RAM as "elbow" room to allow sufficient memory to accommodate the fact that the needs of Mac OS 9 will expand depending on what resources a program might need.

NOTE *You may be able to get away with adding a little more virtual memory temporarily to enable you to use programs for which you normally don't have enough memory. The more you choose in the Memory Control Panel, though, the greater the potential for performance slow-down.*

■ **Make sure you have enough available hard drive space**   A lot of programs can take up 100 MB of hard drive space or more. If you have an older computer with a smaller hard drive, enough room may not exist to complete an installation. And sometimes an installer won't recognize the lack of disk space until you're well into the installation process.

TIP *As explained in the following, some program installers may give you a minimum install option, which enables you to run a program without exacting a big penalty of disk space, usually by grabbing needed components from a CD. However, performance, especially with games, is apt to suffer quite a bit.*

■ **Make sure the program will work with Mac OS 9**   Large changes in various parts of Mac OS 9 made some older programs incompatible. The changes to the File Manager, for example, which allow it to open up to 8,169 files at the same time, affected programs that addressed this resource in ways that Apple warned about through the years. For example, new versions of Adobe Type Manager and Adobe Type Reunion shipped right around the time Mac OS 9 arrived in stores. A good idea is to check with a manufacturer if you have any concerns. A publisher's Web site or versiontracker.com are the best resources for news of updates.

■ **Check the hardware requirements**   Certain programs, like Adobe InDesign, have particularly stiff hardware requirements, even though the hardware may work fine otherwise with Mac OS 9. For example, Adobe InDesign requires a PowerPC 604 or faster processor, such as the G3 and G4 (a G3 or faster is recommended for decent performance). Connectix Virtual PC also specifies a G3 as the minimum platform if you use the version that comes with Windows 95 or Windows 98 installed. If your computer doesn't meet these requirements, then you either have to get an older version of the program (if one is even available) or look for an alternative that can work with your computer.

NOTE

As this book went to press, Connectix was testing a version of Virtual PC that would include Windows 2000. They expected it to require a minimum of 128MB of RAM, and a Mac with a 300Mhz G3 CPU or faster.

■ **Check the ReadMe or Getting Started information first**   Before you install a program, you may be required to do certain things, such as turn off antivirus software or quit all applications (although some programs may do these things automatically). Check any instructions that come with the program to check for these items. You also want to look for news of incompatibilities with programs you are using and how the problem is being addressed. The more complicated the program, the larger the list of cautions you may need to observe.

CAUTION

Even if you buy a brand new product from your local store, don't always assume it's the latest version. Software publishers often post minor updates online, but it may take months for those updates to be included in retail versions of a program.

■ **Make sure the installer isn't installing any programs or extensions you already have**   Some programs automatically install extensions, such as InputSprockets or Open GL, and other programs, such as older versions of QuickTime, which already come in newer versions of Mac OS 9. To keep these from being installed, look for a custom installation option where you may be able to omit these components from the installation. Such options are usually (but not always) shown as a pop-up menu on the main installation screen.

■ **Save installer logs (if any)**   Some programs create installer logs (see Figure 10-1) after you finish installing them, which tell exactly what was installed onto your hard drive. You can often find the logs right on your hard drive (sometimes in a folder called Installer Logs). These documents can be helpful, especially when you decide to remove a program from your hard drive, so you can check to see if you need to trash or disable any extensions in the process.

NOTE

While more and more publishers recognize the benefit of installer logs, not all programs include them. So, if no log is present, don't assume anything is wrong.

**How to Avoid
Installation Pitfalls**

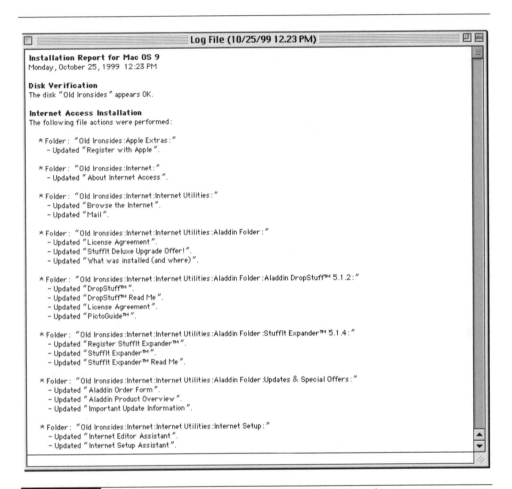

```
┌─────────────────────────────────────────────────────────────────────┐
│ ▣ ▤▤▤▤▤▤▤▤▤▤▤▤▤▤▤▤  Log File (10/25/99 12.23 PM) ▤▤▤▤▤▤▤▤▤▤  ▣▤ │
├─────────────────────────────────────────────────────────────────────┤
```

Installation Report for Mac OS 9
Monday, October 25, 1999 12:23 PM

Disk Verification
The disk "Old Ironsides" appears OK.

Internet Access Installation
The following file actions were performed:

 ✶ Folder: "Old Ironsides:Apple Extras:"
   – Updated "Register with Apple".

 ✶ Folder: "Old Ironsides:Internet:"
   – Updated "About Internet Access".

 ✶ Folder: "Old Ironsides:Internet:Internet Utilities:"
   – Updated "Browse the Internet".
   – Updated "Mail".

 ✶ Folder: "Old Ironsides:Internet:Internet Utilities:Aladdin Folder:"
   – Updated "License Agreement".
   – Updated "StuffIt Deluxe Upgrade Offer!".
   – Updated "What was installed (and where)".

 ✶ Folder: "Old Ironsides:Internet:Internet Utilities:Aladdin Folder:Aladdin DropStuff™ 5.1.2:"
   – Updated "DropStuff™".
   – Updated "DropStuff™ Read Me".
   – Updated "License Agreement".
   – Updated "PictoGuide™".

 ✶ Folder: "Old Ironsides:Internet:Internet Utilities:Aladdin Folder:StuffIt Expander™ 5.1.4:"
   – Updated "Register StuffIt Expander™".
   – Updated "StuffIt Expander™".
   – Updated "StuffIt Expander™ Read Me".

 ✶ Folder: "Old Ironsides:Internet:Internet Utilities:Aladdin Folder:Updates & Special Offers:"
   – Updated "Aladdin Order Form".
   – Updated "Aladdin Product Overview".
   – Updated "Important Update Information".

 ✶ Folder: "Old Ironsides:Internet:Internet Utilities:Internet Setup:"
   – Updated "Internet Editor Assistant".
   – Updated "Internet Setup Assistant".

FIGURE 10-1 Installer logs are helpful, especially when you need to remove a program and its components and there's no uninstall option

■ **Need a floppy?** Not all publishers seem to recognize that new Macs don't come with hard drives. Some still ship their programs in floppy form (even though it's actually cheaper to send out a CD). If your Mac is a recent model that didn't come with a floppy drive, check with the manufacturer to see if it has a version of the program available in a CD. If not, either consider not using the program or buying a floppy disk drive or a SuperDisk drive. A SuperDisk drive reads both 1.4MB floppies and special SuperDisk media that holds up to 120MB of data. SuperDisk drives come from such companies as Imation, VST Technologies (for PowerBooks), and Winstation. Floppy disk drives (which read only the 1.4MB or high-density type) are manufactured by such firms as Microtech International, Newer Technologies, and VST Technologies.

NOTE   *To complicate matters, some programs use installers that require both a floppy disk and a CD. The floppy contains components that serialize the program. Examples include QuarkXPress and older versions of Epson Stylus RIP (a program that delivers Adobe PostScript support for some Epson inkjet printers). If you run across such an installation setup, contact the publisher for assistance and, perhaps, a newer installer set before you invest in a floppy or SuperDisk drive.*

- **Need a dongle?**   Some programs come with a hardware device called a dongle that's needed to, in effect, decrypt a program and allow it to run on your Mac. This is a form of hardware serialization. If you don't have the dongle that is designed for a specific licensed copy of the product, it won't run. The problem is that such devices are designed to connect to a Mac's ADB port, the same place where you connect your input devices, such as the keyboard and mouse. With the general migration to USB, new Macs don't have support ADB anymore. If you run into this dilemma, contact the publisher and see if they have another version of the program that will run without the hardware device, or ask if an ADB to USB converter (such as Griffin Technology's iMate) will serve the purpose.

How to Install a New Program

Once you've taken the time to do your preinstallation homework, the actual process of installing the program on your Mac is relatively simple. These steps apply to most programs:

- As soon as you insert the CD of the program into your computer, the CD's directory, in some cases, automatically opens, giving you access to the contents inside. Otherwise, just double-click the CD's icon to see what's on it.

How to Install a New Program

■ Somewhere in that folder should be an icon, such as the one shown in Figure 10-2, with the word "installer" or "install" somewhere in its name. The example shown here is for Norton Utilities for the Macintosh, a popular set of hard-drive diagnostic and repair utilities. Double-click this icon.

NOTE *A very few installers, such as those used for the latest Microsoft software, resort to the traditional drag-and-drop method. You drag the folder to your hard drive. Then, when you first double-click the application's icon, a special "first run" installer launches and adds any needed components to your System Folder and elsewhere.*

■ From here, you follow the prompts. During the initial stages, you'll probably be asked to agree to the software license agreement. You must accept it for the installer to continue (software makers don't give you a choice).

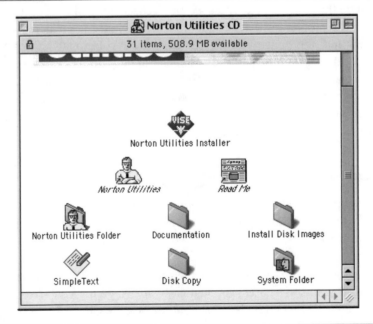

FIGURE 10-2   The installer icon places a set of hard-drive diagnostic utilities on your Mac's drive

■ After you get to the main Install screen, you may have to make some choices as to which type of installation you want (see Figure 10-3):

■ **Easy install**   This type of install is the one you probably want to accept because it will install all the basic applications, support components, and extensions the program needs to run.

■ **Custom install**   This type of installation is more complicated, with several or many choices to make (as shown in Figure 10-4), but you may need to use it. In particular, you may decide you don't want to install all the components of a program right away, or you may want to reinstall something later on that you threw out by mistake. Some programs add components for special purposes in the Custom install screen. If you're in doubt, check the documentation first before you proceed.

TIP

If you click the i icon at the right of the name of a software component, you usually see an information screen as to what that item does.

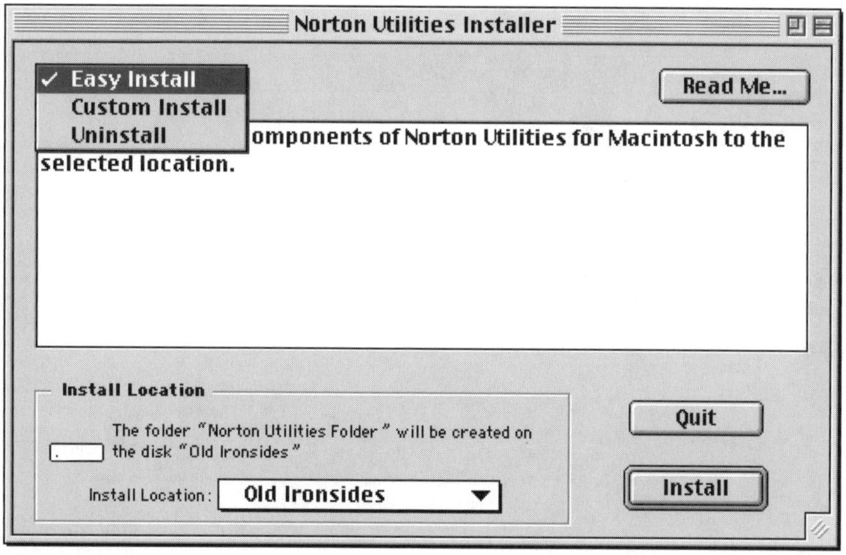

How to Install a New Program

_____
| ≡≡≡≡≡≡≡≡≡≡ Norton Utilities Installer ≡≡≡≡≡≡≡≡ 回目 |
| |
| ✓ Easy Install ▓▓▓▓▓▓▓   [Read Me…] |
| Custom Install |
| Uninstall   omponents of Norton Utilities for Macintosh to the |
| selected location. |
| |
| |
| |
| Install Location |
| The folder "Norton Utilities Folder" will be created on   [Quit] |
| [ ] the disk "Old Ironsides" |
| Install Location: [Old Ironsides   ▼]   [Install] |
|_____|

FIGURE 10-3   You may have to make one of several choices before installation begins

CAUTION

Often a program may need certain extensions to run. If you choose the easy install option, it automatically installs those extensions onto your computer whether or not you have them. While a properly configured installer shouldn't replace later versions of a program on your hard drive, I've seen extra versions of such things as AppleScript, ColorSync, and QuickTime on my hard drive after installing an older program, simply because the installer application wasn't put together properly.

■ **Uninstaller** Not all programs come with this option, but it can be quite useful if the program comes with a large number of components that extend beyond a basic application. As programs become more complex, it's a useful choice. When you select this option, in theory at least, all files originally installed should be removed from your hard drive.

NOTE

Exceptions to a rule always occur and possible exceptions for an uninstaller application are system extensions that may be used by more than a single application. Don't assume everything will be removed when you run the uninstaller application. You may want to double-check the System Folder after the uninstall process is complete.

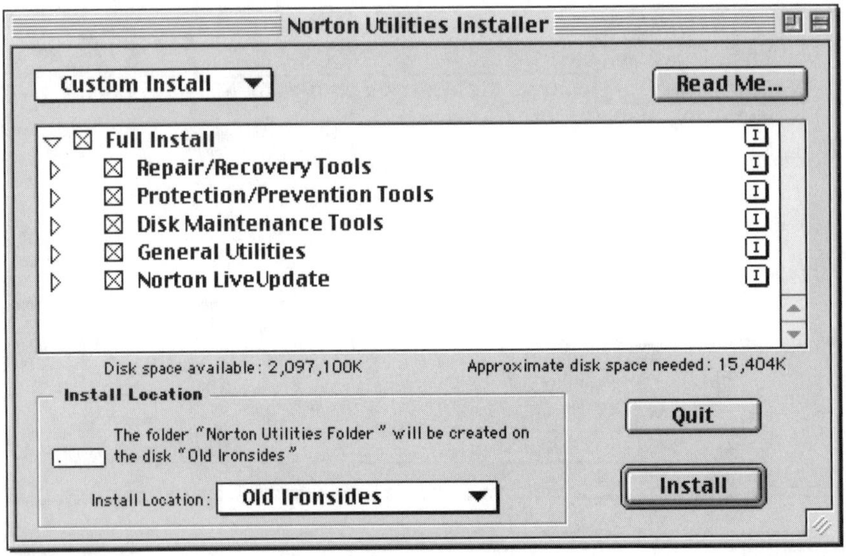

FIGURE 10-4   Custom installs are often used to add another component of a program or to replace it

Types of Custom Installs

If you choose the easy install, as mentioned earlier, it automatically installs all the components and extensions needed for the program to run. Using the custom install, however, you can sometimes choose how much data from a program you want to install on your hard drive (this is a good idea if the program takes up a lot of space, and you don't have the available space). You'll find two main types of custom installations:

- ■ **Minimum install**   This type of custom install only installs the least amount of data you'll need to run the program onto your hard drive. It gives you only the bare minimum. The rest needs to be read from the CD of the program. You'll find this choice present with some Mac games. Although this is a good option for computers with smaller hard drives, especially if the full install of the program can take up half a gigabyte or more (such as the games Caesar III and Falcon 4.0), it can also slow down the performance of that program while it's in use. That's because needed components for the program must be read from the CD, which, of course, must be present in the drive whenever the program is active. You should only accept this option if your hard drive absolutely can't handle a full install; otherwise, go for the whole install.

- ■ **Full install**   This one speaks for itself. It installs everything the program needs to run onto your hard drive, which includes data, graphics files, sound files, and other components. Sometimes these full installs can take up huge amounts of hard drive, but they speed the performance of the program because it doesn't need to contact the CD for data as often (or at all).

After you decide what type of install you want, you can begin to click the Install button. In a moment or two, you'll probably see some sort of progress window (see Figure 10-5) on your hard drive. Some program installers give you the option to install other programs or quit; others force you to restart after you install them, before you can use them (this is only necessary if the installer places items in your System Folder, such as drivers or extensions).

Once you restart your Mac, you should be able to use the program the way the publisher intended. But you still may encounter potential problems, so I describe these possibilities in the next section.

How to Install a New Program

```
                    ═══════════ Installing ═══════════

    Items remaining to be installed:   159
    Installing: PowerBook 170
                                                      ┌──────────┐
    ┌────┬─────────────────────────────────────┐     │   Stop   │
    └────┴─────────────────────────────────────┘     └──────────┘

    This installation was created with Installer VISE from MindVision Software
```

FIGURE 10-5   From here, the installation proceeds automatically, well, most of the time

Updating Your Software

As with death and taxes, software updates are inevitable. Few publishers get it
exactly right the first time. In addition, when Apple releases a new system version,
a publisher may need to change something to address a conflict. Or, the publisher
will fix bugs that weren't eliminated when a program first came out. Or, it may
wish to add new features that make the program work better.

A minor update may be free; you just have to download a new version or get
an updated disk from the publisher. When major features are changed, however,
the publisher often (but not always) puts a price tag on the upgrade.

Check the Manufacturer's Web Site

Having online access has quickly risen from luxury to necessity. Software
publishers regularly post updates for their programs and, as explained in the next
section, Mac OS 9's Software Update feature and similar features from other
companies are bound to become more commonplace.

A good idea is to pay a regular visit to the Web sites run by the publishers of
your most important programs for news of updates. Some even offer you a regular
e-mail newsletter, which gives you news about updates and potential problems
with the program (and even some hints and tips for better performance).

Another great resource is VersionTracker, at http://www.versiontracker.com.
This site provides regular information and direct links to updates. If you check the
site at least once a week, time and a needed update will seldom pass you by.

Apple's Software Update Feature

Apple's Software Update program is a handy feature just introduced with the
release of Mac OS 9. In the past, you had to physically look for news of an update.

Because Apple would release some new component every few weeks, it required regular work on your part to be sure you had the latest and greatest. This new feature, however, automates the process of keeping your system software up-to-date.

NOTE *Currently, Apple's Software Updates feature isn't able to find updates for third-party extensions and applications. However, this doesn't mean that some companies won't eventually choose to work with Apple to make use of this feature.*

Following are the steps required to use Apple's Software Updates feature:

1. Go to the Apple menu, choose Control Panels, and then select Software Update from the submenu (see Figure 10-6).

2. Click the Update Now button to see if any updates for your system software are available. (See Figure 10-7).

| FIGURE 10-6 | Apple's Software Update feature can be used to keep your system software current |

How to Install a New Program

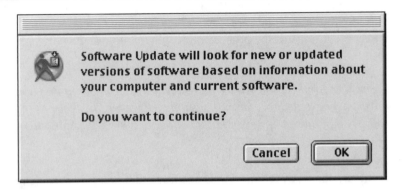

FIGURE 10-7   Your ISP will be dialed to see if any updates are out

3. The Software Update Control Panel works with Apple's Remote Access to dial your ISP and then check for updates from Apple's Web site (See Figure 10-8).

NOTE   *If you have a cable or DSL connection to the Internet, nothing has to be dialed. You always have a live connection. Software Update simply accesses that connection to connect to Apple's Web site to find if software updates are available.*

4. If any software is found, you can click the check box for the software in the window that appears on your screen. Then click the Install button to install that software.

CAUTION   *Because of the way they connect to the Internet, the Software Update feature cannot dial your AOL or CompuServe connection. If you are a member of these services, you need to log on first, and then you can run Software Update to check for new system software updates.*

FIGURE 10-8   Your computer then checks for system updates over the Internet

5. Once the installation is complete, you see a prompt asking to Restart your Mac. When you OK the message, your Mac goes through its normal restart routine, after which you'll be up and running with the new software you've just installed.

Scheduling Software Updates

You needn't remember to check for new updates for Mac OS 9. You can configure Software Update to do the searching for you on a regular basis.

Here's how to set a schedule:

1. Go to the Apple menu, choose Control Panels, and then choose Software Update from the submenu.

2. On the main screen of the Software Update Control Panel, click the Update software automatically check box, which brings up the screen shown in Figure 10-9.

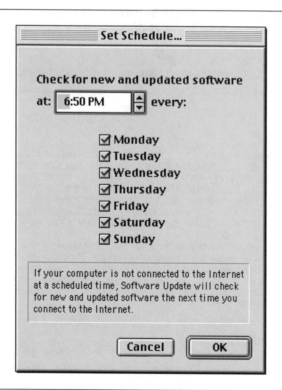

How to Install a New Program

Choose your update schedule from this screen

3. Check Set Schedule.

4. Click the check boxes corresponding to the schedule you wish to establish. You will want to check for updates once a week (checking daily is probably a bit much, though that option is available).

5. Click the close box to store your settings, which will (the first time you set it up), produce Apple's standard software license agreement, shown in Figure 10-10.

Other Automatic Software Update Options

Apple isn't unique in producing the capability to do automatic updates to its software. Other publishers got there first. For example, Insider Software's Update

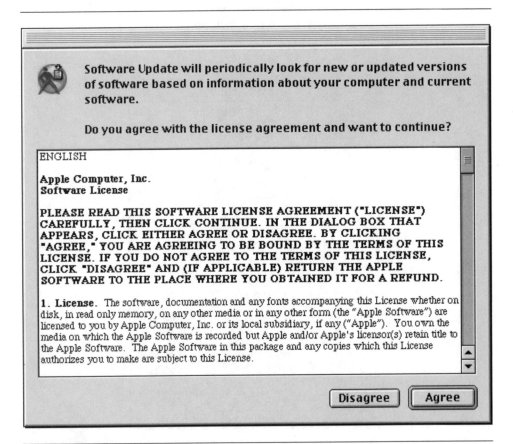

FIGURE 10-10   After installing the new software, you must accept a license agreement before you quit

Agent does Apple one better by automatically checking for updates for thousands of available programs.

In addition, both Network Associates and Symantec have introduced automatic updating features for their key Mac utility programs, such as Virex, Norton Anti-Virus, and Norton Utilities.

You can expect such features will probably spread to other publishers as Internet access becomes more or less universal and automatic software delivery technology continues to be developed.

The Downside of Automatic Software Updates

The ability to keep up to date with your programs without having to dig up information about updates is a real plus. Unfortunately it also has its downsides, especially if you have more than a single Mac in your setup.

When you download an update from the Internet or install one from a CD, you have an installer program you can use again when necessary. This isn't the always case with an automatic update feature. Once the update is complete, there may be no readily identifiable installer that you can run in case the update has to be performed a second time, on that Mac (because you reinstalled the system software) or on another.

The QuickTime online installer manages the feat, leaving a file called "QuickTime Install Cache" in the same folder as your QuickTime Player program. You can use that to reinstall the latest version of QuickTime should the need arise.

Otherwise, you must resort to ferreting out the proper software update components in one Mac's System Folder if you need to have the same updates on another, or run the Software Update Control Panel manually to perform its duties, separately, on each Mac you have.

This is a limitation that does minimize the benefits of automatic updates. Maybe it'll be addressed by the time this book appears in print.

Removing Software Safely

As you see from the previous text, actually installing software should not be a great problem. You just have to do a little advance planning so you don't try to install programs that will not work properly on your Mac.

When it comes to removing software, however, things may not be quite as clear-cut.

You have added more and more software but, for one reason or another, you want to remove some of it.

Removing Software Safely

Perhaps you have a small hard drive with limited space for additional programs. Or, maybe you're tired of using a specific program, or you're dissatisfied with its performance and you want to get rid of it. You can't just dump the program into the trash can, though. Some other hidden components of the program that weren't in its folder may need to be trashed or disabled, or they may cause problems with your computer.

Here are several ways to remove the software:

- **Just trash the folder**   This is the old-fashioned Mac way. You take the program's folder, drag it to the trash, empty it, and it's gone. That's the way it used to work until software became more complicated and elements of a program were also spread through various parts of the System Folder. Some programs add extensions, others add Control Panels, and many items are in the Application Support folder, as well. Also, program settings and support files are within the Preferences folder inside the System Folder, so you may be better off trying one of the other options described here.

- **Use an uninstaller (or remove)**   While not all programs have this option, some, like Microsoft Office 98 and Norton Utilities, offer an uninstall option as a pop-up menu on the installer screen (see Figure 10-11) when you launch the installer. Using this option automatically removes not only the program, but also all extensions and additional components originally installed on your hard drive, along with the program, eliminating the hassle of doing all that work yourself.

NOTE   *Although Microsoft Office is normally installed by dragging the application folder to your hard drive, an uninstall application is, in fact, on the Office CD. It's in the Office Custom Install folder. Just launch the Microsoft Office Installer application, and you'll find a Remove option in the installer's pop-up menu of installation options.*

- **Check the install log**   If the program you installed doesn't come with an uninstall option, you may have to use your installer log to guide you, if that program created an installer log automatically after it was installed. By looking through the log, you can see what other extensions and assorted items that it installed on your hard drive besides the program itself. Then you can locate, and trash or disable them.

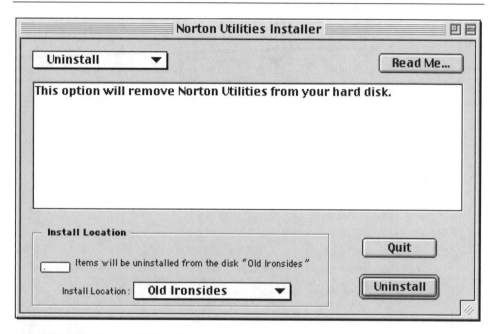

FIGURE 10-11 A complicated program's Uninstall option is the most efficient way to remove it

■ **No installer log?** If the program didn't make an installer log or if you trashed it, the situation may be a little more complicated. You can still locate the various components of the program, though. Apple has the way! Just locate Sherlock 2 in the Apple menu, launch it, and search for items that have the name of the software or its publisher. Figure 10-12 shows an example of a search for components added during the installation of Norton Utilities.

Sherlock 2 can help you locate the right elements of a program, but only if that program installs clearly named components. If those components have relatively obscure names that don't contain the name of the publisher or the program, you may have to do some searching through the heart and soul of your system folder. Never fear, though, because the Apple System Profiler (which can also be found in the Apple menu), shown in Figure 10-13, can help you. When you click the

Removing Software Safely

FIGURE 10-12 Sherlock 2 can sometimes help you find components of software you want to remove

Extensions or Control Panels tab in the System Profiler screen, a list of those items is displayed. That list also tells you whether they are extensions or control panels made by Apple. From here, by process of elimination, you can figure out what you need to trash or disable.

The first step in the process is to eliminate extensions with the names of companies or programs you don't want to delete. This should get rid of much of the list. After that, you can go directly to the extension itself and, by pressing the command and –I keys at the same time, you can get information on that extension,

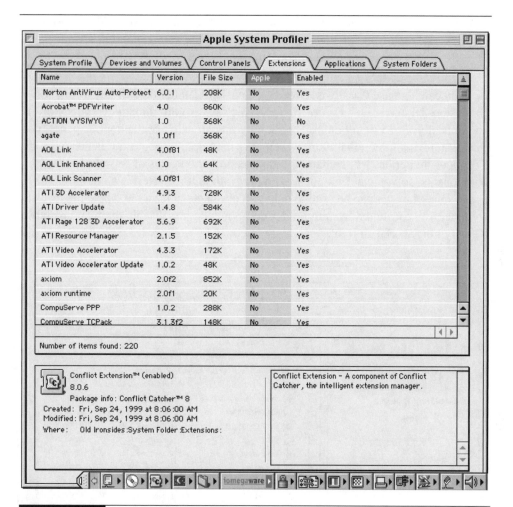

FIGURE 10-13   Apple System Profiler can help ease the task of finding software components that came with software you're trying to remove

which may tell what publisher or program it goes with. If the extension contains the name of the program you want to remove, you can immediately disable it. If the extension only contains the name of the publisher, and you have multiple programs made by that publisher, you may need some time to figure out which programs they work with.

 *A good idea is to disable, rather than delete, an extension that seems to apply to a specific program. That way, if you mistakenly remove an extension needed by another program, you can easily restore it.*

You can also use Casady & Greene's Conflict Catcher (see Figure 10-14) or Extensions Manager (see Figure 10-15), which gives you immediate control of the contents of your System Folder. By clicking an extension or the control panel, you can get information on that item, which may include the program it is needed for. Conflict Catcher has a huge database that records thousands of System Folder components, so you can find out what a program is for, even if it's not Apple's. Extensions Manager can be used to help you eliminate at least the Apple prospects.

Once you locate the System Folder components, just disable them and restart. If everything works all right, you can then consider whether to trash those items.

FIGURE 10-14   In addition to testing for software conflicts, Conflict Catcher gives you information about the source of a particular System Folder component

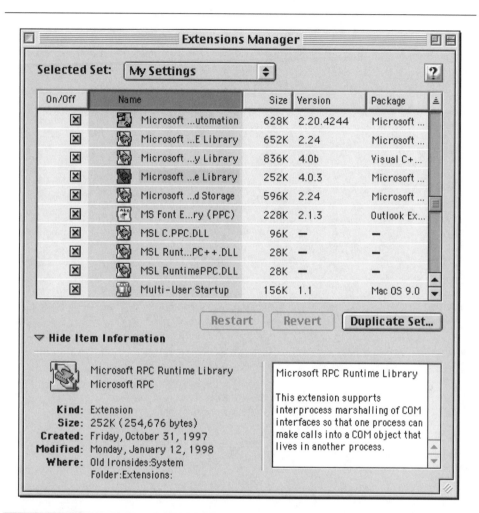

FIGURE 10-15   Apple's own Extensions Manager can deliver information about
Apple-specific items and a few others

Summing Up

This chapter covered the process of installing, updating, and removing software on
your Mac. If you follow the steps with care, you'll avoid most installation hangups.

In the next chapter of this book, I leave behind the simple, everyday tasks of
the Mac OS, and move on to installing and configuring new Mac hardware,
including new computers, printers, scanners, removable drives, and more.

Summing Up

Part II

Installing and Configuring Mac Hardware

Chapter 11

Installing a New Mac OS Computer

This is the experience you've been waiting for. You've just bought a brand new Power Mac, iMac, iBook, or PowerBook. Taking a new computer out of its box and setting it up proudly on your desk can be fun and enjoyable, especially if you're putting it in your home and it's your first Mac (or your first computer, for that matter). If the computer is for your office, you want to get your new Mac up-and-running as quickly as possible, so you can make it a productive tool the minute you start using it.

In this chapter, you learn how to set up a new Mac, whether it's a desktop or a portable, and whether you're setting it up in your cozy home office or a business environment. You'll also learn how to set up your printer or printers on the new system.

> NOTE   *The subject of setting up a new PowerBook or iBook is covered in detail in Chapter 12.*

How to Prepare for a New Mac

The success of the iMac has convinced many Mac users to replace the faithful machines they've used for many years, for the (dare I say, cute) new fruit-colored computer. This success has also been enough to bring over many new computer users to the Mac platform, as well as converts from Windows (a combined total of 45 percent of iMac and one third of purchasers of the iBook are in either category).

If the latter is your situation, then the next section of this chapter is for you. Former Windows users especially will soon realize how different the experience of using a Mac is from using a PC.

Setting up a typical Macintosh, especially with the arrival of the iMac, is extremely easy. In a matter of minutes, you can be up-and-running, surfing the Internet, or doing whatever you want on your new Mac. Literally, all you have to do is plug in the computer, turn it on, and you're off and away. This is most true for the iMac and iBook, where most of the software you need to use daily is already installed on the hard drive for you.

However, you should be aware of some precautions when you install your new Mac, whether you're a first-time user or a veteran of the Mac platform since its early days.

The next part of this chapter gives you some tips to help you start (or resume) your computing experience as painlessly as possible.

Setting Up a New Mac in a Home or Home Office

In this situation, you probably are just starting over. This is either your first Macintosh or it's replacing the one you've owned for years. You need to follow some guidelines, whatever your situation.

For First-Time Mac Users

If this is the first time you are using a Macintosh and the Mac operating system, make sure you carefully heed each step of the installation process. Every new Mac comes with a short, easy-to-follow set of installation instructions to guide you through the simplest steps of unpacking the Mac and plugging in everything. These instructions are so brief you may be confused or frustrated about a number of things after you turn on your new Mac.

NOTE   *In the old days, Macs came with a rather comprehensive set of manuals that covered everything from basic setup and troubleshooting of your new computer to a full tutorial on how to use the Mac operating system. Apple has now confined the latter to the Help menus. The setup and troubleshooting information on a system, which has become more complex than ever, is left to the bare essentials. Computer books have become so popular because they replace the manuals Apple no longer provides.*

Also, if you're a first-time computer user, the thought of adding extra peripherals, like printers, scanners, and hard drives, may seem daunting to you. I'm sure you'll find times where you can use guidance in what may seem, to you, an intimidating situation.

As simple as the iMac or practically any new Mac appears at first, you can't simply turn on your computer and work with it without eventually having to deal with some sort of problem. Your new Mac may work the first day, but after you run some programs for a while, questions can arise and problems can occur. All personal computers are like that.

The following are some tips to help you as you install your new Mac:

- **Try out your computer from stem-to-stern.**   After you turn on your Mac for the first time, make sure all the basic tasks, like using the keyboard and mouse, work properly. Keep a close eye on anything that doesn't seem to work correctly. While you could use a Control Panel setting to change some

How to Prepare for a New Mac

elements of your Mac experience, such as mouse-tracking speed and the display settings, for now you should just know it's there.

■ **Be careful about setting up a printer.**   The Mac OS Setup Assistant, launched when you first turn on your new Mac (or reinstall the Mac operating system) will check your network for the presence of a printer. But Mac OS 9 only includes support for Apple printers. If you have a non-Apple printer (and this is quite likely, since Apple no longer makes printers), you'll need to install the special software that comes with it. If you have a PostScript laser printer, you can use the LaserWriter 8 driver that ships with the Mac OS (unless the manufacturer requires a special custom driver), but you also need to install a special file, called PostScript Printer Description (or PPD for short) that allows the driver to configure itself for your printer's special features. Some printers offer extra paper trays, special resolution settings, and even the ability to print on both sides of the paper (duplexing). All this information is spelled out in the PPD file, which ought to be found on the printer's installation CD. If you cannot locate this file, check with the manufacturer or at Adobe's Web site, http://www.adobe.com/prodindex/printerdrivers/macppd.html. Adobe keeps a repository of PPD files that is second to none. The file is placed in the Printer Descriptions folder, inside the Extensions folder within the System Folder. You don't have to restart when you install a PPD file. Just open the Chooser, select the printer driver, then click the Setup button in the Chooser window to configure your Mac to work with your printer.

■ **Learn your Mac fundamentals.**   This book was written to tell you about Mac OS 9 and the various elements of the Mac user experience that relate to it. But this isn't meant to be an instruction manual for brand-new users. If you're using a Mac for the first time, however, help is there for you. As soon as your Mac finishes starting up for the first time, a friendly desktop appears with a word on the menu bar at the top called Help. Check it for an item called Macintosh Tutorial in the Help menu (Macintosh Tutorial may also be in the Apple Extras folder). The Macintosh Tutorial takes you through the process of learning to work with the mouse and the basic elements of using a personal computer, such as using folders, program windows, and Open and Save dialog boxes. Some of these subjects could be confusing, especially for first-time Mac users. Although it takes about 30 minutes to get through the tutorial, taking the time to learn the basic elements of using a Mac is worth it. I had to learn the same information when I got my first Mac.

NOTE

Once the tutorial is over, don't assume you're now a Mac expert. Developing enough flexibility so the Mac's mouse becomes, literally, an extension of your hand takes time. And, unless you've done a lot of typing, developing good keyboarding skills also takes time. You need to develop the skills so you don't strain your wrists. You may even want to consider an interactive typing course, such as Mavis Beacon Teaches Typing (check with your dealer for a copy).

- **Don't panic if your Mac misbehaves.**   Most of the time, a little troubleshooting should deal with many of the problems you encounter. The reasons for problems include installing a piece of software improperly or not paying careful enough attention to installation instructions. Sometimes it's only a matter of one program not working in harmony with another, and with thousands of possible installation setups, this is something hard to predict. Throughout this book, a number of problems you might face in a wide variety of situations are covered, along with the solutions to fix them (most of the time, anyway). The subject of software installations is covered in more detail in Chapter 10, while tried-and-true troubleshooting techniques are covered in Chapter 31. You may also want to get a copy of another book I wrote for Osborne/McGraw-Hill, *Upgrading and Troubleshooting Your Mac,* which guides you through a whole range of possible Mac and Mac peripheral problems and their likely solutions.

- **Select whichever Internet service provider (ISP) suits your needs.**   Every new Mac enables you to connect to the Internet easily, just as advertised. With Apple's Internet Setup Assistant, you can create a new account on EarthLink, Apple's default ISP, or even use a different Internet service. There's also a setup program for AOL. If you don't want any of these alternatives or if you want to transfer your Internet settings from another computer (even from one running Windows), transferring the settings only takes a few minutes. Usually, they're made in the Internet, Remote Access, and TCP/IP Control Panels. If you need help, the technical support people at your ISP should be able to get you through the process in ten minutes or less, most of the time. You learn more about these subjects in Chapters 3 and 32.

- **Before installing a new device, don't forget to restart your Mac.**   Most of the new Macs come with two types of ports for adding peripherals—USB and FireWire. These ports are called *hot-pluggable,* which means you don't have to turn off your Mac every time you connect a new device to either of them. Whether you're installing a printer or a hard drive, however, you may need to

How to Prepare for a New Mac

install driver software to recognize that device. Because this software loads at startup, you need to restart to make the new device active. Then you can hot plug your peripheral and be sure it runs.

CAUTION *If you're setting up an older Mac, you have a different set of peripheral ports: ADB, serial, and SCSI. You need to shut down your Mac (and any other devices along those chains) whenever you connect something to one of these ports to avoid potential problems (such as short circuits and damage to delicate electronics).*

For People Who Are Replacing Their Macs or Adding New Ones

It shouldn't be hard to set up a new Mac if you've already done it before. The process should be quite familiar to you.

You should be aware of some basic information, though, when you're replacing an older Mac or setting up an additional one.

■ **Find available updates.**   If the Mac you are replacing is several years old, contact the publishers of your software to make sure you don't need an update for the programs to make them compatible with Mac OS 9. While the list of incompatible programs isn't that large, all you need is one incompatible program to bring the system down. A valuable resource for such information, one mentioned often here, is VersionTracker, at http://www.versiontracker.com. VersionTracker keeps tabs on hundreds of software publishers' Web sites for upgrade information. In Chapter 31, a number of updates you may need to make your older Mac compatible with Mac OS 9 are covered. Although this system version doesn't look altogether different from older versions, enough of a difference exists beneath the surface to make some older programs stop working or to cause system lockups.

■ **Reinstall your programs.**   Microsoft's installation for its Office and Internet programs enables you simply to drag the files from the CD to your hard drive. The components needed for those programs can be put directly on your hard drive without using a special installer. As soon as you open any of Microsoft's programs for the first time, a First Run install puts the necessary files in your System Folder. As for other applications, you should consider reinstalling them from scratch, even if you're tempted

user can log
allow for a
tic IP
In addition,
paying a
(...)..or if
erRouter:

ing up
er you
ving

This is especially true for a
...0 processor. You either
...native version of your
...ake advantage of
...set of preference files
...hin the System Folder)
...over to your new computer,

...blisher about getting the latest
...offers a newer version at a reduced
...sers of the product. While many older
...OS 9, others may not. Check this carefully

...to reinstall: Some programs monitor networks
...h a second copy on another computer with the
...mber. Not only do you usually have to buy extra user
...lac you add (except, perhaps, when a single user works
...c and laptop), but each licensed version of a program has
...tal number.

ways to share access to the Internet. If you must connect to
...net from more than one Mac, try to find a way to share your Internet
...ection among all your Macs. Programs that can handle these tasks are
...comsoft's SurfDoubler and IPNetRouter from Sustainable Softworks. You
could also purchase an Internet-sharing Ethernet hub, which enables you to
share one or more modem connections. Another possibility is to consider a
broadband ISP, using cable modems or DSL. If you need access strictly
for e-mail, you may fare just as well using a single e-mail program to share
messages across the network. Another solution is Apple's AirPort wireless
networking system, supported with many newer Apple products. The AirPort
Base Station comes with its own 56K modem and enables you to share your
Internet connection with any Mac that has an AirPort card. You can also use
this product to share a cable or DSL connection via the Ethernet port. Chapter
12 includes complete setup instructions on the AirPort.

How to Prepare for a New Mac

The limitation of this sharing technique is AOL. Only on... on to an AOL account at a time, even if you have maxed o... screen names. You'd have to get a second AOL account to... simultaneous hookup, even with two modems and two Mac... some cable-based Internet services may set you up with a sta... address, which means you cannot use the connection without... separate setup fee (if they require that for expanding your set... the user license permits, using a sharing program, such as IPN...

Setting Up a New Mac in Your Office

You could be switching from the UNIX or Windows platform to the Mac, sett... your first computer, or even adding a new Mac to an existing network. Whateve... need to do, you can find ways to get ready for the computer's arrival, without ha... to deal with any hassles.

Installing a New Mac on an Existing Mac Network

Add a new Mac on to your network shouldn't be hard if several Macs are already... on it, but you need to be aware of the following:

■ **Networking**   If the Mac is going to be on an Ethernet network, you should be sure your hub can handle one more connection. Certain hubs come with an uplink port, which enables you to daisy-chain more hubs if you need to add more. If you use wireless networking with AirPort, you should be sure your Mac can support AirPort. At press time, the iBook, second-generation (slot-loading) iMac, and the AGP-version of the Power Mac G4 could handle AirPort cards. The new PowerBook is also expected to support AirPort. You learn more about Apple's AirPort technology and how to set it up in Chapter 12.

■ **Connecting to the Internet**   While most new Macs have their own internal modems, it may not be good enough if you work in an office. First, a modem has the capability to bypass a firewall on a corporate network, although this may not be a problem with a small office. One or two of your computers can be assigned to deal with the Internet and e-mail tasks. You can set up an e-mail system in the office by purchasing an office e-mail program, such as CE Software's QuickMail. Such a program can enable you to deal with the requirements of both e-mail in your office and across the Internet. You could also use a cable modem or DSL if this option is available. Using either, you can share your Internet connection on a network with an Ethernet hub. After doing this, any e-mail program should work. Eudora Pro, Outlook Express, or Netscape Communicator can be used for communications over both the Internet and throughout the office. You could also use a modem-sharing Ethernet hub, with the capabilities of sharing one or two modems on a network. One such product, the MacSense Palm Router Elite, only requires a normal Internet browser to set up. If you inhabit a bigger office, though, Netopia's line of modems and routers could be for you. One example, the R121 Dual Analog Router, comes with two internal 56K modems and can be shared among 15 different users.

NOTE *A firewall is a hardware or software solution that serves as a traffic cop, putting limits on access to and from the Internet. Such limits may restrict Internet traffic to e-mail or to selected sites.*

- **Software licenses**   If you're adding a new Mac on to your network and you need to use certain software, it may be necessary to purchase an additional software license for each of those programs. Of course, you may not need to get a whole new copy at the retail price. Certain publishers sell licenses at lower prices, especially if you need multiple licenses. Don't forget, also, that many programs won't launch if another program with the same serial number is in use on your network. Third-party font user licenses are more flexible—they depend on the number of output devices you have. So, if you have 20 Macs and one printer, you only need one user license for your extra fonts.

- **Network printers**   If you have a network printer (whether a laser printer or an inkjet with network card), be sure to install any special drivers you need on your new Mac. With a PostScript printer, you need to make sure the proper PPD file is placed in the Printer Descriptions Folder, inside the Extensions folder in the System Folder. This allows the printer's special features (extra paper trays, resolution settings, etc.) to get full support. Macs only come with PPD files for Apple printers. For other models, you'll want to copy the PPD file from another Mac in your network. Once the PPD file is installed, just open the Chooser and select your PostScript printer driver (usually LaserWriter 8). When it shows up in the Chooser, click in the printer's name, then the Setup button to configure the driver to work with the correct PPD file.

- **Serial printers**   With the Printer Share software provided by Apple, you can share one Apple StyleWriter printer across a small network of two or three

How to Prepare for a New Mac

Macs by using one Mac as a print server. A shareware program, EpsonShare, does the same for an Epson serial printer. If you need to generate a lot of work or have a lot of Macs, however, you should probably get an inkjet printer with a LocalTalk or Ethernet card or a regular network laser printer.

CAUTION   *In trying to use an older printer with a newer Mac, you also come up against the lack of a serial port. Conversion methods exist, such as the Keyspan USB Twin Serial Adapter, which enables you to use many serial devices on a Mac's USB port, but not all printers work with such devices. You may find the time has come to consider a real network printer.*

How to Replace a Mac on an Existing Network of Macs

If you get a new Mac to replace an older one you've had for several years, you may need to update some or all of your software. Certain older programs could work all right with newer Macs, like the Power Mac G4 and the iMacs and, of course, Mac OS 9. Other programs may have to be updated to support the new hardware and operating system. Before you put any software on the new computer, check for any available updates first.

NOTE   *One new program I use regularly with my Mac OS 9 is Mac hardware EasyEnvelopes+, a shareware envelope printing program that came out in the early 1990s. The publisher, Ambrosia Software, hasn't updated the program largely because of lack of user interest, but I find the program works fine in almost every respect.*

Besides this and the previously mentioned tips, here's one more:

■ **Don't replace the System Folder on your new Mac with the one on the old Mac.**   Because your new Mac probably comes with Mac OS 9 (or Mac OS 8.6 if the item has been in the store for a while), its system files are optimized for that version of the Mac OS and that specific hardware. Also, different Macs require different files to run, so if the right files haven't been placed in the System Folder, your computer may not work properly.

NOTE   *When you install your new system software, you may want to make sure your Internet and network preferences are copied over from the Mac being replaced in your installation. This way, you needn't repeat the process of doing these setups. If you are upgrading from an old Mac, however, it may be better to start from scratch.*

Tips and Tricks for Safe Setups

While the possibility is slim that your Mac could not work at all when you turn it on (I've never experienced this in all my years of using a Mac, although a few users I know haven't been quite as lucky), this could still happen. You press the power button and your monitor remains dark. Nothing happens at all. Not even any sound of activity coming from the hard disk. If you run into a situation like this, first go through every step of the setup to be sure everything is plugged in correctly and the surge protector is turned on, if you use one.

Before you start calling Apple's tech support people, here are some tips to help you:

- **Double check every connection.**   Sure, you need to be sure everything is plugged in, but you also need to make certain the AC outlet works. Especially if you're working at home, some AC sockets are connected to a light switch. Whenever the light is turned off, the AC power goes off with it. I suppose some architects wanted to make it simple to turn lamps on or off, but they didn't have computers in mind. If you have a power strip, see if it has an on/off switch. Double-check to make sure all connections are tight (do this before turning on the power strip).

- **Switch or replace cables.**   Once in a while, a power cable is bad, which causes your computer not to run properly. If you have a spare cable somewhere, by all means, use it. Then you can check to see if the cables are actually causing your problems.

- **Check every item separately.**   If you put one peripheral in after another, such as in a daisy-chain of SCSI devices, and one device doesn't work, then most likely, the others won't work properly either. Your Mac could even crash when you start it. To deal with this, first check your Mac by itself, along with the keyboard, mouse, and monitor. After you make sure they are working all right, turn them off, and then connect your peripherals.

- **Install necessary driver software for accessory devices.**   Almost every device you connect to your Mac, including printers, hard drives, and scanners, needs special software to work. Although Apple provides some of this software, such as Iomega's software for its Jaz and Zip drives, as well as drivers for certain USB devices, such as the Imation SuperDisk, a lot of the devices won't work unless you actually install the software that comes with the product. And you don't always get a warning, except for USB devices.

NOTE
If you start your Mac or attempt to hook up a USB device for which there's no driver, Mac OS 9 warns you, and then asks if you want it to find a driver on the Internet. Unfortunately, most third-party companies don't support this special feature, so it's best to dismiss the prompt and install the software (or log on to the Internet separately in search of it, if you didn't get software with the USB device).

■ **Don't forget to use the Chooser to select your printer.** Even after you install the necessary printer drivers, your Mac doesn't know which printer you want to use. After you've restarted, following a printer driver installation, go to the Apple menu and select Chooser. When it opens, select the driver in the Chooser window, and follow the prompts to set up your printer port (if necessary) and your printer. Some of the newest HP inkjet printers have a great idea to help this process along: After restart, a special utility is launched that guides you through the initial setup process for the printer. It would be nice if other printer makers would do the same.

■ **This book can help you.** Throughout this book, every essential element of Mac OS 9 is covered. Some chapters include information about many of the program and hardware choices you have to make your Mac perform at its best. If you have problems or questions, please check the table of contents for the chapters that contain the information. Specifically, Chapter 31 covers a number of known problems with the Mac OS 9 and solutions. You also learn troubleshooting techniques in Chapter 25, using both Apple's Extensions Manager and Casady & Greene's Conflict Catcher.

NOTE
A companion book, Upgrading and Troubleshooting Your Mac, is also available from Osborne/McGraw-Hill. This book goes into extensive detail about installing accessories and upgrades on your Mac. It also provides extensive troubleshooting advice, including actual case histories from my own experiences as a Mac consultant.

If nothing seems to work, however, contact either your dealer or Apple Computer directly, and have your computer checked for possible repair or replacement. While dealers rarely replace a computer with a hardware problem, they might consider doing so if your Mac is officially dead on arrival.

What If the Dealer Won't Work with You?

The new warranty for all Apple's desktop computers allows your machine to be serviced free for a year. Any authorized dealer should be able to handle your repair in its own service facility and, for many repairs, this may be exactly the right solution.

If your dealer isn't cooperating, you may try another authorized Apple dealer. Apple dealers are supposed to perform warranty repairs, even if you didn't buy the computer from them (Apple reimburses them for those repairs, regardless).

If, however, there's no other dealer or if you want to have Apple arrange for repairs, you can call Apple directly. Apple's technical support people, as a matter of course, take you through some routine diagnostic steps to make sure it's a hardware, and not a software, problem (be patient, they're only trying to help). For desktop models (other than the iMac), your new Apple computer is eligible for onsite service (as long as Apple didn't change its policy after this book was written).

NOTE

Laptops can be sent directly to Apple to be serviced. Apple even supplies the box to ship it, as well as pays the charges to send it to and from you. First, you have to arrange for the service with the customer service department at Apple, however.

Don't worry about having to ask Apple directly to help you fix your problem (the dealers don't bite). While Apple's requirements for dealers are stricter than they used to be, and while you may need to make your way up the corporate ladder, before long, you should find someone who can help you solve your problem.

A Look at Extended Warranties

You have probably encountered this scenario. You have completed your purchase of a computer or consumer electronics product. The order is written up, but the salesperson has one more thing to offer you.

What about an extended warranty?

Such warranties are designed to extend the new product warranty by an extra year or two, or more. These warranties offer free repairs (or repairs that are free except for a small deductible). They can cost up to several hundred dollars each and they are supposed to deliver peace of mind, so you know your new purchase is protected.

Are they worth it?

That depends. Dealers may make a nice profit from such items, sometimes more than what they get for the sale of the product itself (especially if they have

Tips and Tricks for Safe Setups

done some discounting to get your business). The other consideration is many of these extended warranties don't come from the product's manufacturer; they are, instead, run by a third party, similar to an insurance policy. You may have to use the company's own list of service providers, not just any dealer for that product.

In addition, you have to depend on that warranty service remaining in business long enough for you to use the warranty, if it is necessary.

The other issue is whether your new product is so prone to failure that it would need such a warranty. Normally, if a computer or consumer electronics product, is going to fail, it does so shortly after you purchase it, well within the new product warranty. So, you may never need the protection those extended warranties offer.

On the other hand, Apple has sharply reduced the prices for its AppleCare program. You get an extension from one to three years, free technical support for the period (otherwise, you have to pay a fee for every call after 90 days), and a CD containing TechTool Deluxe, based on MicroMat's TechTool Pro diagnostic software.

If you have a frequent need to call Apple for help, that alone may pay the price for this extended warranty program.

More specifically: When it comes to one of Apple's laptops, which tend to get far more use and abuse than a desktop model, AppleCare may, in fact, be worth serious consideration.

In addition, if you truly plan to keep your Mac running for a long time and you are not in the habit of regularly updating your computer hardware, and if you are uncomfortable with taking your Mac apart and pouring over the insides in search of a solution to a problem, then there's yet another reason to consider Apple's variation on the extended warranty.

How to Transfer Files from an Older Mac

Most likely, you won't move over much in the way of System Folder files from your older Mac. You may have many other files you need to transfer to your newer system (or they might come from an identical Mac in your installation). While I recommend that you try to reinstall all your major programs, some simple utilities may be easily transferred from one Mac to the other without missing any essential system files.

Here are the most common methods of transferring files on your Mac:

■ **Use file sharing.**   This is probably the easiest and fastest way to get your files from one Mac to another, assuming you have an Ethernet network. If you own an older Mac with LocalTalk, but have no Ethernet port, then you need to purchase a LocalTalk to Ethernet adapter (such as an AsanteTalk from Asante) to allow the computers to network. Unfortunately, such file transfers are reduced to LocalTalk speeds, a fraction of Ethernet transfer rates. You may find copying over to a backup drive is easier, and then attaching the drive to the newer Macs. Remember, though, this may not work if your old Mac has a SCSI drive and your new Mac doesn't have a SCSI card.

CAUTION   *While Apple's AirPort technology is a great way to share an Internet connection or the transfer of small files, the Fast Ethernet capability built into newer Macs is much faster. If you are transferring a large number of files with a substantial total capacity, you may find using a wired network to transfer your files more worthwhile.*

NOTE   *If you need to move SCSI devices between the old computer and the new one, a low-cost SCSI card or SCSI to USB adapter may be worth consideration.*

■ **Use a removable or hard drive.**   If you have many files on your Mac and you don't have access to a fast Ethernet connection, you can first copy your files to removable media, such as a SuperDisk, Zip, Jaz, or Orb disk, with capacities ranging from just under 100MB to over 2GB. Or, you can use a large hard drive (affordable models are available with capacities exceeding 50GB). The faster the drive, the more efficient the process.

CAUTION   *If you plan on transferring a drive from one Mac to another and you're still using SCSI technology, be sure all devices are turned off first before moving the drive to another computer. Also, observe SCSI ID and termination settings. Chapter 15 covers the subject of installing and configuring a removable drive in more detail.*

■ **Use optical media.**   Optical media, such as CD-R and CD-RW, are great places to put your files. They can hold over 600MB of data each and you

How to Transfer Files from an Older Mac

can quickly copy them onto a new computer. The only drawback is that if you don't have a fast SCSI or FireWire CD writer, putting your files on a CD, as well as verifying them to make sure the correct files have been installed, could take a while. All new Macs come with a fast CD or DVD drive that reads only. Another possibility is the new DVD-RAM format, which has a maximum capacity of 5.2GB of storage space. At press time, the top-of- the-line model of the Power Macintosh G4 offered a DVD-RAM as standard equipment and Apple's "build to order" program offers it as an option for other models.

CAUTION *Not all CD drives can read a CD-RW disk, so it's best to stick with a plain CD if you're unsure or to make a test disk before transferring all your data to the rewritable variety. The disks you make with a DVD-RAM drive obviously can only be read on another device that supports the same technology.*

NOTE *Another optical-based drive format, magneto-optical, is not nearly as popular as CD writers, but still is useful because of the longevity of the medium. Magneto-optical works the same as any other removable drive, with full read and write capabilities via the Finder or your applications, but it tends to be rather slow (compared to a Jaz or Orb, that is).*

■ **Find newest versions of software.** If your Mac is more than two years old, you should contact the publishers of your software to find out if you need to update their programs to run on a Mac running Mac OS 9 or later. While Mac OS 9 offers good compatibility with thousands of Macintosh programs, some older programs are designed in such a way that they won't work properly (or at all). While you may not want to pay an upgrade fee after investing money in an all-new system, the increased productivity provided by a version that is compatible with your new Mac might pay for itself (and certainly should save you trips to the medicine cabinet in search of relief for your headache). Fortunately, if you need a new printer driver for Mac OS 9, at least that should be freely available from the manufacturer's Web site or via request to their support department.

NOTE *Don't be disappointed if the publisher of your favorite program doesn't have an update. I've run a number of older programs on my Macs with Mac OS 9—programs that will never be updated—and they seem to work fine. It doesn't hurt to try. If the program doesn't run, of course, you need to find an alternative if you still need the functionality it provides.*

■ **Consider reinstalling application software.** Except for the latest versions of Microsoft's Office and Internet software, which use easy drag-and-drop installations, many programs put various files in your System Folder. Knowing which files are needed and which aren't isn't easy because not all manufacturers label their support files so their purpose is clear-cut. The best approach is to install the programs from scratch. This ensures the correct files are placed in their proper locations. You can, of course, consider copying over program preference files if you have a set of complex ways in which you customized software. If you're using programs from a 680x0 Mac, make sure you reinstall your software or purchase the PowerPC versions of the software (if that version isn't already an automatic part of the installation process on the right model Mac). If you use the older 680x0 version, the program won't be able to take advantage of your computer's true potential. This is because the program will run at a much lower speed, especially if it performs complex rendering operations that tax the power of your new Mac's CPU.

Summing Up

Installing a new Mac isn't hard now. Despite the lack of decent manuals, you should be pleased to know the vast majority of Macs are quite trouble-free. If you do run into problems, however, dealing with most of them should be fairly easy. Use the information provided in this book, use your own knowledge of Macs, or use both.

In the next section, starting with Chapter 12, the subject of Apple's popular laptop line, the iBook and PowerBook, is covered. You learn how to harness the power of these marvelous computers at home, in your office, or on the road. You learn how to set up and use your Apple laptop, and you are given detailed instructions on configuring Apple's AirPort wireless networking system, which enables you to run a network with devices up to 150 feet apart without having to hang any wires between your Macs.

Summing Up

Chapter 12

Setting Up a PowerBook or iBook

Apple's laptop computers seem to have always been the underdog of the product line, even after Apple's resurgence in 1998 and 1999. Apple's laptops are trusty and reliable for those who use them. For the most part, the products get top ratings from magazines and newspapers, but they don't quite get the attention they should. Perhaps production nightmares, such as the problems with batteries and the need for an extended repair program on the PowerBook 5300, turned off people. Or, maybe Apple didn't spend enough time promoting its dependable, fast PowerBooks (though the company wasn't doing much to promote any of its products in the days before Steve Jobs returned to Apple in 1997).

All this changed with the release of the iBook in the fall of 1999. Building on the astounding success of the iMac, Apple touted the colorful laptop (tangerine or blueberry or the later release of the graphite Special Edition) as the "iMac to go." Apple also added support for a form of wireless networking called AirPort (which was soon extended to Apple's entire product line).

As a result, the iBook was a resounding success, piling more cash into Apple's coffers, which were already quite filled with the profits on the sales of nearly 2 million iMacs in the product's first year.

Despite flashy commercials of the PowerBook G3 steamrolling lowly Pentium laptops, only 70,000 PowerBooks were sold in the last three months of 1999, compared to over 200,000 iBooks. Will the faster year 2000 PowerBooks, with onboard FireWire and faster CPUs, deliver the goods and get Apple's mainstream laptop line the respect it deserves? Only time can tell.

In this chapter, you learn about setting up a new PowerBook or iBook, and installing the AirPort card and AirPort Base Station to allow your iBook to use AirPort.

You also learn how to make your laptop Mac do double duty as a desktop computer and you learn how to synchronize your files, so the work you do on the road is in tune with the files you have on your desktop Macs.

A Fast Technique to Get Up and Running

Setting up a new PowerBook or iBook is a relatively simple process (at least compared to setting up a desktop computer like the Power Mac G4). You want to follow some steps precisely when installing either, however, to get things going as quickly as possible. These steps are described in the following two sections: one section for the PowerBook and one section for the iBook.

Setting Up a PowerBook

This description is based on the setup process for a 1999 PowerBook G3, the one with the "bronze" keyboard, but it can apply, with the most minor of changes, to the upgraded model that shipped early in 2000.

> **NOTE** *The battery on a new PowerBook is usually spent of power and needs to be recharged. The process described not only gets your PowerBook running, but it also charges the battery (this process takes a few hours).*

1. Put the PowerBook on a flat surface, such as a desk, and make sure the battery is installed in an expansion bay slot.

2. Plug one end of the PowerBook's power cord into the adapter and plug the other end into a power strip or outlet.

3. Plug the power adapter into its corresponding port at the rear of the unit.

4. If you want to use your PowerBook for Internet access, attach a modular phone plug to the modem jack (this may be located at the rear or on the left side, depending on the model). Insert the other end of the plug into your phone jack or the second jack (if one is available) of your telephone.

> **NOTE** *Some older PowerBooks use a combination jack that serves as both Ethernet and telephone jack (with a splitter adapter cable that comes with these models).*

> **CAUTION** *Be careful about plugging in a modem to a digital telephone system, typically used by a hotel or large company. Although newer modems are protected against problems, not only can such a system not work (because your PowerBook modem cannot distinguish which line you want), there's also the potential of damage to your modem.*

5. If your PowerBook is going to be part of a network or connected to a networked printer, snap open the PowerBook's rear panel, and then insert the plug in the PowerBook's Ethernet port, located at the rear of the machine (as shown in Figure 12-1). The exact location depends on which PowerBook you have.

A Fast Technique to Get Up and Running

NOTE *The rear panel of the year 2000 model PowerBook is nearly identical to the one shown here, except for the SCSI device port, which is replaced by two FireWire ports.*

6. Open the PowerBook display by pulling up the latch and spreading the edges apart.

7. Position the display so it is at an angle comfortable for your eyesight.

8. To start the computer, press the POWER key, which is usually located at the upper-right corner of the keyboard.

Battery Wrapped?

Some shipped PowerBooks have a wrapper over the battery to protect the leads or plugs from shorting. If this is the case for your new PowerBook, follow these steps to remove the wrapper:

1. Open the display and remove part of the label on the case of your PowerBook, making sure you don't accidentally tear the wrapper.

2. Close the display.

3. Remove the battery from its compartment.

4. Slowly and carefully, take the wrapper off the battery.

5. Return the battery to the compartment, open your display, and turn on your PowerBook.

FIGURE 12-1   The Ethernet jack on a Bronze PowerBook G3 is the fourth port from the right

Setting Up an iBook

This description is based on the original iBook that shipped in the fall of 1999, but the basic process should apply to any product revision (including the upgraded versions released in February 2000). As with the regular PowerBook, you are plugging this unit into a wall outlet to charge the battery, which ships spent of power.

1. Place your iBook on a desk or other flat surface.

2. Plug in both ends of the power cord: one end into the adapter and the other end into an available power strip or outlet. Fortunately, the plugs have distinctive shapes, so you know what plugs into what.

3. Plug the power adapter into the adapter port on your iBook at the right rear of the unit.

4. If you want to connect to the Internet using your iBook's internal modem, insert a regular phone plug into the modem jack. Then take the other end of the plug, placing it into the phone jack or into a second jack on your phone.

5. If your iBook is going to be on an entire network of Macs or if it must be connected to a printer on a network, insert the plug in the iBook's Ethernet port, which can be found on the left side of the laptop (shown in Figure 12-2).

6. Open your iBook by pulling the top half from the bottom half.

7. Place your iBook at an angle suitable for your eyesight.

8. Boot up your iBook by pressing the POWER key, which can be found at the upper-right corner of the keyboard.

FIGURE 12-2   The iBook's Ethernet jack on this model is the second from the left, next to the phone jack

A Fast Technique to Get Up and Running

Trackpad

Some people (as I do) find Apple has configured the Trackpads on the iBooks and PowerBooks to move too slowly for their taste (in the same way regular mouse response is too slow on a new desktop Mac). You can't use the Mouse control panel to change the speed of the trackpad. Instead, you must use a special control panel named Trackpad (shown in Figure 12-3). Here you can configure the movement and double-clicking speed for the trackpad, as well as other functions you want the trackpad to perform (either dragging and drag lock or the ability to tap twice to double-click).

Setting Up and Configuring AirPort

One of the key features of the iBook and year 2000 model PowerBook is the capability to connect over the Internet or to maintain a network connection without using wires. These models have the capability to transfer data at speeds of up to 11 Mbps (a little over 1 MB). This feature is provided by virtue of Apple's AirPort technology, which supports IEEE 802.11, a worldwide wireless networking standard.

NOTE   *Support for a worldwide standard means other companies can produce products that work in harmony with AirPort to stretch wireless networking features to Macs that do not support AirPort modules.*

FIGURE 12-3   You configure your Apple laptop's trackpad with this control panel

To use AirPort, you must install an AirPort card in each Mac that supports the feature and an AirPort Base station if you want to take advantage of the capability to tie your wireless networking into a regular wired network or to use the airport's internal modem to share your Internet connection.

Installing an AirPort card isn't quite as simple as setting up the computer itself. The setup process involves straightforward steps, of course, but some sensitivities occur with the AirPort system, which you might need to address if connection quality isn't what you expect.

NOTE   *This chapter describes the basic setup process of installing AirPort on the iBook. Similar information can apply to any AirPort-equipped Mac, such as the year 2000 PowerBook line, Power Macintosh G4 series, and the slot-loading, second-generation iMacs.*

Installing the AirPort Card on an iBook

1. Turn off your iBook and unplug the power adapter, as well as the phone cord.

2. Flip your iBook over and take out the battery. This is done by loosening the retaining screws on the iBook's battery cover (you can loosen the screws with a coin). Once you open the door (see Figure 12-4), the battery can be popped out easily.

3. Remove the keyboard from your iBook by sliding the two plastic tabs at the top of the keyboard away from the display.

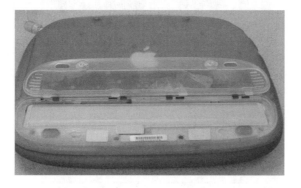

FIGURE 12-4   Here's an iBook with the battery compartment open

A Fast Technique to
Get Up and Running

4. Pick up the keyboard, turn it upside down, and then place it carefully near your iBook.

5. Flip the wire bracket up and attach the AirPort Card to the end of the antenna inside. Be sure the card is tightly connected to the antenna.

NOTE *Apple has thoughtfully provided some diagrams inside the iBook to help you locate the area where the AirPort card is placed.*

6. Put the AirPort Card (with the side containing the AirPort ID number facing you, as shown in Figure 12-5) between the guides, under the wire bracket, and in the slot located beneath the top end of the trackpad.

7. Press down the wire bracket to put the card firmly in your iBook.

8. Reinstall the keyboard, sliding the two plastic tabs toward the display to lock it.

9. Reinsert the battery and then lock the battery cover by tightening the retaining screws.

Installing the AirPort Base Station

To start, place the AirPort Base Station (as shown in Figure 12-6) in a location close to a power outlet or a power strip and a phone outlet, such as a desk or a bookcase.

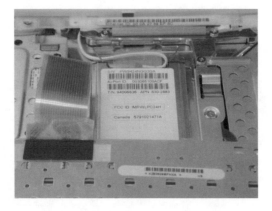

FIGURE 12-5   Make sure the ID number of the AirPort card is facing up when you install it in your iBook

FIGURE 12-6   The AirPort Base Station is the central connecting point for an AirPort network

You may not have enough room on your desk for the AirPort Base Station without completely reorganizing your desk space, something that could take a long time if your desk is piled with papers and magazines (like my desk in my home office). You could place the unit in a convenient location on the floor, perhaps adjacent to your Ethernet hub or switch (if you have one).

You can also attach the AirPort Base Station to a wall. Here is how it is done:

1. Find a place on your wall located near a power strip or outlet and a phone outlet.

2. Using two screws that fit the width of the holes in the bracket, screw the mounting bracket into a wall stud.

3. Find the three mounting bracket openings, which are on the bottom of the base station.

4. Put the cables through the mounting bracket and attach them to the base station.

5. Place the AirPort Base Station carefully on the mounting bracket.

Now you should have installed the AirPort Base Station somewhere close to a power and phone outlet, whether it's on your desk or on the wall. At this point, you need to go through the process of plugging in and configuring the AirPort Base Station.

1. Connect one end of the power adapter to the AirPort Base Station and connect the other end to an open power outlet or power strip. As soon as

A Fast Technique to
Get Up and Running

the base station is plugged in, it turns on automatically. It goes through a startup process that lasts for about 30 seconds. When the middle status light turns green, you know the startup process is complete.

2. If you plan to use the AirPort Base Station's own modem, attach one end of the phone cable to the internal modem port and the other end to an open analog telephone outlet.

3. If you plan to use the AirPort as an access point for a high-speed Internet connection, such as a cable modem or DSL, plug the necessary cable into the Ethernet port on the base station, instead of into the internal modem port.

4. Start your iBook to prepare for the next part of the process, which is configuring your AirPort Base Station. Your iBook may already come with the necessary AirPort software preinstalled. You can find this out by looking for the AirPort Setup Assistant in the Assistants folder. If the AirPort software has not been installed, use the CD that came with the base station to install the needed software.

5. With the AirPort software CD inserted, double-click the installer icon and you will see the screen shown in Figure 12-7.

NOTE *This description is based on setting up version 1.1 of the AirPort software, the one shipping when this book went to press. Later versions will probably have basically similar setup procedures, unless the product line gets a major revision.*

FIGURE 12-7 Click Continue to proceed with the installation process

6. On the next screen, you're asked to specify a location for the installation. This would be your iBook's internal drive (see Figure 12-8).

7. On the next screen, check Apple's Important Information ReadMe for any last-minute information about the installation of the software you're installing. Click Continue to proceed to the main installation screen (see Figure 12-9).

8. Click the Start button to start the installation process.

9. As soon as the installation is done, you see a Restart prompt (see Figure 12-10). Click the button to boot your Mac. Once your Mac has restarted, you can move to the next step of the AirPort setup process.

10. Once the AirPort software has been installed and your computer has restarted (or if the software was already on your computer), the AirPort Setup Assistant launches, so you can configure your base station. During the operation you are asked to specify a password with which to access the AirPort network. Click the next arrow to move through the steps.

11. During the setup process, the Assistant (shown in Figure 12-11) takes you through the entire process of configuring your AirPort network and copying your existing Internet settings (if any) to the AirPort Base Station from your iBook (as shown in Figure 12-12) . You learn more about the

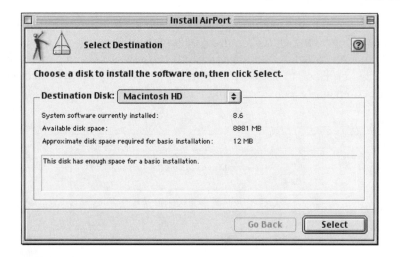

FIGURE 12-8   Select the destination for the AirPort software

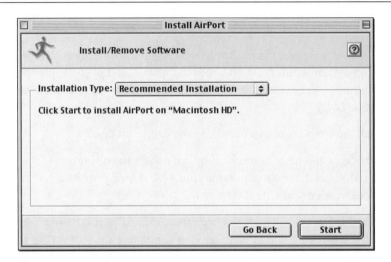

FIGURE 12-9 Begin the AirPort software installation from this screen

Internet Setup Assistant, used to handle the *Internet service provider* (*ISP*) settings transfer process, in Chapter 3.

NOTE *If the AirPort Setup Assistant doesn't launch on the next start, go to the Assistants folder and double-click its icon to begin the setup process.*

The Assistant explains each step you must take to configure your AirPort (this changes, depending on the version you have).

After your AirPort Base Station has been set up (as shown in Figure 12-13), you can use your iBook to access your AirPort network by simply selecting the Setup your computer to join an existing wireless network module option in the

FIGURE 12-10 Restart to activate your AirPort software

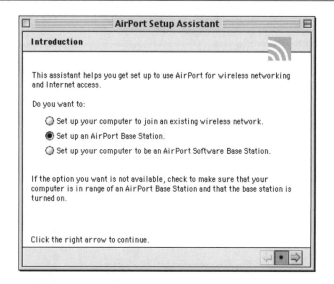

FIGURE 12-11   The AirPort Setup Assistant is used to configure your AirPort
Base Station

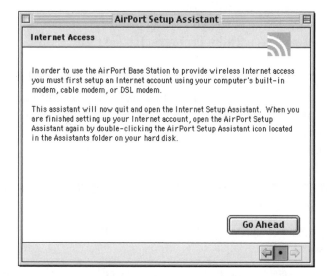

FIGURE 12-12   The Internet Setup Assistant is used to configure AirPort to connect
to the Internet

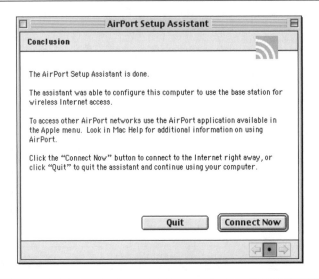

FIGURE 12-13   After you use the AirPort Setup Assistant, you can access the
AirPort network

AirPort application (shown in Figure 12-14), which can be launched from either
the Apple menu or the AirPort Control Strip module (shown in Figure 12-15).

Before you can access the network, you must enter the password (as seen in
Figure 12-16) you specified when you configured the Base Station.

Your AirPort wireless network is now set up and ready for use.

Understanding the Status of Your AirPort Base Station

The process of using the AirPort should be seamless, but problems may, nevertheless,
occur. Understanding the messages conveyed by the status lights on your Airport Base
Station is important.

Here are three instances where you see warning messages:

- **Airport communication is occurring**   One of the status lights flashes
  green to indicate networking is in progress.

- **Power is reaching the AirPort Base Station**   Two of the status lights
  remain green.

- **Ethernet port or modem port is being used**   All three of the status
  lights flash green.

FIGURE 12-14   The AirPort application can be used to join an AirPort network

Connecting to the Internet

To use AirPort for Internet access, you have to launch a program that uses the Internet, which includes e-mail programs such as Outlook Express and Web browsers such as Internet Explorer and Netscape Communicator. An Internet connection is automatically established by the AirPort Base Station whenever any of the computers on the network attempt to use an Internet program.

The Internet connection is automatically terminated by the AirPort Base Station after ten minutes of inactivity. This time-out interval can be changed using the AirPort Utility, which can be found in the AirPort folder of the Apple Extras folder. If you want to disconnect from the Internet manually, click the AirPort Control Strip module and select Hang Up AirPort Base Station from the options in the pop-up menu (as shown in Figure 12-17).

Launch the AirPort application

FIGURE 12-15   The AirPort application can also be launched from its control strip module

A Fast Technique to Get Up and Running

FIGURE 12-16   Put the password you set for yourself here

Remember, the speed at which information can be accessed on your network depends on the location from which you are trying to get that information. As already mentioned, the Base Station can transfer data to and from your iBook at a speed of up to 11Mb or a little over 1MB a second. If you're trying to access the Internet, however, your connection will only be as fast as that of the AirPort Base Station modem, the internal modem on your iBook, or your high-speed Internet connection, if you have one.

Accessing the AirPort Network with a non-Airport Mac

Because the AirPort Base Station has an Ethernet port, it can be connected to a Mac's Ethernet port using an Ethernet crossover cable or to an existing network of Macs with

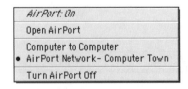

FIGURE 12-17   You can disconnect from the Internet in the AirPort control strip module (the bottom row changes depending on connection status)

an Ethernet hub or switch. If you plan to connect a non-AirPort Mac to your AirPort network, it is unnecessary to install the AirPort software on that computer.

Follow these steps to set up a non-AirPort Mac to access your AirPort network:

1. Connect the Ethernet port on your AirPort Base Station to the one on your Mac. If only one Mac will access the AirPort network, you can use an Ethernet crossover cable to connect the computer and the Base Station. If many different Macs will access the AirPort network, purchase an Ethernet hub, connect the Macs to the hub, and then connect the hub to the AirPort Base Station.

NOTE *You can visually identify an Ethernet crossover cable by looking at the colors of the wires inside the plugs. If the first and second pair of cables are reversed at one end, it's a crossover cable. If they are the same, it's a regular Ethernet cable, which only works with a hub or switch.*

2. Go to the Control Panels in your Apple Menu and select the TCP/IP control panel.

3. In the Connect via pop-up menu, select Ethernet built-in or whatever Ethernet port applies to that particular Mac.

4. In the Configure pop-up menu, select Using a DHCP Server.

5. Close the TCP/IP control panel.

Now this Mac can get all the needed Internet settings to connect to your ISP directly from the AirPort Base Station.

AirPort Problems and Solutions

Because AirPort is a new technology, you are bound to run into some sort of problem when you use it. Here are some of the common problems, as well as their solutions, you can face when you use the innovative wireless technology.

■ **Error message stating AirPort software cannot be found**   This usually appears when you work with the AirPort Setup Assistant. Make sure you have installed the software. If you have, make sure the software has been activated using the Extension Manager control panel in the Control Panels folder of the Apple menu. This message can also show up if the AirPort card has been improperly installed. Make sure your AirPort card has been firmly placed in the slot and that its serial number is facing upward.

A Fast Technique to
Get Up and Running

■ **AirPort network set up by the AirPort Base Station can't be detected**   Double-check to see if the AirPort Base Station has been properly plugged into a power outlet or power strip. Also, make sure your Mac is within the range of the AirPort Base Station (up to 150 feet away from the station). If so, then try restarting your Mac. If you still can't access the AirPort network, make sure both your Mac and the AirPort Base Station aren't close to any source of interference, such as metal walls or a microwave oven. Try changing the position of your computer, and then see if you can access the network. If not, try changing the position of the Base Station.

■ **Trouble accessing the Internet**   To use the AirPort Base Station for an Internet connection, you must first have an account with a standard ISP that uses standard PPP protocols. You can't use AirPort to access the Internet with an ISP that doesn't use standard methods for Internet connections, such as America Online. Unfortunately, this a limit you have to live with, unless AOL or Apple find a way to address this problem.

■ **Can't remember your password or wrong IP address**   If this problem occurs, you need to press the reset button, located on the bottom of the AirPort Base Station, to restore the default settings for the base station password and IP address. To do this, place the end of a straightened paper clip in the tiny opening on the underside of the base station. Hold down the reset button for one second. This restores the base station's default settings for five minutes. Then, using the AirPort Setup Assistant or the AirPort Utility, reconfigure your base station. If you don't do this within five minutes, you must again reset the base station.

■ **Can't access or configure the Base Station**   Reposition your computer in a location closer to the Base Station and be sure no potential sources of interference, such as metal walls or a microwave oven, are nearby. If this doesn't work, restart your computer. If you still can't access the network, try unplugging the power adapter on the AirPort Base Station, and then try plugging it back in again. Finally, try resetting the base station. If none of these solutions work, then it is necessary to reload the base station firmware from your software CD.

Installing RAM on your iBook

Chances are, you may soon find the 32MB of RAM provided with your original iBook is not enough. Even the most basic installation of Mac OS 9 takes from 20MB to 25MB of RAM, and Apple recommends 32MB of available RAM for Mac OS 9 with virtual memory turned on, which can stunt the performance of a laptop computer, such as the iBook. Luckily, installing extra RAM on an iBook is not difficult (compared to installing RAM on the PowerBook, which is a bit more complicated).

NOTE *Apple remedied the RAM shortage on the iBook line when it upgraded the product in February 2000, supplying 64MB RAM standard. But even that may be a bit short if you intend to use a few RAM hungry programs, such as Adobe Photoshop.*

To install additional RAM on your iBook, follow these instructions:

1. Turn off your iBook, close the display, and then unplug the power adapter and phone cord (the second part is a precaution in case the cord snags an item on your desk). Turn your iBook upside down and remove the battery. You need to loosen the retaining screws on the battery cover to extract the battery (fortunately, you can do this with a dime, a nickel, or nearly any coin).

2. Take the keyboard out of your iBook by sliding the two plastic tabs away from your screen.

NOTE *There's a little locking tab at the top center of the iBook keyboard that holds the keyboard down. If it's locked, a small-tipped screwdriver can be used to unlock it (you may have to fiddle with the keyboard, to get it loose, however).*

3. Pick the keyboard up, turn it over, and put it down carefully on a flat surface next to your iBook (see Figure 12-18).

4. If you need to do so, turn the wire bracket up and take out your AirPort Card.

5. Take out the two screws that keep the RAM shield in place (it's at the right in Figure 12-18) and then remove it carefully.

6. Place the RAM in the slot at an angle and firmly press it down to secure it. Then put back the RAM shield, the AirPort Card, the keyboard, and the battery.

TIP *Apple has thoughtfully provided a diagram atop the RAM compartment to show you exactly how the RAM module is situated.*

7. Start your computer.

A Fast Technique to Get Up and Running

FIGURE 12-18 An iBook is open and ready to receive its RAM upgrade

8. Go to About This Computer in the Apple menu to make sure it shows the right amount of RAM. This should be the original amount of built-in memory, plus the amount of RAM you added to your iBook.

NOTE   *The process of installing RAM on a regular Apple PowerBook depends on the make and model of your Mac, but Apple has simplified the process by eliminating the need to buy hard-to-get Torx screwdrivers. Apple has made unlatching the keyboard easy by using twin switches located beneath the expansion bays.*

Using Your Laptop Computer as a Desktop Computer

After a few weeks of using your new iBook or PowerBook, you may find you like it so much you want to use it as your regular desktop computer and retire your trusty old Power Mac after years of reliable use.

The process is fairly easy with the PowerBook. All you have to do is detach your display from your desktop computer, attach it to the VGA display adapter on your PowerBook (see Figure 12-19), and you're ready to go. If your PowerBook doesn't come with a VGA adapter, you need to purchase one from your local dealer (some PowerBooks come with a Mac to VGA adapter plug).

FIGURE 12-19   The VGA display port is second from the right on the Bronze
PowerBook G3

NOTE   *To make the transition to desktop easy, the year 2000 model PowerBook
has a 128-bit ATI graphic chip that provides faster video display than
many older Macs. It'll work fine with just about any regular Mac display.*

NOTE   *If you're using an iBook, there's no way to attach an external monitor to
the computer because it has no VGA port. The 12.1" display is top quality,
though, and in viewable area, isn't much smaller than the display on an iMac.*

Of course, if you have a desktop computer you may find a laptop keyboard and
trackpad don't cut it for intense work. You can use the USB ports of a current Apple
laptop (or the ADB port of older models) to hook up a regular keyboard and mouse.
That, and an external display, can make those speedy laptops serve as a useful desktop
computer replacement. You can even attach external devices to the peripheral ports
(the 1999 PowerBook G3, for example, still had a SCSI port; the 2000 model has
FireWire instead).

You may also find the sound produced by the PowerBook's small speakers is
too tinny or doesn't have enough bass. If you want, you can attach a set of external
speakers to the speaker port on your PowerBook. The subject of adding high-quality
speakers to a computer is covered in Chapter 18.

If you want to use the PowerBook or iBook as your desktop computer, you
will probably want to copy your important files, programs, and settings to your
PowerBook. You can do this in a number of ways. You can use removable media,
such as Zip disks, to copy your data from your old computer to your desktop. Or,
you can network your desktop Mac with your PowerBook, using an Ethernet
crossover cable (or an Ethernet hub if the data is on multiple computers) and use
file sharing to transfer the data. Chapter 8 covers Mac OS 9 networking issues.

Your method of transferring the data depends on how much data you have. If
you have many files to bring over, using file sharing may be faster. If not, you can
use a form of removable media.

Also, you need to decide what data you want to copy over. If you plan to transfer your important documents over to your laptop, make sure you copy over the programs in which they were created or programs that can also convert their formats. Remember, when transferring your vital programs to your laptop, you must transfer any necessary components from the System Folder, including extensions, control panels, and your personal settings for that program. If searching for every component of all your programs (especially if you have many applications) becomes too much of a hassle, then it might be easier to reinstall them from scratch. Sure, getting each of the individual components might save you time, but reinstalling them ensures that all the necessary components are available for you. To learn more about the subject of installing software, check out Chapter 10. You can find more information about transferring data from an old Mac to a new one in Chapter 11.

The software license for most programs enables you to use them on a desktop computer and a laptop, as long as they aren't used by different people at the same time. If you intend to use both your desktop-assembled laptop and a regular Apple desktop computer at the same time, however, you need to contact the software publishers about getting an extra user license.

As long as you take the necessary steps to assure everything is transferred properly, using your laptop as your regular computer can actually be more relaxing than having to sit down in one place all the time.

If your older desktop Mac isn't running Mac OS 9, you should make sure your third-party software is compatible before you transfer any of it to an Apple laptop running Mac OS 9.

Secrets of File Synchronization

The File Synchronization Control Panel (shown in Figure 12-20), which ships with all PowerBooks and iBooks, is a neat little feature that can help you keep different copies of the same file in sync, so the latest copy of that document is always available to you. As a result, this is a useful backup tool if you only need to save a few important files. You can match up different copies of files on your own hard

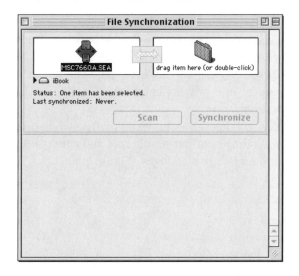

| FIGURE 12-20 | The File Synchronize enables you to keep different copies of the same file in sync |

drive, another hard disk, or even another computer with the one on your iBook or PowerBook. You can then copy the newer version of the file to the computer or disk that has the older version using File Synchronization's simple drag-and-drop interface. All you have to do is drag a file or folder to the open Control Panel, and then click the Synchronize button to get the right version where it needs to go or match up the different versions.

This simple form of backup may not be enough, however, if you're a power user with many different disks and files. Refer to Chapter 29 for more information on different backup techniques and programs.

If you can't find the File Synchronization anywhere on your iBook or PowerBook, use the Add/Remove feature found on the Mac OS 9 installation CD to install the control panel on your computer. This subject is covered in more detail in Chapter 2.

Also, if you're using another kind of Mac running Mac OS 9, feel free to install File Synchronization on that computer as well.

Secrets of File Synchronization

Summing Up

In this chapter, you learned how to set up a PowerBook, an iBook, and an AirPort network. You learned how to install more RAM on your iBook (because its standard allotment on the original version isn't quite enough for Mac OS 9) and how to use your laptop as your primary computer. Finally, you learned tips and tricks about file synchronization.

In the next chapter, you learn about issues you face when taking your Mac laptop on the road, including configuring Internet and network access and keeping your laptop and your data safe from thieves and the elements.

Chapter 13

Using Your Mac on the Road

L et's say your company needs to meet with an important client in New York. Or, you have to help close a multibillion dollar merger in Chicago.

Perhaps you're finally going to take the kids to Disney World or even make your monthly trip to the beach (assuming you're near any water). At the same time, however, you have to stay in touch with your clients or business so things don't get out of control while you're gone. You may even need a way to keep the kids from asking that cliched question "Are we there yet?" every five minutes on your trip.

During the course of this chapter, you learn how to keep your faithful iBook or PowerBook safe while traveling, as well as tips on how to deal with problems with your Apple laptop even when you're at home.

How to Configure Internet and Network Access on the Road

Sometimes when you're traveling with your family you may want to check your e-mail, so you don't get out of touch with the rest of the world for too long. Or, maybe you're on a business trip and you need an important financial research document to close that big deal.

Here are some hints and tips to follow when you desperately need to connect to the Internet while traveling:

- **Be sure your online service can be accessed while traveling.**   The nationwide Internet providers and online services such as AOL and its sister company, CompuServe, AT&T WorldNet, and EarthLink, provide thousands of local access numbers for your use and many of these work outside the U. S. Before you go on a trip, you should check for those numbers and set them down, so you can use them once you arrive at your destination. If you use a local ISP that doesn't provide numbers for access outside your city or state, consider using a Web e-mail service, such as Yahoo! mail or Microsoft's Hotmail service, in case you can gain access to a computer that does have Internet access while on the road. Of course, if you plan to travel a lot, you might want to consider getting a different ISP all together.

- **Make separate dialing profiles for each place you plan to visit.**   Before you leave, you should create separate dialing profiles in Apple's Remote

Access or PPP Control Panels for each place you're traveling. You can do this by choosing Configurations from the program's File menu, copying your current setting, and then putting in the new information. After that, you can rename and save the information for later use. If you're a member of AOL or CompuServe, you can create custom connection (location) profiles in the software used with these services.

■ **Known requirements for voltage and phones outside the country**. If you need to leave the U.S., you'll be pleased to know Apple's products are designed to work in many other countries. Energy requirements range from 100 to 250 volts and current ratings of 50 and 60 Hz. It may be necessary, however, to purchase a special adapter plug to use your laptop in certain places. Also, Apple doesn't officially guarantee that modems sold in the U.S. market will work abroad, although with the right adapters you should be able to use them. Before you leave the U.S., you may want to find a company or dealer that sells international connectivity products. One example listed by Apple Computer is TeleAdapt, whose Web site can be found at http://www.teleadapt.com (or you can call them at 1-877-835-3232). TeleAdapt's product line includes acoustic couplers for phones in hotels that don't come with their own data port modems, line filters, modem and plug adapters, security alarm systems, and testers. TeleAdapt's Executive Telekit, which can be purchased for only $99, enables you to test and hook up your modem at an older hotel whose phones don't come with regular modular phone jacks.

NOTE   *Apple laptops, introduced on or after January 1, 1998, are protected by a worldwide warranty. This means if one of these models needs service, you can visit any local service installation during the warranty period for repairs. As far as older models are concerned, they'd be out of warranty anyway, unless they are covered by AppleCare or another extended warranty program.*

■ **iBook and AirPort**   Now what should you do if you want to connect to the Internet in a hotel room with your iBook, but there's no convenient place to put it near the phone jack? You have a solution. If your iBook or year 2000 model Power Book 93 has an AirPort card and you brought an Airport Base Station on your trip, you can network to it and access the Internet at a distance of up to 150 feet away from the base station. This means you can surf the Internet in your room, on the balcony, or even out on the beach (if one is close by). The Airport Base Station serves as a wireless modem, eliminating the hassle of connecting it to your iBook and forcing you to fiddle and fuss with a phone cable.

NOTE *The wireless modem used in the AirPort Base Station was not considered compatible with AOL or CompuServe at press time. This means you'd have to subscribe to a regular ISP if you want to use AirPort. Both AOL and CompuServe can be accessed atop an ISP connection, however (and AOL, for one, gives you a much lower rate if you access the service exclusively by this method).*

CAUTION *Before you travel overseas with a wireless connection device, you should check to see if the country you plan to visit has any regulations prohibiting the use of such a device.*

Protecting Your iBook or PowerBook on the Road

Lately, it's been rather hard to keep up with Apple's line of laptops, with the exception of the iBook; with its vibrant colors and striking industrial design, it can certainly be easily distinguished from the rest of the line.

This is especially true for products that have the same names, but are distinctly different designs. The four variations of the PowerBook G3 are notable examples.

Regardless of which iteration of the PowerBook G3 you have or whether you have another model in the line—an iBook or a PowerBook Duo—you have a computer that's designed to endure more punishment than a stationary desktop model.

But this doesn't mean they are immune to danger or damage. In the next section, you learn how to take better care of your laptop and how to get the best possible use out of it.

Consider an Extended Warranty

You just placed your order and the computer store salesman smiles and shows you one more thing: an offer for an extended warranty. For an extra fee, you can get two or three years added warranty protection.

Whether such policies are needed is controversial. They are considered big profit items for dealers because most electronic products never need service during the extended period. More than likely, such a product will fail early in its life cycle or long after the warranty has expired.

By the nature of the beast, though, laptops are subjected to far more punishment than a normal desktop. Thus, they are more susceptible to product failures. If you can get a good deal on an extended warranty, you may want to think twice before saying "No." Apple's own AppleCare Protection Plan, for example, extends the new product warranty to a period of three years. You also get expanded toll-free telephone and online support, plus a special diagnostic software CD based on MicroMat's TechTool Pro.

NOTE *Remember, no extended warranty policy can cover your unit for physical damage. If you drop your laptop or if it's wrecked in an accident, no product warranty will cover the repairs.*

Increase Your Battery Life

Batteries have become more and more powerful over the years, but batteries only last so long before they finally give out, leaving you stuck. If you're left in a situation where you're nowhere near a power source, you could be in trouble.

Here are some suggestions on how to handle battery problems and how to get every last inch of power from your PowerBook or iBook battery:

- **Add another battery.** Both the PowerBook G3's and the 3400 come with two expansion bays that enable you to add extra batteries a hard drive. If you don't need a CD-ROM or DVD drive, which will occupy an expansion bay position, then you can add an additional battery to your laptop. As a result, you get more than twice the amount of battery life than you would if you only used one battery.

- **Take out any PC cards.** PC cards, such as those containing modems, can drain a lot of power from your battery. If you don't need the features they provide, you are better off moving them, waiting until you have access to an AC outlet, before you put them back in again.

- **Don't use external or internal devices.** While some external and internal devices, such as hard drives and even CD-ROMs, may use their own power sources or even run on their own batteries, they still need to access the hard drive to communicate with your computer. If you don't need them, turn them off and unplug (or remove) them.

- **Reduce brightness.** Turn the screen display of your PowerBook or iBook down as far as you can without making it impossible to see.

■ **Reduce backlighting.** Reduce any available setting for backlighting as you much as you can because this conserves a lot of energy (although some PowerBooks only come with the standard brightness and contrast controls). Whatever you do, don't have a screen saver running when you're not using your PowerBook because the screen saver regularly calls up data from your hard drive for the images.

■ **Stay away from dark desktop patterns.** Dark patterns on your desktop can eat extra battery life because they use more pixels than light patterns. This is because dark pixels are considered "on," so they require more power than light pixels (which are considered to be "off"). If you need to change your desktop pattern, you can do so in Mac OS 9's Appearance Control Panel.

NOTE *Don't expect a huge benefit from this sort of adjustment. But when you want to eke out every last minute of battery life, everything helps, even if only slightly.*

■ **Use the Energy Saver Control Panel.** Some handy power conservation features are in Mac OS 9's Energy Saver Control Panel (see Figure 13-1). The program can be launched from its corresponding Control Strip module or from the Control Panels folder in the Apple Menu. The default settings are good enough for a fair combination of sleep settings for your laptop, its display, and the hard drive. If you want to experiment with your settings, click the Show Details button. A good idea is to keep your hard drive sleep interval as short as possible. However, some programs, such as Microsoft Word, frequently access data from the hard drive, so putting the drive to sleep isn't practical.

■ **Use processor cycling.** All those extra minutes of battery life are worth it on a PowerBook or iBook, even the newer ones with their claimed battery lives of up to six hours. The less work your processor does, the better. You can choose Processor Cycling in the Energy Saver Control Panel or Control Strip module under its Advanced Settings. While processor cycling can slow your PowerBook, especially older ones, it can give you the extra battery life you need to make it through that plane trip to Tokyo.

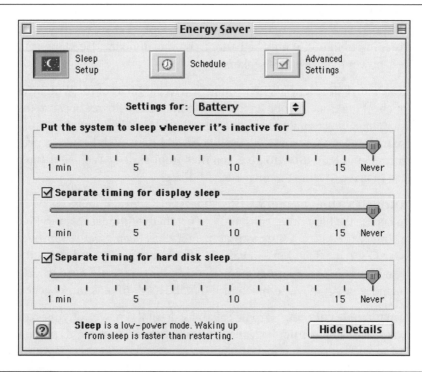

FIGURE 13-1 Mac OS 9's Energy Saver Control Panel provides various methods to prolong laptop battery life

■ **Use a RAM disk.** If you have a lot of extra RAM to spare on your laptop, consider activating the RAM disk in the Memory Control Panel (this needs a restart to activate). You can perform all sorts of functions using the RAM disk, from saving files and storing a Web cache to running programs, while at the same time your hard drive can be kept in Sleep mode. Make sure you select the option to save the contents of your RAM disk upon shutting down or you could lose valuable data.

NOTE *AOL requires its Web cache to be placed in the America Online folder within the Preferences folder in your System Folder. You may be able to get away with making an alias to a RAM disk-based folder, but don't depend on getting it to work reliably.*

■ **Turn the volume down.**   If you want to hear all the sounds coming from the DVD you're watching on your PowerBook G3, or even if you're just listening to music, it may be better to use headphones. Headphones use less power than regular speakers.

■ **Don't surf the Net.**   When you log on to the Internet for Web browsing or checking e-mail, your laptop uses extra battery power because the modem is in use (unless it's an external modem). It's a good idea to keep your connection as short as possible. In addition, Web browsers need to access your hard drive to give you files from various Web sites (unless you can manage to store them on a RAM disk).

■ **Turn off virtual memory.**   Because Apple's virtual memory system has to access the hard drive constantly to get that additional memory, it can be a battery life killer. While virtual memory has been greatly improved under Mac OS 9, it can still take away precious minutes of your battery life. The best idea is to leave virtual memory off unless you truly need to extend memory or you have so much of it that the hard drive is rarely accessed.

■ **Turn AppleTalk off.**   AppleTalk may drain the power of your battery when activated, particularly if it's polling network services. Unless you're using AirPort or some sort of wireless network connection on your iBook or PowerBook, then you have no need for AppleTalk.

PowerBook/iBook Hints and Tips

Many of the problems an Apple laptop can face are quite similar to those affecting desktop models. Other issues are unique to this product class. Here are some common problems when using laptops, as well as their solutions.

Problems with Power Manager

If your laptop's Power Manager is corrupted, it can cause problems. These problems include being unable to boot or charge a battery, or even to wake up from Sleep mode. The Power Manager runs many basic functions on your laptop, including backlighting, energy saver settings, charging batteries, and access to serial ports.

Unfortunately, resetting the Power Manager is not a cut-and-dried process. Various generations of Apple laptops use various types of schemes for this process (I won't presume to hazard a guess why).

Here are the steps involved in resetting the Power Manager on recent laptops:

POWERBOOK G3 SERIES (WALL STREET EDITION)

1. Turn off your computer.

2. At the same time, press the SHIFT, FN (function), CONTROL, and power keys.

3. Wait five seconds.

4. Press the power button to restart your PowerBook.

POWERBOOK G3 SERIES (LOMBARD, BRONZE KEYBOARD, OR YEAR 2000 EDITION)

1. Turn off your computer.

2. Find and press the reset button at the back of the computer. It's located between the modem port and the external video port.

3. Wait five seconds.

4. Press the power button to restart your PowerBook.

IBOOK

1. Turn off the computer.

2. At the base of the display, press the reset button with a straightened paper clip.

3. Wait five seconds.

4. Press the power button to restart the iBook.

IF YOU HAVE AN OLDER APPLE LAPTOP   The previous steps only cover models that were reasonably current at press time. It would take a separate chapter to outline the steps for the rest of the line.

In general, many models require you to take out the battery and disconnect the power adapter before doing the reset process.

A few of these models don't even have a reset button. You have to press the reset and interrupt buttons with two straightened paper clips at the same time for 10 to 20 seconds. The buttons on these models can usually be found inside the rear door. To learn more about the subject, check out Apple's Web site and read the technical information on the subject at http://til.info.apple.com/techinfo.nsf/artnum/n14449.

Protecting Your iBook or
PowerBook on the Road

Apple Laptop Problems and Solutions

In the next section, a slate of common symptoms you may face when using your Apple portable product is covered. Then the most workable solutions for these problems are listed.

- **Computer crashes after awakening**   This annoyance has been plaguing Apple's laptops on occasion for quite some time. While Sleep mode can keep you from having to go through a long startup process every time you boot up your computer, it doesn't always work the way it should. The screen may be blank and it may not even start up at all. The best way to deal with this problem is to use a Base set of extensions under Extensions Manager or Casady & Greene's Conflict Catcher, so you can see if any specific third-party extensions are causing your problems.

NOTE   *You can get a limited-time demonstration version of Conflict Catcher from the publisher's Web site at http://www.casadyg.com.*

- **Trackpad won't work**   The original PowerBooks used a trackball. When trackpads came out, they seemed a revolution in simplicity, at least by comparison. But sometimes problems arise. The arrow on your screen may move slowly or you may not even get it to move at all. The first thing to do if problems occur is to check the settings in the Trackpad Control Panel (see Figure 13-2). Make sure the tracking speed is turned up to the level you want (Apple products ship from the factory with a rather slow setting). You should also make sure the pad is clean and dry because sweaty fingers also cause problems.

- **Battery won't charge**   If you have an older PowerBook, it may be time to replace the battery. If you recently bought a new battery, however, the AC power supply you connected the battery to when you charged it may have been dead or a bad fuse might be on the logic board of the battery.

- **Automatic Sleep doesn't work**   If you own an older laptop or you have to access the Internet constantly, your computer realizes network activity is still occurring and will not go into Sleep mode at the specified time. To fix this, turn off AppleTalk in the Chooser, or disconnect from the Internet using Apple's TCP/IP control panel or its corresponding Control Strip module.

FIGURE 13-2   You can adjust the trackpad's performance with this program

■ **PC Card Irritations**   The small credit card-like devices known as *PC cards* (sometimes called *PCMCIA*) can greatly expand the features of your PowerBook. You can use them to add a FireWire port, video capture capabilities, and expanded networking features. On older PowerBooks, PC cards are also used to provide modem and Ethernet connectivity, but they are not immune to problems. Usually, you can drag the icon of the PC card to the trash to eject it, but the card could get stuck in its slot and refuse to come out. If this happens, restart your computer. If that doesn't help, try to insert a straightened paper clip into the little hole next to the slot containing your PC card, and then push the paper clip in to hit the little button inside, in a manner similar to that of force-ejecting a floppy disk or CD. If this still doesn't do any good and the card still refuses to come out, you may have to take some drastic measures. Please note that drastic measures could damage the PC card! First, try to remove the card with your bare fingers. If this doesn't succeed, take out a set of small pliers and see if you can pry out the card. If the card comes out, use a paper clip to press the little button in the hole next to the slot to reset the spring . . . and then pray a lot.

How to Change an iBook's Battery

On a regular Apple laptop, batteries quickly pop out with a level or a switch.

Life isn't quite as simple if you have an iBook.

To change your iBook's battery, you must use a coin to loosen the screws on the battery cover, located on the botton of the unit. Fortunately, this isn't a serious inconvenience. Just turn the screws counterclockwise, which should be enough to loosen the screws. Once this is done, take out the battery, put in your new one, and tighten the screws.

CAUTION   *Even if you don't have any problems putting in and removing your PC card from its slot, other problems can still keep it from working at all. The new PowerBook G3's come with something called a PC Card Bus slot, which is a revised version of the PC card standard. The older models have regular PC Card slots. Before you purchase a card for a PowerBook, make sure your make and model can handle the product.*

- **Problems with the PowerBook 5300**   The oldest model PowerBook that supports Mac OS 9 was also one that was cursed by problems from the time of its release. When Apple first began to produce these models, they had to do a fast recall because of a few reports that the lithium ion batteries burst into flame. Apple went back to using the older-style battery, and soon re-released the product. Production delays weren't the only problems affecting this model, though. Apple also had to institute an extended repair program to cure a variety of ills. The screen bezels would sometimes separate, logic board problems might cause crashes, and the AC adapters sometimes proved defective. If you still have one of these models, consider having your Apple dealer check the unit if it hasn't already paid a visit to their repair center. Or, consider selling it (as the new owner of my PowerBook 5300ce did after it went back to Apple twice).

- **Memory effect problems**   The NiCad batteries on the older PowerBooks may cause problems because of the so-called "memory effect." If you continue to charge the battery without fully discharging it first, the battery seems to retain the memory of this shorter life cycle and won't last as long before it needs to be recharged. Whatever the cause, the usual remedy is to run the PowerBook all the way down, past all the warning notices that it's about to shut down, right until it shuts itself off completely. This should restore the battery to its normal capacity. The Nickel Metal Hydride and lithium ion batteries available on more recent Apple laptop computers are immune to this effect.

■ **Too hot to place on a lap**   While you're playing an extended game of Civilization II or Age of Empires, while the laptop sits, oh, so innocently on your lap, your thigh starts suddenly heating up for no reason. As you know, though, there's a reason for everything, and the heat is most likely generated by the hard drive, which generally lies at the lower left of the machine. The PowerBook's CPU is also a noticeable source of heat generation. A moderate amount of heat is normal, but if your laptop seems to become unbearably hot, you may want to have your Apple dealer check the unit.

X-Rays and Laptops

You're at an airport and you get to the security gate.

Of course, the standard security check procedure requires that all your carry-on luggage (including your laptop computer) be x-rayed. So, you wonder, will that radiation somehow damage my precious little computer? Or, could it even keep the computer from working at its full capacity ever again? And could radiation wipe the data from your hard drive?

I never say never about anything, but after a couple of years filled with supreme paranoia, I have given up worrying. This after I saw a pilot sending his laptop through an x-ray machine without a look of concern. Even Apple itself says x-rays and other kinds of magnetic radiation will, at most, only cause slight damage to your laptop, and even then, only a small possibility exists of that happening. The only possible danger may be some form of removable media, including floppies, SuperDisks, and Zips. Otherwise, you needn't worry. Feel better now?

Let those security machines do their work and your trusty PowerBook should come out just fine.

NOTE   *If you feel you'd still rather have the security people do a manual check of your laptop, put it in Sleep mode before you leave for the airport. Security folks need to see a normal desktop display, and Sleep mode makes sure it gets to full-operating mode as quickly as possible.*

Protecting Your iBook or PowerBook on the Road

Your Laptop Safety Kit

Despite the fact that crime has been steadily declining in our country over the last decade or so, one type of crime is actually on the rise—the theft of laptop computers.

A firm that specializes in computer insurance, Safeware, reports that over 300,000 laptop computers were stolen in 1998, valued at $900 million.

Even with the runaway success of the iBook, it takes a while for Apple to sell that amount of laptop computers, so the figure is dangerously high compared to many theft categories.

Don't think your Apple laptop is immune. If your insurance carrier offers coverage for a computer on the road, consider getting it. The cost is usually quite modest and the peace of mind is more than worth the price.

Even with proper coverage, you can take some steps to help minimize the prospect of theft.

NOTE   *I wouldn't presume to suggest any options for dealing with an armed thief (unless your combat skills are comparable to, say, Chuck Norris). If you are faced with this frightening prospect, it's usually better to give up the items the thief wants than try to protect yourself.*

Other than a direct confrontation with a criminal, however, you can do some things to help protect your laptop from being the unsuspecting target of such a theft.

■ **Get a good insurance policy.**   As previously mentioned, getting insurance coverage for your entire computer system, including the software, is a good idea. In addition to Safeware, you may find more and more regular insurance carriers have added insurance coverage, either as a rider or a separate policy. When you examine such an insurance plan, make sure the hardware and the software are both covered. If you're using a laptop, make sure coverage away from your home or office is included.

NOTE   *One of our fearless technical editors (and a contributing writer to this book), Pieter Paulson, is a long-time customer of Safeware and recommends the company without hesitation. Knowing what a skeptic Pieter is, this is the strongest possible recommendation a company can get.*

■ **Sign up at a hardware registry.**   O'Grady's Power Page (http://ogrady.com), a popular Web site catering to Apple laptop users, has set up a special PowerBook Registry database. This Web site is designed as a central information center to help the authorities recover your laptop if it's stolen. To register at the site, you need to locate the serial number of your computer. It's either at the rear or on the underside of the unit. You also need to provide the Ethernet hardware (or Mac) address. For more information on registration, check out O'Grady's special registry page at http://www.ogrady.com/registry. Once there, enter the required information where indicated on the Hardware Registry Web site, and click the link to register Apple hardware. When the next screen comes up, give your name and address, plus the requested information on your system. After you enter all the needed information, click the submit record button. Everything you entered is now part of the database.

NOTE   *O'Grady's service isn't only for laptops. You can also register your desktop Macs, each as a separate listing.*

■ **Keep close tabs on your laptop.**   Whether you're at the airport or a car rental agency, make sure you keep your PowerBook or iBook nearby. In only a second or two, perhaps with a bit of diversion, a thief can pick up your laptop and disappear into the crowd. And don't feel protected if the unit is in a bag or case because thieves can easily recognize that case for exactly what it is. Don't put your laptop down and leave it. Keep your hands on the case or the strap. The striking industrial design of the iBook is an obvious theft magnet. While it's designed to withstand the rigors of use by students without extra protection, you should consider getting a special case anyway. While such a case may put a strain on your shoulder muscles, a little pain now can save you a lot more hassle later. If you have to put the case down, sit on the strap with your hand on the case and watch it like a hawk.

NOTE   *As convenient as a laptop case might be as a place to store your computer and accessories, you may also want to think about simply putting the case in a regular overnight bag or suitcase. This can provide added protection because then it won't be identified easily.*

■ **Put your laptop in a safe any time you leave your hotel.**   It isn't as if a maid coming in to clean your hotel room is going to go right in just to do her job and come out again with your laptop in hand. You can never be overconfident, though. An open door while your room is being cleaned can invite unsavory characters to inspect a room for goodies. I've seen this happen in enough James Bond movies not to be cautious about folks in the real world having the same idea. Try to check with whatever hotel you're staying in to see if it has a safe available or some secured area when you can store your laptop while you're away from the hotel. If the hotel has no such accommodation, then make sure the housekeeping staff keeps the door closed both when they're cleaning your room and after they leave.

Traveling with Your Laptop

You always want to do certain things before you take your iBook or PowerBook on the road on a long trip. While some of these things may not be as important in some situations as in others, it's always a good idea to remember them when you take your laptop along.

Here are some suggestions:

- ■ **Break in your new hardware before you leave.** If you recently bought a new laptop, make sure you give it a thorough workout before you leave. You want to make sure potential problems are found and fixed, so you don't get stuck in the middle of your vacation. Even though Apple's product warranty covers such problems, waiting for someone to repair your machine or trying to figure out what your problem is can be a hassle far away from home.

- ■ **Get the right case for your needs.** While a thin, attractive case looks fashionable, it may not have enough room to hold your laptop and accessories. Before purchasing a case, try to examine it in person if you can. Of course, you won't be able to do this if you do a lot of shopping online or through catalogs. See if the case has extra bins and pouches to store such items as disks, peripherals, and cables. Make sure the laptop compartment is sufficient to protect your laptop during a bumpy ride. Also, with the larger screens on Apple's newer laptops, you may have to consider getting a newer, larger case if the older one provides only a tight fit for your PowerBook or iBook. If you get a chance to look at the case, check its specifications for extra features, dimensions, and so on, so you know it can be sufficient to do what is necessary. Make sure you buy the case well before you go on your trip, then if it isn't good enough, you can return or exchange it, and find another one.

■ **Protect your laptop from the elements.** Even though your iBook or PowerBook may appear able to withstand even a hurricane, it can't survive such severe situations. If you plan to go somewhere with extreme weather conditions, make sure your laptop is packed carefully, perhaps in a hard shipping case that can easily withstand the elements. Also, remember to keep your PowerBook or iBook away from extreme cold or heat, or wet areas. TeleAdapt, the company mentioned earlier that supplies international connection adapters, sells a device called a CoolPad that keeps a PowerBook high off a desk to get better air circulation and to keep it from heating up too much. Frankly, it's geared toward Pentium-based PC laptops, which tend to produce more heat than comparable Apple laptops. Under severe conditions, though, the CoolPad may still be useful.

■ **Bring an extra battery and charger.** Even if you don't expect to use your laptop for long, your battery's power can drain quickly, even doing the simplest tasks. This is especially true if you haven't replaced your battery for over a year or two. Also, if the battery goes bad during the course of the trip, you are stuck. If you're traveling to a place where the weather can be unpredictable or whose energy systems are older, you could risk a power outage while your laptop is plugged into an AC adapter. In addition to buying an extra battery, you should also get a charger. Then you'll be ready to go if you need to run your laptop on a battery at a certain time. Batteries, chargers, and other accessories can be purchased for Apple's newest laptops from such places as the Apple Store or VST Technologies (http://vsttech.com).

■ **Don't forget an accessory kit.** Besides bringing an extra battery and charger with you, consider some extra devices, especially if you need access to extra files or possible backup resources. If your Apple laptop has an expansion bay, consider filling it with an extra hard drive, a SuperDisk drive, or a Zip. If you are using SCSI devices, don't forget to get the proper cables and a SCSI terminator. Remember, too, you may need a second terminator for an Apple laptop because of the special termination requirements. If you have the latest Apple PowerBook G3 or iBook, consider getting USB peripherals in the same categories. You also want to bring along a network cable and a longer modular phone cable (if you don't have the capability to use an AirPort). TeleAdapt products may be especially useful.

NOTE *When you buy a cable for a PowerBook's SCSI port, make sure the cable is designed for hooking up extra devices. Remember, the cable labeled SCSI Disk Adapter, while it looks nearly the same, is strictly designed to let your laptop mount as a SCSI device on another Mac. And, if you intend to mount your PowerBook as a SCSI device, consider getting this sort of cable too, or one of those switch adapters that enables you to select both modes at the push of a button.*

- **Take along a separate keyboard and mouse.** If you have to spend a lot of time on your laptop during a trip, the keyboard on your iBook or PowerBook may not be as comfortable as you like. In this case, you should purchase a normal desktop keyboard and mouse. Laptop keyboards and trackpads take a little getting used to, but some people tire of them after an extended period of use. While the keyboard on the iBook is actually quite comfortable, better than any other Apple laptop I've used, a regular keyboard may be better for you. Remember, a keyboard may be too big to put in a regular laptop carrying case, but it will fit well in a suitcase or overnight bag.

- **Send backed up data to yourself.** Just because your files are backed up doesn't mean there's no chance that the files will be damaged or the laptop will be stolen or damaged. If you have to store critical files you need to use later and you have the capability to connect to the Internet wherever you're staying, send these files in an e-mail to yourself. If the original file is somehow damaged, or your laptop is stolen or damaged, you still have a copy of the files, safe and sound and ready to be retrieved when you get home. If you don't want to load your mailbox with these additional files, you can get a second mailbox. For example, AOL lets you set up seven different accounts (meaning seven different mailboxes) for each account. EarthLink gives you a free second mailbox if you upgrade to their optional EarthLink Gold service. They also sell separate mailboxes for all account categories.

- **Get a portable inkjet printer.** If you have to make a printed copy of your documents while traveling, consider checking the Web sites of such printer manufacturers as Hewlett-Packard and Brother to see if they have anything small enough for convenient travel. If you don't want to lug a printer with you on your trip, you can fax a copy to your home computer with a fax modem. Or, consider sending a fax to yourself at the hotel, although your hotel charges a fee for every faxed page. You can also see if a local service bureau or printer shop is nearby that can print documents for you.

■ **Find a place to print your files.**   Check with your hotel's concierge or information desk, or consult a phone directory to see if a local print shop or service bureau is nearby that can help you get printed output. While high-resolution output can be costly just to make a few copies for your personal use, you might be able to get good quality laser output for a dollar or two a page.

NOTE

I recall one instance in which I had to prepare a manual for a product at the company's manufacturing site. I had brought my PowerBook to accomplish the task. Once the job was done, we ran over to a local print shop and I attached the PowerBook direct to their Mac network and commandeered their laser printer for a short time. They were generous enough to charge a small, flat fee to cover their costs, rather than a hefty per-page charge (because I did all the work anyway).

■ **For PowerBook Duo 2300 owners.**   Apple's only PowerPC-based Duo was great for small places, but not enough people bought the machine for Apple to continue releasing it. The problems and concerns for a Duo are the same as any other Apple laptop. If you take your Duo when you travel, you must decide whether you need to use a floppy drive, in which case, you need the Duo MiniDock or Duo Floppy Adapter.

■ **No access to your ISP?**   If you're in an out-of-the-way locale or your online service doesn't have access numbers in that area, another solution may exist. Perhaps you can get Web access from a friend, a business contact, or a local library. AOL, EarthLink, and other services offer Web-based e-mail, so you can access your messages from a Web site without having to set up the computer to access your account. AOL calls it *AOL Mail* and EarthLink calls it *WebMail.* The setup is usually the same. You enter the services's Web site, access the Web-based e-mail area, and then enter your user name and password to bring up the list of your unread messages (see Figure 13-3). You can manage the e-mail in this fashion, from writing responses to building an address book.

Protecting Your iBook or
PowerBook on the Road

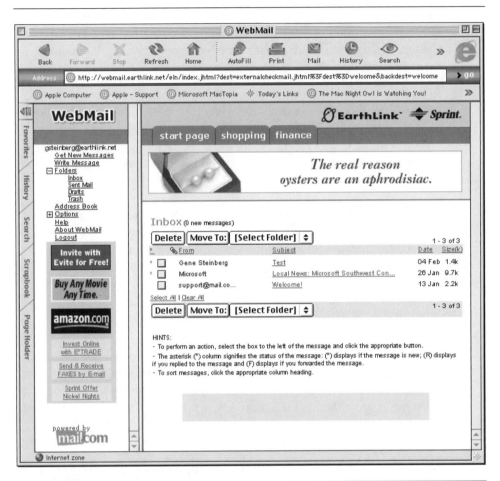

FIGURE 13-3   EarthLink's WebMail feature enables you to access your messages without having to configure a computer to access your account

NOTE   *If you use a Web-based e-mail system for your online service, look for a setup option that leaves the messages on the ISP's server. This way, you can access the e-mail again from your regular desktop Mac and not have to spend time synchronizing messages between the two computers.*

■ **Doing a presentation?**   An Apple laptop works great for company presentations. If such a presentation is part of your travel plan, you can consider using a slide show program, such as Microsoft PowerPoint, and then get a device that can be used to connect it to a TV monitor or projector. One company that makes such products is Focus Enhancements, which even provides a USB interface so your iBook can be used for this sort of project. You can get more information from your favorite Apple dealer or the company's Web site at http://www.focusinfo.com.

Summing Up

With a little extra attention to detail and some caution, you should be able to take your Apple computer on the road and get the maximum benefit from your computing experience. You can get work done or have something to use when you and your family want to play a computer game or surf the Internet.

In the next chapter, Hard Disk Management, you learn how to use Mac OS 9's disk management and repair features. You also discover how to keep your drives happy and healthy ensuring the maximum amount of protection for your files.

Summing Up

Chapter 14

Hard Disk Management

E very Mac needs to run certain components: a CPU, a display (built-in or otherwise), a mouse or other pointing device, a keyboard, and, oh yes, a hard drive.

NOTE   *As our ever-vigilant technical editor, Pieter Paulson, tells us, the earliest Macs, from the 128 through the Plus, could be run from a floppy drive. But, as I reminded Pieter, none of those Macs has any hope of running Mac OS 9.*

Your Mac's hard drive is also the most used and abused device on your Mac. Every second you run your Mac it is whirring, platters turning, reading, and writing files (unless, of course, the drive is allowed to go into sleep mode when it's idle for a period of time). Considering the hard workout the devices get and how small they pack files, sometimes you wonder how they work at all.

The hard drive is absolutely critical to making your Mac work, however, so it stands to reason you would want to do what you can to make sure it behaves itself.

In this chapter, you learn about Mac OS 9's tools for hard-drive maintenance and other methods to help fine-tune your hard drive's performance so you can keep it happy and healthy.

Regular Hard Drive Maintenance Tips and Tricks

Doing nothing is always much easier. You run your Mac, day in and day out, and if everything seems to work properly, why should you bother to expend extra effort to fix something that doesn't seem to need fixing?

For one thing, you cannot really see hard drive damage. You don't observe a scratch on the drive mechanism or a big jagged line on your screen (unless your display has developed a crack).

Everything happens behind the scenes, including the buildup of directory damage.

A Look at Your Drive and Its Directory

At the core, a hard drive consists of several spinning platters, magnetically coated. The contents of the hard drive are written to those spinning planners with heads that move rapidly back and forth to read data from specific spots on the platter. The principle is roughly similar to an old-fashioned tape recorder, despite the ultra miniaturization of the components involved.

In fact, things are so small in there, a hard drive is made in what is called a *clean room,* a place free of contaminants. Even a single particle of dust can cause havoc to your hard drive.

The files themselves are stored on concentric tracks (one inside the other). And the record/playback heads move at rapid-fire speeds from one track to the next, in less than the blink of an eye.

A hard drive's platters run at speeds from 5,400 RPM to 10,000 RPM, and files are packed so small, you'd need a microscope to see how much space they occupy. Each year, it seems, manufacturers find ways to cram more data onto that drive. So the 27GB drive you get in a Power Macintosh G4, for example, is no larger in physical size than a 100MB drive of a decade ago.

NOTE
In fact, it's a lot smaller, being a 1/3 height drive, 3-1/2 inches wide. Those original 100MB drives of over a decade ago were often full height, 5-1/4 inches wide.

It's Not Quite from *A* to *Z*

In the old days of phonograph records (which some folks call *vinyl*), you could always tell where the recording began and where it ended: it was all on a single grove that spanned the disk from beginning to end. And, if you wanted to hear a selection in the middle of the recording, you simply placed the tone arm of your turntable (or changer) on that precise spot. The recording itself was linear, any track on the record occupied a single area.

In a sense, your hard drive's head assembly performs a similar action when you call up or write a file, only it's dealing with lots of tracks, each separate from the other, which is segmented into individual blocks (up to 600 and more per track). Worse, files are not all put in one place. The software on your Mac that sends and receives files from the drive, the File Manager, simply looks for empty space. A file may be made up of one contiguous block of data or it may be spread out in little pieces in different portions of the drive.

Whenever you open a file or save it to your drive, the File Manager goes to work to follow your wishes. For the File Manager to determine where all parts of a file are installed, the hard drive has a catalog or directory on it. It's similar in concept to a book's table of contents or a library catalog card file.

The Parts of a Mac's Directory

Unlike the list of books you see at your local library, you cannot actually see the hard drive's directory. It's there, all right, but it's invisible to the naked eye (although special programs exist, such as Symantec's Norton Disk Editor, which can read that directory). All you need to worry about is telling your Mac by double-clicking or selecting a file that you want it opened.

NOTE *Norton Disk Editor is part of Symantec's Norton Utilities package, discussed later in this chapter.*

- **Master Directory Block**   This is the first step toward locating a file on your drive. *The Master Directory Block* contains information about the name of your drive (even when you change it), the size and capacity, and the available space. Just as important, it knows where your System Folder is placed, so when you start your Mac, the various components of Mac OS 9's System Folder are read into memory.

- **Volume Bit Map**   The next level of information the File Manager needs to consult is the *Volume Bit Map,* which records which portions of a drive are filled and which aren't. Once the File Manager retrieves this information, it knows where to place your file.

- **Extents Tree (or B-tree)**   The job of determining how to assemble the disparate elements into the correct order is the *Extents Tree.* If the information was scrambled, you could see the end of your file at the beginning or in the middle. Only it's a lot more complex than that. A scrambled file is likely to be unreadable because a program expects the elements of a file to be in a certain order to access the file. The Extents Tree includes an index node, so the File Manager can locate the file, and the leaf node, which contains the actual information about the file.

- **Catalog Tree**   This part of the drive's directory contains all the information needed to get the file. The Catalog Tree records the size of the file, the folder it has been put in, or its desktop positioning. This data is needed by the File Manager to answer your request for a file and to open it for you.

NOTE *Despite all the steps the Mac OS must go through to transfer data to and from a hard drive, the actual process of locating the file happens so fast, you can barely sense the process, unless you're using a floppy drive, which is much slower.*

Deleted Files Are Not Always Deleted

When you empty a file from the trash, it isn't actually deleted. At least not at that time. The File Manager simply notifies the Master Directory Block to list the space the file occupied as available. The file is still there, but it can be replaced, partly or completely, when new files are copied to the drive.

Symantec's Norton Utilities can recover deleted files by keeping track of the locations of the files you remove so it can retrieve them for you (at least until the files are overwritten). MicroMat's TechTool Pro actually creates its own storage area for deleted files (up to the size or number specified in its software) and it doesn't allow the files to be deleted until they exceed the amount of storage space you specify.

What Happens and What May Go Wrong

Say you want to open that word processing document you wrote yesterday, the one with an important message you need to send to a client. When you double-click the file's icon or select it in the Open dialog box, Mac OS 9's File Manager gets busy. It looks at the catalog, finds the file's location, assembles each portion of the file in its proper order, puts the contents into your Mac's RAM, and then it appears on your Mac's display.

As soon as you modify the file and save the changes, the File Manager goes back to check where the original is located, and then it replaces the original with the modified version. If the file is larger, additional blocks on the drive are located to store the additional data.

If enough room doesn't exist to contain the expanded file, you get a warning dialog box about it.

The operation of reading and writing files only works when the catalog is accurate and current. If anything happens to damage or remove the little chunks of data that make up the catalog file, you cannot retrieve those files.

This is why you want to make certain your drive's directory is kept in good condition.

What's Partitioning and What Can It Do for Me?

Older Macs used a file system called *Hierarchical File System (HFS),* which divided the drive into 65,000-odd pieces or blocks. This meant, of course, 65,000-odd pieces or blocks was the maximum number of files that could be stored. Unfortunately, as drives got larger, the limitations of HFS became obvious. For one thing, the size of each block was in direct proportion to the size of a drive. So, if you divide a 27GB drive into 65,000, it's a lot bigger than a 1GB drive. Even if your file contains only a sentence or two, the size it consumes on your drive can be no smaller than the minimum size of that single block.

NOTE
The first Macs had an even more primitive file system, Macintosh File System (MFS), which didn't even have the capability of creating nested folders, level upon level deep. Those were the days.

Regular Hard Drive
Maintenance Tips and Tricks

That could be rather inefficient, so folks used to partition a hard drive, or divide it into smaller segments, so small files got smaller as a result.

You can partition a drive with any disk formatting program, such as Apple's Drive Setup, CharisMac's Anubis, FWB's Hard Disk ToolKit, or LaCie's Silverlining.

When you use the software to partition your drive, it, of course, wipes out your data as part of the process. As a result, you must first back up your files and run your hard drive formatter from your System CD or another drive from which you can boot. In the end, you get a separate disk icon for each partition, such as Macintosh HD One, Macintosh HD Two, and so forth.

HFS+ and Partitioning

Apple resolved the problem of small sizes getting bigger, beginning with Mac OS 8.1. Apple introduced a new file system, called HFS+. *HFS+* increased the potential number of sectors to somewhere in the billions, so you can stuff your hard drive with lots of little files and not have them waste lots of extra space.

NOTE *Apple also refers to HFS+ as Mac OS Extended. The older, HFS file system is called Mac OS Standard.*

So, the question arises: Why partition if it doesn't save space? You may want to consider these other advantages:

■ **Faster drive access**   When you partition a drive, it is made into smaller pieces so the drive's heads don't have to move as far to find a file on that partition or volume. In theory, this may speed hard drive performance somewhat, though with drives getting faster and faster, the difference might be too slight to notice.

■ **Organization**   You can create a partition for your System Folder, another for your applications, a third for document files, or however you prefer. This way, you have smaller hard-drive directories to look at when you're trying to locate a file.

■ **Less to recover if a volume is damaged**   If one of your hard drive volumes becomes corrupted or inaccessible, you can sometimes still retrieve the files on the other drive partitions. This doesn't lessen the need for good hard-drive maintenance, however, or reduce the danger that the loss of one partition may signal serious problems with the other. So, if a drive partition vanishes from your Mac's desktop, you should still use the drive repair and recovery tools mentioned later in this chapter to get that lost partition working again. That is, if the drive itself hasn't gone belly-up, in which case all the partitions are lost.

How to Partition a Hard Drive

If you decide you'd like to partition your hard drive, either for more efficient organization of files or to avoid having to upgrade to HFS+, you'll find the process isn't terribly difficult.

You may not need any special software to partition a hard drive other than the disk-formatting software you already have. Apple's Drive Setup can do the job for you, at least for Apple-labeled hard drives. For drives not made by Apple, you may have to use one of the hard-disk formatting programs mentioned earlier.

Once you decide to partition the drive, here's a basic rundown of how the process works:

1. Make a full backup of your files. If you haven't changed the basic system software and programs that came installed on your Mac when you bought it, you can save time by simply backing up your document files and using Apple's restore CD to replace your original files after the drive is partitioned.

2. Restart your Mac using another hard drive (after selecting it with the Startup Disk Control Panel) or with your system CD. To start from your system CD, hold down the C key at startup, after the CD has been placed in the drive, and keep the C key held down until the Happy Mac icon appears.

NOTE   *The latest generation of Macs shipping at press time have a different CD startup routine. For such models as the iBook, slot-loading iMacs, and Power Mac G4, hold down the OPTION key at startup until you see a screen listing startup disk choices. Click the CD icon and then click the right arrow to start from that CD.*

3. Check the Utilities folder on your system CD for a copy of Drive Setup.

4. Launch Drive Setup by double-clicking its icon.

5. Over the next few seconds, Drive Setup looks for drives connected to your Mac and then processes a setup screen (see Figure 14-1).

6. Go to the Functions menu and choose Customize Volumes.

Regular Hard Drive
Maintenance Tips and Tricks

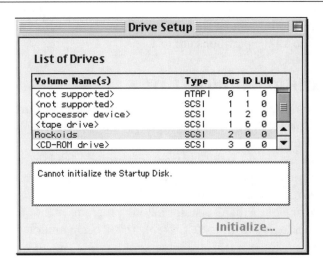

Drive Setup

List of Drives

Volume Name(s)	Type	Bus	ID	LUN
<not supported>	ATAPI	0	1	0
<not supported>	SCSI	1	1	0
<processor device>	SCSI	1	2	0
<tape drive>	SCSI	1	6	0
Rockoids	SCSI	2	0	0
<CD-ROM drive>	SCSI	3	0	0

Cannot initialize the Startup Disk.

Initialize...

FIGURE 14-1   This is the list of drives connected to the author's Mac

7. For fast partitioning, you can use the pop-up menu and select the option indicating how many partitions you want. This is the simplest way, as the correct, equal percentage for each partition is selected. Or, you can drag the rectangles representing the drive partitions to make them bigger or smaller, as you prefer.

8. After you select the number of volumes or partitions you want to make, use the Initialize command to divide your drive. If you have the time, use the low-format option instead because it wipes out the drive's data, not only the directory, and maps out any bad blocks found.

NOTE   *Low-level formatting isn't available for IDE drives, where critical device information is stored. If the drive doesn't support the feature, the option is grayed out in the formatting program.*

9. Once your drive is partitioned, you are ready to restore your files to it. The drive works normally, except it is now divided into two or more parts, which appear on your Mac's desktop as separate volumes.

CAUTION *While you may be tempted to put a second System Folder on one of the other partitions, in practice, this is not a good idea. The Startup Disk Control Panel (even if the selected volume is highlighted) only chooses between disks rather than partitions. Alternatives do exist, however, such as a shareware program, System Picker, which enables you to activate a System Folder on another partition (or even on the same partition, though having two System Folders is usually bad practice).*

THE EASY AND HARD WAYS TO CONVERT TO HFS+   Most Macs that came with Mac OS 8.1 and later came with drives formatted in HFS+, so you may not have to do anything at all. But, if you upgraded to Mac OS 9 with an older Mac, perhaps your hard drive is still in the HFS format, and you haven't had a chance to change.

Here's how you change the file format:

- ■ **Initialize**   Before you convert to HFS+, back up your files because you'll be erasing the drive's directory. Once you've backed up your files, restart your Mac from your system CD. Then select the icon of the drive you want to change to HFS+ and choose Erase from the Special menu (see Figure 14-2 for an example). Click the Format pop-up menu and choose Mac OS Extended. Now click Erase, and the drive directory will be rewritten. This should take, at most, a few minutes. Once the hard drive's icon reappears, you can begin to restore your files.

- ■ **Upgrading to HFS+ Without Initializing**   Some clever programmers have found a way to avoid the drastic step of erasing your files on the road

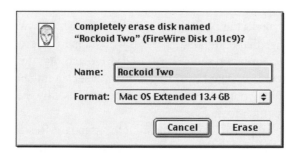

FIGURE 14-2   To change to HFS+, click Erase

to the HFS+ upgrade. Both Alsoft's PlusMaker and Power On Software's Space Doctor enable you to upgrade to HFS+ in place, without having to initialize the drive. And it seems to work quite well, although the publishers of these programs warn you to back up your files first, in case something goes wrong.

What to Do If the Hard Drive Fails

When you stop to think about it, it's truly amazing that hard drives are so reliable. Hard drives are keeping track of thousands and thousands of files, never making a mistake, every single day, every hour your Mac runs. You take them for granted. You open a file, you copy or save a file, and the drive does its stuff without protest, except for those telltale gargling or groaning noises they typically make.

But, as I have pointed out, things can go wrong, dangerously wrong, slowly, behind the scenes, without your noticing it. And then, one day your hard drive reports an error message when you try to copy or save a file, or you get that frightening question mark icon on your Mac's display when you try to start your computer.

NOTE *It should also be mentioned that hard drive failure isn't always gradual. Sometimes a drive stops working, period.*

The dangerous side-effect of a hard drive failure is, with capacity increasing in tremendous steps, when a hard drive fails, a lot more data is at risk than ever before.

Protect Your Drive with a Shut Down

The normal procedure to turn off your Mac is to choose Shut Down from the Special menu, or to press the power key and select the Shut Down button.

When you engage that command, a few things happen before your Mac turns itself off. You observe several seconds of hard-drive activity, during which time the Mac's file system is updated by doing a few housecleaning chores. For example, files stored in your drive's cache and the cache set by the Memory Control Panel are actually written to disk.

The same thing happens if you go through the standard Restart routine.

But you don't always shut down or restart your Mac in the usual fashion. If your Mac crashes, you may just turn it off or on again. Or, you force a restart by pressing a reset button or using the three-fingered salute keyboard combo

(COMMAND-CTRL-POWER ON). When you do this, the File Manager doesn't get a chance to do its normal bookkeeping chores. The drive's directory may not be updated properly or, being interrupted when a file is being written, the directory or file information may be corrupted.

Destroying a file doesn't take a lot. One missing or extra byte of data is enough to scramble the file or make it impossible to open. Different programs may treat damaged files in different ways. Microsoft's Word 98, for example, has a built-in mechanism to help recover a damaged file in a crash by checking the contents of the temporary files it creates when it is running. Those are the files with the dreaded "word work" prefix on them. Conversely, QuarkXPress isn't always as graceful in handling a damaged file. If you use its Autosave option, it refers to a previous version of the file to recover it or maybe the program just freezes when you try to open the damaged document.

And, even if the files themselves seem all right, other problems may be occurring behind the scenes. If parts of the hard drive's directory are damaged, regular reading and writing files may damage it further. More crash episodes may only make matters worse. And one day, you find you cannot open or write files to the drive or that files mysteriously vanish.

An example: If the Master Directory Block, the table of contents to your drive's directory, is damaged, it may, by mistake, overwrite portions of an old file with a new file. So, when you try to open the file, you get a 39 or 108 error.

And one day, the drive itself may not be readable. You get a warning box asking if you want to initialize the drive and, of course, the answer should be No.

A Brief Look at Hardware Problems

This is not to say all hard-drive problems are related to a directory problem. The drive mechanism itself is small and incredibly complex. While it's true drive manufacturers give their products almost unbelievable life-cycle ratings (mean time between failures of several hundred thousand hours), the figures are meant as averages. Some drives can last for years; others fail earlier.

A simple symptom is only a natural consequence of wear and tear. A bad block develops, so data cannot be copied to or retrieved from that block. Disk-formatting programs check and map out those bad blocks when you format a drive, so the File Manager doesn't see them as available.

Other problems are more severe. Some are the result of an accident. Your computer is dropped to the ground and there's a head crash (where the drive's heads strike and damage the drive platter). Or, the drive simply wears out, which can happen at any time, although they usually last for a number of years without trouble.

What to Do If the Hard Drive Fails

Making Sure Your Files Are Safe

The most effective way to be sure a file is safe is to have an extra copy around. This means backing up, whether only your important files or everything. If your files are critical to your business or personal finances, you may also want to store copies in another location for safekeeping. Chapter 29 covers the topic of backups in more detail.

The Real Skinny on Optimizing Your Drive

As you recall from the previous tutorial on how a hard drive works, the File Manager doesn't always put your files in one place. They simply are stored on available blocks on the drive, whether those blocks are adjacent to each other or span from one part of the drive to the other. As you continue to save and remove files, more and more of your new files may become, well, fragmented.

Is anything wrong with that?

If a lot of fragmentation occurs, the File Manager may take longer to retrieve the files, which may slow drive access, thus slowing the performance you get.

When you erase and restore the files to a drive, everything is put back in a single-copying process. No more fragmentation, though that would be an extreme move to take simply to bring your files together.

The other way to bring your files together is less drastic. Several utility publishers have programs that can optimize your drive, a process that moves all the files around so all parts of a file are placed together on the drive. The hard drive doesn't work as hard to get the file and performance takes a boost.

To optimize a drive, you can use the Speed Disk module from Symantec's Norton Utilities (shown in Figure 14-3) or MicroMat's TechTool Pro. Or, you can try a program that performs only that singular function, Alsoft's PlusOptimizer (Figure 14-4).

Be careful how old your disk-optimizing software is. Older versions of Norton Utilities, prior to 4.0, did not support HFS+ drives, and some had the potential of damaging the drive if you tried to diagnose or optimize it.

Is Optimizing Truly for Me?

Now that you see what optimizing is supposed to do, is this something you need? Does losing a few milliseconds in accessing a file help make your hard drive run noticeably faster?

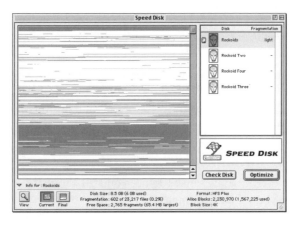

FIGURE 14-3   The author's hard drive is ready to get cleaned up by optimizing it

If that big hard drive on your Mac has only a small number of files on it and you don't replace or add new files constantly, probably not. I have seen Mac users go for years this way without reporting any problems with performance.

But, if you are into graphic design or video editing, you handle lots of big files, and you add and remove files on a regular basis. The fragmentation situation can grow much, much worse.

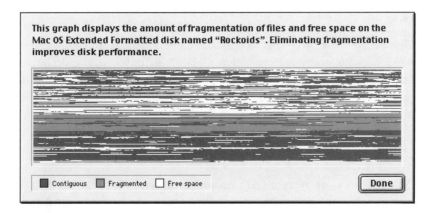

FIGURE 14-4   PlusOptimizer, from Alsoft, only optimizes, nothing else

NOTE
One of the reasons frequent optimization is required for a hard drive that's used for desktop video is because severe fragmentation could result in problems for video recording, such as dropped frames.

On the other hand, if you work with large image files (such as the ones you scan or create in a program like Photoshop), you may find that, indeed, a large amount of disk fragmentation develops and occasional optimizing (about once a month) is probably a good idea.

The Safe Way to Optimize

If optimizing your drive makes sense to you, you still should take a few precautions before you take the plunge.

NOTE
Another term for optimizing is defragging, slang for defragmenting a drive.

■ **Backup your files.** When you optimize a drive, your files are being moved to new locations and the slight possibility always exists that something may go wrong. The publishers of this sort of software have built-in protection mechanisms, such as not removing the old version of a file until the new one is copied and verified. So, while the danger is very slight, having a recent backup is a good idea anyway.

■ **Check the hard drive.** Disk-optimizing programs generally check the drive for problems before they do their stuff and they won't work if problems exist. Running Apple's Disk First Aid or one of the commercial drive diagnostic programs to make sure everything is all right is a good idea. Directory damage could definitely create havoc if you optimize a drive without fixing things first. While the optimizing software normally checks the drives before the process begins, being cautious is best. Run a regular drive diagnostic check first, as I've done with Norton's Disk Doctor component (see Figure 14-5), which actually includes directory optimization as the final leg of its standard drive diagnostic scan.

■ **Start from your system CD or another drive.** You cannot do a full optimization run of your startup disk. At best you can only run a small subset of the program's optimization routines. If your optimization program comes with a startup CD, you should use it, or start from another drive.

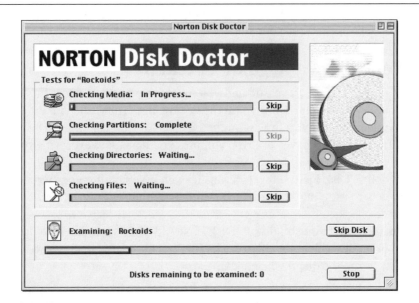

FIGURE 14-5   Norton Utilities checks the drive for directory problems

NOTE *TechTool Pro 2.5.2 and later can optimize a drive that's used as a startup disk from the disk itself, but not for Mac OS 9. The changes made to the File Manager for Mac OS 9 made that feature incompatible (so you're forced to start from another drive or the program's CD).*

■ **If you crash or a power failure occurs, recheck the drive.**   Although the optimization programs have checks and balances to preserve your data, you should run a diagnostic program (see the next section) if your Mac crashes or shuts down during an optimization run. This protects against directory damage that might cause problems later. If the drive checks out all right, resume optimization. If you continue to crash, contact the program's publisher about updates that might address your particular problem.

Your Hard Drive Safety Routine

Your hard drive gets constant wear and tear, and you can do little to prevent a hardware failure, although they are extremely rare. But, you can take steps to make sure your drive's directory is happy and healthy. That, and regular backups, provide the maximum protection for your files.

Give Your Drive a Regular Checkup

If your Mac crashes for any reason and you must force a restart, Disk First Aid can do a check of your startup drive on the next restart. That is, if you don't disable the Shut Down Warning option in the General Control Panel. The process doesn't extend to other drives or drive volumes you have, however, so any damage to those drives will be left unfixed.

Even though Disk First Aid gets a run-through if something goes wrong, a good idea is to run your hard drive through a regular regimen of preventive maintenance checks.

At the minimum, you should run Disk First Aid each week and have it run in its Repair mode, which not only checks for directory damage, but also fixes it. Here's how to run the diagnostic check:

1. Check your Mac OS 9 Utilities folder and locate Disk First Aid.

2. Once you locate Disk First Aid, double-click the program's icon to launch it. You see a screen much like the one shown in Figure 14-6.

3. Click the icon that represents the drive or drives you want to check. If you have more than one drive, you can SHIFT-CLICK each listed drive to have them all scanned by a single process.

4. To diagnose and repair possible problems, click the Repair button. Over the next few minutes, each drive you selected will be checked. If directory damage is located, it will be repaired (assuming Disk First Aid can repair the problem).

5. If the status screen shows disk problems have been detected and repaired, do a second run. This helps guard against the possibility that one form of directory damage hasn't hidden another.

6. If Disk First Aid fails to fix a problem, repeat the Repair scan several times. If a message continues to appear saying the damage cannot be fixed, consider using one of the other hard-drive repair problems, as described in the next section.

7. After Disk First Aid is done, choose Quit from the File menu to leave the program.

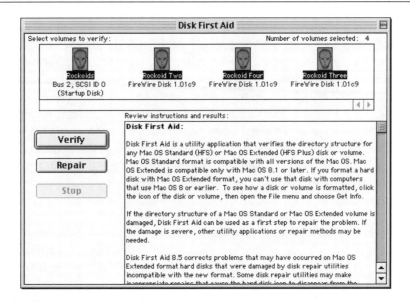

Your Hard Drive Safety Routine

FIGURE 14-6   The author's startup drive and attached drives are ready to be checked

CAUTION

Before Disk First Aid checks your startup drive, it attempts to quit all open programs. If it fails, Disk First Aid won't run. If this happens, go to Extensions Manager, choose a Mac OS 9 Base Set, and then restart and run Disk First Aid again. For example, the AOL Scheduler application that's part of AOL 4.0 sometimes doesn't quit and then Disk First Aid will not run. This problem appears to have been fixed with AOL 5.0 (a free upgrade from AOL expected out at press time). Another culprit is the printer driver used for some Brother laser and multifunction printers.

An Overview of Other Hard Drive Utilities

Disk First Aid has one significant advantage over the other programs and that is, it is free and comes with Mac OS 9. But this doesn't mean it's the best at what it does. Although Disk First Aid has been improved over the years, it isn't nearly as thorough as the commercial hard-drive utility programs in fixing directory damage.

If you run into a situation where Disk First Aid fails, you definitely want to consider the other programs. The following section gives you a brief summary. If you are doing a lot of mission-critical work, you may even want to arm yourself with all the programs, in case one fails.

■ **Norton Utilities for the Macintosh**   Unique among the commercial programs, Norton Utilities from Symantec can scan your startup disk and make directory repairs, the same as Disk First Aid (although one expects other programs may ultimately incorporate the same feature). Norton Utilities shares the capability of the other programs to optimize a drive's catalog or directory, which is said to make it run faster. Norton Utilities' other advantage is that it is multithreaded, which means it can run several disk diagnostic steps at the same time. This speeds the process of checking your drive. Another handy feature of this program is its LiveUpdate component, which it shares with Norton Anti-Virus. You can use this feature to connect automatically to Symantec's Web site to check for and retrieve program updates.

NOTE   *These automatic update programs, whether Apple's or Symantec's, clearly require you to have an Internet connection to function. If you don't have access to AOL or an ISP, you must depend on their support representatives to send you updates (and, more often than not, it takes quite a while for the updates to filter down to an installation CD or upgrade disk). This is only one more good reason Internet access is no longer a luxury, but a necessity today.*

■ **TechTool Pro**   Hard-drive diagnostics and optimization aren't the only tricks under TechTool Pro's sleeves. It also runs dozens of diagnostic runs on many of your Mac's systems, including the cache, CPU, RAM, serial ports, and on and on. Apple has even included a special version of this program as part of its AppleCare extended warranty program. TechTool Pro's latest versions, beginning with 2.5.2, can optimize not only a hard drive, but also the drive's directory.

■ **Alsoft's DiskWarrior**   Al Whipple (the Internet's "Ask Al") and his staff of programming wizards have created a great set of single-purpose programs for your Mac. DiskWarrior (see Figure 14-7) won't fix a hard drive directory's problems; instead, Disk Warrior rebuilds a hard drive directory, using its own routines to optimize performance. Once the directory is rebuilt, you can use its Preview function to examine the drive in its repaired state to make sure it looks all right. If it is, you can use the Replace function to rewrite the directory. This program doesn't fix a startup drive; you have to use the supplied startup CD.

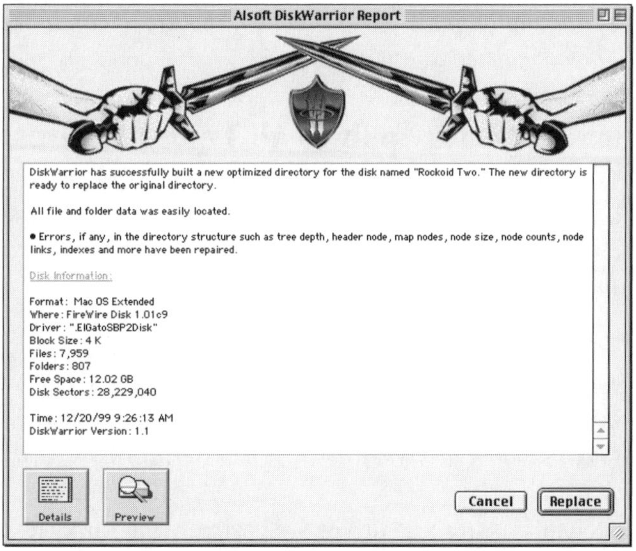
Alsoft DiskWarrior Report
DiskWarrior has successfully built a new optimized directory for the disk named "Rockoid Two." The new directory is ready to replace the original directory.
All file and folder data was easily located.
● Errors, if any, in the directory structure such as tree depth, header node, map nodes, node size, node counts, node links, indexes and more have been repaired.
Disk Information:
Format: Mac OS Extended
Where: FireWire Disk 1.01c9
Driver: ".ElGatoSBP2Disk"
Block Size: 4 K
Files: 7,959
Folders: 807
Free Space: 12.02 GB
Disk Sectors: 28,229,040
Time: 12/20/99 9:26:13 AM
DiskWarrior Version: 1.1
Details
Preview
Cancel
Replace

FIGURE 14-7 Alsoft's Disk Warrior is designed to replace a drive's directory with an optimized, more efficient version

NOTE *At press time, Alsoft had released a new version of DiskWarrior 2.0, which installs a system extension that guards against possible directory damage.*

Those Dates, Unfixed Bundles, and Other Issues

On the last stage of its diagnostic process, Norton Disk Doctor checks so-called Finder attributes, such as whether a file's dates or bundle bits are correct. *Bundle bits* are settings that determine if a file icon is properly shown on your Mac OS 9 desktop. The problem arises with this sort of diagnostic process when two programs disagree as to what forms a faulty bundle bit setting. I've found, for example, the things fixed by Norton Disk Doctor are unfixed by TechTool Pro, which then offers to fix other things.

Unless a file icon doesn't appear correctly, you don't have any reason to fret. Let the program fix what it asks to fix and don't be concerned if another program interprets the results a little differently.

NOTE
In the old days, we used to call the phenomenon of different bundle bit readings dueling bundles. The point is, if the file's icon looks all right, you needn't be concerned about anything.

Disk Directory Problems Apply to All Types of Drives

Mac hard drives come in a number of forms: The older, SCSI drives, plus the newer generation of ATA, FireWire, and USB devices. Each of these standards has its own advantages and disadvantages, but when it comes to hard drives, it really doesn't matter.

NOTE
SCSI is the acronym for Small Systems Computer Interface, and ATA, the drive standard Apple has settled on, is the acronym for AT Attachment. FireWire is also known by its official name, IEEE 1394, or, by Sony, iLink. And, of course, the acronym for Universal Serial Bus is USB.

The basic mechanisms of these drives are basically the same, regardless of which peripheral standard they support. And the potential for drive directory damage is also similar because the file manager treats them all the same. Your regular hard-drive diagnostic regimen shouldn't depend on the changes in peripheral technology.

What to Do If Directory Damage Can't Be Fixed

This problem won't happen too often. The hard-drive diagnostic programs are quite thorough and most directory problems can be fixed or, with DiskWarrior, replaced with a sound directory.

But sometimes, directory problems become so severe, no program can fix the damage. If you get a report of unfixed damage, don't ignore it.

■ **For SCSI drives: Check the SCSI chain.**   Even though Apple has moved swiftly away from the SCSI standard, I know many of you have Macs with SCSI chains. You have scanners, removable drives (Jaz, ORB, Zip, and so forth), and other peripherals. A SCSI chain has room for many problems. First, when your Mac is on, vary all the devices that are turned on and running. And second, make sure no duplicate SCSI ID numbers (except on separate chains) exist and that proper termination requirements are followed. Chapter 15 covers more of the subject of SCSI voodoo.

■ **Don't settle for only one.**   Don't give up if one program cannot fix the problem. Try another one. If Disk First Aid reports a problem cannot be fixed, try one of the commercial programs and see if it does better. If your hard drive regimen includes DiskWarrior, run it ahead of the other commercial utilities. If DiskWarrior gets first crack at the process, it seems to work better to fix the damage Disk First Aid cannot address.

■ **Be wary of recurring problems.**   If hard drive damage is severe, you may find it returns, even after the problem was supposedly fixed. This is a clear symptom of a problem that will only grow worse over time. If the damage reappears, even after regular diagnostic runs, think seriously about backing up your files and reformatting the drive.

A Brief Look at Device Driver Problems

The Mac File Manager "talks" to a hard drive by virtue of a program called a *driver*. When you initialize a drive, the formatting software installs this communication software. A driver is invisible, so you cannot see it.

A system crash could damage the driver software. The consequence? Your hard drive is no longer accessible. If this happens, you want to try updating the drive, a process that rewrites the device driver, to see if this can fix the problem.

Updating a Driver with Apple's Drive Setup

If you cannot boot from your startup drive, restart your Mac from another drive or from your Mac OS 9 CD. To boot from a CD, insert the CD in the drive, and then hold down the C key at startup. For newer Macs, including the iBook, slot-loading iMacs and Power Mac G4, hold down the OPTIION key, and select the CD icon from the list that appears on your Mac's display. To continue with the startup process:

1. Open the Utilities folder on the CD and open the folder.

2. Locate the Drive Setup folder, open the folder, and double-click the Drive Setup icon to launch it.

3. Check the program's directory for the list of available devices and select your drive.

4. Go to the Functions menu and choose Update to rewrite the device drive on your Mac's drive.

What to Do If Directory Damage Can't Be Fixed

5. If the drive does not appear on the list, try running Disk First Aid to see if it can locate and repair the drive before you attempt to use Drive Setup again. If this doesn't work, you may want to try a commercial hard-drive diagnostic program or consider reformatting the drive.

6. If the Update function is successful, go ahead and quit Drive Setup, and then restart your Mac.

CD STARTUP DOESN'T WORK?   The previous process is designed for Apple's own products. Although not officially supported by Apple, Mac OS 9 has been successfully installed on a number of Mac OS clone computers. These include products from APS, DayStar, MacTell, Power Computing, and Umax. Because these models don't use Apple-label drives, the C key startup gambit may not work. If you run into this sort of problem, try using the Startup Disk Control Panel to select a drive.

On the other hand, if you cannot start from the drive, your Mac OS clone then looks for another startup device and may actually succeed in booting from the CD.

Another option to try is holding down the COMMAND-OPTION-SHFIT-DELETE keys. This keyboard combination bypasses the startup drive and may succeed when other methods fail.

Updating a Drive with Non-Apple Software

Apple's Drive Setup is primarily designed to support an Apple-label drive. I say primarily because Drive Setup can actually support a growing number of non-Apple mechanisms. On the other hand, if your non-Apple drive was formatted with a non-Apple disk formatter, Drive Setup's Update feature won't work.

NOTE   *I don't suggest using Drive Setup for an unsupported drive. I've managed to get it to work, but you are usually better off using the program that came with the drive. This is because that program may have been designed to support all the drive's custom features, such as built-in cache, and so on.*

If you need to update the device driver on these products, use the program that came with the product. If the hard drive is an older model, contact the dealer or publisher to see if the formatting software is compatible with Mac OS 9.

NOTE   *Some third-party drives simply don't come with formatting software, not even on the drive itself. If this is the case, contact your dealer and request or order such a program.*

Here's how to update a non-Apple driver:

1. If you can get your drive to mount, you can probably run the program's Update function without starting from another drive. Otherwise, restart your Mac with the CD containing your disk-formatting software or another drive with a System Folder. Hold down the C key to start from the CD or use the Startup Disk Control Panel to pick another drive.

NOTE   *A reminder: You need to use the OPTION key to pick another startup drive if you're using an iBook, slot-loading iMac, or a Power Mac G4.*

NOTE   *If your disk-formatting software didn't come with a CD startup disk, check the instructions to see if they give you directions on how to create one.*

NOTE   *First-generation iMacs and the Blue & White G3 came with USB interfaces that wouldn't support a bootable drive. This was remedied in later USB versions, but Apple's FireWire interfaces, as of press time, still wouldn't support bootable drives. If your Mac doesn't support SCSI, you might consider using a CD writer to make a bootable disk (this takes careful attention to instructions, but it can usually work). Before you make a CD, however, check the manufacturer's software license about this issue. Usually they allow you a backup copy.*

2. After you start from the formatter's CD or another drive, locate the disk-formatting software, and then launch it. In Figure 14-8, FWB's popular Hard Disk ToolKit is used for this example.

3. Check the list of recognized drives and select the drive you want to update.

4. Update the drive using the Update command.

CAUTION   *If the update function is grayed out or it doesn't succeed, you must consider backing up your data and reformatting the drive.*

5. Once the Update operation is finished, quit the program and then restart from your regular hard drive.

What to Do If Directory Damage Can't Be Fixed

FIGURE 14-8 HardDisk ToolKit lists supported devices on the author's Mac

Is It Safe to Leave Directory Damage Unfixed?

Your hard drive may seem to run all right, but you are getting those diagnostic reports that something is seriously wrong.

Should you listen?

The answer is unabashedly yes. Hard-drive problems only get worse over time. As you continue to open and save files to the drive, the directory may get more and more scrambled.

One day you might try to copy a file to or from the drive, and the file won't copy. Maybe you get some sort of disk error message or the file itself may disappear. Eventually, you may be unable to use the drive at all. Instead, you get a warning message asking if you want to initialize the drive (which wipes out everything on the spot).

This isn't meant as an empty warning or only to alarm you. It is a warning based on real-life experience. Even if you have complete backups of all your files, reformatting a drive and restoring those files can take hours if the worst happens.

Do your best to fix the directory problem. If repairs don't succeed, you must seriously consider biting the bullet and reformatting the drive.

Coping with a Hard Drive Failure

The hard-drive diagnostic steps described in this chapter are strictly software-related. They are designed to fix a damaged directory.

But hard-drive mechanisms can fail, too. While this doesn't happen often, it does happen.

If your drive mechanism fails, having a backup at hand is the best insurance. While recovering some or all of the data from a damaged drive is possible, this is a costly process. Such companies as Drive Savers (http://www.driversavers.com) can do the job, but figure on paying a few thousand dollars or more for a reasonably large drive.

And again, no guarantee exists that the process will succeed.

If you have a full backup (see Chapter 29 for more information), however, you needn't consider such a large expense. If the drive fails, you can either have it replaced under warranty or buy another.

Summing Up

In this chapter, you learned about disk drive technology and how to make sure your Mac's drives are running in tip-top shape.

In the next chapter, you learn about removable drives and some of the various peripheral standards available, such as ATA, FireWire, SCSI, and USB.

Summing Up

Chapter 15

Installing a Removable Drive

The original removable drive on a Mac was a floppy drive. Hard to think that those little marvels, which originally stored up to 400K of data, were the way files were transported when you didn't have a networking setup or speedy Internet access, isn't it?

Over the years, this once large amount of storage space soon became less compelling as applications and the files you created from them became larger and larger: 400K became 800K, and then 1.4MB (the high-density or HD floppies).

When these storage methods proved inefficient to handle larger files (unless you could divide them into smaller parts with a compression program, such as StuffIt), other alternatives came along. Among the early efforts were Bernoulli drives from Iomega and SyQuest drives from SyQuest Technologies.

While the underlying designs are different, the idea behind those removable devices was the same. You could put larger files on a mechanism that looks much like a hard drive, but reads and writes data to a little disk that is easily removed and transported to another location. This was a boon to many businesses where the limitations of moving large files (in the days before high-speed networking) were largely overcome.

Over the years, removable drives for the Mac have increased tremendously in capacity, in the same way as the built-in storage devices on your Mac hold more data.

Types of Removeable Drives

Here's a quick look at some of the removable drives now available for a Mac:

NOTE *The now-retired removable formats, such as Bernoulli drives and the various products produced by SyQuest technologies (which folded in 1998), won't be discussed here. Millions of existing users of these products are around and as long as the mechanisms work and drive media is available (and you can use them without problems with Mac OS 9), there's little reason not to continue working with them. This chapter will concentrate on the popular formats you can buy today at most Apple dealers.*

■ **Zip Drive** Iomega's Zip format looks much like a fat floppy disk. Two versions are available: the original, which holds up to 100MB of data, and the newest one, with a maximum capacity of 250MB. Millions of users have Zip drives, which means if you buy one of these products, finding another user who has one and can read your files can be easy. Zip drives are offered as internal drives on new Power Macs and are available as options for other, older models (but not for the iMac, which has no provision for an internal drive). If a downside exists, it's this: the drives tend to be somewhat slow compared to a regular hard drive, but as a file transport mechanism, they're quite convenient.

■ **SuperDisk drive** When Apple took floppy drives from the Mac, another burgeoning removable drive format had a sudden burst of popularity. A SuperDisk drive looks similar to a Zip drive, but it reads both high-density floppy disks and a new type of media (which looks similar to a floppy disk at first glance) that stores up to 120MB of data. A SuperDisk drive is convenient to carry around, but even the so-called 2x version suffers slightly in performance compared to the Zip drive. Having a two-in-one drive is a great plus though, and a good way to keep some of your older floppies in use, as well as for newer programs still packaged in that form.

■ **Jaz and Jaz 2 drives** Iomega's Jaz drives are similar to hard drives, but the actual media is stored in a small cartridge. Capacities range from 1GB for the original Jaz drive to 2GB for the Jaz 2 variation. These products are reasonably fast, and some folks tout the capability to run multimedia presentations, including QuickTime movies, directly from a Jaz cartridge.

■ **Castlewood ORB** Sporting a maximum capacity of 2.2GB, the Castlewood ORB is, in some ways, similar in feel to the SyQuest SyJet, the last product produced by that company before it floundered (the reason for this is that the founder of Castlewood is the same person who also helped start SyQuest back in the 1980s).

■ **CD Writers** These products are discussed in more detail in Chapter 18. Briefly, a CD writer can create a disk that works on a regular CD-ROM drive (the format is called *CD-R*) or you can make rewritable disks (called *CD-RW*). The best thing to be said about one of these products is that the media is super cheap (a buck or two for a blank CD) and they're great for archiving, as the CD can last for many years. I still have audio CDs from the early 1980s around and they work fine, thank you.

NOTE *In respect to our fearless technical editor (and my old friend), Pieter Paulson, I should add that just because a commercial CD works fine after 15 or more years doesn't mean the one you make with a CD recorder will last as long. But, its chances for longevity are definitely better than standard magnetic-based drive media.*

Types of Removeable Drives

■ **DVD-RAM**   Based on the rapidly growing DVD format (that high-resolution format used for high-quality playback of video movies), such drives can use media with a capacity of up to 5.2GB (compared to 650MB for a regular CD). A DVD-RAM media can be used the same as a hard drive. You can copy data simply by dragging the files over to it. Media is available in 2.6GB (Type II) format and 5.2GB.

NOTE   *You can also do this sort of trick with a regular CD writer using Adaptec's Direct CD software. Otherwise, file transfers must be done within a CD creation program (such as Toast) by selecting the files in advance, and then running a session in which your data is written to the CD.*

Setting Up Removable Drives

Although the arrival of FireWire and USB has made such devices simple to hook up, a removable drive doesn't just run in the fashion of a floppy drive or hard drive. You have to install driver software so your Mac recognizes the drive and can mount the media when you insert it into the drive.

NOTE   *Some of these products, such as the venerable Zip drive, can work without installing the software, so long as the media is in the drive when you start your Mac. Then the Zip driver on the disk itself is loaded into memory.*

Here are basic setup tips for an external removable device:

1. If the drive mechanism uses a SCSI interface, check the directions on how to set the SCSI ID number (see Chapter 14 for more information about SCSI setups and problems). Make sure it doesn't conflict with anything you already have on your Mac. A Mac with a SCSI drive usually sets it at ID 0. An internal SCSI-based CD drive is usually set at ID 3 (although it's been a few years since Apple has actually included a SCSI-based CD drive on its computers). SCSI-based Zip drives give you a choice of ID 5 or ID 6. Don't forget to set termination on the last device on the SCSI chain (you learn more about SCSI later in this chapter).

2. Locate the manufacturer's installation CD (or floppy) and install the software (see Figure 15-1). This requires your Mac restart, but it's better to do it now, so the drive is recognized once you hook it up.

FIGURE 15-1   Although Iomega's drivers come as part of Mac OS 9, their latest software has extra features, such as simple backup and disk-cataloging utilities

3. If you're using a SCSI peripheral on your Mac, turn the Mac off, and then turn off all attached SCSI devices.

CAUTION   *No ifs, ands, or buts about this: If you try to hot plug a SCSI device, you risk a nasty crash and potential damage to the Mac or the device's SCSI chips. Hot pluggable terminators are out there if you want to explore the option, but I assume most of you don't have such devices hooked up (the ones I've used aren't always reliable).*

4. If you're connecting an external removable drive, hook it up to your Mac (with FireWire and USB you can do this while the Mac is running without worrying about anything).

5. Once everything is hooked up and turned on, insert the drive's media and test it. Write files to the media and then copy files from it. Make sure everything is all right before you actually copy files you need to keep permanently. You also want to remove and reinsert the media a few times to get used to the way it works. An ORB drive, for example, has a peculiar setup where you have to insert the cartridge and then, for it to work properly, push it down slightly until it spins up.

If your removable drive is internal, the installation process is a bit more complex, but with newer Mac G3 and G4 models, it's not as daunting as it used to be (with fewer opportunities for cut fingers).

Setting Up Removable Drives

CAUTION

Before installing an internal drive, whether removable or fixed, you should consult the instructions that come with your Mac and the ones for the drive. Be prepared to fiddle with delicate cables that seem situated in out-of-the-way corners and to handle tiny screws to get the process done. If you ever assembled a toy or a bookcase, you shouldn't find this process too difficult.

6. Install the software and then restart (you could do this at the end of the installation process if you prefer).

7. Shut down your Mac.

8. Open the Mac's case and locate a spare bay designed for a removable drive (this is at the front).

NOTE

Most removable drive mechanisms require you to get a proper faceplate, so the door of the mechanism is open at the front of your Mac. These little plastic fittings can usually be purchased from your dealer. Or, you can check with one of the popular manufacturers of such faceplates or bezels, Proline Distribution, at http://www.proline.com. You might also find a faceplate as an Apple service part in your dealer's service department, but more often than not, these tend to be more expensive than retail versions (at least they were when I did a few price comparisons).

9. With the Mac still plugged in (but turned off), touch the power supply of the Mac or set up a wrist strap to ground yourself. Once you do this, you can remove the AC plug from your Mac.

10. Seat the drive in the proper drive bay and attach it with the available cabling. Be careful not to pull too hard on those cables. They are delicate and it's not too hard to break them, especially those thin-wiring harnesses found in some Macs.

11. Once everything is plugged in, close the case (don't try to run your computer with the case open).

12. Turn on your Mac. After it powers up, insert the media into the removable drive and test it. Make sure you can write files to it and access files. Also, remove and reinsert the media a few times to make sure everything works properly.

Preparing Removable Drive Media

Getting your removable drive up and running properly is only half the battle. The next step is to get the drive media ready to roll. For some products, this isn't an issue. You can find such products as Zip disks already formatted for your Mac.

If the media comes formatted for the PC environment, or unformatted, you aren't left out, however. You can prepare the media for use in two ways.

If the media comes in PC format, you can use the Mac OS 9 Finder to change it to Mac format by following these steps:

1. Place the removable drive media in the drive.

2. When the media mounts (Mac OS 9's File Exchange handles PC disks), select the disk icon.

3. Click the Finder's Special menu once and select Erase (see Figure 15-2).

4. For a small disk, choose the Mac OS Standard format from the Format pop-up menu. If you have a larger disk, such as a Jaz cartridge, use Mac OS Extended (HFS+ instead) because it greatly reduces minimum file size and enables you to get greater mileage from the media.

5. Click the Erase button.

6. In a few seconds, the media is erased and ready to receive your files.

CAUTION
If the media isn't mounting on your Mac's desktop, you may see a Finder message asking if you want to initialize the disk. Accept this option only if you're sure the disk is empty, otherwise, you'll erase all the files on it. If you know files are on the disk, click the second option on that initialize prompt, which ejects the disk. Then try reinserting the disk and see if it works a second time (sometimes the disk does work on the second try).

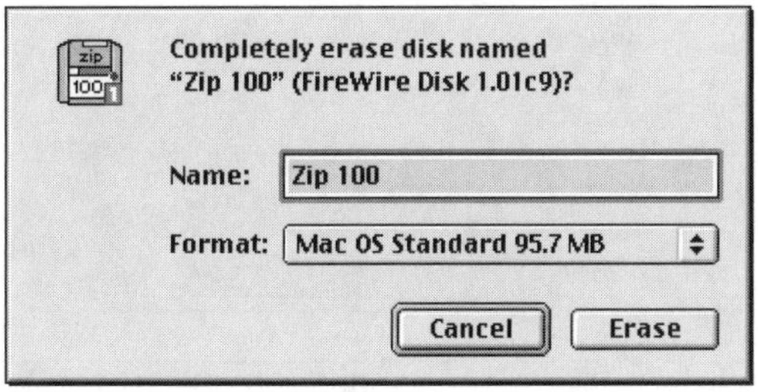

Completely erase disk named "Zip 100" (FireWire Disk 1.01c9)?

Name: `Zip 100`

Format: `Mac OS Standard 95.7 MB`

Cancel | Erase

FIGURE 15-2   Choose your disk format option from this screen

If the drive media doesn't appear on your Mac's desktop, you must go to the formatting program that comes with the drive. Because an Iomega product is used in this example, I use their Tools software, which is part of the standard Iomegaware installation for this description. Some of the general-purpose disk formatting programs, such as FWB's Hard Disk ToolKit, can also be used for many popular drive mechanisms.

Here's what to do:

1. Insert the media or cartridge in the removable drive.

2. Locate and launch your removable drive formatting software (see Figure 15-3).

3. Insert the media you want to format.

4. Click the icon that represents the removable device you have.

5. Then locate and click the button that brings up the formatting screen. In the case of Tools, the icon showing a pencil eraser placed upon a disk, is the second from the left.

6. Name your disk and then choose your disk formatting standard (see Figure 15-4).

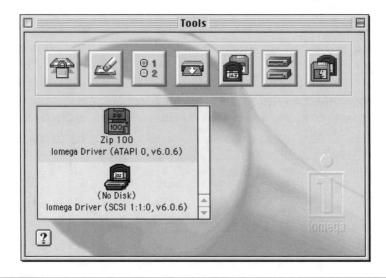

FIGURE 15-3   Iomega's Tools software works with both its Jaz and Zip drives

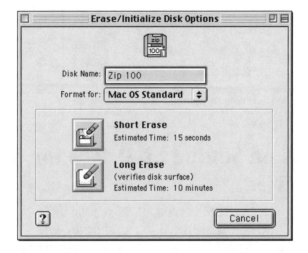

FIGURE 15-4   Because this is only a 100MB Zip disk, I chose the Mac OS Standard format

7. Select the kind of formatting you want by clicking the appropriate button (see Figure 15-4). *A long erase* is the same as a low-level format in other disk-formatting programs. The *short erase* is the same as choosing Erase from the Finder's Special menu and simply wipes out the disk directory, making it ready to receive new files.

8. You will then see a dialog box warning that you will lose any data you erase, as shown in Figure 15-5. Click Erase to begin the process.

9. When the formatting process is over, you see an onscreen prompt (see Figure 15-6). Click OK to acknowledge the message.

FIGURE 15-5   Most disk-formatting programs give you an opt out screen

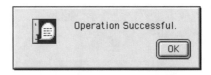

FIGURE 15-6   You have now formatted a Zip cartridge

Hints and Tips on Setting Up Drives for ATA, SCSI, USB, and FireWire

Someone said long ago that SCSI is voodoo. I have used these words so many times, that my publishers are concerned I'm repeating myself.

But Apple's original standard for high-speed peripheral devices, even when set up properly, was fraught with potential pitfalls and conflicts. You could, for example, do everything possible to make sure the SCSI ID numbering and termination setups were correct. The software is installed, the cables are new, no device is left off while the Mac is running, and yet things don't work as they should.

You install an extra device and, either that or another device won't mount, or you start experiencing strange crashes, which no amount of troubleshooting can fix.

In this section, you get some advice on proper drive setup, covering all the Mac peripheral standards currently being supported.

ATA Drives

Apple didn't simply borrow contextual and sticky menus from Windows. Apple also took a PC peripheral standard, *AT Attachment (ATA)*, also known as *Integrated Drive Electronics (IDE)*, and made this its own. As a result, the drives in new Macs are cheaper and have greater capacity, so Apple can deliver bigger mechanisms on its new products and keep costs in line.

A variation on the ATA theme is *AT Attachment Packet Interface (ATAPI)*, which is used for removable devices. Apple's built-in CD, DVD, and Zip drives come in ATAPI form. Newer Macs also come with master and slave support: You can add a second ATA device to each device chain.

NOTE *If you're unsure how your Mac is equipped, first check the technical information leaflet that comes with it. If the leaflet doesn't give you the information you need, point your Web browser to Apple's technical information library (http://til.info.apple.com) and use the search feature to bring up information about your model Mac. Hard drive vendors, such as APS Technologies and LaCie, can also help you get this information.*

FireWire

The ultimate replacement for SCSI and, perhaps, also ATA, is FireWire. *FireWire* is a technology invented by Apple, but only introduced on new Macs with the advent of the Blue & White Power Mac G3 series at the beginning of 1999.

NOTE *The peripheral standard has other names, in case you're looking, such as IEEE 1394 (the official name) or i.LINK (Sony's variation).*

FireWire shares two important attributes with USB: It's hot pluggable, which means you can easily remove and add peripheral devices without turning off or restarting your Mac. The only conditions are that you install necessary software drivers first to recognize the devices and dismount a disk drive icon before you remove it from the chain.

And you needn't play with SCSI ID numbers, worry about termination or any of that because the FireWire chain is self-configuring. The FireWire checks for new devices as soon as you attach something to your Mac's FireWire port or to another device.

If you use a smaller device, such as one of the miniature VST Technologies FireWire drives, you don't even need a separate power supply. The drive derives power from the FireWire bus (the usual limit is two such devices, after which you need the power supply to get enough juice for the drive).

FireWire is capable of up to 400 Mbps and can support up to 63 daisy-chained devices, with a maximum cable length of 14 feet for each device. If this seems somewhat limiting, you can also add a FireWire repeater hub to expand the chain.

Hints and Tips on Setting Up Drives for ATA, SCSI, USB, and FireWire

FireWire has one important limitation, at least at press time: You cannot boot from a FireWire drive, but a future Mac OS system update and firmware update (for new Macs and iMacs) might, conceivably, address this shortcoming.

USB (Universal Serial Bus)

The other Mac peripheral standard is Universal Serial Bus (USB), which is primarily used for input devices, such as a mouse, a keyboard, or a camera. But you can also add USB speaker systems (such as the iSub for the slot-loading iMac series), scanners, and removable drives.

USB can support up to 127 daisy-chained devices, and it's self-configuring and hot-pluggable, the same as FireWire. But USB is much slower, maxing out at 12 Mbps. While this is fine for a relatively slow-speed removable drive, such as a SuperDisk or a Zip, it's downright pokey when you want to use a fixed drive or any other high-speed storage device.

You extend the USB chain with a hub and, by attaching one hub to another, you can, like an Ethernet network, extend it considerably, up to the limits of the technology.

Setting Up Removable Devices

Before you go out and buy a removable drive, you may want to look at all the alternatives. In addition to the drive technologies cited at the beginning of this chapter, you may also want to consider simply buying a second hard drive, whether internal or external. A second drive can, all things being equal, perform at speeds equal to or faster than the drive that comes with your Mac.

If it's portability of media you need though, a removable drive is a good way to go.

Here are some considerations to remember when you get an extra drive for your Mac:

- **For internal devices: Make sure it fits.** It's no fun to wait anxiously for the arrival of your new removable drive, and then, when you open the Mac, you realize there's no place for it. Obviously, adding another internal drive to an iMac is out of the question, but if you have a regular desktop Mac, you may find it's already equipped with a removable device from the factory (usually a Zip drive) and there's just no place to put a second removable drive. So, your answer is external. Check this before you buy.

■ **Get the right technology.**   Does your Mac support SCSI, ATAPI master, and slave mode? Before you buy a drive, check the specifications. If you're uncertain, contact Apple or your dealer to make 100 percent certain you can use the removable drive you're buying. When in doubt, get an external drive, one that supports one of your Mac's external peripheral ports (FireWire and USB for current models).

■ **Does the drive have the proper bracket?**   Apple's most recent models have an internal bay for a removable drive right up front (if it's not already occupied). You don't need a special mounting bracket, but you might for older Macs. Again, if you're uncertain, don't hesitate to consider an external drive. The added benefit of the external model, even if you have room inside your Mac, is that it can quickly be moved to another Mac if necessary (especially if you're about to sell the older model).

■ **You need a new faceplate for a removable device.**   If you want to add a SuperDisk, a Zip drive, or some other device for which you have to remove the media, you need to replace the faceplate on your Mac with one that matches the open slot on the mechanism itself. Your dealer can probably handle your needs (or check with Proline, as previously mentioned). On some Mac OS clones, all you have do is to pop a small faceplate and leave the removable mechanism with its front showing, without a cover.

■ **Need a SCSI card?**   If the drive mechanism you want to add is SCSI and your Mac doesn't support that standard, solutions do exist. For regular desktop Macs, a number of SCSI peripheral cards are available from such companies as Adaptec, AdvanSys, ATTO, Initio, and Orange Micro. They range from just above $50 for a simple SCSI-2 card (with a top speed of 10MB per second, about twice as fast as the fastest internal SCSI port of most older Macs, except for the few models with two SCSI busses) to high-speed SCSI cards, capable of supporting ultra-fast drives suitable for multimedia work.

Hints and Tips on Setting Up Drives for ATA, SCSI, USB, and FireWire

NOTE   *If you have an iMac or iBook, which have no PCI expansion slots, you can still check with your dealer about getting a SCSI to USB converter. Remember, though, you still have to content with all the SCSI chain setup schemes, such as proper ID and termination. In addition, it'll be dreadfully slow, as USB is much slower than even the slowest SCSI standard.*

Removable Drive Troubleshooting Techniques

For the most part, removable drives are easy to install and easy to set up. Nonetheless, problems do occur occasionally(particularly with SCSI devices).

This section should help you deal with any problems that might arise after your installation. If you need more assistance on handling problems with peripheral devices, check out another book I wrote for Osborne/McGraw-Hill, *Upgrading & Troubleshooting Your Mac.*

SCSI Removable Drive Doesn't Work

If your new SCSI-based removable device isn't working, check several possibilities that may have caused the problem:

- **Correct SCSI ID Setting.**   The Iomega Zip drive restricts you on the external model to number five or six. Make sure no conflicts exist.

- **Check termination switch.**   The Jaz and Zip drives have switchable termination. The Castlewood ORB uses a peculiar SCSI termination scheme. If this is to be the device that terminates the SCSI chain, connect your cable to the SCSI IN plug. This step activates automatic termination. If the device is going to be situated in the middle of a SCSI chain, attach cables at both the SCSI IN and SCSI OUT ports (it doesn't matter which is which), which disables the internal termination. This setup is reminiscent of the SyQuest SyJet removable drive.

- **Check the SCSI chain with SCSI Probe.**   Adaptec's SCSI Probe (see Figure 15-7) is designed to show you which SCSI devices are hooked up to your Mac and their ID position. It also has a pop-up menu, so you can switch among multiple SCSI chains, assuming you have a Mac with internal and external SCSI chains, or one with more SCSI peripheral cards. A copy of the program comes directly from Adaptec's Web site at http://www.adaptec.com.

- **Don't forget the software.**   Did you make sure the drive's software was installed? You can get many removable cartridges to mount if you place them in the drive and then restart them (in which case the driver loads from the media). Otherwise, you need to install the manufacturer's software.

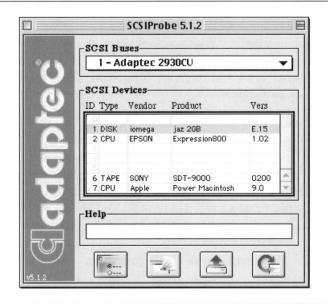

FIGURE 15-7	SCSI Probe enables you to probe the innards of your Mac's SCSI chain

NOTE

I'll amend this in one way. Mac OS 9 includes, as part of the normal installation, the Iomega Driver, required for its Jaz and Zip drives. The software provided by the manufacturer, however, may be more up-to-date and the package will also include bundled software for backups and cataloging disks.

■ **Don't forget the SCSI ID numbers must be unique.**   As previously mentioned, the internal drive on your Mac typically is at ID number 0 (I say typically because I've seen Macs with aftermarket drives set at ID 6). A SCSI CD drive is set at number 3, and an internal Zip is set at number 5. Make sure no duplicates exist in your ID number settings. If your Mac has both internal and external SCSI chains, you can get around this (although scanners sometimes cause problems if an internal device has the same number).

■ **Don't turn off any SCSI devices.**   When your Mac is powered up, all attached SCSI devices should be turned on, and they should be left on till your Mac has been shut down. Even though it's sometimes possible to get a small SCSI chain to work without problems in this way, don't assume this is going to happen every time. Playing by the rules is best, rather than having to contend with potential problems, such as random system crashes or unrecognized devices. If you turn off a SCSI device by error, restart your Mac immediately.

■ **Consider extra termination or an active terminator.** Apple's PowerBook often requires a second terminator for large SCSI chains, and sometimes, you also need an extra one on a regular Mac. Don't hesitate to try if all other configuration setups seem to fail (do remember to shut everything down before you change anything). Another possible solution to a SCSI chain problem is active termination. These termination devices are designed to control SCSI chain voltage more efficiently than regular terminators, and they are sometimes built into a device (such as external drives from APS Technologies). Otherwise, you can buy it from your dealer as an aftermarket item.

■ **Replace the cables.** If the cables are old, consider replacing them. Using cables from the same manufacturer doesn't hurt because you are sure the electrical characteristics are, at the very least, similar, if not essentially the same (it's unnecessary to get high-cost, gold-tipped cables as they don't work any better than the regular variety).

■ **Keep cable lengths short.** The maximum recommended cable length of a regular SCSI chain is a little over 18 feet. For an Ultra SCSI chain, the maximum length is about three meters. When you start measuring cable lengths, you need to add a foot or two here and there for the internal cable harnesses in your Mac, or in each external SCSI device. Performance suffers drastically if cable lengths are too long. With a little preparation, you can equip even long SCSI chains with short cables and stay well within the limitations of length.

■ **Do the SCSI dance.** Don't hesitate to move devices around or change ID numbers (as long as no conflict exists) to see if a particular combination works better. Although Zip drives limit you to two ID settings, you have plenty of freedom with other devices to get the kind of performance you expect. Do remember to shut down everything before you change numbers.

FireWire Device Doesn't Work

I'll say it again: FireWire is definitely the preferred way to go for high-speed storage. Most of the little oddities of the SCSI chain are history when a FireWire device is set up and you won't miss any of the hassles.

This is not to say all FireWire devices are free of troubles, but the range of problems and solutions is much smaller.

For example:

■ **Don't forget the software.**   Even though Apple provides special FireWire drivers with Mac OS 9, you still need to install the specific software that came with your device for it to be recognized. If the drive has been around for a while, check the manufacturer's Web site for needed updates. FireWire is still an emerging technology, and drive makers are working to deliver both better performance and greater reliability.

■ **Slow FireWire drive performance.**   A known conflict exists between FireWire devices and some USB device drivers under Mac OS 9. So, if you find writing a file to your FireWire seems to take forever, go ahead and check your Extensions folder, either with Extensions Manager or Conflict Catcher (if you use Casady & Greene's marvelous software). Disable all the non-Apple USB drivers and restart. Then see if the problem goes away. If it does, turn those extensions on again, one by one, with a restart and see if the problem returns.

NOTE *At the same time, you may want to see if Mac OS 9's USB Device Extension supports your USB devices. If it does, you can forget about extension sleuthing and get on with your work.*

USB Device Doesn't Work

USB technology (which was developed by Intel) is another standard that has simplified management of peripherals. It's also a suitable place for a slower removable drive, such as a SuperDisk or Zip, but room still exists for trouble, as you learn next:

■ **Try Apple's USB drivers first.**   For Mac OS 9, Apple has introduced the USB Device Extension, which supports, among other products, the

Removable Drive
Troubleshooting Techniques

SuperDisk and Zip drives. It may also work with other products. If your USB device isn't working properly, set up Extensions Manager to disable the drivers from your product and see if Apple's USB Device Extension can function.

■ **Check the hub.**   If there's not enough power to work with your drive, use a powered hub (or attach the power cord to a hub that hasn't had one connected). Don't assume that because the hub is lighted, the device should work all right. Sometimes error messages won't display.

NOTE

If you're using a hub that doesn't power up all ports at startup, you might want to consider a different unit. For example, MacAlley updated its hubs to support this feature after problems occurred with some devices with the original version (they'll replace yours under warranty if you have a problem with some devices). You learn more about USB in Chapters 16 and 17.

Summing Up

Removable drives are a great way to extend your Mac's storage capacity and they're also useful for backup purposes. In this chapter, you discovered ways to set up a removable device and how to cope with problems if they occur.

In the next chapter, another popular peripheral device, the scanner, is covered.

Chapter 16

Installing a Scanner

You want to send the family some of the photos you took on your California vacation. Or, you need to touch up a photo for a magazine or book. Perhaps you have a set of legal documents that need editing in your word processing program.

But first you need some means to bring this information to your Mac. This is why you should consider buying a scanner.

Not so long ago, scanners were expensive luxuries. To get even a low-end model would cost you at least a grand. If you wanted to add a few options, such as an automatic document feeder to handle several documents at once (in the fashion of a copying or fax machine), or the capability to handle slides, the price went up accordingly.

As with other computer peripherals, however, prices have come down substantially, to a fraction of what they once were.

A decent scanner can be purchased these days for as little as $100. Although these scanners seem thin and frail, they are capable of capturing artwork with higher quality than products costing many times as much did only a few years ago.

NOTE   *It's fair to say that while scanners are cheap, accessories are not. When you add a document feeder and slide attachment to your scanner, you can easily triple or quadruple the price.*

If you want to consider a scanner in the $1,000 range, you can actually find a product perfectly capable of professional caliber work. In fact, many graphic artists use such products to capture images for ads, brochures, books, and magazines.

Setting Up a Scanner

While scanners may differ from each other in terms of price, features, and capabilities, they all have similar basic instructions for set up that you need to follow. Here is a summary of the steps you need to follow:

1. If you are connecting a scanner to a Mac's SCSI port, first shut down the computer and any connected peripherals. This isn't necessary if you have a FireWire or USB scanner.

2. Take the scanner out of its box along with any needed accessories.

3. Unlock the scanner's optical assembly using the setup instructions provided by the manufacturer.

CAUTION *This is an extremely critical step. If you don't follow it, you risk damage to the delicate optical assembly of your new scanner.*

4. If the scanner must be connected to an open SCSI port, check the ID and termination settings and set them up as necessary. Changing the SCSI ID on a scanner can be done by pushing a button or using a little wheel with a tiny screwdriver.

NOTE *Some SCSI scanners come with termination switches and some don't. If the labeling at the rear of the scanner isn't clear (and, sad to say, that's often the case), you need to consult the manufacturer's documentation to see what's what.*

5. Connect and firmly seat cables that need to be attached.

6. Turn on the scanner and other peripherals and wait for the scanner's on light to turn on. Over the next few seconds, the scanner will groan and slide and slither as it goes through a self-test process. If the activity light is flickering, it'll stabilize when the setup process is done.

NOTE *If this doesn't happen, check the section "What to Do if Something Goes Wrong" to learn how to deal with such a problem.*

7. Once the scanner appears to be working, turn on your Mac.

8. After your Mac finishes starting up, install any necessary software. You may need to restart to get your Mac to recognize the scanner and to have it run.

9. After the scanner software has been installed and you've restarted your computer, if necessary, try scanning a few things first, such as photos or artwork to make sure everything works. If you're not sure what to do, then continue with the next section to learn how.

Dealing with Your First Scan

Low-end scanners come with software that should be easy to install and easy to use, especially for first-time users. While such scanners are used in business environments, they are designed primarily for consumers who want to capture photos for family and friends or to do some simple desktop publishing.

Dealing with Your First Scan

Manuals for most scanners used to be huge, perhaps as big as the manual that originally came with your Mac, with lots of tips and hints to help you start your scanning experience, even if you were doing it for the first time.

Printed documentation of this sort is a rarity now, however, especially when a manufacturer must keep production costs down to compete with other high-volume products. Even higher-cost scanners currently come with the absolute minimum of printed materials. At best, you get a booklet or a foldout card with basic setup instructions and a short set of basic troubleshooting hints.

The software CD usually contains the rest of the documentation you may need. This is because it's cheaper to put the information in electronic form than to print a huge costly manual that cuts into already tight profit margins.

NOTE   *Most electronic documentation comes in Adobe Acrobat format. A copy of the software is either provided on the CD or you can dig up a copy on your Mac OS 9 installation CD (in the Adobe folder), if it hasn't been preinstalled on your Mac.*

Before you start going wild with your scanner and trying to do everything you possibly can with your new toy, it'd be best to scan a simple photo or piece of artwork to get started.

A good way of doing this is to let the scanning software do the work by itself, for the most part. Most scanning software has an Auto or Automatic mode, which is bound to make your entry into the scanning world seem far less daunting. This mode lets your software capture your artwork using its default settings, so all you have to do is click the mouse and wait.

While the results may not be good for professional artwork or pictures, they should be sufficient to get you started. Then you can see how the scanner works and whether it's working properly.

Follow these steps to get started:

1. First, lift the top of the scanner and put your document or picture face down on the scanner.

2. Then, launch your scanning application. If you happen to be using Adobe Photoshop at the time, you can use the Import or Acquire option to launch the software. Adobe's entry-level photo-editing tool, PhotoDeluxe, comes with a Scanner option that serves the same purpose.

3. Once the scanning software is open, locate a button labeled either Preview or Prescan (the name of the function depends on what application you're

using to scan the image). See Figure 16-1 for an example. At this point, the scanner's optical assembly travels across the scanner to transform the image into a digital format your computer can read. Within a short time (this depends on how fast or slow your scanner is), a preview of that image should appear somewhere on your screen, probably to the left or right of the control panels in the program. The preview image gives you the ability to edit the artwork before the final scan is done.

4. Now you have the ability to make the photo look better; for the first time, you should find the automatic exposure mode and click it. The automatic exposure mode is found in different places in different programs, so it may take a bit of searching to find it.

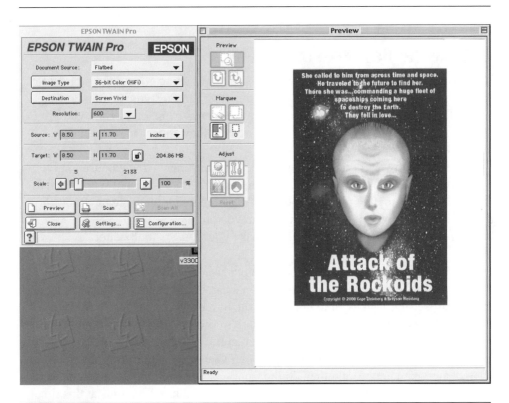

Dealing with Your First Scan

FIGURE 16-1   Your preview image is displayed in the scanner's document window, and now you can edit the image to look the way you want

5. After you make whatever modifications you need to or you took the advice of using the automatic mode, locate and click the Scan button (or however the function to make the final scan is labeled in your scanning software). Depending on the size and complication of the image, the scanned picture should appear fairly quickly.

6. Once the final artwork has been captured, save your photo to your hard drive, if you want to keep it. Some programs come with a direct save option, enabling you to save the image in your scanning program instead of in a photo-editing program. If your scanning exercise is only an exercise, go ahead and close the program without saving your artwork, after you confirm it looks all right.

NOTE *Graphics software and the best file formats for a particular use are covered in Chapter 20.*

Getting the Best Possible Scans

After you try your scanner a few times and you have some good photos saved to your hard drive, you can begin to explore the other features your scanner offers.

Unfortunately, you may not like the way the scans came out. When you print them, and even when you see them on the screen, they appear to be blurry or maybe the colors are all wrong.

Scanning software comes with a number of adjustments you can use to give your image professional quality. If the program only does minimal work, such as scanning and saving the picture, you want to do the touch up chores in Photoshop, Photo Deluxe, or whatever editing program you prefer.

Here are some hints and tips to help make your images look better.

■ **First, try the automatic mode.** Your scanning software uses a technology similar to the automatic exposure on a camera. It examines the artwork and uses its built-in logic to determine the best exposure values. If the preview image isn't accurate, use the software's color adjustments on the scanner to see if you can make it closer to the real thing. Adjustments for brightness and contrast are also there. If you aren't satisfied with the results, return to automatic mode, and then do the final scan of your picture. You can use your photo editing software to make additional modifications at this time.

NOTE *Don't expect perfect color accuracy. It's not an easy task to match up the color you see on your Mac's display with the colors on your printout. A lot of scanners have color profiles, however, which enable you to match up your scan with your display or output device. They may also include special software that allows some level of color matching. Many of these color profiles work with Apple's ColorSync technology to offer better color accuracy. Mac OS 9, for example, includes an improved version of ColorSync that helps the process along. I explain how to set up ColorSync to calibrate your Mac's display in Chapter 21.*

■ **Check the target resolution.**   As a rule of thumb, you should scan your image at twice the resolution you would normally use, to allow for quality loss when you edit or scale the artwork. Let's say you're scanning an image to your computer and you want to set it at 144 dots per inch (the measurement for resolution). The scanner should be set at twice that number, 288 dots per inch, or whatever is the closest available option your scanning software can give you. If the resolution you choose to scan is too high, then it greatly increases the size of your file, causing you to waste unnecessary space on your hard drive. But it doesn't do a thing to improve image quality. You should also remember that the larger the file is, the more memory is required to run the program (because it must load the artwork into memory). Also, if the file is bigger, the software typically uses a virtual memory-type data file on your hard drive to handle the additional data. And this only slows up the performance, sometimes rather severely.

NOTE *As an example of how much storage space and RAM a file can use, a large full-color photo can, depending on the target resolution, take up from 20 to 30 megabytes of storage space. Adobe Photoshop typically requires four or five times that figure in RAM to work with the photo without having to resort to using a disk-swap file to handle the data.*

■ **Make sure the photo or final scan isn't too large.**   If you need to make your photo large, you should scan it at a higher resolution. If have to make the picture eight to ten times larger or more, typical if you're scanning from a slide, you should increase resolution proportionally, so the quality of the picture doesn't suffer as a result. Otherwise, the little dots that make up the artwork get too large, making your photo look bad.

■ **Crop the photo.**   Every scanning program comes with a tool that enables you to select only the part of the photo you want to capture. This is called a *cropping tool,* and it uses an adjustable rectangle or *lasso* to capture whatever part of the image you want.

> NOTE   *When you crop an image, this also makes the automatic exposure feature work better because only the actual portion of the artwork you wish to scan is being checked.*

■ **Save using the right file format.**   If you need to print what you scan, you should use the TIFF format, which provides the best possible quality. This is pretty much an industry standard. If you need to use the art work for a Web site or you want to e-mail the artwork to friends or family, use the GIF or JPEG formats instead. Also keep the needs of users running Windows on their computers in mind and be sure files are named properly. For example, a GIF photo gets a .gif extension at the end of the filename. JPEG is .jpg, and TIFF is .tif.

> NOTE   *Unless you're scanning artwork for Web use, GIF is not a good choice. For one thing, it's limited to 256 colors and, therefore, puts a severe restriction on image quality. If your artwork is going to end up in print form, consider using TIF. Chapter 20 covers this subject in more detail.*

Hints and Tips on Scanner Installations for SCSI, USB, and FireWire

No matter what type of connection port your scanner uses, whether it's SCSI, USB, or FireWire, you should take some basic steps to make sure your scanner is set up properly.

SCSI Settings and Hardware Locking Switches

In theory, you should be able to take any SCSI device, be it a hard drive or scanner or something else, and put it at any free spot on the SCSI chain. That is, so long as no SCSI ID conflicts exist, all devices are powered on when in use, and the last physical device is terminated.

But, when it comes to SCSI, theories and realities don't always coincide. This is one reason we Mac users should relish the rapid switch to FireWire and USB, both of which are free of such considerations.

When it comes to SCSI-based scanners, they are sometimes more sensitive than some other devices to the position they occupy on the SCSI chain.

Before you start playing around with the scanner, check out the manufacturer's setup instructions to see if you should put the device in any certain position along the SCSI chain. As an example, some scanners made by Epson ship with the SCSI ID set to 2. Epson's instructions state this setup is only a precaution because ID 0 is often used for internal SCSI drives, ID 1 is used for another internal device, and ID 3 is typically used for CD drives.

On the other hand, Microtek recommends putting its scanners at the beginning of the SCSI chain, while some users say the scanners work best when placed at the end of the chain. Why this is so appears to depend on the design and the design goals of the manufacturer. The best thing to do is follow the instructions about SCSI chain placement as closely as possible the first time, as this often brings the most successful result.

NOTE   *If you have a Mac, such as the 8500 or 9500, that comes with both external and internal SCSI busses, give the external and internal device the same ID number and you should have no problem. This isn't always true with scanners, however, where the duplication of ID settings on both SCSI ports may cause problems. If the scanner fails to run, consider giving the scanner a unique ID (not duplicated on the other SCSI chain). Chapter 15 also covers the topic of dealing with SCSI chain hassles.*

A Look at FireWire and USB Scanners

When it comes to a scanner that occupies the USB or FireWire port, setup may seem to be a revelation. You don't have to configure ID settings or deal with termination. Once the software is installed, it's true plug and play.

This doesn't mean there's a free ride, however.

Both types of scanners come with special driver software to allow your Mac to recognize and operate these devices. As Apple upgrades its system software, no doubt the driver software that comes with these products must also be changed. For example, the arrival of Mac OS 9 definitely caused problems with some models using older USB drivers. Apple has included support for some popular USB products in its own USB Device Extension (such as SuperDisk and Zip removable drives),

Hints and Tips on Scanner Installations for SCSI, USB, and FireWire

and having another extension doing similar duty often meant the device would work erratically or not at all.

So, if things don't work quite right, check with the manufacturer's Web site or customer support people to see if you need a software update. Even if you bought the product brand new, this doesn't mean the software in the box is the latest. Updates could take months to filter down to the manufacturing and distribution process.

> NOTE   *Once again, I won't hesitate to recommend a popular Mac Web site that has current information on software updates, VersionTracker (http://www.versiontracker.com).*

Be Careful About Hardware Locking Switches

All scanners, whether they're cheap, low-end models, or expensive, professional-grade models, have fragile optical devices that may be damaged if they slide back and forth when they're in transit. To keep this from happening, manufacturers install a special locking switch or screw that keeps the device tight and safe.

If you don't unlock the optical devices before using the scanner, you may not only damage the scanner but, when the scanner locks up, system freezes may also occur.

Make sure you look at the manufacturer's instructions to locate and unlock the switch. Most switches are located beneath or behind the scanner, or under the cover. Even if the documentation isn't quite clear, the switch should be labeled lock and unlock or a small icon should appear, representing whether the switch is locked or unlocked.

If you get a new scanner that wasn't locked, you should verify the scanner works properly first. If any problems occur, contact the manufacturer or dealer as soon as possible to get a replacement. Even though the scanner may have only traveled a short distance from dealer to home, don't forget many of these products are made overseas and they've already endured a voyage of thousands of miles before they arrive at your home or office.

> NOTE   *In all fairness to the scanner manufacturers, I once received a review sample of a popular scanner for a newspaper article on the subject. The scanner came unlocked. Before panicking, I ran the unit through its paces and it worked just fine. But the cautionary note remains.*

What to Do If Something Goes Wrong

Scanners are complex devices that need to interact constantly with the software on your computer. With all their complexity and this constant interaction, conflicts are possible and you may have problems with your scanner as a result.

In fact, it's amazing the scanning process seems to work so well most of the time.

Your scanner can suddenly lock up for several reasons, all of which can cause your Mac to behave in a similar way. One major cause is that old SCSI voodoo, such as incorrect termination, conflicting SCSI ID, or the need to put the scanner in another position in the SCSI chain.

You may also need to deal with other problems. I divided these problems into two categories: SCSI and both FireWire and USB, so you can hone in on the material that applies to your particular setup.

How to Deal with SCSI Scanner Problems

A SCSI-based scanner is apt to have its own unique set of problems. Here are the ones that crop up most often:

- **Scanner freezes when computer is started up**   Whenever a scanner is first turned on, it needs to go through its own self-diagnostic process to make sure it's working all right. If some sort of light is flickering on the device or if it appears to freeze up, you could have a problem. One possible cause is an improperly set up SCSI chain. You should turn off your computer and attached devices, disconnect everything from the SCSI chain except the scanner, and give it the proper termination. Turn on the scanner, let it complete its startup process, and, if everything is all right, boot your Mac. If it still doesn't work, you should contact the manufacturer or a dealer. The unit may be defective.

NOTE   *Also remember, you should check to see if the scanner's optical assembly was correctly unlocked when you set it up the first time. Before checking this out, turn off your computer and then disconnect the scanner.*

- **Activating software causes scanner to freeze**   Now this could simply be a problem with your SCSI chain. Some SCSI chain problems definitely manifest themselves as apparent system or software-related conflicts. If your SCSI chain was set up incorrectly, the scanner could freeze up when the driver software communicates with the device. But the software could also be at fault. Scanning software is constantly being updated by the publishers to deal with the problems caused by the release of new system versions (such as Mac OS 9) to add new features or to fix bugs. You can find these updates at the publisher's Web site or at VersionTracker (http://www.versiontracker.com).

How to Deal with FireWire and USB Scanner Problems

Using a FireWire or USB-based scanner immediately eliminates the annoying ID and termination problems that occur with scanners connected to SCSI ports or chains.

You can even plug the scanner in while your computer is turned on, as long as the scanner software has been installed first.

Unfortunately, there's still no free ride and sometimes problems do rear their ugly heads.

- **The scanner isn't recognized.** First, make sure the device is plugged in and turned on. If it's a USB scanner, connected through a USB hub rather than directly to your Mac, you should first make sure you have connected the hub to the AC outlet (the hub may work with some, but not all, devices without AC power). Also, check with the manufacturer to see if it has a newer version of the hub available; you may want to check with the hub's manufacturer about a revised version. Certain hubs may not open their USB ports until after the parade of extensions begins marching across your Mac's screen. As a result, a problem might occur if the driver software for the device is loaded early in the startup process. If you encounter a problem like this, you should consider contacting the manufacturer or dealer to get a replacement.

NOTE *I encountered much the same problem with an early version of a Macally hub. The Macally hub was set up not to open the USB ports until well into the Mac's startup process, too late to recognize some of the attached devices. The revised version, sent free to users who encountered a problem, works fine with everything I've thrown at it.*

- **Scanning drivers may cause problems.** FireWire and USB scanners can be affected by problems with the scanner's driver software, just as SCSI scanners can. The arrival of Mac OS 9, with all its under-the-hood changes, did render some software incompatible. The publisher's Web site or the ever-popular VersionTracker (http://www.versiontracker.com) should be checked for the latest updates.

- **SCSI is faster than USB.**   While a scanner doesn't require as much bandwidth as a hard drive, a USB scanner is still slower at capturing artwork, especially if it's a big, complicated color picture. If you need to have the best possible speed and you have an available SCSI port or card, you should buy a SCSI scanner instead. If your Mac comes with FireWire ports, then by all means, consider purchasing a FireWire scanner (although such products have been slow to come to market).

NOTE   *The lack of a FireWire port shouldn't deter you completely. Any Mac with a PCI expansion slot and the older PowerBook G3 can be fitted with FireWire ports as moderately priced options. Check with your favorite Mac dealer for the products.*

Multifunction Printers: Do They Make Good Scanners?

Another class of scanner is the multifunction printer. A *multifunction printer* is a device that takes advantage of the similarity of image-capture technologies, for example, used for copiers, fax machines, and scanners. These functions are all combined in one unit, so you can copy, fax, print, and sometimes scan with a single product, rather than buy separate devices to fill all these purposes.

A number of major manufacturers have such products, and more and more of them are appearing in Mac form. In writing this book, I worked with multifunction printers from Brother and Canon, but Epson and HP also offer similar products.

NOTE   *The Epson multifunction printers implement fax features in a somewhat convoluted fashion. They require you to install fax software on your Mac to activate the faxing features on the unit itself. You may find, after all this, a plain old fax modem is enough.*

The question arises: Does combining all these functions into one product entail some compromises or is it a useful way to save some money?

The answer is a mixed bag: For the most part, the multifunction printers I've used make terrific fax machines, but they sometimes fall down in implementing the other functions. For example, print quality may not always match that of dedicated printers, the copy machine manufacturers shouldn't feel their business is threatened yet.

The way these products are set up contributes to the problems, at least as far as copy and scanning functions are provided. Rather than use a flatbed for placing down originals, these units work with a document feeder. This means you can't copy the pages from a document that can't be pulled through the machine (which lets out books or magazines, obviously, unless you tear out the pages).

For scanning purposes, a similar limitation comes to the fore. When you scan a document, you first preview the image, and then you perform your touch-ups to get the artwork properly cropped and the image quality settings just right. Then you do your final scan. When the artwork passes through the scanner on a document feeder, it must be sent through a second time to do the final scan. The chances that the artwork will be in exactly the same place are slim to none (unless you place it just right). So, you can't actually crop the image precisely till you open it in your photo-editing program after its scan and, of course, that entails an extra production step.

On the other hand, this doesn't mean you shouldn't consider such a product. As a second printer or as a low-cost machine for occasional copies, they serve you well, thank you. And, as I said (except for the limits of the Epson product previously stated), they make fine fax machines and are worth considering if you find the regular fax modem on your Mac isn't your cup of tea.

OCR Problems and Solutions

One of the biggest values of the scanner is the capability to capture the text on a document, enabling you to edit it on your Mac. But, because images are captured as bitmap artwork, you need special software to turn that into something you can deal with in your word processor program.

This brings us to *optical character recognition* (*OCR*). OCR is a technology that while not quite perfect in execution can save you the drudgery of hours of extra typing.

OCR software uses various forms of computer-based logic to examine the letterforms and numbers on a printed sheet and convert them to a form you can edit. Years ago, you needed an expensive computer to handle these chores. As with other computer-based technologies, OCR software has come down in price. In fact, some of it is downright cheap.

More to the point, most scanners come equipped with OCR software right out of the box. You don't have to pay extra to begin enjoying this technology.

OCR Trials and Tribulations

As great as it sounds on paper, OCR has some severe limitations. Even those claims of better than 99 percent accuracy should be taken with a grain of salt because all this means is 99 words out of every hundred will be accurate, so long as you supply a high-quality original with clear, crisp letters on it.

And, if the source document isn't in good shape, quality nosedives fast. This is one reason fax software currently no longer includes OCR recognition. Faxes are simply not clear and sharp enough to enable decent OCR recognition.

More important, the errors an OCR program makes are not as consistent or predictable as those a human typist might make. So careful proofreading is necessary to ensure that your final document accurately reflects the finished product. Even simple spell checking doesn't necessarily do the job because the OCR program is as apt to make the wrong choice with a word that looks similar to another word. The word is spelled correctly, it's just the wrong word.

Here are some steps you should take to make sure your OCR program does its best:

- ■ **Use a high-quality original.**   The best possible source document is laser or offset printed, with reasonably large type, using a readable typeface (see Figure 16-2). Such typefaces as Courier, Helvetica, Palatino, or Times are best. Artistic typefaces with flourishes or strange character shapes, smudges on the paper, or pen and pencil marks destroy the accuracy level.

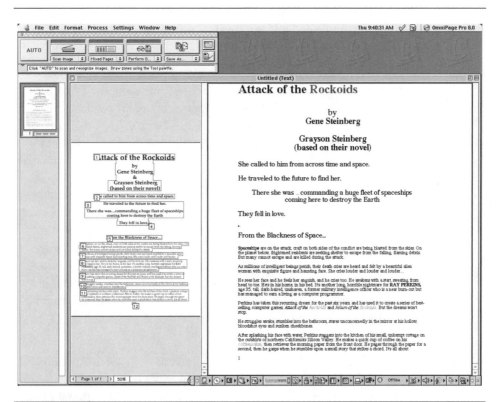

| FIGURE 16-2 | The author used Palatino on this document, which has been captured with near-perfect accuracy by Caere's OmniPage Professional |

■ **Stay away from faxes.**   If you must use a faxed document, insist the sender use the fine-resolution mode on the fax machine, in addition to using a high-quality printed document. This won't guarantee accuracy, but at least it can give you a better head start.

■ **Keep the paper straight and the scanner clean.**   As you place documents in your scanner, no doubt the unit's glass bed will accumulate fingerprints and dust over time. This can affect OCR accuracy. And, even though some scanning software, such as Caere's OmniPage Professional, claim to reorient documents before recognition, it's best to keep them straight.

■ **Newsprint and ultra thin paper troubles.**   If you have a thin printed document with visible text on the backside, don't be surprised if the OCR program captures that, too. The result could be a mish-mash of correct text and irrelevant text. Try backing up the sheet with a few sheets of paper to make it more opaque. You may also want to work with the OCR software's brightness control to see if a lower brightness setting makes the text on the reverse side of the document less visible.

■ **Avoid dot matrix documents.**   Older printers, such as the venerable Apple ImageWriter, used dot-matrix technology, meaning the letterforms were made of visible dots, much like the one on a store receipt. It may look perfectly fine when you read the document, but it can cause problems in recognizing the text. Some OCR programs offer a dot-matrix option but, in practice, I've found the setting doesn't always improve matters much.

TIP   *Another trick worth trying is to make a photocopy of a dot-matrix document. The copying process can smooth the dots and improve recognition accuracy.*

■ **Train the software.**   OmniPage Professional and other programs have training options. This way, you can store common recognition errors in a special file. This can help the program get a more accurate scan. But it's also time-consuming to implement. You may also have to set up separate training files for different types of documents and, if you handle a variety of originals, this may not be worth the effort.

■ **Spell check first.**   OCR software may include its own spell-checking capability, designed to work with the peculiar errors that affect the documents it recognizes. You may want to give it a run through with this feature before you edit the document in your word processing program.

To TWAIN or Not to TWAIN

Most scanning software comes with an add-on or plug-in that allows them to be used with a photo-editing program, such as Adobe Photo Deluxe or Photoshop. But some may also include a TWAIN driver, which is supposed to allow them to work with many more programs.

TWAIN, which is short for Technology Without An Interesting Name (yes, that's really what it means), was designed to extend the usefulness of scanning software. However, not all that many programs support the feature. Even Adobe's flagship desktop publishing products, InDesign and Illustrator, don't support TWAIN. And the other desktop publishing heavyweight, QuarkXPress, doesn't support TWAIN either.

In the end, it doesn't matter if the software comes as a plug-in or as a TWAIN driver. So long as it works with your installation, that's the only important consideration.

You Aren't Stuck with Bundled Software

With all that space to fill, it's no wonder scanners come with so much software. You get image-editing software, OCR software, and sometimes, a document organization program that enables you to keep a searchable database of all your scanning documents, so you can keep tabs on them as the number of files grows.

You aren't limited to those programs, however.

For example, Adobe PhotoDeluxe (a staple with cheap scanners) is great, especially for learning the basics of image editing. Adobe PhotoDeluxe even has a more advanced mode, where you can get an interface closer to that of its big brother, Photoshop. But, perhaps you prefer Photoshop or you want to look into one of the other options, such as the Corel's Photo Paint, which is also bundled with CorelDRAW.

Or, maybe the scanning software is too, well, simple for you. You want to do more of the retouching in the software before the image is captured as a file. You can find some powerful alternatives, for example, LaserSoft Imaging's SilverFast (also bundled with some Epson scanners) and ScanTastic from Second Glance Software (which has made Hewlett-Packard scanners compatible with Macs after a short absence from support for our favorite computing platform).

On the OCR front, some packages include ScanSoft's TextBridge or a bare-bones version of Caere's OmniPage. In either case, you can upgrade to OmniPage Professional or TextBridge Professional to gain new features and better performance.

There's no sense in buying something new until you try the programs that came bundled with your scanner, though. You might find they do exactly what you want and perform great.

What to Do If Something
Goes Wrong

Summing Up

In this chapter, you learned how to make the experience with your newly purchased scanner as trouble-free as possible. In a matter of hours, you can create beautiful documents filled with high-class artwork and photos or, in minutes, you can scan a picture of your first child to e-mail to your parents. No matter what you do with your scanner, it should make your computing experience more productive or rewarding (depending on what it is being used for) for a long time to come (or at least until a better one comes out).

In the next chapter, you learn more connecting input devices, such as mice, keyboards, and joysticks to your computer, as well as potential conflicts you may have with Mac OS 9 when installing such devices.

Chapter 17

Adding Input Devices

With Macs, it used to be so simple, it's almost ridiculous. The earliest Macs just came with a mouse and a keyboard. But then things changed and life became a little complicated.

Apple just gave you a mouse. You were on your own as to which keyboard to buy. That is, of course, unless you got a PowerBook.

This turned around when Apple included its inexpensive AppleDesign keyboards with their Performa line. Eventually, Apple realized this was a good idea, and soon all new Power Macs came with keyboards.

Not all Apple keyboards are to everyone's taste, unfortunately. The soft-touch AppleDesign keyboard, while a favorite of mine, was not quite suited to anyone used to pounding keys on a regular typewriter. They wanted keys with more resiliency, maybe with a bit more springiness.

And then there were those original USB keyboards that came with the iMac, the Blue & White Power Mac G3, and the G4. To make them cool, those keyboards ended up feeling small and cramped. Extra function keys were missing. Even though the keyboard has a feel that mimics that of the Apple Design keyboard, you feel restricted. Page navigation keys are especially difficult to get used to by some folks. The END key, which makes going right to the bottom of a document easy, is missing in action.

NOTE   *Even though my Blue & White Power Mac G3 came with one of those keyboards, I stubbornly continue to use the AppleDesign keyboard instead. Fortunately, this model has an ADB port, so the older keyboards can be used without need of a special adapter.*

As for the round mouse, definitely an acquired taste. You were left turning and twirling the mouse to point it in the right direction. Apple finally put a little grove on the mouse to help you along, but that was only part of the solution. Once again, some folks were left to look for something better.

All this quickly left the marketplace open to opportunities by other manufacturers to fill the gap. If you didn't like the keyboard and mouse Apple gave you free, for a few dollars extra, you could get precisely what you wanted, or at least something that came closer to that ideal.

Installing Keyboards, Mice, Graphic Tablets, Joysticks, and More

When you make the decision that the input devices Apple gave you are not quite suitable, you can buy a standard mouse and extended keyboard replacement with the look and feel you want, or you may decide you want something different.

Perhaps you want to buy a special type of mouse known as a *trackball* and an ergonomic keyboard, which can help people who experience hand or wrist pain with the standard variety keyboard. You can even get a joystick to play 3D games like Quake III: Arena and Descent 3, or a graphic tablet for drawing in such programs as Adobe Photoshop or Adobe Illustrator. Whatever your needs are, the market for such devices that offer these kinds of capabilities is growing rapidly, so you should find a wide selection of products available to meet your needs and work in harmony with Mac OS 9.

Here are some of the input devices currently available:

■ **Regular mouse**   A number of traditional-styled USB mice are now available on the market for iMac and Power Mac users who simply can't deal with that round mouse any longer. Many options are available, and many of these products are essentially similar in look and feel to Apple's original ADB ergonomic mouse. While most of these products do come in both ADB and USB versions, you should check first with the manufacturer or dealer before you purchase any of them.

■ **Mice with two or more buttons**   You PC users extol the virtues of your two-button mice, which give you extra functions when you click the right-mouse button; implying, in turn, that Mac users are losing out by not being able to take advantage of this terrific feature. If you have worked on a PC, or you'd like to see if one or more extra buttons are for you, never fear. Multibutton mice are out there for Macs, too. Companies such as Belkin, Kensington, Macally, and Microsoft produce a number of mice that come with two or more buttons. Most of these products come with special software that enables you to apply various functions to these buttons, enabling you to launch applications automatically or bring up contextual menus. This second function is essentially the same as using the right-mouse button on a PC mouse. Some of these products even come with a scrolling wheel that enables you to scroll through long documents without even clicking the mouse button once. Now, while some mice designed specifically for the Windows operating system work just fine on Macs without the necessary software, the multibutton mice won't be able to perform any of the additional functions without Mac-compatible drivers (see Figure 17-1). In addition, some of these input devices are variations on the standard mouse and mouse pad routine. For example, the Microsoft IntelliMouse line and some of the competitors use an optical sensor rather than a tracking ball, which means you don't have to clean the little ball every so often. You don't even need a mouse pad, just a hard, smooth surface. In fact, some of these devices work less efficiently with a mouse pad.

■ **Trackballs**   Think of a trackball as an upside-down mouse. The little ball you usually find on the bottom of most mice is located on the top of these devices. All you have to do is move the trackball around instead of having

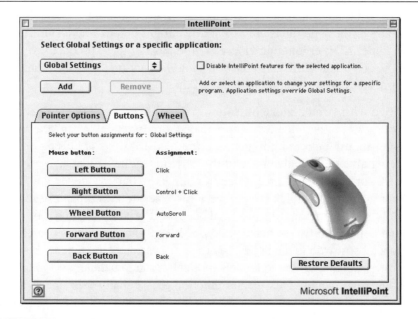

FIGURE 17-1   Microsoft's IntelliPoint software enables you to attach special functions to the extra keys on its IntelliMouse products

to slide the pointing device all around your desk (which may be an advantage if you have limited desk space). Depending on your preferences, you'll either find the trackball easier to use than a regular mouse or more of a strain on your wrist. If you do prefer it, however, a number of trackballs are available from various manufacturers, some of whom also make normal mice. The most famous of these would be one of the first trackballs, the Kensington Turbo Mouse (which is still being produced today), as well as the Orbit from the same company. The Orbit addresses the concerns of some users that the billiard ball-sized trackball of the Turbo Mouse was just too large for comfort. The Orbit's trackball is smaller, more comfortable for some users (such as your author). As with some mouse products, most of these trackballs come with two-to-four buttons, with the extra buttons available for special functions (using special driver software provided by the publisher).

■ **USB mouse extension**   If you just can't stand that annoying little round Apple USB mouse, a little plastic fitting like the UniTrap from Contour Design or the iCatch from MacSense could be what you're looking for. These little fittings attach to the top of the round mouse, making it look and feel just like a regular mouse. Both can be found in different colors, enabling you to match them with your computer whether you have a blueberry iMac or a hot new graphite G4.

■ **Wrist and mouse pads**   While you can't use these products as input devices, you can use them for other purposes. Both can be used to put your wrists in a position so they won't be so strained if you use your computer for a long time. The mouse pad can also make moving a mouse across a rough desktop or other kind of surface easier. Personally, I don't recommend the wristpad because I find it somewhat annoying and uncomfortable, which sort of works counter to its purpose, which is to provide additional comfort and reduce strain. If you do have wrist problems, though, you may find the wristpad places less stress on your wrists.

■ **Trackpads**   If you prefer the trackpad found on PowerBooks and iBook, where you move your fingers across the pad to move the cursor across the screen, you can try to find a stand alone trackpad. Of course, you may not get far. I've seen a number of these types of products shown over the years, but most of them have never appeared in the major Mac mail order catalogs. But, if you look hard enough, you will find some products are out there, such as the Cirque Glidepoint Desktop Trackpad.

■ **Replacement keyboards**   Your keyboard has gone south. One or more keys don't work or stick. If your old keyboard no longer works for you, you can choose from plenty of replacements. Among ADB models, Apple has the AppleDesign keyboard, plus a higher-cost Extended Keyboard II. And the same companies that produce mice and trackballs often have a line of keyboards as well. Many of these keyboards have a look and feel that closely matches those made by Apple, and they should be seriously considered as inexpensive alternatives. Just make sure they're good enough for your needs first.

■ **Ergonomic keyboards**   This keyboard variant is designed to reduce strain on your wrists. These keyboards are divided into three or four sections of keys, with each section facing toward a slight angle to provide better comfort while typing. Not all people may like dealing with these keyboards, however. Those who have serious wrist problems may find these keyboards a savior for their computing experience, while others may be completely unable to deal with them. Before you consider getting such a keyboard, try it out first, if possible, to see if it really is for you.

NOTE   *I understand the value of the ergonomic keyboard, but will only say in passing that I have tried them several times but have never had the patience to endure getting used to them. If you're quite used to a traditional keyboard, you need to be patient and allow yourself to become accustomed to the new routine.*

■ **Combo keyboards**   This sort of keyboard combines the pointing device with the keyboard in a single product. A few products of this sort are on the market. One of these, the Trackboard, is made by DataDesk. This keyboard includes a three-button trackball that is placed right on the keyboard. While some of these models also come with a numeric keypad, others force you to take the keypad out if you want to use the trackball instead.

■ **Joysticks**   This product can make the lives of gamers everywhere much, much easier, especially those playing 3D shooters like Unreal Tournament and flight simulation games like Falcon 4.0. The joystick can be used to perform the normal cursor functions, as well as those in a game. Some may actually find the joystick easier to use than a regular mouse for regular functions, even if they don't play any computer games. Some products worthy of consideration include the Ares Joystick from Ariston

Technologies, the iStick from Macally, and the Cyborg 3D USB Stick from Saitek.

NOTE

When I say some people may prefer a joystick to a regular mouse, I am not kidding. I know of one person who would never touch a computer game, but he was devoted to his joystick for regular mousing chores. He would never touch a mouse. Every time I visited the fellow, a former advertising agency executive who got into magazine publishing, I strived to get used to his joystick when I had to work on his Mac. I ended up begging for a mouse, but that's just me.

■ **Graphic tablet**   If you use your Mac for a lot of heavy graphic designing, you may find the standard mouse or trackball is unable to deliver the precise movements you would get from a pen or a pencil. A graphic tablet, from such companies as Wacom, actually uses a pen-like device, used to draw pictures on a flat panel, whose function is similar to that of a normal drawing pad. These tablets are pressure-sensitive, which means the lines you draw on the tablet become thicker and wider as you push down harder on the device. If you do need one of these products, then you may want to keep your regular mouse nearby for regular work.

Advice Before You Buy

Quite often, people buy a keyboard without even trying it out first. They'll check to see if the keyboard will work with their computer and if it has the features they need, and they'll order it without another thought. Once they get the keyboard home (or it's delivered), they may find they're happy with it. However, some people may also find the keyboard doesn't quite live up to what they expected. The keys may be too springy or too mushy, or they could be positioned in such awkward places, they are a challenge to find, even for the most experienced users.

Whether you like a keyboard depends mainly on your own personal preferences. You may like the feel of the AppleDesign keyboard, but you may be unable to stand the tiny keyboard that comes with the iMac and the later generation Power Macs.

To avoid being stuck with a keyboard you don't like, you should try whichever ones you're considering buying first before taking one of them home You may have to go through several keyboards until you find the one you like, but at least this can save you the hassle of a trip to return the keyboard and to find something that better suits your needs.

Installing Keyboards, Mice, Graphic Tablets, Joysticks, and More

Also, you shouldn't just try out keyboards. The same applies for mice, trackballs, joysticks, and pretty much all other input devices. You should try out the device yourself, at a dealer or on another user's Mac if you can. Make sure the input device lies comfortably in your hand, and that you can move it around, click, and double-click in reasonable comfort. I can see where a dealer might become impatient over the extended trial, but it's your wrist.

Once again, what input device you like depends on your personal preferences. You shouldn't just rely on reviews of certain products because then you are depending on the taste of someone who may have different expectations and needs than you do.

> **NOTE** *I am not denying the value of the review process. Even if you disagree with the reviewer, you may find clues as to whether a product is a real turkey and unsuitable for your needs. You'll want to pay special attention to discussions about special software that comes with an input device, and the potential incompatibilities. But, when it comes to one's preference, your opinion is as valuable as anyone's.*

The Difference Between ADB and USB

Since USB was made standard across the entire Mac product line, it has become much easier to install input devices, no matter what kind it is. You can't just install every single device you want, though, because you need to consider some precautions before doing so.

Also, remember, if you own an older Mac that comes with ADB ports, you may encounter other problems when hooking up and using such devices.

Installing ADB Input Devices

When installing an ADB device on your Mac, some of the same guidelines that apply to SCSI devices also apply to ADB devices.

Before installing any such device, you should first turn off your Mac. Then unplug the ADB product you need to remove and plug in the new mouse, keyboard, or whatever. Like SCSI devices, ADB devices are daisy-chained, so each one comes after the other. If your cables aren't long enough, you may need to find a longer cord or an expansion. If the product comes with special features that a normal keyboard or mouse doesn't have, like programmable keys, you may have to install some software first before you turn your Mac on again.

In the next section, you learn about some precautions about how to add multiple ADB devices safely.

Using Long ADB Chains

A single *ADB chain* is capable of handling up to 16 separate ADB devices. In theory, this should provide some great possibilities to add other input devices. You could have a mouse for all your normal work, a joystick to play the latest games, a graphic tablet for drawing, and maybe even another keyboard if your old one doesn't suit you (or if one of the folks who uses your Mac has wrist problems and you need an ergonomic keyboard).

Of course, even though something may appear to work in theory (as in USB), it just may not be practical. First of all, to get the best performance possible from your ADB chain, especially when you have multiple devices, you need to have enough current with which to run each attached device, not to mention the problem with signal loss as the ADB chain gets longer. If enough current isn't available, the performance of the device may suffer or it just may not work at all. A particularly stingy example is the PowerBook 5300's current capacity of only 200mA for its ADB port. The only practical devices to add are a mouse and a keyboard. That's pretty much all it can handle. If you add any more devices, you could activate the PowerBook's protection circuitry, which will shut down the ADB port. Or, you may even blow the circuit, requiring you to replace the logic board.

NOTE

Even if a single part on a Mac's logic board breaks, it's a rare dealer who will consider a component level repair. They will insist on replacing the entire thing. One main reason is that it can take hours to probe all the delicate circuitry on a modern computer logic board. For another thing, few repair centers are equipped to do so, even if they wanted to do that sort of troubleshooting. It's so much easier to plug in a new board (and if you pay for the service by the hour, it could end up being cheaper).

Different ADB devices have different electrical requirements, although Apple states in its own technical information on the subject that it's best to use only three or four devices at most.

If your Mac is an older model with two ADB ports, then that's good news for you. If your Mac comes with only one ADB port, however, you may be unable to use as many different devices at any one time as you may like.

The Difference Between ADB and USB

TIP   *Older Macs with a PCI expansion slot are not left out in the USB revolution.*
You can purchase a low-cost USB expansion card from such companies
as Belkin and Keyspan, which will enable you to explore the new world
of plug-and-play input devices.

Precautions When Using ADB Devices

You may have once accidentally unplugged the ADB plug from your keyboard or mouse. Once you plugged it back in, however, you noticed response was slow, the cursor took forever to move across the screen. While a simple restart is all that is required to fix this problem, it should serve as a severe warning.

When removing or attaching ADB devices, you should first shut down your Mac. Apple specifically says to do this in its technical information. If you remove or attach an ADB device while your computer is on, you may not only face erratic performance. Whenever you plug in or unplug any ADB device, it could cause a brief short circuit that may damage the input device you're removing or attaching. It may even damage your Mac, meaning you'll have to replace the logic board or use another ADB port.

If you accidentally unplug a device from its ADB port, make sure you restart your computer right away. Even if your Mac works after it starts up again, don't get overconfident. You may just be lucky. While some folks manage to get away with it, I've heard a tale or two of getting a fried ADB port as a result.

Better safe than sorry.

Installing USB Input Devices

Installing a USB device is relatively simple compared to ADB. You just plug it in to a free USB port on your Mac or on a USB hub. If you're using a hub, you need to be aware of some precautions, explained later in this chapter.

After connecting the device, install any needed software, restart, and everything should be all right. If you do encounter problems, however, I recommend you check out the section called "Dealing with USB Device Problems," found near the end of this chapter.

When Apple introduced USB on its product line for the first time with the release of the original iMac, in August 1998, many people with older computers weren't happy. Mac users, who needed them for their work as well as for entertainment, didn't know what to do with all those keyboards, mice, trackballs, joysticks, graphics tablets, and other input devices they had added to their Macs over the years.

At first glance, the question arose, why USB? Actually, Intel tried to get the USB standard accepted on the PC side of the world, but it wasn't terribly successful. With few USB products being released for the PC, it was rather unfortunate, considering USB truly provided plug-and-play unparalleled by anything before it (except perhaps by Apple's FireWire, which didn't become popular until the release of the Blue & White Power Mac G3 in early 1999 with two FireWire ports). Many Windows users never even had the chance to experience true plug-and-play, something that would have made their lives much easier.

The benefits of USB, when it works properly, are significant. Such devices can be attached or removed without restarting or shutting down your computer, unless you need to install certain driver software for the device to work. In addition, you should be able to add up to 127 devices for each USB bus, although several things limit this possibility (I explain this a little later).

A USB chain doesn't only handle input devices, however. You can also add other types of devices like CD writers, Zip drivers, digital cameras, inkjet and laser printers, scanners, modems, and interfaces for monitors and other displays. These are only a few USB products currently available on the market.

The so-called Bronze PowerBook G3, the iMac, Blue & White Power Macintosh G3, and the G4 come with two USB ports each, and the iBook has just one. If you want to add other devices, then you have to purchase a USB hub.

USB Isn't Perfect

Of course, while USB appears to be the perfect technology on the surface, it has flaws, just as everything else does. One USB bus is only capable of a speed of up to 12 Mbps, but even one device that takes up a lot of this bandwidth can severely decrease performance for the other USB devices using the same bus. Products like input devices, such as keyboards and mice, do not tax the USB chain much at all, but a hard drive and removable drive connected to the same USB chain will be unable to perform together at their full capacity. That's because each uses the maximum amount of bandwidth on the bus.

So, you can expect that copying a file from a USB hard drive to a USB Zip drive will take much longer than if you were just using one device at a time or copying from your Mac's own hard drive.

With the release of the Power Mac G4, the new iMac, and the iMac DV's, Apple has tried to deal with this issue by providing one separate bus for each USB port, instead of having two ports share the same bus. The new designs also enable you to boot from a USB removable drive or a hard drive, a feature earlier versions of USB lacked on Apple products.

The Difference Between ADB and USB

Power is also a limiting factor. One USB port only has enough power to run a few low-power devices, such as keyboards. Some USB devices use their own power supplies but, if you add too many low-power devices together, they can serve to exceed the current provided by the USB port and require you to get a hub with the extra ports to provide the additional current (if they're connected to an AC outlet, that is).

Troubleshooting Input Device Problems

Now, when dealing with an input device, whether it uses an ADB or USB connection, you may encounter certain problems that are part of the standard, or typical of the ills that affect any personal computer user.

Dealing with ADB Device Problems

Besides being limited to the number of devices you can put on one ADB chain, you may also encounter other problems as well.

The following are some of the issues you may face when working with ADB devices, along with instructions on how to fix them.

- **Erratic mouse motion**   Where once your mouse moved smoothly, now it just won't work at all. Whenever you try to move it across the screen, the cursor doesn't move in concert or it suddenly jumps to another part of the screen. Usually this is because the mouse or trackball is dirty. With a mouse, you should be able to open the ring at the bottom. You may have to rotate the ring partially to loosen it or it may just snap off. After opening the ring, put the mouse ball in your hand or on some type of soft surface (like a mouse pad). Then use a cotton swab and some rubbing alcohol to clean the mouse ball and the little roller assemblies inside the mouse itself. A trackball's layout is similar, as are the steps to clean it. Check the instructions that come with the input device for the specifics. If cleaning the mouse or trackball doesn't solve your problem, try contacting the manufacturer to get a replacement or buy an entirely new one.

- **Mouse button won't work**   If you have a regular mouse, this probably means it's time to dump your trusty rodent and buy a new mouse. Some manufacturers, like Kensington, used to repair or replace the buttons on their input devices for a small fee, but the lowered cost of input devices makes such simple repair less practical. Contact the manufacturer or look at the product's warranty for further information.

■ **Conflicts with software**   Graphic tablets and mice with two buttons or more need special software to perform their unique functions. You should check the manufacturer's Web site as often as you can, so you can get the latest updates. For example, when Mac OS 9 was released, a number of programs required updates to be compatible. Examples include Kensington's MouseWorks software, used for all their mouse and trackball products. If you can live without the extra button, and the software update isn't available, you can see whether Apple's own Mouse Control Panel will suit. But for the long run, the benefits of having all those extra buttons are lost if you don't have the software to deliver the features.

NOTE   *Input device software conflicts aren't always obvious as to their source. For example, I encountered frequent crashes when opening a message in Claris Emailer when trying an updated release of Kensington's MouseWorks software. A quick visit to Casady & Greene's Conflict Catcher and a short period of work with their Conflict Test produced the culprit. Sure enough, disabling the MouseWorks extension eliminated the problem (a new update was posted soon thereafter).*

■ **Some keys don't work**   You press the letter *T* and nothing happens. Should this occur, you may be unable to do much to address the problem. Not many keyboards let you change individual keys. You can, however, try removing the keytop. Usually a small flat-head screwdriver can pry it off. Clean out the switch assembly and its surroundings as well as you can. Also, Radio Shack and similar stores sell electrical contact spray, which may help solve your problems by cleaning out the electrical contents (they're actually designed for old-fashioned TV tuners and the knobs on a home stereo system). If this doesn't solve the problem, however, you should consider purchasing a new keyboard.

■ **Numeric keypad won't work**   You may like using the numeric keypad to enter numbers or for other special function, like navigating through documents in Microsoft Word. But what should you do if the numeric keypad stops working for no apparent reason? If you use a regular keyboard that comes with a NUMLOCK light, be sure it's glowing. If it isn't, then press the NUM LOCK key on the keypad to see if NUMLOCK lights up before you

Troubleshooting Input
Device Problems

start working with it again. Remember, some programs may not work with the numeric keypad. Check the documentation for the program or an available Help menu if you don't know.

- **Keyboard won't work** If you try to type something on your keyboard, nothing happens. While the mouse keeps working, the keyboard seems to be frozen. Don't automatically assume this is a problem with the keyboard. Check the ADB cables because they can loosen easily. If you find the ADB cables have become disconnected, then use your mouse (assuming IT works) to activate the Shut down command from the Special menu before reconnecting everything else. If the keyboard is plugged in, restart the computer and, as it is starting up, hold down the SHIFT key to load with the extensions off to see if the keyboard works once your computer is finished booting up. If the keyboard still doesn't work, try restarting from your system CD. If that doesn't work, use another keyboard cable if one is available, or use another keyboard if you have one. If you don't have either of these, contact your dealer. Apple's products all have a one-year warranty (unless you've opted for AppleCare or a third party's extended warranty program). Keyboards from other companies may have longer warranties. If the warranty has expired, don't get too angry because keyboards are not expensive and many are available to purchase should your old one should fail you.

- **Liquid on the keyboard** If you accidentally spill any kind of liquid onto your keyboard, whether it's water or coffee, immediately turn off your Mac and any peripherals. Unplug the keyboard and put it upside down on a paper towel or cloth to drain out the extra liquid. Then turn it right-side up again and try to pop out the keys, using a good paper towel or cloth to remove as much of the liquid as possible. In addition, you may want to try to wash the keyboard with distilled water. Make sure you give the keyboard enough time to air dry completely before you attempt to use it again. The cleanup process may not work, however. The keyboard may be completely ruined, so be prepared to purchase a new one.

- **Keyboard beeps instead of displaying character** Go directly to your Mac OS 9 Control Panels folder (from the Apple menu or directly). Check to see if the Easy Access Control Panel is anywhere in sight. This Control Panel is designed to make your Mac's keyboard easier to use by folks with disabilities. If Easy Access is running, holding down the RETURN key for over five seconds will turn it on. If you don't need Easy Access, go ahead and use Extensions Manager to deactivate the program and restart. Your keyboard functions should return to normal.

■ **ADB port or cable is defective**   If nothing else seems to fix your problems, the ADB port itself may be defective. Some older Macs come with two ADB ports, so if one is broken, you can use the other one. That way you don't have to expend the cash to get a new logic board. Although the AppleDesign ADB keyboard (and keyboards similar to it) come with just one ADB port to connect a mouse, others, like Apple's Extended Keyboard and Kensington's Keyboard in a Box, come with two. If one doesn't work, you can use the other. If these steps still don't end your difficulties, use a different keyboard cable (as long as it isn't wired directly into your keyboard, as it is in the AppleDesign keyboard). If all else fails, it's probably time to get a new mouse or keyboard.

NOTE   *Repair shops might offer to fix a broken cable that's hardwired to a keyboard. If such a repair can be done cheaply enough, it's worth it. But it may just be time to give that old keyboard a decent burial.*

Dealing with USB Device Problems

Even though USB has made adding devices to your Mac much easier, the new standard doesn't come without its problems, a few of which have already been mentioned briefly. For the most part, adopting this industry-standard connection port has been one of Apple's best decisions in a while. If you do encounter problems, though, your Mac will, at least sometimes, display an error message telling you about the problem. Here are some of the most common error messages.

■ **No Driver Found**   Should this message appear, it won't be this general. The message will also give the name of the USB device for which there is no driver. Most keyboards or mice perform functions that require special software (such as with multibutton mice) and most other USB devices do need software to run. If you get this message, open Extensions Manager to see if the driver is both there and active. If the driver is not active, turn it on by clicking the check box to the left of the name before restarting. If you can't find the driver software anywhere, however, then find the CD that came with the device and reinstall the software. Remember, with the release of Mac OS 9, Apple has added a USB Driver Extension that supports a number of USB devices, including SuperDisk and Zip drives. To see if the device works with the extension, try it before you install the software. Check to see if the device's features work. If they don't, you need to install the needed software.

■ **Not Enough Power to Function**   As I mentioned earlier, a USB device without its own power supply draws current from the USB bus. If enough current isn't available to power all the attached devices, your computer will exhibit a warning. If the USB device is connected to a power supply through an AC adapter, double check to make sure it's plugged in and the USB device is on (some of them have power switches and others don't). If the product doesn't come with its own adapter, attach it directly to an open USB port on your Mac, instead of daisy-chaining it. You can also purchase a hub that runs on its own power when it's plugged in, which should provide enough power to make that additional device work.

■ **Not Enough Power for All Functions**   This error message can be considered another aspect of the previous one. This message means the device only partially works. The solutions for this problem are the same as for the previous one. If the product comes with its own power supply, double check that it's plugged in and turned on. If the product doesn't have a separate power supply, plug it directly into a self-powered hub or a free USB port on your Mac.

■ **USB peripheral connected through hub isn't recognized**   Certain USB hubs, like the early ones produced by Macally, will not open a connection port until the driver software actually recognizes the device connected to it. Because not all USB devices work in the same matter, this may result in problems when using certain devices. If you have an open USB port available from your Mac or keyboard, hook the device up to it directly, instead of through the hub (or you can do it the other way around). If this doesn't solve the problem, check the manufacturer's Web site for any software updates that do fix it or contact them to get a newer version of the product that eliminates the problem.

■ **Check for software updates constantly**   As USB continues to develop for the Mac, you should check the Web site of the manufacturer that produces the USB products you use often for updates to their driver software. A great source for software information and links is VersionTracker (http://www. versiontracker.com). Some of the conflicts are especially irksome because they're not always readily identifiable as belonging to one USB driver or another. For example, I once worked on an iMac that would freeze solid shortly after the startup process (USB extensions load into RAM early on). It was finally isolated to a conflict with the USB driver used for the client's scanner (fixed soon thereafter with an update from the manufacturer). Other conflicts result in disabling the function of one USB device, even though the driver is used for another device. This is not entirely predictable, so the best remedy is to turn off all of your USB device extensions in Extensions Manager (or just use Conflict Catcher and run its Conflict Test), except for Apple's, then enable them one by one until the problem returns.

■ **Liquid spilled on the keyboard**   You can fix this problem using the same process I described for cleaning a wet ADB keyboard. Once again, hope the process works, and realize if it doesn't, you need to get a replacement or a new keyboard.

Summing Up

While many people are not fond of the recent offerings in terms of input devices that Apple has been shipping with its newest machines, plenty of alternatives are available right now. And switching to USB, assuming you don't have older input devices you need, can be a big plus, especially as it continues to develop in the future.

In the next chapter, I deal with installing and using other devices you can add to spruce up your Mac, including CD writers, speakers, and digital cameras.

Summing Up

Chapter 18

The Extras: CD Writers, Digital Cameras, Speakers, and More

A mong the list of Mac peripherals, removable drives, hard drives, and input devices seem to serve more of a functional purpose than a creative one. Usually, these peripherals are necessities rather than fun, unless you think copying files back and forth to and from disks is fun. Other devices do enable you to expand your creativity, though, with the only limit being your imagination (and, perhaps, how deep your pockets are).

These other devices include digital cameras, CD writers, and speakers. All of these are described in detail in this chapter.

Adding a CD Writer

A CD writer uses optical media (CD-R and/or CD-RW) and can serve both a functional and a creative purpose. If you want to store files for a long period of time, you can copy them to a CD and they can last for many years, as almost any CD outlasts a removable disk or hard drive (both of which are more prone to damage and dust). A CD can hold between 600 and 700 MB of data, enough room to keep not only your text documents, but complicated images and graphics documents as well.

NOTE *CD-R is a write-once CD-writing format, meaning you cannot rewrite the contents of a CD (although on some CD products, you can write multisessions, which enables you to write additional data if space is available). CD-RW, or CD rewritable, is a format that enables you to rewrite a specially designed CD up to 1,000 times.*

As for the creative (and, frankly, entertainment-oriented) purpose, the CD can be used to hold and play your favorite songs. It's still true some albums have only one or two hit songs, and the rest is fluff and filler. No doubt, you may be tired of switching from CD to CD to hear one song on several different albums. So, to save yourself the hassle, you can put all your favorite tunes on one CD, the same as you used to do with a tape cassette.

CAUTION *I'm not suggesting you make pirated copies of a music recording. I expect you'll be using the CD the same way a tape cassette is used, to make personal copies for your own use. Attempting to sell or distribute copies of such a CD can definitely run you afoul of the law.*

As a result, you never have to worry about rummaging through your collection again.

Before you can do either of these things, however, you need special software to copy your files or songs to a CD, and then to record them on the CD itself. Most CD writers come with such software, the most popular of which is Adaptec's Toast CD recording software (as shown in Figure 18-1). This program enables you to perform the necessary functions to *burn a CD* (another name for putting data on a CD).

NOTE   *When you order a CD recorder, double-check to see that the software is actually provided and that it isn't an extra cost option. If the software is an extra cost option, look at a competing product with bundled software to see which is the better value.*

CD writers have grown cheaper and more popular, and now cost little more than a nonrecording CD-ROM drive of only a few years ago. You can get CD writers from such manufacturers as APS Technologies, EZQuest, LaCie, QPS Inc., Mitsubishi, Panasonic, PowerUser, Ricoh, Sony, Yamaha, and Xtreme.

NOTE   *Other than the major electronics manufacturers, many of the companies who sell CD recorders are simply using mechanisms made by other companies, in custom cases with custom documentation and bundled software.*

Adding a CD Writer

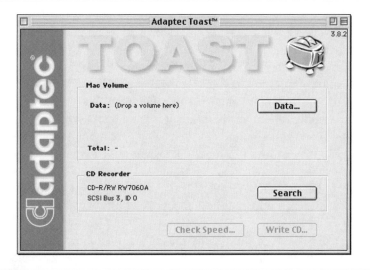

| **FIGURE 18-1** | Adaptec's Toast is one of the most used CD writing programs available for the Mac |

Performance levels range from 1x (meaning the drive spins at the normal CD rate of approximately 74 minutes for 650MB of data, plus time to verify or read back the data to check for integrity) to 12x (meaning the drive spins twelve times faster), and no doubt faster CD recorders will be out by the time you read this book.

The speeds you can achieve depend on the kind of interface your Mac supports. USB is the slowest, limited to 12 Mbps, barely capable of supporting a 4x CD writer (because of overhead in handling the copying of data to the drive). FireWire and SCSI, with much higher maximum data rates, can support the fastest drives available.

CD Writer Formats

The regular CD format records audio and data on a blank CD, which typically costs from one to three dollars at a local computer store, depending on the brand and quantity. If you are buying blanks for a faster CD writer, check the label for its performance rating.

I'm not about to recommend a specific brand of CD, except to suggest you try a couple from a particular manufacturer with noncritical material. If that brand performs to your satisfaction, you can consider buying larger quantities if you need them. Also, make certain your CD media is rated to handle the maximum speed of your drive. 8x CDs, for example, because of their tighter tolerances, may be a bit more costly than other CD blanks.

The standard CD media can be written on once, but a multiple session feature enables you to write separate blocks of data to the same CD, up to its maximum capacity. Each segment or session appears on your Mac's desktop as a separate drive icon.

The other CD format is CD-RW, which supports blank media that can be used in a fashion similar to a regular removable hard drive (but typically at a slower speed). You can erase and rewrite data up to 1,000 times. CD-RW media costs roughly five times the price of a regular CD. This format is worth the extra cost if you actually intend to reuse the disk more than five times. Otherwise, you may as well use regular CDs and toss them out if you no longer need them.

The other negative about CD-RW is that many regular CD-ROM drives and some DVD drives may not read these discs. The best way to check this out is simply to try it.

Also, the CD-RW format typically maxes out at a 4x recording speed, while the regular CD-ROM format can deliver up to 8x and *12x* performance levels (with SCSI and FireWire versions) in recording mode.

Installing the CD Writer

CD writers either use an ATA, SCSI, USB, or FireWire connection. The choice of what to buy depends on the kind of Mac you have. If your Mac has FireWire ports, of course, you want to buy a CD writer with that interface because it provides the fastest possible performance.

> NOTE   *If you want to install an ATA-based CD writer as a second internal device, make sure your Mac supports the "slave" mode (the name for a second device installed on the ATA bus) and has a front slot in which to insert the mechanism that so you can, with a special front bezel, insert the CDs.*

Before you install the device, make sure you have an open port that the writer requires. Then install any driver software that comes with the device on a CD, as well as any CD burning software, such as the previously mentioned Toast, which you need to record data on your CDs.

Installing CD software is no different from installing any Mac program. You put the CD in your regular Mac's CD drive, launch the installer, let it do its thing, and then restart. The subject of software installations is discussed in more detail in Chapter 10.

> NOTE   *A restart is required only if the installation software puts items in the System Folder.*

Once you install the software and restart, you're ready to plug in the device. But if you are installing a SCSI device, turn off your computer and peripherals first. Make sure you pay careful attention to proper SCSI ID numbers and termination (if that applies) as you install the device. If the SCSI device uses USB or FireWire, however, shutting down your Mac is unnecessary. To learn more about SCSI, USB- and FireWire-related issues, also check out Chapters 15 and 16.

> NOTE   *If you are plugging a SCSI CD writer into a SCSI-to-USB adapter on a newer Mac, such as an iMac or Blue & White Power Mac G3 or G4, I still recommend you turn off your computer. While the adapter is plugged into a hot-swappable USB port, the SCSI issues you have to deal with, such as termination and IDs, are present.*

After following these simple instructions, you are ready to roll. You can start recording your favorite songs or critical data you need to keep for many years almost immediately.

Adding a CD Writer

Here's the basic setup to make a CD:

> **NOTE**   *Depending on the sort of CD you want to make, Toast offers several options for writing a recording session. The steps described here cover the most basic process of copying files to your blank CD.*

1. Launch your CD writing program (such as Adaptec's Toast), as shown in Figure 18-2.

> **NOTE**   *Turning off file sharing is recommended, if you have file sharing on, for maximum performance with your CD writing software. This is because possible network activity could affect the writing speed you can achieve with the CD recorder.*

2. Insert a blank CD into the drive.

3. Locate, and then drag-and-drop files, folders, or disks to CD software window or use the appropriate command to add files you want to copy to the CD (see Figure 18-3).

4. Click the Data button to check the files.

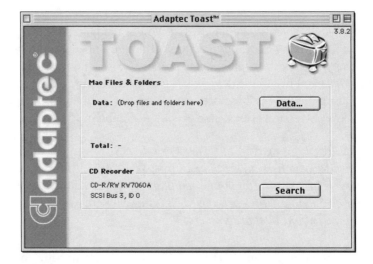

FIGURE 18-2   Toast is up and running and ready to record your CD

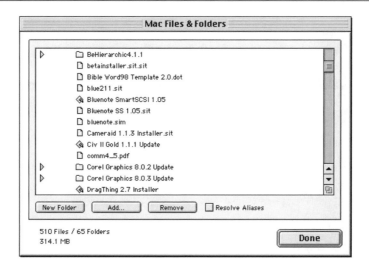

FIGURE 18-3 Here's a typical list of files you might want to archive on a CD

5. To change the CD's name from untitled, double-click the name CD (see Figure 18-4).

6. When you're satisfied the list of files is correct, click Done to close the window.

7. To write your CD, click the Write Session button (see Figure 18-5) and then choose the CD writing parameters, such as the speed at which the

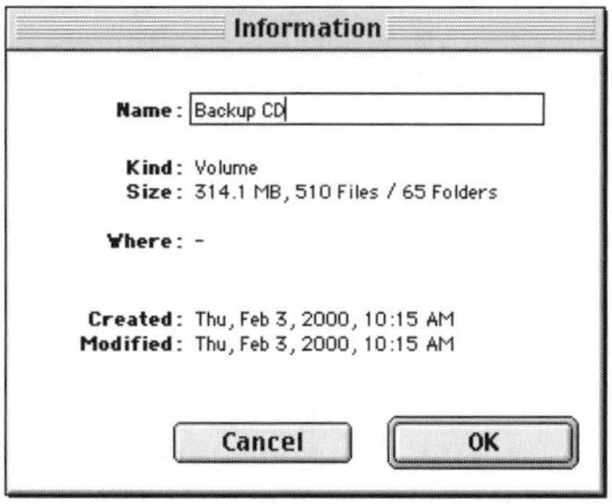

FIGURE 18-4 Name the CD in a way that suits the contents

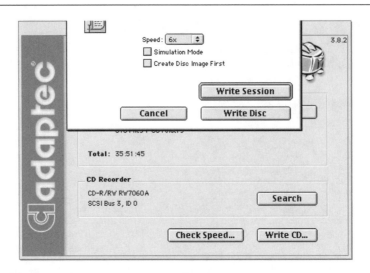

Speed: 6x
☐ Simulation Mode
☐ Create Disc Image First

3.8.2

Write Session

Cancel   Write Disc

Total: 35:51:45

CD Recorder

CD-R/RW RW7060A
SCSI Bus 3, ID 0   Search

Check Speed...   Write CD...

FIGURE 18-5   Select your CD write options here—defaults are a good starting point till you have a chance to test the process a few times

drive runs. This may be a matter of trial and error. If you get error messages when trying to verify a CD, slow it down. Also, expect to run an audio CD at a slower speed than a data CD.

8. Now it's time to write your CD. Toast, for example, gives you the option of saving everything to a disk image file first, which results in a better job of copying data to the CD.

9. If you are writing data to the CD, allow the program to verify the files, so you know everything was copied properly.

10. After the session is finished, check the CD in your Mac's regular CD drive to make sure it can be read and files can be read from it.

CD Writer Problems and Solutions

As you saw in the previous section, CD software, such as Adaptec Toast, come with a simple drag-and-drop interface. You drag files, folders, or disks on to the program's main window to have them added to your CD recording session.

Following this simple procedure, with attention to the proper file format, is usually enough to get you rolling. But you might run into an occasional difficulty.

As you see from the following information, writing a CD involves many complex steps, even though the basic setup procedures are easy. Plenty can go wrong with a particular writing session, so you can use the following description of some of the problems you can face, specifically when using Toast, to help solve them.

■ **While a hard drive that isn't filled completely seems totally defragmented, Toast still shows a message saying the volume is filled.**   If you have Norton FileSaver, turn it off for the volume you're copying before recording any data onto a CD. The hidden files are then deleted by FileSaver and the right amount of space used on your hard drive is reported by Toast.

■ **This message shows up: The Apple CD-ROM driver could not be found. Would you like to look for it?**   Click OK to this message, and then choose the Apple CD/DVD Driver from the Extensions folder of the System Folder on your startup disk.

■ **Whenever you mount a CD, some of the windows are open, even though you closed them on the original disk.**   Eject the CD and then put it back into your CD-ROM drive before doing anything else. The Finder saves information on each disk that's mounted on your desktop and automatically saves the current positions of all your windows.

■ **Although the amount of data you place on the CD-R from a hard disk doesn't fill the CD, you still get a message saying there isn't enough room left for that data.**   With a commercial disk optimizing program, such as Alsoft's PlusOptimizer, Norton Speed Disk, or TechTool Pro, defragment the volume you want to copy to the CD. Or, you can choose the Optimize option in the Volume Selection window.

NOTE   *The minimum size of the files on a CD may differ from those on your Mac's hard drive, which may also account for the disparity.*

■ **Even after checking Optimize for Size, the size of the data you're writing, which is displayed in the main window, seems too large.**   Within the main window, click Check Speed. Before the speed is checked, the data is optimized. This allows the data to be retrieved faster from the CD you record, and then its real size is displayed in the main window.

■ **When you try to choose a volume, this message appears: "Your Volume" could not be unmounted. All open files and programs on this volume must be closed first.**   Do exactly as the message says. Quit any currently running applications and close any open files. Or, you can select the Optimize option. This enables you to write files and applications currently open and also allow for faster access when they're retrieved from the CD.

■ **If you try to drag files or folders onto the selection window, this message appears: Please insert disk…At the File Server "The Server" registered as…Some aliases cannot be resolved.**   Make sure the Resolve Aliases check box has been unchecked. This means aliases will be loaded as aliases and they will not be resolved.

■ **If you try to drag files or folders onto the selection window, this message appears: Couldn't complete the last command because the volume could not be found. Error code=-35.**   Make sure the correct hard disk has been mounted already (check the icons on your Mac's desktop) or uncheck the Resolve Aliases check box.

NOTE   *If you're copying files from a removable disk, such as a Jaz, Zip, or SuperDisk, and you cannot get the disk media to mount, make sure Apple's USB Device Extension (part of your Mac OS 9 installation) or the correct drivers provided with the product are installed.*

■ **When a disc in the format "Mac Files & Folders" has been inserted, the icons of files created in certain programs don't appear as they would usually look.**   Before you try to write a CD with files from a certain program, place a folder containing that program on your hard disk so the Finder records the icon. You may also have to rebuild the desktop for the changes to take.

■ **When you're making an audio CD and you put an audio file into the window, this message appears: Only 16 bit/44 kHz sound can be written. "Your File" is not in this format.**   Make sure your sound file is saved in one of the following formats: 16 Bit, 44.1 kHz, stereo, or mono.

■ **The word "Mono" in brackets is displayed along with the file's name when you're making an audio CD.**   This means the audio track isn't in the correct format. You need to convert the file to stereo format.

■ **When you try to duplicate an audio CD on a disc replicator, it reports something is wrong with the master.**   You might consider a program such as Toast CD-DA to write your audio master.

■ **Noises are heard between the various audio tracks, although you correctly copied all the data onto your CD.**   Check the Web site of the manufacturer of your CD writer for any updates to the software for the device. Some CD writers, for example, need upgrades to make them fully compatible with Mac OS 9.

■ **Before you try to write an audio CD, this message appears: Your recorder does not support index generation. All index markers will be ignored.**   If having index points on your CD is necessary (they aren't used often), use a program such as Toast CD-DA, which has the capability to write in disc-at-once mode.

■ **A SCSI hard drive has been recorded on to your CD, but the disc can't be read whenever you put it into your CD-ROM drive.**   Mount the original drive on your desktop and write the data over again, this time in the ISO 9660 format, instead of the using SCSI Copy mode.

■ **The tracks on one disc need to copied to other discs, but an error message appears whenever you try to check the speed or to write the data.**   Use a program such as ASTARTE CD-Copy to take the individual tracks off the CD, so they can be copied to other discs.

■ **A bootable CD was copied, but the copy is not bootable.**   Before you try to write the data on your CD, make sure you have used the bootable option and Clear Driver Description Map has been unchecked in the Options.

NOTE   *Before you make a bootable CD, be certain you have the software license to do so. You can, for example, make a single backup copy of most programs for your own use, including an operating system upgrade, without going afoul of the license restrictions.*

■ **When you try to mount a disc image, this message appears: "Your File" is fragmented. Please use a commercial Disk Optimizer to defragment the volume "Your Volume." You can also try to duplicate the file or to copy it to another volume.**   This one is self-explanatory.

Adding a CD Writer

Use a program such as Alsoft's PlusOptimizer, Norton Speed Disk, or TechTool Pro to defragment the hard disk that has the disk image itself. You can also make a copy of the image or put it on a different volume.

> **NOTE** *You may also see the previous error message if enough free space isn't on your Mac's hard drive to write the actual disk image.*

■ **This message appears: The drive reported an error: Sense Key=... Sense Code=0x Description**. This isn't something I can solve for you in this book because so many CD drives are available. If you get any error like this, make sure the Sense Code and Description have been written down, so you can give this information to technical support people at Adaptec (if the product is one of Adaptec's), or the publisher of whatever program you're using, for them to help you.

■ **This message appears: A RAM cache of *x* MB was requested, but only *y* MB could be allocated. To make more memory available, try quitting other running applications (if any).** For the RAM cache used to write the session, Toast needs more than the amount of RAM available on your Mac. Do as the message says and quit any other applications currently running.

■ **This message appears: Couldn't complete the last command because of a Mac OS error. Error code=2.** Using software such as ASTARTE CD-Copy, take the various tracks off the CD separately.

■ **This message appears: The SCSI connection is not stable. Please check the cables and termination.** Do as the message says. Check to make sure all your cables are properly connected and termination is correctly set. Chapter 15 covers the subject of SCSI voodoo (situations where the SCSI chain isn't working well in your setup) in more detail.

■ **This message appears: You cannot write this disk with the selected recorder.** This problem usually only occurs when you're trying to use your CD writer to record in less-common formats, such as CD-I, Multitrack CD-ROM, and Video CD. Go to the manufacturer's Web site to see if it has an update to the software that allows your writer to work with these formats.

■ **This message appears: An unknown driver is installed for SCSI ID x. If you run into problems, please remember to disable the driver next time.** Turn off any system extensions you don't need to use. At the least, you need your Mac OS 9 CD software, plus any extensions required for your CD writer and Toast to work. Another instance in which this error might appear is if you are attempting to write to a rewritable CD on a drive that doesn't support that format.

■ **You don't have the option to Write Session in the write dialog box.** This means you don't have enough room left on the disk for any more data. If you do have sufficient room, either use another CD-R or in the ISO dialog settings, select the CD-ROM XA format.

■ **Whenever you select the option to Write Disc or Write Session, this message appears: Failed to allocate x MB of temporary hard disk cache on "Your Volume." Please use the "Preferences" menu item to select a different volume.** If you see this message, go to the Edit menu of Toast and choose Preferences. Then select a different disk volume with enough space to carry your cache file. Otherwise, you can use your Toast session option to make a disc image of that data, so you needn't have a temporary hard disk cache.

■ **Description=BUFFER UNDERRUN.** A number of possible solutions exist. Disable any unnecessary system extensions. Disconnect any SCSI devices on the same chain that you don't currently need to use. Make sure all cables are properly connected and the proper termination has been set. Select a lower speed to write the data. In Preferences in the Edit menu, increase the RAM cache.

■ **Description=TRACK FOLLOWING ERROR.** A number of possible reasons exist for this problem. The CD writer is not level. The CD you're recording data on could be damaged. The brand of that CD could be incompatible with your CD writer. The calibration device of the writer may be defective.

NOTE   *In all fairness, this could also be a symptom of a method used by the publisher to prevent you from copying the software to the CD.*

Adding a CD Writer

■ **Sense Key=HARDWARE ERROR.** If this type of error occurs often, contact the technical support people at Adaptec immediately.

■ **Sense Key=MEDIUM ERROR.** Use a different brand of CD-R. The quality among different brands varies even if they have similar prices and specifications.

■ **During the verifying process, this message appears: Mismatch at byte** *x*/**sector** *y*. **Verification failed.** Go to Toast's Utilities menu and then select the option to verify your media.

■ **You can't use the Verify button.** If you aren't using a disk that can be read by your Mac, it cannot be verified, unless you use the SCSI copy mode (for Macs with SCSI devices, of course).

Installing and Using a Digital Camera

Traditional cameras with film may soon be dinosaurs.

A new breed of digital cameras is gaining ascendancy. Such cameras can now deliver picture quality that can, unless the print is extremely large, rival that of film.

While digital cameras may look much like the film variety, with high-caliber lenses, automatic exposure, focus settings, and so on, they are closer in concept to a camcorder. They use a *charge-coupled device* (*CCD*), same as a camcorder, to capture pictures, pixel by pixel. But instead of recording pictures on tape or film, such cameras generally use a memory storage device, such as a FlashCard or disk, to store the digital data of the pictures you take.

If you want to put the pictures from a regular camera on your Mac, you first must have your film developed, get the prints back, and use a scanner to capture the image of the print and to make a file. With a digital camera, you can plug it in directly to your Mac, and then download the images to your hard drive.

> NOTE *The other alternative in getting disk files from a film is to have your photo finisher create a Photo CD, a process that may take several days or more.*

Once the images are on your Mac's drive, you can edit them in your favorite photo-editing program, such as Photoshop, and then use them in your documents or send them on to friends and family by e-mail.

Choices, Choices, Choices

Generally, the more expensive the digital camera, the better the quality. The cheapest digital cameras start below $100, but quality suffers. The pictures may look fine on your Mac's display, with its native resolution of 72 dots per inch, but try to print them and you see that they don't come up to the quality level of film.

If you want to approach film quality for prints of 5" × 7" or 8" × 10", be prepared to spend several hundred dollars for a quality camera. The best ones cost up to $1,000, and much more than that for the models used by pros.

Many of the same companies who make regular cameras and camcorders have jumped into the digital camera field with both feet. They include Agfa, Canon, Epson, Kodak, Nikon, Olympus, and Sony.

Digital cameras, such as the Nikon CoolPix 950, come with software used to copy the images to your Mac's hard drive, and, perhaps, perform some basic image-editing operations and scaling. You can also use these programs to manage a photo gallery or to save the pictures in different formats (such as GIF or JPEG) so others can use them

Some camera makers have some bundled programs, such as Adobe PhotoDeluxe, to help you get more than the basics in managing your budding photo library.

Most digital cameras use either a serial or USB connection to hook up to your Mac. A few, such as products from Sony, have a FireWire interface.

If the digital camera is a USB digital camera, it is fairly easy to install and use. First, you install the software and then plug the camera into your Mac's USB port.

You launch the software and set it up to download or mount the contents of the camera's FlashCard (or other storage device). Then you engage the playback mode and soon the pictures appear on your Mac's drive.

NOTE *Some manufacturers, such as Olympus, also market USB-based FlashCard readers, which usually provide faster throughput than simply capturing the images from the camera itself.*

If it's a serial connection, an added factor exists. Turning off your computer before plugging the camera into an open serial port is always a good idea. Make sure AppleTalk is turned off for the serial port you're using (this isn't a factor if you use the modem port for your digital camera). Then, be certain the proper software is installed and you're ready to bring those previous photos over to your Mac.

Installing and Using a Digital Camera

If you use a USB-to-serial adapter, such as the Keyspan USB Twin Serial Adapter, you can plug the digital camera into one of the two serial ports on the device without having to turn off your computer at all. Make sure the software provided with the adapter is installed, however, and also be certain the software is compatible with Mac OS 9. More information on USB is in Chapter 17 and Chapter 31 covers a number of known software compatibility issues with Mac OS 9.

Digital Camera Problems and Solutions

As with everything in the Mac computing world, you may run into problems trying to mount your digital camera on to your Mac or retrieving the images from it. The following is a list of some common problems you may face, as well as their solutions:

■ **Camera files will not mount.**   Make sure all the cables are properly connected to your camera and to your computer. Be certain the proper software has been installed before you attempt to mount the camera. Also, if you're using a serial connection or a serial-to-USB adapter, be sure the correct serial port (modem or printer port) is selected. If you're using a USB connection, double-check to make certain no conflicts occurred with other USB drivers. For example, if you're using an Imation SuperDisk, be sure you have version 3.2 of its driver software at the least. Older versions are known to cause conflicts with other USB devices (and sometimes, strangely enough, with FireWire devices as well).

If you attach a serial-to-USB adapter to a USB hub, make certain the hub is powered, as such adapters usually need extra juice to work properly.

■ **Pictures on the memory card cannot be accessed by the camera.**   Be sure your Mac has not somehow renamed or overwritten the files. If the files are not in a format that can be read by your camera (perhaps you used a FlashCard from a different brand?), then the camera won't be able to read them.

■ **Pictures on the memory card cannot be accessed by the computer.**   Make certain all the necessary cables have been properly connected and the software needed to use the digital camera has been installed on your Mac. Also, double-check to see if your program can read image files. Even if you prefer another program, using the software that comes with the camera as a starting point is best. Also, be sure the software is compatible with Mac OS 9. At press time, for example, Nikon was in the process of delivering a Mac OS 9 update to its CoolPix Mounter software.

TIP *If you cannot get your digital camera to work with the software provided by the manufacturer, check out this shareware product: Cameraid. The program can be used to download pictures from most popular cameras and to perform basic image-editing and management functions. You can get a copy from the publisher's Web site: http://www.cameraid.com. I can't recommend it enough because Cameraid enabled me to continue using my Nikon camera till the manufacturer could produce its own software update for Mac OS 9.*

■ **When the camera is connected directly to your computer, an error occurs when you try to view images.** If this happens, make certain the camera has been properly connected to your Mac and the right software has been installed on your computer.

NOTE *If you're using a serial-to-USB adapter to connect the camera to your Mac, be sure you plug it in directly to your Mac's USB port or a powered hub.*

How to Make Your Mac Into a Stereo System

A Mac comes with one or two speakers, but most Mac speakers are, to be perfectly blunt, plain awful.

The speakers sound tinny, scratchy, no better than the cheapest pocket radio. This is not only a problem when you hear your Mac's startup sound and some error alerts. This is also a problem when you want to listen to the audio track of a QuickTime movie or to play your favorite Mac computing game. You confront the limits of the Mac's built-in audio system quickly.

Fortunately, Apple saw the wisdom of doing something with a Mac's sound system when it teamed up with the well-known audio manufacturer, Harman Kardon, to design a sound system for the second generation or slot-loading iMac line. In addition to delivering sound quality far better than what Macs usually provide, an optional woofer system, called *iSub,* takes the sound to quality levels formerly achieved only with separate sound systems.

For most Macs, though, sound was secondary in its design and you probably want to get a better set of speakers if sound is important to you. A basic set of desktop speakers, which I prefer to call *satellites,* greatly enhances your listening experience. Adding a three-piece system with a woofer module can deliver sound quality that comes close to a low-cost home audio system.

The thrill of hearing and feeling the terrible rumble of warships in the famous *Star Wars: The Phantom Menace* QuickTime movie trailer, the thrill-packed action games that have attained renewed popularity on Macs, or simply listening to your favorite CDs, can definitely make the purchase price of such a system worth every penny.

NOTE
Many new Macs come with DVD drives, which can also be used to watch your favorite DVD movie. A high-quality speaker system can greatly enhance your enjoyment of these videos.

The Speakers

Computer speakers typically come with built-in amplifier systems, tailored to provide the highest quality sound. Prices begin at around $25 and range to over $600. Quality varies and the cheapest computer speakers hardly deliver sound quality any better than your Mac's built-in speakers. Other models extend to full-fledged affairs that include such features as Dolby Surround Sound and rival the quality of some regular home audio systems.

The manufacturers of these speakers include some of the same companies that build speakers for the home audio market. They include Advent, Bose, Boston Acoustics, Cambridge SoundWorks, Harmon Kardon (manufacturer of the speakers for the newest iMac, as well as its companion woofer module, iSub), Labtec, Monsoon, and Sony.

Installing a two-piece speaker system is a relatively straightforward process. You place the speakers on your desk: one on the left and one on the right. Then you plug in the necessary cables, including the one that plugs in directly to the sound out jack on your Mac. Once connected, look for an on/off switch of some sort and a volume control. Some may also include a balance control to match left and right levels and a switch to activate a special feature, such as a bass boost or surround-sound effect.

NOTE
I'm not ignoring the three-piece systems with woofer modules. They're covered in the next section.

Choosing the speakers themselves, however, is a much more difficult process. Reading the reviews of various speakers in magazines such as *MacHome*,

MacAddict, Macworld, and even *Stereo Review's Sound & Vision* is probably a good idea. These magazines mention specifications, including price and features, and give you a rough idea of which speakers sound better.

Remember, a loudspeaker system that sounds great to someone else may be absolutely grating on your ears or make no impression on you at all. Unlike the rather large living room audition areas of a stereo store, however, you seldom have a chance to audition computer speakers at a dealer. And, even if you did, they probably would sound differently in your home or office environment anyway (even though listening to the speakers in another location might help you eliminate those apt to sound the worst).

And, for the most part, the saying "you get what you pay for" is still true. Yes, the more expensive systems do sound better.

Subwoofers and Woofers

A *woofer* is a speaker devoted to reproducing the lowest frequencies of the audible spectrum. Some of the more expensive computer speakers include a separate woofer module, which frees the desktop speakers—the satellites—of also having to reproduce low frequencies. This makes the speakers play louder with less distortion and the overall sound quality is superior. With the right system, you can even feel, not just hear, the low-frequency sounds from your favorite Mac computer game or DVD.

Unfortunately some speaker companies label their woofers as subwoofers, which isn't quite correct. A *subwoofer* is designed to plumb the lowest depths of the frequency spectrum, not only the normal bass range of, say, 40Hz to 60Hz, which regular woofers handle. A real subwoofer can often reproduce the low fundamentals of organ music (about 16Hz), which is felt, rather than heard, and can be quite expensive (sometimes costing several thousand dollars each), far more than any normal computer system.

NOTE *A hertz (once called a cycle) refers to the number of vibrations a sound makes in a single second.*

For the sake of accuracy, I call a spade a spade and label the low-frequency module that comes with a computer speaker system as strictly a woofer—nothing more.

Some speakers come equipped as three-piece systems. Other companies offer a woofer module as a separate purchase. A case in point is Harman Kardon's iSub, designed to work with the slot-loading iMac to deliver higher quality sound.

How to Make Your Mac Into a Stereo System

A good woofer section truly makes the sounds emanating from your computer richer, fuller, and more vibrant, making your listening experience on your Mac, no matter if you're playing games, a DVD, or music, much more enjoyable.

Setting Up a Woofer

The process of installing any woofer module is different for every model. To learn how to set it up, check the manual that comes with the device. Normally, the satellite speakers plug directly into the woofer. In some cases, the satellite speakers derive power from the woofers and are controlled by them (the Monsoon M-1000 flat-panel speakers I use on my desktop Mac are a prime example).

Most woofers have a separate level control so you can match their level to your satellites. Setting them up so you get a big, bloated, thumping bass is easy, which makes your Mac seem as if it's located in a dance club, serving up the audio from your favorite local DJ.

For balanced sound, this could be a bit much, though. The usual rule-of-thumb is to set the level of your woofer module till you hear it on music with a good low-end. That's all. This is enough both to provide the proper reinforcement and to give you the most enjoyable and least fatiguing experience.

Positioning is another matter. Putting speakers on the floor between and behind the desktop speakers is common. If you want to fill a room with vibrant bass, however, you may want to put the woofer in a corner of the room, as is commonly done with regular audio systems. Let the manufacturer's recommendations be your guidepost.

NOTE   *You needn't buy a set of computer speakers to get good sound from your Mac. If your computer is in the same location as your home audio system, you can buy a set of adapter cables and use one of your receiver or preamplifier's "line" inputs to receive the audio signal.*

Summing Up

In this chapter, you learned about several devices that can enhance the experience of using your Mac. These include digital cameras, CD writers, and speakers.

In the next section of the book, you learn about the various kinds of software you can use on your Mac. In the first chapter of that section, you can find information on the major word processing programs—AppleWorks, Microsoft Word, Nisus Writer, and Mariner Write —and their major features. You also learn how to get the most out of a word processor and how to use it with your other programs under Mac OS 9.

Part III

Using the Software

Chapter 19

Mac Word Processing
Made Simple

You may have to type a simple letter to a client telling him of a new business proposal. You could be a teenager writing an essay for your English class. You could even be writing the great American novel, hoping someday it could bring you great fame and fortune. Whatever your purpose, you're going to require some sort of software to type the documents you need every day.

A *word processor* is, at its core, a program that enables you to type and edit text, although the basic feature-sets of such programs extend far beyond these basic capabilities. Apple even gives you a free bare-bones word processor, SimpleText, which also enables you to change the size and style of type, but not much more.

If you want to get beyond the task of simply editing notes, you want to look into a dedicated word processing program. The programs covered in this chapter all offer most of the features you need in such a program. In addition to managing basic text-editing tasks, you can create documents with multiple columns for a brochure or newsletter and insert pictures. You can even track revisions, if you handle a document that must go through several editing passes or is worked on by more than one person.

The programs covered in this chapter are top dog: Microsoft Word, a quirky but uniquely featured competitor, Nisus Writer, plus Apple's mainstay AppleWorks, and a low-cost contender, Mariner Write.

In general, word processing programs aren't hard to use, although complicated options may make the task of mastering a program seem daunting.

In addition, some of the programs you're apt to encounter in each of these programs are quite different. What one does wrong, another does right . . . well, most of the time.

This chapter isn't designed to teach you how to use any of these programs. That task would require an individual book for each of them. Instead, the programs are compared, from ease-of-use to general features. You also learn how to deal with problems when they arise.

Major Word Processor Programs Compared

As mentioned, several commercial word processing programs are available for the Mac. All of them come with many of the same basic features to help you construct your documents as you want, as well as additional features to help you spruce up even the simplest word processing document. Let's begin our survey.

Microsoft Word 98

This often too complete word processor (as shown in Figure 19-1) comes with almost all the features you would ever need in such a program, whether you're typing a simple one-page document or constructing an entire novel with hundreds of pages, embedded outlines, editor comments, and marked revisions.

Although Word began as a Mac program, Microsoft fumbled badly with Word 6, which they essentially developed by taking the Windows version and converting it (not too efficiently) to the Mac platform. However, the company recovered mightily with Word 98. This program (which also comes as part of the Microsoft Office 98 program suite) is tightly integrated with the Mac OS, including support for such features as Contextual menus, sticky menus, and the overall appearance of the Mac operating system. Word 98 also has support for Apple's very own QuickTime

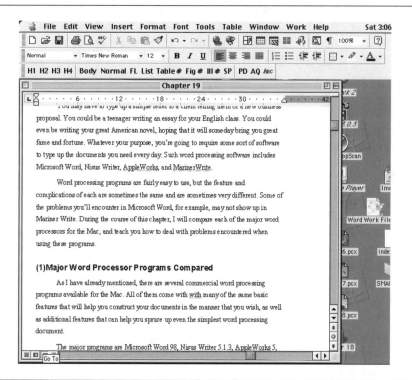

FIGURE 19-1   Microsoft Word 98 is a complete program to serve nearly all your word processing needs

Major Word Processor Programs Compared

technology, enabling you to add QuickTime movies or even QuickTime VR panoramas to your documents. The program enables you to move information easily from one document to another or from one application to another through support for the Mac's drag-and-drop capability.

> **NOTE** *The VR in QuickTime VR stands for virtual reality. VR is the equivalent of seeing all sides of an image: front, sides, and rear.*

Word comes with a *What You See Is What You Get* (*WYSIWYG*) font menu (the fonts are shown in their actual style, set as a program option) enabling you to see how a font will look before you choose it for your document. The grammatical and spelling errors you make when writing your document are automatically highlighted by the Grammar Check and Spell It features. The Quick Thesaurus (available by control-clicking a certain word) enables you to choose synonyms for a word, if one is available. If you want, you can use the option to change the menus to the way they looked in an older version of the program, Word 5.1. Office Assistant (see Figure 19-2), helps guide you in performing various tasks in the program. Office Assistant even has the capability to take you through all the steps of a certain process.

> **TIP** *If you tire of the little assistant jumping, prancing, and making noise whenever you perform a Word function, you can click the close box to turn it off. A quick click of the HELP key brings it back. You may find yourself getting used to the little guy, however, as he is there to help make you access the incredibly vast feature set of Word easily. Lest I seem to be contradicting myself, I should say, in passing, that I use this program with the Assistant turned off.*

> **NOTE** *Word 5.1, which came out in the early 1990s, had a simpler, less cumbersome program toolbar, which some Word users prefer. The nice thing about the feature is that you can easily switch back and forth to see which interface you like.*

With the Word-Table Drawing Tool, you can construct custom tables with columns, rows, and cells for your documents. Also, if you make a number of different mistakes and want to correct them, you have the option to undo and redo your actions multiple times, as opposed to only once, as with most Mac programs.

Using its basic drawing components, you can enhance your documents with all sorts of different effects, including shadows, multicolored fills, textures, and

FIGURE 19-2   A little two-legged Mac is here to help you make Word run better

Bezier curves. While this won't replace a professional drawing program, it's fine for business documents and school reports.

The Letter Wizard (see Figure 19-3) automatically performs some of the more mundane tasks when writing a letter, such as formatting and addressing, enabling

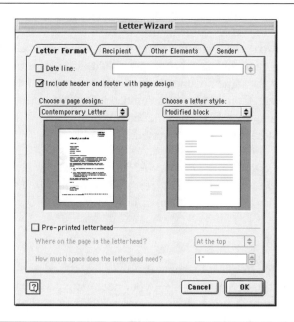

FIGURE 19-3   Let a Word wizard help you format a complex document

Major Word Processor Programs Compared

you to deal with the letter itself, instead of its appearance. *Visual Basic for Applications* (*VBA*) enables you to create your own special business solutions based on the Visual Basic programming system.

The program also has advanced features for the Internet and cross-platform compatibility. The Internet Assistants help you through the process of creating your own Web pages, and you don't even have to work with the sometimes arcane *HyperText Markup Language* (*HTML*) commands. The Web Toolbar enables you to move efficiently through your Word documents using hyperlinks. You can also use the hyperlinks to jump directly to a Web page (your default browser is launched, and you're connected to your ISP as part of the process). Within Word, with its support for creating Internet content, you can create HTML documents, and then prepare them for the Web. HTML documents can be brought directly into Word without even having to reformat them.

The powerful macro feature (which uses VBA) enables you to automate common tasks, so you can quickly format your document the way you want. The only downside of this capability is that macros are vulnerable to that wide strain of viruses that infect both Mac and Windows versions of the Microsoft Office software. Fortunately, the latest virus detection programs can eliminate these infections.

Many other useful features are also in Word. You can track the changes you or others have made to your documents in Word and have those changes highlighted for you. You can also decide whether you want to accept or reject those changes (this is how many books, such as this one, are edited). The information dealing with different versions of the same document are stored within that document, making them easier to manage. Comments can be embedded within your documents without changing the original text. Files produced in Word 97 for Windows can be opened without first having to be converted.

NOTE *Although the file format for Word 2000 for Windows is the same as the older version, some of the features, such as an updated table-formatting capability, do not transfer from different versions of the program.*

AppleWorks 5

AppleWorks 5 comes free on your new iBook or iMac, and you may find you needn't go beyond this program to meet your document processing needs. It's Apple's very own suite of productivity programs (shown in Figure 19-4), which includes word processing, drawing, painting, spreadsheet, and database modules. The program can be found on every single iBook and Revision B iMac (a minor update that came with more default video memory) or later (including the slot-loading second-generation models).

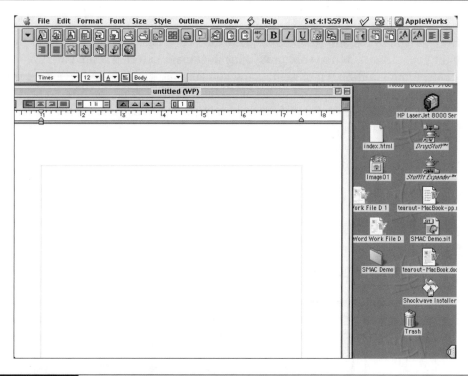

FIGURE 19-4 AppleWorks is Apple's own suite of productivity programs. Among these are word processing, spreadsheet, painting, and drawing modules

NOTE *An older version of this application is known as ClarisWorks 5.0, and it shipped on some of the early iMacs with that name, but it is basically the same program when you get past the labeling.*

The word processing module doesn't have the vast array features found in Microsoft Word, but it does have quite a lot for the money. It enables you to drag-and-drop your text across your documents. You have the ability to check the spelling of your documents and to find synonyms for various words in the thesaurus. You can use footnotes to cite sources for a report and you can save a Web page as an HTML file. You can use a macro record to automate various tasks and support exists for AppleScript if you want to create a custom applet for the program (see Chapter 9 for more information about AppleScript). You can change the formatting and style of your document. You can even set up hyperlinks to access other documents and Web pages.

The drawing module provides simple but useful tools (see Figure 19-5). You can create various shapes and edit them. You have a wide array of colors available to you, as well as patterns, gradients, and textures that can be edited. You can import your artwork into a word processing document to turn a simple text document into a full-blown presentation with elaborate graphics and text. And you can use the library of images to spruce up your document. You can turn your drawings into one big presentation, transforming them into a slide show.

The painting module is similar to the drawing module; in fact, it has many of the same features. The painting module also provides paintbrush and pencil tools you can use to create fine artwork with a variety of shapes and colors. You can paint small parts of a shape or fill the space all at once. You can select parts of images and use them, instead of using the entire graphic. Finally, you have the

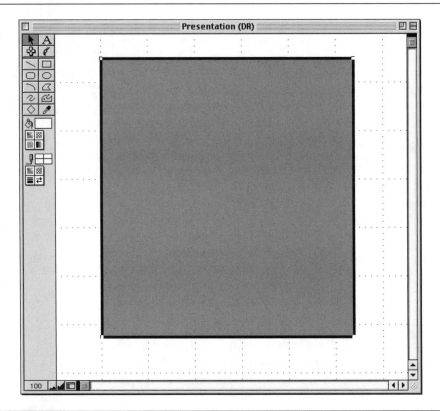

FIGURE 19-5   For presentation quality graphics, AppleWorks can do the job

ability to distort, rotate, and add a number of other effects to enhance your artwork and to give it a professional quality.

The spreadsheet module (see Figure 19-6) may not seem useful to you at first (in fact, it doesn't quite rival Microsoft Excel in terms of features). But if you haven't used a spreadsheet before, you soon realize how good the spreadsheet module is at helping you manage your finances and keeping your checkbook balanced. You can use it for such things as creating business invoices, keeping your financial statements under your care, tracking your stocks, and setting up your schedule for the entire month, or even for the entire year. If you want to see information in a visual format, you can transform it into a chart or graph. You choose what type of graph you want and AppleWorks does the dirty work.

Finally, the database module (kind of a reduced version of FileMaker Pro, the industrial-strength database program produced by Apple's FileMaker subsidiary) can help you do such things as manage an address book or keep a list of important clients close at hand. You can store all sorts of information, however, whether it's for your business or your personal pleasure. AppleWorks enables you to customize

Major Word Processor Programs Compared

	A	B	C	D	E	F
	Accounts Payable Report (SS)					
	A1 ▼ fx × √ ☐					
1	[ ] Spreadsheet showing all accounts payable to vendors by due date.					
2	[ ] Replace the blue text with the names of your vendors and the amounts you owe them.					
3						
4	Accounts Payable Aging Report as of: **8/2/01**					
5						
6		*Outstanding Accounts Payable (in number of days)*				
7	**Vendor**	0 to 30	30 to 60	60 to 90	90 to 120	over 120
8	Vendor A	40,599	36,562	22,717	0	0
9	Vendor B	46,154	31,595	20,037	0	0
10	Vendor C	26,199	25,256	13,484	4,919	0
11	Vendor D	57,987	47,256	26,983	13,418	0
12	Vendor E	22,695	34,158	21,854	6,188	0
13	Vendor F	32,553	28,576	18,733	0	0
14	Vendor G	28,645	13,255	12,203	0	0
15	Vendor H	13,245	8,002	7,043	0	0
16						
17	**Total Accounts Payable**	268077	224660	143054	24525	0
18						
19	**Percentage of Total Accounts Payable**	*40.6%*	*34.0%*	*21.7%*	*3.7%*	*0.0%*
20						
21						

FIGURE 19-6   For simple financial statements, AppleWorks can easily handle the job

your database in any way you want. You even have the ability to add color and pictures to your database. One of its more useful features enables you to merge information from a database into a word processing document or spreadsheet.

> NOTE *Near press time, Apple was preparing to ship AppleWorks 6.0, which includes over 100 new features, including a presentation module similar to that of Microsoft's own PowerPoint presentation software.*

Nisus Writer 5.1.3

Nisus Writer (shown in Figure 19-7) is a powerful, but somewhat strange, word processor that boasts a number of odd features not found in any other programs. Like Microsoft Word and AppleWorks, Nisus Writer integrates the platinum appearance of Mac OS 9. While the command set library is not as vast as that of Word, you can customize keyboard shortcuts for various tasks in the Preferences

FIGURE 19-7   Nisus Writer is a quirky word processor boasting features not found in any other programs of its kind

dialog box. Nisus Writer has a WYSIWYG font menu, as well as live scrolling. QuickTime movies and other types of multimedia can be inserted into documents for full-length, elaborate presentations. Although Nisus Writer doesn't have a grammar checker like Word, it does boast an 80,000-word dictionary for the spell checker and a large thesaurus.

Live scrolling simply means when you scroll through a document, you see the full image on the screen, intact, as contents travel up and down.

The program's vast features don't end there, however. You have the ability to open not only one file, but multiple documents at once using the Catalog feature. Like Word, multiple undo's are available if you happen to make mistakes when creating or editing your documents. Your layout page window can be viewed while you are modifying the document and it can be updated immediately.

Another unique feature addresses the limitation in Apple's single clipboard feature. Nisus Writer has ten clipboards, each fully and separately accessible and editable (see Figure 19–8). This way, you can have multiple pieces of text available for insertion in various parts of your document at the same time.

Along with Nisus Writer's multiple clipboard capability is its advanced file selection capability. Not only is drag-and-drop supported, but you can also select separate, nonconnected pieces of text at the same time, and copy or drag them as a single unit.

Major Word Processor Programs Compared

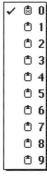

FIGURE 19-8   Use this menu to paste text and pictures into as many as ten separate clipboards in Nisus Writer

One of the most distinctive features of Nisus Writer is its powerful find/replace feature, which has the capability to search for phrases, words, or page numbers in any documents whether it's active or inactive, opened or closed (see Figure 19-9). You can also get extremely specific when you do your searches. Nisus Writer provides a macro recorder that can be used to automate various tasks. You simply start recording, perform whatever tasks you want to be done, and the steps are recorded automatically. After you record those complex steps, you can play them back when you want.

Nisus enables you to move directly to a specific piece of text. It also updates cross-references automatically, so whenever you change the page for the reference, it is updated immediately.

If you need foreign language capability, you may find Nisus Writer the program of choice. Right out of the box, it supports a number of languages, including Arabic, Hebrew, Japanese, and Russian, without having to add extra costly modules.

NOTE   *The foreign language capability feature of Nisus Writer is extraordinary, considering Arabic and Hebrew are read right-to-left, and the Asian languages up and down.*

The other features of Nisus Writer are relatively minor to most people, but some of them are useful. You can place a graphic image found in one Nisus file and place it in any other document within the program. When typing legal documents, you can use the Line Numbers feature to number your lines on the screen. Finally, the tracking (letterspace) feature enables you to adjust the space between characters precisely, which is extremely helpful when doing page layout work. While this isn't quite a match for a real desktop publishing program, it comes fairly close.

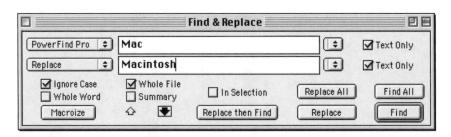

FIGURE 19-9   Nisus Writer's find feature has three levels of complexity, depending on how extensive you want to make your searches

NOTE
If Nisus Writer lacks anything, it's the capability to zoom the text in your document so it appears larger on the screen. This is a limitation that has existed in this program from the start. If you create your documents in larger type styles, it's not a major factor; otherwise, it can be an inconvenience.

If you're curious about Nisus Writer, experiment with an older, free version that you can download directly from the publisher's Web site at http://www.nisus.com. If you find its exceptional feature set suits your needs, upgrade to the latest version.

Mariner Write 2.0

If you only want the word processing basics, without extra frills or fluff, and you don't want to spend a lot of money, consider Mariner Write 2.0 from Mariner Software (see Figure 19-10). Mariner Write isn't bare bones either.

This little word processor doesn't put a great strain on your computer, and requires little of your RAM and free hard drive space. This is good, especially if you have an older Mac with a smaller, slower hard drive and a lower-powered CPU. Mariner Write's features are vast and many. They include the capability to move your toolbar across the screen, ten levels of Undo, seven degrees of magnification, kerning (in rather a crude fashion), split windows, support for WorldScript, text wrap-around graphics, import and export compatibility with some of the other major word processing programs (including Word and AppleWorks), a WYSIWYG font menu, and the capability to drag-and-drop text throughout your documents. Mariner Write even has support for AppleScript commands.

A number of other strange little features are also in Mariner Write. It has a huge dictionary available to check spelling, although it doesn't come with a thesaurus. The widow and orphan feature keeps one line of text from coming up on the top of a page, but that's a little different from the similar paragraph-formatting capabilities of Microsoft Word.

NOTE
The benefit of this feature is that it gives your text a more professional look, but unless you intend to distribute a printed document and can accept that some pages will be a little short as a result of moving whole paragraphs, you might not find this feature useful.

Both a color for the text and a color for the background surrounding the text can be chosen. Noncontiguous pieces of text can be selected, the same as Nisus Writer. The Open Recent command shows the last eight documents you've worked with in the program (in contrast, Microsoft Word displays up to nine). The

Major Word Processor Programs Compared

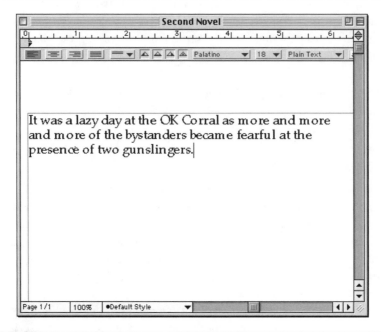

It was a lazy day at the OK Corral as more and more and more of the bystanders became fearful at the presence of two gunslingers.

FIGURE 19-10   Mariner Write isn't on everyone's Mac, but it does most of the chores you expect from a word processor

Dynamic Scrolling feature enables you to see your text going by when you drag the thumb of the scroll bar. Mariner Write also comes with four types of underlines, small caps, strike-throughs, and a style that can place a rectangle around any selected text.

> **NOTE**   *You can get a shareware version of Mariner Write, bearing a Lite label or buy the retail version from the publisher's Web site at http://www.marinersoft.com. You should also find out about the next version of the software, 4.0, which is supposed to add a large number of new, more powerful features.*

Deciding Which Is Right for You

If you need to share documents with others in your company or with other Mac users elsewhere, the key ingredient is compatibility. And, in this respect, you may not have a choice. While the other word processing programs do, for example, open older-version Microsoft Word documents (and Word is the industry standard), not all of the custom formatting features, such as revision marks, are supported.

If you have a consumer Mac, the iBook, or the iMac, you may only want to give AppleWorks a complete workout to see if it meets all your needs. Despite being a bundled program, it doesn't short-change you on the necessary features for creating and editing your documents.

Otherwise, feel free to experiment with the free version of Nisus Writer or the shareware version of Mariner Write to see if you acquire a taste for either program.

Unfortunately, the other major alternative in the word processing arena, Corel WordPerfect (not covered in this chapter), is no longer being developed by its publisher. You might still be able to download your free copy of the last release version, 3.5e, from the publisher's Web site at http://www.corel.com. But that version is apt to be withdrawn from circulation at any time, according to Corel.

How to Handle Format Problems

While word processing programs aren't hard to use, the more complex your formatting, the more often you're apt to encounter problems. You may need to figure out how to get the format you want, or even if you follow the steps to the letter, you might find the document doesn't quite look the way you expected.

Here are some common formatting tips, problems, and solutions in each of the four programs.

Microsoft Word 98

Microsoft Word is so powerful, its feature-set may seem almost impossible to grasp at first look. But, as you gain experience with the program and pour through its Help menus and assistants, you find you can do almost every task without going through a long learning curve.

Here's a list of common word-formatting issues and their solutions:

- ■ **Justifying the last line of a paragraph**   To justify a short line of text at the end of a paragraph, which spreads the letters all the way from left to right on the line, press SHIFT-RETURN.

- ■ **Placing different types of alignment in one line of text**   First, be sure the paragraph with the one line of text has been aligned to the left. With the ruler, use the tab stops that refer to correct alignment, such as a centered tab stop at the center and a right tab stop at the right, for the one line of text you want. Before every part of the line you want to have aligned, press TAB.

- **Cutting off graphics or text in one line**   Sometimes, if exact line spacing has been specified between one line of text and the next one, it may not be large enough to hold a lot of text or a large amount of graphics. To fix this, either make the spacing larger in the At box or choose an option besides Exactly in the Line spacing box in the Paragraph dialog box.

- **Changing text formatting when text is deleted**   If the mark for a paragraph has been deleted, the next paragraph merges with the one before it, causing its formatting and style to change to the previous one. Choose Undo from the Edit menu to restore the paragraph mark and its original formatting.

- **Turning off automatic formatting, but the program still automatically formats the document**   Make sure you are on the right tab when you choose AutoCorrect (shown in Figure 19-11) in the Tools menu. If you

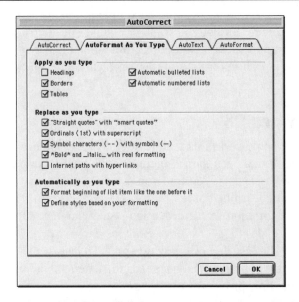

FIGURE 19-11   AutoFormat As You Type can be used by Word to make changes as you're typing your document and AutoFormat can automatically make a number of changes at once

want to choose which automatic changes you want Word to make while
you type, choose the AutoFormat As You Type tab, and then choose or
clear whichever options you need. If you want to choose which changes
Word makes automatically to selected text in a document or an entire
document, choose the AutoFormat tab, and then select or clear whichever
options you need for the text.

- ■ **Text formatting of list is off**   Make certain the Format beginning of list
  item like the one before it check box has been chosen in the AutoFormat
  As You Type Tab.

- ■ **Inserting en dashes and em dashes**   Make sure the Symbol characters
  (- -) with symbols (—) check box has been selected in both the
  AutoFormat and AutoFormat As You Type tabs. Word automatically
  places an en dash whenever you type text, a space, either one or two
  hyphens, one or no spaces, and then more text. The program automatically
  inserts an em dash only when you type text with two hyphens after it, and
  then more text.

- ■ **Showing printed text that doesn't match the text onscreen**   Several
  reasons exist for this. The program could be showing the text as draft fonts.
  Make sure the Draft font check box is not selected in the View tab of the
  Preferences in the Tools menu. Also, your printer may not support the font
  you're using in your document. Either change the font you're using to a
  TrueType font or a font your printer does support. Finally, realize animated
  text effects don't print. Only the underlying text formatting is printed.

- ■ **Showing incorrect font in the document**   The reason for this problem is
  that either your computer or your printer doesn't have the font. To fix this
  problem, first make your way to the Compatibility tab, located in the
  Preferences in the Tools menu. Click Font Substitution. Then choose the
  name of the font that is supposed to appear under Missing document font.
  Finally, choose a different font in the Substituted font box.

AppleWorks 5

Many users get AppleWorks free, but free doesn't mean lack of power. And, Apple
choosing to bundle AppleWorks with its consumer products simply means you can
access a full-featured word processor without having to buy anything extra.

**How to Handle
Format Problems**

Here's a look at some hints and tips to get the program to do all the things you want:

■ **Changing margins** Select Document in the Format menu. In the dialog box that appears (as shown in Figure 19-12), type in the margin widths you want for the document in the boxes. Then click OK.

■ **Showing or hiding margins and page guides** Check or uncheck the Show Margins and Show Page Guides check boxes in the Document dialog box.

■ **Inserting a header or footer** In the Format menu, choose Insert Header or Insert Footer. In the area for either, type or paste in the text you want for the header or footer, and then click back into the main text area to continue typing the rest of your document.

■ **Removing a header or footer** In the Format menu, choose either Remove Header or Remove Footer.

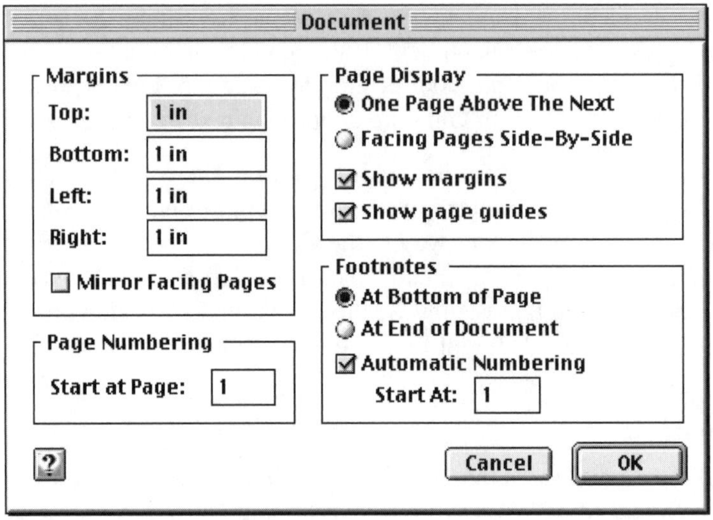

FIGURE 19-12 The Document dialog box in AppleWorks can be used to change the margin widths of your document

- **Inserting page numbers to be updated**   Place the insertion point where you want to put the page number. If a page number needs to show up on every page, place the insertion point in a header or a footer. In the Edit menu, choose Insert Page #, and from the dialog box that appears (shown in Figure 19-13), select your options.

- **Inserting fixed page numbers**   When selecting Insert Page # from the Edit menu, hold down the OPTION key.

- **Changing the starting page number in a document without sections**   In the Edit menu, select Document. Type a page number in Start at Page.

- **Changing the starting page number in a document with sections**   Place an insertion point in the section that must be renumbered. In the Format menu, choose Section, click Restart Page Number, and then type a page number.

- **Inserting a date or time that is updated**   Click the place where the date or time should appear in your document. In Edit menu, select Insert Date or Insert Time. The one you choose then appears in the place you specified.

- **Inserting a fixed date or time**   When selecting Insert Date or Insert Time from the Edit menu, hold down the OPTION key.

- **Creating a title page**   In the Format menu, select Section. Choose Title Page from the Headers and Footers section of the dialog box (as shown in Figure 19-14), and then click OK.

How to Handle Format Problems

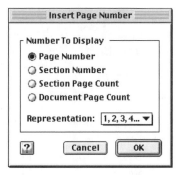

FIGURE 19-13   The Insert Page # dialog box can be used to insert page numbers, section numbers, and more in your document

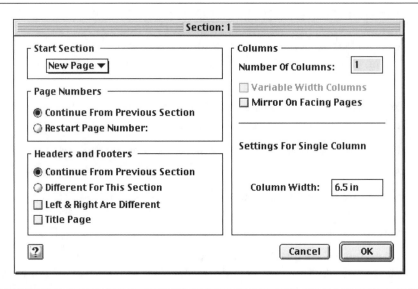

FIGURE 19-14   The Section dialog box can be used to create a title page in your document or to divide it into sections

■ **Putting a footnote in your document**   Place the insertion point at the end of the word where you want the footnote. In the Format menu, select Insert Footnote. Then type the required information for the footnote in the footnote area. To return to the main text area, click it, or press the ENTER key.

■ **Removing a footnote from your document**   Select the number of the footnote in your document and press DELETE.

■ **Inserting a page or column break**   Click at the end of the text where the page or column break should appear. In the Format menu, select Insert Page Break or Insert Column Break.

■ **Removing a page or column break**   Click the beginning of the line that comes after the break and press DELETE.

■ **Printing an envelope**   Type the address that should appear on your envelope and select all of it. In the Help menu, select AppleWorks Assistants. In the dialog box that appears (like the one in Figure 19-15), make sure the selected category is General. From the list of Assistants, select Address Envelope and click OK.

FIGURE 19-15	AppleWorks Assistants can automatically take you through the process of performing certain tasks

- **Setting up columns with equal widths**   Select Section from the Format menu. Type the number of columns you need in the Number of Columns box in the Columns area of the Section dialog box. Be sure Variable Width Columns was not selected. Then click OK.

- **Setting up columns with different widths**   Select Section from the Format menu. Type the number of columns you need in the Number of Columns box in the Columns area of the Section dialog box. Make sure Variable Width Columns has been selected. Choose Mirror On Facing Pages if the left and right sides must mirror each other. In the Settings for Column pop-up menu, select the column that must be resized. Select your options and then follow these same steps for every column that must be changed. Then click OK.

Nisus Writer

Quirky doesn't mean impossible, so while Nisus Writer has some unique features, some of which may take some practice to appreciate, you should find it is not hard to access.

Here's a list of common Nisus Writer formatting issues and the solutions:

- **Inserting a ruler**   You insert a ruler to transfer formatting from one paragraph to another. Click the place where you want to put a ruler. Then, from the Insert menu, select Paragraph Ruler. Now you can make the necessary changes to the Text Bar.

How to Handle
Format Problems

- **Setting the indent or outdent for the first line of a paragraph** Drag the First Line In/Outdent Indicator across the ruler and then release it wherever you want to place the first character in your paragraph.

> **NOTE** *With an outdent, Nisus Writer is making the first line of text extend to the left or right of the rest of the paragraph.*

- **Creating the text wrap area** Drag the Left or Right Line Wrap Indicator across the ruler and then release it once it is in the position where you need to wrap the lines of your paragraph.

- **Setting a leader tab on a ruler** Click the Leader bar. Then click a Tab Indicator and drag it across the ruler. Once you put the Tab Indicator in place to line up the tabbed text, release it.

> **NOTE** *A leader is a row of dots or a line that you may place between two items on a line, such as a price list or a bill.*

- **Defining styles** From the Style menu, select Define Styles. The dialog box shown in Figure 19-16 appears. Select New in the Style pop-up menu. Give your new style a name in the Style box. Check the boxes for the style attributes you want for your style. These include the font, the color, the size, and the style and language. After you select all your attributes, click Set, and then click Done. Now your new style is shown as a command at the bottom of the Style menu.

- **Creating a style library** This is a fast way to retrieve complex document styles. Create a file and define the styles, exactly as you would for any other file. Save the file in the Style Libraries folder in the Nisus Writer Tools Folder and give it a name, preferably something to help you remember its purpose. Now every time you launch Nisus Writer, the style library files shows up at the bottom of the style menu for every one of your documents. This feature is similar to the template files you create in Word.

- **Setting up a stationery file** Stationery files form templates that you use to form the basis of your new documents. The technique in Nisus Writer is somewhat more convoluted than other programs, which is why it's described here. From the File menu, choose New. Choose whichever rulers, font, size, and styles you want to have in the template. Add any needed text, including a header and footer, as well as variables and

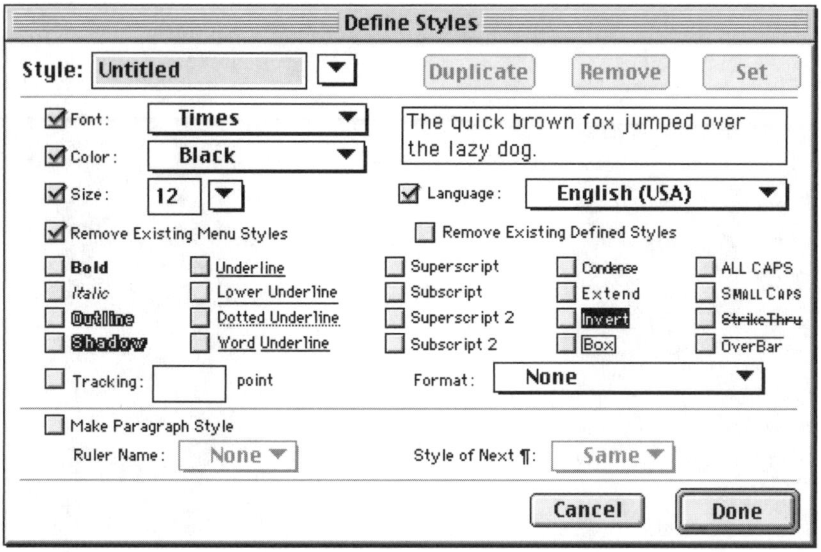

FIGURE 19-16   The Define Styles dialog box enables you to design your own styles, based on a variety of different attributes

graphics. Prepare the window in the manner that you want to open it. If you use a PostScript printer, select As PostScript in the Display Attributes pop-up menu in the Horizontal Button Bar at the bottom of the window. This reassures you that your PostScript printer will print the same document currently on the screen. From the File menu, select Save As and name your template. Select Nisus Stationery from the pop-up menu and then click Save.

■ **Creating a graphic that extends beyond the edge of the printed page**   In the File menu, select Page Setup in the Print submenu (see Figure 19-17). Decide what attributes you want to have for custom paper size. Check the Printer Cropping Marks check box. Select Layout Page in the File menu, and then select Layout Options in the Layout Menu. Check the check box Printer Limits in the Clip Graphics To: area located in the lower-right corner of the Page Layout Options dialog box. Now, close the window and return to the graphics layer. Put text on a colored background, and then rotate or change the text as you want. The next steps depend on whether you want the document to go from left-to-right or right-to-left.

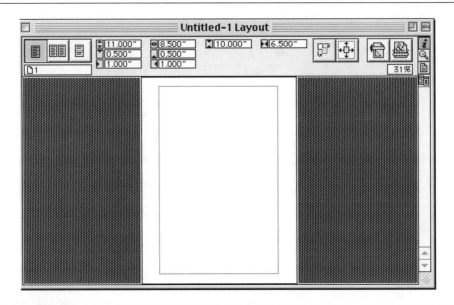

FIGURE 19-17   Using the Layout Page dialog box, you can make a graphic extend beyond the edge of one page

NOTE   *Another term for extending a graphic past the printed page is bleeding. Bleeding provides the effect of the graphic filling the full width of the page, including margins (without a little gap at the edges, assuming the printer can handle that width).*

If you want the document to go from left-to-right, drag the graph to a place just a few pixels beyond the gray region on the graphics bar. If you want the document to go from right-to-left, then drag the graphic beyond the left margin while pressing the SHIFT key.

Mariner Write

Not to be outdone, Mariner Write has its own array of features you should master to experience exactly what this low-cost word processor can do for you.

Here's a list of common formatting issues:

■ **Changing the paragraph margins on rulers**   Place the insertion point in the area of the paragraph whose margins you want to change. Then, from the Format menu, select Paragraph. Enter the numbers for Left, Right, and First-Line spacing in the Paragraph Spacing section of that dialog box.

- **Changing the spacing of paragraphs**   Place the insertion point in the area of the paragraph whose spacing you want to change. Then, from the Format menu, select Paragraph. Type numbers for Before Paragraph and After Paragraph spacing in the Paragraph Spacing section of that dialog box.

- **Setting up a new tab**   Select the paragraph for which you want to set up a tab stop. In the Document menu, select Tabs. Click the New Tab button. In the box labeled Position, enter the ruler location where the new tab should be placed. If you want, you can put a tab leader character in the box called Leader. Select an alignment for the tab (right, left, center, or decimal). Then click the Insert button, and this new tab is added to your list of tab stops. Press OK and the new tabs are placed within your document.

NOTE   *A right tab aligns the contents on the right side of each tab field and the left tab aligns the contents on the left side. The center tab aligns the contents in the middle of the tab stop. With decimal alignment, used for number displays, the alignment is on the decimal, regardless of the number of digits on each side.*

- **Adding columns to a page**   From the Format menu, select Columns. Type in however many columns you want (you can have up to ten). If you want to place a one-point, solid, vertical line between every column, check the Lines Between Columns check box. If you want to change the amount of space between each column, type in a new value in the Space Between box.

- **Setting up a style sheet**   Select or place an insertion point before whichever text you want to use a style sheet. In the Style pop-up menu at the bottom of the document window, select Choose New Style. After the next dialog box is displayed, you can choose the various attributes for your style sheet. You can then choose a name for your new style sheet. Click OK and your style sheet is created. If you want to apply it to the text you just selected, choose the style sheet from the style sheet menu at the bottom of the document window.

- **Adding style sheets to a document**   Create a new document by selecting New in the File menu. In the Style pop-up menu, select Choose Import Styles. In the Open dialog box, choose the document with those styles you want to add to this new document. Then select Save as Default Document in the Preferences submenu of the File menu.

How to Handle
Format Problems

Summing Up

In this chapter, you learned about the various Mac word processing programs, including Microsoft Word, AppleWorks, Nisus Writer, and Mariner Write. You also learned about the various formatting features of these programs and how to fix formatting problems.

In the next chapter, you learn about the graphics software available for the Mac, the various formats for graphics files, and problems when dealing with graphics files and programs.

Chapter 20

Exploring Graphics Software

The Mac has become the graphics powerhouse because the computer is easy to set up and use but, just as importantly, you can find a rich variety of available graphics programs. They start from the basic drawing features of AppleWorks, FileMaker Pro, Microsoft Excel, PowerPoint, and Word 98, and extend to powerful illustration programs used in the art departments of major entertainment and publishing centers.

> NOTE
> *The graphics modules of such programs as AppleWorks, Microsoft Word, and Nisus Writer are covered in Chapter 19.*

Drawing and Painting Programs Compared

In the first part of this chapter, some of the major graphic programs available on the Mac are profiled. This isn't intended as a complete listing or a tutorial on how to use these programs. By learning the basic features, however, you can narrow your search to the right tool to use, along with Mac OS 9, to create the graphics you want for your documents.

Adobe Illustrator 8.0

The first professional illustration program for the Mac continues its dominance. Adobe Illustrator (see Figure 20-1) can be used to create illustrations from scratch or it can work in concert with Adobe's other products, such as InDesign, PageMaker, Photoshop, and ImageReady, to produce a complete project.

Unlike the older drawing programs that built pictures with pixels, Illustrator and its competition are vector-based programs, where the objects you create are made up of contiguous lines. This allows the illustrations you create to be viewed and printed in any size without affecting quality.

In addition to its popular native format, Illustrator documents can be easily exported to many other formats that support one of its various export options. Illustrator also supports Mac OS 9's drag-and-drop feature, which makes moving elements easy from one document to another, even to other programs—Adobe's or others—that support the feature. Multiple undos and redos are supported, so you can easily switch back and forth among various changes you've made.

Illustrator supports all the most popular file formats, including CorelDRAW, EPS, Photoshop, TIFF, GIF, JPEG, PICT, and Macromedia FreeHand. Files can be shared easily between the Mac and Windows platforms with any programs that can read files in those formats.

> NOTE
> *The various graphic file formats described here and in the next few sections are defined in more detail later in this chapter, in the section entitled "Graphic Formats Compared."*

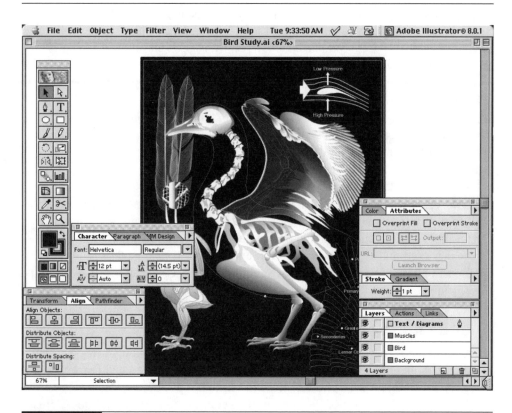

FIGURE 20-1   Illustrator's multipalette interface matches that of other Adobe programs

If you're a new user of Illustrator or if you haven't worked with it for a while, the program is bundled with tutorials and training movies to help you learn it quickly. With the new Pencil Tool, you can draw and edit smooth free-form curves, which almost look like you're sketching on a piece of drawing paper with a real pencil. This feature is especially valuable if you add a graphics tablet (such as one of Wacom's products) to your Mac. You can then work on an illustration in a fashion similar to traditional pen and pencil.

NOTE   *The subject of adding input devices to your Mac is covered in detail in Chapter 17.*

Objects can be easily selected and scaled with Bounding Box handles, similar to those available in Microsoft Office, Adobe PageMaker, and other applications. The objects can then be organized and aligned with Smart Guides and snap-to

Drawing and Painting
Programs Compared

grids. Colors and patterns can be easily chosen and added, and the Eyedropper functions can help you add color to your text. You can then place text anywhere in your document, put it around a shape if you want, or even link text blocks with total control over where they go and how they look.

The amount of blends, colors, gradients, and patterns provided in Illustrator allow for nearly unlimited possibilities. Only the limit of your imagination can stop you. With the addition of a Gradient Mesh feature, you can blend colors in nearly any direction by creating strange airbrush or watercolor effects. Artwork can be scattered or stretched almost anywhere in your document with many new brush options that can provide all kinds of results.

Among the enhancements you can make are embossing text, adding drop shadows, or even creating your own 3D effects with the Actions palette, Illustrator's built-in macro-type function that stores a set of repetitive or complex tasks. These can be chosen from your Illustrator Action Sets or the program's predefined macros, or you can even make your own. You can also correct your mistakes easily with an almost unlimited amount of undos. Wouldn't it be nice of the Mac OS offered this feature?

Adobe PhotoDeluxe 2.0

Although it's now up to version 4.0 on the Windows side, Adobe's low-cost consumer photo editing program, PhotoDeluxe, hasn't been updated for the Mac in nearly two years. Adobe appears more interested in promoting Photoshop LE (a limited function version of Photoshop) than continuing to develop PhotoDeluxe.

On the other hand, you are still apt to find PhotoDeluxe bundled with a number of low-end scanners these days, but don't attribute price to quality. Unlike Photoshop (described in the next section), PhotoDeluxe is specially designed to be used by novices. Its interface almost appears to be something out of a child's computer game. It's colorful and simplistic, enabling all of its features to be easily accessed. PhotoDeluxe has something called Guided Activities (similar to the setup wizards found in Microsoft's products), which can help you get through the various tasks of photo editing.

PhotoDeluxe also includes a number of templates, photo images, and clip art specifically meant to be used by consumers, not professionals. The program supports many different formats, including BMP, EPS, GIF, JPEG, PCX, Photoshop, and PICT.

PhotoDeluxe has a number of fine features. Like Photoshop, filters enable you to change the look of images and the program also supports Photoshop plug-ins (add-on modules). You can frame photos as well as change them into a calendar or a greeting card. With the Hold Photo feature, you can set up your own special scrapbook to keep your photos.

If you only want to scan photos and do simple image-editing chores without having to learn complex and powerful features you won't ever use, PhotoDeluxe may be your program of choice, regardless of whether Adobe ever upgrades it for the Mac. Even under Mac OS X, PhotoDeluxe should run in a satisfactory manner as a *Classic* application, Apple's definition for older Mac OS programs.

Adobe Photoshop 5.5

The industry-standard photo-editing program is Adobe Photoshop (see Figure 20-2). Adobe Photoshop is used in both the entertainment and publishing industries, yet it's easy enough to use that you can master the basic features in a short time.

Drawing and Painting
Programs Compared

FIGURE 20-2   Photoshop's palette-driven interface provides fast access to many of its powerful features

Photoshop 5.5 may look similar to the previous version (in keeping with Adobe's intent to provide a similar look and feel among its product line), but you see a great many changes once you explore the features. Many of these improvements make Photoshop 5.5 more Web-savvy and provide an easier path to creating dazzling Web pages.

This is accomplished by combining the vast creative capabilities of Photoshop with the Web tools of Adobe's ImageReady Web illustration software. While the programs are separate, they are tightly integrated. A handy Jump-to command makes switching back and forth easy between the two programs. When you switch from Photoshop to ImageReady, the key features of your document, as well as its layers, are fully preserved. Adobe's standard user interface, similar to the one in its other programs, provides a vast variety of image-manipulation tools, keyboard shortcuts, and palettes to satisfy your needs. Files can easily be shared among Adobe's other products, Acrobat, InDesign, and Illustrator, as well as between the Windows and Mac platforms.

NOTE   *Think of layers as separate sheets of paper, placed one on top of another, which make up the entire illustration. When you switch to a different layer, you are accessing the parts of the illustration on that layer.*

You can also export Photoshop documents to other programs, using a variety of formats, including EPS, GIF, JPEG, and TIFF.

Many different masking tasks can be performed using the Background Eraser, the computer equivalent of a pencil eraser, or the new Extract tool can be used to mask your images with complex edges and to retain a quality rivaling that of graphics professionals. You can change an image into paint strokes automatically with the new Art History brush.

You can set up contact sheets or picture packages with all the images in a folder, along with their captions, for your Web pages. Your colors appear accurately with the Color Management Assistant. As with Illustrator, multiple undos and redos are available in the History palette if you make a mistake. This enables you to move back to a prior version of your document easily if you find that version more suitable for your needs.

Text-formatting features are enhanced, although they are still limited compared to Illustrator, for example. Text is still entered within a limited-function dialog box, a less-than-welcome feature that persists in this program. However, you may place text and graphics on separate layers, and easily move from one to the other for direct editing of the text in your document.

> **CAUTION**   *To save a document in anything other than standard Photoshop performance, you must use a command (available from the Layer menu). This operation combines all the layers of your document into one. Once you do this, you cannot edit the separate layers that make up your original working file. You may, however, get around this by using the Save As function to make the "flattened" version and to keep the original version for changes that may be needed later.*

Photoshop has many Web-savvy features in version 5.5 that make it a much more powerful tool for Web authoring.

Here's a brief overview of Photoshop 5.5's Web-savvy features:

- You can set up JavaScript rollovers (a Web object that changes its look when the cursor passes over them) immediately, and you can even animate the behavior of those rollovers.

- You can transform Photoshop or Illustrator files into GIF animations.

- You can optimize your graphics for the Internet with easy-to-use compression and export options. You can slice complex images with many layers and give each area different format and compression options.

- Whenever you export your images, the HTML code is automatically generated for you to ease the transfer to your Web site.

- Up to four side-by-side live variations of a file can be previewed in Photoshop, so you can easily choose the happy medium between the quality of your images and the sizes of your files.

CorelDRAW 8

Although CorelDRAW has been hugely popular in the Windows market, it is still a relatively new and untested commodity in the Mac marketplace. But despite the publisher's widely publicized troubles in its executive office and stock market performance, they seem intent on capturing a respectable marketshare on the Mac marketplace.

CorelDRAW 8 (see Figure 20-3) is a feature-packed bundle that consists not only of Corel's flagship illustration program, but also of Corel's competitor to Photoshop, PHOTO-PAINT. The package also includes 1,200 clip-art images in EPS format, digital photos, and 1,600 PostScript and TrueType fonts.

Drawing and Painting Programs Compared

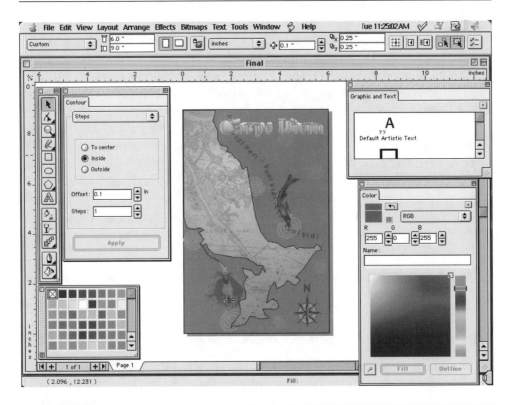

FIGURE 20-3   CorelDRAW, though ported from the Windows version, retains a distinct Mac look and feel

In fact, the package is almost worth the price for the fonts alone, but having a powerful graphics suite is a real plus. You can do almost any graphics task here, illustrations, page layout, photo editing, and bitmap conversions.

The CorelDRAW 8 application is, on the surface, decidedly different from Illustrator, but it has a wealth of powerful features. You can work with fine precision with its vector-editing tools. Moreover, you can have total control of how your text appears using such text attributes as leading, kerning, and connecting text to a shape or a curve. Text can also be flowed among frames.

A number of complex tools also exist to create elaborate special effects, bearing such names as Distortion, Blends, Envelopes, Fills, Transparencies, Transforms, and Grids. Such tools give you a variety of methods to alter the look of your illustration substantially without having to go to great lengths to reshape each separate element manually.

The Live Drop Shadow Tool enables you to make realistic-looking shadows on any object. With PowerClip, an object or group of objects can be put inside other objects or groups of objects. Fractually generated texture fills can be put on objects to make them look more natural. It also supports AppleScript, which enables you to perform common tasks automatically.

That alone should be enough to justify the purchase price of CorelDRAW 8, in addition to the artwork and fonts. And then there's Corel's answer to Photoshop, PHOTO-PAINT 8, which handles painting and image editing. The program supports Adobe Photoshop and MetaCreations Painter formats, enabling you to move files easily among these various programs. You can use many third-party plug-ins because PHOTO-PAINT 8 is compatible with the Adobe plug-in standard. The multiple undos feature enables you to fix your mistakes easily in the Edit menu. With Orbits and Symmetry, you can make spectacular special effects, like rope strands. You can soften or change effects with your brush using a number of features, including Smudge, Sharpen, Smear, and Blend. You can make realistic effects with your brush strokes with the natural media paint tools.

More than 70 built-in effects filters enable you to alter any image. You can also edit individual frames in QuickTime movies, QuickTime VR scenes, or objects in those scenes.

If you're crossing computing platforms, you should be pleased to know the two programs are fully compatible with the features and files found in the similar versions on the Windows platform. A special preference option enables you to alter the interface of both programs to look similar to those of Illustrator and Photoshop. You can also change objects and their properties with the context-sensitive Property Bar, which allows the capabilities and attributes of the selected tool or object to be displayed automatically.

NOTE   *At press time, Corel announced its renewed, expanded support for my favorite computing platform and was busy working on CorelDRAW 9 for the Macintosh, which was promised to offer improved stability, speed, and more comprehensive support for Macintosh-only features. In addition, the program will ship supporting Carbon, an application-programming interface being used for Mac OS X. The promised delivery date is summer 2000.*

Graphic Converter

If your graphic needs are modest and all you want to do is open and save files in a variety of formats, GraphicConverter (see Figure 20-4) may be your cup of tea. Unlike the other programs mentioned so far, GraphicConverter is shareware. You

Drawing and Painting
Programs Compared

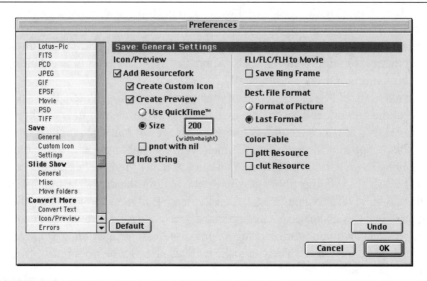

FIGURE 20-4   Describing all the graphic file formats GraphicConverter can handle would take pages

can try GraphicConverter, access all its incredibly robust features, and then, if you like it, pay the small fee to its author (which will get rid of that recurring reminder about paying).

Among the key features of GraphicConverter are the capability to import 120 graphic file formats and export 40 graphic file formats, which include PICT, TIFF, JPG, GIF, BMP, and PCX. GraphicConverter can also convert multiple files simultaneously, as well as other actions. In fact, I use GraphicConverter regularly to process the illustrations I create for my books. I can't recommend this program highly enough. It's fast, reliable, and does its specific tasks with utter precision and efficiency. In addition, GraphicConverter is regularly updated by its author, Thorsten Lemke, so it gets better and better.

If you like GraphicConverter after trying it, don't hesitate to pay your shareware fee. This encourages the author to continue developing the program.

NOTE *You can find GraphicConverter and many other shareware programs plus software updates on the popular VersionTracker Web site (http://www.versiontracker.com).*

FreeHand 8

Originally, FreeHand was the brainchild of Altsys, a Texas-based developer of a font creation program, Fontographer, but marketing and distribution were handled by

Aldus, who also created PageMaker. When Adobe purchased Aldus, part of the agreement included spinning off FreeHand to another publisher (to avoid Justice Department concerns). Macromedia grabbed FreeHand and continued developing it.

At one time, FreeHand seemed no better than a handmaiden to Illustrator. It was slower and more of an acquired taste. But as Macromedia has continued to develop the program, many artists have come to prefer FreeHand over Adobe's illustration product. In fact, graphic artists debate which program is better almost as enthusiastically as they debate the issue of QuarkXPress versus Adobe PageMaker (or Adobe InDesign).

Some of FreeHand's most significant features are covered here.

First, FreeHand doesn't save documents as pure PostScript files, which Illustrator does. Instead, the files are saved in FreeHand's own native format, which supposedly gives it a greater level of options to create professional-grade illustrations. You can decide if this feature is of any value or not.

On the surface, the user interface of FreeHand probably isn't the most orderly one out there. It has a main toolbox, two palettes for holding all the Xtras (its answer to a plug-in module format), three predefined buttons bars, five inspectors with multiple panels, and many palettes of random sizes.

If FreeHand's interface looks a little too cluttered or confusing to you, you can customize it to make yourself more comfortable. You can make your own keyboard shortcuts or use a list of predefined settings, so the shortcuts are equivalent to those in Adobe Illustrator, InDesign, PageMaker, Photoshop, and QuarkXPress. You can't move the Xtras menu anywhere else in the program to make it more convenient for you, however.

FreeHand has a number of interesting illustration-handling features. Several Lens effects are available for your use. You can apply translucency to an object and you can magnify a large number of objects, invert them, and even make them all the same color. The focal point of effects can be modified, so its source is placed somewhere other than directly behind the lens. You can easily enter the transformation mode by double-clicking one or more selected objects and then dragging the handles at the corners to scale them or drag them out of the selected area to rotate them.

A number of Xtras special effects are included as well. With the Graphic Hose, for example, you can deposit a number of objects when you drag them across a page. The Emboss command enables you to bevel the edges of objects. With the Shadow tool, a hard or soft drop shadow can be added to an object. The Mirror tool allows a selected object to be reflected a number of times, so a Spyrograph effect is created.

Other features of the program include the capability to rasterize objects in place, to see your work in a preview mode, to fill open areas of a page, to save

Drawing and Painting Programs Compared

custom views, and to export graphics in the EPS format without having to deal with a special dialog box.

On the Horizon: FreeHand 9

At press time, Macromedia announced FreeHand 9. As with the competition, the publisher is intent on improving Web integration with its new version. Direct support exists for Flash, Macromedia's Web-based animation tool.

Other program enhancements include the capability to save documents in HTML format, including URLs and embedded Flash files, and with formats that support Macromedia's flagship Web-authoring program, Dreammaker.

You can develop 3D-type illustrations in the program's traditional 2D environment with the Perspective Grid feature. Your illustrations can be warped and distorted with a live-action enveloping tool. The autotrace feature has also been enhanced to provide more accurate conversion of bitmap graphics to vector objects.

Macromedia promises across-the-board enhancements to all the program's major features, including typography, drawing control and precision, and color management. Once again, the bar has been raised in the quality and flexibility of illustration software, and it is expected that Adobe will attempt to answer the competition's new features with Illustrator 9 (no release date announced).

Graphics Formats Compared

It might be easy to assume the most common problem Mac users have to deal with is related somehow to your system software, perhaps a conflict between extensions or an extension incompatible with Mac OS 9. Because users of personal computers have to deal with crashes occasionally, this would probably be correct. Check Chapters 25 and 31 for more information on learning about system-related troubles.

Problems with graphic files are among the most annoying problems I encounter. The Internet boom has made sending and receiving files much easier. This can cause problems, however, because the Windows, Mac, and other major computing platforms all deal with such files in a different fashion.

I hear constant complaints from people who get graphics files from others by e-mail or on disk that they can't read.

The following is a brief overview of some of the most popular graphic formats you may have to work with, whether you receive them from the Internet or share files with

Windows users. The list also includes the DOS file extensions, so you can be sure to name the files correctly when transferring them to that "other" platform.

■ **ART (.art) files**   This graphics format (from Johnson-Grace Company) is used to process images from the Internet on AOL, using its proxy server network, and is supposed to make Web pages come up faster on AOL by providing an extra layer of compression. But quality suffers and animated GIFs aren't supported. You also need AOL's software simply to open these kinds of images. GraphicConverter doesn't even understand this type of file. Even more annoying, converting the file won't change the extension, such as .gif or .jpg, which comes after its name. The only way to know if it's in the right format is to attempt to open it. To eliminate the annoyance of dealing with these problems, turn off the option to compress graphics from the Internet if you use AOL. This option is located among the WWW preferences in AOL's software.

NOTE   *A proxy server works as an intermediary between the AOL member and the Web site. Frequently accessed Web pages are stored on the proxy server which, along with the built-in compression, is supposed to improve Web speed for that service. The downside, however, is a delay might occur in getting the latest versions of a Web page that's frequently updated.*

■ **AVI (.avi) files**   This is Microsoft's movie format, intended as competition for QuickTime. QuickTime 4.0, via the QuickTime Player application, can easily read these files, though, so you don't need a separate AVI converter.

■ **BMP (.bmp) files**   This is the DOS or Windows equivalent of PICT. If you use the print screen feature on a Windows computer, the captured image is saved in this format. Because this is a bitmap format, it can be scaled downward, at the same time, increasing the resolution. The quality of the image declines, however, when the dot size grows larger if the image is scaled upward.

■ **EPS (.eps) files**   The name of this format stands for *Encapsulated PostScript*. Within EPS files are PostScript instructions that need a PostScript printer for the produced image to be of adequate quality. Only a low-resolution PICT version is produced if you don't have a PostScript printer. High-end graphics programs, such as Illustrator and FreeHand, are used to create EPS files and they are imported into desktop publishing or word processing files. This is the

Graphics Formats Compared

only vector format listed among these formats. An EPS file can be scaled to any size and yet retain its full resolution when reproduced on your printer or other output device.

■ **GIF (.gif) files** This compressed graphic format is a term meaning *Graphic Interchange Format*. GIF began on CompuServe. You can find good points and bad points when you deal with these files. They can be good for images on the Internet, but you can only use 256 colors (unlike JPEG). Besides being better for the Internet, GIF files produce better-looking text than JPEG.

■ **JPEG (.jpg) files** This is another compressed graphic format that stands for Joint Photographic Experts Group, which is a popular format for artwork on the Internet. The JPEG format employs a technique called *lossy* to compress files, in which portions of the files are removed, although a large amount of compression is necessary to make the quality of the images suffer noticeably. Most programs that save a picture in JPEG format give you various compression options, so you can trade off file size against the ultimate quality of your artwork. While JPEG files are great for photos (in fact, quality is so close to the original, it's often hard to tell the difference except by direct, close comparison), they don't do so well with graphics that have text in them.

■ **MOV (.mov) files** This format is used for QuickTime movies. It can be opened in QuickTime Player or any other program that can open QuickTime files.

■ **PCX (.pcx) files** This format is used in PC Paintbrush and other applications for bitmapped graphics on the PC side of the world. Four different versions of this format exist, but the so-called version 5 is the only type that supports millions of colors.

■ **PICT (.pct) files** This format for bitmap files is proprietary to the Mac platform. Whenever you save an image file to your clipboard or capture an image on the screen (by pressing COMMAND-SHIFT-3 or by a separate screen capture program, such as Ambrosia Software's SnapzPro), the file is saved in this format. The PICT format has to deal with the same disadvantages as other bitmap image formats. If you need to send a file to a person using Windows, don't use the PICT format.

■ **PNG (.png) files** Many believed this format would eventually succeed GIF. *PNG* stands for *Portable Network Graphics* and it allows a file to be compressed better, along with better quality for graphics and support for millions of colors (also known as 24-bit color). Internet browsers that support HTML 4.0 are also compatible with PNG. If it isn't, then you simply receive the GIF version of the image.

■ **SGI (.sgi) files**   This format is used for images on *SGI* (also called *Silicon Graphics*) workstations. You might have to deal with this type of image file occasionally because SGI computer systems are used often when creating complicated graphics and special effects for movies.

■ **Targa (.tga) files**   Truevision (now part of Pinnacle Systems) originally created this format for its Targa and Vista video capture boards. It's a bitmap format for files with high-quality graphics and is supported by a variety of graphics programs.

■ **TIFF (.tif) files**   The name of this format standards for *Tagged-Image Format*. If you really want to know, the *tagged* part of the name enhances an image to make it look better. TIFF files are often used for photos and other high-quality graphics. However, a complicated TIFF photograph with lots of colors can occupy a number of megabytes on your hard drive (even if you use a program's TIFF compression feature). For this reason, programs such as Photoshop need a lot of RAM to work with these files.

NOTE   *Unlike the compression feature used in a JPEG photo, the compression feature offered for TIFF photos in such programs as Adobe Photoshop is* lossless, *meaning no actual data from the picture is lost during the compression and decompression process. As a result, quality remains the same, though the file size is reduced.*

■ **WMF (.wmf) files**   This format stands for Windows Metafile Format and is used for exchanging graphics between programs on that "other" platform.

Troubleshooting Graphics Files

As previously stated, the explosion of the Internet has created the climate for more and more trouble with graphic files. Here are some of the main problems you can encounter and their solutions:

■ **Message saying "Application not found"**   If such an alert appears on your screen telling you no application can open a document, look in your Control Panel folder in the System Folder to double-check File Exchange

Troubleshooting Graphics Files

has been installed. If File Exchange has been disabled for some reason, open Extensions Manager and reactivate the extension. If you can't find File Exchange, do an Add/Removal reinstallation of Mac OS 9 to restore it. Chapter 2 covers the various approaches to a system installation.

NOTE   *Another possible solution to this problem is simply to rebuild the desktop on the drives you're using on your Mac. A corrupt desktop file can cause the loss of application/document links. Hold down the* COMMAND-OPTION *keys after your Mac boots, before the last startup icon appears. Release the keys when you see the prompt asking if you want to rebuild the desktop and OK the prompt. This message is repeated for each drive you have connected to your Mac.*

- **The wrong application is launched**   If you open a file by double-clicking it and it opens in the wrong program, you should trash your File Exchange preferences in the Preferences folder in the System Folder. If this doesn't do anything, rebuild your desktop by following the technique described in the previous note.

- **Use the Open dialog box**   If nothing seems to work, attempt to launch the application, and then select Open in the File menu of the program. Then select the file from the list. If the file doesn't appear in the dialog box and there's an insert, import, or place feature, use it. If the program supports a certain kind of graphic file format, this feature should help you.

NOTE   *I won't attempt to list which program supports a specific format, as the possibilities are vast. If the file you want to open doesn't seem to work with that program, check the program's Help menu or documentation to see what files it can read.*

Getting Mac Graphics Ready for a Windows Computer

If graphics files could be read immediately on different platforms, without changing the format or fixing the file's name, everything would be a lot easier.

Unfortunately, this isn't the case. With a Mac, the Finder automatically identifies the format of a file by using the invisible desktop files that tell what type of file it is and in what program it was created.

As for Windows, UNIX, and other computing platforms, however, the operating system tells what type of file something is by including a three-letter extension or suffix after the file's name. If you don't add this extension, the platforms won't understand how to deal with these files. Also, make sure the file has been saved in the correct format. If not, the file could end up being damaged or opened in the wrong format when someone using a different computing platform attempts to open it.

If you're going to send a JPEG file to a non-Mac computer, the .jpg extension must be added after the name of the file for the user to open it. Windows computers automatically add the necessary file extensions when you save your file on that platform.

The following explains how to prepare your files so Windows users can access and use your files with ease.

File Is in Right Format

If the file has been saved in a format that can be understood by the Windows platform, but hasn't been given the correct name, follow the next few steps:

1. To select the file's name, click it and then press the RETURN key.

2. Put the necessary file extension after the end of the name of the file. For example, if a file is in the JPEG format and the name of the file is zanther, you would rename the file **zanther.jpg**.

Now a Windows user who needs to access the file can easily open it in any program that supports its format.

File Not in Correct Format

If you haven't saved your file in a format supported by a computer running Windows, you must convert to a format Windows can read, as well as give the file the proper extension after its name.

Here is how to do this:

1. In the graphics program you want to use, open the file.

2. In the File menu, select Save As. A screen appears where you can choose whichever format you want to save the file. If your graphics program doesn't have a feature like this, select the Export command, if it has this option.

3. Select the proper format from the list. GraphicConverter, for example, automatically puts the proper file extension after its name (make sure its preference option to use DOS file extensions is checked).

4. Click the Save button to change the file's format and its name.

Getting Mac Graphics Ready for
a Windows Computer

Now, once you've sent the file to the Windows user, she should be able to open the file without any problems.

Summing Up

During the course of this chapter, you learned about the most prominent graphics software available for the Mac: Adobe Illustrator, PhotoDeluxe, Photoshop, Macromedia Freehand, and CorelDRAW and Corel PHOTO-PAINT. You also discovered how to handle problems with graphics files, especially when sending them to Windows users.

In the next chapter, you learn about desktop publishing in programs such as InDesign, QuarkXPress, and PageMaker, as well as getting documents ready for commercial printing.

Chapter 21

Publishing on Your Mac's Desktop

A revolution began on the Macintosh and spread throughout the publishing world. This revolution was desktop publishing. Before the Mac and a certain program from Adobe, called *PageMaker,* most folks who created typeset documents had to use dedicated computer systems and learn complex command codes. And many of these systems wouldn't even display the finished results, so you were apt to experience a nasty surprise if the printed result didn't meet your expectations.

NOTE   *This is an understatement. Some of those older dedicated computer systems didn't even have a data storage system. If you made a mistake, you had to do the job over or apply little patches on printed copy using tape, hot wax, or rubber cement.*

Can You Do Desktop Publishing on a Word Processor?

Long, long ago, a word processing program performed only a single set of functions having to do with writing a document, and then edited that document by removing and adding words, or moving them around. But through the years (some call it feature-bloat), word processing has taken on multicolumn creation, the capability to insert and edit pictures, and similar functions that take it closer to the traditional image of desktop publishing.

NOTE   *By feature-bloat, I mean today's word processor has literally hundreds of features beyond the basics. Those features include drawing tools, the capability to read and write Web (HTML) files, create outlines, track document revisions, and check not only spelling but also grammar.*

As you saw in the previous chapter, all word processing programs have a basic set of functions that appear to make them suitable for desktop publishing. You have a full range of text editing functions, you can edit character styles to include a slew of typeface, style, and text size options. You can create multiple-column documents with a look similar to a magazine or newspaper. You can also insert illustrations in those same documents.

And when you print the material, it looks pretty good, but is it suitable for commercial publishing? Well, you're part of the way there, but not completely. Let's look at some of the differences:

■ **Precision**   A desktop publishing program enables you to place text and picture elements with pinpoint accuracy, down to hundreds of an inch. This may not seem like a big deal to you until you look at a magazine, brochure, or other high-quality publication, and you see the exactness with which all the elements are placed. You cannot approach this measure of precision with word processing programs, though they come closer than they did in the past.

■ **Master pages**   When you create a document with complex designs that recur throughout a publication, master pages enable you to set up the default parameters, such as the basic layout of the page and recurring pictures, and then apply them to the specific sections of the document. This is way beyond simply setting up a stationery or template document, as extra master pages can be created to address-specific design problems.

■ **Refined character spacing**   Although some word processing programs offer this to a limited degree, a good desktop publishing program has powerful tools that enable you to adjust the way characters look in a document. One of the key features is *kerning,* in which one letter is tucked into another to make it look better to the naked eye. A common example of kerning is to place a lowercase *o* inside the capital letter *T*. This tucked-in effect, when you get used to looking at it, is the hallmark of good quality typography. While word processors can sometimes manage this in a rather crude fashion, once you get used to the look, you see a vast difference exists.

■ **Refined word spacing and justification**   A desktop publishing program also has tools to control the space between words so a paragraph of text is properly balanced. A notable example is the multiline composer feature that distinguishes Adobe InDesign, which lets the program check the line breaks for six lines (this is the default setting) to provide the best overall look. In addition, all the programs described here enable you to adjust such parameters as how many words in a row can be broken by hyphens and how many letters before such a break should be considered by the software's algorithm.

■ **Color controls**   This is far beyond simply applying a color to your text or picture. Desktop publishing programs are designed to support both spot color and process color, so you can create true separations for full-color work. With process color, a document is printed in four parts: cyan, magenta, yellow, or black. Combined, negatives in each of the four colors produce a true full-color print job. Spot color features enable you to specify the actual color ink used by your printer from the same color palette. Such colors come from several firms, including Focaltone, Pantone, Toyo, and Truematch. Another color option is called *trapping,* which is a scheme designed to compensate for paper and printing plates for a multicolor job not lining up precisely (it's considered out of register). Trapping is a process of compensating for the small gaps that might appear in the printed page as a result of this condition, by expanding the lighter colored areas of a document to overlap the darker ones slightly. Unless the registration problem is severe, this usually compensates for the problem.

Comparing Desktop Publishing Software

As with any program category, there are many reasons why you like one desktop publishing program or the other. Newsgroup message boards and computer magazines are littered with debates about the benefits of, for example, Adobe PageMaker versus QuarkXPress. And, the arrival of Adobe's InDesign, which was referred to in the computing press as the *Quark killer* (because it was designed to challenge that program's dominance in the publishing industry) has only intensified the discussion.

In this section, some of the major features of each program are discussed so you can have a basis for comparison. The big factor, however, is whether you need to be compatible with users in your company, in another company, or whether you intend to have your documents printed commercially. In the last case, the program the printer prefers to work with may dictate your choices.

Adobe PageMaker Plus

Adobe PageMaker (see Figure 21-1) was the desktop publishing program that, with the arrival of PostScript and laser printers, caused a revolution in the publishing industry. Adobe PageMaker gave the Mac dominance in these areas (a dominance that still exists, despite the heavy market penetration of Windows in other business categories).

NOTE   *To be quite technical, PageMaker (then published by Aldus, which was later taken over by Adobe) wasn't the first publishing program. That honor went to Ready,Set,Go, which is discussed in more detail later in this chapter. But even at its best, the earlier program never gained anywhere near the popularity of PageMaker.*

PageMaker uses the same design metaphor as the traditional paste-up artist who used to generate artwork and text layouts for printing. In those days, artwork (including typesetting proofs and pictures) was assembled on a large piece of thick paper and pasted down with hot wax or rubber cement. The thick paper would

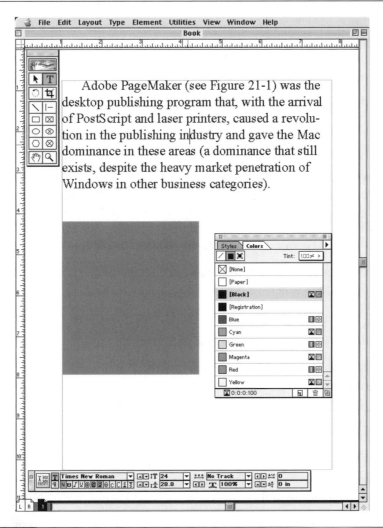

FIGURE 21-1   Adobe PageMaker Plus put the desktop publishing industry on the map

normally have guidemarks (printed in a so-called nonreproducible color) the artist would use, along with various sorts of rulers to place the artwork in position as accurately as possible.

PageMaker enables you to do the same thing on your Mac, by letting you drag-and-drop the elements of your page into position. You can also use fixed guidelines to align multicolumn text. The latest versions of the program support a frame-based metaphor, similar to the ones used with Adobe InDesign and QuarkXPress. It uses text and graphic frames that are, simply stated, containers that hold this material, so it conforms to a specific design concept.

Here, with pictures, are some of PageMaker's key features:

- **Fairly modest system requirements**   PageMaker can work on any Mac that can run Mac OS 9. It needs 12MB of RAM for itself and consumes close to 60MB of disk storage space, plus the space consumed by the templates and artwork provided.

- **Easy integration with Adobe's products**   If you're used to working with Adobe Illustrator and Adobe Photoshop, you should find PageMaker's working environment an easy adaptation. Adobe has strived to give a similar look across the board with the program's menu bar labels and various and sundry floating palettes. This helps reduce the learning curve.

- **Hundreds of prebuilt templates**   In keeping with PageMaker Plus's business document orientation, Adobe offers a large number of templates covering a number of business categories, so you needn't waste your time designing your publication from scratch. You can easily adapt one of the existing designs to match your requirements.

- **Extensive selection of export and import filters**   PageMaker makes it easy for you to import text and artwork from a wide variety of formats. In addition to Adobe Illustrator and Photoshop, you can import files from such programs as Microsoft's Excel and Word, plus bitmap files created on both Mac and Windows computers.

- **Hotlinks to Adobe programs**   When you import (PageMaker calls the process *place*) a graphic file made with Adobe Illustrator or Photoshop, you can easily open these files directly from PageMaker for further editing.

- **Multiple master pages**   This is a feature all the programs discussed here share. It enables you to create custom designs, including column guides, margins, and repeating backgrounds, so they can easily be applied to specific pages in your publication.

- **Large document publishing support**   PageMaker Plus can handle anything from a one-page brochure to a book with up to 999 pages in a single document. It includes indexing and table of contents generation, so you can prepare complete books or magazines in this program.

■ **Story Editor**   This is a feature unique to PageMaker (see Figure 21-2). The Story Editor is a sort of miniature word processor where you can enter your text and handle such normal chores as spell-checking. As you write text, it flows through your actual page layout. The theory behind this feature is that editing simple text is much faster than working through the text in a complex document, but this isn't a feature that has any support in the other programs.

■ **Automatic Layout Adjustment**   This feature aids in the precision of your publication, making it possible to position and resize the elements automatically that make up the document. As you change master pages to conform to a new design, the contents of your document based on those master pages also changes. This helps enhance the freeflow nature of this program.

■ **Frames for graphics and text**   As with Adobe's other desktop publishing program, InDesign and QuarkXPress, you can set up your publication using text or graphic frames to contain the contents of some parts of your design. This feature, by the way, works in concert with PageMaker's freeform design motif, giving you more design options.

■ **Plug-ins**   Add-on modules, called *plug-ins,* can be used to enhance the core capabilities of PageMaker. While not as extensive as those available for QuarkXPress, this means you can extend the features of the program beyond the standard range of capabilities.

Comparing Desktop Publishing Software

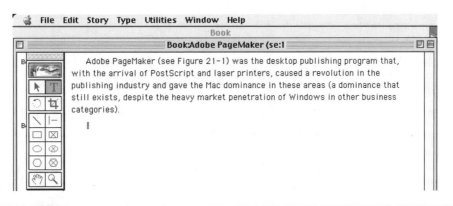

File   Edit   Story   Type   Utilities   Window   Help

Book

Book:Adobe PageMaker (se:1

Adobe PageMaker (see Figure 21-1) was the desktop publishing program that, with the arrival of PostScript and laser printers, caused a revolution in the publishing industry and gave the Mac dominance in these areas (a dominance that still exists, despite the heavy market penetration of Windows in other business categories).

FIGURE 21-2   PageMaker's Story Editor amounts to a simple word processor

- **Internet integration**   In keeping with the migration toward the Internet, you can export a PageMaker publication to HTML format, while retaining reasonable fidelity to the original design. You can also embed hyperlinks in your publication, pointing to other parts of your document or to any Internet URL.

- **Save as PDF**   You can save your finished PageMaker publication in Adobe's *PDF* format (the acronym for *Portable Document Format*), the popular format used for online documentation. This allows your document to be printed on nearly any output device.

Although PageMaker is widely used in the publishing industry, it has never generated quite the impact as QuarkXPress.

Adobe InDesign

In the months before the release of Adobe's new high-end desktop publishing program, InDesign (see Figure 21-3), its publicity engine was working at full steam. Reports were published about a product with the code-name *K2,* dubbed the *QuarkXPress killer.*

The goal of the QuarkXPress killer was obvious: to compete head-on with QuarkXPress and gain ascendancy in the professional publishing industry and in advertising agencies. The first release of InDesign, the one described in this chapter, appeared in the summer of 1999.

NOTE   *At press time, an update to InDesign was expected spring/summer 2000, which would provide new features and, perhaps, address some of the limitations of the previous versions of the program.*

The following are some of the major features of InDesign that make it a compelling alternative and a few areas that may create problems for you:

- **Hefty system requirements**   InDesign has a lot of core features, as you see in the following pages, but it also extracts a high degree of system resources. It works fine with Mac OS 9, but you need to devote at least 20MB of RAM to the program (it needs twice that to get optimum performance), a Mac with a 604 or faster CPU (G3s and G4s are much better), and the basic installation consumes over 90MB of disk storage space.

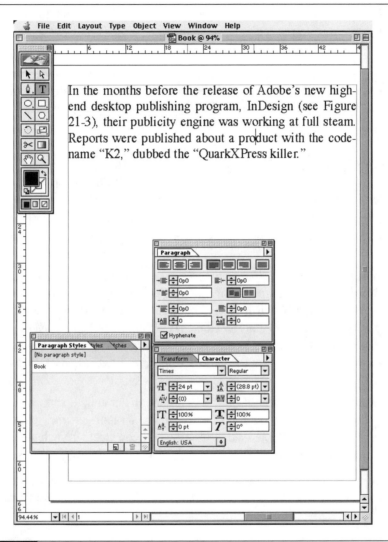

In the months before the release of Adobe's new high-end desktop publishing program, InDesign (see Figure 21-3), their publicity engine was working at full steam. Reports were published about a product with the code-name "K2," dubbed the "QuarkXPress killer."

Comparing Desktop Publishing Software

| FIGURE 21-3 | InDesign has a basic look that resembles other Adobe programs |

■ **Opens PageMaker and QuarkXPress documents**   If you're migrating to InDesign from PageMaker or QuarkXPress, take heart. You can open files created in either program. The process isn't quite seamless, as some design elements may be changed. But, even if you have to edit your design to fix a few problems, it's a far more pleasant process than building a new document from scratch.

NOTE *In my experience, InDesign was actually able to open several complicated QuarkXPress documents with reasonable fidelity. The biggest change was the way text flowed because the hyphenation and justification settings in InDesign differ considerably from those in XPress.*

- **Easy integration with Adobe products** InDesign has the look and feel of other Adobe products, such as Illustrator and Photoshop, so the learning curve is fairly easy. I can open native Illustrator and Photoshop documents without having to save those documents in any special way (such as EPS or TIFF), and it also supports PDF files, both importing and exporting.

CAUTION *While InDesign can export a file to PDF format, the format is strictly Acrobat 4.0, which means you cannot view the documents in older versions of Acrobat. In addition, the files InDesign creates do not work well with printers that use a PostScript clone, rather than licensed Adobe PostScript technology. This causes problems for recent printers from HP and other makers who support emulated PostScript rather than the real thing.*

- **Extensive file import options** In addition to handling documents created in Adobe's graphic programs directly, you can import a variety of graphic formats, such as EPS and TIFF, plus the text you create in such industry-standard programs as Microsoft Word (Mac and Windows versions).

- **Integrated drawing tools** InDesign incorporates a subset of Illustrator's drawing tools, so you can edit an Illustrator document or simply build one from scratch.

- **Multiple master pages** As with the competition, InDesign enables you to create separate master pages to incorporate different styles in your publication. This way, you can make complicated documents without having to re-create involved designs.

- **Unlimited undo and redo** This feature sets InDesign apart from the competition. You are no longer limited to Mac OS 9's standard single undo and redo capability. You can easily compare multiple degrees of changes until you hone in on the actual look you want.

■ **Advanced kerning controls**   This is definitely worth some discussion. The automatic kerning features of PageMaker and QuarkXPress use fixed measurements to bring two characters together (such as the tucking of the lowercase *o* under the capital *T,* as mentioned previously in this chapter). InDesign adds an optical kerning feature, which adjusts spacing, so instead of only measuring well, it looks good. This is extremely useful for advertising agencies, who insist on the nearest thing to perfect letter fit. The capability to do this automatically, rather than depending on manual adjustments, is a big plus.

■ **Multiline composer**   This feature is my favorite (see Figure 21-4). Normally a desktop publishing program handles its justification of text one line at a time. This means that the look of a paragraph may be unbalanced, with some lines having words spaced too far apart, others too close together. In its normal form, the multiline composer compares six lines at a time, making sure that the line breaks are optimized for the best possible look.

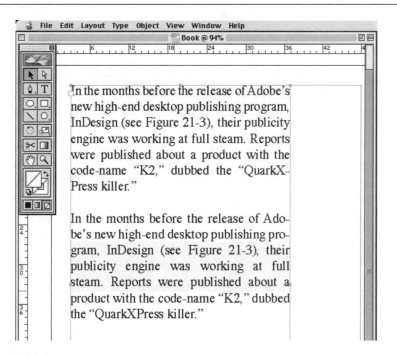

Comparing Desktop
Publishing Software

FIGURE 21-4   This picture shows the same paragraph with (above) and without (below) multiline composer applied

■ **Character-based styles** You needn't create styles for an entire paragraph. You can also create a special character-based style, so you can easily convert words to italic, bold, or underlined form without affecting the entire paragraph.

■ **Frame-based layout** InDesign uses text and graphic frames for your design. As previously described, frames, or text and picture boxes, are containers that hold the elements of your publication.

■ **Flexible grids and guides** You can use InDesign's handy snap-to feature so text and graphic elements easily line up to your grids. This ensures a virtually exact fit, resulting in the maximum degree of precision in your document.

■ **Internet integration** You can save InDesign documents in HTML format for publishing your documents on the Web.

■ **Plug-in architecture** The program is heavily dependent on plug-ins, those add-on modules that provide many of its basic features. This makes supplying program updates easy for Adobe, and it also makes it possible for third-party software companies to make plug-ins to provide features missing from the program, such as indexing and table of contents generation.

■ **Built-in preflighting** A *preflighting feature* gives InDesign the capability of double-checking all elements of your publication to be sure everything is correct, and then copying it into a single folder (a package), which makes sending your publication to a prepress or a printing establishment easy for you.

Adobe InDesign packs a lot of wallop for a first-generation product. Its multiline composer sets it a breed apart from the competition, but this feature also makes the program run slower, even on a speedy G3 Power Mac. InDesign's lack of long-document features, such as indexes and table of contents generation, can be filled by outside providers, but having this as part of the core program, as it is in PageMaker and QuarkXPress, would definitely help to endear this program to publishers.

Then again, I'm covering version 1.0 here and, no doubt, some of the program's shortcomings will be addressed as it continues to be developed.

QuarkXPress

Although Adobe PageMaker is popular among small business users, advertising agencies and publishers have given the nod to QuarkXPress (although exceptions can be found anywhere), as shown in Figure 21-5.

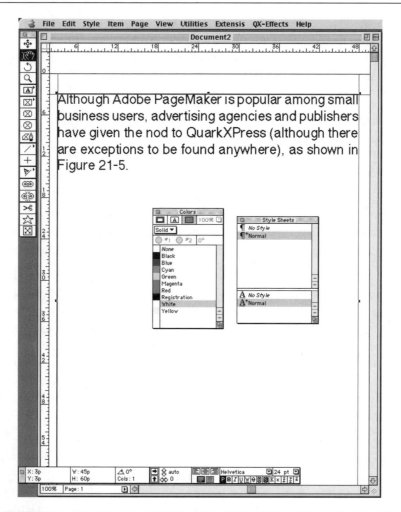

FIGURE 21-5   QuarkXPress is used to create many of the books and magazines you buy

Comparing Desktop
Publishing Software

While PageMaker uses the design metaphor of the paste-up artist for its basic design features, QuarkXPress appeals to the commercial typography in its insistence on precision and control. Depending on which sort of approach you like, XPress may be simple or difficult to master.

Here's a list of some of the program's notable features:

- **Small system requirements**   QuarkXPress runs easily on any Mac that can handle Mac OS 9. It's even reasonably fast on a basic Power Macintosh 6100, which has a 60 MHz PowerPC 601 CPU. The program needs 12–13MB for itself (less with virtual memory on), and takes less than 20MB of disk storage space on your hard drive.

- **Integrated drawing tools**   With Adobe Illustrator in mind, QuarkXPress added extensive drawing tools to the core program. This enables you to create complex artwork without needing to resort to another program to create that material.

- **Frame-based elements**   All text and graphic elements are put into containers or frames, which can be resized by a mouse or a dialog box to the size you want. Although you specify a separate text or picture box before you write or import your text, you can switch the type of frame from one form to another (with appropriate changes to the contents).

- **Advanced color trapping controls**   Although Adobe PageMaker and InDesign provide support for color work, whether it's spot colors or separations, QuarkXPress prides itself on having more extensive capabilities to adjust trapping and other color management settings (including color style sheets for the components of your document). The downside to all this flexibility is that someone who is inexperienced on color work can easily make the wrong setting. In the hands of the experienced professional, though, it is a big plus.

- **Quark XTensions**   Quark's add-on technology is called *XTensions*. Because this program was one of the first of its type to support plug-ins, hundreds of QuarkXTensions are available. Some are free, directly supplied by Quark Inc. Others come from a variety of publishers around the world. They address everything from the basic program features to handling advanced table creation workflow management for large organizations.

- **Up to 127 master pages**   You can apply only one or up to 127 master page pairs (left and right side) in a single document. The program's document layout palette (see Figure 21-6), similar to one provided in InDesign, helps you create new document and master pages, and apply specific master pages to a document page.

■ **Long document format features**   QuarkXPress has a built-in indexing and table of contents generation feature, which enables you to handle large documents easily, such as books and technical manuals, without having to buy extra software. You can make a single document up to 2,000 pages in length, compared to 999 with PageMaker and an awesome 9,999 in InDesign (though that program lacks indexing or table of contents features).

■ **File import capabilities**   Graphic files can be imported in the standard formats, such as EPS, JPEG, and TIFF, and you can also import text in such programs as Microsoft Word.

■ **Both character and paragraph styles**   As with Adobe InDesign, you can have separate styles for characters and styles, so you can easily switch typefaces for individual words or letters in a paragraph without affecting the entire paragraph.

■ **Collect for output**   Although the process has some limitations, it enables you to collect the original document easily, plus put all linked graphics into a single folder, along with a text report of its contents and the files used.

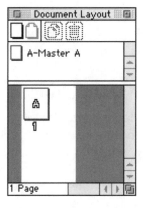

FIGURE 21-6   QuarkXPress uses a document layout palette to add and move pages around

Comparing Desktop Publishing Software

Unfortunately, the process doesn't include the fonts, and that's where many of the common problems with outputting a job occur.

■ **Internet Integration** Beginning with QuarkXPress 4.1, you can save your XPress documents in HTML format for publishing on the Web without a special XTension.

■ **Save to PDF** QuarkXPress has a special filter (included with version 4.1 or later) that enables you to convert your documents to Adobe's PDF format. The filter has its limits, however. For example, you need to buy the full Adobe Acrobat retail package, which includes its Acrobat Distiller application, to use this feature.

QuarkXPress provides a speedy, responsive environment and lots of precision features that have made it a standard-bearer in the desktop publishing industry. The learning curve may be a little difficult for beginning users, though, because QuarkXPress doesn't look like the competition in many respects. The exact nature of the way you create elements for the program mimics the approach taken by a typographer, for example.

If you have experience in desktop design, you should find QuarkXPress isn't terribly hard to master. It also has extensive support on the part of the printing and service bureau industry because it provides reliable, predictable performance.

NOTE *This is a brief exception to the previous paragraph. If you're using the early releases of QuarkXPress 4, you could find printing performance is unpredictable. Version 4 was a major update with lots of new features and it shipped with its share of bugs (many related to printing). But Quark Inc. has also provided several free updates, including the one to version 4.1. These updates have all but vanquished many of those early release problems.*

Other Publishing Program Choices

The big three desktop publishing programs described here aren't the only options for your books, brochures, magazines, newsletters, and other publications.

A number of Mac users have stuck by a program called Ready,Set,Go through the years. This program is similar to QuarkXPress in some respects because it's based on a framed-metaphor, with textboxes and picture boxes.

Ready,Set,Go was started by a New York-based printing company, Manhattan Graphics, but it never caught on, either with users or commercial printers, or the big three desktop publishing programs. It is still being published, however, by London-based Diwan Software Limited. You can get more information about Ready,Set,Go from the publisher's Web site at http://www.diwan.com/ready/prsg.htm.

Another alternative made only a brief appearance on the Mac platform, but failed to capture a sizeable user base: Corel's VENTURA, a descendant of the original Ventura Publisher that was distributed by Xerox for a number of years.

Still available on the Windows platform, VENTURA is especially suited for large documents, such as books. In fact, this book was put together using VENTURA. The program relies heavily on formatting documents using *tags,* which are commands specifying how an item in your document is to be formatted. In this respect, it's somewhat reminiscent of the HTML language used for Web pages.

NOTE   *Adobe's other page layout program, FrameMaker, continues to be produced for the Mac, Windows, and UNIX environments. FrameMaker excels in preparing long technical documents because of its capability to insert links and cross references, but it hasn't had a substantial update in several years.*

Preparing Documents for Commercial Printing

When you complete your document, you're used to using the Print command to get a printed copy. That's fine and dandy, even with a desktop publishing document, unless you want to take it to a commercial printer. Then all sorts of design considerations crop up. And you can expect to have times when the document you send to the printer doesn't come back as you expected (or you have to field frantic telephone calls from the printer's production staff).

The following is some basic advice on preparing your document for commercial printing. This can help you get past the major problems. But the best advice I can offer is to take the time to discuss the job with your service bureau or printer, or both, before you start working on your publication. This way, you can take steps to avoid problems and last-minute changes that might cause unexpected mistakes in the printed piece.

Comparing Desktop Publishing Software

Print Shop and Service Bureau: What's the Difference?

Before the era of desktop publishing, you'd typically take your artwork directly to the printer, who would handle everything from color separations to the printed pages and binding.

With the advent of personal computers and desktop publishing, another sort of business has come into play, serving as an intermediary between you and your printer. That's the service bureau (or prepress house). A *service bureau* handles a number of elements you may need to prepare your document for printing. These may consist of high-resolution color proofs, film, or paper output on a high-resolution imagesetter, or additional design services such as color preparation (trapping and separations).

True, some printers offer all these services under one roof. But others expect to receive the artwork ready for press, and that's where the service bureau comes into the picture.

- **Don't take color lightly**   Doing color correctly in a printed document isn't always easy. And the arcane points of proper trapping and color selection definitely require training and attention to detail. Unless you have the experience in handling color documents, the best suggestion is to work with your printer to pick the right colors and color setup for your publication. If necessary, you should consider paying for the printer's production staff to put the final touches on your document. This may be a lot cheaper than having to reprint a job because the colors didn't come out the way you wanted.

- **Calibrate your colors**   Apple's ColorSync enables you to calibrate your Mac's display (even the ones on the iBook and PowerBook). Many scanners and color printers support the technology. This enables you to get the closest possible match to the colors you specify on your screen.

NOTE   *Calibrating color is nothing to take lightly. The colors you see on your Mac's display use a different color method (RGB) than, for example, your printed full-color documents (which use a four-color method). Depending on the level of mismatch, the printouts may be darker or lighter, or the actual colors themselves may look different.*

■ **Use PostScript fonts**   Although Apple gives you TrueType fonts with your Mac and many great designs are available in this format, the commercial printing industry long ago standardized on PostScript. While newer, high-resolution output devices should handle either format without a problem, this isn't true with every establishment. Again, communication with your printer is essential.

■ **Check your own printed copy carefully**   Don't assume what you see on the screen is what will be printed. Remember, your Mac's display typically has a resolution of 72 dots per inch. Even the oldest laser printer prints at 300 dots per inch, and most current inkjet printers and laser printers handle 600 dots per inch and greater. In addition, problems with fonts and graphics may not be obvious till you look at the output. Obviously, the image you see on the printed page is a much more accurate representation of what comes off the press.

■ **Give a printed copy with your job when submitting it**   Whether you go to a service bureau or a printer directly, you should give the company a printed copy, even if you have the lowest cost inkjet printer available. They need a reference point to check against possible mistakes. Don't assume that because it looks perfect to you, the job will also be perfect at their end. If you upload your publication directly to a printer's Web site or FTP site, you should still try to fax or ship them a printed copy so they have a rough approximation of how the job should look.

■ **Don't forget the job information form**   Printers and service bureaus have special forms where you need to be specific about your material. You need to list the exact program and version number used to make the document, and to provide information about linked graphic files (this is explained in the next section) and fonts.

■ **Send the graphic files, too**   Word processing programs embed the graphic elements of your publication that were created in other programs as part of the document. With a few exceptions (small graphics in a PageMaker document), desktop publishing programs do not. All they do is store the links to the original files. This means you must also include those graphics files with your document. If you don't, all you'll see is a low-resolution version of the image (and this can be a horrible surprise if your job is printed that way).

Preparing Documents for Commercial Printing

■ **Be careful about graphic file formats**   The standard Mac graphic format, PICT, looks fine on the screen, but it isn't so fine when printed out on a high-resolution output device (because the printed resolution is much higher). You should consider using the TIFF format for bitmap graphics and EPS for vector artwork (artwork consisting of contiguous lines, rather than only individual pixels). This would include illustrations created in such programs as Adobe Illustrator, CorelDRAW, and Macromedia FreeHand.

NOTE   *More information on the various graphic formats and which ones are most useful is in Chapter 20.*

■ **Make sure they have the same software as you**   Printers and service bureaus typically have the mainstays in desktop publishing, such as Adobe PageMaker and QuarkXPress. Adobe InDesign is still quite new and not all firms support this program. Finding a shop with Deneba's Canvas or Ready,Set,Go is rare (contact the publishers of those programs to see if they have information on companies in your area who do support those products).

■ **Consider saving the files in PostScript format**   With a little planning, this is an option that could save you grief. You needn't worry about supplying the correct graphics or fonts. The actual file contains all the information needed to output the job. The limitation is if the file must be edited. The process of editing a PostScript files requires a trained technician and can be expensive. You also want to check with your printer or service bureau about special Page Setup requirements because you may have to configure the job in a special way to work properly on their output devices. To save the job as a PostScript file, you need to have your Mac set up to use LaserWriter 8, and then, in the Print dialog box, click the Destination pop-up menu and choose File (see Figure 21-7). Once you do this, you see a regular Save As dialog box where you give your print job a name.

■ **Also consider Adobe Acrobat format**   Adobe's InDesign (with the limitations previously noted) can save a document in Adobe's PDF, the same format used for all the online documentation that fills so many software CDs these days (including the one you get with Mac OS 9). A PDF file can be easily output on nearly any printer, whether or not it supports PostScript. And your graphic files and fonts can be easily embedded in the document. The biggest limitation for Acrobat format is

| FIGURE 21-7 | Saving a file in PostScript form may be a good choice for high-resolution output |

color, which is still a work in progress. Again, consulting with your printer or service bureau on this is the best approach.

■ **Use a preflight program**   A preflight program examines your publication, including all linked graphics and fonts, and assembles everything in a single folder so you can easily copy all the needed files to the disk you send to your service bureau or printer. One useful example is Extensis Preflight Pro (see Figure 21-8). This program also checks your document for potential printing problems, such as improper page settings or missing linked graphic files, so you can fix what's wrong before you make an expensive mistake.

A Fast ColorSync Tutorial

When you need to match the color of your document from screen to printed copy, you must spend some time calibrating all the devices used in the job. Apple's ColorSync feature enables you to do that by creating and using special profiles for each device.

When you install Mac OS 9, a selection of color profiles already exists for Apple's own displays and color inkjet printers. Many manufacturers of such

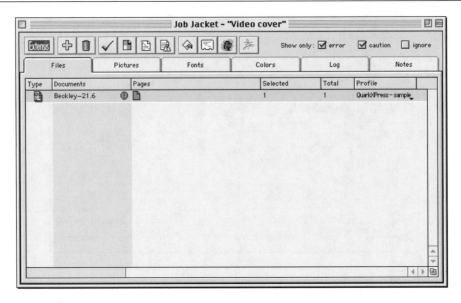

FIGURE 21-8   Extensis Preflight Pro can take some of the guesswork out of submitting your files to a prepress outfit

products as scanners and printers include their own ColorSync profiles, so you can easily match the colors you see onscreen to the ones in the printout, that is, if you calibrate your display first.

> NOTE   *The standard calibration scheme of ColorSync is easy to do, but depends somewhat on guesswork. If you need exact matching, especially if your Mac is located in an art department generating work for the advertising or publishing industries, you might want to contact the manufacturer or your dealer about a hardware calibration device, which actually measures the display and gives you more accurate results.*

How to Calibrate Your Display with ColorSync

With Mac OS 9, Apple includes an enhanced version of the Monitor Calibration Assistant, which enables you to customize your display in minutes.

To use this feature, follow these steps:

1. Go to the Apple menu, choose Control Panels, and then select Monitors from the submenu.

2. Click the Color icon (see Figure 21-9).

3. You see a list of default display profiles. Pick one that appears to match your Mac's display. If you don't see one that includes the manufacturer's name, simply pick the type of display (such as Trinitron).

4. Click the Calibrate button, which brings up the Monitor Calibration Assistant (see Figure 21-10).

5. Click the Expert mode to give you the full range of options.

6. Use the Next button at the bottom of the screen, and follow through each step of the process. Use the instructions provided to guide you. The first setup screen is used to set your display's brightness and contrast. The next screen you see is used to determine your monitor's current gamma (see Figure 21-11), or midtone adjustment. You have to move back from your display a bit now. Try to line up the colors so the Apple logo in the center matches up with the color of the rest of the square. This may take a little trial-and-error to get it right, so be patient.

7. Once you've determined your display, select a Target gamma (see Figure 21-12). Again, you use the slider control to adjust this setting as precisely as possible.

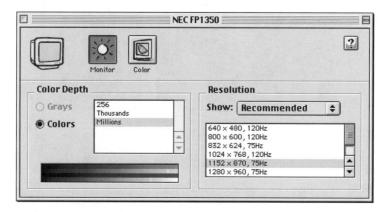

A Fast ColorSync Tutorial

FIGURE 21-9   Set your Mac's display settings from this Control Panel

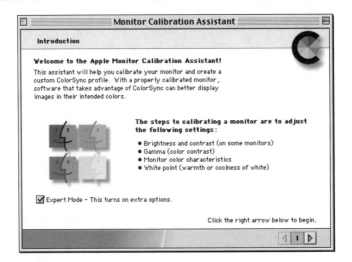

FIGURE 21-10   Begin calibrating your Mac's display here

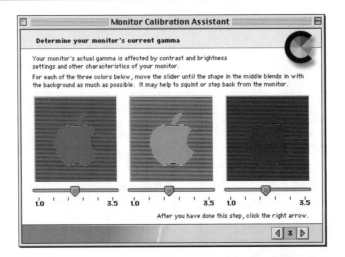

FIGURE 21-11   Drag the slider to make the display's gamma settings

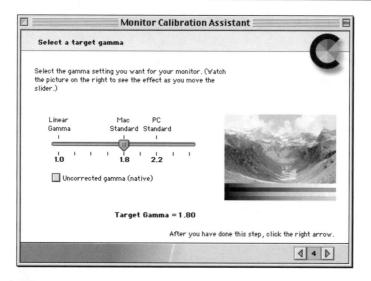

FIGURE 21-12   Use this screen to set the target gamma

8. On the next screen, you set your display's white point, again using a slider to customize your settings.

9. When you finish, you can save the calibrated profile under any name that identifies it quickly for you. This profile is stored in the ColorSync Profiles folder inside the System Folder.

NOTE   *While you might be tempted to use the calibrated profile to set up a similar display on another Mac, I suggest you don't. Each display, even of the same make and model, has enough of a variance in adjustments to make doing a separate profile for each Mac more productive. Besides, the process only takes a few minutes to complete.*

Summing Up

In this chapter, you learned about the major programs used to create documents in the publishing world: Adobe InDesign, QuarkXPress, and Adobe PageMaker. You

A Fast ColorSync Tutorial

discovered the major features of each program and received hints and tips about preparing your documents for printing on a regular laser printer or by commercial printing.

In the next chapter, another important area of desktop publishing is covered, one that is often the cause of annoyance, or worse: fonts.

Chapter 22

The Magic, Mystery, and Aggravation of Fonts

No matter what, you always need fonts on your Mac, whether you're making a word processing document or an entire presentation. You even need them for the menu bars and display.

The Macintosh was attractive to the graphics industry in its early years because not only were fonts easily available, but also because of the invention of the PostScript page description language, fonts written for PostScript, and laser printers.

Considering that the Mac was supposed to be the easiest personal computer to use, realizing that font management is no cakewalk often comes as a shock. Keeping tabs on your fonts and handling them properly, especially when you have a lot at hand, can be a chore.

This chapter helps you organize fonts and conflicts you may face when dealing with them.

Exploring TrueType versus PostScript Fonts

In the early days of the Mac, fonts were bitmapped. Different fonts were checked for different sizes, and whatever was produced onscreen was then reproduced on the page, at least as well as the ImageWriter and similar dot-matrix printers available at that time could do it.

Everything changed, however, when Adobe invented PostScript, which reduced the various elements on a page into math. Coming along for the ride were PostScript fonts. If you needed to have fonts that would print in any size at the full resolution of your printer, then PostScript was for you. But, as you see throughout this chapter, all that marvelous technology had its shortcomings.

Exploring PostScript Fonts

For people doing computerized typesetting back in the early days (before personal computers), the fonts you used came with two parts. First were the actual forms of the letters, which came on a thin piece of film or a floppy disk. Then the second part, a printed circuit card or floppy disk, contained the width values for the fonts. In those days, this was usually called a *width card* or a *width disk*. This information was used to let the computer know how wide a character must be.

When Adobe introduced scalable fonts to the world, they stuck to this idea. First was the screen font, which clearly displayed the font on your screen in a single size, The screen font also included the font's width values. As with the older typesetting systems, this insured that the letter *m* would be wider than the letter *i*—except for fonts (called "monospaced") where all width values were the same.

The other component of a PostScript font was the printer font, which has the outline information for the font. This component of the font is what enables you to use the size you want, while getting the same quality as you would at any other size. Figure 22-1 shows one of Adobe's PostScript screen fonts at the left and the printer font at the right. Icons do differ, depending on who makes the fonts. In some cases, the printer font's icon matches its purpose (that of a printer).

You must install both parts of the font. The screen font is used to build font menus in your programs; the printer font is needed for high-quality output. Otherwise, the screen font is used, and you are limited to a low-resolution version of the font. This low-resolution version gets worse when you pick a size that's different from the size of the screen font. Screen fonts usually come in a single file that contain several sizes and several styles. The file is called a *suitcase,* which explains its icon (see Figure 22-2).

NOTE   *To make matters more confusing, the original font management utility (currently published by Extensis) was also called Suitcase. And when you ask someone about a suitcase, it's common to have the suitcase file confused with the program of the same name.*

The biggest shortcoming of the screen font was that it only looked good if you selected a point size that matched the size of the screen font. Depending on how far you moved from that size, the quality got progressively worse, until the letters were impossible to recognize. Apple's QuickDraw display technology tried to fill in the gaps with little success.

Exploring TrueType versus
PostScript Fonts

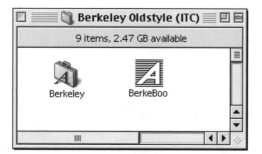

FIGURE 22-1   The components of a typical PostScript font (the printer font is at the right)

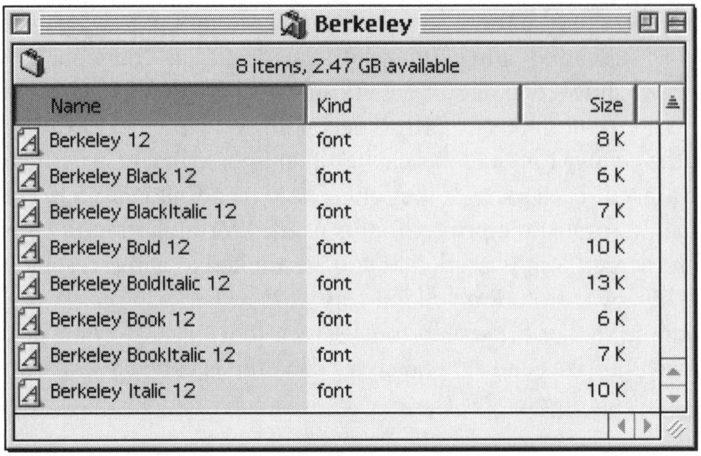

FIGURE 22-2 A suitcase file contains several screen font files and, perhaps (as you discover later in this chapter), a TrueType font

Adobe finally managed to find a solution to this problem. In the fall of 1989, Adobe released *Adobe Type Manager* (*ATM*). ATM worked its miracle by taking a single-screen font size, and then accessing the printer font to generate clear font displays on your screen in all available sizes.

You cannot imagine how budding desktop publishers at the time appreciated the ability to see what the fonts looked like on the Mac's display (to be fair, Adobe also eventually developed a Windows version that accomplished the same thing for the other computing platform).

ATM also did the same thing for non-PostScript printers as it did for screen display. You could take a cheap inkjet or dot-matrix printer and get pretty good text output because ATM was acting as the processor or rasterizer, converting the font information to a form it could reproduce clearly even if a PostScript printer wasn't used.

The End of ATM?

Maybe not, but Adobe has begun to install ATM technology into some of its graphic programs. A case in point is Adobe's high-end desktop publishing tool, InDesign. When you use InDesign, you don't need to have ATM around to get a clear display of your PostScript fonts.

In addition, Mac OS 9 includes an extension called Type 1 Scaler, which is designed to deliver clear screen display of Type 1 PostScript fonts for programs that use *Apple Type Services for Unicode Imaging* (*ATSUI*). *Unicode* is an international standard for double-byte character generation. Only programs that provide support for this technology (used basically to create computer readable character sets for ideograph-based characters, such as those used in Asian languages) benefit from this extension.

> **NOTE**   *Type 1 and Type 3 PostScript fonts are discussed later in this chapter.*

> **TIP**   *If you are not using a Unicode program, you can dispense with the Type 1 Scaler and reclaim about 1MB of RAM on your Mac.*

Installing a PostScript Font

Installing a PostScript font is a simple process. Drag the files to your Mac OS 9 System Folder icon. The clever Finder recognizes what the files are and will, after asking you to OK a dialog box, put them in the Fonts folder.

> **NOTE**   *You can avoid the Fonts folder and manage a big font library more efficiently. This is covered later in this chapter.*

The Types of PostScript Fonts

Two types of PostScript fonts actually exist. The one most commonly used is Type 1.

The other kind of PostScript font is Type 3 (there's no point in mentioning whatever happened to Type 2, except to mention there aren't any!).

You don't find Type 3 fonts around much, though they do turn up occasionally. The basic value for Type 3 fonts was for custom-designed logos, and the capability to handle shades and fills better than Type 1. On the other hand, Type 3 fonts use more disk storage space and occupy more of your printer's memory to work. And worse, they aren't supported by ATM, so you must have screen fonts in all the sizes you plan to use for good screen display.

From here on, when PostScript fonts are mentioned, it'll be strictly Type 1.

Introducing TrueType

Font management got either simpler or more confusing (depending on your point of view) when Apple introduced TrueType in 1990. Originally, the new font format was produced, in part, to avoid paying licensing fees to use Adobe's fonts. The TrueType font also was easier to handle because both screen and outline fonts were integrated into the same file. You didn't have to worry about missing or losing one or the other.

Although Apple originated TrueType, its biggest boost has probably come in the Windows world, where TrueType fonts are widely used.

Like PostScript, TrueType uses scalable facts. But, unlike PostScript fonts, the scaler is built right into the system software. You can view and print such fonts on any output device without having to worry about ATM or two separate font files.

As with screen fonts, a TrueType fonts can be placed within a suitcase file. In some cases, the font manufacturer includes extra screen fonts, which are said to provide better quality display in smaller point sizes.

The Prepress Community Doesn't Take to TrueType

In theory, TrueType seemed to be a breath of fresh air, a single font file that would free users of having to install extra software for display and printing to non-PostScript printers. In theory, TrueType even had other advantages over PostScript, such as added hints, which are little elements of a font that optimize display or print quality. This added benefit was seldom realized in practice, though.

Worse, the advent of TrueType delivered many headaches for the regular printing community.

Those high-priced typesetting machines (imagesetters) were designed to work with PostScript, not TrueType. While the Mac OS had its built-in TrueType feature, those output devices were built to support PostScript. When you put a TrueType font into a document, the device may take longer to print a document, stop processing altogether, or produce a poor quality result.

In many cases, this wasn't something you could fix with a simple downloadable update. Sometimes you had to replace or upgrade the device's raster image processor (RIP) at a cost of several thousands of dollars (assuming the upgrade was available).

No wonder the firms who used such devices balked.

PostScript or TrueType—Which Fonts Should You Use?

From almost the beginning, PostScript fonts became the standard for the publishing industry. Despite the confusing aspects of keeping tabs on two separate font files, PostScript fonts delivered professional quality, which is what the industry needed.

TrueType fonts, on the other hand, only worked if the printer had output devices that supported the technology. Before you send your work out for high-resolution output, ask the firm what font format they support. Don't take chances.

NOTE   *I cover the subject of firms who provide high-resolution printouts, called service bureaus, in Chapter 21.*

On the other hand, if you intend to print your documents on a personal printer (inkjet or low-cost laser) or a regular laser printer, it doesn't matter which font format you use. If you plan to exchange files with Windows users, you may even be better off sticking with TrueType.

Introducing OpenType

Wouldn't it be nice if you could have a single font file that included both TrueType and PostScript fonts, without needing separate screen fonts for the latter?

It sounds like a miracle may be in our future. Or maybe another headache.

Adobe and Microsoft have developed a new font format called *OpenType* that promises to do just that.

Another nifty feature enables you to place fonts on a Web page, which is used to give a general look and feel for Web pages, no matter what browser or platform is used. In addition, OpenType has built-in support for extended characters, such as special ligatures and elaborate letterforms, which can add flourishes and special effects to the letters and better character kerning.

It can go a long way to improve the usefulness of fonts. That is, if Apple chooses to support the technology. And currently, that is by no means certain.

QuickDraw GX and Mac OS 9

Mac OS 9 put the nail in the coffin of another failed technology: QuickDraw GX.

Introduced in the early 1990s, QuickDraw GX was supposed to create a revolution in the way fonts and images were handled on a Mac. You'd have extended character sets, the capability to create desktop printers, and support for graphic technology brought in, which would enable software publishers to create a new generation of Mac drawing programs.

QuickDraw GX got bogged down by hefty RAM requirements and bugs. In addition, many software publishers expected to develop programs that worked on both platforms. Without a Windows version, no point existed in spending time and money to deliver a product that couldn't work on the platform with the majority of users.

Apple realized QuickDraw GX wasn't going anywhere. It first adapted its desktop printing technology to the regular print drivers. You can keep tabs on a print job by checking the icon on your Mac's desktop, and you can switch from one printer to another by a Printing menu, a Control Strip, or even in the Print dialog box.

Once you set up a printer in the Chooser, you didn't have to return—well, with the exception of a few inkjet printers that don't have desktop printing support.

Beyond that, QuickDraw GX is history.

Multiple Master Fonts

Adobe's Multiple Master Fonts fared a little better than QuickDraw GX.

A Multiple Master font basically enables you to take a single font and make a number of variations on it. You could make the characters thinner and smaller for use in headlines, or taller, wider, and thicker for text-based applications.

In practice, the technology can be confusing. Because you can manipulate a font in any number of ways, you must include the exact font with a document when it's transferred to another Mac. And, while typographers pride themselves on the ability to recognize a font and style by sight alone, the subtle variations you create with a Multiple Master font make the task of recognizing it nearly impossible.

Today, Adobe has a small number of Multiple Master fonts available. For the most part, however, they use the technology for font substitution. A basic set of Multiple Master fonts come with Adobe's Acrobat software and ATM. They are used as part of Adobe's font substitution technology. When you open a document using a font you don't have, ATM looks at a database of Adobe font information and uses the Multiple Master fonts to build a simulation of the missing font. ATM spaces the same way and even resembles the original to some extent.

While it wasn't quite as good as the real thing, the font simulation was useful to help deliver some of the look and feel of the original. This helped you check a document on different Macs without having to install the same fonts on each.

How to Deal with Font Conflicts

When I say "font conflict," no doubt you think of a battle royal between two files. The reality is more subtle, but no less annoying.

Font problems have been the bane of desktop publishers for years, and any Mac user who needs to work with a reasonable number of fonts may occasionally encounter such problems.

In the next few pages, you learn how to use some of Mac OS 9's tools and, perhaps, some other programs to help you resolve these problems.

The Search for Damaged Fonts

Finding a damaged document is rare, unless your Mac has a severe hard drive directory, or a disk drive problem, or your Mac crashed right in the middle of saving the document. The story is quite different when it comes to fonts. Damaged fonts seem to turn up with alarming regularity. And this isn't always an easy problem to pin down.

The Symptoms of a Damaged Font

Whenever you launch a program on your Mac, one of the things the program does is load the list of available fonts. If one of those fonts is damaged, it could cause the program to crash just as it's getting underway.

NOTE   *In some situations, a damaged font may also prevent your Mac from completing its startup process if the font is used by the Finder for system display purposes, such as an icon title or title bar.*

And even if the program starts up all right, the possibility still exists that documents won't print properly, or the printer itself could fail to process the job.

While many Mac problems are usually because of System Folder-related blues or application conflicts, fonts do enter the picture more than they should.

How to Fix the Problem

Whether a font is damaged isn't always obvious. The icon can stay the same or the installation process goes through smoothly, although the symptoms previously listed display themselves quite openly.

Here are some ways to check for damaged fonts:

- **Use a font management program**   Adobe Type Manager Deluxe, Alsoft's MasterJuggler, DiamondSoft's Font Reserve, and Suitcase 8's FontAgent can all search for damaged fonts. These programs check your font files to see which ones are damaged. When you get the report, the simple solution is to replace the damaged files with clean originals.

- **Use virus software**   Virus programs aren't only for checking computer viruses. Both Network Associates' Virex and Symantec's Norton Anti-Virus also look for damaged files as part of their standard scanning process. Make sure you constantly update the virus programs to have the best possible protection. Even if you have a copy of the now-defunct free virus program, Disinfectant, you can still use it to scan for damaged files, although you should use one of the two commercial programs to check for the presence of a computer virus.

How to Deal with Font Conflicts

- **Use Norton Utilities or TechTool Pro**   Both of these programs check for damaged fonts whenever they do a full scan of your Mac's hard drive for problems with the directory. If any of your fonts are damaged, delete and then reinstall them.

> NOTE   *If the damaged font file is located inside a suitcase file, only the font management programs can detect the damage. The rest simply look at the main file and report what they see.*

More Font Conflict Troubles and Tribulations

If conflicts exist between two or more system extensions, you needn't be a fortune teller to predict what might happen. Applications might suddenly quit or your Mac might crash. Fixing such problems is relatively easy, although it may take a little time to isolate the source. You can check Chapter 31 for more information on this subject.

Besides having fonts in both PostScript and TrueType formats, or having a font from the wrong manufacturer, for example, other problems can be equally annoying. In this section, you learn about some of the common problems with fonts, their causes, and their solutions.

FONTS DON'T APPEAR IN FONT MENU   If it hasn't been put in the font menu, there's no way to use it. Here are the main causes for this problem and how to fix them:

- **Software doesn't update font menus**   Certain programs, like QuarkXPress and Adobe InDesign, know whenever you install new fonts. The font menu is updated automatically, but it could take a few seconds. Most programs aren't smart enough to realize when these changes occur. If a font you just installed doesn't appear in the font menu, quit the program and start it again. If the font still doesn't appear, restart your computer.

- **Bitmap font is missing**   Even if the PostScript printer font has been placed on the Fonts folder, font menus in Mac programs also require the presence of the bitmap (screen) font. If you install a new font, but it isn't listed in the menu, make sure the bitmap font has been properly installed (it is either a separate file or in a font suitcase).

- **Remove preference files for font menu**   The programs you use to modify your font menus, and to organize and clean up the fonts displayed on your screen need preference files to keep a database of the fonts you have installed on your Mac. Such programs include Adobe Type Reunion Deluxe and Action WYSIWYG Menus. If you add or remove fonts, but the font menus don't reflect these changes, find the preference files in the Preference folder inside the System Folder and trash them. If you can't find the preference files for the program, find a folder with the name of the publisher who produces the software (like Power On Preferences for their Action Utilities line of products).

■ **Reinstall the font**   If the font has been checked for damages and nothing comes up, you should reinstall it anyway. If the printer font has been damaged, it's easy to detect, but if one screen font size in a font suitcase has been damaged, programs like Norton Utilities and TechTool Pro won't be able to find it.

FONT CHARACTERS ARE MISSING OR APPEAR AS SQUARE BOXES INSTEAD OF LETTERS   The answer is simple, but the solution may not exist. Some of those cheap font packages, from companies, such as FontBank and KeyFonts, didn't include the complete set of characters. While all the letters and numbers where there, the percentage signs and copyright symbols and their like were not. And, if the font had all capital letters, the lowercase positions would only display square or rectangular boxes. If you don't know if a certain font comes with a complete set of characters, use Apple's KeyCaps programs from the Apple Menu, or a shareware program called PopChar Pro, both of which can check the characters available with a certain font.

TIP *If a specific character doesn't come with a certain font, don't hesitate to switch to the Symbol font or another typeface and use the character in that font instead, if it's available.*

POSTSCRIPT FONTS ARE BITMAPPED ON THE SCREEN   If you type something on your computer, you expect the letters to be clear and sharp when it appears on the screen. Instead, the edges are jagged and the text may appear as a set of large rectangular bricks. As you change point sizes, the effect only gets worse.

You want to look at these solutions:

■ **ATM isn't installed**   When working with PostScript fonts, they only look clear on your screen in all point sizes if ATM is installed. Fortunately, the so-called Lite version is free with Acrobat Reader or it can be downloaded directly from Adobe's Web site. If you installed Acrobat Reader, but you

How to Deal with Font Conflicts

don't have ATM, search the folder in which Acrobat was installed. Often it's in a folder called Fonts inside the Acrobat application folder.

- **Reinstall the font**   If you installed a font properly and ATM is working, try to install the font again. The original may have been damaged.

- **Check for conflicts with fonts**   Even if you did properly install a font, room for mischief still exists. If you have both the PostScript and TrueType versions of the same fonts (like PostScript Times and TrueType Times), or versions of the same font from different manufacturers, expect some unsavory effects on your display or in the printed document. Look at the section called "Tips and Tricks to Efficient Font Management," in the last part of this chapter to learn about some software that can help you avoid this problem.

- **Printer fonts are missing**   Make sure you have the accompanying printer fonts for the bitmap fonts you use. Screen fonts can be found easily. They are free at Adobe's own Web site, but they don't do much good if you don't also have the printer fonts (and that requires buying the font or getting software with the fonts included as part of the package).

- **ATM needs PostScript printer fonts**   If you use Adobe Type Manager, Extensis Suitcase, Alsoft's MasterJuggler, or DiamondSoft's Font Reserve, be sure the bitmap (screen) and printer fonts have been placed in the same folder. ATM has no way to find your printer fonts in another location. Fortunately, these programs can help you locate orphan font files, so you can make sure they are in the right locations.

POSTSCRIPT FONTS ARE BITMAPPED WHEN PRINTING   If your printer displays good quality with documents, but the display of fonts on your screen is poor, you may be able to live with that. If it's the other way around (screen display is good and printing display is bad), however, that's not good. Here are some solutions to deal with this problem:

- **Non-PostScript printer needs ATM**   The inkjet printers you can purchase from companies like Epson and HP produce good-quality photos and artwork, but they can't deliver PostScript output without some help. They are fine for TrueType fonts, but if you have to use PostScript fonts on these printers, you have two options. The best option is to install ATM (as mentioned earlier, this can be downloaded free from Adobe's Web site and it also comes with Adobe Acrobat Reader). If you need to work with

PostScript graphics, such as those created in a program and saved in the *Encapsulated PostScript* (*ESP*) format, consider purchasing PostScript software, which can turn your Mac into a *raster image processor* (*RIP*). These programs can be bought from companies such as Adobe, Birmy, Epson, and Infowave.

NOTE

Not all printers are supported by these software programs. You'll want to consult the list of printers they work with before you pick one of these products.

- **Conflict with fonts**   If you have both PostScript and TrueType versions of a font, or two fonts from different manufacturers with the same name, your Mac may not download the right font information to your printer. You may not get only poor letter spacing, the characters themselves could be bitmapped. To fix this symptom, you should organize your font library (see suggestions later in the chapter) and be more cautious when you mix various fonts.

- **PostScript printer font is missing**   Even if ATM has been installed, good-quality printouts are not produced unless the PostScript printer font has been installed properly in the same folder as the screen font (normally in the Fonts folder).

Tips and Tricks to Efficient Font Management

You just can't escape from fonts. You can buy them in inexpensive packages and they can even be found with various applications from Adobe, Corel, Microsoft, and other companies. In the old days, when you wanted to buy a lot of fonts, it either took a big chunk out of your available credit line or you were left with low-quality rip-offs that didn't offer acceptable quality and didn't have some of the more obscure symbol-type characters (even foreign accents weren't available).

These days, though, you can get hundreds or even thousands of fonts without a substantial investment from all sorts of places. Now the question is: What should you do with them? Should you install them on your Mac and use them when you need them? Unfortunately, it isn't that simple.

Mac Font Folder Limits—Not Anymore

With the release of Mac OS 9, Apple has dealt with some of the big limits that plague font-handling capabilities. First, the 128-font resource limit (applying strictly to screen font and suitcase files) that existed through Mac OS 8.6 is gone. The limit is now increased to 512.

NOTE   *You could, of course, drag-and-drop font suitcases on each other to get around this limit. But consider the length of your font menu and the speed with which you select fonts.*

Also, the maximum number of files that can be open at any one time has been increased from 348 to 8,169. While this may seem unimportant to most people who believe they almost never need 348 files open at the same time, it is a relatively simple limit to surpass.

When you start up your Mac, all the various components in your System Folder necessary for your computer to work can account for over 100 open files. Lots of applications are made up of various components that are run as soon as you double-click the program's icon. Software that can handle plug-ins and other types of add-on modules that add more features are the main reason for this. It's not hard to see that having even three or four programs open at once can get you to that 348 file limit, especially if you have lots of fonts loaded.

With these changes, Macs running Mac OS 9 are much more stable because you have plenty of additional system resources to handle extra open programs, and you can run many more fonts than you'll probably ever need, unless you are a dedicated graphic designer or desktop publisher.

This change does have a disadvantage, however. It, along with a number of other changes, has made certain programs, including ATM, incompatible with Mac OS 9. Luckily, Adobe and the other companies with incompatible software quickly posted updates to fix these problems.

If you reach the point where you definitely want to add a huge number of fonts, consider a font management program for efficiency and flexibility. Imagine navigating through a font menu with 512 separate entries, even if your software can use that number (and many are limited to 256 fonts).

Overview of Font Managers

Mac OS 9 is so far removed from the heady days of System 6, it seems hard to remember the way things were. In those days, you couldn't just drag fonts to the System Folder. Back then, you had to use a clunky, unintuitive application called Font/DA Mover to take bitmap fonts in and out of your System file. The program would often crash your computer, especially if you had to do a lot of adjustments to your fonts all at once.

Finally, a programmer named Steve Brecher invented a clever solution for Mac users everywhere. Known as Suitcase (see Figure 22-3), it had the capability to open and close fonts, whether or not they were installed in your System Folder.

Suitcase does its little tricks by fooling the Mac OS into believing the fonts are in the right location, the Fonts folder. While some could call this program a good hack, I wouldn't use that term. Suitcase is just a smart way to make font management more efficient.

All you have to do is put the fonts in a special folder and use Suitcase (or another program that performs a similar function) to turn your fonts on and off. You needn't spend endless amounts of time searching for a font in a long font menu or tie up a program's font-handling limitation.

When you finish with the font, you turn it off, pure and simple, without physically having to move anything.

Besides Suitcase, there's also Adobe Type Manager Deluxe (see Figure 22-4) and Alsoft's MasterJuggler.

Font Reserve

DiamondSoft's Font Reserve, another font management program, works by placing all your fonts (except for those in the System Folder) in one big database.

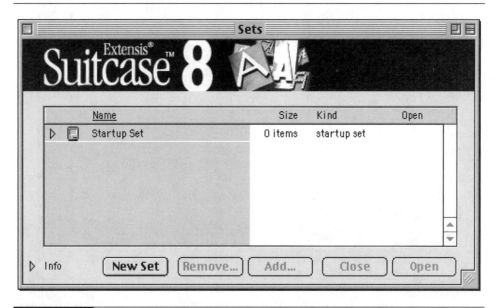

FIGURE 22-3   While Steve Brecher has long since retired from the software game, Extensis continues to develop Suitcase

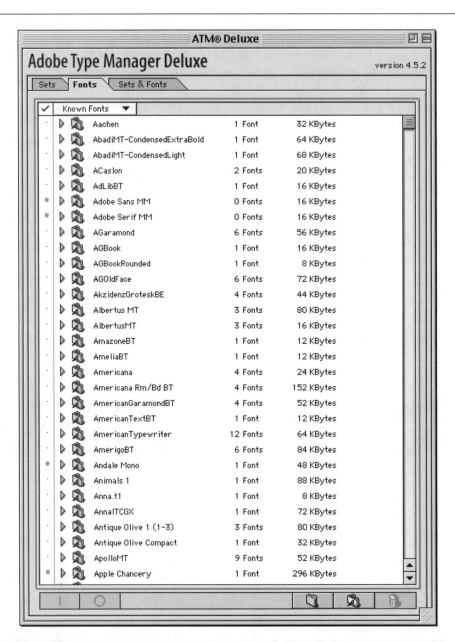

From its humble beginnings as a font display helper, ATM now also manages your entire font library

Font Reserve examines all of them, discovering any conflicts between fonts and whether any of them are damaged. Font Reserve can also let you know if either screen or printer font is lacking in your PostScript font library.

From the standpoint of organization, Font Reserve yields its greatest benefit for a larger font library.

How to Organize Fonts Without a Font Manager

If your library doesn't consist of, say, more than 100 fonts, then you probably don't need to get a separate program for managing your fonts. You do need to be aware of some things, however, as you take on the job of organizing your font library by yourself.

- **Merge font suitcases**   Although the limit for the number of font resources has risen to 512 with the release of Mac OS 9, a good idea is to combine the font suitcases of fonts from the same family. You then have fewer files to deal with in your Fonts folder, which makes seeing what you have available easier.

- **Get rid of fonts you don't have to use**   If you aren't planning on using specific fonts anytime soon, you should move them out of your Fonts folder. One way to do this is to create a folder called Fonts (Disabled), which can correspond to the folders where disabled Control Panels and Extensions are put. Place whatever fonts you don't need to use in that folder.

NOTE   *Casady & Greene's great extension management program, Conflict Catcher, can also manage your font library by doing the same trick it does with extensions, but you have to restart your Mac whenever you change the font lineup.*

- **Quit programs before removing any fonts from the Fonts folder** Without font management software, you can't take a font from the Fonts folder until all other open applications have been closed first. If you believe you have quit all your programs, but you still can't remove any fonts, check your Mac OS 9 Applications menu. Click it and see what programs are left open and, in turn, switch to them and quit them. Mac OS 9 even lists the venerable Launcher as an open application and, if you don't quit Launcher, you can't remove your fonts. If that still doesn't work, open the Extensions Manager Control Panel, choose a Mac OS 9.0 Base Set, and

Tips and Tricks to Efficient Font Management

then restart. This should quit any other hidden or background applications being used on your Mac.

How to Organize Fonts Using a Font Manager

Let's say you have a lot of fonts and you need to turn them on and off quickly as you move from one document to another. The following are some ideas on how you can organize your fonts to avoid nasty conflicts, such as problems when launching programs.

When you use a font-managing program, you needn't put all your fonts in the Fonts folder. The software does all the work for you. All you must do is keep your basic set of Apple-installed fonts in the System Folder. Among these are Charcoal, Chicago, Capitals, Gadget, Geneva, Impact, Monaco, New York, Sand, Textile, and Techno. You should also leave fonts you need all the time, such as Courier, Helvetica, and Times. If you use Adobe Acrobat, then you should have these additional fonts in your Fonts folder as well: AdobeSerMM, AdobeSanMM, Adobe Serif MM, and Adobe Sans MM (the MM stands for Multiple Master). These are needed to provide font substitution capabilities for ATM and Adobe Acrobat.

As for the rest, you can put them elsewhere.

Leaving out the essential fonts, place the rest of your font library in a new folder, which you can call anything you like, Resources or Suitcase Fonts, or whatever. You needn't put the folder in the System Folder. It only has to be on a hard drive mounted on your Mac when you have to use the fonts.

Now organize your fonts by their manufacturers. This should make organizing your fonts much simpler if your font library is large. In your new Fonts folder, create little subfolders with the names of the manufacturers of your fonts, such as Adobe, Bitstream, Monotype, or whichever companies make them. Doing this can make watching for any conflicts between your fonts easier, as previously mentioned, which can occur if you have more than one font with the same name active. If you can't find the manufacturer of the font just by looking at the icon, use the Finder's Get Info command (choosing Get Info from the finder's File menu on a selected icon). Look for the copyright notice and you should find the company. If you don't, make a folder for the fonts without specific companies called Miscellaneous or something to tell you that you don't know who made the font.

Next, make separate folders for each family of fonts. This is especially useful if you have a large library. After dividing your fonts by their manufacturers, make a separate folder for each type family, such as one for Times, another for Bookman, and so forth. Just make sure you don't mix fonts of the same name from different manufacturers.

The following are some additional precautions you should be aware of when organizing your fonts:

- **Disable fonts you don't need**   Enjoy the convenience of the font menu manager. Disable any fonts you don't need. Then your font menus are kept short and your application launch times are as brief as possible.

- **Be careful when using TrueType fonts for professional printing**   If you want to use a TrueType font for a printed document, contact the printer or service bureau that is going to take care of your high-resolution output. Take that company's advice on compatibility with various fonts. If the printer or service bureau doesn't give you the help you need, try contacting another firm.

- **Be careful when using PostScript fonts for a Web site**   While TrueType fonts may not be good for professional output, it is exactly the opposite for the Internet. Many people may not have some of the fonts you have because the primary system fonts for both the Mac and Windows platforms are TrueType fonts. Using those basic TrueType fonts provides better quality when displaying text on the screens of most Web surfers.

Using FontSync to Match Fonts

Mac OS 9 includes the tools to help you synchronize the fonts you use from one Mac to another.

This feature is called FontSync (see Figure 22-5).

You find FontSync in Mac OS 9's Apple Extras folder, in a folder called Font Extras. To install, drag to the closed System Folder icon and restart.

Here's how to make a profile of your font library:

1. Locate the AppleScript labeled Create FontSync Profile, located in the same folder in which you found FontSync.

2. Double-click the script to make the profile, and then name the profile you create.

3. Once your profile is created, you can take that same script to another Mac and use another Font Extras script, Match FontSync, to compare the fonts

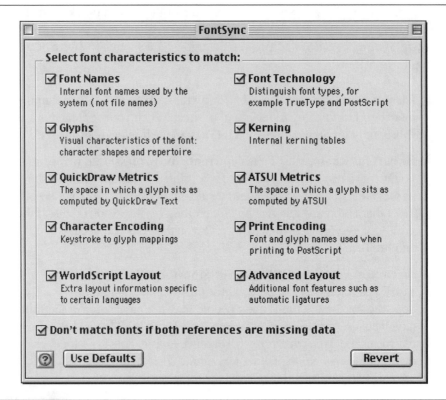

FIGURE 22-5   FontSync does for font matching what ColorSync does for color output

on that Mac. The script checks that Mac's Font library and reports on the fonts that do not match.

As you can see, FontSync is a great help if you want to sync the fonts on your various Macs so they can handle your font library without missing font reports, or weird display and printing artifacts.

Summing Up

Throughout this chapter, you learned about the various font formats on the Mac, how to manage them, and how to deal with problems that come up when working with fonts.

In the next chapter, managing your finances on your Mac is covered, from managing your checkbook to handling online trading and even preparing your tax return.

Summing Up

Chapter 23

A Shortcut to Financial Management on the Mac

Keeping your finances in control and balancing your checkbook can be a hectic process. Even if you are careful about entering all figures exactly, a single mathematical error can result in bouncing a check or making an incorrect financial decision.

Preparing your tax statements can be even more of a hassle, trying to figure out which tax laws, out of thousands, apply to you and which deductions are appropriate to your particular situation, and, of course, which deductions might flag a possible tax audit.

Of course, all this is necessary to keep your financial well-being in order. Ways do exist, though, to help make the process less painful.

In earlier chapters, some of the most significant Mac software in such categories as word processing, graphics, and desktop publishing software was profiled. In this chapter the focus is on some of the most popular financial software products, such as Intuit's Quicken Deluxe 2000. This type of software can manage your checkbook and track your assets, and there's even support for doing all your financial management online.

You can even discover a Mac software product to help guide you through the treacherous minefield of tax laws and prepare your tax return.

> **NOTE** *The software described is not intended to replace a good accountant or experienced financial manager. But it can help you get your financial information highly organized, and then, even if you do take it to an outside advisor, that person's job should be far easier.*

Doing Your Books on a Mac

As already mentioned, you can balance your checkbook, keep your financial statements in order, plan your budget, and even more on your Mac without having to write a single thing (except perhaps sign a check with your signature).

In fact, every iMac comes with a program to do all this, Quicken from Intuit.

Quicken Deluxe 2000

This program (as shown in Figure 23-1) has a vast amount of features not only for keeping your finances in control, but also for recording your tax-related information, online banking, and online trading.

> **NOTE** *The version of Quicken included on the iMac is Quicken 98. This chapter, however, focuses on the latest shipping version (available as a modestly priced upgrade for users of earlier versions).*

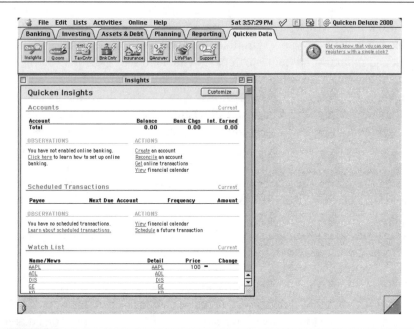

FIGURE 23-1 Quicken Deluxe 2000 helps ease the burden of managing your personal finances

As with most Mac programs, Quicken 2000 comes with a convenient one-button installer, which quickly gets the program up and running on your Mac. What's more, Quicken is designed to import all your financial data easily from previous versions of the program, even as far back as version 3.

The first feature discussed is the one that made Quicken famous, its checkbook feature.

If you ever dread that chore of balancing your checkbook when your monthly statement arrives from your bank, you can appreciate how easy the task becomes with Quicken. In addition to keeping an accurate running tab on your bank balance, you can assign categories to your recurring expenditures and income, so you always know for what purpose your money is being spent, or the source of your cash. You can also print your checks, the same as a large business can, using preprinted check blanks from Quicken and other companies. Or, you can make your payments from the Internet without having to worry about a payment getting lost in the mail.

Quicken can also remind you whenever those payments are due, and then you never have to worry about those dreaded late charges that come because you forgot to get the car or house payment in on time.

You can set budgets, so if you only have a specific amount of money to spend, you can use it more wisely. You can customize the reports of your finances and decide exactly what you want them to include and how you want them to look.

Stock and mutual fund quotes can be downloaded into Quicken. Using this information, the program can generate many different kinds of charts, graphs, and other reports, and then you can have an overview of your investments and other financial assets. You can compare your investments by how much you've gained or lost from them, how much they add to your income, and a lot more using the Portfolio View (shown in Figure 23-2). You can search for stocks and mutual funds that fit your needs with online tools that enable you to find that information.

Records of your tax-related income and expenses are kept whenever you enter them into Quicken. Using the Tax Planner, you can examine a number of strategies to see which one can save you the most money. With the Tax Deduction Finder (as seen in Figure 23-3), you are logged into your ISP and connected direct to the publisher's Web site, where you can search for any possible deductions that can enable you to save more of your precious cash.

Quicken can help you shop online to compare insurance rates and to get in-depth comparisons between the companies and policies. You can also search for the best mortgage rate from the top lenders. You can also find the current rates on bank loans, CDs, and credit cards in your hometown.

The interface of the program is extremely easy-to-use and customizable. Your screen in Quicken can be configured to access frequently used accounts and activities easily. You can find helpful tips and comments in the Tip Area. The toolbar is also

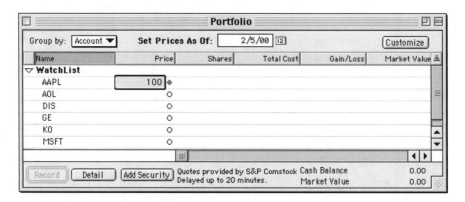

FIGURE 23-2   The Portfolio View enables you to check stock quotes and your entire financial portfolio

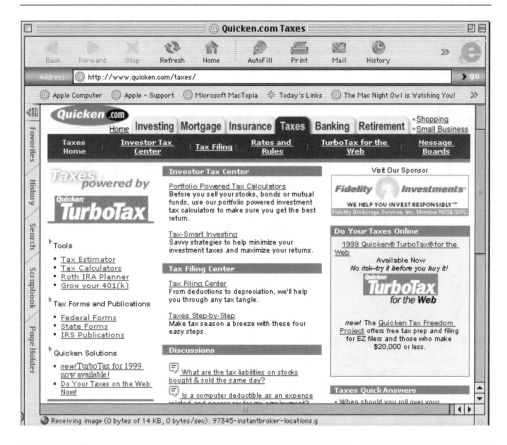

FIGURE 23-3 The tax features of Quicken can help you save some precious dollars when tax time is near

customizable, enabling you to access only the functions of the program you need to use and to hide the ones you don't want to see.

You can use QuickAnswers (as shown in Figure 23-4), calculations to get estimates for a variety of things. You can plan for a new car, college, retirement, buying a new home, or other major financial decisions. Various options can be tested before you make an investment or other major financial decision. You can use the calculations to find out how you can save by reducing your spending on certain discretionary items (maybe you can see how much you save if you stop smoking).

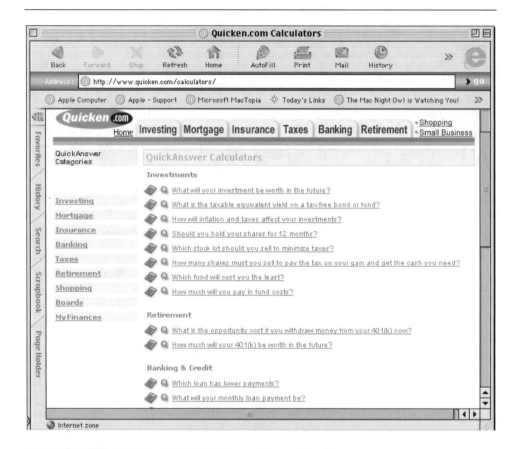

FIGURE 23-4 QuickAnswers can help you calculate a number of financial scenarios

Quicken can also help you create a balanced investment portfolio. You can get the latest investment news and updated analyst ratings. Older quotes can be downloaded up to a period of five years for stocks and mutual funds. This enables you to track the trends of specific investment prospects easily before you make your decision about whether they are worth your money. New opportunities that might make you money can be researched as soon as they are available. Strategies for buying, selling, and diversifying your investments can be compared.

Banking and paying your bills online is much easier with Quicken. You can contact a growing number of financial institutions that provide online financial services. Once you sign up, account balances and other records can be downloaded from your bank directly into Quicken from your bank or credit cards. You can even transfer funds among the various accounts at your bank (as long as your financial institution supports the feature).

NOTE   *Most financial institutions require you to install a Web browser that supports 128-bit encryption before they let you access their services. The two major Web browsers, plus a young, scrappy contender, are covered in Chapter 33.*

More is explained about online banking and stock trading later in this chapter in the section titled "A Brief Look at Online Banking and Stock Trading."

A Cautionary Tale About Quicken 98

Quicken 98 comes preinstalled on the iMacs that shipped at the time this book was written. While no problems occur running the program from your iMac, if you don't want to upgrade to Quicken 2000 right away, be careful if you ever decide to reinstall it from the CD provided with your iMac

When you run that installer, it puts an older version of AppleScript onto a Mac running Mac OS 9 and overwrites the version you have. Unfortunately, no custom install option eliminates System Folder items. You see this problem when you restart after Quicken 98 has been installed, and the AppleScript icon has a big red *X* over it.

To solve this problem, use the Add/Remove feature of the Mac OS 9 CD. AppleScript is found in the Utility folder of the Mac OS 9 Custom Install screen. To keep your installation as brief as possible, make sure only this item is selected for your custom install. Chapter 2 covers Mac OS 9 installation options in more detail.

Doing Your Books on a Mac

Microsoft Excel 98

A spreadsheet isn't available only to manage your personal finances. Such a program does its duty by displaying a variety of information for you to compare, such as the specifications of a new product, a project schedule, and other data.

But Microsoft Excel 98 (as shown in Figure 23-5) still has plenty of available features to keep your finances in control if you only need a simple program to do

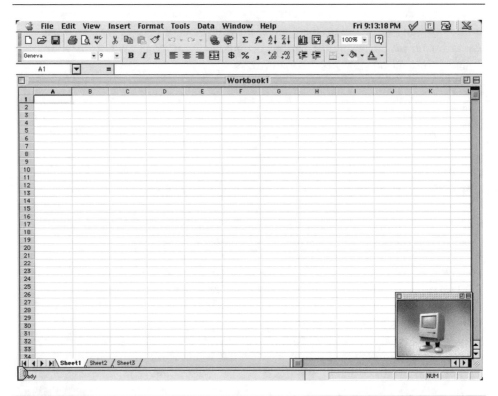

FIGURE 23-5 Excel's useful features help you keep track of financial information

the work of displaying the information you need without a hassle. In addition, Microsoft Excel 98 can help you with project billing and purchases.

In this section, some of the important features of this most popular spreadsheet program are covered. You can use Excel as a standalone product or as part of Microsoft Office 98.

The spreadsheet you create in Excel is called a *workbook*. The information you put into a spreadsheet is put in separate text blocks called *cells*. Excel's Range Finder feature uses different colors to make building mathematical formulas for calculations and editing much easier. The range of cells that makes up the formula is color-coded, as is the cell that has the formula itself.

Excel's convenient Template Wizard enables you to set up online forms for your workbooks without having to spend much time learning complex cell formatting. A number of templates are also included with Excel that enable you to create invoices and purchase orders more easily.

The program's Page Break Preview feature enables you to see which part of your sheet will print and where the page breaks are located, so you can conveniently scale it down in your Page Setup box if it comes out too large.

Certain cells can be formatted automatically, depending on the values in your spreadsheet. The formatting tells you if your budget has been exceeded or when a certain goal has been accomplished. Specific cells can also be formatted to highlight or organize your information. Cells can be easily resized to 409 pixels high and up to the width of your screen. They can be one row or one column, making it much easier to add titles or notes to your worksheets, or for table layout or setting up forms.

As with many programs, Internet integration is part of the picture with Excel.

Hyperlinks can be added to cells or objects, or even to other documents created in different Office 98 programs. You can also save your workbook in HTML format to put it on your Web site. Rules can be configured for the information in your cells so only certain values can be entered. Input and error messages appear to help you enter the right values. This helps you avoid costly errors if you attempt to enter the wrong sort of information.

Excel is also set up to accommodate multiple users that work together on one workbook at the same time, using the Share Workbook setup window in the Tools menu network (shown in Figure 23-6). The Advanced tab is used to set revision

FIGURE 23-6   The multiple users feature enables a workgroup to manage a single spreadsheet

Doing Your Books on a Mac

tracking options. You can also insert comments (the feature is available from the View menu), so your coworkers can review additional information about the data that must be shared.

If you decide to share a workbook, you should also appreciate the Protection feature (it's available from the Tools menu), which enables you not only to track revisions to the workbook, but also to prevent revision tracking from being removed.

The Chart Wizard (shown in Figure 23-7) more easily enables you to create exactly the kind of chart you need to display your financial picture more efficiently. You also have access to tips that can help you learn more about a certain element of your charts. The program's Office Assistant can give you step-by-step information on a certain process. A number of new 3D charts are included with Excel, such as pyramid, conical, cylindrical, and a bubble chart that make your data easier to read.

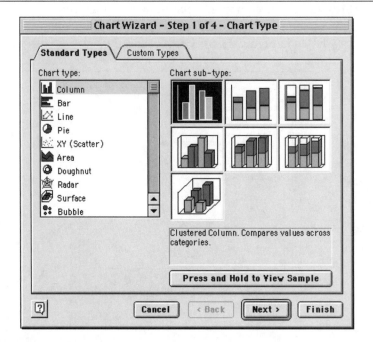

FIGURE 23-7   The Chart Wizard makes it much easier to create the kinds of charts you need

TIP

If the prebuilt charts provided in Excel aren't sufficient for you, you can easily export your Excel data into special purpose charting programs, such as Adrenaline Chart Pro, a 3D program from Adrenaline Software (see http://www.adrenaline.ca/ for more information) or DeltaGraph, currently being published by SPSS Software (see http://www.spss.com/ software/DeltaGraph).

Office Assistant Help Feature

The Office Assistant help feature enables you to learn more about the various features of Excel and about performing different tasks in the program. The drawing tools have been greatly improved compared to previous versions, enabling you to create many kinds of graphics, including 3D effects, fills, and sets of predefined shapes. The Formula AutoCorrect feature enables you to identify and correct the 15 most common formula errors automatically. When building formulas, your own row, column labels, and headings can be used without having to set up named ranges first. The Formula Palette combines the Function Wizard and the formula bar into one easy-to-use tool (shown in Figure 23-8). The Formula Palette enables you to access a menu containing the most common functions you used more easily, such as SUM, AVERAGE, HYPERLINK, COUNT, and MAX.

Doing Your Books on a Mac

Mac Accounting Software

Another financial management program available from Intuit is QuickBooks Pro. Unfortunately, because of what the publisher reports is poor demand on the Mac platform, the program hasn't had more than a few minor updates beyond version 4.0 for the Mac, compared to QuickBooks 2000 on the Windows side. Many small companies, however, still rely on the Mac version of QuickBooks. Fingers are crossed that the program can remain compatible with future versions of the Mac OS.

- **Aatrix Accounting**   This accounting package features Navigation Aids and Smart Guides to help users easily tap its most sophisticated features. All the essentials are here, such as inventory tracking, general ledger, invoicing, payables, receivables, payrolls, budgeting, job and project tracking, plus multiuser capabilities. The program offers a three-step

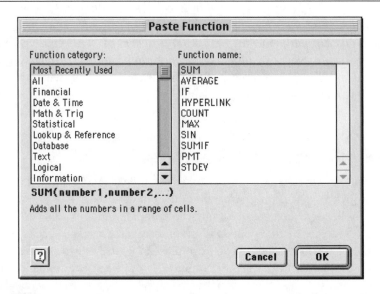

FIGURE 23-8 Commonly used functions are easily accessed via Excel's Function Wizard

New Company Setup procedure, so you can easily transfer your company's books to this program.

- **M.Y.O.B. Accounting Plus**   From MYOB, this program offers quick wizards and 100 templates to help even inexperienced users get started putting their books on their Macs. The program includes such features as inventory tracking, invoicing, purchase orders, general ledger, payables, receivables, payrolls and other financial requirements of the businessperson. A multiuser feature is invaluable for a larger accounting department.

- **MultiLedger**   This program, from Checkmark, supports up to ten users. All the essential features of your business are supported, such as inventory management, invoicing, general ledger, trial balance, income statements, budgets, payables, receivables, commission tracking, customer credit limits, and more. The publisher reports the program is designed for easy setup, so your accounting department can get up and running with the minimum amount of fuss and bother. An add-on program, CheckMark Payroll, covers that aspect of your company's requirements.

Using Macs for Tax Preparation

Only two things in life are certain: death and taxes. Taxes can be extremely irritating, especially if you have many expenditures and financial assets that take your returns beyond the single postcard category. Never fear, though, your Mac is here to save you. The most prominent tax program available for the Mac at this time is MacInTax 99, from none other than Intuit Software, the maker of Quicken 2000. The following is a summary of MacInTax's major features.

NOTE *MacInTax is updated annually for a specific taxable year. So the next version will mostly likely be MacInTax 2000 and so on.*

Intuit MacInTax Deluxe 99

This program (shown in Figure 23-9) boasts many useful features to prepare and manage your taxes and to help you avoid special attention from the IRS when the time comes for it to pick candidates for possible audits.

In only three multistep processes, you can get your taxes ready to sign and mail.

The first part of the process is to ask questions about your financial picture for the tax year. As you answer those questions, MacInTax automatically places your answers on to IRS-approved forms, as well as performs all the necessary calculations. Only the questions necessary for your return are asked, based on the information you provide.

This initial question-and-answer process is designed as the interactive equivalent of a tax preparer sitting across from you and asking you key questions as you pluck the information from your receipts. This is probably the most difficult part of the preparation process, but the neat thing about it is, if the information is already entered in Quicken, MacInTax can easily import it from any recent version of the program. This way, the most difficult part of the tax preparation process is made much easier (so long as your financial information in Quicken is complete).

NOTE *The MacInTax CD also includes a number of videos to help explain the purpose of a particular question or to guide you through the process of assembling the information or choosing the deductions that help you most.*

These two features help simplify the most difficult parts of the tax preparation process. Once the information is entered, MacInTax goes to work to search for any

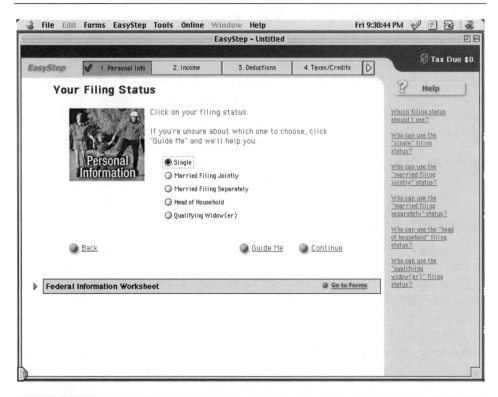

FIGURE 23-9   MacInTax enables you to prepare and file your taxes in a few fairly easy steps

errors, including overlooked deductions and entries that might cause an audit to occur. Finally, you can electronically file your taxes with the IRS to get your refund more quickly or the return can be printed onto IRS-approved forms (along with your worksheets, so you can easily review the information used to generate your return).

All the features of previous versions of the program are still there. MacInTax has been revised and updated to include all the latest tax law changes to help you prepare your taxes better and to take advantage of any more deductions. Information can be brought over from the previous year's return, so you needn't reenter the data. The Tax Advisor gives you custom money-saving tax advice as you go through the process of completing your return. A customized, printable action plan can be used as a reference point to help you save money when you prepare your taxes the next year. The Refund Monitor constantly shows you the refund amount or tax due, and it is updated whenever you enter new information. You can also get an overview of your taxable income and your deductions along with your bottom line by clicking twice on the Refund Monitor to see your Tax Summary. The Final Review (shown in Figure 23-10) checks your return for errors, missing information, or entries that cause an audit to occur. The TaxLink imports any tax-related data from Quicken into MacInTax to save you time when entering your data. Your returns can be printed directly onto IRS-approved forms, so all you have to do is sign the form and then mail it. Or, you can file your return over the Internet for $9.95.

MacInTax also has a number of other features. You can access tax information directly from IRS itself or from a variety of other information sources, including financial advisors and financial magazines. Integrated onscreen videos help you understand complex tax laws more easily, so you can make better-informed tax decisions. The Life Events Planner helps you discover how major changes in your

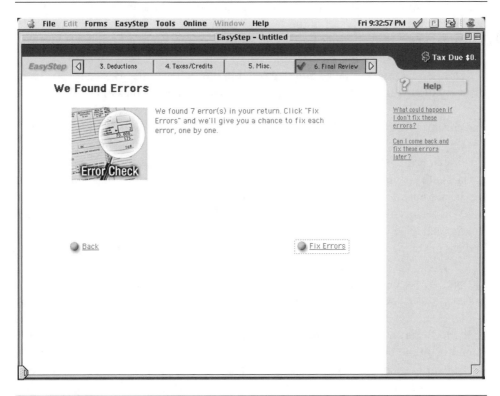

FIGURE 23-10   The Final Review feature searches your tax return for errors to make certain your return is as accurate as possible

life, such as a new home or a child can impact your taxes. Finally, the Roth IRA Planner can help you find out if you are eligible for the Roth IRA, if you can rollover funds into a traditional IRA, and which IRA suits your needs best. The Roth IRA Planner can even show you how your contributions to your IRA can grow over time and how much income should be available to you once you finally retire.

NOTE
A standard version of MacInTax doesn't include the CD tutorials. You can also purchase a state version, which automatically transfers the federal tax data for easy preparation of your state's tax return (if your state has an income tax).

A Brief Look at Online Banking and Stock Trading

Online banking and stock trading are relatively new fads. With the rapid rise of the Internet over the last few years, both Mac and Windows users alike have gained access to many new ways of doing business and daily tasks never before available to them. Doing certain things has become much easier, such as buying Christmas gifts and getting the latest stock quotes.

Online banking may sound complicated, but it is quite simple. Basically, you can do everything you would do with your bank on a normal basis, plus more. You can have access to the latest information on all your accounts, and learn which deposits and checks have cleared. You can get access to the most recent information on your banking and credit card transactions directly from your bank, no matter the time of day. Funds can be transferred among the different accounts at your bank. You can stay in contact with your bank on a regular basis through e-mail and your credit card transactions can be automatically sorted by their categories.

You can even pay your bills to anyone in the U.S. over the Internet, which is much quicker and more efficient than using regular mail. The hassle of having to write checks, address envelopes, and buy stamps is then eliminated, as is the occasional problem of a payment getting lost in the mail. You can learn about how your account will be changed by paying certain bills. Online payments can be scheduled in advance, so you are notified before you need to pay them. Payments can even be cancelled online.

Of course, while all these features are useful, some people may not have access to them. Before you can use them, you must make sure your financial institution supports online banking. You can check the Web site of your bank or see a full list of the banks (as shown in Figure 23-11) that support online banking at Intuit's Web site (www.intuit.com).

If for some reason, your bank doesn't support online banking, you have other options. You can apply for online payment with Intuit Online Payment using your

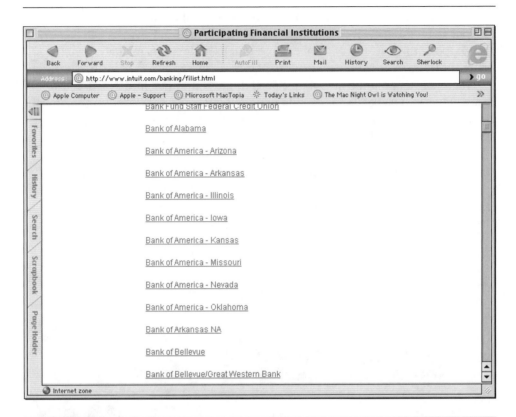

FIGURE 23-11   Intuit's Web site gives you a list of banks that support Quicken for online transactions

own account or you can apply for a credit card download with the Quicken Credit Card, offered through Travelers Bank. And, of course, you can look for another bank that offers support for online transactions.

Online stock trading and investment tracking is nearly as easy to learn. Like online banking, it gives you nearly all the features of the real thing (with the possible exception of personalized service, and even then online support is getting better), plus more, which you'd have a hard time getting from a brick-and-mortar installation.

You can get the latest statements for your account directly from your financial institution (so long as they support Quicken), no matter the time of day. You have access to information on your latest transactions, holdings, and balances. You have neither the hassle of waiting for a paper statement to arrive in the mail every month nor the bother of busy signals and complicated voice mail menus when you try to get help over the phone.

Information on all your investments can be viewed in one place, along with all your regular financial data (assuming you use a program such as Quicken 2000 that supports these features). You can use graphs and reports to analyze your entire portfolio.

Managing an accurate investment portfolio becomes much easier. If you're using Quicken, you needn't manually put in updates, as the program automatically does this for you. You can get direct access to the stocks that you trade through links to your financial institution's Web site.

Besides the banks, many brokerage firms support online trading. Brick-and-mortar brokers, such as Charles Schwab and Donaldson, Lufkin, and Jeanrette, enable you to trade stocks online. There are also pure Internet brokerage firms, such as E-Trade (shown in Figure 23-12) and Ameritrade that enable you to do the same. At either, you can set up accounts enabling you to access the online stock

FIGURE 23-12 Many brokerage firms, including E-Trade, offer the ability to trade stocks online

trading features, receive real-time quotes for your stocks, get important tips from professional stock analysts, and much more.

Stock quotes are usually delayed 15 or 30 minutes. For the specifics, check the information at the financial Web site itself.

Setting up Quicken for Online Financial Services

While online banking is extremely easy, before you can start accessing the useful features of online banking, you must first go through these steps:

1. Make certain your bank supports online banking. You can either visit the bank's Web site or check the full list of financial institutions supporting the features of online banking at Intuit's Web site (www.intuit.com).

2. Be sure the version of Quicken you're using supports online banking. Quicken 98 and 2000 both support online banking. If you're using an earlier version of Quicken, contact Intuit about upgrading to Quicken 2000.

3. You must have Internet access before you can use the Online Financial Services offered in Quicken 98 and 2000.

4. Make sure your Web browser has 128-bit security. You can get secured versions of Internet Explorer and Netscape from the publisher's Web sites. AOL enables you to download a 128-bit version of its program as an option when you access the Upgrade area (at keyword Upgrade) while you're logged on to the service.

The 128-bit version of these Web browsers is only available to residents of the U.S. and Canada.

5. Contact your bank by phone to learn about pricing and to apply for access to the online features. You can also apply using Quicken itself.

The steps for applying for the online features of Quicken 98 and Quicken 2000 are somewhat different from each other. The following describes both processes:

Quicken 98

1. Launch Quicken 98.

A Brief Look at Online Banking and Stock Trading

2. In the Online menu, select Getting Started with Online Banking.

3. Use the guide to complete your application (as shown in Figure 23-13).

4. After your application is processed, a Welcome Kit is sent to you containing all the necessary information, so you can start using the online services offered through the program.

Quicken 2000

1. Launch Quicken 2000.

2. In the Online Menu, select Getting Started with Online Banking.

3. To complete your application, select the icon in Step #3 of the online guide.

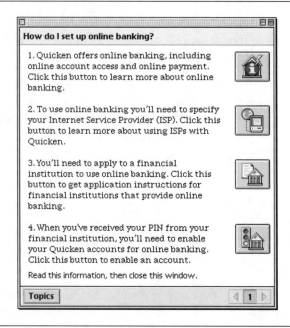

FIGURE 23-13   Quicken Deluxe 98 provides a guide to help you set up the program for accessing its online banking features

4. After your application is processed, a Welcome Kit is sent to you containing all the necessary information to start using the online services offered through the program.

Summing Up

In this chapter, you learned about financial management software, such as Quicken Deluxe 2000 and MacInTax, which enables you to keep your finances in order, prepare your tax returns, and more. You also learned a little about online banking and stock trading, as well as how to set up Quicken 98 or 2000 to access those features.

In the next chapter, you learn about capturing and editing videos on your Mac. Most models that run Mac OS 9 can be equipped to perform some level of video capture. You see what you need to accomplish the task and receive tips to help you give your masterpieces that special professional touch.

Summing Up

Chapter 24

The Fast Route to Desktop Video Production

Almost from the beginning, Apple Computer marketed Macs as multimedia computers. The products were rapidly embraced by musicians, who were quick to take advantage of its capability to support *Musical Instrument Digital Interface* (*MIDI*) connections.

Musicians were then able to take anything from simple electronic keyboards to full-blown synthesizers and hook them up to their Macs. The end result was a computerized multitrack recording studio. No doubt many commercial recordings were produced on Macs as a result.

NOTE   *In addition to being compact, the early Macs had no cooling fans. As a result, they were ideal for a recording studio environment, where even the slightest, most barely audible sound comes through loud and clear when you hear the finished recording. Early adopters of CD technology were surprised to hear air conditioner noises on some early music recordings (the sounds were otherwise buried in the surface noise on the vinyl or LP version).*

As with sound, video production also took a foothold on the Mac platform. In this chapter, you learn about the video editing options you find on your Mac and how to get the best possible quality for your productions.

Capturing Video on a Mac

No doubt you've seen Macs in front of the cameras on TV programs and movies alike. Of course, it's true this is largely a result of clever product placement by Apple's public relations staff. But it's also true Macs now have a unique industrial design. Their striking, colorful appearance can enhance a movie or TV set better than the bland products most PC-oriented companies produce.

But Macs aren't only fixtures in front of the cameras. They are found behind the cameras, too, in postproduction houses that do the actual editing of commercials, TV shows, and movies. The Mac's ease-of-use and setup is a key factor, and this is a reason many creative professionals have embraced the Mac for much of their work.

Major motion pictures do still use special effects generated on workstations from such companies as SGI, but as Macs get faster, their presence is being felt.

In fact, you may find Macs show up in more places than you imagine. For example, Macs were used to generate some of the new special effects footage added to the Special Edition versions of the first three *Star Wars* movies.

NOTE *It's interesting to note that one of the major special effects wizards at George Lucas's Industrial Light and Magic (ILM), John Knoll, is a long-time Mac advocate (one of Apple's AppleMasters). John and his brother Thomas formed the original programming team that created Adobe Photoshop.*

As with other technologies, desktop video editing began on high-cost computers, but quickly filtered down to more affordable products. Personal computers with performance rivaling that of super computers has come to the masses in the form of Apple's Power Mac G4 line. And, high-quality video is available to consumers at affordable prices as well, in the form of growing numbers of digital video camcorders and lower cost Macs with the editing hardware as standard equipment.

For example, with the iMac DV series, you can take your digital camcorder and Apple's brilliantly conceived iMovie software, and easily create video movies that, at least in terms of picture quality, can rival those done by professionals.

Linear versus Nonlinear

Capturing and editing video production is done by two basic methods, one of which is not widely used these days.

- **Linear editing** This technique involves taking segments of your video production and assembling each, one after the other, in making up your final production. This can be time-consuming, especially when you have to put together footage from different video sources.

- **Nonlinear editing** This is the most flexible choice. You can easily assemble segments from disparate sources. For example, you can mix video clips, sounds, special effects, transitions (the video effect you see when you move from one scene to another), and titles in any order you want. Once the project is assembled, you output (copy) to your video recording device in a single, seamless presentation.

Capture Hardware versus FireWire

Once you get the hang of it, editing videos on your Mac can be an enjoyable, rewarding process. You can create your own projects (to use the technical term) for friends and family. As your skills grow, you can produce business presentations, documentaries, and, perhaps, even commercials and other productions.

Capturing Video on a Mac

NOTE *Stephen Spielberg learned his craft with a relatively primitive home movie camera long before consumer video tape recorders and camcorders were around. Imagine what Spielberg could have done if he had the sophisticated tools available for Mac users in this day and age?*

If you only need a system for your family or a local small business, an iMac DV is probably good enough. All you need to start making your creations is a digital camcorder (which you can currently purchase for under $1,000) and software (if you own an iMac DV, the computer comes with Apple's iMovie video editing software at no extra cost).

NOTE *Macs without FireWire ports aren't left out. Adaptec, Orange Micro, and other companies make cheap PCI-based FireWire interface cards for many of these computers. Newer Technology, for example, offers a FireWire to Go PC card for the PowerBook G3 (the year 2000 Power Book comes with Fire Wire).*

Older or lower-cost analog camcorders are not being abandoned by new technologies either. A low-cost video capture board, a product that converts analog video to digital and transfers it to your computer, is available for almost any Mac with a PCI video slot. Once you edit the video, the capture board can convert the digital data back to analog, and enable you to transfer it to a VCR or camcorder.

Of course, if you want professional-caliber production for broadcast or movies, you still have to spend a fairly sizeable sum, notwithstanding the experience of *The Blair Witch Project,* which was done on relatively low-cost video equipment.

NOTE *If The Blair Witch Project shows anything, though, it's that a lot of creativity can often overcome limitations in other areas of the production process.*

Video Editing Options

Once you make the decision to edit video on your Mac, you are faced with a bewildering array of choices as to what to buy and what's suitable for your needs. Here are the basic elements.

A Camcorder

Once consumer video decks became popular, the logical next step was a *camcorder,* a product combining both the camera and the recorder into a single device. These too were once costly, but as production techniques and technologies improved, you could get higher quality at lower prices.

Unfortunately, with so many formats to choose from, sometimes it's difficult to separate them. The basic consideration here is the quality of your video can be no better than its weakest link, and you want to consider the best possible picture from your source footage. Here's the basic list of home video formats:

■ **VHS**   The dominant home video platform is cheap and convenient, but quality is a few notches below even regular broadcast television. Further, when you copy (*dub*) a video to make duplicates, you lose quality. The end result may not be totally satisfactory. In addition, because the cassettes and transport mechanisms are large, the camcorder is correspondingly big. Resolution is rated at about 240 lines.

■ **VHS-C**   It's only VHS in terms of quality, but the tape comes in a miniature cassette to allow for use in a smaller camcorder. The same limitations apply.

Special VHS Features You Want

If you decide to stick with regular VHS, you want to consider two more features. One is VHS-HiFi, which delivers near CD-quality sound. Otherwise, expect the audio reproduction barely to approach that of a good FM table radio. The other is flying erase heads. With normal VHS equipment, the erase head is separate. *Flying erase heads* are on the spinning drum that contains the regular video heads. The net result? When you stop and start the unit during the recording process to add new elements, you don't see that "splotch" or "blip" effect on your screen as you do with the regular erase head.

■ **SVHS**   Although it never became super popular, SVHS is much sharper than regular VHS (between 380 and 400 lines). Not many SVHS camcorders can be found, but having an SVHS deck is good for making a master tape because the duplicate is still higher in quality than VHS.

NOTE   *An updated version of SVHS, with the moniker SVHS ET (available mostly in JVC's line of decks), lets you use regular VHS tape and still get superior picture quality. The older version of the format requires special video tape, which costs two or three times more than the normal variety.*

■ **8mm**   Using small tapes and camcorders, this is a popular alternative, though quality isn't altogether different from regular VHS, at roughly 240 lines.

Capturing Video on a Mac

■ **Hi8**   This format delivers what SVHS did to VHS. It offers near-broadcast quality (up to 400 lines resolution) and because digital camcorders became reasonably affordable, prices have come down to the level of what regular 8mm camcorders sold for not long ago.

■ **Digital 8**   Coming from Sony (inventors of the 8mm video format), this new standard puts digital video on regular Hi8 metal tapes, offering up to 500 lines resolution. In addition, these camcorders can also play back regular 8mm or Hi8 tapes.

■ **DV**   Digital video camcorders started out at two grand and more, offering stylish looks, compact form factors, and extraordinary video quality, again in the 500 lines area. The technology has developed, and prices are now comparable to what a Hi8 camcorder cost only a few years ago (maybe I should have waited). Many of these models come with FireWire ports, so they can connect to any FireWire-equipped Mac.

NOTE   *Not to be confusing, but FireWire isn't always called FireWire on non-Apple products. For example, some manufacturers use the technical name, IEEE 1394. Sony refers to it as i.Link.*

Decisions, Decisions

If you already have a camcorder, there's no sense tossing it out because technology has advanced. Solutions to the dilemma do indeed exist, as you learn shortly.

Should You Toss Your Analog Camcorders?

All right, you have an analog camcorder around and a Mac with FireWire. Should you retire it in favor of the new DV products? Or, is there an alternative? Fortunately, a solution exists that won't set you back a great sum.

Check with your dealer about getting an A/V-to-FireWire converter module. If one is available for your camcorder, you can hook it up to your Mac's FireWire port. Check with the manufacturer's Web site, or your local consumer electronics or camera store.

If neither has what you want, think about the options: getting a new camcorder or a video capture board.

If you're starting from scratch, however, consider that Apple has been switching its line to support FireWire. Getting a camcorder similarly equipped can save you the bother of having to buy special video capture hardware.

With a FireWire-equipped DV camcorder, all you have to do is plug it into your Mac's FireWire port. That, and some video editing software, can make it possible to capture video, right then and there.

Video Capture Cards

As explained earlier, a video capture board converts the analog output of your video source (be it a camera, camcorder, or tape deck) to digital, so you can transfer it to your Mac. In a sense, a video capture board acts with video as a modem acts with a phone's analog signal.

Once you edit your video, a video capture board converts it back to analog, so you can then copy it back to your camcorder or video deck.

A number of video capture cards are available, some are fairly cheap, others are costly, but they can deliver broadcast-quality output. Here are some of the choices:

Lowest Cost

ATI's Xclaim VR128 is one of the lower-cost video capture solutions at only $239 (based on the company's retail price). It fits into an open PCI slot on nearly any Mac, yet it has a lot of potential.

The card includes ATI's Rage 128 2D/3D graphics acceleration chip, similiar to the one used on the latest iMacs timessign. It also has video inputs and a TV output and is designed to perform real-time video capture with resolutions up to 640 × 480 at 30 frames per second. This is the standard resolution for broadcast video, though quality may not quite match that standard. It should work fine on a regular SVHS or Hi8 video deck or camcorder.

Moving Up the Line

If you want higher quality, consider a product such as Pinnacle Systems' MiroMOTION DC-30plus. This PCI video capture board retails for around $700. It employs Motion-JPEG video compression, which is supposed to deliver high quality while keeping the size of your video files manageable. You also get a copy of Adobe Premiere, a video editing program, which is widely used by both amateur video buffs and professionals alike. Unlike lower-cost cards, this model also has an onboard sound chip. This helps you make sure your audio and video are in sync, which isn't always the case on a longer clip, when your Mac's sound hardware is used.

Pinnacle Systems also markets the TARGA 1000 and TARGA 2000, for the semiprofessional and professional marketplace.

If you are producing videos for commercial use, you also should consider systems from Avid and Media 100. Both these products have loyal followings in postproduction studios around the world.

If you want to learn more about any of these products, point your browser to the manufacturers' Web sites:

ATI: http://www.atitech.ca
Avid: http://www.avid.com
Media 100: http://www.media100.com
Pinnacle Systems (MiroMOTION and TARGA): http://www.pinnacle.com

USB Video Capture

Unfortunately, the non-DV iMacs and the iBook didn't come with FireWire or any PCI feature. While third-party companies might do something about the iMac, you needn't depend on that solution for video editing, at least not at the hobbyist level.

While it's true the USB ports on those computers won't break any speed records, at 12 Mbps per second (quite a bit below what you need for high-quality video capture), the XLR8 branch of Interex has a product called Interview USB, which manages to deliver VHS quality, at 320 x 240 pixels.

This is perfectly fine, however, for home-based video production. If you want to learn more, visit the Interex Web site at http://www.xlr8.com.

An Overview of Video Editing Software

To record video on your Mac and edit it, you need a video editing program. Such programs produce the computer equivalent of an editing machine. But instead of splicing together each element of your production, they enable you to put the raw footage and extra effects in place, usually by simply dragging-and-dropping them into the proper order before you copy them back to your video source.

Some video capture boards already come with software. If the video capture board isn't a proprietary product, such as the software that comes with the Media 100 system, it's most likely Adobe Premiere (see Figure 24-1). Premiere has become an industry-standard program that attracts casual users and pros alike.

Adobe Premiere is designed so you can learn the basics in a short time. Its sometimes dense manual, however, should be studied if you want to learn all the ins-and-outs of this sophisticated program.

FIGURE 24-1   You can use Adobe Premiere to make full-fledged video productions

Another powerful desktop video product comes directly from Apple, and it's positioned more as a tool for professionals. Final Cut Pro (shown in Figure 24-2) comes with system requirements that definitely make it suitable only for faster Macs. Final Cut Pro requires a 266 MHz G3 CPU or faster, a minimum of 128MB of built-in RAM, a 6GB A/V capable hard drive, and Mac OS 8.5 or later. It's also free with the year 2000 Power Book live.

CAUTION   *If your Mac meets the hardware requirements and you intend to use a video capture board, make sure it's compatible with Final Cut Pro before you take the plunge. The manufacturer's support people should have this information.*

Apple's second software option is free on the iMac DV and iMac DV Special Edition. It's iMovie and it's designed strictly for consumers who want to edit

FIGURE 24-2   Professional video editors can look to Final Cut Pro to deliver high-quality projects

high-caliber videos with little fuss and bother. The interface (see Figure 24-3) is designed for the novice user. You attach your DV camcorder to the iMac DV, capture the video, and drag-and-drop all the elements, from raw footage to titles and other effects. Then, you output to your video source and you're ready to view your finished production.

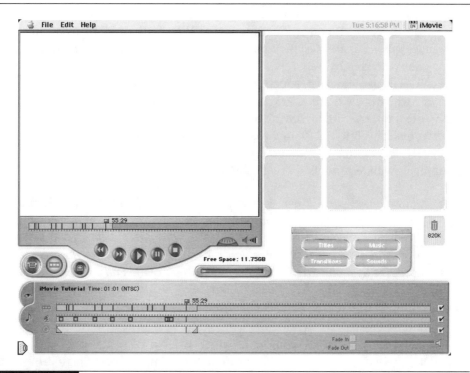

FIGURE 24-3   Apple's iMovie brings desktop video editing to the masses

> **NOTE**   *At press time, Apple hadn't released iMovie as a separate product, though in theory, it should work on any FireWire-equipped Mac. Unless iMovie is officially supported by Apple (and in light of the usual software licenses), however, you'd be using it at your own risk.*

An Overview of Desktop Video Requirements

Video requires a tremendous amount of hard drive storage space. You can expect, for example, a production to be as little as 100MB in length, up to 2GB and higher. Apple upgraded the Mac OS 9 File Manager to allow for video footage larger than 2GB in size, but not all video software supports the expanded capability.

> **NOTE**   *If your video clips are more than eight or ten minutes long, you may want to consider editing a piece at a time, at least until your software is capable of supporting bigger file sizes (assuming you have enough hard drive space, of course).*

At the very least, you should have a fast hard drive at hand and a Mac with at least 64MB of RAM. Whether the drive is FireWire, IDE, or SCSI won't make a difference, so long as it's fast enough to handle the uninterrupted data transfer rate of your video hardware.

If you have an older Mac, which may have come with a slower hard drive, determine whether the drive is A/V capable. An A/V hard drive can sustain lengthy file transfers without having to go through a process called *thermal recalibration*. This brief pause in the copying process can mean lost frames. Fortunately, most of the larger hard drives now available can easily sustain such output levels without trouble.

NOTE   *The older A/V-style drives were optimized for speed on larger file transfers, but were somewhat less capable on smaller files, such as regular text documents. Two of the popular hard drive formatters, CharisMac's Anubis and FWB's Hard Disk ToolKit, can be optimized for different drive purposes by modifying a device's mode pages, which adjusts a drive's low-level behavior. As a result, a drive may be able to sustain larger file transfers with a greater level of performance than the normal configuration.*

If you have any questions, you can usually check the Web sites run by the major hard drive makers for more information. Even Apple-labeled hard drives use standard drive mechanisms for which specifications are available. Unfortunately, Apple's own product information doesn't usually contain this information, because Apple is apt to change drive suppliers during the production cycle because of unit availability.

NOTE   *Removable media, such as an Iomega Jaz or Castlewood ORB drive can, in theory, sustain fairly video capture rates. But such solutions are best suggested for archiving purposes only. A removable drive is usually not recommended for full-time use.*

A Look at RAID

Professional video editors use RAID drives to record video footage. *Redundant Array of Inexpensive Disks* (*RAID*) employs two or more hard drives that function as a single drive. As a result, you get extremely high video transfer rates.

In addition, large RAID systems are also set up for mirroring, which means the same data is written to two drives. If one drive fails, the file is still there on the second drive, ready for use.

Because of their high degree of performance, a RAID system requires a speedy SCSI accelerator card (particularly one that supports RAID) or FireWire.

Tips and Tricks for Good Quality Video

It may be easy to drag-and-drop video clips and special effects. But desktop video can also have its problems and pitfalls. You need to make certain your system is fine-tuned and set to run at the highest possible speed without interruption.

In this section, you learn what you should consider to maximize the quality of your projects.

- **Choose high-quality video sources**   VHS camcorders may be all right for a birthday party or another family event, but the quality isn't terribly good, especially when you make a copy for friends and family. Each generation of dubbing exacts a big penalty in quality. You should consider a high-band source, such as SVHS and Hi8, or one of the new digital camcorders.

- **Don't forget a fast hard drive**   For good video quality, you need a drive that can handle a sustained read/write rate of 3.5MB per second. A hard drive must be capable of working at least twice that fast to handle that rate. If hard-drive speed suffers, you encounter dropped frames in your production or you have to scale back the transfer rate. And this, of course, means lower quality.

- **Hard drive must be optimized**   The jury is out about the value of optimizing a hard drive regularly, but when it comes to desktop video editing, the word is yes. This sort of work involves a tremendous amount of writing and removing of large files, which can cause fragmentation. In addition, you need to eke out the best possible performance from your drive. Hard-drive optimizing utilities include Alsoft's PlusOptimizer, MicroMat's TechTool Pro, or the Speed Disk component of Symantec's Norton Utilities.

CAUTION   *If your video capture board came with Alsoft's Disk Express Pro, be careful. At press time, the program hadn't been made compatible with Mac OS 9. Visit the publisher's Web site at http://www.alsoft.com.*

■ **Keep your system lean and mean** Some system extensions function in the background, slowing the performance of your Mac. You should build a new extension set based on your Mac OS 9 Base configuration for Apple's Extension's Manager or Casady & Greene's Conflict Catcher. Then add whatever video drivers you need. If you're using PostScript fonts for titles, you should also activate Adobe Type Manager.

> **NOTE** *If you are concerned about being vulnerable to computer viruses, remember you can easily scan a disk directly with your virus application without having to use the system extension or Control Panel. Those extra items are designed strictly for automatic or scheduled scans.*

■ **Switch AppleTalk off** This process should be automatic, done via your video editing software. But checking via the Chooser or the AppleTalk Control Panel never hurts. Network activity may cause a brief interruption of your video capture stream, resulting in lost frames.

■ **Switch off virtual memory** Mac OS 9's virtual memory works quite well. You scarcely notice a performance drop under normal use. But it's not recommended for video editing. To switch off virtual memory, go to the Memory Control Panel, turn it off, and then restart. You can turn it on again when you finish with your video editing chores.

■ **Fill the slots on removable drives** The drivers for removable drives probe the bus (CD or FireWire, SCSI, or USB) to check for the presence of media. Floppy drives are not immune. The only way to stop this is to place media in those drives.

Live Video Tips

Most video editing is done with a camcorder or video deck, but you can also capture live video from a video camera or camcorder.

Here are some operational tips to consider:

1. Make sure the unit is properly hooked up to your Mac's video or FireWire port.

2. When you switch on a camcorder, be sure it is set to the camera mode and place the Lock/Standby switch in Standby position.

NOTE *The previous information is designed as a general guideline. Your unit's documentation explains the proper steps to take.*

3. Remove cassette from a camcorder. When a cassette is present, a camcorder usually switches to a sleep mode after a brief interval when something isn't actually being recorded on it.

4. Watch for a demo mode on your unit and make certain the feature is not active. If it goes into demo mode, your video image may be interrupted.

Tips and Tricks for Video Capture Software

Although these programs are not hard to get up and running, you occasionally need to address pitfalls and potential problems.

The following is a brief list of common problems and solutions for the three video-editing programs described in this chapter.

iMovie: Problems and Solutions

Apple's iMovie software straddles the line of being powerful and easy-to-use at the same time; so easy, in fact, you may forget you are doing some sophisticated work in its simple interface.

If you run into trouble with your video editing, consider this information:

- **Missing audio**   If you don't hear a soundtrack or if voices and music drop out, do this: open the project file and decrease the volume of the clip using the volume slider in the audio viewer. Then export the movie again.

- **Video doesn't display when in capture mode**   If you can control your camcorder via iMovie, disconnect the FireWire cable while the unit is running. Then reconnect it and try again. This usually fixes the problem.

- **Device Too Slow warning when capturing to a FireWire drive**   Early versions of FireWire hard drives were slow, as was Apple's FireWire software. Mac OS 9 addressed some of the limitations of Apple's FireWire feature. You may also have to visit the drive manufacturer's Web site for updates.

TIP *Although MacTell, manufacturer of FirePower drives, is defunct, you might be able to use VST's FireWire drivers with the product. You can also format the drive with Drive Control from El Gato Software.*

Final Cut Pro: Problems and Solutions

For professional caliber video editing, Apple's Final Cut Pro is extremely powerful.
Final Cut Pro is also complicated and requires a bit of a learning curve to master.
Problems you may encounter include the following:

- **Video source not recognized**   Check the FireWire cable to make sure it's
  properly connected. You should also confirm your camcorder is in VCR
  mode (the manual can help if the setting isn't clear). Once the settings are
  checked, quit Final Cut Pro and launch it again. Also check the Device
  Control tab in the Preferences dialog box to see if the proper protocol for
  your camcorder has been selected.

- **No video on external NTSC display**   The first step in diagnosing the
  problem is cables. Don't be surprised if, for example, your S-video cables
  pop-out. I've had that happen with camcorders occasionally. Also, you
  need to make sure your camcorder is in VCR mode. Launch Final Cut Pro,
  check the General Preferences tab, and be sure the proper hardware has
  been selected in the View External Video Using pop-up menu. You have to
  choose Rendered Frames from the menu, so the frames are displayed
  before they are output to an NTSC video source. Finally, select All frames
  or Single frames from the External Video submenu in Final Cut Pro's
  View menu.

- **Dropped frames during DV playback from Timeline on NTSC
  display**   First, try reducing the project's Canvas or Viewer display size to
  50 percent. Turn off Mirror on desktop during Playback in the General
  Preferences tab. Second, open the View pop-up menu and disable the View
  as Sq. Pixel feature. Finally, reduce the display's bit depth to thousands of
  colors (16-bit) from millions of colors (24-bit). You probably won't notice
  any difference at all.

- **No video on display**   Check the cables first. You should also examine
  Final Cut Pro's Capture preferences tab and double-check that your
  QuickTime video settings are correct.

- **Poor quality or stuttering video playback**   If these problems crop up
  when you edit your project, make sure you aren't using keyframe
  compression options, such as Cinepak or Sorenson, when working with
  your media.

- **No sound on Mac when footage is transferred from camcorder or deck**   Check the cables first. Standard RCA-type audio cables can also come loose. Check the Capture preferences tab and make sure your QuickTime audio configuration is correct.

- **No sound from camcorder headphones or speakers**   Check the Sound Control Panel and make sure the correct audio inputs are selected. Then confirm that your cables are correctly sealed. If you are scrubbing (scanning) audio using the Audio tab in the Viewers menu, raise the output volume.

- **Camcorder or desk functions don't work**   Check the cables to make sure your connections are tight. Also make sure the correct protocol needed for controlling the camcorder is selected in the Device Control tab in the Preferences. If your video device uses FireWire, try switching from Apple FireWire to Apple FireWire Basic, and then see if the problem has been fixed.

Adobe Premiere: Problems and Solutions

As you progress through the list, you see that many of the problems and solutions that apply to the other programs also apply to this program.

The following list adds some Premiere specific issues you sometimes confront:

- **File isn't displayed in Import dialog box**   At the start, you want to make sure Premiere supports the file format of the video clip. You may also want to try to open the file in another program that may support the format, such as QuickTime, and see if it looks all right. If you can open the file in another program, perhaps one of Premiere's plug-in modules may be damaged or missing. If this is the case, reinstall the program. If the plug-in is from a third party, you need to use the installer for that plug-in instead.

- **Imported image only displays first frame**   You can probably attribute this problem to your configuration. Check Premiere's Import dialog box and check to see if the first file in the sequence and the Numbered Stills option are both selected.

- **Exported or previewed images display poor quality during playback**   You can often trace this to the source. Perhaps the picture itself is blurred or distorted. You should also specify the proper data rate if you're using Motion-JPEG as your compression codec. Check the setting of the Quality slider and enter a specific data rate (check the instructions for your capture device to find the best settings).

■ **Project audio and video lose sync during playback or export**   Go back to Premiere's Project Settings dialog box. Set the timebase to 29.97 and set the frame rate to 30. If the timebase is set to 30 (even if this seems to be the correct choice), it shifts the audio out of sync with the video, making your film appear poorly dubbed.

NOTE   *If you are using a video capture board without an onboard sound chip (hence, it uses your Mac's audio circuitry), try to limit the size of your video clips or edit smaller segments. As the clips get larger, the audio and video sync might drift.*

■ **Tracks out of sync**   Look at Premiere's project window for red triangles at the In locations of the audio and video clips that are out of sync. Click each of the red triangles and choose the timecode that appears onscreen. This should enable you to resynchronize audio and video.

■ **Export, playback, or preview operation seems slow**   Make certain the frame size is properly set. Check your Export Settings or Project Settings and make sure they match up closely. Also check your audio and video filter settings. Go to the Export Settings or Project Settings dialog box and find the Keyframe or Rendering. Choose Ignore Audio Filters and Ignore Video Filters to see if that fixes the problems.

■ **Video flickers during playback**   Return to your source clip and see if it flickers. If the source clip is all right, select In. Then apply Premiere's Flicker Removal option. If the problem continues, recheck your hardware and software configuration to make sure everything is set up properly.

■ **Audio or video clip cannot be dragged into timeline**   Check to determine if the track you want to move isn't adjacent to another audio or video track. If this is the case, there's no place to move the track. Also make sure the track wasn't "locked" by accident.

■ **Video clip runs short or long, or it is the wrong segment**   Check the Range option in the General Settings panel of the Export Settings dialog box. You want to make sure the proper project work area was specified.

Summing Up

With such a collection of weird problems, you may think editing your own videos is a daunting task. But actually, once you master the basics of dragging-and-dropping raw footage, special effects, sounds, titles, and the rest in your project window, you'll find it's not hard at all.

Of course, as with any artistic pursuit, producing professional-grade material requires a lot of attention to detail, talent, and training. But with such high-quality video capture tools available to you with the Mac OS 9 and your Mac, you'll be off to a running start.

In the next chapter you learn how to get the most value from installing utilities on your Mac with Mac OS 9.

Summing Up

Chapter 25

Using Utilities for Fun and Profit

Mac OS 9 gives you some basic tools to enhance the look and feel of your Mac and to run basic hard disk diagnostics. But your options don't end there. Plenty of other programs can enhance what your Mac does.

On the other side of the coin, adding too many of those enhancements can work in reverse. They can make your Mac run slower or crash often.

In this chapter, you learn about some of the options, from standard options to some of the enhancements a lot of clever Mac programmers have devised for you.

Dealing with the Appearance Control Panel

If you're upgrading to Mac OS 9 from a version of the Mac OS that precedes Mac OS 8, you should be rather surprised at how the options to change the look of your desktop have changed.

Apple has a nifty application, the Appearance Control Panel, which gives you a number of options to make your Mac look the way you like. Previously, some of those features required a third-party program, which tended to increase the possibility of a system extension conflict.

Like everything else, though, the Appearance Control Panel (shown in Figure 25-1) is not free from its own little quirks. And there's a limit to what it can do, which means you may still want to look into some of the third-party options.

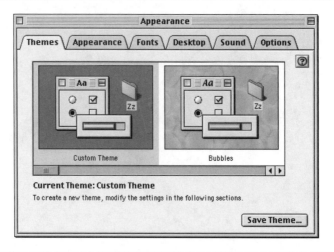

FIGURE 25-1   Apple's Appearance Control Panel can completely change the look and feel of your Mac

Here's a look at the features of the Appearance Control Panel and just where it may go wrong:

■ **Problems with font anti-aliasing** The text on your screen may seem cleaner and more reader-friendly if you decide to use the Smooth All Fonts option (see Figure 25-2). Instead, the letters may appear to look smeared. You should definitely notice this if you're using an LCD screen, like that of a PowerBook or an iBook. This could cause problems with your font display in older programs. When you install Mac OS 9, the smoothing option is turned on by default, but you may prefer (as I do) to leave it off. Sometimes, things are better left alone.

> NOTE *In addition to the smearing effect, you will find font smoothing doesn't work with PostScript fonts.*

■ **Pictures on the desktop look smudged or blurry** If the pictures are less than 128 × 128 pixels, they are placed side by side so they fill your screen. In other words, the Appearance Manager sets them up like tiles. If the picture isn't large enough, it is scaled upward and you're apt to find the reduced quality of the picture has made it completely unusable. If you want

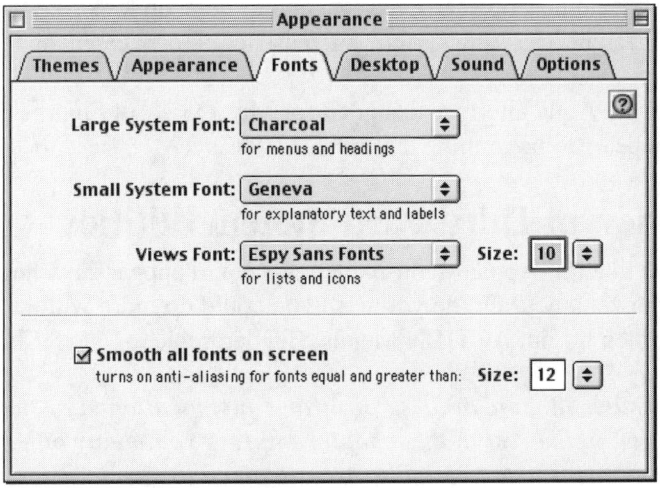

Dealing with the Appearance Control Panel

FIGURE 25-2 Font smoothing could cause your letters to look smeared or better, depending on your point of view

to have only one picture on your desktop, be sure it's big enough to fill your screen without having to make it any larger.

NOTE *If the picture you want for your desktop pattern is too large, you can have it centered and cropped by the Appearance Manager without resizing it. This gives you added flexibility in using different pictures for your desktop.*

■ **Screen redraw sluggish** If you don't have Apple's best and fastest computer right now (this being the Power Mac G4, as of press time) or a fast graphic card, your computer could take a long time to display a complicated picture. This also occurs if your Mac doesn't have enough system or video memory. If this happens, consider a regular desktop pattern, rather than a picture.

Programs That Make Your Desktop Look Better (or Worse)

Apple's Appearance Control Panel can't do everything to satisfy your decorative needs. Other programs may be able to provide for those needs, however.

One of these programs is a shareware program called Kaleidoscope (see Figure 25-3). This can do much more for your Mac's desktop than the Appearance Control Panel. Kaleidoscope can even make your desktop look like that of a completely different operating system, such as BeOS, or it can even take on some of the aspects of the Aqua interface designed for Mac OS X. In Figure 25-4, my son's iMac appears to be running the BeOS . . . or is it?

An Overview of Third-Party System Utilities

Wouldn't you like it if Apple Menu-like menus could appear anywhere on your desktop for convenience? Or, do you wish you could do more with just your Apple Menu? If so, then try out ACTION Menus, BeHierarchic, or MenuChoice.

NOTE *Remember, if none of these programs just mentioned or the ones I mention in the rest of this chapter impress you, many other system enhancements are available. A good place to check is VersionTracker at http://www.versiontracker.com.*

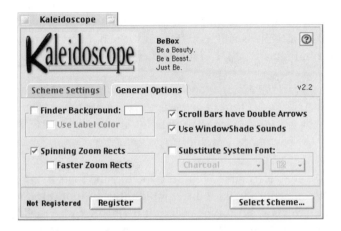

| FIGURE 25-3 | Kaleidoscope takes desktop enhancements way beyond the Appearance Control Panel |

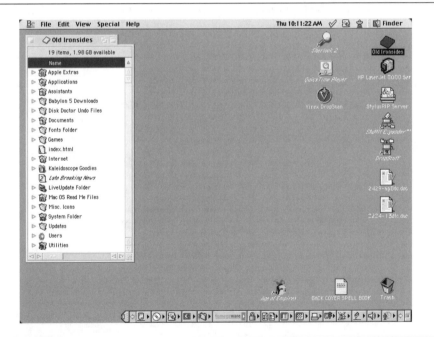

| FIGURE 25-4 | An iMac's desktop has been made to simulate the BeOS, an alternate operating system that supports pre-G3 Macs and Intel-based PCs |

Dealing with the Appearance Control Panel

The Open and Save dialog box provided by Apple may not impress you if decoration is your thing, but a number of applications can improve the look of your dialog boxes, as well as add more features. Such programs include ACTION Files (as shown in Figure 25-5), Default Folder, or DialogView.

NOTE *If you've used the Mac for a while, no doubt you've noticed how the various ACTION Utilities components resemble those from Now Utilities. While Power On also acquired the old Now products, ACTION Utilities was, at the beginning, developed separately.*

How about your font menus? Wouldn't you like the fonts to appear as they would in your documents and have different families of fonts grouped together? What if you want to know what type of font it is (PostScript, TrueType, and so forth)? Then ACTION WYSIWYG Menus, Adobe Type Reunion Deluxe, MenuFonts, or TypeTamer would be good for you.

NOTE *While some programs, such as AppleWorks and Microsoft Word 98, have a WYSIWYG-type font menu, they lack many of the features included in these programs, such as grouping fonts into family submenus.*

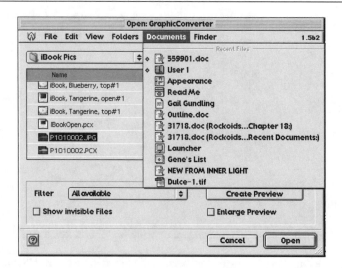

FIGURE 25-5   With ACTION Files from Power On Software, the old and new Open and Save dialog boxes get a thorough makeover

What about Apple's Launcher? Do you wish it didn't fill up so much of your screen (especially if you have a lot of programs)? Do you want an easier way to find files, disks, and programs you placed in the launcher? Wouldn't it be nice if the Launcher had more features? Then consider DragStrip, DragThing, OneClick, Power Launch, SmartLaunch, Square One, or the Tilery.

Do you want to make it easier to capture images from your screen for presentations or other documents? Do you wish you could actually name your documents (instead of having them appear as Picture 1, Picture 2, and so forth)? Don't you want to save your pictures in other places on your hard drive? Programs with these features and more include SnapzPro and Captivate.

> **NOTE** *My personal favorite is SnapzPro, a shareware program from Ambrosia Software (http://www.ambrosiasw.com). It enables you to save your screen captures in a number of different file formats and you can capture difficult images, such as those from many games. SnapzPro even supports QuickTime movies.*

Whatever you can think of, whatever system enhancement you wish you had, somewhere, some programmer has developed it to give your Mac more capabilities. The downside is that every time Apple releases a major system upgrade—Mac OS 9 has major under-the-hood changes even if it doesn't look so different from recent system versions—those enhancements may need updates to stay compatible.

> **NOTE** *An older program may seem to work fine, but it may cause your Mac to behave in a less-than-stable fashion, with frequent lockups.*

System Enhancement Problems and Solutions

While most of the system enhancements work fine with Mac OS 9 (though you may need an update or two), an opportunity for mischief always exists. While many of the programmers who make these programs handle them with meticulous care, some of the others release programs without checking them as thoroughly as they should.

If you're careful about adding one of these system or desktop enhancements, however, you can make your Mac-using experience much more enjoyable.

■ **Take care when using older system enhancements with newer system versions.** While the application that gives you extra menus in the finder may have worked fine under Mac OS 8 or earlier, it could not work

Dealing with the Appearance Control Panel

anymore under Mac OS 9. If no updated version is available, you should think about taking it off your computer and finding a newer, similar program, which can work as well for you. A case in point is NowMenus, part of the now-discontinued Now Utilities suite. Many of NowMenus' best features have been updated for Mac OS 8 and 9 in ACTION Menus, from Power On Software.

■ **Pay for shareware.**   Many of the better system utilities and enhancements are shareware. This means you needn't pay for them right away after putting them to use. If you continue to use the program beyond 15 to 30 days (depending on the program), however, you are expected to pay a small price to the creator of the product. If you like the product and you want it continually to be improved, as well as made compatible with the latest Apple system releases, you should pay the fee. Imagine, for example, if you spent weeks or months working on something, only to have your customers refuse to pay you for your work.

■ **Be on the lookout for updates.**   Whenever Apple releases updates for its system software, the components the system enhancements require to work could have been modified. Especially programs that give new functions to the Finder may not work if such changes are made. You should always check Web sites, such as VersionTracker or the publisher's Web site, for the latest updates to those programs.

NOTE *Mac OS 9's Software Update feature would be great for third-party programs, but as of press time, it was only designed to support Apple system software.*

■ **Don't use two or more enhancements that perform the same task.** It doesn't matter if the enhancement does something for your dialog boxes or font menus or provides protection against computer viruses. If you have installed two system extensions that perform the same function, they could interfere with each other (because they access the same Mac OS resources). Sometimes, they could even cause your Mac to crash. If you can't decide which of the programs you want to use, then use each one separately before making your decision. Be sure the other programs have been disabled with the Extensions Manager first.

Why Rebuild the Desktop?

The Mac OS Finder is constantly keeping an eye on file icons, documents, and the programs in which you use the files and documents with desktop files. These files are marked by the Finder as *invisible,* which means you cannot see evidence of

Apple's Better Idea

The previous tried-and-true desktop rebuilding scheme works fine in most cases. But Apple has another idea about rebuilding your desktop, which isn't quite as simple as the one suggested. Apple states that, first, you should disable every system Extension in the Extension Manager except for File Exchange. Then you have to follow the previous steps to rebuild your desktop.

After the desktop has been rebuilt by Apple's recommendation, reactivate your needed extensions in Extensions Manager and then restart.

If your desktop does not rebuild correctly, you may have to use a program such as Alsoft's DiskWarrior, MicroMat's TechTool Pro, or Symantec's Norton Utilities to repair directory damage on your hard drive. They deal with problems with so-called *bundle bits,* too, which could cause icons for files or folders to be incorrect or missing.

You could also use the desktop rebuild features of TechTool Pro or Conflict Catcher, which rebuilds your desktop better and more thoroughly. Instead of only rebuilding or updating the desktop files, the desktop rebuild feature in these programs deletes them first and the Finder then rebuilds the desktop from scratch once you restart your Mac.

Dealing with the Appearance Control Panel

their presence without a program that can view such files. The Finder's desktop files store information about the two criteria used to identify programs and files: what type of file it is and the program in which the file was originally created.

A typical example is Microsoft Word 98, the same program used to write this book's manuscript. A document created in this program has a file type listed as W8BN, which identifies the version of Word that was used to create it. The file's creator is MSWD, which stands for Microsoft Word. The Finder uses this information to launch Microsoft Word 98 whenever you double-click a document made in this program (or, for that matter, in a previous version of Word).

Everything may work fine as you add and remove programs on your Mac. But one day, things might go awry. The icons for such files suddenly turn to white-colored documents. If you try to open them, you could receive an alert saying the application in which the file was created can't be found or it may not be opened in the right program. This could happen if you have a system failure or damage to your hard drive's directory, and the desktop file is corrupted.

To fix this, you need to rebuild the desktop file. First, restart your Mac. As soon as the last extension icon zips onto your desktop, hold down both the COMMAND and the OPTION keys at the same time.

As soon as you are asked if you want to rebuild the desktop, click OK. If more than one disk is loaded on your Mac, you receive the same message for each disk, until all of their desktops have been rebuilt.

A progress bar moves along as the desktop is rebuilding. If you have a small hard drive or a number of small hard disks, this could only take a matter of seconds (or longer if you have a slower computer). If you have many big hard drives or one with many files, this could take up to several minutes or more.

Coping with Utility Software Conflicts

If your Mac crashes (and no Mac or any personal computer is completely immune to crashing), this can be both annoying and frustrating. You could be on the verge of finishing your great American novel (like the *Attack of the Rockoids* series of novels I wrote with my son Grayson) before mailing it off to eager publishers looking for your kind of material. And, as you finish the last sentence, you save the document and your Mac suddenly freezes. What in the world should you do?

Problems like these can occur with the wide variety of software and system and hardware combinations. Everything that can cause problems for your Mac could take years to list, and even then, I couldn't find every single problem. You can find out what is causing you problems, though, and then you can either stop using the program or extension that's causing your frustrations, or you can get an update or help from its publisher.

What Causes a System Crash?

What could cause problems with your system? The answer constantly changes. While one minute, Microsoft Word 98 may work fine, the next day, AOL 4.0 could suddenly cause your Mac to crash. Unfortunately, you can't avoid this type of problem when you use a Mac or any personal computer. Bugs are in software, hardware, and operating systems simply because the humans who write these programs aren't perfect.

Such problems should not be part of your daily Mac experience, however. Mac OS 9 is designed to be more reliable than previous operating system versions. One significant reason is its capability to access more open files (8,169 compared to 348 with older versions of the Mac OS). While 348 may seem like a lot, when you consider that more than 100 files are opened each time you boot your Mac (before you run a single program, which may have dozens of support files), you can see how you can easily run up against the limits.

NOTE   *A possible answer to the age-old problem of Mac OS stability is the consumer release of Mac OS X, which will greatly enhance your protection against system crashes. Among these are protected memory, which means each program receives its own address space, providing in essence, a wall of protection from other programs. This way, if one program freezes when you're using it, you can go on with your computing lifestyle and use other programs without having to restart your Mac.*

If you encounter problems, the following methods can help you isolate most problems:

Isolating Problems in Extensions Manager

Included with Mac OS 9 is Extensions Manager (shown in Figure 25-6) to manage your system extensions. You can turn individual Extensions on and off when you need to do so, and you only need to restart to implement your changes.

Extensions Manager can't handle these problems nearly as well as a commercial utility program called Conflict Catcher from Casady & Greene. But first, you learn how to deal with system problems using Extensions Manager. In the next section, you learn how to deal with system problems using Conflict Catcher. You can discover the causes for recurring problems (like repeated crashes in the same program when you're doing the same thing every time). If a problem happens at random, though, it can be a bear to solve. Follow these steps to deal with basic problems:

FORCING A RESTART   If your computer suddenly won't do anything at all or if it won't respond to your mouse movements, you can deal with this problem.

Here are the common solutions:

- **Force quit**   Press COMMAND-OPTION-ESC at the same time. A message asks if you want to force the program to quit. The program will do this if the process works, and then you can restart your Mac normally before going on to the next step.

- **The Three Fingered Salute**   This was once a common method used to restart Macs, but the newest Macs with USB input devices did not, at press time, support this feature. If the attempt to force-quit your Mac doesn't work, or if your Mac freezes as soon as the program has been quit, then press COMMAND-CONTROL-POWER ON. If you have a USB Mac, check the next section.

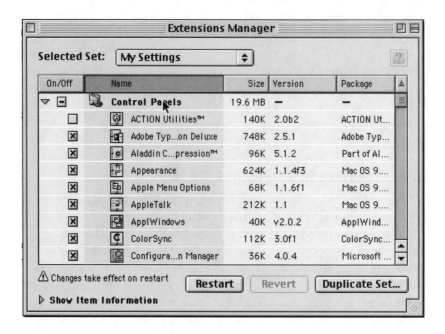

FIGURE 25-6 Apple's Extensions Manager is a great tool for finding problems related to your system software

■ **Press the Reset button** This can be in any number of places, depending on what kind of Mac you own. To restart an older Mac, you must use a small button with a small left-pointing triangle. Where is it? This depends on which model you have. With a Blue & White Power Mac G3 and the Power Mac G4, the button is directly under the power button on the computer. Sometimes, however, the reset button itself is recessed, located in a little hole just beneath that little triangle. The first-generation iMacs and some PowerBook models met this description. To access that switch, straighten the end of a paper clip, carefully put it into the hole, press down the button, and release it.

NOTE *Another solution for early-generation iMac owners is the iMac Button, a $9.95 paste-on device that rids you of paper clips forever. You can order direct from the manufacturer's Web site at http://www.theimacbutton.com.*

CREATE YOUR SYSTEM PROFILE FIRST Before taking steps to fix your problem, you should create a record of the way your Mac's System Folder is set up. By doing this, you have a point of reference when you try to discover the cause of a problem you're encountering. From the Apple menu, choose Apple System Profiler. A screen similar to the one in Figure 25-7 should appear.

| FIGURE 25-7 | Apple's System Profiler can help you isolate the causes of problems |

In the File menu, select New Profile (as shown in Figure 25-8).

Check whichever items have to do with the System Folder Controls (found on the right side of the screen). On the left side, uncheck the ones you don't need. After you click OK, a report is created. This could take from as little as 30 seconds to one minute or longer to appear on your screen, depending on how much you have on your hard drive. Once the report appears on your screen, choose Print One Copy in the File menu, so you have a hard copy available.

This is only the beginning, though. Now you actually have to isolate the cause of your Mac's problems.

MAC CRASHES WHEN STARTING UP   Examine your Mac when it is going through the startup process before doing anything else. If your Mac crashes before all the Extensions have been loaded, look closely at whichever icons appear just before the crash occurs. An extension that loads immediately after that icon could be causing your problems.

After you identify the file that loads before the crash happens, restart your Mac. If you have to do a force restart, then do so. As your Mac is starting up, hold down the SPACE BAR key. This action brings up the Extensions Manager window. Once it is displayed, check your list of Extensions and Control Panels to find which ones load after the icon you identified. After finding the extension you saw, disable the next two or three extensions, as long as they aren't Apple's, and resume the startup process. You can do this by closing the Extensions Manager window.

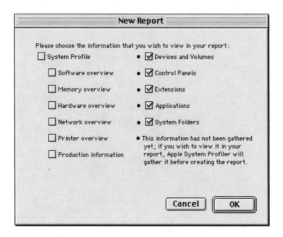

FIGURE 25-8   In this screen, you can choose your options for a system profile

Coping with Utility
Software Conflicts

> NOTE *You can change Extensions Manager preferences to use a different startup key, but you might as well leave it as it is.*

Assuming your Mac survives the entire startup process without a single crash, then try to find the files you disabled in the System Folder. If you can't find them, use the Finder's Get Info command to identify them. Once you have the necessary information, you can stop using the file or contact its publisher about getting an update to solve your conflict.

If the crashes keep happening, however, repeat the previous steps. Not everything in your Extensions and Control Panels folders appears as an icon during the startup process. You might be forced to dig deep into your System Folder for a file that loads later in the startup. Remember, Extensions usually load alphabetically.

MAC CRASHES AFTER STARTING UP If your Mac crashes as soon as the startup process is compete or if it freezes whenever you're trying to accomplish a certain task, such as opening a program, then the information in the following paragraphs should help you discover the problem.

1. If your Mac crashes whenever you're performing a certain function, such as launching a program or even booting up your Mac, choose Extensions Manager from the Control Panels submenu in the Apple menu. If your Mac didn't crash immediately after the startup process was completed, then you're fine. If this isn't the case, hold down the SHIFT key at startup to load with extensions off, until your Mac's startup screen displays a message labeled Extensions Disabled. Now you can release the keys. If the startup process works, consider reinstalling Mac OS 9, which is covered in depth in Chapter 2. Otherwise, go on.

2. If the startup process does work, however, open Extensions Manager and select Duplicate Set in the File menu, which should cause the following image to appear on your screen (see Figure 25-9).

3. Name the duplicate set so it's identified for system diagnostics. You can call it anything you want, but it should be something that has to do with the situation, such as Test Set (feel free to stretch your imagination). The duplicate set starts out with the same settings as your Mac OS Base set, but you change it in whatever way you want (you can't modify the built-in Mac OS 9 Base and All sets, which is why you must make a duplicate set).

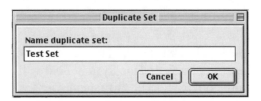

FIGURE 25-9   Use this screen to make a new startup set

4. Check your list of Extensions and Control Panels, and then turn on half of those that are turned off. Look at the report you created in System Profiler to get the information you need. Also, make sure you keep a record of what you're doing, in case you need to restart and go through the process again several times. Then restart.

5. After your computer finishes starting up, perform whatever function initiated the crash. Let's say, you're going to open an application, but it needs a certain extension to run. Go back to Extensions Manager, turn on the necessary extensions, and then restart.

CAUTION   *If you are using one of Microsoft's Office-based or Internet programs, you want to activate anything labeled Microsoft or MSL. If you don't do this, these programs automatically replace the missing Extensions, giving you both active and disabled copies (and more headaches to resolve later).*

6. Once the problem has disappeared, return to Extensions Manager, and turn on the rest of Extensions that you didn't activate before, and then restart. Once you finish booting up, try to reproduce the crash. Next, turn on half of the remaining Extensions every time you restart until the problem returns. As soon as the problem comes up again, use the steps in the following section.

IF THE SYSTEM CRASH HAPPENS AGAIN   Before long, you'll discover the source of your problem. By this time, you know at least one of your active Extensions or Control Panels has caused your Mac to crash. If this happens, first restart your Mac. As soon as your Mac has done this, press the SPACEBAR down until Extensions Manager appears on your screen. After Extensions Manager comes up, disable half the Extensions and Control Panels that were turned during the previous restart, and then resume the startup process.

Now take the necessary steps to reproduce the crash. If the crash continues to happen, repeat the previous steps and make sure you deactivate half of the remaining Extensions and Control Panels (besides the files provided by Apple in the Base Set). Once you find the source of your problem, use your computer without the Extension or Control Panel to determine if the problem disappears. You should be overjoyed (or, at the very least, satisfied) that you deal with a potentially nasty problem. You can now use your Mac reliably and well (at least until a new problem appears).

You can now switch back to your regular startup set. If you have to use the disabled Extension or application, contact the publisher to see if it has an update that fixes the problems or try to find a different program that performs the same or a similar function.

Conflict Catcher—A Better Choice

While the Extensions Manager provided by Apple with the Mac OS is free (and who would not accept something free?), trying to find the source of a system problem is a lot of trial and error. While you can probably find the source of your problem, this may take lots of restarts and guesswork to determine what went wrong.

Another way is out there—a program that guides you deftly through the system-diagnostic process—Casady & Greene's Conflict Catcher, by Jeffrey Robbin. Conflict Catcher had its humble beginnings in the early 1990s and it has been steadily updated to fill nearly anyone's wish list of what such a program should do (and then some). Some of the most important Conflict Catcher features, based on the Mac OS 9 savvy version 8.0.6, follow:

- ■ **Conflict Test**   This is the linchpin of Conflict Catcher's large feature set. Using a clever set of fuzzy logic-type algorithms devised by Robbin, Conflict Catcher can systematically turn system extensions off and on, taking you to a reasonably fast answer about the cause of repeatable system crashes.

- ■ **Reference Library**   If you're trying to find the source of a problem, a good idea is to know the purposes of the files in your System Folder. While the Extensions Manager only has information on Apple's software, Microsoft's, and a handful of others, Conflict Catcher provides a large reference database telling about thousands of third-party programs. It also provides links to the Web sites of the publishers, so you can search for updates to your programs.

- ■ **Merge System Folders**   If you decide to perform a clean install of MacOS 9, Conflict Catcher helps you with the process of taking stuff from your Previous System Folder and putting in the one newly installed by the system installer. This can be done in minutes and you don't even have to do the grunt work yourself. For information on performing a standard or clean system installation, read Chapter 2.

■ **Rebuilds the desktop efficiently**   When you rebuild your desktop the normal way, only your existing desktop files are updated. If the files are corrupt, however, Conflict Catcher won't fix the problem of opening the file in programs and displaying its icon. When Conflict Catcher rebuilds your desktop, it actually deletes the desktop files already there and creates a replacement, instead of only rebuilding them during the next restart.

■ **Finds corrupted system files**   When you do a Conflict Test, Conflict Catcher also searches for damaged or corrupted startup files in your System Folder (as shown in Figure 25-10), among them fonts and Preferences files. Corrupted Preference files can especially cause recurring system crashes. Conflict Catcher gives you the option of fixing the problem if it discovers a damaged file, but it can only fix minor damage.

Using Conflict Catcher's Conflict Test Feature

If your Mac crashes whenever you perform a specific task, Conflict Catcher's power can be harnessed to discover the source of the problem. Make sure you have the latest version of Conflict Catcher (8.0.6 as of the time this book went to press) before you do this. Then you can follow the steps in the following paragraphs to focus the program's power on solving your problems.

1.   First, restart your Mac and then press the SPACEBAR until the Conflict Catcher window appears on your screen (as shown in Figure 25-11).

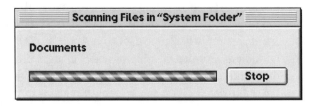

FIGURE 25-10   Conflict Catcher checks for damaged system files

| **FIGURE 25-11** | Conflict Catcher can be used to discover the source for constant crashes on your Mac |

Coping with Utility
Software Conflicts

2. After Conflict Catcher comes up, click the Conflict Test button and the screen shown in Figure 25-12 appears.

3. Now get ready to work with the program, so you can do the test. First, Conflict Catcher scans your files during the startup process to search for any damaged files in your System Folder. After Conflict Catcher gives you a report on the status of the System Folder, click OK and then you can go on to the next step.

4. When the next screen comes up, you are queried by Conflict Catcher as to whether you are currently dealing with a system problem. If you are, click Yes (I assume you will be doing this).

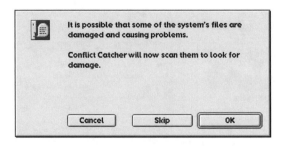

FIGURE 25-12 Select your Conflict Test options

5. Then you have to type in a short description of the problem you're encountering (as shown in Figure 25-13). This helps you to keep track of the original problem. Conflict Catcher itself doesn't need to use it. Click OK once you're done.

6. The next part of the process is crucial. You are asked to click the Needed Files option, so you can choose which system Extensions you have to use every day, such as those files relating to the programs in Office 98 with the word Microsoft in them. After you select the needed files, click OK to continue.

7. If you want to try to guess which item in the System Folder is causing you problems, choose the Intuition button, which causes the screen shown in Figure 25-14 to appear. To get Conflict Catcher to focus on that file first, click its name. Now Click OK to move to the last part.

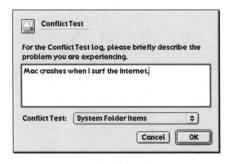

FIGURE 25-13   List the problem you're having with your Mac

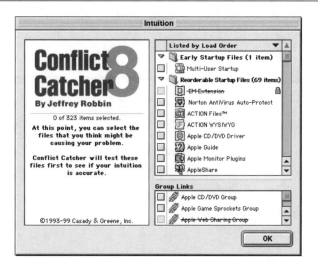

FIGURE 25-14   If you think you know what file is causing your problems, tell Conflict
Catcher so it can check that file first

Coping with Utility
Software Conflicts

8. Before long, you are done with the setup process. Click the Start Conflict
    Test button and then click Restart on the screen to begin the test itself.
    Now Conflict Catcher's true power is revealed to you. After your Mac
    restarts, recreate the conditions that resulted in the crash, such as opening
    or launching a program, or opening a certain file.

9. After you finish this, restart. If your Mac crashes again, force a restart.

10. Once the restart occurs, Conflict Catcher asks if the problem has disappeared
    (Click Problem Gone) or if the problem is still there (Click Problem
    Exists). With this information, Conflict Catcher can continue to vary the
    lineup of the System Folder. Finding the source of your problem could take
    ten or more restarts.

11. After Conflict Catcher has found a suspect, you will be asked if you want
    to deactivate it and then do another test to find out if any other programs
    are related to the problem you're having.

The Conflict Test process is neither perfect nor can it help if your system-related
problems are hard to reproduce. But in most cases, Conflict Catcher can guide you
to a solution to some of the nagging problems you may encounter with your Mac
and Mac OS 9. If you want to sample Conflict Catcher, visit the publisher's Web

site at http://www.casadyg.com. You can download a limited-time demo and put the program through its paces. If you like what you see, you can order the program directly from the publisher or buy a copy from your favorite Apple dealer.

Summing Up

In this chapter, you learned about adding system enhancements to your Mac, as well as how to check for problems that may accompany those neat additions.

In Chapter 26, you discover the wonderful, exciting world of Mac games (I even introduce you to a few of my favorites).

Chapter 26

Playing Games on Your Mac

Young or old, many people buy Macs for only one reason: to play games. A computer game can be educational, just plain fun, or some combination of the two.

The arrival of Mac OS 9 has enhanced the Mac's game-playing capabilities in several ways. For one thing, Apple offers better OpenGL performance, which is a prime requisite for maximum performance on some games.

NOTE   *OpenGL is a 3D graphics display technology that Apple licensed from Silicon Graphics. With OpenGL, publishers of games can write software for multiple platforms, using the same basic graphics display routines. To take advantage of this feature, your Mac needs a graphics card (such as the ones from ATI and Formac and the developing series from 3dfx Interactive), which support the technology.*

In addition, Apple includes its game sprockets technology as standard issue. This allows built-in support for the use of special input devices, such a trackballs and joysticks. This helps enhance your Mac gaming experience.

In this chapter, the key players in the Mac games industry are covered. You learn hints, tips, and tricks about how to get the maximum possible performance when playing games on your Mac with Mac OS 9.

An Overview of Mac Gaming Software

A common misconception is that no software is available for the Mac, especially for games. This is incorrect, of course.

The fact of the matter is that thousands of games are available for the Mac, both old and new, and lots more are on the way. If anything, the success of the iMac, iBook, and Power Macintosh G4 has caused Apple's profits and market share to skyrocket, which has given game developers more reasons to have faith in the future of the Mac platform.

Also, Apple's decision to embrace industry standards, such as OpenGL and *Accelerated Graphics Port* (*AGP*) technologies, has made the climate for Mac development much more favorable. This means a gaming graphics card, such as 3dfx's Voodoo, can be easily modified to work on a Mac. This also makes bringing games out in a Mac OS version easy for game developers and assures the maximum possible level of performance.

Mac Games Categorized

Among the top-selling games for the Mac are real-time strategy games, such as Age of Empires I and Starcraft. In these games, you gather resources to build your civilizations and armies (Starcraft mainly has you building up the latter), and then trying to defeat or appease your enemies using diplomacy, advanced warfare tactics, or simply overwhelming them through sheer force.

In other city-building games, such as Caesar III and SimCity 3000, you build and manage a city, balancing all the issues of real cities and maintaining order, while trying to keep your citizens constantly happy.

Turn-based games, such as Civilization II and Alpha Centauri, involve building an empire over a long period of time. You eventually win the game as you juggle politics, economics, and diplomacy to become the most powerful country in the world.

In dazzling 3D shooters, such as Unreal Tournament and Quake III: Arena, you get to frag everybody in sight (and all your friends over the Internet), while attempting to survive yourself.

Even while many games, such as Unreal Tournament, Civilization: Call to Power, Rainbow Six, and Quake III: Arena, have recently been released for the Mac, they still appear first on that other platform.

The reason for this, whether or not you want to accept it, is that Windows holds a significant majority of the market over the Mac, as well as a greater portion of the hard-core gamers out there, making it far more profitable to release games on the PC first. Porting code from Windows to Mac is a hard task, even with Apple's support of OpenGL, and it can take a long time, especially considering that the features in both versions of the game must be made as equal as possible. In addition, the performance and interface must be acceptable to a Mac user. Microsoft's experience when it produced the PC-like Word 6 for the Mac shows users reject a program that is not ported properly to the platform.

Games Market Realities

Although I don't care to admit it, sometimes doing all that work isn't worth the cost. Although Apple sold 2 million iMacs in its first year and sales continued to soar for the iMac and iBook as this book was written, Mac games sales haven't necessarily risen in proportion.

A typical Mac game sells only 25,000 to 35,000 copies at most, which is exactly the same as it was back in 1997, when Apple's very survival seemed doubtful. Some game companies won't take the time to port their games to the Mac because selling so few copies would not allow them to recoup the cost they need for programming and testing.

> NOTE *Some companies do give the Mac the attention the platform deserves in their product releases. For example, Ambrosia Software, the shareware company, only programs for Macs. Bungie is known for releasing its new games for the Mac and Windows market simultaneously. Sometimes the Mac versions even get out the door first.*

Despite the uncertainties of the market, though, many more games are being developed in Mac versions. The use of industry standard technologies has helped reduce the cost. With a wide variety available, the hope is that more Mac users will pay attention to the choices and buy the products they like. This, of course, can make it easier for software publishers to decide whether a Mac version is a worthwhile effort.

Popular Mac Games Profiled

So many different games are available on the market right now, it's hard to provide more than a basic list for this chapter.

The following are brief descriptions of some of the most prominent games now available in Mac form (omission of any particular game is not meant as a comment about its quality one way or the other):

- **Age of Empires (MacSoft)**   This is a real strategy game (see Figure 26-1), so the computer doesn't give you a chance to mull over your decisions while you wait your turn. Everything proceeds in real-time, so you better have good response time or your civilization can fall when you're not looking. In this game, you play one of 12 ancient civilizations, including the Greeks, the Egyptians, the Yamato, and others. You start out by collecting resources, such as gold and wood, for your civilization, using your loyal villagers to build up your society, researching new technologies, and building powerful armies to crush all your enemies to become the most powerful empire in the world.

FIGURE 26-1   Age of Empires requires you to think fast and keep up with rapidly changing events

■ **Alpha Centauri (Aspyr)**   This next-generation strategy game (shown in Figure 26-2) was created by Sid Meier, who also created Civilization and Civilization II. You are the leader of one of seven unique factions on an alien planet. You can fully customize your military units, along with many aspects of the game play, including a random 3D world generator, many strategies and paths to victory, and a full map editor, enabling you to keep playing for hours. Diplomacy is extremely advanced, as various personalities in the game react to your actions. You even have the ability to transform your landscape radically, either making it better for you or harsher for your adversaries.

FIGURE 26-2   You are a faction leader in an alien world

■ **Baldur's Gate (Graphic Simulations)**   This game was still in beta test form as of press time, but the descriptions available at the publisher's Web site show great promise. The product is designed as a genuine tour de force with five CDs (a DVD-ROM version is inevitable). This is a sword-and-sorcery style role-playing game that takes place in a land called The Forgotten Realms. The publisher says the game includes over 10,000 scrolling screens, meaning you could play for hours and hours without ever revisiting a set.

■ **Caesar III (Sierra Studios)**   The goal of this game is to build a prosperous city in Ancient Rome (see Figure 26-3). You must build up your infrastructure and make sure your citizens are kept constantly happy. This can be done by either advancing through a series of increasingly difficult missions with preexisting conditions, eventually to become the Emperor of Rome in the Career Game, or to set your own goals for a thriving, prosperous city in the City Construction Kit. Either way, the game features beautiful graphics and can easily be played over and over again.

FIGURE 26-3   Journey back in time as you construct a Roman city

- ■ **Descent 3 (Graphic Simulations)**   This is the third version of the popular
  3D flight simulation game in space for the Mac. The game features over
  30 new robots with almost human-like artificial intelligence and 20 new
  weapons to crush your enemies. You fly through all sorts of landscapes
  and use your lethal weapons to destroy enemy forces both on the ground
  and in the air. Using the new Fusion Engine, even more realistic game play
  is provided with nearly seamless movement through the landscapes
  featured throughout the game.

- ■ **Escape Velocity: Override**   Ambrosia Software is unique among Mac
  game publishers. It markets its products strictly as shareware, yet it has a
  full-time staff and office. Although people tend not to pay shareware fees,
  somehow this company has survived by publishing high-caliber software,
  fully the equivalent of commercial varieties. Escape Velocity: Override is
  the sequel to the hit game Escape Velocity and gives you the chance to
  make your way up the ranks from a lowly shuttlecraft pilot to the hero of
  the United Earth territories with your own battlecruiser to prove it. Or, you

can stake it out on your own as a pirate, mercilessly raiding trading routes wherever you go. Whatever you do, this game is open-ended, meaning you decide your fate, depending on your actions, as well as what missions you complete.

In addition to publishing games, Ambrosia Software is adept at Mac utilities. In fact, its multimedia screen capture utility, SnapzPro, was used to create the screen illustrations used in this book.

■ **Falcon 4.0 (MacSoft)**   In this flight simulator, you portray a pilot flying an F-16 war plane during the Korean War. You can do this in single engagements or in the campaign mode, which features a series of missions. Each mission of the campaign is linked to the other and the decisions you make and the time you need to make them affect how the game progresses, meaning each campaign is different from the next or the previous one. The game has steep hardware requirements, however, and unless you have a G3 or later, along with a high-performance graphic card, such as an ATI RAGE 128 or Formac ProFormance 3, 96MB of RAM, and plenty of hard drive space, this game is nearly unplayable.

■ **Heroes of Might and Magic III (3D0 Company)**   This turn-based strategy war game, which takes place in the fantasy world of the Might and Magic, is a spectacular role-playing adventure. Heroes 3 has a number of features, including a rich magic system, fully developed characters, many different allies and enemies, a large mysterious world to discover, and intense storylines. The game focuses on elements of strategic conquest, however, which include building powerful armies, expanding your territory, siege warfare, and fighting your enemies in battle.

■ **Madden 2000 (Aspyr)**   This is the first football game ever to be ported to the Mac. It features play so realistic, it's almost like the real thing. You can control your players accurately, sending one player to dive across the ten-yard line, while another player is spinning his way through an incoming block. The graphics of the game are phenomenal, and the players look almost exactly like their counterparts in real life. You can also play games over the Internet, so your friend can control one team, while you control the other.

■ **Multiplayer Civilization II: Gold Edition (MacSoft)**   Civilization II (shown in Figure 26-4) is one of the most popular strategy games ever released for the Mac. Unlike Starcraft and Age of Empires, it is turn-based, meaning once you make all your decisions in one round, the play is turned over to the computer to allow your enemies and allies to respond to your actions. The goal of this game is to take over the world using diplomacy or conquest, or to be the first civilization to colonize a distant star system within 6,000 years (or 30 to 40 hours of playing the game). This new edition of the game features 40 additional scenarios not found in the original release, plus the ability to play Civilization games with other people.

■ **Civilization: Call to Power (MacSoft)**   The sequel to Civilization II is a greatly improved version of the game. It now spans 7,000 years, taking you into the wild and unknown future of 3000 A.D. You can discover many new technological advancements, military units, and Wonders of the World. You can also build colonies in the sea and in space once you discover the technological advancements necessary to do so. The game's look is greatly improved over the original, featuring animated, high-resolution, 16-bit graphics. The game even comes with a Map Editor to create your own worlds.

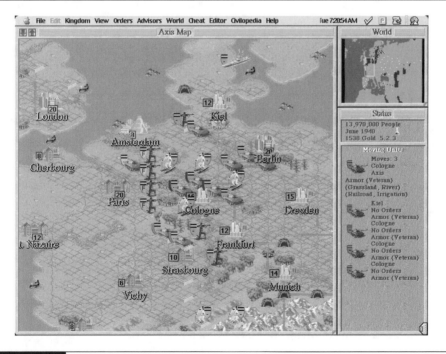

FIGURE 26-4   Nurture your civilization to power and conquer the world

■ **Myth II: Soulblighter (Bungie)**   This sequel to the wildly popular 1997 game pits you, the commander of the forces of light, against the evil leader of the forces of darkness, Soulblighter. Through a series of missions and battles, you lead archers, dwarves, journeymen, and warriors against Soulblighter's quest for world domination. During the process of the game, you forge alliances, uncover treachery, learn things once forgotten, and much more.

■ **Quake 3: Arena (id Software)**   This third installment of the Quake series is the first-person shooter to be multiplayer-only. It includes both simulated and online death matches. In the second installment, you get the chance to connect to the Internet and to attempt to kill your friends as many times as you can using a wide variety of weaponry. Whoever has the most kills at the end, wins the game. For simulated play, you play against a series of bots (robots) that act very much like real players, so much in fact, they seem almost completely indistinguishable from the real thing.

■ **Rainbow Six (MacSoft)**   Based on the novel by Tom Clancy, you are the leader of an elite group known as RAINBOW, a top-secret antiterrorist force that features only the brightest and best America has to offer. The game is realistic, as even one bullet from a terrorist can kill you and your men, although it also goes the same way for killing the terrorists. The game features such situations as rescuing hostages from an embassy and a biotech facility in the Congo, and is also bundled with the Eagle Watch expansion pack, which includes additional missions.

NOTE   *The appearance of a Tom Clancy game on the Mac is significant itself. But more to the point, he is a big Mac advocate. Clancy writes his books on a Mac and he is one of Apple Computer's AppleMasters, a group of notables who help evangelize the platform.*

■ **SimCity 3000 (Electronic Arts)**   This is the third edition of the popular city-building game, SimCity. You are the mayor and sole decision-maker for your city. As your city continues to grow, you must decide how it grows, how and where its inhabitants live, and you must control the budget, city ordinances, and transportation, as well as all other aspects of real-life cities. Besides making the cities you build more visually appealing than previous versions, SimCity 3000 also adds a number of features and enhancements to make your cities much more realistic.

NOTE *Sim City 3000 fans will appreciate that a Mac-only add-on, The Apple Campus, is available for free download directly from Apple's Web site. The URL is: http://www.apple.com/hotnews/features/sim3000.*

■ **StarCraft (Blizzard Entertainment)**   Like Age of Empires, Starcraft is also a real-time strategy game (see Figure 26-5). Its play is mission-based and involves a complicated, but thoughtful and interesting plot. StarCraft revolves around three races, the Terrans, the Zerg, and the Protoss, as they struggle for dominance in the galaxy. At its most basic, the game requires you to gather resources to build up your military forces and crush all your enemies. At its most complex, the game contains some difficult, but well thought-out missions to provide you with hours and hours of rewarding gameplay.

FIGURE 26-5   Battle for galactic superiority with StarCraft

An Overview of Mac Gaming Software

■ **Star Wars Episode I: Racer (LucasArts Entertainment)** This is the first Mac game from this software company in over two years, when Apple was in the doldrums. Racer puts you in the seat of one of the pod racers from Episode I: The Phantom Menace, in which you compete against many different opponents in several worlds. You have the ability to choose the character you play and the pod racer you use to zoom your way to victory over your opponents. Even if you weren't a fan of the movie (I wasn't), this gives you an excellent chance to race up to 600 mph in the safety of your own home.

■ **Tomb Raider III (Aspyr)** This is the third installment of the popular third-person shooter starring Lara Croft, the most famous woman ever to appear in a game. This time around, Lara is once again spanning the globe, from the islands of the South Pacific to the North Pole, searching for lost artifacts. Unlike her previous adventures, however, the play in Tomb Raider III is not as linear. You can choose how the story progresses by playing each of the four huge levels in any order you want. Each level provides multiple routes to the same ending, but you must make the right choices or you will lose.

■ **Total Annihilation: Gold Edition (MacSoft)** This real-time strategy game puts you right in the middle of the long war between the Core and the Arm. There are 25 missions for each side, in which you play one or the other, and you try to conquer your enemy. Between the two, you have a choice of over 150 3D-generated land, air, and sea units The game also has support for multiplayer games and the Internet. Besides the game itself, this special edition also includes two add-on packages with over 100 additional missions, as well as new maps, units, worlds, and more.

■ **Unreal Tournament (MacSoft)** This game, the sequel to the landmark first-person shooter, Unreal, is like Quake 3: Arena because it is only a multiplayer game. However, unlike the original version, Unreal Tournament emphasizes team work and group communication skills, enabling gamers to work together to kill each other. It also has more elaborate and interesting maps than Quake, and is a more complicated game overall. Sometimes you may have to use your brain to defeat your enemies, rather than just blow them up. Unreal Tournament also has a completely new graphics engine, so under the right hardware, it could look absolutely beautiful.

The Perfect Gaming Machine

Many of today's games can stretch your Mac to its limits, with prodigious system requirements and the best 3D-acceleration hardware possible needed to play them with reasonably satisfactory performance.

For example, the Revision A iMac, although earmarked for consumers who would likely consider games, came with a relatively weak ATI Rage IIc graphics acceleration chip and only 2MB of VRAM (though it could be upgraded to 6MB). This was all right for less graphic-intensive games like Riven and Age of Empires, but unplayable for Quake III: Arena and Tomb Raider III, where high-frame rates are required for full motion and fluid display.

The so-called Revision C and D of the iMac came with the more powerful Rage Pro chipset and 6MB of VRAM. Still not the best, but far more usable than the original.

Contrast this with the AGP versions of the Power Mac G4. They are outfitted with ATI's Rage 128 or Rage 128 Pro with a 2*x* AGP bus, sufficient for even the most demanding games. AGP first made its debut on the iBook, although that model doesn't include the speedier ATI graphics chip. In addition, Apple's slot-loading iMacs and the latest PowerBook, released in February 2000, also include a Rage 128 chip with AGP, making these computers more appealing to gamers who need the best possible performance.

> NOTE
>
> *While playing games on a Mac that isn't quite state-of-the-art is possible, the requirements for heavy-duty gaming are little different from doing graphic arts when the work you are doing requires 3D capability.*

Here are the minimum requirements all you Mac gamers should consider when buying or upgrading your Macs:

96 or 128MB of RAM

Most games today hog RAM like crazy. Even those with more modest requirements, such as Starcraft and Age of Empires, require at the very least 32MB of RAM. More graphic-intensive games like Falcon 4.0 and all the 3D shooters need 64MB of available RAM and even more to get the best performance.

Because Mac OS 9 needs a minimum of 32MB of RAM just to run, your best bet would be to have at least 96, and preferably, 128MB of RAM, so you can get reasonable performance from your games of choice.

Luckily, the high-end Power Mac G3s and G4s, the iMac DV Special Edition, and the PowerBook G3/500 already come with 128MB of RAM, eliminating the need to buy extra memory. As for older Mac users, RAM prices have fallen from their highs after a terrible earthquake in Taiwan disrupted production and sent prices skyrocketing, but remained volatile at press time. Watch the market closely when you decide it's time to make your RAM purchase.

NOTE *While RAM is essentially a generic product, you should buy from a reputable dealer who offers customer support and a good warranty if the product is defective.*

6GB Hard Drive

Does 6GB of hard drive seem like a lot, considering only a decade ago drives of 100MB and 200MB were considered positively huge?

Most of today's games take a minimum of 50MB of storage space and some take upwards of 100MB of space. Certain games, such as Falcon 4.0 and Caesar III, fill 600MB if you decide to take the full-install option. This choice is recommended for the best possible performance because you don't constantly have to pull files from the CD, which runs much slower than a hard drive.

The 6GB hard drives on the original iMacs don't seem quite so large when you install a few games, a fully outfitted Mac OS 9 system folder, and a few productivity applications.

Fortunately, any Mac with a SCSI or FireWire port can easily accommodate an external hard drive. Considering you can get huge drives for only a few hundred dollars, you shouldn't have to worry about insufficient space for storage-hungry games, except maybe on the iBook, which has a smaller hard drive and only a slow USB port as an expansion option.

NOTE *The updated version of the iBook released in February 2000 has a 6GB drive and extra RAM, making it more suitable for gameplay. However, Macs that are only equipped with USB expansion ports aren't really good candidates for adding extra drives (except for occasional use and backup), because speeds are so slow.*

ATI Rage 128 with 8MB of VRAM (minimum)

A graphics chip that doesn't provide super-speed 3D display, such as the older Rage and Rage Pro chips, may work fine for casual gaming. But when you have to install one of the heavy-duty games, you might find slow display speeds and low-frame rates make some games unplayable.

The ATI Rage 128 with 8MB of VRAM is probably the absolute minimum for these kinds of games, putting the second-generation iMacs and year 2000 PowerBook models in contention.

But experienced gamers, especially those using the Windows platform, do not regard the Rage 128 (Pro or not) as the best possible graphics chip for dedicated games. Instead, they prefer the Voodoo 3 cards from 3dfx Interactive or the even more powerful cards based on nVidia's Riva TNT2 chipset (especially the recently released GForce 256). Although graphics cards from nVidia hadn't been made available officially for Macs when this book was published, 3dfx Interactive was hard at work developing Mac versions of its ultra fast Voodoo 4 and 5 cards, making this the first time the company has developed its own Mac-specific version of any of its products. Before this, you either had to get a Mac version of the cards from companies such as ixMicro or VillageTronic, or download special beta drivers from 3dfx's Web site, which could be used to convert the PC versions of their Voodoo 2 and 3 cards to work on our favorite computing platform.

While the existing Voodoo cards are extremely powerful, as already mentioned, something even better exists: cards based on the Riva TNT2 chipset (at least until the next generation of Voodoo cards are released).

nVidia's graphics processor, the Riva TNT2, can be found in graphics cards from Diamond Multimedia and other companies. Its 3D performance is considered first-rate, faster even than the Voodoo, but one little problem exists . . . it's only for Windows. Lucky for Mac users, though, nVidia is working with Mac developers to develop Mac versions of drivers for its graphics cards. It's possible that the software may be available by the time you read this book, meaning you may have yet another option for superlative game performance on your Mac.

Great Speakers—The Other Equation

Macs have not traditionally had the best quality loudspeakers. Some models have included beefier woofers and the first-generation iMacs had pseudo-surround sound.

When it comes to games, however, high-quality sound greatly enhances the presentation, especially for space and shoot-'em-up gaming. And superior speakers tremendously enhance the mystical atmosphere of Broderbund's Riven.

Beginning with the second generation of the iMac product line, Apple finally recognized the need for superior audio when it incorporated a sound system using hardware and technology from Harmon Kardon, a well-known manufacturer of audio equipment. An accessory product, the iSub, beefs up the low-end and provides near high-fidelity quality.

The Perfect Gaming Machine

The other models in the Apple line haven't benefited from a similar level of attention. The sound is tinny, the bass is almost nonexistent, and stereo sound is rare, except on a few models.

You do have choices, though. Many computer speaker systems are available these days. The top models come in three pieces, with two desktop or satellite speakers positioned at each side of your Mac, with a woofer module on the floor for enhanced bass. A few systems offer surround sound as well, which can greatly enhance a game's special effects.

Many of these products, in fact, emerge from the same companies that provide equipment for regular home audio systems. They include Advent, Bose, Boston Acoustics, Cambridge SoundWorks, JBL, and Monsoon. A visit to your favorite computer store and a little time spent auditioning a few models are bound to produce satisfactory results and a much more enjoyable Mac gaming experience. Chapter 18 covers the subject of computer speakers in more detail.

Input Devices

The round mouse and keyboard that come with the iMacs and the Power Mac G3 (Blue & White) and G4 may look cute, but they're not the most comfortable ones available. Some games require a lot of rapid finger movement, especially the first-person shooters, and that small USB keyboard may not be your best choice.

If you have an older Mac, it probably came with an extended ADB keyboard and a more ergonomically designed mouse. You aren't without choices on Macs with USB ports either. A number of third-party mice and keyboards are available in a variety of configurations. In addition, trackballs and joysticks are available (see the following). Chapter 17 covers this topic.

17-inch monitor (minimum)

Well, this isn't written in stone. You can definitely get useful gameplay with the iMac's 15-inch monitor and the ultra-clear active matrix displays of the iBook and PowerBook G3 line give you picture quality that belies their small size.

In addition, the iMac DV and DV Special Edition have VGA ports for external displays that mirror the built-in display, giving you the screen area you crave. Most recent PowerBooks can also hook up to external displays.

If you have a regular desktop Mac and a small display, don't feel left out. A few hundred dollars can buy you a top-quality 17-inch display, and larger displays aren't that much more costly.

If you want to explore the ultimate in computer displays, you might even want to look at one of the costly LCD models. The best example of the breed is, no doubt, the gorgeous Apple Cinema Display, a 22-inch wide screen model designed to work with the Power Macintosh G4 (its initial selling price was just shy of four grand).

Optional: Joystick

While some games work perfectly well with a keyboard, some programs, most notably shooters and flight simulators, may work better with a joystick, which enables you to respond more quickly to the movements of monsters in Quake or enemy fighter planes in Falcon 4.0.

Most joysticks can be plugged into an available ADB or USB port, depending on what kind of Mac you have. These include the Ares Joystick from Ariston Technologies, the iStick from Macally, and the Cyborg 3D USB Stick from Saitek.

Setting Up Your Mac for the Best Game Performance

All right, you have acquired the perfect Mac game machine or its closest equivalent. You have boxes filled with the latest games, such as Tomb Raider III, Unreal Tournament, Age of Empires, and Caesar III, all pleading to give you hours of nonstop fun. You want to make sure you can get the best possible performance from your Mac, even with all the goodies you probably outfitted it with. Here are some quick hints and tips:

■ **Allocate as much RAM to your games as possible**   As previously mentioned, even the most modest games, like Age of Empires and Starcraft, require a minimum of 32MB of RAM just to run. Assuming you have the RAM to spare, give them as much RAM as you possibly can, especially more graphic-intensive goodies such as Descent 3 and Quake 3: Arena.

■ **Turn off virtual memory**   Even though virtual memory has been greatly improved under Mac OS 9, and unlike previous system versions that can slightly speed up your computer in certain functions, virtual memory may bog down graphic intensive games and make them seem less responsive. Virtual memory can also lower the frames per second, which can be critical if your Mac is not one of the high-end models. If you have the available RAM to spare, turn off virtual memory.

■ **Turn off File Sharing and AppleTalk**   Sometimes network processes can decrease the performance of your games. Make sure both these functions are turned off before you begin to play. Even if you're playing a game across a network, you can use your regular TCP/IP connection. Unless you are networking across an Ethernet connection, consider leaving AppleTalk off.

■ **Quit all other programs** Other programs running in the background can hog CPU time. As a result, game performance can suffer. While this problem will probably be substantially less significant when the consumer version of Mac OS X comes out, for now you should consider quitting programs you're not using (even if you have enough free memory to accommodate them).

■ **Make sure your game is optimized for the best possible graphics** Some games, like Descent 3, offer high-quality and low-quality image modes. These high-quality modes may offer special effects like fog and lightning, while the low-quality modes generally don't. If you have enough RAM and a dedicated game-oriented graphics card, these high-quality modes can make your games look even better than they already do.

Coping with Weird Screen Displays and Crashes

Games are among the cheapest-priced software around, but they are complex affairs, exercising every element of your Mac system. As a result, the tendency to crash may exist.

Here are some hints and tips to enable you to deal with such problems:

■ **Make sure your game is compatible with Mac OS 9** Although Mac OS 9 doesn't appear altogether different on the surface, under the hood are vast programming changes. Certain games may be vulnerable to the system components that were updated and may not perform their best or crash frequently. If your game doesn't seem to work for no apparent reason, check the publisher's Web site to see what updates or patches are available.

■ **Make sure your game is compatible with the display resolution you use** Some games may be unable to support certain monitor resolutions. If you see a blank screen or the game acts weird when it's in a certain resolution, check the manual for the game to see which resolutions are compatible with it.

■ **Don't be surprised if the color depth changes** Not all games are compatible with the thousands or millions of colors settings. Usually the games put up a notice offering to reduce color depth to 256 colors (or they do it anyway). But if you experience weird color artifacts, check the manual or online help information for the correct requirements.

■ **Make sure your game is compatible with your graphics card**   Some games may be only playable with certain graphic display technologies, such as OpenGL and Glide. Today, most games are compatible with both formats. Before you play a game that may require Glide, however, check to make sure your graphics card supports the technology (it was developed by 3dfx Interactive, manufacturers of the Voodoo cards).

■ **Make sure your graphics card has the latest driver updates**   Sometimes, for certain games, the drivers of your graphics card may need to be updated to support it. Check out the manufacturer's Web site for conflicts and problems using that graphics card, as well as the latest updates and patches.

■ **Make sure your game has the latest updates**   Many times after a game's initial release, the publisher posts patches and updaters to fix bugs that weren't squashed before the program was released. Problems you may be having with a certain game may already have been solved; you'll want to check for the updates to see.

Summing Up

With some attention to detail, you can make your Mac into a first-rate game machine. Many of the newest models even come that way, right out of the box. And, because Mac OS 9 provides superior support for gaming technologies, you are in for a fun-filled experience.

In the next chapter, an aspect of the Mac OS 9 experience you encounter when you tackle a multiplayer game is covered: networking.

Summing Up

Chapter 27

Sharing Files with Other Macs

Personal File Sharing was one of the great inventions on the Mac. It was first introduced in Mac System 7.0 (they didn't call it Mac OS in those days). You didn't need to install any special software or buy a model with advanced networking capability. With just a few simple setup procedures, you could easily exchange files with other Macs on your network. And, with some extra steps, you could also share files with folks who use computers on other platforms.

For Mac OS 9, Apple has given you additional File Sharing features, making it significantly more advanced than the previous versions. For one thing, you can now share files across the Internet as easily as you can share files on your local network. This is part of Apple's Internet strategy, which is designed, in effect, to blur the distinction as to whether a shared Mac is on your local network or located somewhere on the other side of the world.

This chapter covers Mac OS 9's File Sharing features, from setting it up and activating it to handling the more advanced features so you can exchange files with the maximum possible security.

Setting Up File Sharing Using Mac OS 9

Setting up File Sharing on your Mac using Mac OS 9 doesn't involve many steps so you can get be and running in only minutes. If you are just exchanging files in a small office or at home, this may be quite sufficient for your needs. File Sharing can take a long time to fine-tune, though, so it doesn't become the all-consuming monster that drags down your Mac's performance. Fine-tuning File Sharing requires you know the various options you can set up on your Mac to secure the files you are sharing, as well as how to make sure those files are only available to people with whom you want to share them.

Turning on File Sharing

The first thing you should do to start sharing files with your Mac is to turn on File Sharing. When you first installed Mac OS 9, you ran through the Mac OS Setup Assistant and gave your Mac a name for its owner and for the computer. If those settings are not made, you cannot turn on sharing.

This setup process is covered in Chapter 3. If you didn't use Mac OS Setup Assistant at the time, you may want to review this chapter because those settings are essential if you wish to use File Sharing.

NOTE   *A common reason for the failure of file sharing to work is indeed the fact that the basic identifying information was never entered in the File Sharing, either because the Mac OS Setup Assistant was dismissed when it was launched or the information was removed later on.*

Assuming all settings are correct, follow these steps:

1. To turn on File Sharing, click the Apple menu icon, and then scroll down to Control Panels. Then move your mouse over to the right and select File Sharing from the list of Control Panels.

NOTE   *You can also save yourself a visit to the File Sharing Control Panel simply by clicking on the File Sharing Control Strip (the one with the folder icon), and selecting Turn File Sharing On.*

2. Once the File Sharing Control Panel is open, click the Start button located under the File Sharing section of the dialog box, as shown in Figure 27-1. Your Mac will seem to slow down for a minute or so while File Sharing is starting.

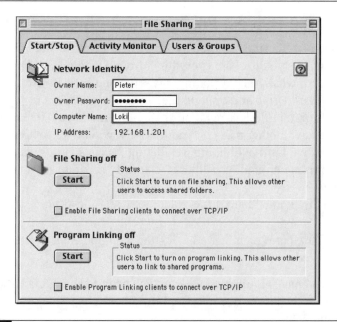

FIGURE 27-1   Use the File Sharing Control Panel to turn on File Sharing

TIP   *Another method to open the File Sharing Control Panel when File Sharing is turned off is to click a volume, folder, or file. Then click the file menu, select Get Info from the list, and then select Sharing from the Get Info submenu. You are then presented with a message that tells you File Sharing is currently turned off and asks if you want to open the File Sharing Control Panel. If you click the OK button, Mac OS 9 opens the File Sharing Control Panel. Clicking the Cancel button dismisses the dialog box.*

As you may have noticed, a small check box is located under the File Sharing Start button that lets you enable File Sharing to be used by clients connecting via TCP/IP. This feature is brand new in Mac OS 9 and allows clients located on the Internet to connect to your Mac and share files, just like the users located on your network. For more information regarding this feature and other tips on how to use File Sharing over the Internet, please see Chapters 8 and 35.

CAUTION   *Be careful about putting a Mac whose files are being shared on the network into sleep mode. At best, sleep mode makes the shared volumes inaccessible. But if a file or folder is being accessed at the time, the Mac accessing that file may crash.*

Sharing Hard Drives, Folders, and Files on Your Mac

Once you have File Sharing started on your Mac, it's time to start sharing files. File Sharing enables you to share everything, from a whole Hard Drive to a single file. Regardless of what you are sharing, the setup and security are fundamentally the same for a Hard Drive and a single file.

When you turn on File Sharing, you are simply making available all the files on all the drives to all other users on your network without exception. This may be convenient in a small office or home installation, but in a larger installation where security concerns are around, you'll want to specify separate sharing privileges. Here's how:

To share an individual hard drive, folder, or file, follow these steps:

1. Once File Sharing has started, click the item you want to share so it is highlighted.

2. Once you have highlighted the item you want to share, click the File Menu and move the cursor down to Get Info. Then select Sharing... from the Get Info submenu.

3. From the sharing portion of the Get Info dialog box (see Figure 27-2), you can enable File Sharing for this item and set the security options you want to use.

4. To share this item, simply click the check box that says "Share this item and its contents."

5. Once you have shared the item, you need to set the security options you want to use with this item. If you want to protect the file from people making changes to it, then you should lock the item by clicking the "Can't move, rename, or delete this item (locked)."

NOTE   *You can lock a Hard Drive, folder, or file by clicking the "Can't move, rename, or delete this item (locked)" check box even without having to share the item you want to lock.*

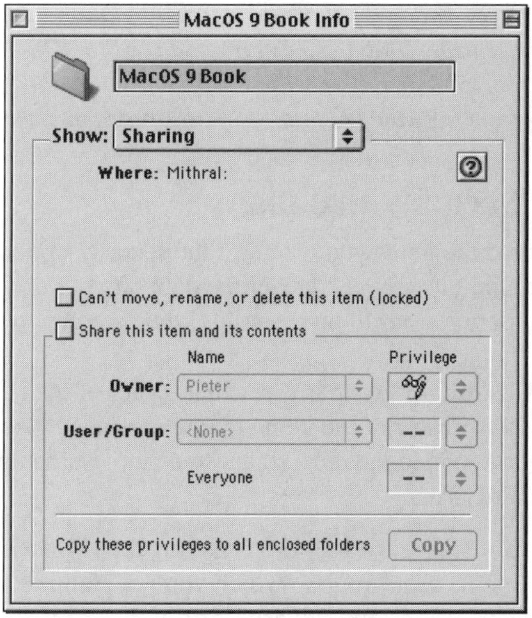

FIGURE 27-2   From the Get Info dialog box, you can share files and set their security options

To allow users to run applications from the shared volumes on your Mac, you need to turn on Program Linking.

1. To turn Program Linking on, click the Start button located under the Program Linking portion of the Start/Stop tab in the File Sharing dialog box.

2. Once you click the Start button, your Mac will be busy for a second and then the button will change from Start to Stop. If you want to allow users on the Internet to execute programs on your Mac, then you need to click the check box labeled, "Enable Program Linking clients to connect over TCP/IP."

NOTE *I'm including the information on activating Program Linking simply for your information. As a practical matter, it's not a terribly efficient way to run your software (aside from any software licensing issues). For one thing, performance across a network is going to suffer, perhaps a lot, compared to running the program on your own Mac. In addition, many programs just won't run in this fashion, because they require the presence of certain files in your Mac OS 9 System Folder. You are better off installing the program on each Mac for which it will be used. The exception to this is a situation where you are using Mac OS X Server and the Mac OS "Network" booting feature supported by many recent Macs. That setup allows you to run everything from the Mac OS to all of your programs from a server.*

File Sharing Security Groups

After you have shared the items you want, set the security options you wish to use. This enables you to limit access to some of the data on your drive.

You can assign permissions to three groups when setting up security.

- **Owner** This user or group is the actual owner of the Mac that's sharing files and/or the creator of the item you are sharing. Normally, this user/group is assigned the most rights since the user is the actual owner of the file you are sharing.

- **User/Group** This is the user or group to which you are granting access. Depending on the user/group to which you are granting access, you may want to give the user/group full access or only a limited amount of access.

- **Everyone** As its name implies, this group includes everyone on the network that is not granted permission to the files as either the Owner or a member of the User/Group assigned permissions. Normally, this group is assigned the most restrictive rights because you do not have any control over who is a member of this group.

File Sharing Permission Levels

After you decide which users or groups to set up in the Owner and User/Group portion of the sharing dialog box, then you need to set the permissions you want them to have when accessing this item through File Sharing. Mac OS 9 enables you to set one of four levels of access, which you can grant to the Owner, User/Group, and Everyone.

- ■ **Read & Write**   This permission level allows users to read and write to the shared file. Because the user has the ability to both read and to write to the file, the user or group is given the ability to modify and/or destroy the file being shared.

- ■ **Read Only**   This permission level only allows users to read the file and not to make any changes to it. This level of security enables you to make files available for users on your network to review, but protects your files from being changed or damaged.

- ■ **Write Only (Drop Box)**   This permission level is designed to create a drop box where users on the network can drop off files on your Mac for you to review. Because users can only write files, this permission level only makes sense to use with hard drives and folders you are sharing.

- ■ **None**   As the name suggests, this permission level denies access to the item being shared. If you are sharing items you don't want shared with everyone on the network, this is the appropriate permission to set on the Everyone group.

NOTE   *By default, the owner of the shared item is granted Read & Write access. All other groups are set to None, denying access to the item.*

Once you set all the File Sharing permissions you want to (see Figure 27-3), click the close box to close the Sharing dialog box to implement the changes you made.

Setting Up File Sharing Using Mac OS 9

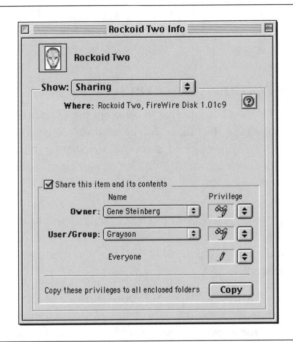

FIGURE 27-3   This example shows various degrees of permission levels granted to users of the author's Mac network

NOTE   *If you are sharing a large number of files or folders (which is the case on a large drive), expect the Sharing box to take several minutes to close. Don't think you've crashed. This is a normal part of the setup process.*

Monitoring File Sharing Activity

After you finish setting up the items you want to share with File Sharing, watch it so you can see who is using the files you have shared and the load it is placing on your Mac.

1. To see how much impact File Sharing is having on your Mac, click the Apple Menu and move your mouse down to Control Panels.

2. Then, from the Control Panels submenu, move your cursor to the right and select the File Sharing Control Panel.

3. From the File Sharing dialog box, click the Activity Monitor Tab, as shown in Figure 27-4.

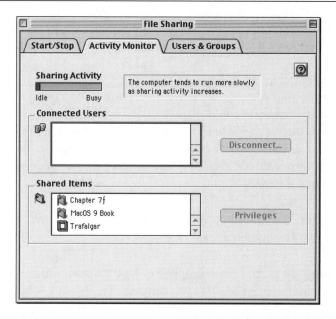

FIGURE 27-4   Click the Activity Monitor tab to see how busy File Sharing is

4. Using the Activity Monitor, you can disconnect a user connected to your Mac; simply click the user you want to disconnect, and then click the Disconnect button.

5. Once you click the Disconnect button, you are presented with a dialog box asking you how many minutes you want to wait until disconnecting the user, as shown in Figure 27-5.

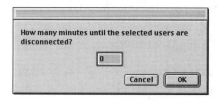

FIGURE 27-5   Select the length of time before disconnecting the selected user

Monitoring File Sharing Activity

6. Select how long you want to wait before disconnecting the user, and then click OK or Cancel to cancel the disconnection. This terminates the user's connection to your Mac and closes all files the user has open on your Mac.

CAUTION   *It is important to notify the other user, if you can, that you are disconnecting them from your Mac. If they are transferring or reading a file at the time, a sudden disconnect could cause their Mac (and yours) to crash. In addition, there's the potential of actually damaging the file being copied. This may be difficult with Internet networking, of course, but it is not something you should dismiss because notifying the other user may prove less than convenient.*

Likewise, using the Activity Monitor, you can change the permissions you have assigned to a given item you are sharing.

1. To change the permissions assigned to a given item, simply click the item you are sharing from the list and then click the Privileges button.

2. The Sharing dialog box is then opened to enable you to make all the changes you want to the security settings you applied to the item you are sharing.

3. Once you set all the security settings for this item as you want them, click the close box to save the changes you made.

Creating New Users and Groups with File Sharing

Unlike previous versions of Mac OS, Mac OS 9 has moved the management of users and groups from the Users and Groups Control Panel in to the File Sharing Control Panel. By combining this functionality with the other parts of the File Sharing Control panel, you should find that managing the users and groups on your Mac is easier.

To manage the users and groups on your Mac, follow these steps:

1. Open the File Sharing Control Panel, as previously described.

2. Once the File Sharing Control Panel is open, click the Users & Groups tab to display the Users & Groups dialog box, as shown in Figure 27-6. From the Users & Groups dialog box, you can create new users, create new groups, open an existing user or group, duplicate an existing user or group, or delete an existing user or group.

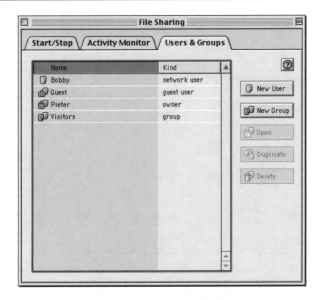

| FIGURE 27-6 | The Users & Groups dialog box enables you to create and manage users and groups |

Creating a New User with Users & Groups

Now you are ready to create your additional users, as the following describes:

1. To create a new user on your Mac, click the New User button.

2. From the New User dialog box, type in the new user's name and password, as shown in Figure 27-7.

3. If you want to let the user change their password, then you will want to click the "Allow user to change password" check box.

Once you finish typing in the new user's name and password, you need to assign this user to the groups where you want them to belong. To assign the new user to your chosen groups, follow these steps:

1. Click the Show menu in the New user dialog box and select Sharing from the pop-up menu, as shown in Figure 27-8.

FIGURE 27-7   Type in the new user's name and password

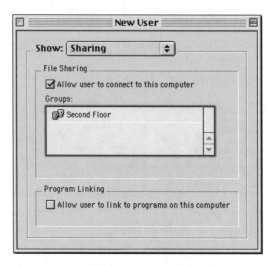

FIGURE 27-8   The Sharing portion of the New User dialog box shows to what groups the new user belongs

2. To assign a user to a group, simply select the group you want this user to belong to from the list of groups in the Users & Groups dialog box. Then drag it into the Groups window of the new user dialog box.

From the Sharing portion of the new user dialog box, you can also allow users to connect to the shared volumes located on your Mac. To do this, click the check box labeled "Allow user to connect to this computer." Likewise, if you want to allow this user to run programs from your Mac, click the check box labeled "Allow user to link to programs on this computer."

NOTE   *Again, I'll emphasize that program linking has its disadvantages in terms of performance, and the fact that some programs might not work without the proper elements in the System Folder of the Mac trying to access that program across the network. In practice, this option is not something you'd want to consider, except in a rare situation where installing the program directly isn't convenient (and you don't run up against a software licensing restriction).*

The last thing to do when setting up a new user is to click the "Show:" pop-up menu again and select Remote Access from the list of options. Looking at the Remote Access part of the New User dialog box, you have the option of allowing users to dial in to your Mac, provided, of course, it is equipped with a modem, or having your Mac call them back, as shown in Figure 27-9. Normally, you do not set up this option unless your Mac is also set up with a modem so users can dial in to the network.

Creating a New Group with Users & Groups

The process of creating new groups of users is quite similar. Follow this process:

1. To create a new group of users, click the New Group button located in the Users & Group dialog box.

2. After you click the New Group button, you are presented with the New Group dialog box, as indicated in Figure 27-10.

3. Type in the name of the new group you are creating and then begin adding users to it.

Creating New Users and Groups
with File Sharing

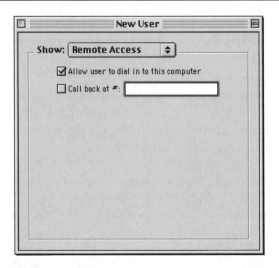

FIGURE 27-9   The Remote Access portion of the New User dialog box enables you to grant dial-in access

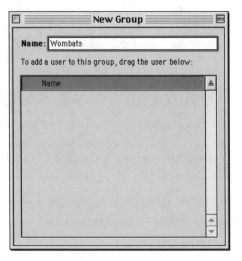

FIGURE 27-10   Adding users to a group is as simple as dragging-and-dropping

4. To add users to your newly created group, select the user(s) you want to add to the group from the list of users in the Users & Groups dialog box, and then drag them into the space provided in the New Group dialog box.

User and Group Management

Once your roster of users and groups is set up, you may find you want to change the lineup over time.

From the Users & Groups dialog box, you can also Open Users and Groups to modify them, Duplicate Users and Groups for the easy creation of many similar users and groups, or Delete the Users and Groups already created. Follow these steps:

To open a user or group, highlight the user(s) or group(s) you want to open and then click the Open button. You can then modify the user or group as you want, and then save them by clicking the close box. Or, you can double-click on a user or group to open it.

NOTE *The one user you won't be allowed to duplicate is the owner of the Mac on which you are working.*

Duplicating users and groups is also a simple procedure. All you need to do is highlight the user or group, and then click the Duplicate button to create a copy of the selected items.

Deleting users and groups is also a simple procedure. Select the users and groups you wish to delete and then click the Delete button. You are then asked if you want to delete the users and groups you selected. Click the Delete button to complete the deletion of the selected users and groups, or click the Cancel button to keep the selected users and groups.

File Sharing's Impact on Your Mac

Like most things in life, sharing files using Mac OS 9's File Sharing is not a free ride. Like any other service, File Sharing draws on your Mac's resources and, if used heavily, it can drag down your Mac's performance. File Sharing's impact on your Mac is directly related to the number of people who connect to your Mac to use or copy files. As such, users whose Mac is being used by a large number of people to store and share documents see a greater impact on their Mac's performance than a user who only shares files intermittently.

File Sharing's Impact
on Your Mac

Quick Guest Access

If you just want to give other users on your network simple access, without having to remember a user name and password, there are ways to simplify the process.

CAUTION   *This simple sharing option works fine for home use or in a small office where everyone freely shares their Macs, but otherwise, I do not recommend it, as it could compromise a company's security.*

One alternative is just to remove the password from the File Sharing Control Panel before you activate File Sharing. That way, when another user connects to your Mac, they just have to enter the user name, then click OK to bring up the list of shared volumes.

An even faster method is just to make it easy for a guest user to access your Mac. Here's how it's done:

1. Go to the Apple Menu, choose Control Panels, then File Sharing from the submenu.

2. Click on the Users & Groups tab.

3. Double-click on Guest.

4. In the dialog box that will appear next, click on the Show pop-up menu and select Sharing.

5. Check the box labeled "Allow guests to connect to this computer."

6. Click the close box on the dialog box, then the File Sharing Control Panel to store the setup.

From here on, when the user attempts to access your Mac, the "Guest" radio box will be available. They can connect to you just by checking that box, without having to log on.

TIP   *Once you've accessed a shared volume on your Mac, just make an alias to the disk icon, and place it on your desktop or in the Apple Menu Items folder. This will let you quickly log on to that shared Mac without having to make a return trip to the Chooser.*

> **NOTE** *File Sharing can also consume a few hundred kilobytes of RAM, but this isn't a significant issue unless your Mac is already tight for memory.*

When you set up File Sharing on your Mac, look at what you want to share and what impact it will have on your Mac's performance. The first thing you should think about when setting up the files and folders you want to share is how many users will use these files and how often they will use them.

If many users plan to use these files on a regular basis, you should look at placing these files on a dedicated file server. On the other hand, if the files will only occasionally be used by a few users, then sharing them from your Mac will not impact your Mac's performance much.

The second thing you should think about when setting up File Sharing is the size of the files you plan to share. The larger the file you are sharing, the greater the impact File Sharing will have on your Mac, particularly your hard drive. As such, it is easier on your Mac to share a number of smaller files than it is to share a few large files. Likewise, using Program Linking to allow applications on your Mac to be run by remote users can impact your Mac's performance quite a bit. Of course, the performance degradation you incur by letting someone run an application being shared by your Mac is dependent on the size and type of application.

The impact on your Mac of someone running a small program like SimpleText should be quite minimal for most Mac's and may well be unnoticeable. Letting a user run Word 98 from a shared volume on your Mac, however, can cause all but the fastest Mac's to slow down to a crawl.

While letting others on the network run applications from your Mac is possible, in general, this is not a good idea. If you must share applications on your Mac, make sure they are all relatively small and do not demand a lot of resources on your Mac by opening a large number of support files. If you do this, the impact on your Mac should be low enough that it does not make your Mac unusable when users actually run the applications.

> **NOTE** *We aren't going to guess how badly various File Sharing steps slow down your Mac. This can depend on networking speed, traffic on the network, the speed of your Mac's hard drive, and the CPU. You should examine the degree performance degrades and consider other options if the hit is too much for you.*

File Sharing's Impact on Your Mac

Creating an Inbox on Your Mac

When using File Sharing, you may find just setting up a folder where users can drop off documents to review and edit is easier. This method of sharing files is frequently referred to as an *Inbox* and, as the name implies, it is like a physical Inbox, where users simply drop their files off into a folder whose contents they cannot examine.

Inboxes are useful when you have a large number of users who need to give you documents, but you do not want to let them see the documents already given to you. Perhaps you are doing this for security reasons, so no one can see the other files and then delete some of them. Or, perhaps you simply do not want users to be able to read the other files in your shared volume.

Setting up an Inbox on your Mac is a simple procedure that can be done in only a few minutes. Once created, users can then begin depositing their files on your Mac without you having to worry about them or seeing the files other users have placed there. To create an Inbox on your Mac, follow these steps:

1. Make sure that File Sharing has been started on your Mac.

2. Go to the location where you want to place the Inbox on your hard drive, and then create a new folder by clicking the File menu and selecting New Folder.

3. Once the new folder has been created, rename it to the name you want to use.

4. After you create the new folder, make sure it is highlighted and click the File menu once again. Scroll down to Get Info and then select Sharing... from the Get Info submenu located to the right.

5. Look at the Sharing part of the Get Info dialog box, then click the check box labeled "Share this item and its contents." Then type in the name you want users to see when they connect to the Inbox.

6. Once you click the Sharing check box, you will want to set the permissions levels you assign to each user and group. By default, the owner of the Inbox (you), is granted Read & Write access to the contents of the shared volume, so you can manage them as you want.

NOTE   *Because no User/Group is specified by default, it will be set to None, as will the permissions level. If you want a group of users to have access to this shared item, you need to assign a user, or group of users, and then set the permissions you want them to have.*

Because this will be an Inbox, the permissions for Everyone should be set to Write Only. Then people can only write files to the shared volume and they cannot look at files stored in there.

Once you finish setting up all the permissions the way you like, click the close box to close the dialog box and save the changes you made.

Creating an Out Box on Your Mac

The idea behind an Out box is that you frequently have a number of files you want to share with a large number of people. Because a large number of people may be looking at these files, however, you probably do not want to allow everyone to be able to change them.

Creating an Out box on your Mac using File Sharing, like the procedure for creating an Inbox, is a quick and easy task. When you create an Out box, think about what files you want to share with everyone and whether you want to give a certain user or group greater rights than you plan to give everyone else. To set up an Out box on your Mac, follow these steps:

1. Go to the location where you want to place the Out box on your Mac and create a new folder by pressing Command-N, or by clicking the File menu and selecting New Folder from the list of options.

2. Once the new folder is created, rename it to the name you want to use.

3. After you create the new folder, make sure the folder is selected and then click the File menu once again.

4. Scroll down to Get Info, and then select Sharing… from the Get Info submenu located to the right. Or, you can select the item and then press Command-I to bring up the Get Info dialog box. Then click the Show: pop-up menu and select Sharing….

5. If File Sharing is not currently turned on, you will see an error dialog box informing you of this. If you see this error dialog box, click the OK button to open the File Sharing Control Panel, and then click the File Sharing Start button to turn on File Sharing.

6. In the sharing portion of the Get Info dialog box, click the check box labeled "Share this item and its contents." Then type in the name you want users to see when they connect to the Out box.

7. Once you have clicked the sharing check box, you want to set the rights you grant to each user and group. By default, the owner of the Out box (yourself), is given Read & Write access to the contents of the share, so you can create and delete files as you want. Because no User/Group is specified by default, it is set to None, as are the rights assigned to it. If you want to grant a group of users access to this shared item, then you must select a user or group of users by clicking the User/Group pop-up menu. Select the user or group you want to give access to, and then grant them the proper permissions.

8. Because this will be an Out box, the permissions for Everyone should be set to Read Only. This way, all the users not in the Owner or User/Group you specified are only able to read files in the shared folder and cannot write new files into the Out box.

9. Once you finish setting up the Out box the way you want, click the close box to close the dialog box and to save the changes you made.

Connecting to a Shared Volume from Your Mac

Connecting to a shared volume located on another Mac can be done in a few seconds. But first you need the correct user name and password set up on the other Mac. Once you have this information, you're ready to proceed:

1. Click the Apple menu, and then select Chooser from the list.

2. With the Chooser open, click the AppleShare icon, and then click the name of the Mac you want to connect to from the list of servers listed in the window to the right, as shown in Figure 27-11. If you do not see the Mac you wish to connect to, then you can click the Server IP Address... button. Then simply type in the IP address of the Mac you want to connect to and click the Connect button.

NOTE *If your company has a system administrator, you may have to consult with her to get the list of IP numbers for other computers on your network.*

3. Once you select the Mac you want to connect to, click the OK button.

4. Next, your Mac asks you to enter the user name and password you want to use when connecting to the remote Mac, as shown in Figure 27-12.

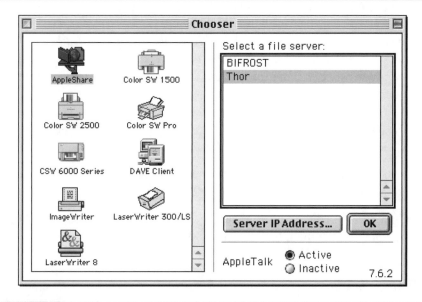

FIGURE 27-11 The Chooser isn't only used to select printers. It allows your Mac to connect to other shared volumes on the network

FIGURE 27-12 Enter your user name and password to log in to the Mac containing the shared volume

Connecting to a Shared Volume from Your Mac

NOTE *One valuable feature present in Mac OS 9 is the capability to add passwords to your Keychain. The Mac will remember your passwords for you, which means you only have to remember the password needed to unlock the Keychain itself. To enable the Keychain to record your password, click the check box labeled "Add to Keychain" located to the right of the space provided for your password.*

5. Once you enter your user name and password, click OK to log in to the Mac that hosts the shared volume to which you wish to connect.

6. You are now presented with a list of the volumes available for you to connect and use, as shown in Figure 27-13.

7. Click the shared volume you want to connect to and then click the OK button to mount them on your Mac's desktop.

TIP *If you want to have this shared volume mounted each time you boot up your Mac, click the check box located to the right of each volume's name. By doing this, each time you boot up your Mac, you are asked to log in to the Mac(s) housing the volumes you have set to be mounted upon startup. Just remember, the networked Mac must be running for you to access its drives.*

8. Once you have the shared volume mounted on your Mac's desktop, you are ready to use it. If you have read and write access volume, you can treat it

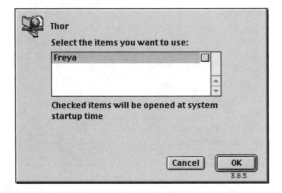

FIGURE 27-13 Select the volume you want to mount from the available list

just like the hard drive in your Mac. If, however, you have only read or write access, then your ability to work with that drive's files is limited.

NOTE   *If you only have read access on the shared volume you have mounted, then you can only read the files present and not modify them in any way. Likewise, if you only have write access to the shared volume you are using, you won't see any of the contents of the volume; you can only drop files into it. Of course, users with No Access cannot do anything with the drive.*

File Sharing Problems Diagnosed

Apple's File Sharing feature is easy to set up and usually works fine, even under heavy network traffic conditions. But sometimes, sharing won't start up, or if it does, the shared volume is inaccessible.

Here's a list of some of the more common File Sharing problems and some solutions:

- **File Sharing can't be turned on**   Open the File Sharing Control Panel and then reenter the Owner Name, Owner Password, and Computer Name. If sharing still can't be activated, open the Preferences folder, inside the System Folder, remove the File Sharing folder and restart. If this does not restore File Sharing, also remove the Users & Groups Data File from the Preferences folder. Also make sure your networking extensions haven't been disabled via Extensions Manager by mistake (reactivating them requires a restart). As a final alternative, you may want to consider reinstalling Mac OS 9 in case some of your network software was damaged or deleted.

NOTE   *Some third-party removable drives may prevent File Sharing from activating. One example is the SyQuest SyJet drive, which may prevent File Sharing from turning on if a disk is in the drive. The best solution is not to insert a disk until after File Sharing is on.*

- **Item can't be shared**   Even if File Sharing seems to work, you may be unable to share a folder or volume. If your Mac's drive is formatted with non-Apple software, you may want to contact the publisher to see if 'a compatibility problem exists and whether a new version can solve it. Also, remember that some removable devices cannot be shared. The same holds true for floppy disks. In addition, if the disk is quite full, make sure at least 1MB of space is available for File Sharing to work.

NOTE *As a practical matter, avoid filling a drive to more than 90 percent of its capacity. This allows for replacing documents with larger versions and, for a startup drive, you need space for printer files if you print your documents using the background printing feature.*

■ **Shared Mac not visible on network**   If you have more than one Mac in your installation, you may want to see if another Mac has the same problem. This way, you can check to see whether it's your Mac or the one being shared. Once you isolate the culprit, check that Mac to see if AppleTalk is turned on in the Chooser and that network cabling is attached and working. With an Ethernet hub, you see a light indicating a connection is established, although this may be misleading if the system software on the Mac itself has a problem. If the Mac can be accessed, but the shared volume you want can't be, make sure you have the proper user name and password, and, even more important, proper access privileges. If all the settings seem all right and network software is activated, consider reinstalling Mac OS 9 on the Mac that's having the problem.

NOTE *If your Mac is part of a large network, no doubt one or more of your fellow workers is responsible for network management. You may want to make sure the network is properly configured and the users have been granted the access privileges they need.*

Summing Up

Sharing files via Apple's File Sharing has been one of the most exciting aspects of the Mac OS. Now, Mac OS 9 has taken the already excellent File Sharing capabilities present and extended them to work over the Internet. By enabling users to share files and applications over the Internet as easily as they share them on their local network, Mac OS 9 has greatly improved upon the capabilities provided by File Sharing.

The subject of Internet file sharing is discussed in more detail in Chapters 8 and 35. In the next chapter, you learn the ins and outs of sharing files with users of the Windows platform.

Chapter 28

Sharing Files with PC Users

No Mac is an island. It's a fact of life that the Windows platform has far more users than Macs, as much as we'd like to see that change.

As such, you sometimes need to share files with PC users either on or off your network. Fortunately, this is not a difficult task.

Several good utilities can help make the movement of files from your Mac to the PC a quick and painless procedure. These utilities range from Mac OS 9's File Exchange, a utility bundled with the Mac OS to mount PC disks and the map PC file extensions to their Mac equivalents; to *DAVE,* a utility from Thursby Systems that allows your Mac to become a member of an NT network. Many different tools enable you to exchange files with your peers on the PC.

Depending on your needs, File Exchange might be the perfect tool for you. But, if you need more sophisticated file conversions or network connectivity, then you need to look at some of the other products described in this chapter.

Preparing Files for Cross-platform Use

The key to successful file sharing between your Mac and a PC is making sure you create your documents with sharing in mind. This means you must choose your applications and file formats with care. You don't want to end up choosing ones that are unavailable on the PC or, after conversion, you'd lose information in the file.

The first thing you should consider when moving files between the Mac and the PC is what application you plan to use to create the file you want to share. When you choose an application to use, be sure to see if a version exists for the PC, and if the file formats used on both the Mac and the PC are compatible. What this means is that the PC version of your program should read files you have created on the Mac without needing any special filters or utilities. Likewise, you can read files created by the PC version of your program without having to convert them.

One of the best examples of a program that is available on both the Mac and the PC is Microsoft Office. Microsoft Office 98 on the Mac and Microsoft Office 97 share much of the same user interface and functionality, with only a few differences. Fortunately, the file formats used by the various programs in both versions of Microsoft Office are fully compatible with each other, allowing for the easy transfer of files.

Even with a program as compatible as Microsoft Office, however, sometimes you can lose information when transferring files between different versions of the same program. This occurs when you create files that contain features that aren't present in the other version. For example, Office 2000 for Windows introduced certain features unavailable in the Mac version of the program. When you convert the files to the Mac platform, you lose this formatting capability.

NOTE   *The next version of Microsoft Office for the Mac was under development at press time and may appear some time in the latter part of 2000. Because the Mac and Windows versions of the program tend to leapfrog each other, this means the advanced features of the later version on one computing platform won't translate to the older one on the other platform.*

Moving Files Between Mac and PC Versions of the Same Program

Even when a version of your program is available on the PC and you have made sure it can read the files you created on the Mac, you need to make sure the version on the PC supports all the features you intend to use. This is normally not a problem when both your Mac and the PC are running the same version of the program, or when the PC is running a later version than your Mac.

If, however, your Mac is running a later version of the program than the PC, then you need to make sure all the features you intend to use are supported by the PC version of the program.

A quick way to see if the PC version of the program supports the features you intend to use, is to create a small sample file containing those features, and then see if the PC version can read the file properly. If you can see the document the way it should look, then you should not have any problem moving files. Even when the PC version of the program supports all the formatting features you want to use, you need to make certain the PC also supports all the fonts you are using in the document. If you are using PostScript-based fonts, make sure the same font you are using on the Mac is installed on the PC.

NOTE   *Another useful resource is the publisher's Help menu or printed documentation. Microsoft, for example, has information about conversion compatibility with its various versions of Office. By consulting these documents, you have written confirmation of what you see when you convert the document.*

If the PC cannot read the file, then you need to see if you can save the file in an older format the PC can read. Normally, this is performed by selecting Save As

Preparing Files for Cross-platform Use

from the File menu, and then selecting a file format the PC version of your program can read. In Microsoft Word, this is accomplished by clicking the File Menu, and then selecting Save As... from the list of options. Once the Save As dialog box is displayed, click the Save File as Type pop-up menu and select Word 6.0/95 to have the file saved in the older Microsoft Word file format (as shown in Figure 28-1).

Moving Between Different Mac and PC Programs

If a version of the program you are using on the Mac does not exist on the PC, then you need to save your files in a format available on both the Mac and the PC. Because a wide variety of file formats are available to ease the transport of files between the Mac and the PC, you need to choose the one that best suits your needs.

NOTE   *To save space, you can compress Windows-based files in Zip format, which can be easily translated by the Aladdin's StuffIt programs for the Mac. In addition, Aladdin provides a DropZip application with StuffIt Deluxe and StuffIt Expander 5.5, which enables you to open the files easily on a PC. Aladdin also offers a Windows-based StuffIt expansion program, but the Zip format is recommended, as it doesn't require a PC user to install extra software beyond the standard Zip utilities.*

When choosing the proper file format for transferring files between the Mac and PC, you need to look at the type of data you are moving back and forth. If you

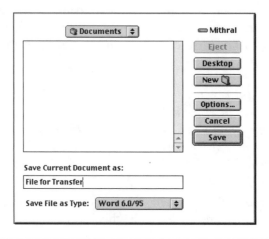

FIGURE 28-1   Microsoft Word gives you a variety of options with which to save files

are moving only text, then you can choose among a variety of formats from saving the file as pure unformatted text to using a format such as *Rich Text Format (RTF)* to transfer both your text and the formatting you have applied to it.

NOTE   *Microsoft's RTF is supported by a number of programs that can retain most of the basic formatting of your document. You learn more about RTF later in this chapter.*

Choosing the proper file format to move graphics files is a more complex task because a large number of graphic file formats is to you, each with its own strengths and weaknesses. The trick to choosing the proper graphics format is to find one your program can read and write, and one that can transfer your data in the way you want. This means you can choose between a file format that sacrifices disk space to store an exact copy of your graphic or a file format that uses much less disk space, but sacrifices some of the image quality.

Other programs, such as music software, video software, and others tend to use a few well-defined file formats aside from their native file formats. Formats such as the WAV file format for sound and QuickTime or another video format almost always involve converting the file to the Windows format, and not using a format that is easily readable on both the Mac and the PC.

An Overview of Cross-platform File Translators

Getting accurate file translations between a Mac and PC program is usually not terribly difficult. Such programs as Adobe Photoshop and Microsoft Word 98 for the Mac include a healthy number of file translation formats. These translators enable users on both platforms to see all or most of the formatting of a document intact.

But file translation isn't always seamless, especially if the versions of a program differ when moved from one computing platform to the other. For example, a Word 98 file for a Mac looks essentially the same on the Windows platform, including the key editing features that make it easy for manuscripts, such as the one for this book, to be seen by writers and editors on both sides of the computing universe.

When one platform has a later version of a program, however, new formatting features may be lost in the translation. For example, the file formats of Microsoft's Office 98 for the Macintosh and Office 2000 for Windows are identical. But certain features, such as the advanced table and text-wrapping features of Office 2000, simply do not accurately translate when the document is opened on a Mac. The formats convert to the older formats and the new features do not display. This will be remedied when the next Office for the Mac version is delivered at the end of 2000.

Another approach to file translations comes from DataViz. MacLinkPlus Deluxe can handle a large number of Windows file formats, including Windows 2000, and convert them so they can be read not only in Word for the Mac, but for other programs, such as AppleWorks and Nisus Writer. When you send files in the other direction, DataViz' MacOpener handles the chores. As with a program's built-in file translators, of course, conversions aren't seamless. They need to be adapted to the features of a specific program rather than the one for which they were created. This means complex formatting is apt to disappear.

In general, if you don't have identical versions of a program on both platforms, try to simplify your document as much as possible. Check the publisher's documentation about what is lost when documents move to another program or another version of a program.

The other great issue of cross-platform file translations is fonts. A Mac document created in common Mac system fonts, such as Helvetica or Times, won't look the same under Windows if the user only has the Windows variations, Arial and Times New Roman. Line breaks and even the fundamental size and shape of letterforms differs.

If you need to retain font compatibility for both platforms, two basic approaches exist. One is to create your Mac documents with the versions of the fonts used on the Windows platform. This is made simple because Microsoft's Internet programs, Internet Explorer and Outlook Express, install those basic fonts (such as Arial and Times) as part of the setup process. Another approach is to buy identical commercial fonts for both platforms from the font libraries of such companies as Adobe and Monotype.

Common Cross-platform File Formats

While you can use literally hundreds, if not thousands, of file formats when you move files between the Mac and the PC, only a few are used widely on a daily basis. I've already described the RTF format above, in the section entitled "Moving Between Different Mac and PC programs." The following is a listing of some other common file formats you see used when transferring files between Macs and PCs.

HTML—Hypertext Markup Language

Hypertext Markup Language (*HTML*) is a text file format that encodes its formatting in a series of codes or *tags* that are embedded into the text of the document. Thus, when read by a program that can understand these codes, the document is displayed with all its formatting in place, just as it appeared in the original document. Because HTML is a newer format than RTF and is constantly being extended, it contains many more formatting codes and, as such, is likely to better represent a document that uses many of the newer formatting features present in modern programs. Also, because HTML is the file format used to create documents for the Web, you can easily share documents by posting them on the Internet for someone else to read.

GIF—Graphics Interchange Format

Graphics Interchange Format (*GIF*) is a format developed by CompuServe in the mid-1980s to allow for the transfer of graphics files between different graphics applications. GIF is also commonly used on Web sites or simply for families to exchange photos by e-mail. GIF stores each image exactly, bit for bit, which can create extremely large files. To offset the size problem, GIF files are compressed as they are saved to help reduce the amount of disk space they take up. Because GIF was created back in the early days of computing, the original version of GIF was only capable of storing images that contained 256 or less colors. A newer version of GIF exists (called PNG) that does not have this limitation, but it has not seen the same level of acceptance as the original.

TIFF—Text Interchange File Format

Tagged Interchange File Format (*TIFF*) is a text-based graphics file format. While this might seem like an oxymoron, TIFF files encode the contents of a graphics file in text form so it can easily be transferred between different computers. Like GIF files, TIFF files are an exact copy of the original image and can be extremely large. Unlike GIF files, however, TIFF files do not contain compression as part of the file format. Compression is, instead, up to the application that creates the TIFF files. On the PC, standard procedure is to compress a TIFF file upon creation, while on the Mac, this is not always the case. TIFF files are commonly used in the publishing industry because the images are of extremely high quality, but the file size can sometimes run tens of megabytes for a large color photo.

BMP—Bitmapped Picture

Bitmapped Picture (*BMP*) is the PC equivalent to the PICT file format on the Mac. BMP files contain a binary image that contains an exact image of the graphic on which you are working. Because BMP files contain an exact copy of the image, they tend to be rather large, especially when working in thousands or millions of colors. While BMP images were popular in the early days of Windows on the PC, they have been largely supplanted by JPEG and other file formats for graphics work. The format is still useful, however, for capturing screen images for use with instruction manuals or computer-related books.

JPEG—Joint Photographic Experts Group

The Joint Photographic Expert Group (JPEG) is one of the most common graphics formats you encounter. JPEG was designed in the early 1990s by a group of photographic experts to provide a high-quality file format for the transfer of photographic images between computers. Because the people who designed JPEG realized it was impractical to create a huge file for each picture, they decided to have JPEG use a lossy compression routine. What *lossy* means is, when JPEG stores an image, it uses a compression scheme that throws away the part of the image detail, the amount of detail thrown away being determined by the level of compression you chose. JPEG throws away only the least significant detail. Because of this, the visual difference is quite minimal between a JPEG image with little compression being performed on it compared to one that uses a much higher level of compression. JPEG files are commonly used for photos on the Web and the format is ideal for transferring family photos via e-mail.

MPEG—Motion Picture Expert Group

Motion Picture Expert Group (*MPEG*) is a file format designed to store motion pictures and other video sources. Like JPEG, which was designed to store still pictures, MPEG was specifically designed to store video information in a compact and easily transferable file format. Like JPEG, the authors of MPEG quickly realized they needed to build compression into their file format to prevent the files from growing too large. As with JPEG, MPEG uses a lossy compression scheme that throws away the least significant parts of the video image. MPEG also incorporates a system that looks for which elements do not change from frame to frame, and then ignores them until they actually change. This allows MPEG files to maximize the amount of data they store. MPEG technology is used for DVD video, so a full-length movie can fit on a single 5-1/4 inch disk.

MP3—MPEG Layer 3

MPEG Layer 3 (MP3) is a sound file format that has grown explosively in the last few years. Based on the sound compression technology built into MPEG—hence, the name—MP3 files contain high-quality stereo sound in an extremely small and portable file format. MP3 is commonly used on both the Mac and the PC to store copies of music CDs and other sound recordings, so they can easily be shared with people over the Internet or played on either a computer or one of the many new

portable MP3 players. Such players include Diamond Multimedia's Rio. Like
MPEG and JPEG, however, MP3 is a lossy file format, in that it does not quite
match the sound quality of the original. In practical terms, MP3 provides close
to CD-quality sound when used in its highest resolution mode.

WAV—Wave Files

Wave files (*WAV*) are another popular sound format on the PC. Similar in most
respects to the sound files available on the Mac, WAV files, like sound files,
encode small snippets of sound digitally in such a way that they can be played
back on the PC. Unlike MP3 files, WAV files are not well suited to long pieces
of music because they do not support stereo sound or contain compression to
keep the file size manageable. Because WAV files can be used to replace common
system sounds on the PC, you will find most WAV files are being used to
customize Windows sound schemes.

Moving Files Between the Mac and the PC

Once you prepare your file for transfer to the PC, it is time to move it over to the
PC. As with the choice of file format, you can move files between the Mac and the
PC in many different ways, ranging from good old sneakernet to uploading your
files to the Internet.

Choosing the right method(s) for you depends on the type of Mac you have
and how you are connected to the PC to which you want to send the file. For users
of Macs with a floppy drive, SuperDisk, or Zip drive, the simplest solution may
be *sneakernet,* the copying of a file to a PC-formatted floppy disk, SuperDisk, or
Zip disk, and then simply walking the file over to a similarly equipped PC. For
users wanting to send a file to someone over the Internet, the best solution might
be sending the file via e-mail or uploading it to a server on the Internet for the PC
user to retrieve.

For users sharing files on a local or wide area network, the options available to
you are much greater. From using good old-fashioned sneakernet, to using DAVE to
tie directly into the Windows NT (or Windows 2000) file servers, being on a network
enables you to exchange files easily between your Mac and the PCs on the network.

Moving Files When You Are Not Connected to A Network

For users who are not connected to a network, the number of ways you can share
files between your Mac and a PC is somewhat limited. If your Mac has a floppy
disk drive, a SuperDisk drive, or a Zip drive, you can simply format either a
floppy disk or a Zip disk as a PC or DOS-formatted disk. To do this, simply insert

the floppy disk or Zip disk into your Mac and wait until it appears on the desktop. Then click the Special menu and select Erase Disk from the list of options.

In the Erase Disk dialog box, enter the name of the disk, up to 11 characters, and then click the Format pop-up menu and select DOS, as shown in Figure 28-2. Then click Erase and your Mac will format the floppy or Zip disk so it can be used on a PC. Once you finish formatting your floppy or Zip disk, you can simply drag the file you want to move to the PC on to the PC, provided the file is small enough to fit on the disk.

Before you send the file to the PC, either by disk or by some other method such as e-mail or copying it to a network shared volume, it may be necessary to rename the file so the PC can understand it. Before the advent of Windows 95, PCs were limited to filenames that were no longer than eight characters, followed by a period, and then a three-letter file extension. After Windows 95 was released, the length of the filename was increased from eight characters to (in theory, at least), 252, plus a three-letter file extension.

NOTE *The actual path of the file (the folder in which it is located) is subtracted from the filename to give you the maximum number of characters available to the file itself.*

If you are sending your file to a PC that is running MS-DOS or a version of Windows earlier than Windows 95, then you need to make sure your file's name is no longer than eight characters.

A Look at PC File Extensions

On a Mac, the desktop files record information about which applications open which document. On the PC side of the computing universe, the file must be

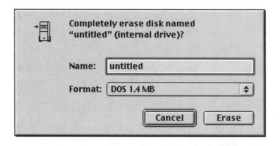

Mac OS enables you to format Floppy and Zip disks for use on a PC

identified with the information that tells the computer what sort of file it is, and that's the three-letter file extension at the end of the name.

The following are some common file extensions you see on the PC. If you do not see one for the file format you want to use, then you might want to open the File Exchange Control Panel and check the various PC file extensions and the Mac applications to which they map, as shown in Figure 28-3. If you still cannot find an appropriate PC file extension, check with the manufacturer of the program you are using.

Common File Extensions for PC-Based Files

■ **.BMP**   Bitmapped Picture, this is one of the more common, if older, graphics formats on the PC, similar to the PICT format on the Mac.

■ **.DOC**   This extension usually indicates the file was created by Microsoft Word, however, some older word-processing applications have also been known to use it.

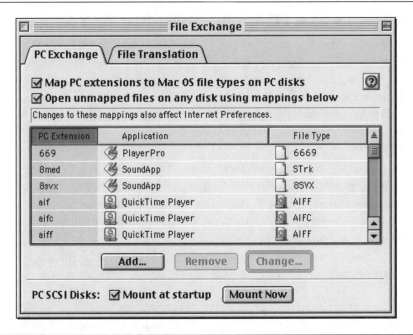

| FIGURE 28-3 | File Exchange contains a large number of PC file extensions and the Mac applications mapped to them |

Moving Files Between the Mac and the PC

- **.JPG**   This is the extension used to denote a JPEG picture. Many different applications can open this document, however, Windows frequently defaults to choosing Internet Explorer or some other Web browser to open these files.

- **.MP3**   This file extension tells Windows the contents of the file are MP3-encoded sound.

- **.PDF**   This extension is used by Adobe Acrobat. Acrobat is a platform-independent document description program frequently used to distribute electronic manuals or books.

- **.RTF**   This file extensions informs Windows that the file contains a text document stored using the Rich Text Format.

- **.TIF**   This is the extension used to denote a TIFF graphics file.

- **.ZIP**   This extensions tells you the file contains another file that has been compressed using PKZip, WinZip, or one of several programs capable of creating ZIP files.

Moving Files to a PC When Connected to a Network

Transferring files to a PC that shares the same network as you do provides you with even more choices than you would have as a stand-alone Mac. Depending on the type of network to which you are connected and the services the PC is running, you can choose to move files by sneakernet, e-mail, uploading to network server, or uploading to a shared volume on the PC you want to use the files.

Sneakernet

As discussed earlier, one option for Macs with a floppy disk, SuperDisk, Jaz, or Zip drive is simply to put the file on a disk, walk it over to a similarly equipped PC to which you want to transfer the file, and let them copy it. The downside, of course, is you actually have to get up and walk over to the destination, something that might be hard if the PC in question is located across the campus, or worse, in another city, state, or country. The other major limitation to sneakernet is that you are limited to moving files no larger than those that can fit on the type of disk you are using.

> **NOTE**   *Another alternative is to install Aladdin Systems' StuffIt Expander for Windows, and then segment a large file so it can be copied to more than a single disk. This tends to be cumbersome, however, compared to networking the file.*

E-mail

For users connected by e-mail, sending files from your Mac to the destination PC by your network's electronic mail system is one of the simplest and most reliable ways of transferring a file. The most common problem you may encounter when sending a file, especially a large one, is that the mail system has limits on how large a file can be sent. Some e-mail systems are set up simply to reject a mail message that contains a file exceeding a certain size, while others simply trim off the attached file and deliver the rest of the message.

If you have trouble sending a file to the PC user you want, check to see if the mail has been rejected–a rejection notice should be sent to you by the mail system–or if the PC user got the message without the attached file. If either of these things happen, then you need to find a different way to move the file to a place where the PC user can access it.

NOTE   *If you're sending files by an online account, you'll be pleased to know AOL lets you e-mail files of up to 16MB to fellow AOL members. The limitation is 2MB for files sent to addresses outside the service. EarthLink's file limit is 10MB. Contact your ISP for specifics on file size limits.*

File Servers

On most larger networks, you can use one or more file servers to share files with other users on the network. The way you access and store files on these file servers, however, depends on the type of file server.

Users on UNIX-based networks can use utilities like MacNFS from Thursby Systems to mount a UNIX *Network File Share*, also known as a *NFS volume,* and then copy files to it just like it was another Mac volume. For users without a NFS client on their Mac, you can use Fetch or another FTP program to transfer files to a FTP server on the UNIX server. Users on the PC, likewise, can use an NFS client on their computer to read the files on the UNIX server, just as if they were on another networked-shared volume. Similarly, if an NFS client is not available, they can use an FTP client to upload and download files located on the UNIX server's FTP server.

MacNFS enables Mac users to connect to NFS-shared volumes located on the various UNIX servers, and then to upload and download files to them. MacNFS makes the UNIX-shared volume look exactly like a Mac volume, including storing Mac files in their native format. Thus, if you intend to make a file on the NFS-shared volume available for use by a PC, you need to make sure the version you save on the NFS share is in a format the PC can read and understand.

Moving Files Between the Mac and the PC

Uploading files from your Mac to an FTP server located on the UNIX servers on your network is another, if more complex, solution to sharing files. Using a program such as Fetch from Dartmouth University, you can log in to the server, and then upload and download files (see Figure 28-4). Once you log in to the FTP server, you can use Fetch to upload files by clicking the Put File… button, and then selecting the file you want to upload. Files can also be dragged-and-dropped into the Fetch window to initiate the file transfer.

Likewise, to download files, simply select them from the list of files on the left-hand side of the dialog box and then click the Get File… button to start the download. One key thing to remember is FTP servers do not preserve the two-part Mac file format. You must convert the files into either a PC-file format or a format like BinHex, which will not damage the files you upload.

Mac users on Windows NT- and Windows 2000-based networks have a variety of options available. Depending on how the Windows NT file servers are configured, you can connect directly to a Mac-shared volume located on the NT Server, use DAVE from Thursby Systems to allow your Mac to connect to the Windows-shared volume, or use FTP to access a FTP file server located on one of your NT Servers or Workstations.

Windows NT Server and Windows 2000 Server and Advanced Server come with File and Print services for Mac. These services allow Windows NT servers to

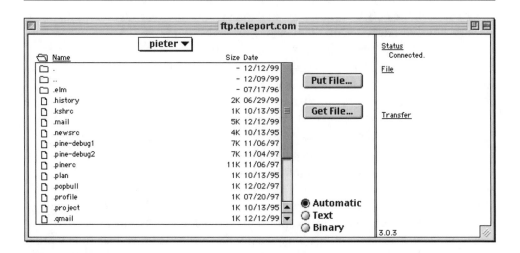

FIGURE 28-4   Select the files you want to transfer from the Fetch window, and then click Put File to begin the file transfer

communicate directly to your Mac using AppleTalk and to support Mac-shared volumes that can be accessed by all the Macs on the network. Because the Mac-shared volume is located on a Windows NT server, PC users can connect to the server and, if they have the proper permissions, access the files the Mac users have stored on the server.

To connect to and use a Mac volume on a Windows NT file server, all you need to do is click the Apple menu, and then select Chooser. Once the Chooser is opened, click the AppleShare icon and then click the name of the file server you want to connect to from the list displayed in the box on the right and click OK.

When you click OK, you are asked to enter your user name and the password you want to use when connecting to the NT or 2000 server, as shown in Figure 28-5.

Once you log in to the NT server, you are presented with a list of the Mac-shared volumes currently available on the NT server (see Figure 28-6). Select the volume you want to connect to, and then click the OK button. If you want to open the shared volume each time you start up your Mac, then click the check box located to the right of the shared volume you want to open.

NOTE   *In order for the Mac to mount the shared volume at startup, the server containing that volume must be up and running first.*

Once you mount the NT-shared volume, you can use it like any regular Mac drive. But if you want to share those files with PC users by storing them on the Windows NT server, then you need to make sure the files are stored in a format the PC can read.

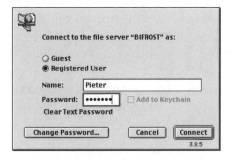

FIGURE 28-5   Logging in to a Windows NT or 2000 server on your Mac is no different than connecting to another Mac

Moving Files Between the Mac and the PC

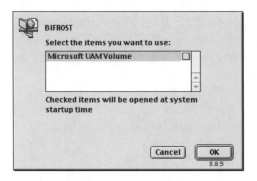

FIGURE 28-6 Select the Mac volume you want to use

DAVE

Another option Mac users have when connecting to Windows-based networks is DAVE from Thursby Systems. DAVE is a utility that allows Macs to communicate directly with Windows computers using their native file-transfer protocol, NetBIOS. Like its UNIX equivalent, MacNFS, DAVE enables you to mount Windows NT-shared volumes, and then use them just as if they were standard Mac volumes.

When DAVE is running, you can mount a Windows NT-shared volume as simply as mounting any other AppleShare volume.

To use DAVE to mount a Windows NT-shared volume, click the Apple Menu, and then select Chooser. Once the Chooser dialog box has opened, click the DAVE Client icon, and then select the server you want to connect to from the list of servers located in the box on the left-hand side of the Chooser dialog box.

If you do not see the Windows NT servers to which you want to connect, select the item named Mount Manually, and then click the OK button. DAVE then asks you the name of the server you want to connect to and the shared volume on the server you want to use (see Figure 28-7).

Once you enter the name of the server and the shared volume you want to connect to and click OK, DAVE asks you to enter your user name and password (see Figure 28-8).

Once you enter your user name and password and click the OK button, DAVE connects to the NT server to make sure you have the proper rights to mount the shared volume.

Once your access is verified, you see the icon for the NT-shared volume on your Mac's desktop.

| FIGURE 28-7 | Enter the name of the server to which you want to network |

As with a Mac-shared volume on a Windows NT server, if you intend to share files with a PC by storing them on the Windows NT server with DAVE, you need to make sure they are in a format the PC can understand (see the section on transferring files across platforms earlier in this chapter). Otherwise, DAVE enables you to treat the Windows NT file shares as a normal Mac volume.

NOTE *DAVE will work with a Windows 2000 server as seamlessly as it works with one using Windows NT.*

Connect to the server
"BIFROST" as:

User name: Pieterp

Password: •••••••

Domain: NIFLHEIM

Cancel   OK

| FIGURE 28-8 | Enter your user name and password to connect to the server |

Troubleshooting Mac and PC File Sharing

Sometimes when you are moving files between the Mac and the PC, things do not go quite the way you expected.

Look at what went wrong, and then see if you can determine the reason. The two main areas where you encounter problems in moving files from the Mac to the PC is in the preparation of the file and in the actual moving of the file between the two computers.

When the file gets to the PC, but the PC cannot seem to read it properly, the first thing to check is if the file became corrupted during the transfer or if it is in a form the PC simply cannot read.

If the PC looks like it is trying to read the file, but then displays an error message saying the file is unreadable, a good chance exists that the file was damaged during the file transfer process. If, however, the PC tries to open the file and then displays garbage or a message saying the file cannot be read, it is likely the file was saved in a format the PC cannot understand.

If the file appears to be damaged, try saving the file again on your Mac, and then sending it over to the PC. Now have the PC try to open the file again. If this fails to work again, look at how you are saving the file to make sure the way you are sending it does not corrupt the file. Make certain the file is being saved in the proper PC format, not in a Mac format. Many Mac files use the standard two-part file format, which is not understood by the PC.

If the file is transferring correctly, but still is not readable by the PC, you need to look at the file to make sure the format in which the Mac is saving the file is compatible with the PC program you are using to try to open the file. As explained earlier in this chapter, some file formats are slightly different between the Mac and the PC. As a result, the files saved on the Mac may not always be usable on the PC. If you believe this is the case, try saving the file in another format that both computers understand, perhaps by saving it in an older version of the program you're using.

If the file has reached the PC and is readable by the user's program, but it does not look as it should, you need to look at the way the file was prepared. One of the most common problems you see when moving files between Macs and PCs is a font mismatch. This results from using fonts during the creation of the document that do not exist on the PC reading the document. Another common problem occurs when you use formatting present in one application, which is not understood by the application reading the file on the PC.

Font mismatches are one of the most common errors you encounter when transferring files between the Mac and PC. The simplest solution to this problem is to use a font common to both the Mac and the PC, such as Arial or the other fonts that come with Microsoft Office 98. Or, you can make certain the proper Postscript fonts are installed on all the PCs that will read this file.

CAUTION   *Having fonts of the same name isn't quite enough to ensure that they will work on both platforms. You also need to make certain the fonts were made by the same manufacturer. One company's Times font, for example, may look different from one made by another company. Letterspacing may be different and the actual size of the characters may vary, even if the fonts are used at the same point size.*

If the PC program cannot understand some of the formatting options you used when creating the document on your Mac, then it will not look correct when you open it on the PC. Changed line breaks usually indicate a font-related problem. But other problems may not be as easily observed. Check all the elements of the documents, such as tables, margins, and special format features.

If you notice the formatting is being lost or changed when you open the file on the PC, try to isolate exactly which formatting elements are being lost. Once you identify what parts of the formatting are being lost between the Mac and the PC, try to restructure the document so it does not use the formatting elements that are being lost. Or, you might want to try saving the file in a different format to see if the PC program is then capable of reading the formatting properly.

Summing Up

In this chapter, you learned that transferring files between the Mac and PC environments may have a few problems, but in the end, you can usually make the transfer work.

In the next chapter, you learn the value of doing regular backups of your data.

Summing Up

Chapter 29

Solid, Safe, Backup Techniques

No mincing words now: You should always make more than one copy of the files you create on your computer, simply for protection.

Macs are prone to crashes. This is a fact of life, no matter what and how many precautions you take. Most of the time, crashes can be irritating, but they're relatively minor occurrences. The chance of losing any documents and files you were working on before the crash is slim.

Sometimes you have to prepare for the worst, though. Many of your most critical files could be lost and, if you don't have copies of them somewhere, you could be out of luck. For example, you think nothing happens when you save your file. After you save it, the new version replaces the old version of the file. Unfortunately, there's no telling what could happen in those few precious seconds when your computer is vulnerable. What would you do if your Mac crashes during those critical seconds?

The How's and Why's of Backups

Documents on computers are extremely vulnerable, perhaps even more so than their paper cousins. If one of your files gets corrupted, you may be unable to open it at all. Certain programs, such as Microsoft Word 98, have the capability to open only slightly damaged files, but more often than not, you may simply be unable to open the document. Always prepare for the worst and take some precautions to make sure you have copies of your critical files if the worst does occur.

A file could be damaged or lost for a number of reasons. The following lists the major causes:

- **Power goes out**   If the power goes out while you're saving a file, the file, or even your hard drive, can be damaged. A UPS device, which gives you surge protection and battery backup, is a good measure of protection. Backup batteries only last a short time (about 10 to 20 minutes), however, depending on the capacity of the battery and the power your system requires. If a series of short power outages occur, such as during a storm or because of a construction project, you may lose the chance to turn off your computer before your battery life is spent so you can protect your critical files.

- **Problems with Software**   You can face a number of potential conflicts when you use the software running on your Mac. Some may only cause minor symptoms, like cosmetic and performance degradations. But some could crash your Mac. If this happens when you save a document, you may be unable to recover the file once you restart.

- **Damaged hard drive directory**   The more times your Mac crashes, the better chance of your delicate hard drive directory getting damaged. As your drive gets older, your files can be damaged by bad blocks or your hard drive might simply fail. Whatever happens, though, a chance exists that you won't be able to recover your critical files.

NOTE   *The subject of hard drives and how to cope with drive directory problems is covered in more detail in Chapter 14.*

- **Viruses**   With the Mac now more popular than ever, a resurgence of new strains of viruses for the platform has occurred. Some of these viruses might only produce silly message or screen backgrounds, but others could also crash your computer or even damage your files or your drive's directory. To learn more about this subject, read Chapter 30.

- **Theft**   Even if your house is protected by the best available security system, a chance exists that nasty burglars can break into your home or office and steal your computer. On the road, your Apple PowerBook or iBook is also vulnerable to theft. Learn about ways to protect yourself against laptop theft in Chapter 13.

- **Earthquakes**   An average earthquake of even three or four on the Richter scale may be sufficient to shake things up quite a bit. Assuming your Mac doesn't fall off your desk, the hard drive may encounter a head crash, which occurs when the heads strike the spinning platters (admittedly, it would take a pretty long drop to cause this sort of damage). This could cause you to lose critical files.

NOTE   *Our ever-vigilant technical editor, Pieter Paulson, reminds me that he lives in Oregon, near two active volcanoes. Pieter wanted me to suggest this is yet another source of potential catastrophe (although not one that happens quite as often as an earthquake).*

- **Fire**   Even if the fire is extinguished before spreading, your Mac and peripherals can be damaged by heat or by the water used to put out the fire.

- **Flooding**   If the area you live in rarely encounters floods, heavy rains and other unexpected types of weather can still cause problems. If your computer sustains water damage, expect a disaster.

The How's and
Why's of Backups

How Large Corporations Backup Files

Most of the world's large companies, including the banks, manufacturers, and the computer corporations, realize they may lose critical data on the computers they need to run their businesses. As a result, these large companies constantly back up their important files. Some use *file mirroring,* which makes copies of files on separate drives at the same time. Backup sets may also be stored at other locations, in case of damage to the plant where the main computers are located.

NOTE
A particularly unfortunate example occurred in the wake of the World Trade Center bombing some years back, when some companies went out of business because they lacked offsite backups to restore their business records.

Naturally, the Internet services you connect to have a regular backup regimen to ensure the services you access are available even if a disaster strikes.

Of course, the companies know no alternative exists. If a new Internet start-up company (common these days) is getting ready to present a new strategy to a group of investors with large pockets and it loses the information on its computers without having backups, the company could be in deep trouble.

How You Can Conduct Backups

The very idea of doing a backup may seem like drudgery personified. Imagine having to remember what file to duplicate, and where and when to duplicate it. This sort of drudgery doesn't match in the least what you'd have to go through to rebuild damaged files, though.

Two basic backup systems exist, which are described next. Later in this chapter, you learn about the best backup strategies.

- **Back up manually** This is probably the easiest way to back up your files. First, you must have some sort of removable drive or additional hard drive available. Then you drag the icons that represent whichever files and folders you want to back up to the icon of that drive. Unfortunately, you have to specifically select which files you want to copy over and you can make a mistake. Also, if a file is mistakenly put in the wrong folder, you may miss it.

- **Automatic backup** You can also back up your files at specified times using backup software, such as Retrospect and other programs mentioned later in this chapter. You simply have to prepare the media to which you're copying your files. As long as you don't have to switch the media after the first one is full (assuming you don't have a tape changer, which can swap the media automatically), then you needn't be around while your files are being backed up.

What Should You Back Up?

When backing up your files, you can choose from an number of methods, depending on whether the process is manual or automatic. Here are some of those options:

- **Easy backup**   If you have the original Mac OS 9 installation CD, as well as those for your programs, you may not need to make copies. You can simply make copies of your most critical files and the settings you created for your programs in the Preferences folder.

- **Incremental backup**   If you don't want to back up everything on your hard drive all the time, you can simply back up all the files you changed since your last back up. This technique works most efficiently with a dedicated backup program.

- **Full backup**   Here you can make copies of everything on your startup disk. This could take several hours, especially if you have many big files, but it's a great advantage to restore all the files on your Mac without having to create them all over again in case a disaster strikes. The full backup includes all the documents you created, the settings and changes you made to programs, and unique desktop patterns, as well as everything else that makes your experience as a Mac user much better.

NOTE   *One of the great features of Retrospect, mentioned later in the chapter, is its capability to use a snapshot to literally restore your drive's contents precisely as they were originally. This includes even the desktop icons you have and the folder hierarchy.*

Choosing Backup Media

You need a place to put your critical files before you can back them up. Don't simply copy those files to the same drive as the original. Backups are a measure of protection in the worst-case scenario, where not only the file, but also your hard drive is damaged, meaning it may affect only one file or all of them. A wide variety of backup media is available at press time, all having advantages and disadvantages. The following is an overview of what you can use to back up your data.

- **Removable media**   Removable media has names like SuperDisk, Jaz, Orb, and Zip, although all perform similar functions. While the drives that use these media may look and act like floppies, you can simply remove them after they are full and insert another one for your files. You can use as many as you need until all your files are backed up. Removable media can have capacities of as little as 100MB to 2GB or more, just like a regular hard drive. Even better, though, you can put the media in a safe place.

NOTE   *While some of these removable devices use technology based on hard drives, they are not as quick or reliable because the drive will be more affected by dust than a regular hard drive.*

- **External or internal hard drive**   It doesn't matter whether the hard drive uses a USB, SCSI, or FireWire connection, or whether it is nestled in your Mac. Hard drives are useful storage areas for large amounts of data. Of course, using a hard drive in a place where it can regularly be backed up may be impractical. While you could divide the drive into multiple segments (also known as *partitioning*), it isn't efficient. If your hard drive fails, all your partitions will be gone.

- **Tape drive**   Various kinds of backup tape drives exist. Among the more popular is *Digital Data Storage* (*DDS*), based on *Digital Audio Tape* (*DAT*) technology. Other tape formats include the more costly *Digital Linear Tape* (*DLT*) or *Advanced Intelligent Tape* (*AIT*) mediums. While these tapes are inexpensive, they aren't quite as robust as other types of media. These tapes can also be much slower, though some of the newer tape drives provide faster and more reliable performance. Locating one file could take a long time. As with a regular tape cassette deck that you use on a stereo, random access of files isn't possible. The tape must be manually run back and forth to locate a specific file. Another shortcoming except for Optima Technology's DeskTape Pro, is that the contents of the tape don't simply show up on your Mac as another drive icon. Your backup software has to access those files directly through its special interface.

- **Data mirroring**   Certain software packages that support *Redundant Array of Inexpensive Drives* (*RAID*) include a feature that mirrors or duplicates the files you placed on two or more drives. So, if one of the drives happens to fail, you have another identical file at your disposal on the other drive.

■ **Magneto-optical drive**   Some drives use an optical disk technology, like the one used by CDs, which enables you to keep backed up files for a long time, even several years or more. This option (or a CD writer) ensures unparalleled longevity. While a magneto-optical drive is faster than all but the fastest CD writers and most forms of removable media, it isn't as fast as a hard drive. At the same time, though, it could be worth the effort for a backup that lasts a long time.

■ **CD-R or CD-RW**   Like the optical disk drives previously mentioned, these two methods are based on the technology used on compact discs, just like the music CDs you listen to all the time. An obvious advantage is longevity. CDs are not prone to failure (though they can be physically scratched or otherwise damaged, of course). I still have my first audio CDs, purchased 16 years ago, and they work flawlessly. If you need to keep certain files for a long time, one of these two CD-writing methods could work for you. The downside is that you need special CD software to write files and it's not as fast as other types of backup media. Typically, expect the special CD software to take from 15 to 45 minutes to fill a typical 650MB CD, depending on the speed of the CD writer. Those $2x$ and $4x$ figures are meaningful because they tell you how much faster than normal speed (approximately 74 minutes for a CD) they run. Once you get past the speed penalty, however, you should find the media itself is cheap, less than two dollars a disc in quantities of five or more. Unfortunately, you can only write files once to a CD (though you can use multiple sessions to lay them down). The alternative is CD-RW, for which media costs several times that of a regular CD. This format enables you to rewrite files up to 1,000 times, but the rewritable versions may not work on many older CD drives.

■ **DVD-RAM**   A DVD-RAM disk, based on DVD, the high-quality video disk format, has the capability to hold more than 5GB of data. It might be a while before this technology takes off, though, because at press time, competing technologies were still being evaluated.

■ **Network drives**   If you use a Mac at an office, you could use the networked drives or servers to back up your files. Before using a networked drive to store file backups, however, consult with your network administrators about their special backup strategies. The subject of sharing files across a network is

The How's and Why's of Backups

covered in Chapter 27. Copying files to a Windows-based system, is covered in Chapter 28.

- **Floppy disks**   These were used to back up files on Macs from the time of the earliest Macs. While floppy disks may have been good for older Macs, using your floppy drive doesn't make sense if you have an older Power Mac or getting an external floppy or SuperDisk drive doesn't make sense if you have a newer Mac or iMac. Considering that floppies can only hold 1.4MB, think how long backing up everything on a 3GB hard drive would take and how many floppies you would need to do it. If you only need floppy disks to back up a few documents or if you're going to put the file on another computer, this should be fine. For heavy-duty backups, however, you might want to consider another method.

- **Backing up over the Internet**   With the release of the iMac, Power Mac G3 and G4, and the iBook, this has become a more popular option because of the absence of a standard floppy drive on all these computers. Instead of buying an external floppy or a SuperDisk drive, you can upload your critical files to an Internet backup service, which provides security and a place to keep your files. This can be a good thing if the service backs up its files every day, but you must realize how long it can take to upload your files to a distant location. If you don't have access to a high-speed Internet connection, like DSL or a cable modem, uploading even the smallest files could take hours. Also, you may only get a small amount of space to store your files (most of the time, it's only 10MB), so you could only use it to back up small files.

> NOTE   *One of the iTools features offered for Mac OS 9 users at Apple's Web site (http://www.apple.com) is iDisk, which gives you 20MB of free storage space for your personal Web page, shared files, and your own personal backups.*

- **Upload data to someone else's computer**   Instead of using an Internet backup service to store your files, you could upload them to the computer of a friend or family member by Apple Remote Access, so the files can be kept safe for you. Make sure the person who has your files for safekeeping regularly backs up his files, in case something bad happens at his side of the backup world.

Choosing Backup Software

The selection of backup software for the Mac used to be much greater, but many programs went by the wayside for marketing and sales reasons. In addition to,

Retrospect, which now dominates the market, there was also FastBack and Redux, to name a few The utility software, like Norton Utilities and MacTools, also came with their own backup functions.

However, when Fifth Generation Systems, the publisher of FastBack and FastBack Plus, was bought by Symantec, FastBack and its sister product were scrapped. When Symantec bought out MacTools, it took out the backup module from the program, as well as the one in its own program, Norton Utilities.

Redux remains available as a freeware program.

Fortunately, several excellent backup options are available for the Mac, so don't panic because a few other programs have been lost. Even if you are using discontinued backup software on your Mac and it works fine for you, by all means, keep using it. Of course, the program won't ever be updated by its publisher or whatever company succeeded or took it over, and forget about tech support. Also, remember that, after you upgrade to Mac OS 9 or get a new Mac running that version of the Mac OS, the program may not work. If this happens, you need to consider a newer backup option.

Retrospect Express and Retrospect Desktop Backup

If you purchase a backup tape drive, it may include a copy of the backup program, Retrospect Desktop Backup from Dantz Development, or the low-end version, Retrospect Express. Dantz constantly updates the software, so it works with the latest Macs and system versions. With each version, more features have been added, and the program has proven its worth with individuals, small businesses, and even large corporations. The following are some of the features offered by Retrospect:

NOTE   *The name Retrospect Desktop Backup applies to version 4.2 and later. Upgrade to this version for full Mac OS 9 compatibility.*

- **Supports a wide variety of backup media**   Whether you use a tape drive or a Zip drive to backup doesn't matter (unless you're using Retrospect Express, which can't support backup tapes); Retrospect most likely supports it. As the manufacturer of the product releases new versions, it probably will also release an update allowing it to work with Retrospect.

- **Simple interface**   After Retrospect has been set up, you can easily access all its major features from its simplistic interface (see Figure 29-1). The commands are clearly labeled in normal English, not in "geekspeak," and the online help enables you to deal with the more complicated aspects of backing up your files.

- **Backup over the Internet**   If you want to back up your files online (limits that you should be aware of do exist, such as the speed of file

The How's and
Why's of Backups

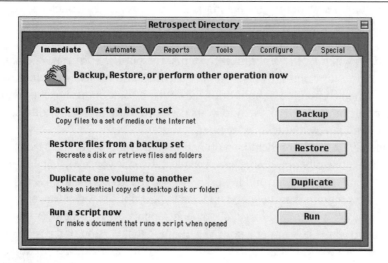

FIGURE 29-1 Retrospect has an easy-to-use interface that isn't daunting to first-time users

transfer and the file size limits for such transfers), Retrospect can easily handle this for you, just as well as it can for a regular backup.

■ **Backup over a network**   Retrospect also comes in a version known as the *Retrospect Workgroup Backup,* which enables you to back up files over an entire network, no matter what the size. If you work in a cross-platform environment with both Macs and PCs running Windows, don't worry. The Windows version of Retrospect has similar features.

NOTE *When you set up a networking backup routine with Retrospect, you need to install a client program on each computer on the network from which backup files are retrieved.*

■ **Retrospect's EasyScript**   Using this feature enables you to back up automatically without having to deal with scripting or programming language. When using EasyScript (see Figure 29-2), Retrospect carefully guides you through the process. All you have to do is answer some questions and you can back up everything from a lone Mac to an entire army of the latest iMacs and Power Macs.

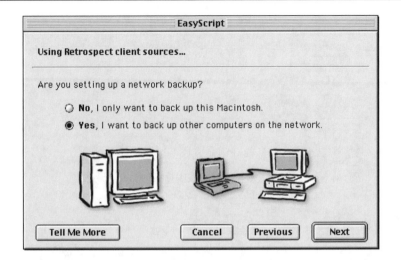

FIGURE 29-2   EasyScript is a good solution for those who don't want to deal with the
inner complexities of backup software

NOTE   *Although EasyScript certainly simplifies the process of creating a backup
routine, you can do it manually without a lot of practice. Retrospect comes
with a thorough manual and Help menus.*

Using Personal Backup

If you own only one Mac, or even two, and you want something to do the job easily,
then ASD Software's Personal Backup could be for you.

All of Personal Backup's features can be accessed from only one screen (as shown
in Figure 29-3). After the program is set up, you can conduct backups whenever you
want with the program's useful menu bar command. You can also use the automatic
schedule setting to set up backups at specified times and days. If you use an Apple
laptop, one of the most useful features is the program's automatic synchronization
feature, which ensures that both your iBook or PowerBook and desktop Macs have the
latest versions of your files.

NOTE   *Personal Backup can also be set up to record keystrokes of the text you
type. This way, if you lose any files before you have time to do the next
backup, at least you can retrieve that text to bring a document up-to-date.*

The How's and
Why's of Backups

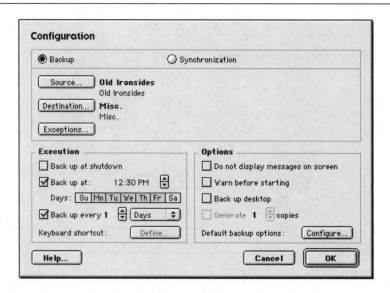

FIGURE 29-3   Personal Backup offers ease-of-use and power, all in one package

Using AppleScript for your Backups

AppleScript is an extremely handy tool that makes the various mundane functions of your Mac occur automatically, without having to purchase special programs or to learn computer programming. In the following paragraphs, you learn how to use this useful application to back up your files.

First, be sure that whatever media you are backing up your files to is ready to receive them. If you're using a removable drive, make sure you insert the disk and that its icon is visible on your Mac's screen before you begin.

Now follow these steps:

1. Make a new folder on your Mac where you can put the backed up files. You can name the folder whatever you like, but make sure you give it a name that describes what it contains to make things easier.

2. Next, click the folder once. Hold down the CONTROL key at the same time, which activates contextual menus and brings up a list of things that can be done with the folder.

3. Now click the option called Attach a Folder Action.

4. When the Open dialog box appears, you can choose the AppleScript related to the folder.

NOTE *If the Open dialog box brings up the wrong folder, find the folder called Folder Action Scripts, which is nested inside the Scripts folder in your System Folder. If you can't find the folder, use the Add/Remove feature of your system installer to reinstall AppleScript.*

5. Then choose the script called add-duplicate to folders. The folder where you are putting your files should now have a script icon, which tells you a Folder Action can be performed with it.

6. Now click the icon of your backup disk once. Make an alias of the disk using the Make Alias option in the File menu of the Finder. Click the name of the icon to select it. Then add the symbols ~! before the name of the disk. This is what identifies the disk as the one to which backups are directed. Next, drag the alias icon with the new title to your backup folder.

From now on, whenever you put a file or folder in your special backup folder, the files are automatically copied to your backup disk.

CAUTION *Make sure you open the backup folder first, otherwise, AppleScript is unable to function correctly.*

Using the File Synchronization Control Panel

The iBook and iMac are bundled with a backup utility called *File Synchronization*. Using this control panel enables you to match a version of a file on your Mac with a different version on a network. While it doesn't come with the full-blooded features of Retrospect or Personal Backup, it does quite well if you have two computers and both must have the right versions of your files. In fact, File Synchronization began as a way to match up the files on a PowerBook with a desktop computer.

File Synchronization is also easy-to-use. All you have to do is drag a file or folder to the screen of the control panel, allowing it to be compared with the other version. Whichever one is newer then replaces the older version of the file.

Make Sure Your Backup Works

You shouldn't just back up your files and then hope you can restore them when it's necessary. In a sense, this sort of test is similar to what large corporations did when facing the possible dangers of the Y2K bug, a minor issue with Macs (because only a few programs were vulnerable). To test for the possibility of a bug, they ran their systems after setting the date to any time after January 1, 2000 to see what might happen.

To check your backups, you want to see if the files are still usable, so you have to restore some of them.

Here are a few ways you can run this test:

1. If you're backing up manually or using a backup in Finder format (this means the backed up files are in the same form as the originals), copy a few files in a different location from their originals back to your drive. Here you can make sure they work, without worrying about overwriting them. Open the files to make sure they correspond with whatever is in the originals. If you can open the file without a problem, everything should be fine.

2. If the file doesn't open, however, use your backup strategy and the tips in the next section to deal with this and related problems.

3. If you use a backup program like Retrospect, then just try out the Restore function in the software, and choose some files to restore on your drive. Just make sure that you don't replace an existing file; you only want to be reassured that there is a good copy of a file available just in case something goes wrong later on.

CAUTION *As part of its normal backup routine, Retrospect verifies the backup against the original files and will report any problems in the program's log file. This is an option you should not turn off, as it can alert you to potential problems with your backup media, backup drive, or the peripheral bus you're using (such as the SCSI chain).*

Your backup strategy should work just fine if this test works correctly.

Make a Plan to Regularly Back Up Your Files

Backups can be a severe irritation for those who don't like taking the time to do them. Instead of spending the whole night fragging your friends over the Internet in Unreal Tournament, you have to endure painful hours making extra copies of your files. Just dealing with the concept of backups could make people want to just ignore them and hope for the best. Unfortunately, if you haven't a made a clear plan for when you want to backup your files, you could easily lose a critical file while you're trying to decide.

A simple plan is provided below for backing up your files. You just need a separate drive on which to put your files.

- **Make extra copies of important files.**   Whenever you're working with a file, drag a copy of its icon to a different disk. You can also choose Save As from the File menu and save an extra copy of the file on another disk.

- **Make sure your files are stored in a safe place.**   The same things that can happen to your original files can happen to those contained on the backup media as well. As a precaution, large corporations will put a copy of their backed up files in a different location. For maximum security, you could put your files in a secure location like a bank vault. Of course, you could even put them in the home of a trusted friend or family member. Just make sure you have another copy of your files somewhere else, just in case the other copy is damaged or stolen.

- **Backup important files after you're done working for the day.**   This can be done manually with a backup program like Retrospect. Also remember that these critical files should include the Preferences folder in the System Folder. This folder has the settings for all your programs, including those dealing with your Internet connection.

- **Do a full backup every week.**   You've probably made numerous changes to your Mac over the years, whether you've simply changed the background on your desktop or the settings in programs or installed entirely new software altogether. To re-create everything that's made your experience with your Mac a pleasure would take a long time. If you create a complete backup of everything on your startup disk, you don't have to deal with any hassle (except when copying the files back to your disk) if you lose your files for any reason.

- **Take advantage of your software's AutoSave or backup feature.**   Take a look at the preferences for the programs you use to see if either or both of these options are present. If you see an option to save a backup to a different drive or partition, then use it if you can.

- **Recycle old media.**   If you have disks with files that you don't need anymore, you can use them to backup your newer files. Of course, if the disk is very old, it would probably be better just to get new ones.

The How's and Why's of Backups

■ **Don't overuse media.**   Removable media, whether tapes or Zip disks, can wear out after constant use. To deal with this, you should use several different disks to conduct your backups.

■ **Manage the labeling of your backup media efficiently.**   If you have to replace a lost file, searching through dozens of different backup disks to find a few files can be a hassle. Make sure you give each backup media a distinct, descriptive name. You can even print a directory of the contents of a disk.

■ **Make a backup of your storage catalog.**   An important feature of Retrospect is its storage set, a file that contains the table of contents of your backup. While the program can re-create a lost storage set from the backup media, if your Mac's drive can't be accessed, a good idea is to copy these files (which usually run several megabytes each) to another drive to speed recovery of files.

■ **When you leave home, take a copy of your files with you.**   Make sure you do this as a precaution. Just in case the worst happens while you're away, you can get back up to full capacity when you return. While insurance companies do replace stolen computers and peripherals, replacing your missing data can take a long time, especially if you have a lot of it. And the chances you can recover all your files are little to none.

NOTE   *If you have to keep files for a long time, traditional removable disks may not be good enough. On the other hand, optical-based media can last for several years. If you have to use a file for a long time, consider purchasing a CD or DVD writer or a magneto-optical drive. While traditional disks and tapes may wear out over time, optical-based media can last for many years. If you anticipate that you might need that file five years from now, a CD or DVD recorder or a magneto-optical drive may be something to consider as an extra backup tool.*

Backup Features in Various Programs

Besides backing up your critical files to one location, such as a hard drive or some form of removable media, another option is at your disposal.

You can, of course, manually back up files using a program's Save As option to make another copy to another drive or to copy the files in the Finder. But other, more convenient methods exist, as preference options for some programs, which have the added benefit of being done without your intervention. When used, these automatic backup or automatic save options, create another copy of a critical document for you, just in case the original file is damaged or lost. Here are two of the most notable examples:

Word's AutoSave/Backup Option

If you use Microsoft Word 98 for the Mac often, this feature located in the Preferences settings of the program will keep your documents safe in case they are damaged or lost. There is a similar option in PowerPoint 98, but not for Excel. Here's how to activate the automatic backup feature: Select Preferences from the Tools menu. As shown in Figure 29-4, click the Save tab, which brings up another screen.

To make an extra copy of a file, click the check box called Always create a backup copy. This creates an extra copy of your document in the same folder as the original (it has the prefix Backup of).

| | FIGURE 29-4 | This is where you can select Save options for Word 98 |

The How's and Why's of Backups

If you want to restore a file after crashing while saving it, choose the Save AutoRecover info every... check box, and type in the time. Ten minutes, which is the default setting, should be all right. After this option is active, whenever you open a damaged file, Word can use the AutoRecover feature to restore it to the way it was before your Mac crashed (or no more than ten minutes before that). Click OK to make these options active.

QuarkXPress's Secret Backup Feature

While QuarkXPress is used widely on the Mac for the production of books, magazines, and newspapers, many people don't know about its backup feature. This option is extremely critical because XPress can sometimes corrupt a document if it crashes while a document is open or being saved. Although some of these problems can be traced to other reasons, like problems on the SCSI chain, they can still be annoying and the sensitivity of the program to such ills is troublesome (though recent versions of the program are better able to deal with minor document damage).

Follow these steps to save and backup the documents you create in QuarkXPress automatically:

1. First, open QuarkXPress. Then select Preferences from the Edit menu and choose the first option on the list, which is Application Preferences. The dialog box shown in Figure 29-5 then appears.

2. Then choose the Save tab, which causes the screen shown in Figure 29-6 to appear.

3. Choose Auto Save and select how often you want your documents to be saved automatically. The default setting is five minutes. Next, choose Auto Backup and how many different versions of the file you want to have. The default setting is five, but you should choose one or two instead. Otherwise, you will have a lot of extra copies of your files that you don't need.

NOTE *If you choose to make too many copies of your QuarkXPress backup files, your hard drive will be littered with many versions of the same document. This program doesn't remove older backup files when it creates newer ones. You can also create an AppleScript to perform this function, using the information provided in Chapter 9.*

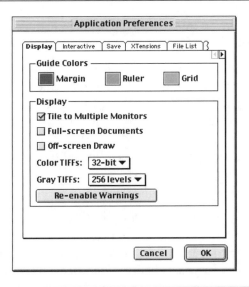

FIGURE 29-5   The Application Preferences dialog box in QuarkXPress 4.1 is just like
the one in earlier versions of the program

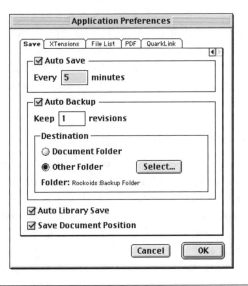

FIGURE 29-6   Pick up your backup options from this dialog box

4. Then choose the destination for the backup. Don't stick with the default Document folder, in case something happens to your hard drive. Instead, click the Other Folder button.

5. When the next dialog box appears, select whichever drive or folder you want to use for the backups. You can also use the option to make a new folder with a descriptive title that easily lets you know what it contains. If you have an external drive attached to your Mac, you could put backups there as well. If you are connected to a network or a server, you can use them to back up your documents. This could slow you down when your document is being saved, however, especially if your office doesn't have access to a high-speed network connection.

6. After you select these options, click the OK button to store your settings.

From now on, every document you make or modify in QuarkXPress is saved and/or backed up whenever you want. The Auto Backup files have the original filename with a suffix that begins with a number to show how many backups of the files have been created.

A Useful Way to Restore Damaged QuarkXPress Files

If you run into a situation where a file you create in QuarkXPress has somehow been damaged and the backup doesn't work either, a solution is available from MarkZWare, a company that creates QuarkXTensions, or add-ons, for the program. MarkZWare also has a product called MarkZTools, which enables you to restore damaged XPress documents. You can find out more about this product at MarkZWare's Web site: http://www.markzware.com.

How to Deal with a Bad Backup

If your hard drive has just crashed and you've lost all your files, it can be very, very, very annoying to realize your savior, your backup media, has also failed you, making it impossible to restore your files. Whether you use the Restore function within your backup program or you manually copy the files back to your hard drive, you receive a message that a disk error occurred or a warning telling you that something is wrong with your backup program's storage set.

While this may, at first, seem like a serious problem, you should be able to restore at least some of your files. For example, Retrospect offers tools that enable you to repair the backup directly, even if the table of contents, the Storage Set file, is damaged.

The steps described here can recover any available files, but they don't do anything to fix a bad disk.

Repairing a Damaged Storage Set in Retrospect

Retrospect won't keep you in the dark when you attempt to restore a damaged file or disk.

You receive a warning if Retrospect is unable to restore one, some, or all of your files. Most of the time, this means the contents of the Storage Set are not the same as the actual files on the backup media. This can occur if your Mac crashes during a backup, though the same message appears when a Storage Set file has been damaged.

Remember, the Storage Set files of Retrospect are kept in the same folder of the original application. You should make copies of your files on another hard drive or a different form of removable media as a precaution. If the original drive is damaged or fails, the sets can be re-created, although doing this takes a while.

The following describes how to deal with the problem using Retrospect 4.2, the most recent version of the program.

1. First, be sure the first or only disk for your backup has been placed in its drive.

2. Next, open Retrospect. Select the Tools tab, which causes the screen shown in Figure 29-7 to appear.

3. Now, select the Repair button, which brings up the dialog box in Figure 29-8.

4. Whatever you decide depends on whatever warning message came up when you attempted to restore a file. If the catalog wasn't the same as what was on the backup, choose the first option. If a Storage Set doesn't exist, you can re-create it with the files on your backup media by choosing the option in Figure 29-8 that applies to it.

5. If you need more disks for your backup, a prompt appears to insert those disks when the first one is full. Most of the time, the previous disk is ejected first, but you may have to press the Eject button to eject it. If you don't need any more backup disks, then just respond according to the dialog box and you'll see a message that the storage set has been re-created.

Re-creating or building the files could take from as little as a few minutes to several hours, depending on how badly the Storage Set catalog was damaged.

The How's and Why's of Backups

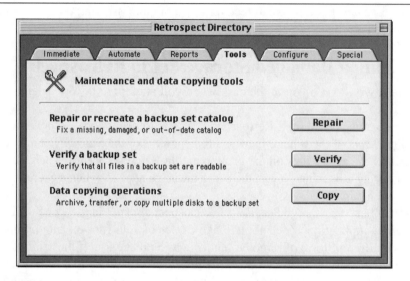

FIGURE 29-7   In this screen, you can choose your catalog repair options

> **TIP**   *To avoid dealing with a bad backup you should have more than one backup set; use two or more disks in regular rotation. In case a fragile backup disk fails you, you have another recent one at your disposal so you can restore your files.*

More Ways to Recover Your Backup

Sometimes it may not be the backup catalog causing you problems. The actual backup disk or tape could be the culprit. However, the prospects of restoring the

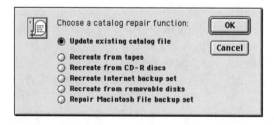

FIGURE 29-8   Here you can decide to re-create or update your Storage Set catalog

backup from damaged media are generally slim to none, so make sure you create extra backups.

NOTE

You should do this especially if your backed up files are on a tape, which needs special software to be read, such as Retrospect. If the disks fail, then your normal file recovery and repair programs cannot help you in this situation.

CAUTION

When you use a tape drive as a backup tool, make sure you follow the manufacturer's recommendation about keeping your tape heads clean by using cleaning disks. If you have a DDS drive, for example, it should be cleaned after every 15 hours of use. If you're using Retrospect, it can be configured to remind you when you need to clean the drive. If you don't regularly clean the disks, read/write errors could occur on your backup, meaning your files could be lost or corrupted.

A Helping Hand from Abbott Systems

Abbott Systems, a long-time publisher of utilities for the Mac, has two applications that can enable you to restore damaged or lost documents. The first, CanOpener, can open almost any file and restore its contents, even if the program in which the file was created can't open it. If you have complicated documents with many graphics and fonts, restoring them to their original form may be hard, but documents with only some text and a few pictures can be retrieved.

The other restoration program, Rescue TXT, enables you to track text from files you trashed by accident. This is probably a last resort, in case your attempt to use a hard disk recovery program, like Norton Utilities, to restore your files doesn't help.

You can learn more about the products of Abbott Systems from its Web site: http://www.abbottsystems.com/.

Dealing with SCSI Chain Backup Problems

If you can't restore a backup from a SCSI device on a chain with several other devices, follow these steps.

1. First, examine the SCSI chain to check if all devices on the chain are turned on. Also check to see if the termination is turned on or attached to the device at the end of the chain.

The How's and
Why's of Backups

2. Before moving devices to different positions, turn off your computer and any attached SCSI devices. Make sure you give them the correct termination and SCSI ID configurations.

3. If the backup drive still doesn't work properly and you have an available removable drive, such as a Zip or Jaz drive, use a hard-drive diagnostic program. Before using the program, however, look at the manual or ReadMe file provided by the publisher. Making the situation worse isn't a good idea, unless the media is useless. Even then, however, taking the risk may be worth it.

TIP   *Also, here's another alternative to consider if the backup drive doesn't work. If you own another Mac that can work with that drive, you can set the drive up there and try to get the file from that computer, as long as you have installed the backup software first. Then, if it works, you can network the two Macs to get the files or put them on another available drive.*

NOTE   *You find more coverage of SCSI issues and solutions in Chapters 14 and 15.*

Summing Up

In this chapter, you learned a number of ways to back up your Mac's files and to develop a robust backup strategy that can go a long way to protect you if you have a problem with the originals.

In the next chapter, you learn about another sort of protection against catastrophe: how to protect your Mac from an infection by a computer virus.

Chapter 30

Secrets of Virus Protection

When you buy a new Mac, you get your system software and, with a consumer Mac (the iBook and iMac), you get a great selection of productivity software. You have an office suite (AppleWorks), Internet software, games, and educational software, enough to start using a Mac without buying anything extra.

But one type of program seldom provided is virus detection software.

The Myths and Reality of Mac Viruses

Computer viruses are not something to take lightly. They aren't funny, and they aren't instruments by which the good guys manage to give the enemy their comeuppance, even though some popular movies have conveyed that impression.

Computer viruses can attack your Mac's operating system and cause minor or serious problems, just as real viruses can attack the human body and do various degrees of harm (of course, you a cold instead of a system crash).

The symptoms of a computer virus vary. A virus may put up a silly message on your computer and promptly remove itself. Or, it can do real harm by slowing down your Mac's performance, causing system errors and crashes. At its worst, a virus may destroy files wholesale.

Because these viruses are designed to spread to your computer, they're difficult to deal with unless you get a little help (as I explain shortly). A typical computer virus contains computer instructions allowing itself to spread to your files. Some viruses attack certain applications and others generally cause havoc with all your documents or system files. Other viruses can first infect a system file before spreading to other files. A new brand of viruses (the Melissa virus and others of its ilk) do not actually infect files, but instead, perform other annoying actions, such as sending e-mail en masse.

You can get a virus in a few different ways. You may transfer a virus-infected file from someone's computer to your own and, if the original owner doesn't have an antivirus detection program, he wouldn't know his file was infected. (This is discussed a little later in the chapter.) Or, you could download a file from an obscure e-mail containing the virus. The first instance is probably the most common situation in which Mac viruses are spread.

An unscrupulous programmer can insert a potentially lethal virus into a file, and then send you a message saying "Hi, this is the file you've been waiting for," or something similar, to make it seem like the file is something you want or need.

Once you download the file and launch it, the virus's power is unleashed on your computer, doing whatever it was originally designed to do.

NOTE   *One of the most dangerous viruses in recent years was the infamous Melissa virus and its successors. This virus was primarily a Windows issue, infecting Microsoft's Outlook e-mail software, and was propagated by e-mail, appearing as a file from someone you knew. Damage caused by this virus was estimated in the millions of dollars. This is one of the chief reasons I recommend that confirming an unexpected file from one of your online contacts is genuine.*

Luckily, Mac viruses are less common than Windows viruses. The benefit for Mac users is that we are in the minority in the computing world. Macs don't attract as many virus authors. Additionally, the process of creating a virus on a Mac presents a greater challenge to the would-be virus maker. As you've no doubt noticed, most of the viruses you hear about on the news usually affect Windows 95, Windows 98, Windows NT, and, no doubt, Windows 2000. You don't hear much about malignant Mac viruses.

But this isn't a reason to become overconfident. Cross-platform viruses, affecting macros used in Microsoft Office programs, remain a threat. In addition, some new virus strains affected Mac users after a period of relative quiet. This seems an unfortunate side effect of the Mac platform's renewed popularity.

Every time you read about Apple's remarkable sales growth, its string of quarterly profits and the good marks it gets from Wall Street and the popular media, consider that the malicious folks who write computer viruses are reading the same stories. This is an invitation to them to bring their dirty work to our favorite platform.

Virus Myths

Some of the most annoying viruses actually manifest themselves as e-mail warnings about a virus. One popular example was "Good Times," which appeared as an e-mail message warning about the dangers of such a virus. The warning was couched in language that made it seem as if it originated from an official source.

The message asked people to pass the e-mail on to alert others of the dangers from infection by this alleged virus, which supposedly did its dirty work soon as you opened an e-mail that contained it.

The Myths and Reality of Mac Viruses

The message was actually a hoax. No such virus existed, but the spread of this e-mail alarmed many people unnecessarily. In a sense, the spread of the warning about a bogus virus was the actual infection.

If you receive messages of this sort, ignore them. Don't pass them on to others. In fact, *America Online* (*AOL*) and most ISPs prohibit the spread of chain letters and unsolicited e-mail. So, not only do you cause distress to others by sending such warnings, you also place your online account in jeopardy.

Protecting Yourself Against a Virus

Even with the relative paucity of Mac viruses, you should not be overconfident. So long as you access files from outside your Mac (from the Internet or from a disk someone sends you), there's the danger of virus infection.

Consider the following to protect yourself from this problem of computer viruses.

Buy Virus Protection Software

This is the best possible and easiest way to guard your Mac against those nasty viruses. The older free and shareware programs, such as Disinfectant and Virus Detective, are history. The range of Mac viruses became too involved to allow these simple programs to remain up to date. And, sad to say, shareware programs seldom yield enough income to justify their development.

NOTE   *Virus Detective was actually the first virus program I used. Author Jeff Schulman kept it alive for a number of years, getting great reviews for his work. The software continued to be updated even though many of the folks who downloaded and installed the product never sent in their checks for their copies. Finally he read the handwriting on the wall and realized the sad fact that many shareware authors face—only a small percentage of users pay for shareware even though they continue to use the product beyond the trial period.*

But two powerful commercial virus programs can get the job done.

Norton AntiVirus from Symantec and Virex from Network Associates can protect you from nearly any known virus. In addition, they warn you against so-called "suspicious" activities that may indicate an attempt to spread a virus on your Mac.

You should, however, not be content just to install the software. Both programs incorporate the capability to check automatically for updates, so you can be assured you have up-to-date protection. This is important because the capability to protect yourself against a virus depends on being able to detect the specific way in which it affects your Mac and to provide an antidote against that effect. Mac virus software developers are constantly on the alert for new virus strains. Once they discover such viruses, they analyze them, isolate what they do, and find a way to stop them in their tracks.

NOTE   *In addition to being protected against new viruses, you want to make sure your virus software remains compatible with your Mac as you upgrade your system software to new versions or buy new Mac hardware. A case in point is Virex 6, which came out shortly before Mac OS 9 was released. Unfortunately, it wasn't compatible with Apple's new operating system (you'd get a crash as soon as the Virex Control Panel loads during startup). As this book went to press, Network Associates was putting the finishing touches on Virex 6.1, the Mac OS 9 compatible version.*

Don't Forget Regular Backups

In addition to arming yourself with the latest virus protection software, it's important to have a spare copy of a critical document, in case the original is infected by an unknown virus.

While virus programs attempt to remove infections from a file, no guarantee exists that the removal process is perfect. In some cases, the file itself may be damaged.

You can manually back up your files to another drive. Or, you can use a dedicated backup program such as Dantz's Retrospect. Then, even if your original file is damaged by a virus, you can use your backup to get back to work.

Chapter 29 covers the entire subject of backups in more detail. Once your virus detection software is set up, you want to consider a regular backup regimen for additional protection.

Watch Out for Strange E-mail

As previously mentioned, some viruses can infect your computer through a program downloaded to your computer from an e-mail someone sent you. The safest procedure is only to download files from people you know well. Even then, you should scan the file using your virus protection software to be safe. As an added measure or protection, contact the sender to confirm a file is genuine if you receive an e-mail you didn't expect.

If you get a message from someone you don't know offering you a file you didn't know you were supposed to get, avoid the message at all costs. Deleting the file right away is best.

The Myths and Reality
of Mac Viruses

> CAUTION
>
> *AOL has a feature called Automatic AOL, which allows it to schedule sessions to log on and send and retrieve your e-mail and message board postings. One of the options available is to automatically download files attached to e-mail (it's a preference setting when you set up Automatic AOL). AOL is also designed to expand compressed files when you log off. I suggest disabling the option to automatically download files. You can easily retrieve files attached to e-mail when you go online if you really want them.*

Online Services Scan Files

AOL, CompuServe, and most ISPs and software publishers routinely scan the files they offer for the presence of viruses. However, that doesn't mean you shouldn't be protected as well. For example, no way exists to check against a virus that hasn't been isolated yet.

In addition, it's important to note that some services, such as AOL, depend in large part on unpaid volunteers to scan files before they are posted. While these volunteers are dedicated and responsible, they may not always have access to the latest virus protection programs.

Take comfort that the files are checked; however, it never hurts for you to check again when the files are retrieved. Fortunately, the major virus protection programs I describe in this chapter can do this checking for you automatically.

AOL E-mail Viruses

Because AOL is the largest online service, it is a target for junk e-mail and Trojan horse viruses. A Trojan horse is, as in the classical myth, something that masquerades as something it is not. In the case of a virus, it may come as a benign or helpful application or document file.

Almost daily, thousands of AOL members get e-mail containing files that purport to enhance the user experience. Fortunately for Mac users, most of these files are Windows-only, but they are designed to steal your password and send it to the unscrupulous developer of the program. Just ignore the files, whether or not you think they are Mac files.

Here's another chronic problem: You get e-mail or an instant message from someone purporting to be from AOL's customer service department. A network problem has occurred, they say, and they need your password and, perhaps, your billing information to fix the problem. Otherwise, you will lose your account.

AOL puts up warnings here, there, and everywhere that no one will ever ask you online for your password or billing information. These instant messages are there strictly to steal your password and your credit card numbers, nothing more, nothing less. If you receive such a notice or an instant message, report the problem to AOL. The AOL keyword **Notify AOL** can be used to bring up report forms.

Another online scheme involves a message that actually takes you to another Web site to give out your information or check alleged unread Web-based e-mail. Once again, it is a scheme to extract your personal information. If you receive any message on AOL with a Web link you're not sure about, just CONTROL-CLICK the link, and select the View Address command in the Contextual menu. This information will show you whether or not the link points to an AOL area or not.

NOTE *Although the warnings about giving out personal information are prominently displayed all over the service, it's a sad fact that lots of folks fall for these password-stealing schemes. There's something about couching a request in official language, with an official signature that makes them seem authentic.*

Lock Removable Media

You cannot infect a locked disk. If you receive a file on a removable disk, such as a floppy, SuperDisk, Jaz or Zip, check it for viruses. If the disk is clean, lock it. When the disk is locked, you cannot write files to it, and viruses cannot infect it. For floppy disks and SuperDisks, there's a convenient lock switch.

Zip and Jaz disks cannot be locked via a switch. You need to use Iomega's Tools software or whatever program you use to format those disks.

How to Choose Virus Protection Software

You can never know when a virus will strike your computer. Programmers are constantly designing new viruses that can do nasty things to your Mac. Even if no viruses have shown up on Macs in a while, this doesn't mean one won't occur again.

The best way to protect your Mac from viruses is to buy virus protection software. Make sure you constantly update your software whenever new versions

How to Choose Virus Protection Software

are released by the software's publisher. Although older versions of many programs work just fine with Mac OS 9, that's not the case with virus software.

Virus software is tightly integrated with the operating system. It must be, to detect the presence of virus strains. As a result, major system software changes are apt to render such programs incompatible.

In addition, software publishers often remove support for their older programs. Part of the reason is to encourage the purchase of updates, an important source of revenue. While this may not be a significant issue when it comes to other programs, the need to keep virus software compatible with the Mac OS to detect new virus strains means you often have to bite the bullet and upgrade when new versions are released.

In the interim, as explained below, the publisher will make downloadable virus detection string and bug fix updates available, at least until the new version is ready to roll (and sometimes shortly thereafter, so long as the old version supports the same sort of virus detection updates).

Setting Up a Regular Virus Protection Program

The best way to be protected is to keep your virus software extensions running and to make sure the programs are configured to scan the disks you insert into your Mac's drives and the files you download from Internet sources.

Here's a brief overview of the two popular virus detection programs and how to take the best advantage of their features.

Norton AntiVirus

Norton AntiVirus 6 (see Figure 30-1), which shipped shortly before Mac OS 9 was released, not only includes the capability to scan your computer for viruses, but also includes several other useful features:

- **Auto-Repair** This feature automatically repairs any infected or damaged files on your hard drive. This process isn't perfect, though, and realizing some files may simply be unusable once infected is important. This is one reason I emphasize the need for backups.

- **Scheduled scans** You can set up the program scan your Mac completed at specified times by clicking the Tools menu and choosing the Scheduler option (see Figure 30-2). Then you can decide what times and dates you want your computer to be scanned, as well as what disks you want to be scanned.

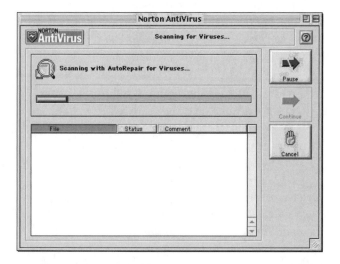

FIGURE 30-1   Norton AntiVirus enables you to scan for viruses on your computer and more

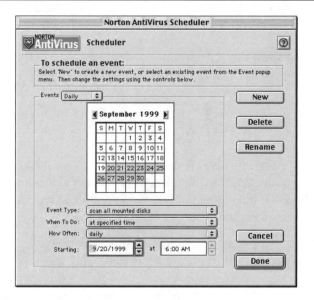

FIGURE 30-2   The Scheduler enables you to choose when you want to have your computer scanned for viruses

Setting Up a Regular Virus Protection Program

The virus programs discussed here speed up performance by keeping a tracking record of the files already scanned. Once that's done, they only need to scan for new or changed files the next time they run, which sharply reduces the time it takes for rescans.

■ **Scans compressed files**   Files compressed in any of the most popular compression protocols can be checked by Norton AntiVirus automatically. The process is clever. The files are expanded into RAM and then checked. This way, your actual files aren't constantly being expanded and recompressed on disk (which can generally add to file fragmentation).

When a virus program checks for compressed files, its scanning process takes much longer to complete. Also consider that a virus in a compressed archive can do nothing till you expand the file. Then the virus program will detect the infection and stop it from doing its dirty work. So as a practical matter, you should consider turning off this option if you wish to get better scan performance.

■ **Scan for strange activities**   AntiVirus doesn't just check for the presence of known viruses on your computer, it also checks for activities that may result from an infection by the unknown strain of a virus.

Part of the price you pay for good virus detection is that fairly routine activities, such as expanding a compressed file containing software, can trigger a warning about a suspicious file. You should examine the warnings and see what they refer to, but most of the time, you can simply allow the action to take place.

■ **SafeZone**   You can also choose a location on your hard drive where scanning occurs automatically. If a file is copied to that area, whether it comes from the Internet or another hard drive, the program will scan for the presence of viruses.

■ **LiveUpdate**   This features, similar to Apple's own Software Update feature, searches Symantec's Web site automatically to find updates for the program to fix bugs or to guard against new viruses. You can configure this feature to work automatically at scheduled intervals (at least once a month is best).

The LiveUpdate feature also works for Norton Utilities and, if you also have that program installed, it searches for updates for both.

Virex

The other virus protection program is Network Associates' Virex 6. Like Norton AntiVirus (see Figure 30-3), Virex can scan for the presence of viruses and activity that may be caused by viruses.

CAUTION   *You need version 6.1 of the Virex Control Panel or later for Mac OS 9 compatibility. Version 6.0 simply crashes at startup. Check with the publisher's Web site, http://www.nai.com, for the latest version.*

Here are some other features:

■ **Infected File Repair**   Virex can automatically repair or delete infected files. As with Norton AntiVirus, you should be cautious about using files that have been repaired because the repair process isn't always successful. It's best to revert to a backup, if you have one.

■ **Schedule Editor**   You can set up this function to scan your Mac's drives at specified intervals (see Figure 30-4). This can by done by choosing this option from the Schedule menu. At this point, you cannot only decide what days and times you want your computer to be scanned, but also what kind of scan you want to do (scan for viruses, repair infected files, or update the software) and what disks you want to scan.

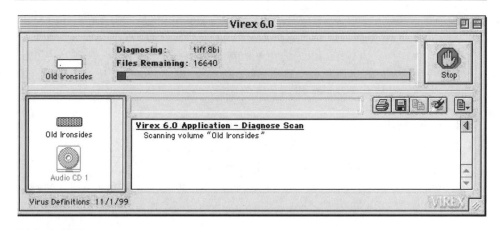

FIGURE 30-3   Virex scans for viruses and virus-related activity

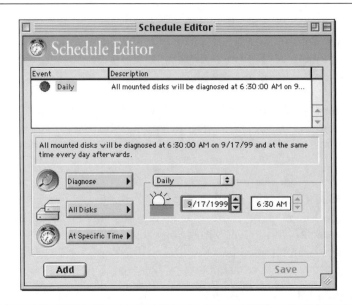

FIGURE 30-4   You can set up a schedule for Virex to check automatically for viruses, repair infected files, or update the software

- **Scan compressed files**   This feature is limited to StuffIt files only. It's not quite as comprehensive as the one offered by Norton AntiVirus, which can handle compressed files in a number of formats.

> **NOTE**   *In all fairness, I should point out that a virus residing in a compressed file won't do any damage until you actually expand the file. At that point, you don't need the capability to check compressed files to reveal the presence of the virus. It's also important to point out that Virex tends to be a little slower about scanning compressed files than Norton AntiVirus, so turning off this option can be a huge time saver.*

- **Scan-At-Download**   Virex checks files downloaded from the Internet or retrieved from a disk or network.

- **Support for Control Strip and Contextual Menus**   In addition to the handy Control Strip, you can summon many of the features of Virex via Apple's Contextual menus.

- **Use Heuristics**   Virex can use its internal logic to scan for any activity caused by viruses on your computer and return the report to the user. This is similar to Norton AntiVirus' capability to check for the presence of suspicious files or suspicious activities.

- **Updates Over the Internet**   Similar to Symantec's LiveUpdate feature, Virex can be configured to check the publisher's Web site for updates to the software to fix bugs or to guard against infection from newly discovered viruses or strains. Virex can also work with Virex's Schedule Editor, so it automatically checks for updates on a regular basis.

Problems with Virus Programs

As previously explained, virus software works closely with your Mac's system software because it needs to check for any activity related to viruses, as well as the presence of virus strains on your computer.

So, when Apple releases an update to its system software, virus programs are among the first culprits for incompatibilities. In addition, because virus programs work with so many parts of the Mac OS, they may also interact unfavorably with other system extensions.

In this section, I cover some of the problems you may encounter with a virus program. Remember, though, the price of protection may sometimes result in a performance hit. You want to be on the alert for some of the issues.

- **Extensions load slowly at startup**   This problem is more evident with Norton AntiVirus than with Virex. Symantec's program scans all your system extensions for any viruses during startup, and it slows the pace of the startup process rather severely. Just let the program work and clench your teeth as the march of extensions drags by slowly.

- **Applications slow to launch**   If the program is large, requiring lots of support files (such as Adobe and Microsoft products), it takes longer for your virus software to scan all those components to make sure no viruses exist. Once again, you should just be aware of this problem and accept it as another inevitable symptom of constant vigilance.

NOTE   *You can speed performance by turning off the option for your virus software to scan items as they're opened. But that also reduces the flexibility of the protection they offer. The latest generation of virus programs have managed to reduce the slow-launch symptom to manageable levels.*

Problems with Virus Programs

■ **Starts scanning floppies or other removable disks when inserted**
This is perfectly normal behavior and the sort of behavior you want. You can disable the option (they are separate for each program). But because removable media, such as floppies, Jaz and Zip disks, and SuperDisks are common entry points for viruses, you want to keep this protection active.

NOTE *If you have a floppyless Mac, such as the iBook, iMac, and Power Mac G3 and G4, the floppy drive or SuperDisk drive you connect is considered a removable drive. You want to make sure the option is appropriately configured to allow for scanning such media.*

■ **Strange crashes after installing a new version of system**   If you experience strange crashes after installing a new version of Apple's system software (even the Mac OS 9), check the publisher's Web site for any available updates. For example, as mentioned earlier, when the Mac OS 9 was released, Virex was incompatible with the new system version. This problem required Network Associates to release a 6.1 update to the software to allow it to work with Mac OS 9.

NOTE *Sometimes Apple's Mac OS ReadMe file alerts you to known updates, but quite often, the documents are prepared some time before the actual system comes out, so newly discovered conflicts aren't listed.*

Do You Have a Virus?

Even if you do take the precautions previously listed, and you do whatever is possible to avoid the inevitable, sometimes even the most careful Mac user may eventually be confronted with a virus. Here's what you should do:

■ **Make sure it's a real virus**   If you encounter constant crashes, slow performance, or other problems in a specific program, this may not be a virus at all. This may be a conflict between extensions, a corrupted preference folder, or using a program that isn't working properly with Mac OS 9. Try running the program with only a base set of extensions, as well as those needed to make the program work, and see what happens. Then, one by one, activate all your extensions to see if you can isolate your problem. If this doesn't work, try throwing out all the preference folders for the program and try launching it again. If this doesn't work, check Chapters 25 and 31 for more detailed troubleshooting information.

If you've been infected with a virus while connected to a network using Ethernet or AppleTalk, turn off AppleTalk so others who may access your computer across the network are protected.

- **Replace infected files** Use the virus protection software on your computer to pinpoint any files infected by the virus. Once you locate those files, trash them immediately, or move them off your hard drive before they become a problem for the uninfected files and programs remaining on your computer. Then, assuming you back up your files every day, copy the most recent versions of your infected files from your backup tape, or wherever you're storing your critical files, to your computer. Put them on your computer one-by-one, and scan them before you do so, just in case the virus is still around and can attack these files. While this can take a while if you have a slow computer and/or lots of files, it's better to do this slowly than to make a mistake and have the virus infect your files all over again.

A Short List of Known Viruses

Through the years, a number of Mac virus strains have been discovered. Some of these aren't especially relevant to Mac OS 9, or they haven't been reported in years. But, as point of reference, you may want to be aware of their names, in case you encounter them in your travels:

- **MDEF Virus** This virus is also known as Garfield and Top Cat. It infects application files, causing them to beep once you open them.

- **CODE 252 Virus** Obviously, it must have been April Fool's Day when the programmer designed this virus. It only occurs if you launch an infected application or system file between June 6 and December 31 in any year. It displays the following message (and despite what it says, it doesn't erase your disks):

You have a virus.
Ha Ha Ha Ha Ha Ha Ha
Now erasing all disks…
Ha Ha Ha Ha Ha Ha Ha
P.S. Have a nice day
Ha Ha Ha Ha Ha Ha Ha
(Click to continue…)

■ **CODE 32767 Virus**   This virus can apparently trash documents once every month, but it hasn't spread.

■ **CODE 1 Virus**   This virus causes strange system crashes by renaming your startup disk "Trent Saburo."

■ **Scores Virus**   This virus is also called Eric, NASA, San Jose Flu, and Vault. It changes the icons for the Note Pad and Scrapbook files in your System Folder to blank sheets of paper with turned-down corners. They won't go away even after you rebuild the desktop. Although they can spread to your other applications once your computer has been infected, this virus doesn't do any serious damage.

■ **Flag Virus (also called WDEF C)**   This virus attacks system files and can overwrite a WDEF resource of ID 0 in your system, potentially causing problems with certain files.

■ **Macro viruses**   Because Microsoft Office programs, such as Excel and Word, are so popular on the Mac, macro viruses are common. They are also cross-platform, meaning both Mac and Windows users can be infected (as previously mentioned, though computers running Windows have far more virus infections to protect against). The system files on PCs may be corrupted as a result of a macro virus. On the Mac, the symptoms are not as severe, but they are still quite irritating. The usual symptoms are sudden password-protection of a document and being unable to save a document as anything except a template.

NOTE   *If you run a Windows emulator on your Mac, you want to arm yourself with Windows antivirus software. While a Windows emulator won't be susceptible to many low-level viruses that may do nasty things to a PC's bios (or ROM), enough mischief can still be wrought to get protection. The publishers of the major virus programs also have Windows products.*

■ **AutoStart Worm**   This virus turned up in 1998. It's called a "worm" because it doesn't actually use programs and files to spread itself. Instead, it duplicates itself between disks and adds invisible files to your hard drive, causing strange activity on the drive. Some of your data could be overwritten by random data. A fast way to protect yourself is to turn off the AutoPlay feature in the QuickTime Settings control panel or in the control strip module with the little CD on it. If you believe you're computer is already infected, use your antivirus software to pinpoint the virus and eliminate it.

NOTE

The AutoStart virus came so quickly and was so unexpected, some infected commercial software CDs actually shipped. Fortunately, the publishers managed to isolate the problem and recalled the disks before they could damage anyone's Mac.

■ **CODE 9811 Virus**   The virus is extremely serious because it replaces all your applications with files containing names that seem to be nothing more than gibberish. The background on your desktop appears to look like electronic worms and a message says, "You have been hacked by the Praetorians." This virus seems to appear only in 25 percent of infected installations and only appears on a Monday.

■ **nVIR Virus**   nVIR is a virus that infects your system files. Every time you run an application, it will also be infected. Another system is a voice message saying, "Don't panic," which can be heard if Talking Alerts is turned on in the Speech Control Panel.

NOTE

nVIR was the first virus I encountered face to face way back in 1989. It was only a few days after I installed a new Mac that this virus reared its ugly head. I hadn't installed virus software yet (didn't think about it), and I was forced to reinstall the system software and a number of applications (after I downloaded a shareware virus program to dispose of the actual infection). I may be a slow learner, but I try not to make the same mistake twice, and no Mac I've owned since then has ever run without active virus protection.

■ **The SevenDust Virus**   This dangerous virus, also called MDEF 9806 or MDEF 666, consists of a series of strains. Two of the strains may erase nonapplication files on your startup disk. Another strain of SevenDust appeared to be a video acceleration extension called *Graphics Accelerator* (with a nonprinting file prefix, which causes it to load first when you start up your computer). At the time, however, the virus caused a lot of confusion because one of Apple's own extensions, used for Macs with ATI graphics cards, was named Graphics Accelerator. The real extension was later renamed ATI Graphics Accelerator, however, removing the confusion. If any chance exists that the fake is still there, any modern virus protection program can find it.

■ **MBDF Virus**   This is a Trojan horse virus. While these files or programs may appear to do something good for your computer, they may instead infect or damage files when you use them. This particular virus can be spread through games like 10 Tile Puzzle, Obnoxious Tetris, and Tetricycle. After your computer has been infected, MBDF can damage both application and system files. You need to do a clean installation of Mac OS 9 if any of your system files are damaged.

- **INIT-M Virus** This destructive virus can damage files and folders, but it only appears on Friday the 13th. File names are changed to random combinations of only eight characters, while folder names have from one to eight characters. Worst of all, the file type and creator information (this is needed for the Finder to link documents to the applications they were used or created in) are changed, and the creation and modification dates become January 1, 1904. Also, one or more of the icon names on your computer may change to "Virus MindCrime."

- **T4 Virus** This Trojan horse virus was hidden in a game known as GoMuku. After infecting your Mac, this virus can also infect your programs, including the Finder, and attempts to change the System file. Programs infected by this virus can't be repaired and, if the system file is changed, extensions are unable to load when starting up your computer.

- **ZUC Virus** This virus infects your programs and causes the mouse cursor to move all across the screen whenever you launch an infected application. It can also change your desktop pattern and cause mysterious disk activity to occur. Macs connected across a network can also be infected.

Summing Up

Computer viruses are nothing to take lightly, and Mac users are definitely vulnerable to infections. If you buy the latest antivirus software and keep it current, however, you can keep the risk of infection to a minimum. You should be extremely wary of downloading any files from the Internet unless you know the source who sent you the file.

In Chapter 31, you learn how to become a troubleshooting ace with Mac OS 9 and a few tried-and-true procedures.

The Mac Troubleshooting Guide

How would you feel if you switched on your microwave oven and the display said "System Error?" No doubt, you wouldn't believe it and you would never expect such a thing to happen, except in a rare instance of hardware failure.

Yet we tolerate this same sort of behavior with personal computers. A stable Mac or Windows computer is one that doesn't freeze several times a day or where applications don't constantly quit.

Must it be so?

The Mac operating system, even from its humble beginnings in 1984, has always been apt to crash occasionally (as is the consumer version of Windows, for that matter).

Your Mac works by a complex interaction among a number of hardware and software components, made all the more complex because literally millions of possible system combinations exist. Even if all the Macs in your company use Mac OS 9, it doesn't mean they are the same. Different models, different memory capacities, and different options could be available and surely, they don't all run the same software, have the same files, or have the same document files.

When the interaction breaks down (whether because of a conflict with the software or hardware), a program quits, your Mac freezes, or, on a rare occasion, it simply refuses to start.

In this chapter, the focus is on common hardware and software problems, with a special emphasis on the new problems wrought by the major changes in Mac OS 9 over previous versions.

Troubleshooting in Brief

While the potential for system-related conflicts is huge, isolating the causes is usually a simple process of trial and error (even if you don't have a direct clue to a specific program as the cause of the problem).

The vast majority of issues are simple software conflicts. One program or system extension doesn't play nicely with another, or it has a problem with the newer system version or new Mac hardware. When a program is being designed, there is no way to predict how future products might impact it. In general, if a program is designed strictly to Apple's guidelines, it should work most of the time, but for good reasons, publishers may have to take a few shortcuts to get something to work. While you can criticize those shortcuts as bad programming practices, the capability to write software isn't a cut-and-dried process. Many highly creative elements are involved and, sometimes, you must bend the rules to accomplish a difficult task in an efficient way.

In fact, many old programs run fine with Mac OS 9. I have software from the early 1990s that I still use nearly every day without a lick of trouble and, more often than not, you may find the same thing is true.

If you do find a program has stopped working, look at the information in the next two sections about known problems with Mac OS 9 and solutions.

In addition, consult Chapter 25, which guides you through the process of using Apple's Extensions Manager (see Figure 31-1) or Casady & Greene's marvelous Conflict Catcher (see Figure 31-2) to help you find the cause of repeatable crashes.

If you follow those steps, you can cope with most Mac software and system hassles with a reasonable chance for success. I use these same techniques when I encounter problems with my systems. Even Mac book authors aren't immune to troubles; in fact, we're often more prone to them because an author often has to look at a wide variety of products, even prerelease versions, to complete a book on time.

Coping with System and Hardware Conflicts

As explained in Chapter 1, Mac OS 9 is, under the surface, a major update to the Mac operating system. In part, it's paving the way for the migration to Mac OS X,

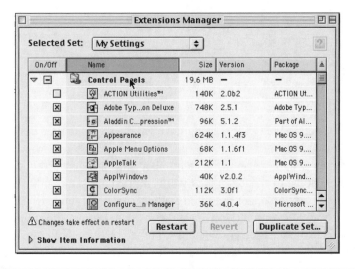

FIGURE 31-1   Extensions Manager comes free with the Mac OS and it enables you to manage your system extensions

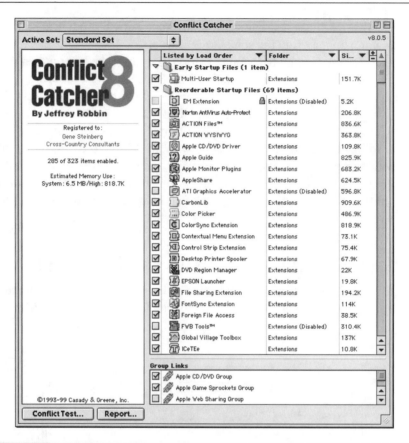

FIGURE 31-2   Casady & Green's Conflict Catcher has a Conflict Test to help you isolate conflicts

but in other respects, Mac OS 9 is designed to make the Mac user experience more efficient and more reliable.

By the same token, this also means a number of programs need updates to work with Mac OS 9. Some of these updates were shipped at the same time the new operating system version came out, while others came out later. If you upgraded from an older Mac OS version, you should consider some of these updates.

While this is by no means a complete list, I assembled a list of known problems with Mac OS 9 and with Apple and other third-party system components. The list, along with the most common solutions, follows.

■ **Apple Color StyleWriter 4000 and HP Inkjet Printers**   The last Color StyleWriter was basically just a relabeled HP printer. This printer's software is removed by the Mac OS 9 installation. In addition, many HP inkjets have drivers that do not support Mac OS 9. The best solution is to contact HP or visit its Web site (http://www.hp.com) to look for software updates for your particular model. The Color StyleWriter 4000, by the way, reportedly works fine with DeskJet 600 series software.

■ **Apple CD-ROM Extension and Third-Party Drives**   The Apple CD/DVD drivers are designed to work with CD drives from Apple and they do not support non-Apple products. Because the installation of Mac OS 9 includes the Apple driver, you should remove it from the Extensions folder after the installation is complete and you restart your Mac. Then you should reinstall the CD software you normally use with that drive. Also check with the publisher to make sure the CD software is compatible with Mac OS 9.

■ **At Ease Doesn't Work with Mac OS 9**   Apple's new Multiple Users feature is an outgrowth of At Ease in many respects. You'll want to disable At Ease and stick with Multiple Users. If that solution doesn't suit your environment, you might want to consider moving to a third-party security program. Options include DiskGuard and FileGuard from ASD Software, and DiskLock and OnGuard from Power On Software. You want to confirm the program you're buying is Mac OS 9-compatible first, however, as some of these programs were in the update state at press time.

■ **ATI Graphic Cards**   Although Canada's ATI Technologies supplies the graphic cards and controller chips for many Macs, its retail cards have had problems with Mac OS 9. The solution is to look for the latest ATI Universal driver from VersionTracker.com or at ATI's Web site (http://www.atitech.com).

NOTE   *This problem doesn't affect the ATI graphic cards Apple provides with its computers as standard issue. The ATI drivers installed as part of Mac OS 9 or the latest version of Open GL are fully compatible.*

■ **Color QuickCam**   The Color QuickCam, from Logitech (formerly a Connectix product), is a neat desktop video camera. The driver software may be incompatible with Mac OS 9, though. If you get one of those Type 119 errors, consider contacting the manufacturer about an update or check with VersionTracker.com.

■ **Display resolution changes**   If you do a clean installation of Mac OS 9, whatever resolution setting you had previously is gone, and the default setting, whatever that is, is going to be used on your first restart. You can

Coping with System and Hardware Conflicts

easily switch it back by the Monitors Control Strip or Monitors Control Panel. If you had a number of desktop icons on view, be prepared to rearrange your desktop icons.

- **Don't Forget Your Firmware Updates** If you attempt to install Mac OS 9 on an iMac or Blue & White Power Macintosh G3, you'll be asked to run an update if you have an older firmware version. These updates are in the Utilities folder of your Mac OS 9 installation CD. Before you attempt to run the update, read the instructions carefully.

- **DSL Connections** DSL is still an emerging technology. Some of the software used for DSL products, such as MacPoET 1.0 (a program used to provide PPP connections over an Ethernet network), may be incompatible. One solution is to make sure your Mac runs with virtual memory turned on (which is, for most Mac OS 9 users, a good idea anyway). Or, contact your DSL provider about getting version MacPoET 1.1 or later.

- **GeoPort Telecom Adapter Doesn't Work** The now-discontinued GeoPort was designed to allow a Mac to emulate the functions of a modem. The GeoPort never caught on, though, and a real modem works much better. Mac OS 9 is the nail in the coffin for this feature. If you need to use a modem, consider buying one. 56K modems are usually less than $100 and they work much better than the GeoPort ever did.

NOTE *If you have one of the original 56K modems, it may need a manufacturer's firmware update to support the final V.90 standard. The original models supported preliminary standards, either K56Flex or x2, and, unless the ISP also supports the older standards, you may not be getting the performance you should expect.*

- **The Case of the Disappearing Desktop Items** When another user logs on to a Mac set up using the Multiple Users feature, the items you put on the desktop are not present. This is because this feature gives each Normal user (within the limits you grant as owner) his own desktop, onto which he can deposit his own choice of icons (beyond the standard disk icons, of course).

- **Global Village PC Card Modems and Mac OS 9** If you're using a PowerBook with a Global Village modem installed, expect a Finder crash when you boot with Mac OS 9. If you encounter this problem, check with

Global Village for a downloadable update to its PC Card Enabler software. This can address the problem.

■ **iMac Update 1.0 Warning**   This update replaces the MacOS ROM file on the iMac with a version incompatible with Mac OS 9. Don't use this because it causes your iMac to freeze on startup.

■ **Iomega Driver**   The Iomega Driver is used for both Jaz and Zip drives (including the expansion bay version for PowerBooks). The exceptions to this rule are the USB-flavors of Zip drives, which require separate USB extensions (or Mac OS 9's USB Device Extension). If you want to run Mac OS 9 from a Jaz or Zip disk, be sure you have virtual memory run directly from a fixed drive (such as your Mac's regular hard drive). The location of the virtual memory swap file, used to handle unused data, can be changed in the Memory Control Panel.

■ **LaserWriter Fax No Longer Works**   Apple's LaserWriter 8f printer driver actually enables you to send and receive files with a few Apple printers equipped with fax cards. This feature and the accompanying printer driver aren't supported under Mac OS 9, so instead, you need to use the standard LaserWriter 8 driver. This also means your printer's fax card is rendered useless, so you must look for another fax alternative, such as a fax modem or a standalone fax machine (or multifunction printer).

■ **LocalTalk and Serial Printer Conflicts**   The usual setup is to disable AppleTalk when you switch from a LocalTalk printer to a serial printer, if the two are connected to the same serial port. Unfortunately, the port may not always reset when you turn off AppleTalk, even though the AppleTalk Control Panel indicates it has been disabled. The solution is to restart your Mac.

■ **Multiple Users and Epson Printers**   Epson's popular line of color inkjet printers are top sellers in the Mac marketplace. If you want to use one of these printers in a Mac configured with the Multiple Users feature, the owner must give users access to All Printers. The second step befalls someone with Limited or Panels access. Such a user must also set up the printer driver to send print files to a spool folder placed in that user's folder. This is done by invoking the Epson print dialog box. Then you click the Tools button and after that, click Configuration. You can then specify a new location for the Temporary Spool and Temporary High Speed Copies folders so they are accessible in that user's environment.

■ **PowerBook 3400/G3 Ethernet Problems**   If you have problems accessing the Ethernet port, check for the presence of the PowerBook 3400/G3 Modem extension. Even if you don't intend to use the modem on these models, the extension is also required to activate the Ethernet port. If the file is missing, open Extensions Manager and see if it's there. If the file isn't there, you need to run your Mac OS 9 system installation, using the Add/Remove feature and a customized installation to restore this component. Read Chapter 2 for more information about Mac OS installation options.

■ **PowerBook, Zip Drives, and the Control Strip**   This problem affects only some PowerBook models (your mileage may vary). If you're using a VST Technologies Expansion Bay Zip drive, the Zip disks won't show up in the Media Bay Control Strip menu. This is nothing to be concerned about, as they should appear on the desktop (assuming your Iomega Driver is properly installed).

■ **Missing StyleWriter Printer Drivers**   The StyleWriter drivers have been renamed with Mac OS 9, which is bound to complicate matters because the older versions of these drivers isn't compatible. If you have a StyleWriter, StyleWriter II, or StyleWriter 1200, use the driver labeled Color SW 1500. For the StyleWriter 2200 and 2400, use the one labeled Color SW 2500.

■ **Processor Upgrade Card Software**   Most of the processor upgrade cards, such as G3 and G4 upgrades, require special software to activate some hardware features, such as the upgrade module's backside cache (a major factor in improved G3 and G4 performance). Check with such manufacturers as Newer Technology and Sonnet Technologies about updates for their software. Again, VersionTracker.com is a good source to locate such updates.

NOTE *The Encore line of G3 and G4 updates from Sonnet work in the ZIF slots of Power Macintosh G3s without the need of any software at all, so you don't have any concerns about compatibility issues.*

■ **SCSI Accelerator Products**   If you have a SCSI card from Adaptec, AdvanSys, ATTO, Initio, or Orange Micro (to name a few recent product lines), check with the manufacturers about the need for hardware (firmware) updates. Some cards can be flashed, which means you download a utility from the company's Web site and run it to update the card. Others actually require you to swap out the ROM chip on the card itself (or have the manufacturer do it for you). If you experience startup problems or frequent crashes with one of these cards installed, consult the manufacturer for assistance or check its Web site for upgraded compatibility information.

■ **SuperDisk and Mac OS 9**   The popular Imation SuperDisk line offers compatibility with HD floppy disks and the 120MB SuperDisk format on USB-equipped Macs. But the software that comes with the drive may conflict with Apple's USB Driver Extension included with Mac OS 9. The solution is to disable the SuperDisk drivers (the drive works anyway) or, better yet, get version 3.2 or later of the SuperDisk software from Imation's Web site (http://www.imation.com).

■ **TCP/IP File Sharing Doesn't Work**   One of the great features of Mac OS 9 is the capability to share files over the Internet. This way, regardless of where any two Macs are located in the world, an Internet connection is all that's necessary to connect the two. If your setups are correct (see Chapter 27), look in your Mac's Extensions folder to see if ShareWay IP Personal Bgnd is present. If not, make sure it's enabled or consider doing an Add/Remove custom installation of the networking components of Mac OS 9.

NOTE   *This is one of the reasons I suggest you should be careful about throwing out stuff in your System Folder. It's so easy, with such strange labeling of system components, to toss the wrong thing and suffer with a system-related problem as a result.*

■ **Type 119 Error**   This new Mac OS 9 system error rears its ugly head on a few programs that do not support a key change of the new operating system. This system error is, in part, due to the increase in the maximum number of open files supported from 348 files to 8,169 files. In the past, Apple has warned programmers against certain practices in setting up their programs to recognize this file limitation. For whatever reason, some programmers engage in those practices anyway and the result is this system error. The solution is to disable the extension that produces this error via Extensions Manager, and then contact the publisher (or use the resources mentioned at the end of this chapter) to get the new version.

Coping with System and Hardware Conflicts

NOTE   *Because a programmer does something that isn't 100% in compliance with Apple's guidelines doesn't mean they did something wrong when they created a program. Sometimes a programmer may have to be inventive when trying to make a special feature work, even if they have to bend the rules a little bit.*

- **USB Driver Problems**   You install the software and then plug in a USB device, such as a SuperDisk or CD drive, and it doesn't work. The first solution is to stick with Apple's USB Driver Extension, part of the standard Mac OS 9 installation on a USB-equipped Mac. The USB Driver Extension provides native support for both the SuperDisk and Zip drives (both 100MB and 250MB versions), plus a variety of other mechanisms. If you install a manufacturer's driver instead, the conflict might prevent the device from working.

- **Voice Password and PowerBook 5300**   The PowerBook 5300 series was one of Apple's most troublesome lines. It had a smoking beginning, literally, when a few of the initial production units apparently overheated because of a defect in the lithium ion batteries originally provided (they were removed from production before the 5300 series got wide distribution). In addition, Apple had to set up an extended warranty program to fix various and sundry product defects. When it comes to Mac OS 9's capability to store a password as a voice in the Multiple Users Control Panel, the ill-fated 5300 series doesn't support the feature. If you have one of these models, you must enter a password the old fashioned way, by typing it.

Coping with Application Conflicts

One reliable survey shows that over 17,000 Mac products are available. These include everything from word processing software to dedicated programs designed to run professional offices or handle scientific calculations.

There is plenty of room for conflicts, and it's a tribute to the thousands of dedicated programmers worldwide that the number of known problems, while seemingly large, isn't as daunting as it could be.

Here's a list of some known problems with popular Mac software and add-ons, and the solutions that usually address these problems:

- **Adaptec Toast and Mac OS 9**   The popular CD writing program Toast comes with a large number of CD writers. Compatibility with Mac OS 9 isn't a certainty, unless you have version 4.0.1 or later. Because older versions are often bundled with various drives, contact the driver's manufacturer or Adaptec to get the update (you probably will have to pay the standard upgrade fee).

NOTE *Our alert technical editor, Pieter Paulson, tells me he's had good luck with Toast 3.56 and Mac OS 9 (and I have used version 3.8.2 of the same program without trouble). So your mileage may vary. On the other hand, Toast 4.0 offers a bevy of new features and you may want to consider updating if you want to go beyond the basics of CD ripping and gain some new capabilities. Adaptec's Web site (http://www.adaptec.com) has information about the product upgrade.*

■ **Adobe Type Manager, Adobe Type Manager Deluxe and Adobe Type Reunion Disabled**   For the same reasons other programs fail with 119 errors (see the previous item labeled Type 119 Error), any version of ATM prior to 4.5.2 or Type Reunion prior to 2.5.2 won't run under Mac OS 9. ATM is needed not only to run PostScript fonts, but it is also required by Adobe Acrobat. Because many manuals are in electronic form now, using Adobe's PDF format, Acrobat is an essential installation. Fortunately, an easy solution exists. Go to Adobe's Web site at http://www.adobe.com and download the free updaters (for ATM 4.5 and 4.5.1, and ATR 2.5 and 2.5.1). You'd need to buy the retail upgrade for prior versions. At press time, Adobe was developing newer and later versions of these programs.

NOTE *If you don't have the free Acrobat Reader on your Mac, check the Adobe folder on your Mac OS 9 CD. The installer is there. You can also visit Adobe's Web site to get the latest version. Also, later Mac OS 9 CD's include the ATM update.*

■ **AppleWorks**   Check the CD Extras folder on your Mac OS 9 installation CD for the AppleWorks 5.0.4 updater, designed to provide full compatibility with Mac OS 9. The updater is designed to update version 5.0.3 of AppleWorks. If you have an older 5.x version (including the one originally called ClarisWorks) check with Apple's support Web site (http://www.apple.com/ support) for the 5.0.3 updater before you attempt to apply the 5.0.4 update (otherwise, the update won't work and the software will be left alone).

■ **Aladdin StuffIt Products**   Mac OS 9 installs a compatible version of DropStuff and StuffIt Expander when you go for a default installation

Coping with Application Conflicts

(which includes Internet software). Earlier versions may not work with Mac OS 9. If you didn't get the new versions of the program, you can either install the Internet access programs from your Mac OS 9 CD or visit the VersionTracker Web site (see the final section of this chapter) to check for newer versions of Aladdin's utility products.

■ **AOL 4.0 and Palm Desktop 2.5**   If you're using a Palm Pilot handheld computer and access AOL via the standard dial-up connection, you might find they don't get along well together. You can expect a port in use error message when the two programs are set up. The solution is to locate the Palm Desktop icon in the menu bar (located to the right of the Applications menu), and then launch HotSync Manager. Go to the HotSync menu, choose Setup, and turn off Palm Desktop HotSync. Version 5.0 of AOL's software, due at press time, may fix this problem.

■ **Applications Fail to Open**   Some older Mac programs do not recognize a system font other than Chicago. This setting can be easily changed in the Appearance Control Panel by clicking the Fonts tab. If the program still won't open, use the Finder's Get Info command to increase application memory by at least 300K. If neither solution works, contact the publisher of the software (or use one of the resources mentioned in the next section) to see if any updates are available.

■ **Connectix Speed Doubler Disabled**   Connectix Speed Doubler, a program that offers faster file and network transfers, and a version of the 680x0 emulator (used to run older Mac software) that's supposedly faster than Apple's, is disabled when you install Mac OS 9. At press time, Connectix hadn't decided if it wanted to do an update for the problem, but many users were clamoring for development to continue. One of the best features of Speed Doubler was its Smart Replace option, which only copies files that have actually been changed. This is especially useful for no-frills backups if only a few out of hundreds of files in a disk or folder have been changed.

■ **Connectix Virtual PC Crashes**   According to Connectix, you need version 2.1.2 or later of its popular PC emulator program for full compatibility with Mac OS 9. And upgrading to version 3.0 or later (3.0.1 was the version shipping at press time) affords you support for your Mac's USB peripherals on the Windows side (at least if you have Windows 95/98 or Windows 2000).

■ **Digital Cameras and Mac OS 9**   In addition to the Nikon View software, which I use for my Nikon CoolPix 950, drivers for other digital cameras may not function with Mac OS 9. Problems may occur with cameras from Agfa, Ricoh, Toshiba, and other manufacturers. A quick solution is to get Cameraid, a shareware program (check VersionTracker.com for a copy) that supports a number of models.

■ **Extensis Suitcase**   Suitcase was the first font manager for the Mac and, though it's moved from publisher to publisher, it continues to be updated. You should find that Suitcase 8 is mostly compatible with Mac OS 9, except for the Limited or Panel user option you set with the Multiple Users Control Panel. If you intend to set up your Mac in this fashion, you want to contact Extensis about a possible product upgrade. In addition, if you want to continue using Suitcase, you might want to see whether some of your users can be elevated to Normal user status or manually install the fonts these users require for the work they do.

■ **Final Draft**   Many screenwriters, budding or otherwise, use Final Draft to create their cinematic masterpieces. If this is your program of choice, look for version 5.0.2d or later. If you use an earlier version of this program, a danger exists of possible file corruption or loss of data, not to mention a possible freeze when you attempt to launch the program on some Macs.

■ **Kensington Input Devices and Mac OS 9**   Be on the lookout for newer versions of Kensington's MouseWorks software after you install Mac OS 9. Older versions don't support the scrolling wheel mechanism of some of Kensington's mouse replacements. Check Kensington's Web site at http://www.kensington.com or VersionTracker.com for product updates.

■ **Microsoft Office 98**   In most respects, Microsoft Office 98 is compatible with Mac OS 9. Updates do exist for Microsoft Excel and PowerPoint. These are available via VersionTracker.com or Microsoft's Web site (http://www.microsoft.com/mactopia). Microsoft Office 4.2.1, according to Apple, is incompatible with Mac OS 9 and the only solution offered is to upgrade to Office 98.

■ **Multi-Ad Creator**   Multi-Ad Services products are useful for creating retail ads and other documents. Version 4.0.4 or later of this program is considered compatible with Mac OS 9. The program also requires ATM to work with PostScript fonts, so make sure you also installed your ATM upgrade.

■ **Multiple Users and Program Preference Files**   Apple's Multiple Users feature is a great boon for home or business users who have more than one

Coping with Application Conflicts

person working on any Mac. But it also creates a few problems for some programs developed before Mac OS 9. If you set Limited and Panel access (see Chapter 6 for more information), you may have to put a program's Preferences files in the appropriately labeled folder inside the Users folder established by the Multiple Users Control Panel. AOL is one example of a program that suffers from this problem.

NOTE *One unsupported technique is to place an alias in a program's preference file, instead of placing the original within the Users folder.*

■ **Network Browser Dials Your ISP Whenever You Open the Program**   This is perfectly normal behavior. Network Browser is checking for TCP/IP services because of its capability to support file sharing, FTP, and Web file transfers. It happens if you set the TCP/IP Control Panel to make a PPP connection and Remote Access has been configured to connect automatically when you start a TCP/IP aware program. If you don't intend to use Network Browser for Internet-based file transfers, consider disabling the DNSPlugin, LDAP Client Library, LDAPPlugin, and SLPPPlugin extensions (via Extensions Manager). These files should not impact any of your Internet access, but they can prevent the automatic dialing.

CAUTION *The previous fix fits into the unsupported category, meaning it's not sanctioned by Apple. Because it's so easy to enable the extensions, if they don't do what you want, however, trying to avoid the automatic dial-ups is definitely worth trying.*

■ **Netscape Communicator and TalkBack**   When you install Netscape, a utility called *TalkBack* is part of the package. TalkBack is designed to enable you to send information automatically to Netscape's quality control people if the program has a problem. But, through version 4.7 of Communicator, TalkBack isn't compatible with Mac OS 9. Netscape recommends you remove this utility.

NOTE *Netscape 6.0 was announced as this book was being prepared for release some time in the spring or summer of 2000. Perhaps that version will include a version of TalkBack that works with Mac OS 9.*

■ **Network Cards**   If you use an Ethernet card from Kingston and other manufacturers, consult the Web site or VersionTracker.com for information to see if a new set of drivers is needed. Problems affect Ethernet 10/100 cards and similar products. Also check with manufacturers of Token Ring or ATM networking cards for possible conflicts with Mac OS 9.

■ **Norton AntiVirus** Version 6.0 or later of Symantec's virus detection software is fully compatible with Mac OS 9. If you are using an older version, it may be a good time to upgrade, as Symantec eventually stops doing virus string updates for older versions of the product.

■ **Qualcomm's Eudora** Major e-mail programs are covered in Chapter 34, which discusses how these programs compare in terms of their main features. If you find Eudora Pro suits you, make sure you have version 4.2.2 or later, to avoid a problem that occurs when you try to check your e-mail. Otherwise, you may get a –3216 or –7160 error.

NOTE *As this book went to press, Qualcomm had released version 4.3 of Eudora Pro, the one that would include ad displays for the full version if you don't pay for an upgrade. This new version runs just fine under Mac OS 9.*

■ **Retrospect** Retrospect and other backup software are covered in Chapter 29. This is my program of choice. I use Retrospect for network backups of all the Macs in my rather crowded home office. For Mac OS 9, you need version 4.1E or later, available as a free update for 4.1 users from VersionTracker.com or the publisher's Web site (http://www.dantz.com). Or, even better, get version 4.2 (it's free for users of version 4.1).

■ **SoftWindows** FWB's SoftWindows needs an update for Mac OS 9 compatibility. When you launch the program, once the Windows 95 or Windows 98 environment is present, you find the desktop icons do not respond, among other problems. Check with VersionTacker.com or FWB's Web site for the update that fixes this problem.

NOTE *If you have an older version of SoftWindows, note that the publisher is listed as Insignia Solutions. FWB, publisher of CD and hard drive software, acquired the SoftWindows product line in fall 1999.*

■ **TechTool Pro** If you want to get the most value from TechTool Pro, MicroMat's integrated disk and hardware diagnostic program, be sure you get version 2.5.2 or later. Version 3.0, which includes a virus-detection component, was due for release shortly after the publication of this book.

■ **Virex**   The issue of compatibility with Virex is rather confusing. Version 5.9 or earlier causes crashes unless you turn off the option to Scan Files When Opened. Unfortunately, this severely reduces the program's effectiveness in tracking the presence of viruses. Version 6.0, released shortly before Mac OS 9 came out, freezes at startup. Look for version 5.9.1 or 6.1 for Mac OS 9 compatibility.

NOTE   *I'm not listing a link to Network Associates' Web site to look for the update because it is, quite frankly, confusing to navigate. Check with VersionTracker.com for any downloadable updates for Virex.*

CAUTION   *Another Network Associates product, McAfee VirusScan, was available in a Mac version for a short period of time, but it has not been updated for Mac OS 9. Even if you manage to get the program to work, no virus string update exists, which makes McAfee VirusScan a less-than-satisfactory solution if you want the best possible protection from computer viruses.*

■ **Watch Out for Old Application Installers**   While most Mac OS 8 savvy program installers should be able to handle Mac OS 9 without incident, it's not always the case. And older installers, ones designed to work with the System 7 Mac environment, are apt to do some strange things. They might replace your Mac OS 9 version of AppleScript or QuickTime, or they might put ObjectSupportLib (a potential cause of system lockups) in the Extensions folder. The solution to the latter problem is simple. Trash the file; it is not needed for Mac OS 9. For the first two problems, you must run the Mac OS 9 installer, click the Add/Remove option, and then do a customized installation of Mac OS 9 to restore the missing items.

NOTE   *A recent offender happens to be Intuit's Quicken 98, which is standard issue on the iMac. If you install the program from scratch, it can wipe out the Mac OS 9 version of AppleScript and dutifully install a much older version. Quicken is described in more detail in Chapter 23 (along with steps on what to do if this problem confronts you).*

How to Check for Updates Before It's Too Late

Wouldn't it be nice if someone called you on the telephone each time a new update came out for your Mac? Or, if you got an e-mail and then you simply logged on to your ISP and got the update?

Apple has taken an important step in the right direction with its Software Update feature (see Figure 31-3), first introduced in Mac OS 9. Chapter 10 discusses the subject in more detail, but briefly, this feature enables you to get automatic updates of your system software. You can set the Software Update Control Panel to connect to Apple's Web site at regular intervals. The Software Update Control Panel locates a list of new software, if available, and then gives you the chance to download and install the new version.

If anything is missing from this feature, it's that the Software Update is limited to Apple's operating system and related software. But thousands and thousands of Mac software products are out there, and many of them get updates on a regular basis.

How can you possibly track all these updates without spending the better part of your day surfing the Net?

Fortunately, more and more programs are designed with automatic updating in mind. Two examples come from Network Associates—Virex and Symantec— the LiveUpdate feature incorporated in Norton AntiVirus and Norton Utilities.

Another solution is Update Agent, from Insider Software (see Figure 31-4). This program comes in two forms. One is a quarterly CD, which contains the actual updates for a number of popular programs, except for Apple's programs. The other is an application that simply links you to the publisher's Web site, from which you can retrieve the updates.

FIGURE 31-3   Mac OS 9's Software Update feature helps free you from having to hunt for the updates yourself

How to Check for Updates Before It's Too Late

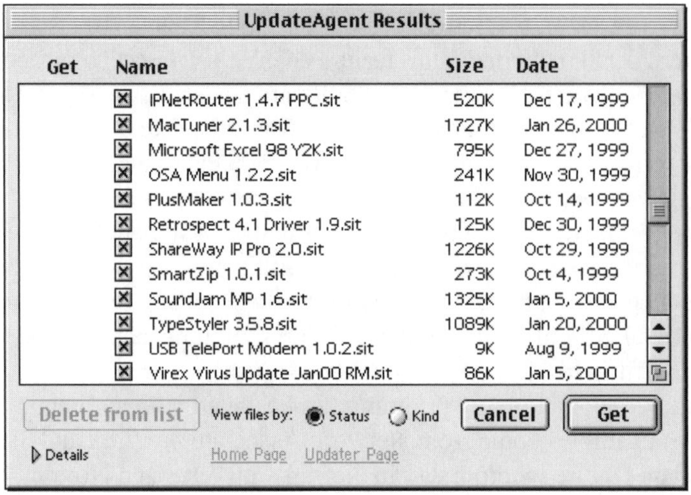

Get	Name	Size	Date
☒	IPNetRouter 1.4.7 PPC.sit	520K	Dec 17, 1999
☒	MacTuner 2.1.3.sit	1727K	Jan 26, 2000
☒	Microsoft Excel 98 Y2K.sit	795K	Dec 27, 1999
☒	OSA Menu 1.2.2.sit	241K	Nov 30, 1999
☒	PlusMaker 1.0.3.sit	112K	Oct 14, 1999
☒	Retrospect 4.1 Driver 1.9.sit	125K	Dec 30, 1999
☒	ShareWay IP Pro 2.0.sit	1226K	Oct 29, 1999
☒	SmartZip 1.0.1.sit	273K	Oct 4, 1999
☒	SoundJam MP 1.6.sit	1325K	Jan 5, 2000
☒	TypeStyler 3.5.8.sit	1089K	Jan 20, 2000
☒	USB TelePort Modem 1.0.2.sit	9K	Aug 9, 1999
☒	Virex Virus Update Jan00 RM.sit	86K	Jan 5, 2000

FIGURE 31-4 Here's a list of updates needed for the author's Blue & White Power Mac G3, as provided by Update Agent

NOTE *It's Apple's policy not to let third-party companies distribute their updates anymore, unless that update is needed to make a vendor's product work.*

When you run Update Agent, whether automatically by a predetermined schedule or manually, it not only delivers the list of available updates, but it also enables you to retrieve them directly from the program.

Another option is to pay regular visits to the popular VersionTracker Web site (see Figure 31-5). This site is unique among Mac-support Web sites. While other sites (such as my MacNightOwl.com support page) have a mixture of news and update information, VersionTracker supplies nothing but update and new product links.

Run by the same company that brings you *Macworld* magazine and MacWeek Online, VersionTracker is updated several times a day. You needn't fret over missing an update either. The site maintains a search engine, so you can easily search for a specific update that may address a problem you're having with a particular software product.

Store a link to VersionTracker in your favorite Web browser and revisit it every few days to check for the updates you might need.

FIGURE 31-5   VersionTracker combs the Internet in search of information and links for updates and new product information

Beyond these resources are the manufacturers themselves. If you run into a problem you feel is related to their product, don't hesitate to telephone the technical support people. Manufacturers do not, as a rule, notify customers of minor updates because sending out mailings for every minor fix can become quite expensive (though some manufacturers do mail critical updates that might cause serious problems to their users).

NOTE *Although a local dealer might seem to be a good source for this information, as a practical matter, a dealer only sells the normal retail versions of a product. When minor updates are produced, the changes may take several months (and additional time for those updates to get to the dealer) to filter down to retail versions of the product. In addition, it's fair to say that not all dealers are up-to-speed on the latest issues or updates for all the products they sell.*

Summing Up

In this chapter, you learned some tried-and-true techniques for isolating and troubleshooting problems with Mac OS 9 and your Mac. If you want more information on the subject, read another book of mine, *Upgrading & Troubleshooting Your Mac* (Osborne/McGraw-Hill). This book should be available at your favorite bookstore.

In the next chapter, the focus switches to the Internet, as AOL is compared with the ISP alternative, and you learn new ways to get better online performance.

Part IV

The Road to the Internet

Chapter 32

Your Online Options: AOL or an ISP

S ome day, almost every man, woman, and child will have some level of Internet access. We're almost there now, with a proliferation of opportunities to get online. They extend from the simple, controlled, comfortable environment of AOL to the new, uncharted waters of an ISP.

And between these distinct choices, others are muddying the waters, such as free ISPs (if you can stand a constant display of ads on your Mac), cable modems, and DSL.

This chapter is designed to focus on helping you choose which online option is for you, your Mac, and Mac OS 9.

You learn about AOL and how it compares with the other Internet offerings. Then you learn tips and tricks to make your online access go faster. And finally, you learn about the new world of broadband access, where your cable TV provider or phone company can deliver you performance up to 100 times faster than you get with a regular modem.

AOL Compared with an ISP

The ads flow back and forth. AOL's custom online environment is easy-to-use, so "no wonder it's number one." EarthLink's ads dismiss AOL as an online kindergarten, more or less, and promote that it provides a direct Net connection, saying "it's your Internet."

You have many, many choices of how to access the Internet. Just because AOL is top dog doesn't mean it's your only choice or even your best choice.

The EarthLink advantage is this: As a result of Apple's $200 million investment into the company (and its merger with MindSpring), it is the default ISP on the Mac platform. You can also expect that a future version of Apple's access software could have better integration of its Internet components. This has already begun with version 5.0 of EarthLink's Windows 98 software, which accesses all its main features from an integrated interface.

The beauty of the Mac, however, is you can use one of many online options, without having to run through vast hoops to configure the software or Mac OS 9, and still get the best possible online connection.

Here's a quick comparison of AOL versus some of the alternatives, with the focus on EarthLink simply because I'm a member of both:

■ **Custom content** AOL wins out here. AOL is an online service, not an ISP in the purest sense. Although it does have a Web browser, e-mail, FTP, newsgroups and other Internet features, it also delivers custom channels, forums, chat rooms, message boards, and information resources unavailable to nonmembers (see Figure 32-1). Even if you have misgivings about the quality of the software and the limitations when you want to use non-AOL software as part of your connection, the exclusive content may be a compelling reason to stay with the service.

■ **Safe for kids**   AOL CEO Steve Case has made a big deal about the service's Parental Controls feature (see Figure 32-2). This enables parents to establish custom online environments for children, restricting them from some Web, e-mail, chat room, and instant message access. You can customize a Web browser, such as Microsoft Internet Explorer, to deliver restricted content using the options in the Preferences panel, but this also restricts your access. As a Mac OS 9 user, however, you can access the iTools feature at Apple's Web site (http://www.apple.com) and take advantage of the KidSafe function (see Figure 32-3). KidSafe, when used in concert with the Multiple Users Control Panel, restricts your kids only to Web sites approved by a panel of educators.

■ **Integrated software**   AOL's proprietary software is the only way to access the service. It builds in chat, e-mail (see Figure 32-4), Web browser, and other features into a single program with a unified interface. An ISP gives you the

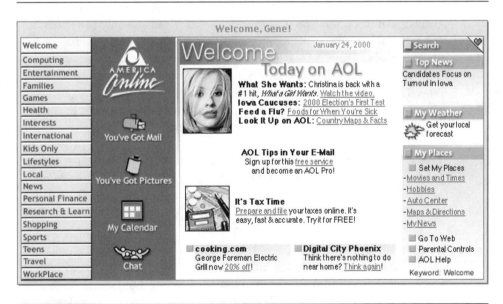

FIGURE 32-1   AOL offers a custom software and custom content in a controlled, easy-to-use environment

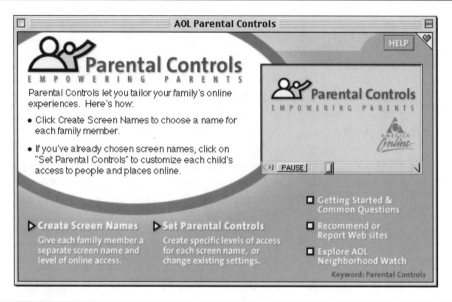

FIGURE 32-2   AOL's Parental Controls feature enables you to put severe restrictions on the online areas your child can visit

freedom to use any Mac Internet program with little or no restriction. The advantage of this is that you get the software you want and only that software. You aren't forced to accept a program you don't like. While AOL enables you to use other browsers and FTP software while online, its e-mail and newsgroup systems are proprietary and cannot be retrieved by other programs (other than the now-discontinued Claris Emailer for e-mail). In addition, a separate browser is unable to access areas available through AOL's Favorite Places feature or by direct links from one of its forums.

> **NOTE**   *Technically, such components of AOL's software as e-mail and its Web browser are offered as a number of separate, related files that load into memory when these functions are used. This lets AOL deliver online bug fix updates to its software occasionally.*

■ **Customized Start Page**   Although EarthLink, for example, isn't providing a lot of exclusive content, it does offer you a Personal Start Page (see Figure 32–5). You can customize the page to provide links to your favorite Web sites, and collect only the news and other information that appeals to you. The

FIGURE 32-3   Use Apple's KidSafe feature to help your kids only visit safe Internet sites

Personal Start Page also provides links to the service's Shopping, Personal Finance, and Support sections, so you can get a heavy dose of your online experience from a single area. At press time, EarthLink had released version 5.0 of its access software for Windows 98, which offers Web access and e-mail in a single, custom interface. A Mac version is expected to see the light of day fairly soon, perhaps by the time you read this book.

■ **AOL software isn't compatible with Mac OS 9's automatic software updating**   Apple's handy Software Update Control Panel can be set to log on to your ISP at predetermined intervals in search of program updates. This feature doesn't work with an AOL connection, however. Instead, you must first connect to AOL, and then run your Software Update session

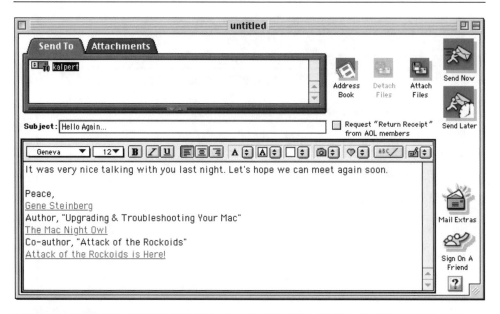

| FIGURE 32-4 | AOL's e-mail client gives you the basics, but few of the advanced customization options of a program such as Microsoft Outlook Express |

manually. The same is true for the automatic update features of such programs as Network Associates' Virus and Symantec's Norton Anti-Virus and Norton Utilities.

■ **Some financial institutions have problems with AOL's Web browser** AOL's Web browser is based on Microsoft Internet Explorer, reduced to its component parts and with a reduced feature set. Even if you get the 128-bit version for maximum online security, some financial institutions may not support this service. This is something you might have to check yourself with the financial agencies.

Obviously, I haven't tried to cover all the scenarios of AOL versus a separate ISP, but you can try both without incurring a big expense. AOL sends out millions of CDs with free access software every month. In addition, the software is also located in the CD Extras folder of your Mac OS 9 CD.

AOL's standard plan gives you one month's free service, and then you can decide whether to stay (you have to actually cancel, though, if you wish to avoid billing after the initial free month).

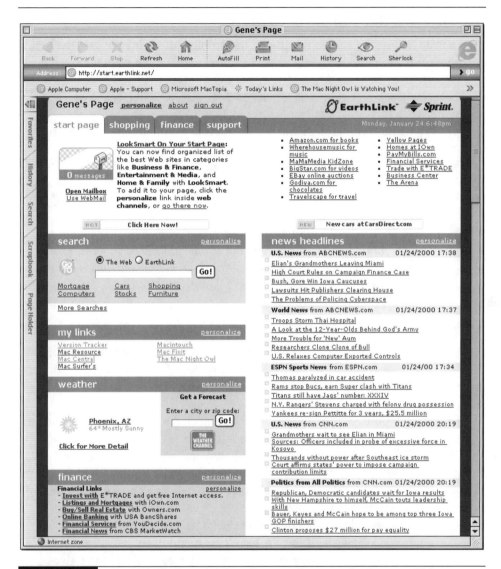

FIGURE 32-5   EarthLink's Personal Start Page can be customized to your liking

In addition, EarthLink and other ISPs frequently offer special discount offers. That way, you can take the time to sample various online alternatives before you decide which ones to keep.

And as you see in the next section, it's not only one or the other.

Getting the Best of Both Worlds

AOL has an interesting way to get around the problem of giving the user the best of both worlds. If you like some of what AOL has to offer, but want the freedom of a separate ISP, consider AOL's Bring Your Own Access Plan.

This special account gives you a reduced price for AOL (the cost was $9.95 per month when this book was being written) so long as you access the service by way of a regular ISP, through that ISP's network. If you do this, AOL's costs for maintaining your account are less.

The downside is, if you do choose to log on to AOL's dial-up network after establishing this account, you pay an extra hourly service charge for the time you spend using their network.

NOTE   *If you can handle the limitations of a free ISP, you might even want to consider joining one of those services, if they have Mac support, and then signing up for Bring Your Own Access to get the maximum bang for your bucks.*

Apple's KidSafe Protects Your Kids from Internet Evils

Installing Mac OS 9 puts you in an exclusive club when it comes to visiting Apple's Web site. While anyone with Web access can learn about Apple's product line or make a purchase at The Apple Store, taking advantage of Apple's iTools feature is another issue entirely.

iTools (see Figure 32-6) is a set of add-ons that enables you to take advantage of some extra special features provided free by Apple.

The one discussed here directly impacts how your kids interact with the Internet. It's called KidSafe. This iTools component works along with Mac OS 9's Multiple Users feature (as described in Chapter 6) to deliver a custom, safe Internet experience for your children.

With KidSafe installed, your children are only granted access to special educator-approved Web sites. If the site hasn't been approved, they cannot get to it. The idea takes the concept of Parental Controls used on AOL and moves it to the Internet.

Unlike Web filtering software, you needn't spend extra time configuring a program to block specific sites. Instead, KidSafe does the work for you.

Here's how to set it up:

1. First, sign up and install the iTools software. To do this, go to Apple's Web site at http://www.apple.com, and click the iTools tab (look again at the previous Figure 32-6).

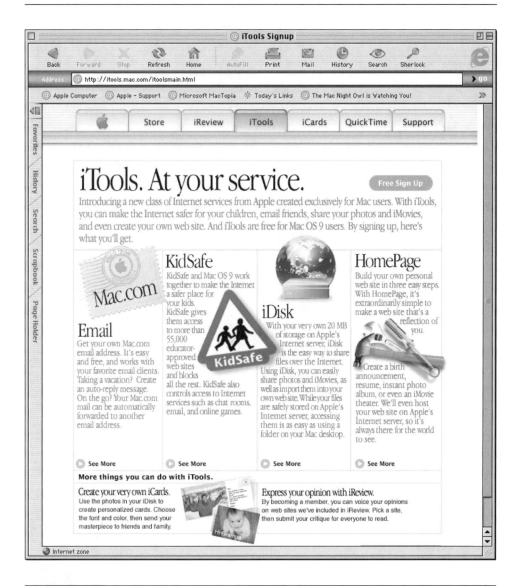

AOL Compared with an ISP

FIGURE 32-6   Choose the iTools you want from this screen

---

2. Click the Free Sign Up button (see Figure 32-7).

3. Click the Start button to download the small installer that adds iTools capability.

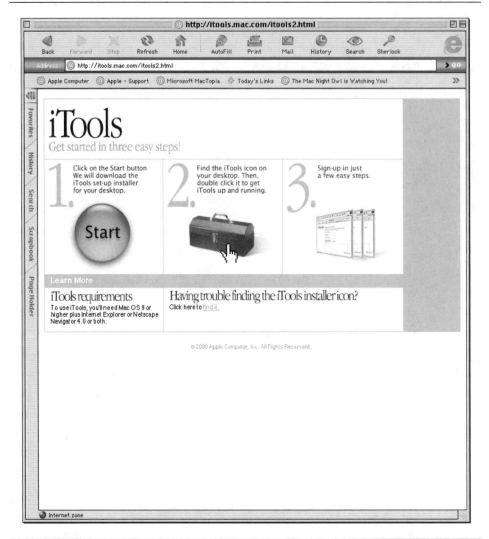

FIGURE 32-7   A simple one-two-three process gets iTools running on your Mac

4. Once the download is done (it takes a few minutes to finish), double-click the iTools icon on your Mac to continue the setup process.

5. You are returned to the iTools page at Apple's Web site where you enter your name and other information. You can also give yourself a mac.com user name, which enables you to use mac.com as an e-mail address (mine is genesteinberg@mac.com, naturally).

6. Once you're set up, you are returned to the main iTools page where you click the button labeled Setting up KidSafe to begin the process of downloading the component you need to use this feature.

7. You are taken to a second Web page with instructions on setting up the feature. From here, click Start to download the setup component.

8. Once the software has been downloaded to your Mac, double-click the KidSafe installer to launch it.

9. After the installation is finished, your Mac restarts.

10. To take advantage of KidSafe, you need to set up an account for your child in the Multiple Users Control Panel. Go to the Apple menu, select Control Panels, and choose Multiple Users from the submenu (see Chapter 6 for more information).

11. With Multiple Users open, set up your child as a New User.

12. Enter your child's name and password, and then specify the kind of account you want to establish. For KidSafe, it's best to pick Limited or Panels, so your child cannot disable the program.

13. To expand the setup window, click the triangle adjacent to Show Setup Details.

14. In the User Info tab, click the check box labeled Enable KidSafe. This activates the feature and provides full protection for children when they visit the Internet.

NOTE   *You may want to provide a separate Multiple User account for each of your children to give them their own custom environment (even if the setups are basically the same).*

AOL Compared with an ISP

Is Free Internet Worth It?

You see the ads. You don't have to pay for online access anymore. By signing up with the appropriate service, you get free Internet.

What are the advantages and the disadvantages?

At press time, the largest free ISP, NetZero, still hadn't delivered Macintosh software, but it had promised a version. The experience reported on here is from FreeiNet (check http://www.freeinet.com for information).

The service comes with a custom installer, called FreeiClient, which you download from the service's Web site, after registering your user name and password.

The basic setup process is little different from a paid ISP, all done by the installer once you register. You can continue to use your favorite Web browser. e-mail software, or any other Internet access program.

The lone difference is a floating window, several inches long, which displays recirculating ads (see Figure 32-8). Even if the ads don't disturb your online access, having them float above all other active programs on your Mac means you can be disturbed by their presence throughout your online visit, whether or not the Internet software is the active window.

Actual connection speeds, in my experience (based on encounters in the Phoenix, Arizona metropolitan area), were no different when compared to AOL or EarthLink. Don't expect speedy customer service if you encounter a problem with the service, though. I have e-mailed them several times and never had a response. This may only be an indication of early growing pains and nothing more.

Regardless, it's clear free ISPs are not going away. Some, in fact, such as the one run by Excite@home, are designed as loss-leaders to help interest you in eventually subscribing to their cable Internet service (assuming the service is available in your city).

NOTE
Free Internet service is common in the United Kingdom, but this doesn't mean surfing the Net is free. Even if you sign up for such a service, you have to pay for your local phone connection, on a per-minute rate. So you gain in one area and lose in another, unless the ISP can also deliver a special telephone rate (which also happens on occasion).

How to Speed Online Access

Online access isn't a cut-and-dried process. Many intervening factors, beginning with your Mac, the modem, the phone lines, and extending to the vast network that comprises the Internet, may contribute to problems in getting connected and staying connected.

You can control some of these intervening factors. Others you can't control. The next sections separate the two, so you know where problems exist that you can control directly.

Frequent Disconnects or Bad Performance

Most Macs currently come with built-in modems, so there's nothing special to configure. Even AOL probes your modem and stores default settings to provide the maximum level of good performance with your online connection.

But with an older modem, you may enter a strange world where plug-and-play is only a pipe-dream, and you are left to discover if that modem is the cause of your online grief. The usual answer is to make sure the right make and model modem is selected in the Modem Control Panel under Mac OS 9 or in AOL's Setup box.

Even with the modem working properly, other causes may sabotage online performance:

■ **Incorrect TCP/IP Control Panel Settings**   Under Mac OS 9, the TCP/IP Control Panel (see Figure 32-9) is used to store connection protocols and IP numbers. If the settings are incorrect in either category, you may find you cannot connect or, when you do connect, you cannot get your Web browser to access a site or send e-mail. If you are certain your modem is set up properly, check with your ISP for the correct numeric settings. This

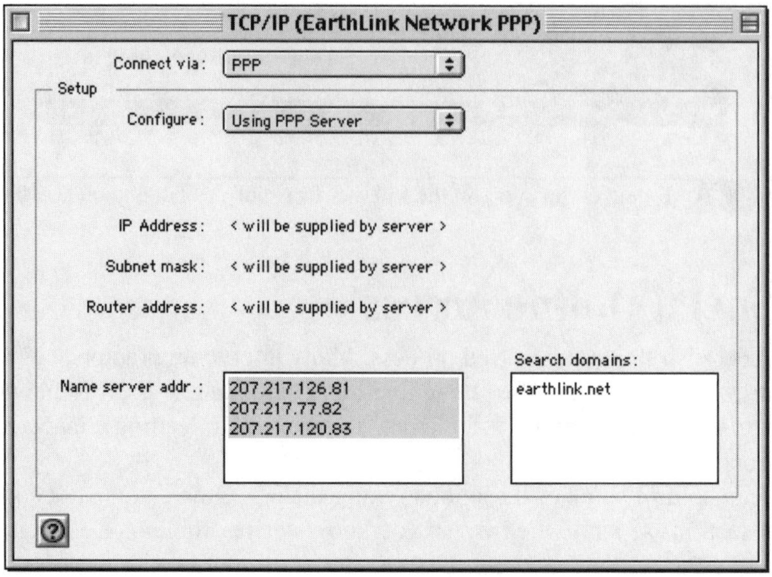

FIGURE 32-9   The settings you see in the author's TCP/IP Control Panel cover
EarthLink. Expect your mileage to vary with another ISP

isn't something I can describe in this book because thousands of these
services exist, each with a different set of IP numbers that must be set.
Some come with an installer to take care of all this behind the scenes.
Otherwise, you have to sit back and get the numbers right, digit by digit.

NOTE   *AOL automatically configures TCP/IP Control Panel settings as part of
its software installation process. IP numbers are handled dynamically
by the service and you need enter nothing once installation is complete.*

■ **TCP/IP Settings Are Absent**   This could be the consequence of a new,
clean system software installation. In Chapter 2, the various elements you
need to restore the settings to your Mac are covered, if you choose this
installation option. In general, when you choose this sort of installation
process, be sure the TCP/IP Preferences from the Preferences folder inside your
Previous System folder are carried to your new System Folder. This can take
care of the issue promptly. Quit TCP/IP Control Panel, copy the settings, and
they'll be there immediately the next time you open the program.

■ **TCP/IP Settings Are Damaged** This doesn't happen often, but it does happen. Sometimes it's the consequence of a bad software installation with your ISP's software. Other times, this happens when you make several changes, such as removing and adding a setting. Other issues, such as a system crash or hard-drive directory catalog problems may cause this problem. If the settings are not there, even though you have the right TCP/IP Preferences file, you may want to delete the file and enter the correct settings manually. A check of your hard drive (see Chapter 14) can help diagnose and fix any directory issues.

TIP *Once your Internet settings are correct, make a backup of the files, separate from your regular backup routine, in case the problem occurs again. You only need to make a folder with those files and put them on another drive or removable disk. You can label the folder, as I do, Internet settings.*

■ **User Authentication Failed** The process of hooking up to your ISP requires your user name and password to be checked against the account records of the service. The information is normally placed in Mac OS 9's Remote Access Control Panel (see Figure 32-10). If the file becomes corrupted, simply entering the information again should be sufficient. If this solution doesn't work, contact your ISP. On occasion, a service's authentication computers may not be functioning, but such problems are usually addressed quickly.

Mac OS 9 Internet Control Panel

Older versions of the Mac OS required a program called Internet Config to store settings for your ISP. The file was nearly as ubiquitous as Apple's SimpleText. Apple has found a solution, however, by merging the features of the program into its Internet Control Panel (see Figure 32-11).

While AOL doesn't, for example, touch the Internet Control Panel, a regular ISP does. Each of the settings you use for one of those services is stored there. Sometimes the file is updated when you set up the new service. Other times, you have to resort to the information the ISP provides in a small booklet or information sheet or by its telephone support people.

But not all the settings are visible. For example, Microsoft's Internet programs, Internet Explorer and Outlook Express, store settings in your Internet preferences file, which is accessed by the Internet Control Panel. AOL, which uses Internet Explorer (or a reduced subset of the program) as its built-in browser, does the same thing.

How to Speed Online Access

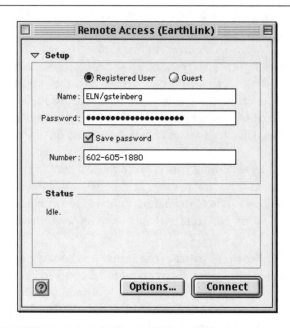

FIGURE 32-10   The author's Remote Access Control Panel shows access numbers to connect to his EarthLink account

Browser issues are covered in the next chapter. I wanted to mention the complexities here in case you see such basic settings as the size and location of your Web cache file change without your intervention.

In the next section, the basic setups for the Internet Control Panel are reviewed, without getting into what secret elements may lie in its preference file.

Configuring the Internet Control Panel

Mac OS 9's Internet Control Panel (as shown in Figure 32-11) carries all your basic Internet settings, aside from actual connection information (used to log on and sustain your connection). These, as mentioned earlier, reside in the Modem and TCP/IP Control Panels.

The Internet Control Panel's convenient tabbed interface makes it easy for you to enter the information for a specific category. Here's how to make those settings:

1. To access the Internet Control Panel, visit the Apple menu, select Control Panels, and then choose Internet from the submenu.

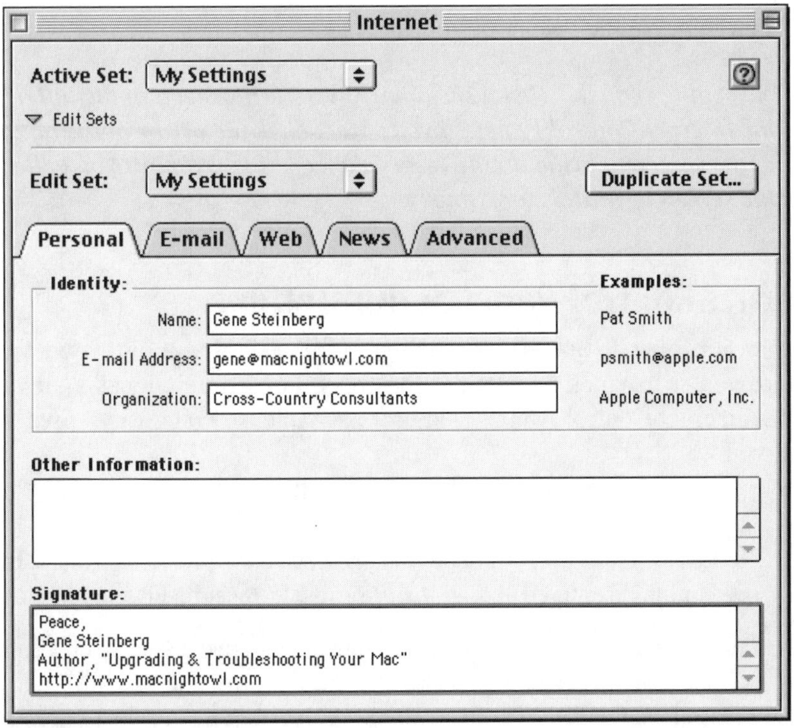

FIGURE 32-11   Mac OS 9's Internet Control Panel merges various ISP preferences in one convenient place

2. The initial settings are usually called Default or My Settings. If you prefer to be more creative in the name, click the File menu, choose Rename, and change the name the way you like. This feature helps if you have access to more than one ISP and need to switch rapidly among them.

CAUTION   *None of the changes you make in the Internet Control Panel have any effect on the settings for AOL. In addition, some of the free Internet services, such as FreeiNet, have custom software to access the service, and some of the settings you make in the Internet Control Panel won't touch them at all.*

3. With your settings onscreen, type the information you want to use to identify yourself in e-mail and newsgroup messages in the Identity column.

How to Speed Online Access

The Other Information column is for additional information you might want to put in the header of your message.

NOTE *No settings panels? If you see a narrow screen instead of the full depth of the Internet Control Panel on your Mac, click the arrow at the bottom left of the screen to bring up the rest of the contents. Perhaps you collapsed the screen by mistake previously.*

Internet Control Panel Setup Options

While most people do not use more than a single ISP, if you find you do (perhaps you're using an iBook or a PowerBook in different locales), make a separate Internet Control Panel setting for each one, so you always have the setups you want.

Here are the choices available to you from the File menu:

- **New Set**   I don't recommend this one because it produces a blank Internet set. Nothing's entered and all the information must be inserted manually.

- **Duplicate Set**   This setting is much better. To make a new set, duplicate the one you have, and then adapt the setup information to conform to the needs of another ISP. This is much faster than putting in all the information again, especially if most of it is the same.

- **Rename Set**   If the set doesn't have a name that properly identifies its purpose, change it.

- **Delete Set**   If you don't need a set, you can easily delete it. But first, you have to make another set active (you can't delete an active set).

4. Storing a signature for e-mail and newsgroup messages is common. If you want to do this, insert the signature in the appropriate field.

NOTE *Microsoft's Outlook Express 5 has its own custom signature settings, as does Claris Emailer and AOL 5.0 (due for release around the time this book is set to appear). The signatures you set in the Internet Control Panel won't impact these programs.*

5. The next setting you want to make is needed to access your e-mail because you need to log in with the correct user name and password. To make those settings, click the E-mail tab ((see Figure 32-12). You also need to type in the information your ISP provides for incoming and outgoing mail servers (once again it's different for each one and the two settings might not always be identical).

6. The next selection is a matter of personal taste. When you click the Web tab (see Figure 32-13), you can set default Web home pages and the Web search site you prefer (such as Excite, Yahoo! and any number of similar Web portals).

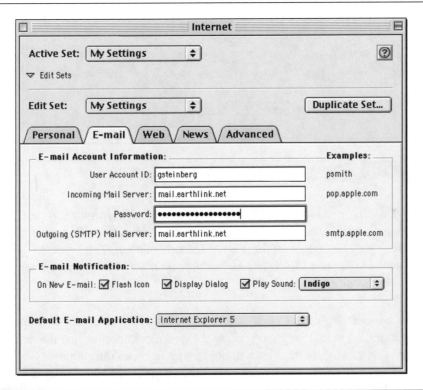

FIGURE 32-12   The text fields here are needed to place your ISP's e-mail log in information

How to Speed Online Access

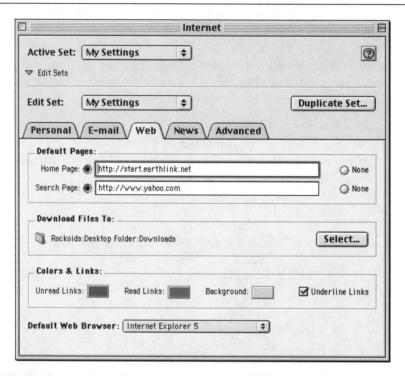

FIGURE 32-13 Insert your preferred Home page and search page choices

NOTE

If you're an EarthLink member, you want to stick with http:// start.earthlink.net, which accesses your Personal Start Page, a useful jumping point for a lot of Internet content. You want to check with your ISP as to whether they offer a similar service and what settings are needed.

7. Your next setting is to pick where you want to put files you downloaded from the Internet. A good place is the desktop folder (or just the desktop), so you can locate the files without having to comb through miles and miles of nested folders. Click the Select button in the Download Files To field and pick the location where you want to place the files.

8. You'll now want to select your default Web browser, the one that launches whenever you open a program that connects you to the Web (such as clicking a hyperlink in Microsoft Word 98). If the Default Web Browser setting isn't the one you prefer, click the pop-up menu to the right of that label to see the available browsers on your Mac.

> NOTE
>
> *If the browser you have and want to use isn't shown in the pop-up menu, click the Select command to bring up an Open dialog box where you can choose the right one. You cannot select AOL's embedded browser this way, however (although you can have it launch AOL's software, after which you connect to the service manually).*

9. The next category depends on whether you have any interest in Usenet newsgroups. If you do, click the News tab, and then put in the information required to connect to your ISP's news servers.

> CAUTION
>
> *To combat spam and other unsavory use of their newsgroup servers, EarthLink and some other services require you to enter your user name and password to access these features.*

10. This should be it for most purposes. If you want to customize your Web settings still further, however, click the Advanced tab (see Figure 32-14). You can set a number of sometimes arcane parameters in this tab. The following bulleted points list these parameters:

> NOTE
>
> *You seldom, if ever, have to visit the Advanced tab for custom settings under normal circumstances. By default, installation of any of your Internet software brings with it a number of default settings. You can easily live with and never have to change these settings, except in rare circumstances where you decide to explore something new or a new program requires a changed setting.*

- **File Transfer**   Use this setting to list default FTP servers. This is useful if you travel outside the U.S.

- **Helper Apps**   Your browser and other Internet applications often need to operate in concert with other programs to perform certain functions. For example, if you want to open compressed files automatically, StuffIt Deluxe or StuffIt Expander (if you have either) may be called on to do the chores.

- **Fonts**   Choose the fonts you prefer to use with your Internet software.

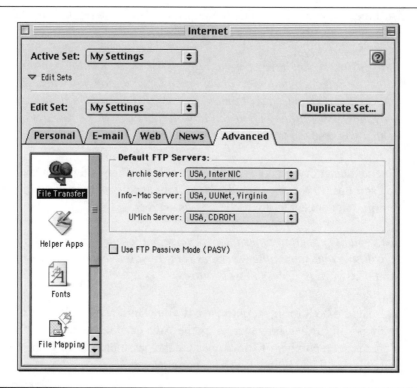

FIGURE 32-14   Change fonts for Internet programs, choose Helper applications, and make other settings in the Advanced tab

■ **File Mapping**   You can select Mac programs to automatically open files of specific types, such as .doc for Microsoft Word.

11. After you finish the setup process, simply click the close box of the Internet Control Panel. Then, click the Save button on the next dialog box to store your changes. If you want to return to your previous Internet Control Panel settings, click Cancel instead.

Coping with Internet Software Crashes

The programs you use to surf the Internet are called into play to perform a variety of functions over and over again, such as sending and receiving all your e-mail to browsing the Internet seamlessly to deliver your favorite Web sites to your Mac.

Through it all, most of these programs run fine, but because of their complex interaction with the Mac operating system, they are sometimes the prime cause of system crashes. From simple program quits to hard freezes, don't expect all your Internet visits to be totally perfect.

> **NOTE** *Just because the programs you use to visit the Internet are largely free doesn't mean the publishers or authors have taken less pains in making them stable and reliable. In fact, such publishers as Microsoft have large-scale software developing and testing projects to make sure their programs work well.*

In this section, some of the common causes of problems with Internet software are listed. If the problems persist, you should read Chapter 31, which covers working solutions to system-related problems. You should also read the next chapter, which focuses strictly on Web-browser issues.

> **CAUTION** *Even if a program simply quits, continuing to use your Mac without a restart is a bad idea. A program quitting causes the operating system and your other programs to be less than stable. If you continue to work on your Mac, you are asking for a much more severe crash sooner or later.*

Here's a list of usual suspects of Internet-related system problems and their solutions:

- **ObjectSupportLib** In older versions of the Mac OS, this system extension was placed in the Extensions folder to provide support for AppleScript and other functions in various programs. Apple has been working harder to manage System Folder clutter, so it merged ObjectSupportLib into the System file instead. Older program installers don't detect its presence, however, and install it in the Extensions folder, regardless. In theory, the version in the System file should override the functions of the separate version. In practice, its presence may also cause unexplained system crashes and should be removed if you discover it.

> **NOTE** *Apple's Extensions Manager doesn't always reveal the presence of ObjectSupportLib, so checking the Extensions folder manually doesn't hurt anyway.*

- **Web Cache corruption** The stored artwork for your browser can deliver a crash if corrupted. Chapter 33 covers the issue of purging the Web cache.

- **Preference file corruption** Most Mac programs store custom settings in a separate preference file. These files are always open and accessible whenever you use the programs and they are often changed to some degree (even if you don't actually do something with a preference setting). If a crash or hard-drive directory corruption harms this file, you may find your program fails to store custom settings or crashes when you launch the program. If this happens, pay a fast visit to the Preferences folder, inside the System Folder, and see if you can locate such a file. Not all programs put preferences there. Some programs put them in the application folder directly or separate the settings into several files. If the location is not readily apparent, see if the program copied an installer log file to your drive. Maybe you can determine what files are involved.

CAUTION *To avoid an almost certain crash, don't remove a program's preference files till you quit the program. When you launch the program the first time (after you delete the preferences), be prepared to go to the Preferences dialog box to make your settings again or even to plough through a setup assistant to set things right (Netscape Communicator and Outlook Express are prime examples of this).*

- **Give the program more memory** Your Web browser, for example, is set to work fine with the standard amount of RAM allocated to it. But, as soon as you add some plug-in files, those add-on modules that deliver QuickTime video, RealAudio video, Shockwave animations, and more, the memory requirements creep up. You should add at least several megabytes of additional memory with the Finder's Get Info command to cover these needs.

- **Internet software has conflicts** Whether it's a browser, an e-mail client, or a program you use for chatting, the programs are updated frequently. Some programs need updates for Mac OS 9, while others only need to fix general problems. Check the publishers' Web sites or VersionTracker.com for the latest news.

■ **A Conflict with a System Extension** This is nothing more than the standard scenario. Internet programs, such as Microsoft Internet Explorer and Outlook Express, put various and sundry files in your System Folder. A conflict could exist with another program. Chapters 25 and 31 show you how to diagnose such problems.

The Road to Speedier Online Performance

So far in this chapter, you learned how to set up your Internet software to deliver correct performance. Yet, you might be able to do other things to get speedier delivery of Web pages via your browser or more efficient retrieval of a mission critical file for your business.

The following points explain ways to optimize your online experience:

■ **Pick the fastest dial-up access number.** You just bought a 56K modem, but you're lucky to connect at half that speed. Check with your ISP and see if you can choose from additional local access numbers. And make sure the numbers are rated for 56K performance; not all are, although the number of holdouts are few.

■ **Avoid heavy traffic hours for surfing.** The peak evening hours, considered prime time for TV networks, also bring many people online. In times of heavy traffic, an ISP's network may be hard-pressed to keep up with the load, even if the service works hard to install enough computers to meet the demand. Sites themselves may be clogged and this isn't something your ISP (or AOL) can control. Try to stay away from evenings or weekends for best performance. The early morning hours have the least amount of online traffic in most cases (unless the site is located in another part of the world, where it may get frequent visitors in its native time zone).

■ **Keep the disk cache at its default setting.** You may want to save a few megabytes of RAM, especially if memory is tight. But Mac OS 9 routinely sets the disk cache for the best possible performance. The disk cache stores frequently accessed data from your hard drive, which can provide a slight, but noticeable, performance boost. If you're uncertain if the setting is correct, open the Memory Control Panel and click the Use Defaults button at the bottom of the screen. Then restart. This establishes the disk cache at 32K per megabyte of installed RAM.

How to Speed Online Access

NOTE
A consequence of the Use Defaults setting is virtual memory, which is automatically switched on and set to a total of 1MB above the installed RAM. While virtual memory works much better with Mac OS 9 than with older operating system versions, if you have a lot of RAM installed on your Mac, you might want to switch it off and see if performance is better (and save a reasonable amount of hard drive storage space used to store the virtual memory "swap" file). Remember, both Mac OS 9 and your programs will use a lot more RAM, as a result.

Optimizing Internet Performance

The Web demands a lot in terms of performance. For one thing, more and more multimedia files are at a site or available for download. In addition, the volume of e-mail goes up all the time as more people use it for both personal and business correspondence. Do what you can to provide the fastest possible performance.

Here are some methods to get the fastest possible performance from your Internet experience:

- **Get a 56K modem.** Your old modem may have worked fine in the past and it may still provide virtually flawless connections, but if it's not a 56K modem, you may not be getting all you can expect from a dial-up connection. While many phone lines, especially those in older neighborhoods, can't take you past 28.8K or 33.6K, many 56K modem users do, indeed, manage to speed up performance to some degree.

- **Try broadband Internet access.** In the next section, you learn about cable modems and DSL. Although these are not widely available, they can get you performance up to 100 times as fast as a conventional modem. If you can locate this service in your city, think seriously about it if your Internet performance isn't satisfactory.

- **Get more RAM.** Mac OS 9 is quite demanding of RAM. And the Net software you use will soar with as much RAM as you can give it. If your Mac has less than 64MB of installed RAM, consider upgrading to a minimum of 96MB or 128MB. You should find the investment worth it because you can run more programs at the same time. And your programs can resort less on virtual memory to meet RAM needs (this simply means they won't have to go to your hard drive to run). Remember, your drive runs much slower than real RAM.

- **Speed up your Mac or get a new model.** Even the cheapest iMac had a 350 MHz G3 CPU at press time (and no doubt much faster models may be out by the time you read this book). If a new Mac isn't suitable for you, perhaps a G3 upgrade card is. Many of the recent non-G3 Macs can support such an upgrade and cost as little as a few hundred dollars or thereabouts.

CAUTION *While a G3 upgrade is a great way to spruce up performance for an older Mac, it could be a deadend path. Apple will not guarantee that such an upgraded system will run their next generation operating system, Mac OS X, when it ships (although third-party companies may try to step in and attempt to address that limitation). Mac OS X is only promised to support a Mac that actually shipped with a G3 or G4 CPU.*

An Overview of Broadband Internet Service

The speed of your Internet connection has moved in the same direction as the speed with which your Mac crunches data: Up, way, way up.

Back in the early 1980s, I marveled at how a 300 baud modem enabled me to retrieve files from a client over a telephone line, no less! All I had to do was place the phone headset onto a little black box, and wait, and wait. . . .

Well, we have moved far from 8 MHz and slower CPUs and 300 baud modems. Today, less than a hundred bucks buys a genuine 56,000 bps modem. Well, genuine if you consider that the FCC mandates connections can be no higher than 53,000 bps and normal connection rates are far lower, but a huge amount of progress has occurred, nonetheless.

But, as fast as modem speeds have increased, the data that fills your phone line has also become larger. You have the World Wide Web, QuickTime Movie trailers, and those huge files you retrieve every time Apple updates Mac OS 9.

When you think about it, 56K isn't much after all, not when you have to wait hours to retrieve a single file.

Based on the new technologies now becoming available, your analog modem is about to become a dinosaur.

The final section of the chapter is devoted to the two major replacements on tap for your modem.

Cable Modems

One of the big reasons AOL and Time-Warner got together was *broadband,* the buzzword for high-speed Internet access. Time-Warner has a huge cable television operation, with millions of subscribers, and many of those subscribers can connect to the Internet by cable modem.

A cable modem enables you to call the Internet in the same way as you network your Mac by Ethernet. You attach the cable modem to your Ethernet hub, make a few settings in your Mac's TCP/IP Control Panel to access the network, and install the cable company's access software.

The result? A revelation. Suddenly, data from the Internet literally flies across your screen, with potential speeds of 1,000,000 bps and higher. You don't even have to log on—you're always on, the same as your Mac is always connected to your network hub. Whenever you need to surf the Net, simply launch your browser and, in seconds, your selected home page appears on your Mac's display.

The price? Maybe two or three times what you're paying now (pricing depends on your location), but think about the speed.

The question is, does this miracle of technology truly work in the real world? Let's take a careful look:

- **Performance levels may vary.** You are on a shared network, consider it a zone consisting of your Mac and those of your neighbors. Depending on how many users are surfing the Net and the system's capacity, performance may be nowhere near what the ads promise. But even at its worst, it's bound to be superior to a 56K modem.

- **Cable service throttles upload speed.** You can get those files as fast as the wind, but the breaks are put on when you upload something. How much depends on the fashion in which your cable provider is set up, but it could be a fraction of your download speed. If you intend to send large files by e-mail to a family member or business contact, you should inquire about this before you sign up for the service.

- **Be prepared for a new e-mail address.** Cable television services are contracted to specific ISPs, maybe not the one you're using now, so you might have to obtain a new e-mail address and notify all your contacts.

- **You can't get it—yet.** At press time, I'm still waiting for my cable modem. The local cable provider servicing Scottsdale, AZ, has missed deadlines by months in upgrading the system and in offering such niceties as 200 channel digital cable and Internet access. You should expect the same of your cable provider. Do not depend on deadlines being 100 percent certain.

- **Printing to your neighbor's printer.** The first time I had this experience, I was surprised. I was visiting a client's site, setting up a local network with two Macs (each running Mac OS of course) and two printers. But the Chooser showed two more printers with totally different names. They were used by a nearby company, which also had a cable modem. That night, my client found an unfamiliar job sitting in his office printer's output tray, apparently from someone else who had accessed the network. Now this doesn't mean your network security is necessarily at risk, but you should follow my instructions in Chapter 27 about setting access privileges. In addition, some networked printers have their own custom settings for password protection. Better to be safe than sorry.

NOTE
In all fairness to the cable industry, the local provider I deal with, Cox Cable, automatically downloads a security software (daemon) to the cable modem within a day or two after installation. And sure enough, in a short time, my client neither saw other printers on his network nor did anyone print strange jobs on his printer (even though he had not changed his printer security after my office visit).

Digital Subscriber Lines

The local phone companies have their own answer to high-speed Internet access. It's called *Digital Subscriber Line* (*DSL*) and, while it uses your own phone lines, it exploits digital data to deliver high performance. If early connection delays and performance hassles can be resolved, DSL may be a great alternative to the cable modem.

The miracle of DSL, in effect, is that it provides a second channel of data through a single phone line. You can receive your regular calls as you do now and access the Internet, without having to interrupt your call or even to dial out.

DSL, when offered, promises speeds from 256,000 bps to 7,000,000 bps. The *International Telecommunications Union* (*ITU*), the body that approves international telephone standards, gave the go-ahead for a DSL variant, *ADSL* (*Asymmetric DSL*), which offers maximum performance on downloads, such as retrieving Web artwork and files. But upload speed is limited, in the same fashion as it's limited with a 56K modem. Your local service establishes the limits.

In addition, you may be unable to get the service, even if you want it. To get a proper signal to deliver the high-performance service, you must be located no more than three miles from a phone company switch. And even this doesn't guarantee you DSL because the phone company may also have to install new equipment to accommodate the service. So, if you live in a rural area or a sparsely populated suburban locale, you could be out of luck.

Even if DSL is available, don't expect to call your ISP or the phone company on a Monday and be surfing the net that Friday afternoon. At press time, wide

An Overview of Broadband Internet Service

reports said new subscribers were sometimes waiting months for installation. A widely publicized program from EarthLink to establish nationwide DSL service had been halted temporarily because demand outstripped the ability of local installers to handle the connections.

When all is said and done, you may also have to pay an extra installation charge and a fee for the DSL modem, although some companies may eat the setup charges in exchange for a long-term contract. EarthLink was offering their service for $49.95, complete, after the initial installation. But pricing goes all over the place and your mileage may vary.

Once you're connected, setting up DSL on your Mac is little different from a cable modem. You enter the proper settings in Mac OS 9's Internet and TCP/IP Control Panels, fire up your browser or e-mail software, and you're on your way to enjoy the brave new world of broadband Internet access.

DSL hookups do not seem as vulnerable to possible security problems as cable modems, but you should still password-protect your Macs if you are using Mac OS 9's file sharing feature.

Summing Up

In this chapter, you were given some ideas on whether an online service, AOL, or an ISP is a better choice to fit your needs.

You also learned how to cope with common Internet software and access problems, as well as how to get faster performance by way of a speedier modem or one of the new broadband Internet access technologies.

In the next chapter, we continue to explore the Internet and you learn how to get the best possible performance from your Web browser.

Chapter 33

Using a Web Browser

For several years, you've read about something called the *browser wars,* where two programs were pitted against each other in a battle for supremacy. The two programs were Microsoft Internet Explorer and Netscape Navigator (the version that includes e-mail and Web authoring features is called *Netscape Communicator*). Most analysts now consider the battle to be over.

The victor is Microsoft, and the second place entry, Netscape, has been swallowed up by AOL (which is merging with Time-Warner). While Netscape has had some updates and is still preferred by millions, no serious expectation exists for Netscape to ever again regain the market share it once had (when it literally dominated the browser market).

This chapter, however, isn't designed to analyze market share. Instead, this chapter briefly describes not only these two browsers, but also a scrappy new contender from a European software company. Then you learn how you can maximize the performance of your Web browser.

Mac Web Browsers Compared

What sort of quality can you get for free? Because Microsoft got the upper-hand in the browser wars, you no longer had to pay to get a quality Web browser. Before that, the king of the hill, Netscape, was sold in a sort of shareware arrangement, where you were expected to pay for the program if you used it. In addition, Netscape had a retail version that also included some extra features, such as the capability to join an ISP from those it supported in the package.

But as with e-mail software, you cannot relate quality with cost. Strategic reasons exist why Microsoft and the Netscape subsidiary of AOL make their browsers available free, and the user benefits with high-quality software.

In this section, the basic (basic because feature sets themselves can consume a large chapter) features of the major Web browsers are compared. You are then introduced to iCab, a new product from a German-based software publisher that offers many features, but conserves disk space and RAM requirements.

NOTE *Because AOL's Web browser is based on a reduced-feature version of Microsoft's Internet Explorer, it is not covered here because you cannot change the built-in browser AOL provides. You can run another browser with your AOL connection, however, such as one of the three described here. Just remember, AOL's own direct Web links and Favorite Places features won't work with a separate browser.*

Microsoft Internet Explorer

Microsoft has an extremely active and able development team producing its Mac Internet software. And this development team keeps getting better and better. Although Mac OS 9 comes with Internet Explorer 4.5, by press time, version 5.0 will be out (see Figure 33-1), a free download from Microsoft's MacTopia Web site (http://www.microsoft.com/mactopia). This is the version you learn about here.

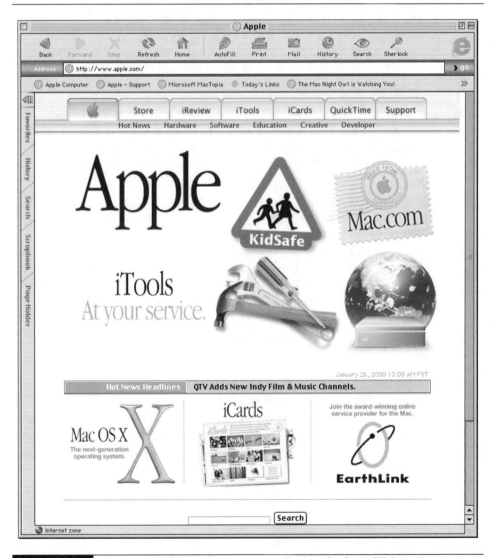

Mac Web Browsers Compared

FIGURE 33-1   Internet Explorer 5.0 sports a new look and a faster Web engine

Key Internet Explorer 5.0 Features

Here are the updated features Microsoft touts for its updated release:

- **Tasman Web-browsing Engine**   Claiming a speed boost of up to 50 percent over the previous version, Microsoft says its Tasman engine, the motor for its browser program, delivers more accurate Web page display. The Tasman engine touts full support for the latest published Internet standards from the World Wide Web Consortium (known as *W3C*). This supposedly provides a more accurate display of pages. Microsoft also claims the new browser can render pages much the same on both the Mac and Windows platforms, which can make the jobs of Web designers easier (except when they also have to offer compatibility with older browsers).

- **New Search Assistant**   Part and parcel of a smooth Web-browsing experience is searching. Unless you have already compiled a list of regular sites (using the program's Favorite's feature) and you don't want to deviate, you want to find convenient ways to get Net information. The feature works by first entering a search category, such as a Web site or a person's address, and after you type your request, Internet Explorer goes to work finding what you want.

> **NOTE**   *In all fairness, Apple's Sherlock 2 search feature works fine with any browser discussed here. Once you set a default browser in the Internet Control Panel, click the search result link in Sherlock 2, and your browser is launched to deliver the page to your Mac.*

- **Related Links**   Internet Explorer 5 supports a Web navigation service known as *"Alexa,"* which provides information to help you locate sites that relate to the ones you're visiting.

- **Address AutoComplete Improved**   Microsoft has given a better *type-ahead* feature, which produces a pop-up list of sites that match what you type (see Figure 33-2). This way, you can quickly scroll to the one you want, rather than having to type the more and more complex site addresses you find as you continue to surf the Net.

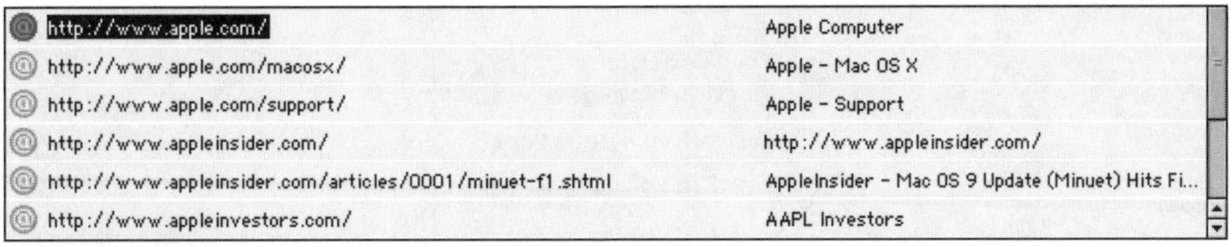

http://www.apple.com/	Apple Computer
http://www.apple.com/macosx/	Apple - Mac OS X
http://www.apple.com/support/	Apple - Support
http://www.appleinsider.com/	http://www.appleinsider.com/
http://www.appleinsider.com/articles/0001/minuet-f1.shtml	AppleInsider - Mac OS 9 Update (Minuet) Hits Fi...
http://www.appleinvestors.com/	AAPL Investors

FIGURE 33-2   Pick a site from the menu by scrolling down the list

- **Improved Tools Menu**   You get a new menu with extra features, chief of which is the new Auction Manager (see Figure 33-3). This feature enables you to track your bids, so you know when someone has posted a higher bid and when the auction is over (then you can see if you won the item). One of the other major features, brought over from the previous version, is AutoFill. *AutoFill* helps you insert some basic personal and address information into an online forum by clicking a button, rather than typing it over and over again.

> NOTE   *In fairness to Apple, Auction Manager also supports Sherlock 2, so you get integrated searching as well.*

- **Internet Scrapbook**   Tired of wasting paper and ink (or toner) printing page after page of Web pages you want to refer to later? The Internet Scrapbook enables you to store the entire content of the page, such as a receipt for an online transaction or an article, so you can retrieve it later. Because the page is stored on your Mac, you can still view it, even if the site has removed the page.

- **Customize the Look**   Microsoft has joined with the full-color generation of Mac products. You can pick from nine color schemes for Internet Explorer 5, from the basic iMac-inspired colors to graphite, plus PowerBook black and PowerBook bronze. The buttons on the program's toolbar can also be customized by adding and removing items from a default palette, or by moving them around to the position you prefer.

Mac Web Browsers Compared

FIGURE 33-3   The Tools menu is a big new feature of Internet Explorer 5

Netscape Navigator

Compared to Internet Explorer, Netscape hasn't been revamped so radically (see Figure 33-4). Netscape has, however, a number of useful features that many Mac users prefer to the Microsoft alternate, particularly because Netscape comes as an integrated suite of Internet software, which can deliver the basic features from a single program. This can definitely save you some time and energy in configuring new software.

Key Netscape Communicator 4.7 Features

Communicator 4.7 was a minor update to 4.5, with mostly bug fixes and a few improvements. Here are some of the major features:

■ **Smart Browsing**   As you type a Web site's address, Netscape attempts to complete it for you. This is a boon when coping with a complicated address that brings you to a page buried down deep at a site. This feature isn't quite as extensive as the one in Internet Explorer 5, however.

■ **Integrated E-mail**   While Internet Explorer requires you to pick another program for e-mail (other than a Web-based e-mail service), Netscape Communicator offers the Messenger module (see Figure 33-5). E-mail software is covered in more detail in Chapter 34. In brief, Messenger offers a host of e-mail features, from simple, pinpoint addressing to filtering that can help you easily manage both your e-mail and newsgroup messages.

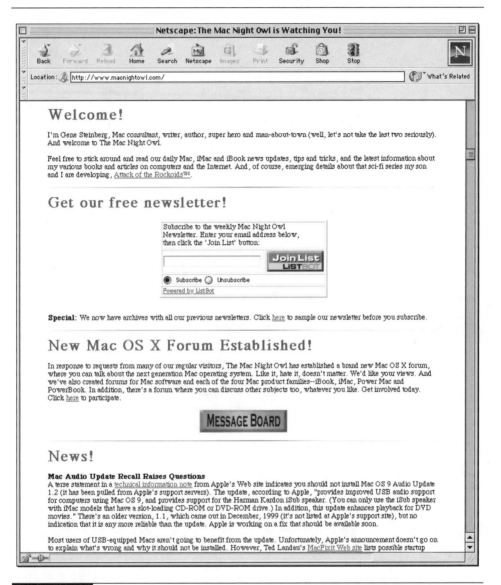

FIGURE 33-4   Netscape Communicator 4.7 offers state-of-the-art browsing

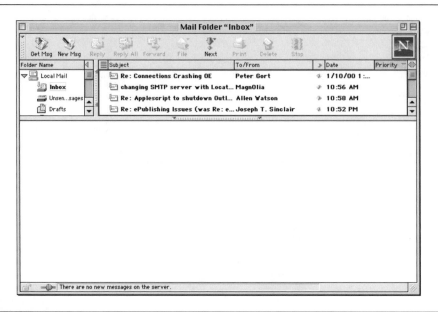

Integrated with Netscape Communicator is the Messenger e-mail program

■ **Instant Messaging** The standard Netscape Communicator installation includes AOL's Instant Messenger software. This software enables you to engage in convenient one-on-one chats with your online contacts (as long as they also have the software installed). Tens of millions of people use Instant Messenger, including all those AOL members. The subject of instant messaging and other online chatting is discussed further in Chapter 36.

> **NOTE** *As this book went to press, AOL announced version 6.0 of Netscape, which will integrate the functions of Instant Messenger as part of the basic application.*

■ **Smart Update** Rather than having to locate and download a new version of Netscape when it comes out, the SmartUpdate feature automatically seeks out and downloads the update for you. Once it's retrieved, your current version is updated, rather than replaced. Because a Netscape Communicator installer can run upwards of 13MB in size, this can save you lots of disk space and download time.

iCab Preview

At press time, author Alexander Clauss hadn't finished development of iCab, but the late preview version of the program available (see Figure 33-6) definitely showed an attempt to offer powerful performance and relief from browser bloat.

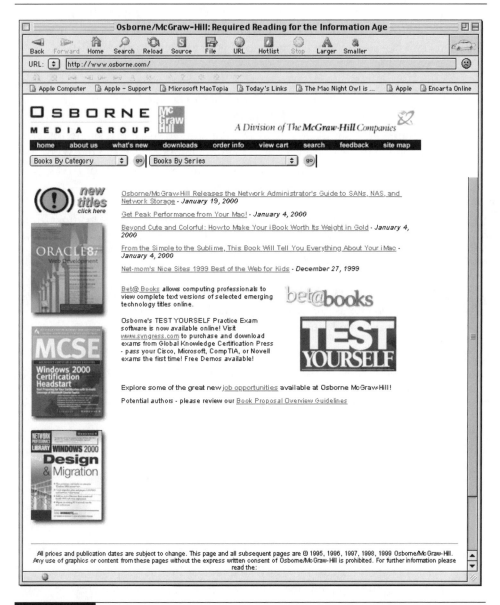

FIGURE 33-6   iCab takes a leaner, meaner approach to browsing the Web

NOTE   *The pricing policy of iCab is currently uncertain. The publisher's Web site says a free version will exist, but a "Pro" version (features not listed) will cost $29.*

Key iCab 1.9 Preview Features

Compared to the competition, the feature set for iCab seems leaner. But, if you want to get a browser that doesn't tie up your Mac's resources, especially if you find Mac OS 9 has already taken a big bite of your available memory, it's definitely worth a try.

- **Small Footprint**   iCab is a revelation in an era where programs keep getting larger and larger, both in RAM and disk requirements. The full installation of iCab fills less than 3MB of storage space in a single folder, with nothing in the System Folder other than preferences and the Web cache. In addition, iCab runs efficiently, using barely 4.5MB of RAM (less than half that if you use virtual memory).

NOTE   *If you have some older Macs around, you should be pleased to know iCab will work with Macs running System 7.0.1 or later, even those with 68020, 68030, and 68040 CPUs.*

- **Mac OS 9 Support**   Unlike its competition from Microsoft and Netscape, iCab supports the Keychain feature, which enables you to store your user passwords in a single location for quick access.

- **Import from Internet Explorer**   When you set it up, iCab will offer to import your Favorites from Internet Explorer or Netscape (it can also bring in your previous browser's Web cache and history files for fast retrieval of your favorite sites). iCab calls its favorites a *HotList,* by the way.

NOTE   *AOL's proprietary setup means your Favorite Places and history files cannot be imported into any other browser.*

- **AutoComplete**   Similar to Netscape Communicator and versions of Internet Explorer prior to 5.0, iCab will offer to complete a URL as you begin to type it.

- **Support for latest Web features**   HTML 4.0 is supported, along with special support for custom HTML features of Internet Explorer and Netscape. An example is the <BLINK> command, which creates the named effect in Netscape.

- **Download Manager**   This feature is similar to the one that's been a mainstay of Internet Explorer, which enables you to keep track of files you downloaded and to reload them, if necessary.

- **Plug-in Support**   iCab can use the very same plug-ins that work with Internet Explorer or Netscape, so you can access the same set of enhanced features, such as Macromedia's Flash animation, QuickTime movies, and so on.

Secrets of Fast Internet Access

Getting a faster modem and making sure it's set up properly, or migrating to a cable modem or DSL (if you're lucky enough to have this available in your neighborhood) is one of the first things you can do to produce the best Internet experience.

But because so much of your Net visits are concentrated on using your Web browser, this section advises you on how you can get your browser to run better.

Examining Your Web Cache

The cache your Web browser uses employs an operating principle similar to other types of cache. Frequently used data is stored and retrieved first. The cache on your Mac's CPU stores frequently used data, as does the cache on your hard drive or the disk cache you set in your Mac's Memory Control Panel.

In each case, the underlying concept is the same. Faster retrieval makes for faster performance.

Your browser's cache is stored on your hard drive, up to the maximum you set in the program's preferences. Whether a separate file, as in Netscape or iCab, or a single file, as in the latest versions of Microsoft Internet Explorer, the browser checks the artwork and other data at the Web site and accesses the cached version if it's the same.

For that reason, revisiting a site with the same artwork (or mostly the same) gets you there faster. The browser also purges older, least-used artwork to make way for new data. The designers of these programs have worked long and hard to optimize the way these browsers work with caches to make browsing faster.

But the system doesn't always work perfectly.

How to Purge a Web Cache

All things being equal, the Web browser can take care of discarding older cached artwork and replacing it with new artwork as you continue to surf the Net. Over time, however, the process is apt to become less efficient and sometimes, a good idea is to empty the cache and start over to get maximum performance.

NOTE *When you upgrade your Web browser to a newer version, the way it examines the cache may change as well. This is another reason to purge the cache.*

Here is how purging the cache is done in the major Web browsers.

Microsoft Internet Explorer Through Version 5.0

1. Launch Internet Explorer.

NOTE *You will be logged on to your ISP, unless you turned off the feature to connect automatically in the Remote Access Control Panel. But there's no reason to be concerned. Emptying the cache won't cause you any problems. Instead, it may actually fix problems.*

2. Go to the Edit menu and select Preferences.

3. Look at the Browser category and click the arrow at the left to expand the view, if the view collapsed.

4. Click Advanced (see Figure 33-7).

5. To clear the cache, click **Empty Now.** It only takes a moment. The purging process is done in the blink of an eye because the cached artwork is contained in a single file called cache.waf. When you empty this file, it doesn't remove anything. It simply marks the file as ready to be written with all new data. The other options in the Advanced window enable you to adjust your history file (tracking the recent sites you visited), to support multiple connections (so you can download and surf at the same time), and to connect you to your ISP to view a site that hasn't been cached.

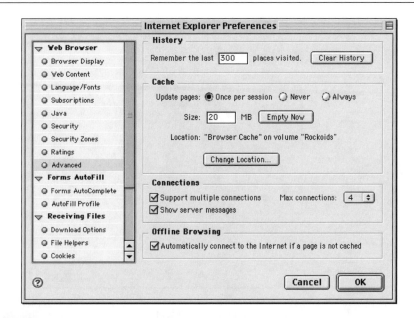

FIGURE 33-7   Adjust Internet Explorer's Web cache from this screen

Netscape Navigator (or Communicator)

1. Launch Netscape.

NOTE

As with Internet Explorer, when you launch Netscape, you're connected to your ISP, unless you turned off the option to connect in the Remote Access Control Panel. Go ahead and empty the Web cache, even though you're online.

2. Go to the Edit menu and choose Preferences.

3. Click the Advanced category (click the arrow to expand the view, if necessary).

4. Look for the item labeled Cache (shown in Figure 33-8).

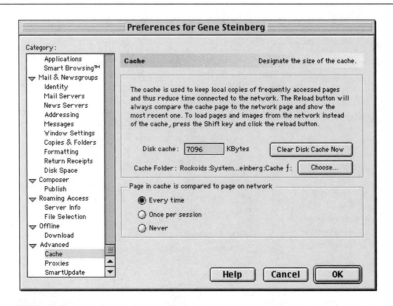

FIGURE 33-8   This is Netscape's cache management screen

5. Click the Clear Disk Cache Now button.

6. You get one of those confirmation messages about the process you must OK. Because Netscape stores all its cached artwork in separate files (and you may have hundreds of them on your hard drive), expect to wait a while for the artwork to be trashed.

AOL 4.0 and 5.0

1. This is one of the many areas in which AOL 4.0 and 5.0 haven't changed a whit. Just launch the program. Unless you click the Sign On button, you won't be connected to AOL.

2. Click the My AOL toolbar button and select Preferences.

3. Scroll down to the icon labeled WWW.

4. With WWW selected, you see your Web preferences (shown in Figure 33-9). Click the button labeled Empty Cache Now. Because AOL uses the same cache.waf file as Internet Explorer, the file is marked as empty, ready for new cached artwork.

5. When you finish, click OK to dismiss the Preferences window.

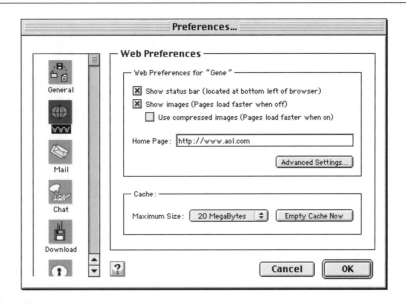

FIGURE 33-9   Click Empty Cache Now to clear AOL's Web cache

iCab

1. Launch iCab. This logs you on to your ISP if the option to connect automatically is set in the Remote Access Control Panel.

2. Choose Preferences from the Edit menu.

3. Scroll down to Caches and click the arrow to point it downward if it's collapsed.

4. Click Web Pages (shown in Figure 33-10) to bring up the display of cache options.

5. Click the button labeled Clear Cache Now. Within a short time, the contents of iCab's cache folder are purged.

6. When you finish, click OK to dismiss the Preferences window.

Deleting Cache Files

Sometimes deleting the cache by the browser's preferences doesn't work. You still experience slow performance or distorted graphics. The next step is to trash the

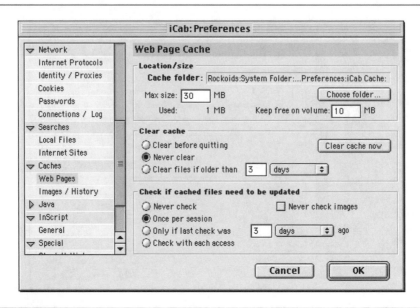

FIGURE 33-10 iCab offers a fairly standard method of deleting the cache file

actual cache file. Before doing so, however, quit the browser. Otherwise, you cannot empty the trash after you drag the files to it.

To eliminate Internet Explorer's cache, use Sherlock 2 to locate the file labeled **cache.waf**. If you're an AOL user, you can find it in the America Online folder, within the System Folder's Preferences folder. Regardless, wherever it ends up, you want to get rid of it.

It's easier with Netscape's cache folder. You can find it in a folder labeled Cache ƒ, usually in a folder with your Netscape user name on it, inside the Netscape Users folder (it was called Netscape ƒ with older versions of the program), which is placed in your System Folder's Preferences folder.

iCab's cache is located in a folder called, naturally, iCab Cache, located in the iCab Preferences folder, within the System Folder's Preferences folder.

In any of these instances, drag the actual cache folder (or the contents) to the trash and then empty the trash.

CAUTION

Restrict your deletion to the actual cache files or the actual folder that contains them. Application folders for a browser typically contain other items you need, such as your bookmarks or favorites (or Hot List with iCab), your preferences, and, in the case of Netscape Communicator, your actual e-mail and address book files You don't want to have to re-create these files if you delete them by error.

Getting a Bigger, Badder Cache

Each browser has its own default setting for the Web cache, and each browser is designed to deliver good performance for most users. Performance may vary, either 5MB or 10MB.

If you browse the Web heavily, however, you may actually get better performance if you double these figures. Experimenting doesn't hurt.

CAUTION

Remember, going too high might have a negative effect. If the browser spends too much time searching the cached files before retrieving new artwork from a Web site, performance suffers. I once saw a user with a 50MB Web cache who complained that browser performance was slow. When I brought it down to 10MB, it was a revelation as to how fast that browser ran.

Boosting the Microsoft Internet Explorer Cache Size

1. Launch Internet Explorer (it logs you on to your ISP if you chose that option in the Remote Access Control Panel).

2. Go to the Edit menu and choose Preferences.

3. To expand the preference view, click the arrow to the left of the Browser category (if it's collapsed).

4. Now click the Advanced category (go back to Figure 33-7 to see the dialog box).

5. Use megabytes to type in the Web cache setting in the Size textbox.

6. Click OK to save your settings.

Boosting the Netscape Navigator (or Communicator) Cache

1. Launch Netscape (this connects you to your ISP if Remote Access has its default setting to connect automatically).

2. Choose Preferences from the Edit menu.

3. Scroll to the category labeled Advanced and click the arrow to provide an expanded view (if it's collapsed).

4. Locate and click Cache, which delivers the setup screen shown back in Figure 33-8.

5. Enter your new cache size in kilobytes (double the original setting for now).

6. To store your settings, click OK.

AOL 4.0 and 5.0

1. Launch AOL. You needn't sign on.

2. Click the My AOL toolbar button and choose Preferences from the submenu.

3. Scroll directly to the WWW option.

4. With WWW preferences onscreen (see Figure 33-11), go to the Cache column at the bottom and select the Web cache size from the pop-up menu (doubling the present figure is fine).

5. Click OK to close the Preferences window and store your settings.

> NOTE   *As mentioned earlier in this chapter, both AOL and Internet Explorer share cache settings. This means the change you make to one affects the other (but sometimes not until both programs have been opened).*

Getting Faster Web Speed with a RAM Disk

If you have a new Mac with a fast hard drive, you won't worry too much over loss of performance from a Web cache. But, with an iBook or PowerBook, or an older Power Mac (where drives were slow), it would be nice if another way existed.

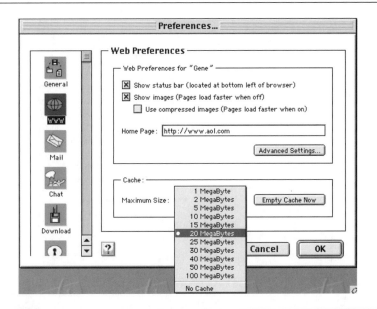

FIGURE 33-11 Choose your Web cache size from the list

And there is another way—it's called a RAM Disk. It's a Mac OS feature that enables you to devote a segment of your Mac's built-in memory to emulate a hard drive. Once you set up the RAM disk, it mounts on your desktop, the same as a hard drive, and you can copy your files to it, including a System Folder.

Every megabyte of RAM you allocate to a RAM Disk is subtracted from available RAM, however. With the Mac OS 9 System Folder usually taking from 200 to 400MB of storage space, using a RAM Disk for a startup disk would be wasteful, even if your Mac is maxed out with RAM.

But you might find using the RAM disk is convenient for your Web cache. You can see if this feature makes the Web cache run better (remember, your Web cache typically ranges from 5MB to 20MB).

Here is how you do it:

1. Pay a visit to the Apple menu, choose Control Panels, and select Memory from the submenu (see Figure 33-12).

2. With the Memory Control Panel displayed, check out the RAM Disk column at the bottom of the screen. Click the On button.

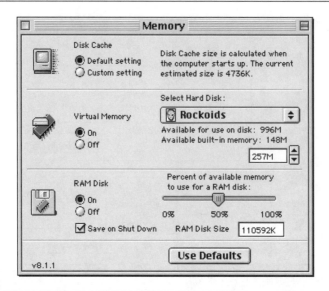

FIGURE 33-12   Create a RAM Disk with the Memory Control Panel

3. Take your mouse and move the slider to allocate a fixed percentage of your Mac's built-in memory for the RAM Disk.

4. If offered, click the Save on Shut Down option. This way, the contents of your Mac's RAM Disk are automatically saved to disk when you shut down your Mac for the day (and you needn't recopy the contents again when you boot the Mac).

> CAUTION
>
> *If a Save on Shut Down option does not appear, don't bother with a RAM Disk. It's not worth the trouble copying these files over every time you start your Mac.*

5. Once your settings are made, close the Memory Control Panel and then restart. On the next restart, a RAM Disk icon is on your Mac's desktop, which you can use in the same fashion as a hard drive and copy files to it.

6. The next step is to put the browser's cache in the RAM Disk. Open the browser's preference panels, precisely as described in the previous section "How to Purge a Web Cache." These settings panels enable you to specify a specific location for the browser's cache.

7. Once you change the location, click OK to store your settings. Now your browser can derive its cache from your RAM Disk

CAUTION

Unfortunately, AOL rigidly insists its Web cache stay in the America Online folder, inside the System Folder's Preferences folder, so this RAM Disk scheme won't work. The same is true if you use both the separate version of Internet Explorer and AOL, as the cache file goes in only that one place. After experimenting with a RAM Disk, if you find it's not for you, return to the Memory Control Panel, turn it off, and that, as they say, is that.

Coping with Internet Access and Performance Problems

The Web browser is the core of the Internet experience for most users, aside from AOL (where it's part of a multifaceted online environment). The Web browser gives you the look and feel of the Internet, by linking you to the sites you want to visit. Also, it is the means by which many of you download files and even check your e-mail (whether Web-based or otherwise).

NOTE

Checking e-mail in Internet Explorer launches your selected e-mail program, but the action can begin with the browser.

In Chapter 32, general Internet setup and connection problems are described. Now the focus is strictly on the browser end of the online equation. The following is a list of fairly common Web-browser problems and their solutions.

■ **Wrong number?**   No room exists for error when you try to access a Web site. If you type a single wrong character, you access a site other than the one you want or you get a warning message indicating the server cannot be located (see Figure 33-13 for a glaring example). If this happens to you, recheck the URL for the site and reenter it, and then press RETURN or ENTER to get to the site.

NOTE

Some larger Web sites buy related domain names, so even people who are guessing or who enter the wrong address somehow manage to get to the right one. But with most of the good names taken already, you can't depend on this. Try to use the right URL the first time.

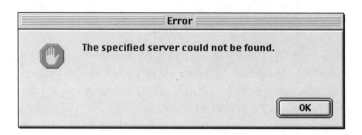

FIGURE 33-13   Microsoft Internet Explorer is telling me the site can't be reached

- **Where's the DNS server?**   When you call up a URL in your browser, behind the scenes your browser checks the Internet to see if the site is accessible. If not, you get a DNS error of one sort or another, usually saying no entry exists for the site (this is a common Netscape error message). The solution is the same as the first, recheck the address or try again at a later time.

- **What's a network socket connection?**   When you attempt to access a site with Netscape, and you're not properly connected to your ISP, you see a message about the failure to make a socket connection. If this happens, try logging off, and then try logging on again to see if this fixes the problem. If not, recheck your Remote Access and TCP/IP Control Panel settings to make sure you entered the correct access numbers and IP addresses for your ISP.

> NOTE   *Because Internet preference files occasionally become corrupt, don't always assume the setup is correct, even if you previously logged on correctly.*

- **The fault lies at the Web site**   In theory, the firms that host Web sites are supposed to be up and running on a 24/7 basis (24 hours, 7 days a week). In practice, equipment breaks down or requires maintenance. If the site is privately hosted, perhaps by a single computer, and that computer crashes, well . . . you get the picture.

NOTE   *In one widely publicized incident, pair Networks of Pittsburgh, a large Web-hosting service that handles a number of major Macintosh Web sites, such as MacCentral.com and VersionTracker.com (and your humble author's MacNightOwl.com), was offline for over a day when it moved to new, larger quarters.*

■ **Out of business?**   Internet startup today, business casualty tomorrow. Or, maybe it changed the site's address or decided to close down for other reasons. Whatever the case, if you recheck the site address and it's still unavailable, don't assume it's anything you've done. You might want to run Sherlock 2's Internet search feature to see if it can find that or a similar site for you. You learn more about Sherlock 2 in Chapter 7.

■ **The fault lies with your ISP**   AOL isn't perfect (you've no doubt read of some of their well-publicized system failures) and regular ISPs also have maintenance problems. You're apt to encounter this situation during the early morning hours, but a system-wide failure can occur at any time. Some services do post news of scheduled outages, however. If you're an AOL member, the keyword **AOL Update** gives you system status information. The Support tab on EarthLink's Personal Start Page carries system information for that service. For other services, check their Home pages for links to support or service update information.

■ **AOL problem: User identification failed**   Despite the obvious meaning of the phrase, more than likely this has nothing whatever to do with your AOL screen name and password. This is usually a system-related problem at AOL's networks: The common solution is to log off and then log on again. If the problem still occurs, try deleting the AOL browser's Web cache (see the following section, "Purging a Web Cache"). Beyond that, you can't do much. If the failure is AOL's, you must wait for AOL to fix it.

■ **Attempt to load failures**   When Remote Access has put you online, it normally puts up a flashing icon in the Apple menu and in the Remote Access Control Strip module. Even if it's flashing, though, you may not be logged on at all. Try another Web site. If the message persists, log off, and then log on again to see if anything changes.

> **NOTE** *If you access the Internet by cable modem or DSL router, check your network hub for a visual indication that you're connected. If you see no indication that you're online, contact your Internet service provider for help*

- **AOL 3.0, 4.0, and 5.0: Attempt to load failures** This problem is often only a matter of reconfiguring AOL if it happens with their service. AOL uses a set of system extensions, with labels beginning with AOL Link, to make an Internet socket connection. Here's a common solution to this sort of symptom. Click the My AOL toolbar button and select Preferences from the submenu. With Preferences open, scroll to the AOL Link icon. First, check whether the option to use AOL Link with your modem is checked. Try unchecking the AOL Link, and then checking it again (sometimes the setting doesn't wake). Then click the Configure button and restart your Mac. You may want to consider reinstalling AOL's software (it has an Upgrade option to retrieve your account information from an older copy), but usually clicking Configure does it.

> **NOTE** *Another possibility exists, which is to disable or discard the AOL Link extensions. If this happens, launch the AOL installer, click the Custom Install option, and check the AOL Communication Files. This installation restores the AOL Link-related extensions.*

- **You need a 128-bit browser** If you're a U.S. or Canadian resident, you can download a version of Internet Explorer or Netscape with the maximum possible security, 128-bit encryption. In fact, some financial institutions, from banks to brokerage houses, require it to ensure that the transactions are conducted with the maximum level of security. You can get the 128-bit empowered updates for these browsers from http://www.microsoft.com/mactopia and http://www.netscape.com. Because actual URLs change occasionally, looking for the browser download areas and following the prompts to get to the one you want is best.

> **NOTE** *AOL also gives you the option to get a version of the software with a built-in 128-bit version of the browser. To get to it, you need to access the Upgrade forum via a U.S. or Canadian dial-up connection. Some financial institutions, however, don't always accept AOL's browser as secure, but this is something between you, AOL, and the firms involved.*

CAUTION

Another update you need covers security certificates, a component of your browser that's required for doing secured transactions on the Internet. In some older browsers, the security certificates expired at the end of 1999. Check with the publisher's Web site about required software updates because you won't be able to do secured transactions without valid certificates.

Fixing Laggard Web Performance

Even if the Web cache has been replaced or expanded, you aren't always guaranteed the fastest possible performance. Other causes of performance problems may exist.

Here's a list of common symptoms and solutions:

- **It's the Web site's fault**   Believe it or not, not all Web sites are run by a huge network of computers. Some are run by a single computer, maybe no different from your Mac. Capacity may be limited and, if too many people try to access the site, performance takes a hit. If it has a system crash, then the site can't be accessed at all. Try the Web site again later.

- **The Web is clogged**   The site you want may be popular or some major news story (such as the Starr Report on President Clinton) might result in much greater Net traffic than normal. Whatever the reason, you can't do much about it, other than to try connecting at a different time.

- **Your ISP is too busy**   AOL is a huge, sprawling enterprise, as is its sister company, CompuServe, and many of the larger ISPs (such as EarthLink). But a finite capacity is all around and, if too many people are trying to get connected at the same time, performance suffers. This factor also prevents you from getting maximum performance with a cable modem. Again, you can do nothing but postpone your Internet visit and see if performance gets better. Try staying away from evening prime-time hours, for example, if performance continues to suffer.

NOTE

I don't want to minimize the benefits of complaining either. If your ISP doesn't deliver the level of performance you want, don't hesitate to call its technical support people about the situation. Perhaps your ISP has already begun a network update to address capacity issues, but if no such update is being done and enough users complain, they have to listen to keep members.

Coping with Internet Access and Performance Problems

NOTE *Another potential cause of a busy signal at a Web site is one of those "denial of service" hacker attacks that have been widely publicized. These assaults involve flooding a Web site with spurious data, so its capacity is quickly overwhelmed. One hopes that ongoing government investigations and cooperation from those who run the major Web portals will reduce these problems.*

Coping with Crashing Internet Software

This is covered, to some degree, in the previous chapter. Internet software tends to be regarded as among the least stable software out there. And, whether Internet software deserves the label or not, it's true such programs have to do an awful lot in a short time. You access a single Web site and one or maybe dozens of graphic files have to be retrieved. You open a second browser window, stop the first, and begin to display another site—you get the picture. All this opening and closing can change program memory requirements, causing an out-of-memory situation or aggravating a possible conflict with another program. Either way, the program may suddenly quit or your Mac could freeze.

Here are some possible causes of these problems, along with solutions:

■ **The Web cache is corrupted** As you download files from the Web, the browser compares them with the artwork cached on your Mac and is supposed to deliver only the changed or new artwork. But if the contents of the cache become corrupt, a crash could result when any one of those items is accessed by the browser. Read the section on removing or deleting a Web cache to see how to address this problem.

■ **System memory soars with AOL 4.0 and 5.0** You look at the memory requirements of AOL software and it doesn't seem so high. But when the program is running, you check the About This Computer window from the Apple menu and you see Mac OS 9 has consumed an additional 5MB or 10MB of RAM. This happens because when you launch the AOL program, it also launches a number of shared components needed to provide basic functionality, such as browsing the Web or e-mail. The only possible solution is to use virtual memory. This way, unused code from the program is left in the virtual memory "swap" file stored on your hard drive.

NOTE

When you install Mac OS 9, virtual memory is turned on by default, to a total of 1MB above your built-in memory. Considering how virtual memory used to impact performance, you may be inclined to open the Memory Control Panel and turn it off. Unless your Mac has a huge amount of RAM (and even 256MB, as I have, isn't huge anymore), I suggest you leave it on for all but critical multimedia work. You'll find performance isn't impacted at all in most cases. In fact, it enables a program to use less RAM, and, once you quit the program, it may in some cases relaunch faster.

Getting Clear Web Graphics

The cornerstone of your Web browsing experience is clear, sharp artwork. Whether it's a news site or an online merchant, you want the pictures to be as clear as possible, with bright colors, easy-to-read lettering, and so on.

But even if you carefully adjust your Mac's display and the brightness, contrast, and color sync settings are perfect, you may find the Web artwork isn't what it should be.

You cannot, of course, do anything about the way the site has been designed. That's up to those who maintain that site. All you can do is hope they share your concerns about delivering the best quality artwork.

However, you can do a few things to give Web graphics a better look.

AOL's .ART Format

Before AOL standardized Microsoft's Internet Explorer for Web browsing, it tried to make its own browser, which, frankly, didn't perform all that well. One of AOL's efforts to speed Web access was to use a proprietary format to compress Web artwork on the fly, as it passed through their network of proxy servers. The intention was to get the page to display faster on your display.

But this had its side effects. For one thing, the speedup is slight—for another, the act of converting a GIF or JPEG to the .ART format (acquired from a company known as Johnson-Grace), which AOL uses, kills Web-based animation graphics and can sometimes cause image quality to nosedive.

The best solution is to remove the setting to compress the artwork. Here's how this is done:

1. Don't sign on AOL, simply open the program.

2. Click the My AOL toolbar button and select Preferences from the submenu.

3. Scroll directly to the WWW icon and select it.

4. Look for the option labeled Use compressed images and uncheck it (see Figure 33-14).

5. To store your settings, click OK. Now you can sign on.

Once the settings are made, AOL won't deliver subpar graphic quality and now you can get the best the Web has to offer.

General Suggestions to Improve Web Artwork

Fixing AOL software won't necessarily repair all your problems with Web-based artwork. Here are more problems and solutions:

- **Purge the Web cache to improve artwork.** If the Web cache is damaged, you might find graphics don't display properly. Worse, your Mac crashes or the browser application quits. You want to follow the instructions earlier in this chapter on removing the cache.

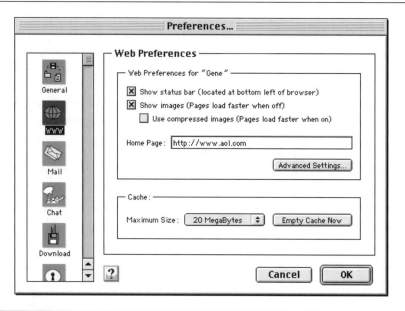

FIGURE 33-14 Rid yourself of the problem of subpar Web graphics on AOL

■ **Try the Refresh button.**   Sometimes Web artwork isn't delivered properly. Perhaps you have a bad connection or too much network traffic exists. If the artwork does not display completely, or if it looks blurry, click the Refresh (or Reload) button on your browser. The site is then called up again and the artwork is downloaded. More often than not, this fixes the problem (but not if the site has a problem or if heavy Net traffic still exists).

> NOTE   *If you're using Netscape, hold down the OPTION key when you click Reload. This invokes the program's Super Reload function, which supposedly provides a more thorough reload process. Sometimes it works when the regular Reload function fails.*

■ **Don't hesitate to use another browser.**   Experienced Web designers know that creating a good-looking Web site can be, in part, a chancy process. This is because different browsers, different versions, display the pages somewhat differently. And sometimes the changes are rather severe. It's not a crapshoot, as you eventually learn how to compensate for most problems. But if you aren't satisfied with how a site looks on, Microsoft Internet Explorer, for example, don't hesitate to try Netscape. Or, use the new one mentioned at the start of this chapter, iCab. Each program interprets Web standards differently. See what you like.

■ **Don't forget the display settings.**   Web sites, when properly designed, not only have to look good with different browsers, they also must look good on computers from different platforms. Not only Macs and Windows computers, but those running UNIX, as well. If the site doesn't look good to you, check your display settings. You might also want to use Mac OS 9's ColorSync Control Panel to run a screen calibration. This way, you can be assured of getting a reasonably accurate color display. The rest is up to the site.

Summing Up

In this chapter, you were introduced to the major Web-browser options, including a new kid on the block, iCab. You also learned how to get the most reliable performance when you visit the Web.

In the next chapter, you learn how to harness the power of e-mail and you get a brief look at the various software options. You don't have to stick with the ones that came with your Mac.

Chapter 34

Discovering the Power of E-mail

Y ou just can't live without e-mail in this day and age. E-mail is the fastest,
easiest way to communicate, and without it, you're cut off from much
of society.

While writing and sending e-mail on a Mac should be easy, problems can occur.
Mail cannot get to its destination or your e-mail program may crash after a few
sessions. You should also be aware of other issues, such as handling the onslaught
of junk e-mail, dealing with files attached to e-mails, and being wary of the
prospects of computer viruses hidden in e-mail.

    This chapter shows you how to get the maximum benefit from your Mac's
e-mail software and how to avoid some of the problems.

Mac E-mail Programs Compared

You can use a number of different programs to send your e-mail on your Mac. Most
are free or, in the case of one, mostly free. But each program has its own strengths and
weaknesses. You want to consider all the options before you try an e-mail program.

> **NOTE**   *With the exception of the first program mentioned here, the AOL user
> is stuck with AOL's own e-mail software or, perhaps, the somewhat
> cumbersome Web version offered. However, AOL's software has
> gained one nifty new feature with version 5.0, which is covered shortly.*

Claris Emailer

Apple's Claris subsidiary is history. FileMaker has been spun off into a new
company, and the older Claris programs have been abandoned, except for the
newly christened AppleWorks.

    Claris Emailer began with a lot of promise, but never quite made the hoped for
splash in the marketplace. This is unfortunate, as it's the only e-mail program that
enables you to retrieve e-mail from America Online and CompuServe, in addition
to regular ISPs, all from a single, simple interface.

    And, at least up to and including Mac OS 9, Claris Emailer runs compatible
with almost any Mac that meets its 3.5MB RAM requirement.

> **NOTE**   *Even though Emailer is officially no longer being produced, it is such a
> good program that the author absolutely refuses to abandon it. You may
> still find it available at a local Mac user group or auction, or from a
> dealer with some older stock in a storage room somewhere. Emailer is
> definitely worth trying to find.*

For first-time users, Emailer has an Easy Setup Wizard, which gets you up-and-running in minutes by enabling you to configure all your online accounts at once.

The interface is easy to use (as shown in Figure 34-1), with one two-paned window. The folders holding your mail are on the left, while the contents of each folder appear on the right when you click them. Messages can be sorted by subject, from/to, date, priority, and account. Within each folder, you can also have subfolders with even more messages.

A toolbar has the features you will probably use most often. You can easily attach files to messages by dragging-and-dropping them into a message. You can also move text between different windows or even between other programs.

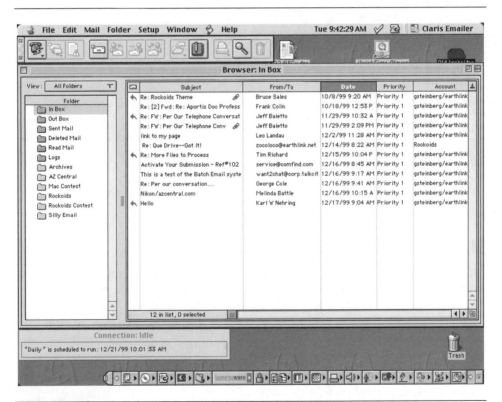

Mac E-mail Programs Compared

<table>
<tr><td colspan="2">FIGURE 34-1</td><td>The simple interface of Claris Emailer has been duplicated to some
extent in other programs, but never exceeded</td></tr>
</table>

Emailer has a feature called *mail actions,* which filters your mail by the rules you specify. One mail action can cause several things to occur at once, like indicating the priority of a message, putting a message into a certain folder, running a script, and adding the person who sent you a message to your address book. This feature is especially useful if you want to eliminate junk mail or sort messages from the mailing lists you subscribe to in a special location, so they don't clutter your main window.

AppleScript gets direct support and you can activate a few already built-in scripts from the scripts icon in the menu bar. A number of third-party scripts are currently available for the program from the original publisher (who sold it to Claris just before it came out), Fog City Software, at http://www.fogcity.com.

All the mail in the program is stored in an internal database, instead of in separate files. This means your messages take up less space on your hard drive, the program is faster and more responsive, and it takes much less time to find a specific message. Other features included a spell-checker and Help menu, as well as support for multiple signatures. Emailer can also handle as many different online or ISP accounts as you want. And, you can set up Emailer to connect to AOL, CompuServe, or your ISP to check your e-mail at specified times, so you needn't go through the hassle of checking manually every time.

> TIP
>
> *Claris Emailer's mail database can sometimes get corrupted and crash your Mac when it gets too large. If this happens, launch the program, hold down the* OPTION *key, and select one of two database rebuild options. The first, Typical, cleans up the database for most purposes.*

Finally, you can change and store various access numbers for your area and the connection information required when you leave home.

Microsoft Outlook Express

Microsoft's *Outlook Express 5* (see Figure 34-2) is a free download from the Internet. Outlook Express makes you think twice about paying anything at all for an e-mail program. Too bad it doesn't support AOL e-mail.

Outlook Express has an extremely wide list of features to suit many people. Account Setup Wizard makes setting up your existing accounts easy and it can even create a Hotmail account. You can import your messages, contacts, signatures, and other account information to Outlook Express from a number of different e-mail programs, ranging from previous versions of Outlook Express, to Claris Emailer, Eudora, and Netscape Messenger (part of Netscape Communicator).

The program's handy Preview pane enables you to see everything from a single window, including your new messages. You don't have to double-click a message title to open it, as you do with Claris Emailer. You can format a letter in the Preview pane, as well as change the size of text, move it around, and so on.

You can also configure Outlook Express to perform various tasks automatically, such as checking your e-mail account at specified times. The program has support for computers used by more than one person, with separate Inboxes, account information, and Preference settings for every user. Outlook Express also supports Mac OS 9's Multiple Users feature. Managing a number of different e-mail accounts is easy, and you can switch between POP, IMAP4, and Hotmail accounts. You can also search for messages by a number of criteria using the Advanced Find feature.

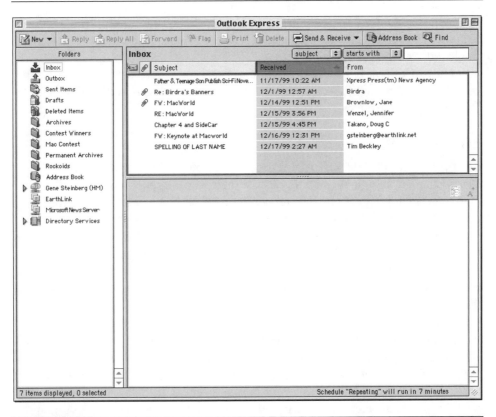

FIGURE 34-2   Outlook Express has become the program to beat on the Mac platform

Mac E-mail Programs Compared

Sending and receiving e-mail with attachments is simple, even if the sender or recipient is using a different e-mail program or computing platform. You can add and remove attachments, and change the settings in the Attachments pane, as well as encode your files in a number of different encoding formats.

Another feature is the Junk Mail Filter, which helps you automatically pinpoint suspected junk e-mail.

> **NOTE** *Junk Mail Filter is described later in this chapter, as part of the section on setting such filters in the various e-mail programs.*

Besides storing e-mail addresses, home, and work addresses, plus phone and fax numbers, the Address Book feature enables you to add other contact information you may need. Also, whenever you address a message, all the contacts in your Address Book are automatically available to you. When someone sends a message to you, it's easy to add their e-mail address to your Address Book.

If you're interested in participating in Usenet newsgroups, you'll find Outlook Express is perfectly capable of managing your messages, using the same interface employed for e-mail.

Finally, Outlook Express enables you to keep your address book in sync with your 3Com Palm Pilot (if you have one). Unfortunately, support doesn't extend to the messages themselves.

Eudora Pro

Eudora Pro from Qualcomm is also used widely on the Mac platform. Unlike Claris Emailer, though, it can only receive Internet or intranet-based e-mail. The program has a great set of features, however, perfect for almost anyone. The interface for Eudora Pro is simple (see Figure 34-3), and it's not hard to attach files and work with the mailboxes, folders, and messages. You have the ability to do several things at once in the program. At the same time you're downloading or sending e-mail messages, you can also search for an address in your address book or even create a filter to block out junk mail. You can also group together the windows you use most often into their own container windows. This enables you to put the windows somewhere where you have easy access at any time.

The message preview pane enables you to see what is inside a message without actually opening it. You can also send and receive messages with graphics or photos in them, so you needn't open a program like Graphic Converter or Adobe Photoshop to see them. Eudora Pro also has a built-in spell-checker, using Working Software's SpellSwell, which helps eliminate the errors you made in your messages. A unique feature of the program is the capability to exchange messages using your voice. However, you need to download the PureVoice plug-in from Qualcomm's Web site (www.qualcomm.com).

You can also set up multiple e-mail accounts and access them all from the same interface. Eudora enables you to send and receive Internet mail quickly and easily: it supports the POP3 and IMAP4 protocols. For each account, you can set up different signatures to personalize your letters. You can also create automated responses to use if you get many of the same types of messages every day (for example, if your name is Bob, and many people mistake you for a different Bob). Eudora Pro also supports a number of encoding methods, such as *MIME* (*Multipurpose Internet Mail Extension*), BinHex, and UUENCODE, to process your attachments in a form that's easily interpreted by the recipients.

The address book is easy to customize, and you can set up more than one address book for all your different contacts. Finally, you can use filters to identify and put your mail where you specify, put messages in different folders, forward messages, or use automated responses to answer them. You can also use filters to block messages from different sources or automatically trash them when they are sent to you.

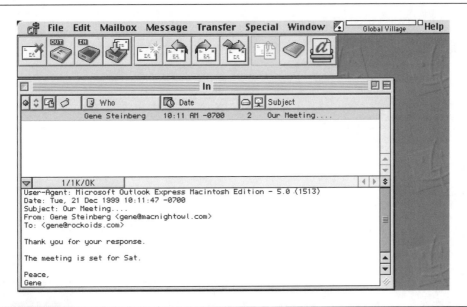

FIGURE 34-3   Eudora Pro is slowly moving from a commercial program to a hybrid, with a full-featured version that's free if you select advertising as part of its interface

Mac E-mail Programs Compared

Netscape Messenger

Netscape's Messenger module is part of its Communicator Web-browsing software (see Figure 34-4). While its features are not quite as extensive as those of the other three programs, it still offers quite enough for casual e-mail users. Its interface is simple, with three panes to make it simplify message management. The address book provides two panes, with support for more than one address book and better management of your lists. Using Pinpoint Addressing, you can accurately and quickly address your e-mails. The program's search feature enables you to find e-mail address in your own address books or in a corporate directory.

If you also use Eudora or Outlook Express for your e-mail, you can import your messages, folders, address books, and preferences from those programs. Messenger supports the IMAP standard.

To round out its features, you can participate in UseNet discussion groups, in the same fashion as Outlook Express, using a single convenient interface.

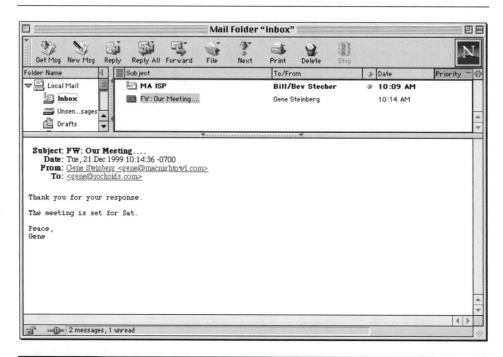

FIGURE 34-4   A familiar, simple interface makes Netscape Messenger easy to use

Messenger also has templates you can use for message formatting. Finally, you can keep your e-mail and address books in sync with that of your Palm Pilot.

AOL

If you're an *America Online (AOL)* member, aside from Claris Emailer and an AOL's Web-based e-mail feature, you have to use AOL's software to handle your e-mail.

But this shouldn't necessarily limit you from doing the essentials in sending and receiving messages. AOL's mail feature offers an easy-access graphic interface (see Figure 34-5) with most of the basic functions accessible with clearly labeled buttons.

AOL 5 for the Mac, which was due to ship when this book came out, adds the capability to store an online signature for each screen name on your account (it's available from the Mail Center toolbar button). You can send e-mail to single or multiple recipients and attach files, but multiple attachments must be compressed by AOL's built-in StuffIt compression tool.

Mac E-mail Programs
Compared

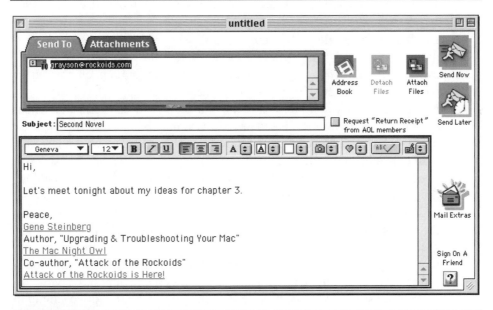

FIGURE 34-5   Beginning with AOL 5 for the Mac, you can also store your online signature

The coolest AOL e-mail feature, though, is the capability to insert photos or embed them in the background. This is a useful feature when communicating with a fellow AOL member, but it doesn't work when you send the message to a service outside AOL (or to users of very old versions of AOL's program). You can also insert a Favorite Place hyperlink and adjust text styles and colors, but again, these features are restricted to members only.

A Common Sense Guide to E-mail Attachments

Times may occur when you've just completed a cool advertisement for a company, and you need to submit the document to your boss for approval. Or, maybe you finished the latest chapter of a book you know will be a candidate for the best-seller list, and you need to deliver it to the publisher immediately.

Whenever you need to attach a file to your e-mail, you can click the Attach button and send the file where it needs to go.

You may think nothing can go wrong now. But, to your surprise, you receive a message saying you have the wrong e-mail address. Or, the recipient complains the e-mail never arrived at all.

What do you do now?

Here is some information to be aware of before you send e-mail with attached files:

- **Don't send large files.**   Some *Internet service providers* (*ISPs*) and online services impose restrictions on how large files attached to e-mails can be, but sometimes they may not have that information in an obvious place. AOL, for example, lets you send messages of up to 16MB to members, but only up to 2MB to nonmembers. EarthLink's file attachment limit is 10MB. If your file is too large, it is simply bounced or returned to you, which can come as an uncomfortable shock if you just spent an hour uploading it during an e-mail session. One way to reduce file size is to compress it, using StuffIt. Depending on the type of file you're sending, StuffIt (or the shareware version, DropStuff) may reduce it to only 10 or 20 percent of its original size. You may also find it convenient to divide the file into several pieces or use your ISP's free Web or FTP storage space for the file. AOL gives you 2MB, which is no better than what they give you for sending file attachments beyond the service. EarthLink offers 6MB. If you intend to transfer large files on a regular basis, you might even see if a Web hosting service can give you a low price simply to establish an FTP transfer site. One Internet hosting service, pair Networks (http://www.pair.com), which hosts many of the most popular Mac Web sites, only charges $5.95 per month for FTP-only service. Otherwise, you can transfer the files to a floppy or a Zip disk and take it directly to the person, or send it through old-fashioned snail mail.

NOTE *Another possibility for handling large files is iDisk, one of the iTools features offered by Apple at their Web site for Mac OS 9 users. With iDisk (which allows you up to 20MB of storage space), you can place files in a Public Folder to make them accessible to others with Internet access (with the attendant lack of security, of course, but it is an alternative).*

■ **Try resending it.**   Even if the file meets the size restrictions, it can still get bounced during transmission and be sent back to you. Perhaps you used the wrong e-mail address when you sent the files, or a problem related to your ISP could have stopped the file from reaching its correct destination. If you really need to get a file somewhere, then try again and see what happens. If the person you're sending the file to has more than one e-mail address, send it to one of the other addresses or to all of them at once.

When E-mail Doesn't Reach Where It's Going

No matter how careful you are, your e-mail may sometimes not reach the right place. You probably only made a silly error in the process of addressing the e-mail, such as forgetting a letter, a number, or giving the wrong domain name. Most of the time, you get a message telling you what happened and why. Then you can fix the mistakes you made and resend the message.

Of course, you won't always get a message. Sometimes, the Internet services won't let you know a problem exists in the e-mail. Here are some ways to deal with this problem:

■ **Make sure you have the right address.**   Putting only one wrong letter or number, or an incorrect domain name in an e-mail address causes problems when you send your e-mail. You may get a message that no such person exists or it may go to someone who happens to have that address, who may send you a nasty note saying you sent e-mail to the wrong person. Or, the recipient may just ignore it, and then you'll never know where the message went or if it was received.

■ **Use another address.**   If the person you're sending e-mail to has more than one e-mail address, try sending the e-mail to one of the other

When E-mail Doesn't Reach Where It's Going

e-mail addresses. E-mail accounts have finite limits and perhaps one of the recipient's mailboxes was full. AOL, for example, limits you to 550 messages. This may seem a lot, but not when you consider that some folks may receive dozens or hundreds of messages a day as part of their business.

■ **Remove attached files.**   As previously explained, ISPs limit the size of file attachments (in some cases they may limit transfer of self-expanding files). The message will be returned, but the message you see may not clearly explain what went wrong. Try sending the message without the attachment. If it arrives, consider other methods to get your files to your recipient.

■ **Just send it again.**   The Internet is a huge place where millions of messages are transferred each day. An ISP, or even a complete network segment, may have an outage. It's amazing the system works as well as it does, considering the chances for something to go wrong. If the message doesn't get to your recipient after a day or so, resend it.

■ **Use a different e-mail program.**   If you don't use AOL, your only option is Claris Emailer, if you can find a copy. With a regular ISP, there's no such limitation. If Netscape Messenger doesn't do it for you, there's always Outlook Express or Eudora, to name two of the options.

■ **Be patient.**   Realize that with the Internet, an e-mail can take as little as a few seconds to as much as several hours to reach its destination. The Internet is unpredictable. Be willing to grit your teeth and wait a while.

A Realistic View of E-mail Viruses

You've probably heard about the warnings not to open certain e-mails because you could damage your files, or worse, destroy your hard drive. But is there really any reason to worry over something like this?

Well, no . . . sort of.

The only way to make a virus active or to transfer it to your computer is to download and open an infected file. E-mail programs, other than AOL, download the file when you receive the message containing it (it's a separate step on AOL), but as long as you don't open the file, it shouldn't do any damage. Your Mac won't suddenly crash when you open e-mail with an infected file. You have to watch out, though, when dealing with attached files.

The curse of the Melissa virus comes to mind. That particular virus spread itself by masquerading as a genuine e-mail from someone you know. While Melissa's worst damage was to users of the Windows platform, there's no telling what future virus authors might think of to disrupt Mac users.

So the point is this: If you receive an e-mail with a file attached that you didn't know was coming, but you do know who sent it, make sure to reply to the message and confirm that this person did send the file to you. When you send a file to someone else, include an explanation in the e-mail of what the file is and what its purpose is, to reassure the recipient that the file is genuine.

Dealing with E-mail Annoyances

Let's say you sent your e-mail to the right address and took every precaution possible to make sure the message gets to its recipient. Even then, however, you can never be entirely sure the person will receive it in the form it was intended. He may not even get the e-mail. You can control a few of the things that cause these problems, but others have to do with what e-mail software you're using or even the e-mail service you use.

Be aware of some precautions when sending e-mail through AOL and an ISP. The major precautions are described in the next two sections.

AOL E-mail Problems and Solutions

AOL has grown by leaps and bounds over the past few years, with over 20 million members all over the planet, and still more coming in every day. Much of the e-mail on the Internet is being sent and received by members of AOL, which is the undisputed number-one online service.

You should be aware of some things, however, when dealing with e-mail on AOL.

- ■ **Address e-mail from AOL to the Internet very carefully.**   AOL deals with e-mail addresses in a different manner than other ISPs. First, AOL's type of e-mail address, known as a *screen name,* enables you to put a space between words, which isn't allowed by other online and Internet services. If you use the Internet to send e-mail to a person who has a space in his screen name (like joe smith@aol.com), make sure you put an underscore between each word (joe_smith@aol.com). If you don't, then it's likely your e-mail will be sent to the wrong person (in that example, smith@ aol.com, since the first name will be dropped).

■ **Don't freak out if you receive a message from MAILER-DAEMON@ aol.com.** These messages don't contain viruses and they won't hurt your computer in any way. They are there to tell you your e-mail cannot be sent to its destination, and the message itself tells you why that can't happen. Read the message before you panic.

■ **Don't send large files outside AOL.** At press time, AOL imposed a limit of only 2MB for files attached to e-mails being sent to and from the Internet. If you use AOL and you're sending a file to another AOL member, then you get 16MB. If you have to send a lot of large files to AOL members often, then you should also consider getting your own AOL account.

■ **Never send more than one attachment to AOL or ISP members.** The MIME protocol is not supported by AOL in the same fashion as other services. In other words, you can't send more than one file with your e-mail, unless you use its built-in compression software to create an archive. The best format is StuffIt for the Mac and Zip for Windows users. If you get an e-mail with more than one attachment, it will come all in one file, which must be run through a decoding program to access its contents. Luckily, the most recent versions of StuffIt Expander and shareware programs, such as Decoder, can extract the contents of a MIME file, although sometimes it may not work. If you must send more than one file through an ISP to an AOL member, first compress the files into one file using StuffIt.

■ **AOL restricts the sizes of its mailboxes.** On AOL, you can only have 550 messages in an incoming mailbox at any time. Older e-mail sent to you is deleted after seven days and e-mail you sent remains for thirty days (even sooner if you get a lot of messages). If you receive hundreds of e-mail messages in a short while, you could receive a "mailbox is full" message. If you get a lot of e-mail often, be sure you check it and read it as quickly and as often as you can. You can use AOL's Personal Filing Cabinet feature to store e-mail you need to save past the time limit.

■ **When sending e-mail to non-AOL members, don't use special formatting.** AOL provides several message formatting features, which include font, style, size, and color. But AOL doesn't use the same type of HTML for formatting as such programs as Outlook Express, for example. Rather than concern yourself over what formats will translate and what formats won't, limit your message to nonmembers to straight, unformatted text.

AOL versions 4.0 and 5.0 for Mac and Windows enable you to embed photographs in the background of your message. But none of this translates to older versions of the software or to messages sent to users who are not on AOL. Use this feature with caution or just send the picture as an e-mail attachment.

Why AOL Crashes

AOL's Personal Filing Cabinet enables you to store e-mail sent to you, so you have a copy even after AOL's e-mail servers scrap it. The Personal File Cabinet is susceptible to file corruption, however, and large File Cabinets could even crash your Mac.

Methods of dealing with this problem do exist, though. You can compact your Personal Filing Cabinet occasionally. By doing this, you can rebuild the file's database, which removes deleted files, and allows it to work better. AOL should do that automatically whenever you quit the program, but it may not always occur.

Follow these steps to compact the Personal Filing Cabinet in AOL 4.0 and 5.0:

First, open AOL. You needn't sign on. Second, select the My AOL menu from its icon in the toolbar and choose Preferences. Go to the Filing Cabinet option, which causes the screen shown in Figure 34-6 to appear.

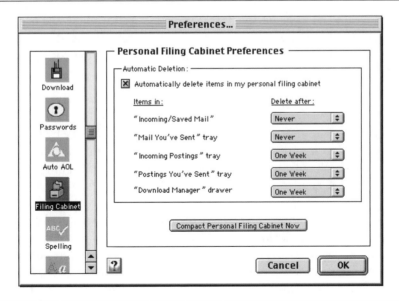

FIGURE 34-6   This screen enables you to clean up your Personal Filing Cabinet in AOL

Dealing with E-mail Annoyances

And third, select the button called Compact Personal Filing Cabinet Now, and then click OK to close the Preferences window.

You can also protect yourself in another way. You can back up your Personal Filing Cabinet file so you have a copy if the original is damaged or lost. Remember, each screen name has a separate Personal File Cabinet file.

The file is located in a folder with the name America Online in the Preferences folder inside the System Folder. Open the America Online folder and find another folder called Data. Within the Data folder is a file for your screen name with the words Filing Cabinet after it. This file will be something like Zeuther's Filing Cabinet, for example. Then, using the Finder's Duplication function, you can make a copy or you can put a copy of the file somewhere else on your Mac by holding down the OPTION key.

Internet E-mail Problems and Solutions

All ISPs are prone to some of the same problems that occur in AOL, although the problems don't get the same level of publicity (simply because the services are much smaller). The following mentions some of these problems:

■ **Message indicating the mailbox is full**   Other services besides AOL impose limits on how large an e-mail box can be. If you're sending a file to someone whose e-mail system is running while she's on vacation, and she hasn't had a chance to check her e-mail in a few days, the mailbox could be filled. You can wait and send the e-mail late, send your e-mail to another e-mail address if the recipient has more than one, or try to contact her by phone.

■ **Program quits for no reason**   E-mail software is sensitive to how much memory you allocate to it. If your Mac has sufficient available built-in memory, you can give the software more memory by using the Finder's Get Info option in the File menu. Increase the memory allotment by 1MB each time, but make sure the program is closed before you try to make this change (otherwise you cannot change the memory allocation).

TIP   *Both Outlook Express and Claris Emailer, which were developed, in part, by some of the same programmers, enable you to rebuild a corrupted mail database file, a potential source of crashes. Hold down the OPTION key when you launch either program and OK the message to rebuild the database. Remember to manually remove the database files with the word "old" in the file name later.*

- **Watch out for ObjectSupportLib**   The extension known as ObjectSupportLib is not needed for Mac OS 9 (or any Mac OS 8 version, for that matter). This is because its functions were put in the System file. Older programs may still install this extension. In theory, this shouldn't make a difference. In practice, it has been blamed on performance anomalies or system crashes. If you find this file, trash it.

- **Crashes occur when opening Netscape Messenger**   One of the features of Netscape Messenger enables you to compact a message folder, which then enables you to eliminate deleted data and to optimize the file. As with other e-mail programs, cleaning up this file may remove a potential cause of slow performance or system crashes. To compact a message folder, choose the e-mail folder you want to compact, and then select Compact This Folder from the File menu (this option is only available if Messenger is open). You should also use Messenger's Empty Trash Folder feature every once in a while because a lot of trashed e-mail causes your e-mail files to become bloated.

Use an E-mail Forwarding Service When You Travel

Many people have more than one e-mail account, while others use more than one e-mail service. You can use whichever provides the best performance and services for your own needs.

Whatever your needs, an e-mail forwarding service may be just the thing for you. Places that provide this service give you an e-mail address and you can decide where you want your e-mail sent at any time.

The three most prominent places that offer this service are Pobox (http://www.pobox.com), Bigfoot (http://www.bigfoot.com) and iFORWARD (http://www.iforward.com). If your e-mail service is based on the Web, you may already get automatic forwarding.

How to Cope with Junk E-mail

Junk e-mail can be a bad thing and can quickly clutter your mailbox. Junk e-mail includes such things as misleading advertisements, get-rich-quick schemes, pornography ads, and a lot more. All of it is extremely annoying, however, and can make your e-mail experience an unpleasant one.

How to Cope with Junk E-mail

Luckily, e-mail programs provide methods to filter your junk mail. Beginning with Outlook Express 5, the process became more or less automatic. For other programs, you need to create separate filters for each domain or sender who sends you junk mail.

Here's how you can attack the junk mail problem with AOL and the four popular e-mail programs mentioned.

America Online

Because AOL is the world's biggest online service, it is more prone to junk mail than any other service. Luckily, AOL's lawyers have fought heated court battles to fight junk e-mailers and have won several significant legal victories. This has discouraged a lot of junk-mail senders and reduced the problem to a level far below what it once was.

Also, AOL has a Mail Controls feature that enables you to filter out the most offensive e-mail you get and block e-mail from those senders who often bother you online. This is how to work with AOL's Mail Controls:

1. First, sign on to AOL with your master account name. This one appears first in your list of screen names and it's also the first one you use after you create your AOL account.

TIP
If you use another name frequently on your AOL account, you can also give "master" status to your other AOL screen names. The setting is made in the Mail Controls area. By doing this, you can also set Mail and Parental Controls for that name.

2. Once you're logged in, type in the keyword **Mail Controls**. A screen similar to the one in Figure 34-7 should appear.

3. Now, select the Set Up Mail Controls button, and the screen shown in Figure 34-8 appears.

4. Select the screen name for which you want Mail Controls, and then click the Edit button. The screen where you can actually edit your controls now appears (see Figure 34-9).

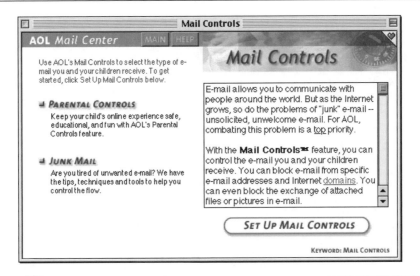

FIGURE 34-7   AOL's Mail Controls enables you to block mail from senders or whole domains

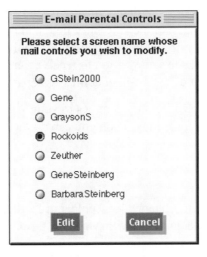

FIGURE 34-8   Choose from the list of screen names to customize e-mail settings

How to Cope with Junk E-mail

Many features and settings are available in AOL's Mail Controls

5. Type the e-mail address, domain, or Internet service from which you don't want to receive e-mail in the text entry field and then click Add to include it or select a setting for all your e-mail. If you only want to get e-mail from certain people, use the same option to receive e-mail only from those people. Enter each of their e-mail addresses separately in the text field.

6. After you make the necessary changes to your Mail controls, click the Save button to store your settings. Then you can do the same for all your other screen names.

Claris Emailer

Yes, Claris Email has been orphaned by Apple, but I still unhesitatingly support it anyway because it works just fine with Mac OS 9. And with any luck, you may locate a dealer who still has a copy.

Here's how to set up Emailer's powerful filtering capability:

1. In the Setup menu, select Mail Actions, and then the screen shown in Figure 34-10 appears.

FIGURE 34-10   In this screen, you can make an Emailer action

2. Now, choose the New button, and then the screen shown in Figure 34-11 appears.

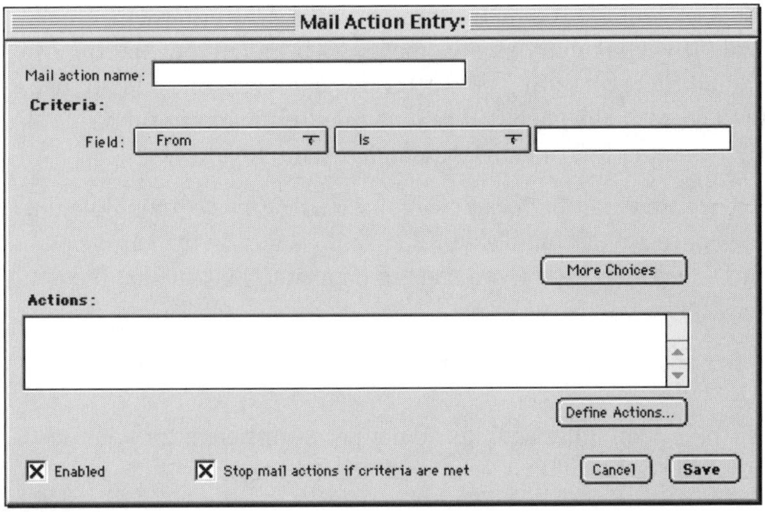

Mail Action Entry:

Mail action name:

Criteria:

Field: From   Is

More Choices

Actions:

Define Actions...

☒ Enabled   ☒ Stop mail actions if criteria are met   Cancel   Save

FIGURE 34-11   In this window, you can configure your Mail Actions

How to Cope with Junk E-mail

3. Name your mail action something to identify its purpose, such as junk mail. Put the required information in the fields. You should include one or more keywords that might be in the average piece of junk e-mail. Next, under action, click the Define Actions button. When the next window appears, choose an option for messages that meet your specifications. You should probably place the messages in the Deleted Mail folder, which automatically eliminates the mail.

Outlook Express

Among the new features in Outlook Express 5 is a Junk Mail filter. By using the program's internal logic, it can decide what e-mail you consider junk. Among the specs are forged e-mail addresses, which happens a lot in junk mail. To get this new version of Outlook Express, you can download it free of charge from Microsoft's Web site at http://www.microsoft.com.

Follow these steps to use the Junk Mail filter:

1. Open Outlook Express and select the Tools menu. Choose Junk Mail filter, and then the screen shown in Figure 34-12 appears.

2. To activate the junk mail filter, select the Enable Junk Mail Filter check box. Then, using the Sensitivity slider, you can decide how thoroughly Outlook Express should examine e-mail for the criteria that makes it junk mail. If you regularly receive messages from Internet mailing lists, you should choose a setting between Low and Average, so legitimate e-mail isn't accidentally specified as junk mail. If you don't subscribe to any such mailing list, though, try a higher setting.

3. To be sure the filter doesn't search e-mail from a certain domain, enter it at the bottom of the Junk Mail Filter setup screen in the corresponding text box. Then select what you want to happen to junk mail at the bottom of the screen.

4. After you finish, click OK and your settings are then saved.

If your Junk Mail Filter settings do not prove sufficient for your needs, change the settings and see how they work under normal use.

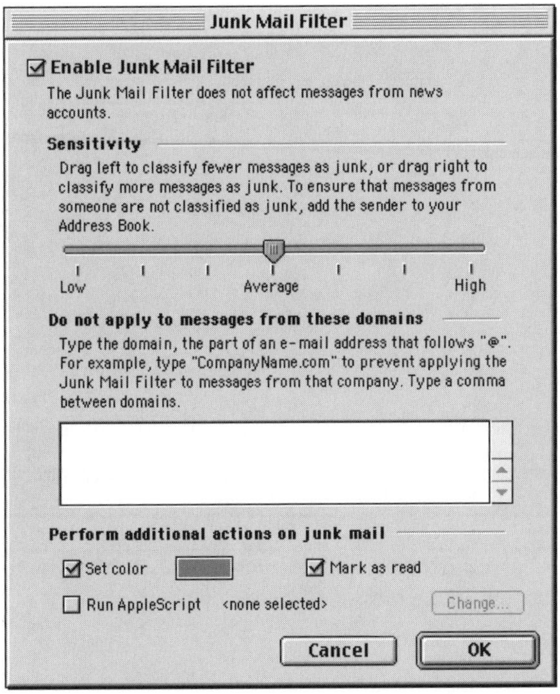

FIGURE 34-12   The Junk Mail Filter in Outlook Express helps clear your mailbox of unwanted e-mail

You can also have more powerful filters for certain kinds of e-mail. Here's how:

1. First, open Outlook Express and, from the Tools menu, select Mail Rules. The screen shown in Figure 34-13 should appear.

2. Choose whichever tab has to do with the Rule you want to add. You should select Mail (POP) for regular Internet e-mail addresses. Depending on the type of service you have, though, you need to choose other e-mail categories (Outlook Express also supports office e-mail systems). The screen shown in Figure 34-14 then appears. In this case, the category has been filled out already.

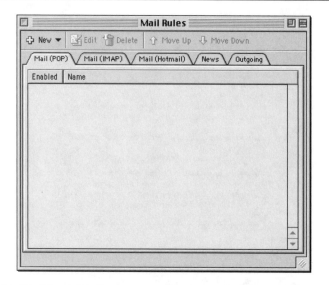

FIGURE 34-13   Outlook Express's Mail Rules feature enables you to apply specific actions to the messages you receive

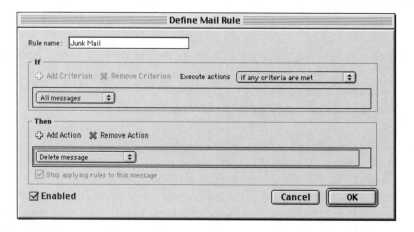

FIGURE 34-14   Configure Mail Rules in Outlook Express from this screen

3. Now put a Rule name in the text field at the top. In the If category, you can choose what conditions the filter uses to decide what to do with the junk mail.

4. In the pop-up menu, select the criteria which have several categories, including From and Subject line.

5. Type the keyword or keywords you want the filter to search for in the text field.

6. Next, under the Then category, which is what the filter will do if it finds an e-mail that meets the criteria, choose an action from the pop-up menu. In addition to an option simply to delete the message, a number of other choices exist, such as transferring the message to another folder. Then, click the Enabled check box to activate the rule. After that, click OK to save your settings.

Eudora Pro

Although most e-mail programs are free and offer lots of good features, Eudora Pro wins out because of its mail-handling features. You can also apply filters to block mail from various people and places.

NOTE *At press time, Qualcomm was experimenting with a new way to distribute Eudora. A limited-feature version, successor to the freeware Eudora Lite, will be available. Two full-featured versions will also be offered (one will include paid ads). If you want to forego the ads, you can buy the software and get all the features without the ad banners.*

1. First, open Eudora Pro and choose Filters in the window menu, causing a screen like the one in Figure 34-15 to appear.

2. Now, select the e-mail category the filter corresponds to under Match. Next, enter the words that cause the filter to become active under Header. From the pop-up-menu right next to the keyword, choose a category.

3. Under Actions, select what should happen to the message from the pop-up menu. You could put the mail in another folder or have it trashed immediately.

4. Finally, click the close box to save your new settings.

How to Cope with Junk E-mail

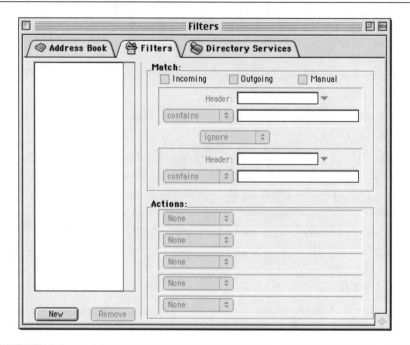

FIGURE 34-15   All the filters for Eudora are placed in one convenient window

Netscape Communicator

Aside from Outlook Express's Junk Mail Filter, Netscape Communicator's Messenger module is just as capable when filtering junk mail. You can block a lot of unwanted mail with a reliable set of e-mail actions.

Follow these steps to use the Message Filters in Netscape Messenger:

1. First, open Netscape. From the Edit menu, select Message Filters, which should cause a screen like the one in Figure 34-16 to appear. In this case, I already entered the information for my Junk Mail filter.

2. Choose where your rules should be in effect in the pop-up menu at the top of the screen.

3. Make up a name for the rule in the text box, and then select the Enabled check box to put it in action.

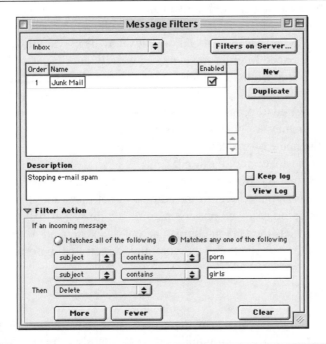

FIGURE 34-16   Netscape Messenger's filters enable you to deposit junk mail in another location

4. Next, create a description that gives the purpose for the filter under Description. If the arrow on the left of the Filter Action label has been collapsed, click it. Choose from a variety of categories in the pop-up menus.

5. Finally, under the Then category, select an action (such as Delete) from the pop-up menu. After you click the close box, your settings are saved for later use.

Complaining About Junk Mail

If you are still getting waves of junk mail, even after you set up powerful filters, you can do something else to stop it. You can complain to the ISP where the e-mail appears to have originated. I use the word "appears" because the address in the From line could have been forged, which means someone is trying to blame someone else for sending you (and, most likely, others) this unwanted e-mail.

E-mail programs have an option that can enable you to show Internet headers (this occurs automatically in AOL). This can help the people who investigate junk e-mailers find who the true culprit is. Forgeries may be clever enough to fool most people, but experienced Internet travelers can usually dig out the telltale clues about the service that originally produced the message by looking at those headers.

To send the e-mail message and comment or complaint, use the Forward command in your e-mail program. Send the message to either of these addresses: abuse@<domainname> or postmaster@<domainname>. Where it says "domain name," place the name of the domain where the junk e-mail appeared to have originated, such as aol.com or earthlink.net.

But don't even bother sending a complaint back to the place where the junk e-mail seemed to originate. Even if the address is not fake (and this means an innocent person could receive your complaint), sending an e-mail to the sender of the junk e-mail lets the person confirm he got the correct address, and this could make you the recipient of even more junk e-mail than before.

Summing Up

In this chapter, you discovered how to master your e-mail so you can get the benefit of this great way of communicating as efficiently as possible.

This chapter included coverage on handling e-mail attachments. In the next chapter, the focus is extended to general Internet file transfers, including Mac OS 9's Internet File Sharing feature.

Chapter 35

Internet File Transfers

Transferring files over the Internet used to be a fairly complex process where you would log in to remote servers and then use *Telnet* (a method to access another computer, usually via a text-based interface) to copy files. As time went by, the process of copying files from one computer to another became progressively easier, as FTP was developed and quickly spread around the Net.

Over the last few years, we've seen the growth of the Internet simply explode as the World Wide Web became more and more popular and Web browsers were developed that enabled you to move files easily between your computer and a server on the network. Finally, with the introduction of Mac OS 9, Apple has made file transfers even easier by making sharing files over the Internet via regular File Sharing possible.

In this chapter, you learn about the various Internet File Sharing methods and the easiest ways to set them up on your Mac.

Internet File Transport Protocols

While many different protocols can be used to transfer files over the Internet, only three have significance to Mac users. These three protocols are FTP, HTTP, and the new Internet-enabled version of Mac File Sharing introduced with Mac OS 9. Using any one of these three protocols, you can easily and quickly move files to and from your Mac.

FTP, the First Real Internet File Transfer Software

File Transfer Protocol (*FTP*), was first developed in the early 1980s as a way of transferring files easily from computer to computer over a network connection. FTP was a major step forward as it allowed for the easy transfer of both text and binary, machine-language files between two computers connected to a local network or even over the Internet. FTP servers also enabled you to post files that might be of interest to the public and allowed anyone to connect to your server anonymously to retrieve them.

Today, most FTP servers are used to transfer files that are too large to be transferred efficiently via HTTP, the standard protocol of the Web, say, 5 MB or over. Because FTP servers can be accessed either by a dedicated FTP-client tool like Dartmouth University's Fetch or by a Web browser like Microsoft's Internet Explorer or AOL's Netscape Navigator, transferring files is a simple process.

HTTP: The Protocol That Runs the Web

Hypertext Transport Protocol (*HTTP*) was first developed in 1990 by Tim Berniers Lee when he developed the first Web server. HTTP has grown and expanded over the years with the introduction of HTTP version 1.1, which added significantly more functionality to the protocol. HTTP allowed for much easier file transfers between servers and for greatly improved navigation when browsing around the remote Web server. Like FTP, HTTP is capable of transferring files between computers; however, because of the way HTTP is designed, it is not as efficient at moving large files, greater than 1 megabyte.

Today, HTTP is one of the most heavily used protocols on the Internet. It is used by all the Web servers currently running on the Internet. The amount of HTTP traffic on the Internet and local area networks is expected to continue to grow as the number of Web sites and their users continues to grow.

> **NOTE**   *An estimate published as this book went to press indicated that there are over one billion active Web sites on the Internet, which means an almost incalculable amount of HTTP traffic.*

Mac File Sharing Protocol

The latest addition to transferring files over the Internet is the File Sharing component included in Mac OS 9. Mac OS 9 has taken the File Sharing protocol that was originally developed for AppleTalk and has extended it to work over the Internet. This allows your Mac to connect to and share files with another Mac located either on your local network or half a world away. This makes sharing files between different Macs much easier. You can now connect to any Mac that has File Sharing running and has an Internet connection.

> **NOTE**   *The downside to this, of course, is that you need to make sure you have properly secured your Mac's shared volumes so no unauthorized users on the Internet can access your files.*

Using Microsoft Internet Explorer to Download Files via FTP and HTTP

Another common tool to move files between computers on a local area network and the Internet is to use a Web browser such as Microsoft's Internet Explorer. Internet

Explorer, like almost all Web browsers, enables you to download files using either the *File Transport Protocol* (*FTP*) or *Hypertext Transport Protocol* (*HTTP*).

As you may have suspected already, using Internet Explorer (affectionately known simply as *IE* or *MSIE*) to download files from a Web site using either FTP or HTTP is much simpler than using Fetch or some other dedicated FTP client. Using IE, all you need to do to download a file is click the link to the file and then let IE do all the rest. The Web server then tells IE what type of server will deliver the file, an FTP or Web (HTTP) server, and in what format the file will be transferred. The file is then downloaded and stored in the folder where you have told IE to store downloaded files.

To connect to a Web server and download a file, follow these few steps:

1. Launch IE or your favorite Web browser and wait until it starts. Once IE has started, click the File Menu and select Open Location.

2. Enter the location you desire. For this example, let's go to http://asu. info.apple.com because this is the Web site that contains Apple's software updates.

3. Once you connect to Apple's Software Update page, scroll down to the list of featured software and then click an item. For this example, please click the link that points to the AppleShare Client.

4. Once you are looking at the Web page for the AppleShare client, click either the link for the MacBinary version of the file or the BinHex version of the file to download, as shown in Figure 35-1.

NOTE *While MacBinary versions of the file are going to be smaller, and thus, faster to download, they do not always transfer properly, depending on how the server sending you the file is configured. BinHex files, on the other hand, are larger and take longer to download, but they generally transfer without any problem. If you have trouble downloading files in MacBinary format, you should try downloading the BinHex version of the file to see if the problem was just an issue with MacBinary.*

5. IE then displays its Download Manager window to show you what files you have downloaded, as well as the progress of the files you are currently downloading. Once IE has indicated the file is finished downloading, go to the folder that stores your downloaded files and double-check that the file was downloaded properly.

6. Once you finish downloading the files you want, simply quit IE, or use it to continue browsing the Web.

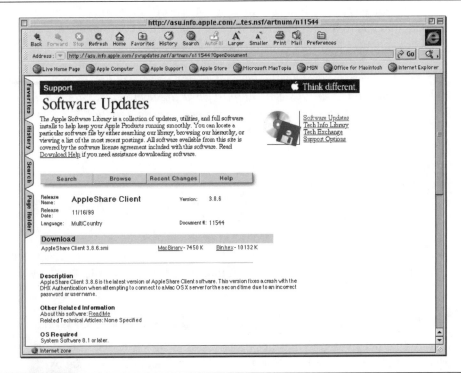

FIGURE 35-1   Click the file you want to download from the Web server

Using Microsoft Internet Explorer to Download Files from an FTP Server

One of the nice things about IE and other Web browsers is that you can also use it to log into and download files directly from a FTP server without having to use Fetch or needing to go through a link on a Web server. To connect to an FTP server using IE, follow these few steps:

1. Launch IE and wait until it has started.

2. Click the File Menu and then select Open Location from the list of available commands.

3. In the Open Location dialog box, enter the location of the FTP server you are connecting to by using the following command style: ftp://ftp.microsoft.com. This will connect you to the FTP server whose

name you have specified (in this case, Microsoft's). If this FTP server requires you to log in, then you need to modify the command that you use to connect to the FTP server.

TIP   *For FTP servers that need a user name and password for access, change the command to ftp://user name:password:ftp.gizmo.com, where the user name and password are the ones you need to access the FTP server. This process kills the login dialog box and gets you right to the directory where the file you want is stored.*

NOTE   *When a URL has a prefix that indicates its type, such as the ftp in ftp.microsoft.com, you don't even have to enter ftp://. The browser will figure it out and do it for you when it accesses the site.*

4. Once you finish downloading the files you want from the FTP server, then you can either quit IE or use it to continue browsing other sites on the Web.

Configuring Internet Explorer's Download Options

Setting up Internet Explorer's various preferences so they are customized just for your needs is an easy procedure. For most things, the default values set by IE when you first start it are good enough. But you might want to change some settings to match your specific needs.

To configure IE to meet your specific needs, follow these few steps.

1. Start Internet Explorer and wait until it has finished launching.

2. Click the Edit menu and select Preferences… from the list of available options.

3. In the Preferences dialog box, scroll down the list of options, click the little triangle located just to the left of Receiving Files, if it is not already expanded, and then click Download Options.

4. When you look at the Download Options dialog box (see Figure 35-2), you see a list of the download options you can configure in IE. The main options you may want to set are the location where you store the files you download, the maximum number of files you can download at one time, and whether the program should automatically decode MacBinary or BinHex files as you download them.

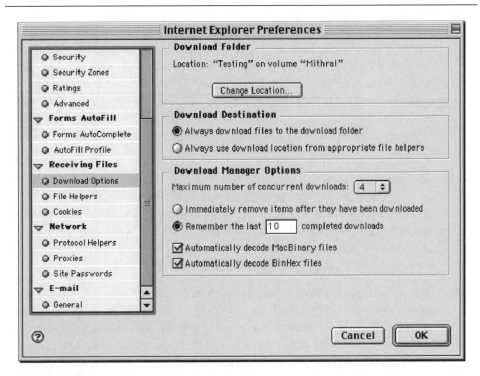

FIGURE 35-2 Set the file download options you want in the IE Preferences dialog box

5. To set the folder where you want your downloaded files to be stored, click the Change Location… button located near the top of the dialog box. IE then brings up the standard Mac Open File dialog box, enabling you to locate the folder where you want to store the downloaded files.

6. Once you have located the folder, click it and then click the Save Files Here button.

7. Next, you want to set the maximum number of files you can download at any one time. Normally, leaving this set to four is best, however, you may want to lower this number to improve the transfer of individual files. This way, you can focus the browser on only downloading a few files, rather than downloading many files. If you don't mind slowing things down a bit, you might feel the need to set the browser to download many files at once to make life a bit easier. Then you needn't wait for one set of file transfers to end before you begin another.

8. The other thing you should look at is the two check boxes that allow IE to decode MacBinary and BinHex files automatically once they are downloaded. Usually, leaving these two check boxes selected is best. But if you find IE is not decoding certain files correctly, you may want to turn off this option and decode the files manually. You can use a variety of utilities, like Aladdin's StuffIt Expander (which is included as an Internet utility with Mac OS 9), StuffIt Deluxe (the commercial version), or some other program capable of converting MacBinary or BinHex files back into their original format.

9. Next, you want to set up your firewall or proxy server settings if you are located on a network that uses one to protect your network from the dangers of the Internet. You need to know a few things about your firewall to configure IE properly to work with it. To set IE to work with your firewall or proxy server, click Proxies, located under the Network portion of the Preferences dialog box, shown in Figure 35-3.

10. To enable IE to go through your firewall to access the Internet, click the radio button labeled Enabled. Once you have done this, enter the IP address or the name of the firewall that you are going through to reach the Internet. The other options you can choose when setting up your firewall or proxy server are which protocols you will use with the firewall or proxy server; normally this is set to All. The other option you want to set is the method IE uses when going through the firewall or proxy server. The default setting for this is Normal, and unless your network is using a SOCKS or another type of proxy, you should leave it this way.

NOTE   *The key thing to remember when configuring IE to work through a firewall or proxy server is to talk to your network administrator and ask him how you should set it up. No room exists here for guesswork.*

11. Once you set up the download and proxy settings the way you want them, click OK to save your settings.

Using Fetch to Move Files via FTP

Fetch is the most popular FTP client available for the Mac. Developed at Dartmouth University, Fetch has spread throughout the Mac world and is now considered the default FTP client used on the Mac. Over the years, Fetch has

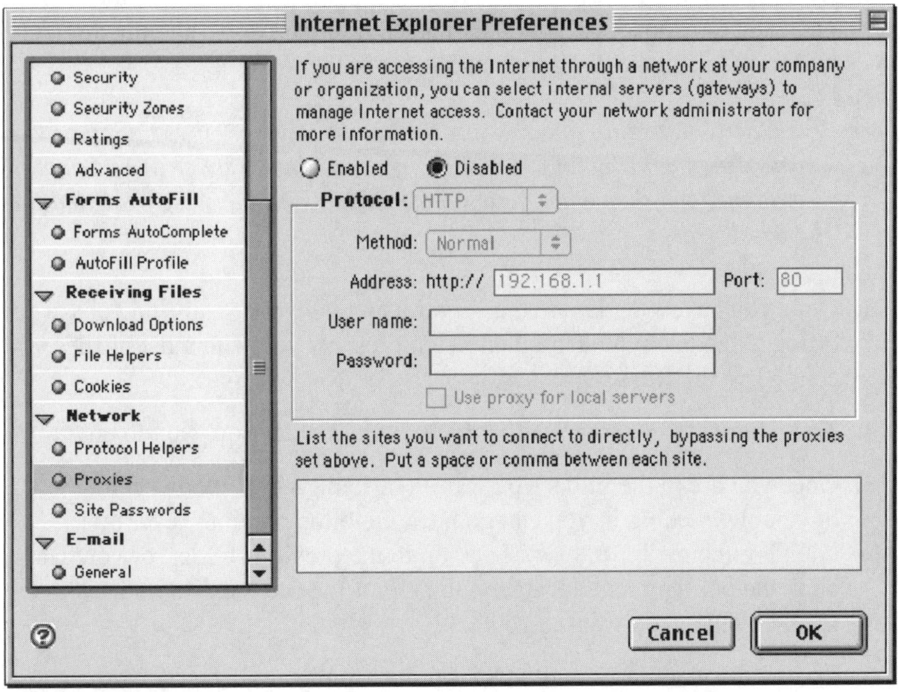

FIGURE 35-3   Use this dialog box to configure IE to work through your network's firewall or proxy server

evolved from a somewhat crude program with a fairly limited feature set to the current version, version 3.0.*x,* which offers a wide variety of features.

> **NOTE**   *You can find the latest version of Fetch from the author's Web site, http://www.dartmouth.edu/pages/softdev/fetch.html. The program is shareware, but free user licenses are available for educational users and non profit organizations.*

Using Fetch version 3 to send and receive files from FTP servers on your network or on the Internet is a simple process. To use Fetch to copy files to and from an FTP server, please follow these steps:

1. Double-click the icon for Fetch to launch the application and to have it display the New Connection dialog box.

2. Looking at the New Connection dialog box, enter the name of the server you want to connect to, your user name, your password, and the directory you want to connect to, if any, as shown in Figure 35-4.

NOTE *If you are connecting to a server anonymously (the FTP variation of guest access), then you should enter "anonymous" in the space provided for user name, and then enter your e-mail address in the space provided for the password.*

3. Once you have logged into the server using your user name and password, or logged in anonymously, then Fetch presents you with a list of files you can see on the file server.

4. To go into a folder, simply double-click the Folder you want to enter.

5. Once you are in the folder you want, you can go into another folder by double-clicking it, you can go back up to the previous level by double-clicking ".." to move back up to the previous folder, or you can click the pop-up menu located at the top of the file window and select the level to which you want to go back.

6. To download a file from the FTP server, simply click the file you want to download and then click the Get File… button to start the download process, as shown in Figure 35-5. Fetch then displays a circular counter

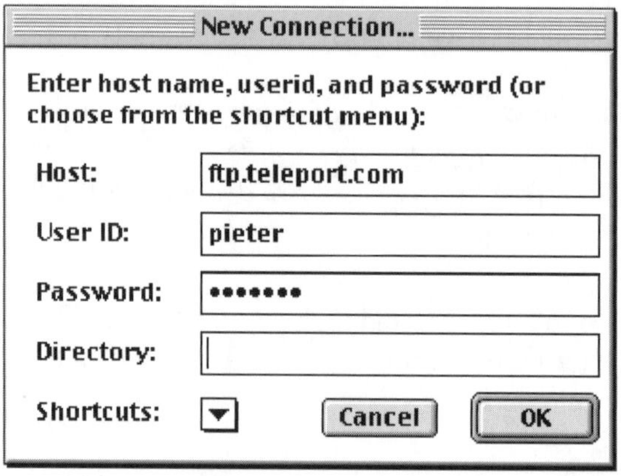

FIGURE 35-4   Enter the name of the FTP server you want to connect to, along with your user name and password

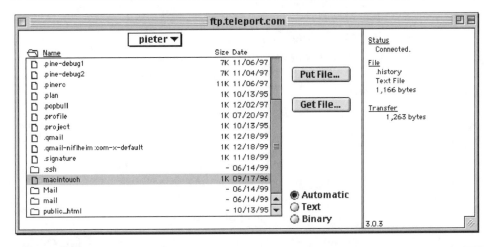

FIGURE 35-5   Click the Get File… button to download a selected file

showing you how much time is required to download the file. For smaller files, this may occur so quickly it is a blur, but for larger files, this display can give you a good idea as to how fast your connection is and how long the file will take to download.

7. Uploading a file to an FTP server is also a simple procedure. All you need to do is locate the area on the FTP server where you want to place the files and then click the Put Files… button. Fetch then brings up the standard Mac Open File dialog box, so you can select the file you want to upload to the FTP server and then click OK. You are now presented with the Put File dialog box showing the name, with the file extension, either a .bin for MacBinary II files or .hqx for BinHex files, and the format by which the file will be transferred. If everything looks the way you want, then click OK to start uploading the file.

NOTE   *You can also drag-and-drop one or more files to the Fetch connection window to transfer them. In addition, you can drag a file from a list in Fetch to transfer it to your Mac.*

8. Once the file has finished downloading or uploading all the files you want, you can simply Quit Fetch.

Using Fetch to Move
Files via FTP

TIP

If you want to transfer multiple files via Fetch, go to the Remote menu. Check the commands labeled Get Directories and Files, and Put Folders and Files. Each one brings up a dialog box where you can select more than a single file to add to the download or upload process. Once files are selected, Fetch will retrieve them, one at a time, until the file retrieval process is done.

Configuring Fetch

Fetch 3.0.*x* offers you a variety of options you can choose to configure to meet your specific needs. To configure Fetch, follow these few steps:

1. Double-click Fetch to start up the application.

2. This brings up the program's standard New Connection dialog box. Click the Cancel button to dismiss it.

3. After you have dismissed the New Connection dialog box, notice that all the items in the Menu bar are now available. Click the Customize menu and then select Preferences from the list of options.

4. Look at the General tab, where you see a variety of options you can set (see Figure 35-6). The key options you should look at are the check box that

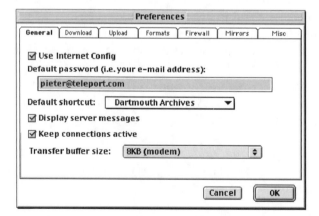

FIGURE 35-6 Configure Fetch to match your needs using these options

enables you to use the Internet Config, the space provided for you to enter your e-mail address, and the pop-up menu that controls the size of the transfer buffer used by Fetch. Because the size of the transfer buffer is dependent upon the speed of your connection, those of you with connections to the Internet faster than a 56K modem should probably click this pop-up menu and select the option closest to your actual connection speed.

5. When you click the Download tab, you see the options you can set for downloading files, as shown in Figure 35-7. The key option you want to set in this dialog box is the location where the downloaded files are going to be placed. By default, downloaded files are stored on the Desktop as they are downloaded. Because the Desktop on most Macs is already a crowded place, however, you probably should store them someplace else.

6. To change where you plan to store files you download, click the check box labeled Use download folder: and then click the button located just to its right. Fetch then presents you with the standard Mac File dialog box. Locate the folder where you want to store your downloaded files, highlight it, and then click the Save Files Here button.

7. Next, you want to click the Upload tab and set the various options you want to use when uploading files, as shown in Figure 35-8.

Configuring Fetch

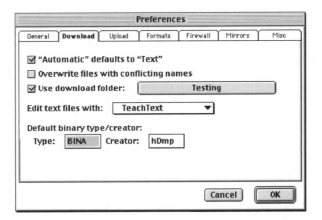

FIGURE 35-7   Choose the folder where you want to store the files you download

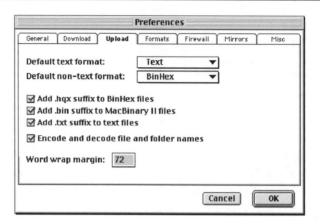

FIGURE 35-8 Choose the file formats you plan to use when uploading files to an FTP server

8. When you check the Upload options, the ones you need to pay close attention to are the two default file formats you use when uploading files. For almost all applications, uploading Text files works. But for some servers, you may need to choose one of the other options, such as Wrapped Text or Raw Data. While the choice of a Text format is not normally important, the selection of a Binary file format is important. If you are going to send all your files to UNIX-based or Mac-based FTP servers, then use MacBinary II format to upload files. If, however, you plan to upload files to Windows or Windows NT-based FTP servers, then you need to upload files using the BinHex format because Windows based FTP servers cannot handle MacBinary II.

9. Once you finish setting up your download and upload options, then you want to click the Formats tab, shown in Figure 35-9.

10. In the Formats dialog box, you see a list of the various file formats Fetch can recognize and automatically decode after downloading the file. Make sure all the file formats you intend to use are selected. In general, simply selecting all the file formats is best, and then have Fetch do all the work of determining with what format a file is encoded.

11. If you are located on a network, you may need to click the Firewall tab to set up Fetch so it can go through your network firewall and access the Internet (see Figure 35-10). If you are on a corporate network and you do not know if a firewall exists or what its settings are, then you should check with your network administrator and ask her for the information you need.

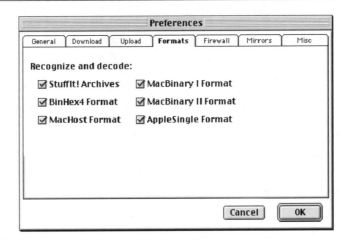

FIGURE 35-9   Choose all the file formats you want Fetch to decode automatically

NOTE   *To configure Fetch to use a firewall, you need to know if your firewall uses passive mode transfers, or Pasv, the IP address of the firewall; and if the firewall uses a SOCKS proxy, the IP address of the proxy. Once you click the check boxes for the various options you must use, enter the appropriate IP addresses.*

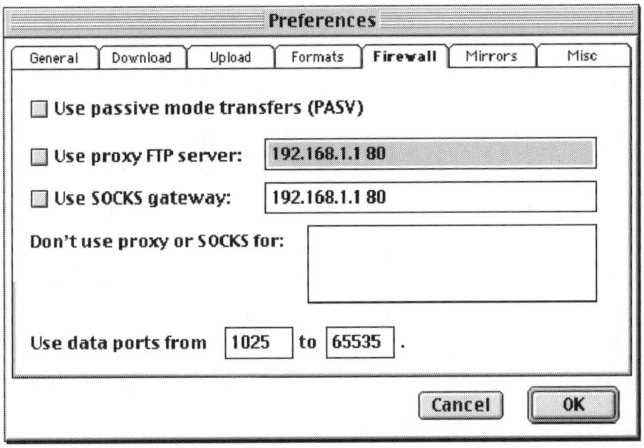

FIGURE 35-10   Configure Fetch to access the Internet through your firewall

Configuring Fetch

12. When you click the Mirrors tab, you see two pop-up menus that enable you to choose which predefined mirror for the Info-Mac and UMich, University of Michigan, Mac file archives you want to use. Click either pop-up menu, and then select the server from the list best suited to you. For normal use, the default settings are fine.

13. Last, click the Misc tab to set up some minor configuration options, shown in Figure 35-11. The only interesting features in this dialog box are the filename cache size, the option to send a Type I command to the server before sending a binary file, and the option to bring up the New Connection dialog box upon startup. The Maximum file list cache size is the amount of memory Fetch can use to store the filenames it gets from the FTP server to which it is connected.

NOTE   *If you are connecting to an FTP server with a lot of files on it, you may need to increase the amount of memory you allocate to this cache. The Use Type I to transfer binary files option tells Fetch to send a Type I command to the FTP server, setting the server into binary file-transfer mode, before sending a binary file to it. This is important when working with some older FTP servers that do not automatically switch between text and binary mode. The last option you see is Show sign-on dialog at startup, which simply causes Fetch to display the New Connection dialog box when you start it. If you do not want to see this dialog box, just uncheck this option.*

14. After you finish configuring Fetch to meet your needs, click the OK button to save your changes.

Setting Up Mac File Sharing for the Internet

The other option Mac users can use to transfer files easily over the Internet is the new Internet File Sharing capabilities present in Mac OS 9.

For Mac OS 9, Apple has extended the already useful File Sharing capabilities of your Mac so they now extend to the Internet. As previously discussed on sharing files with other Macs on your network in Chapter 27, setting up File Sharing on your Mac is quick and easy. To configure Mac File Sharing so it can be used over the Internet, simply follow these few steps:

1. Click the Apple menu and select Control Panels. Then select File Sharing from the submenu.

2. Look at the File Sharing Control Panel, shown in Figure 35-12. You see there are two small check boxes, one located beneath the File Sharing section of the dialog box and the other located under the program-linking portion of the dialog box. These check boxes enable File Sharing to work over the Internet.

3. To make File Sharing work over the Internet the same way it works over your local area network, simply click the check box that says Enable file sharing clients to connect over TCP/IP. Once you click this check box, File Sharing begins accepting clients who are using TCP/IP to connect to your Mac.

4. To enable users on the Internet to run programs located on your Mac, click the check box that says Enable Program Linking clients to connect over TCP/IP. Once this check box is selected, users on your network and the Internet can launch programs shared on your Mac.

5. After you finish enabling File Sharing over the Internet, click the close box to save your File Sharing settings.

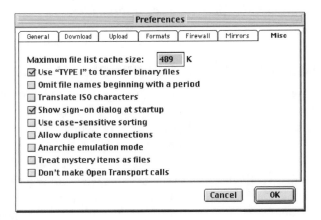

FIGURE 35-11   Set up the various miscellaneous configuration options for Fetch

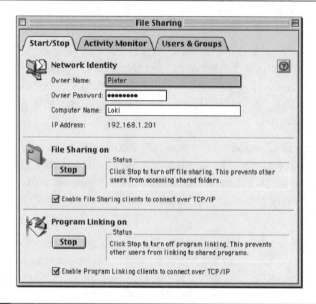

FIGURE 35-12 Enable Internet File Sharing from this setup screen

CAUTION *Unless you have a broadband Internet connection, program linking via the Internet is not really a good idea. Performance is going to be very slow, probably not acceptable for most users. General file sharing is also apt to provide unacceptable performance for large files on a regular dial-up connection.*

Securing your Shared Files from Internet Hackers

When you use File Sharing over the Internet, one of the most important things you should think about is security. Opening your Mac up to every Mac user on the Internet may sound like a great idea but you must remember that many users out there do not have your best interests in mind.

When you think about sharing files over the Internet, you should decide what files you want to share and what access rights you have to protect them. If you want to make some of your files available to everyone, then you should probably configure the file share on which they are located with only Read rights for the Everyone group. This prevents users unknown to you from having the ability to change or delete the files you are sharing. Likewise, to protect yourself from having users on the Internet run programs from your Mac without your permission, you should set the file permissions on the shared volumes that contain applications so the Everyone group has no access.

When you set up your Mac to share files over the Internet, you should also use strong passwords and make sure you are locking down all your sensitive shared volumes, so the files on them cannot be changed or destroyed without your permission. If you do these two simple things, you can substantially improve your Mac's capability to repel hackers and other Internet intruders.

Using strong passwords means your passwords should contain a combination of uppercase and lowercase letters, numbers, and special characters. For example, while the password "Mac" might seem like a nice password, it is not secure because it is easy to guess. The password "mAc1nt$h" is a much harder password for a hacker to decipher. While strong passwords are more difficult to think up, remember that they provide you with much greater protection.

> **TIP**
>
> *After setting up passwords, use Mac OS 9's Keychain feature to store them all, which enables easier access. This feature is described in detail in Chapter 6, which also details Apple's Multiple Users feature.*

Locking down your shared volumes is another thing you should do to help protect your Mac from being victimized by hackers. To make sure this does not happen, go through your shared volumes and set them to prevent users from changing or deleting files.

To do this, select the folder you are sharing and then click the File menu. Scroll down to Get Info and then select Sharing from the Get Info submenu. Looking at the Get Info dialog box, click the check box labeled Can't move, rename, or delete this item (locked). Selecting this option makes sure your files are protected from unauthorized changes.

Chapter 27 has more information on setting up security levels for File Sharing, which is even more important when you're planning on sharing files on the Internet.

> **CAUTION**
>
> *If your network is hooked up to a cable modem for Internet access, you are, in effect, opening your Mac's network to outside users, unless the cable service has some sort of Firewall protection to offer you. You are best advised to password protect all your shared volumes and even your printers. It is not uncommon for people to see and be able to access printers on your network with a cable modem. Fortunately, more and more cable providers, such as Cox Cable, are offering additional security with their installations to help forestall such security issues.*

Setting Up Mac File Sharing for the Internet

What to Do When You Finish Downloading Your Files

Once you download files from the Internet, you need to know what to do with the files you have just acquired. While most modern Internet applications, like Internet Explorer and Fetch, convert files they download in MacBinary or BinHex format back into the native Mac file format, not all applications do. Likewise, some files you download are stored in a format your Mac does not normally read. I'll discuss those situations below.

You can use a few good utilities to convert files encoded using MacBinary and BinHex back into the normal Mac file format. The most popular commercial program available on the Mac to convert files from MacBinary and BinHex back into their normal form is Aladdin Systems StuffIt Deluxe. While most users know StuffIt as a compression product that creates the ubiquitous .sit and .sea files, it is also capable of encoding and decoding MacBinary and BinHex. One of the cool components of StuffIt is the StuffIt Expander utility that comes with the retail version of the product and as an Internet utility with Mac OS 9. Using StuffIt Deluxe or StuffIt Expander, you can simply drag-and-drop the BinHexed or MacBinary file on top of the applications icon to have it decoded.

Likewise, to encode a file, launch the StuffIt Deluxe application and then click the Translate menu to select the protocol you want to use to encode the file.

1. To encode a file with BinHex, simply click the Translate menu, scroll down to the listing for BinHex4, and then select Encode from the submenu that appears to the right.

2. Next, StuffIt Deluxe presents you with the standard Mac Open File dialog box enabling you to select the file you wish to encode. Select the file you want to encode and click OK.

3. You then see the standard Mac Save dialog box with the name of the file you selected and a .hqx attached. Click OK to save the file with the .hqx extension. Once you have done this, then you can upload the file to a server on the Internet.

While MacBinary and BinHex are by far the most common type of file encoding used for Mac files on the Internet, you may also encounter others. These include the older UNIX formats of UUCode and Tar, along with the Apple-only format, AppleSingle. Fortunately, StuffIt Deluxe is capable of encoding and decoding files in nearly any format you might encounter when digging around on the Internet.

While StuffIt Deluxe is a wonderful application, not everyone owns a copy. For those of you looking for a freeware or shareware application capable of encoding and decoding the files you download from the Internet, many different applications exist from which you can choose. Unfortunately, most of these applications are designed only to encode or decode one specific format. For users who want to decode files using BinHex and MacBinary, you can use the free version of StuffIt, *StuffIt Expander,* which can handle nearly any file download you may encounter. It comes preinstalled with Mac OS 9 (when you select the default installation, which includes a selection of Internet software).

Another useful and free program is MindExpander from MindVision software. To encode and decode files using UUCode, one of the better utilities you can find is UULite 3.0. Copies of these utilities are readily available on many of the shareware and freeware sites that cater to Mac users.

NOTE
MindVision is the publisher of Vice, the installer utility used in many of the most popular programs. MindExpander is designed to compete head-on with the leading free expansion program, StuffIt Expander.

Even after decoding, some files may be in an unfamiliar format. Usually these files are designed for use on a Windows-based computer and, as such, are stored in either a .zip format or in some file format you have never seen. Programs like StuffIt Deluxe and MacZip are capable of creating and expanding Zip files you find on the Internet. Other file types you may encounter while browsing the Internet include .pdf files, Adobe Acrobat, .doc, and Microsoft Word, along with a myriad of others. Most of these files can be read by applications on your Mac, such as the Mac version of Adobe Acrobat, and Microsoft Word 98.

For more information on reading files created on the PC, please look at Chapter 28.

What to Do When You Finish Downloading Your Files

Summing Up

Transferring files to and from your Mac and the Internet is a simple procedure with tools like Fetch, Internet Explorer, and the Internet-enabled File Sharing present in Mac OS 9. Using and configuring applications like Fetch and Internet Explorer, you can explore the Internet and easily transfer files to and from your Mac.

Now, with the advent of Mac OS 9, you can even share files between different Macs across the Internet, using the Internet-enabled version of Mac File Sharing. Making your Mac a source of files on the Internet is not without its risks, however, and, as such, you should always make sure you protect yourself from hackers and other dangers. Finally, once you have downloaded the file, you may need to use a utility to convert it into a format your Mac can understand.

In our next, and final, chapter, you discover the secrets of Internet chatting.

Chapter 36

Secrets of Internet Chats

In recent years, an explosion has occurred in the number of tools that enable users to chat with each other over the Internet. Unlike e-mail where you send off a message to a friend and then wait for them to send an e-mail back to you, Internet chat software enables you to have a conversation in real-time between yourself and another user or users on the Internet.

Using these tools, you can talk with your coworker across the room or a friend located across the globe, just as easily as you could pick up the phone. For users who want to participate in a chat with many different users, *Internet Relay Chat* (*IRC*) provides a forum where users from around the world can converge and talk about any topic under the sun (or beyond).

Instant Messaging Clients for the Mac

Currently, four major instant messaging services are available for users around the world to use. The oldest of these instant messaging systems is called *ICQ,* shorthand for *I seek you.* ICQ was developed in the late 1990s by Mirabilis, now a subsidiary of AOL.

After ICQ began to take off and dominate the market for Internet instant messaging, AOL, Microsoft, and Yahoo! all decided they wanted to get into the act. Fortunately for Mac users, all three companies make a version of their software for the Mac, so you can take advantage of their instant messaging systems.

All instant messenger software is based on the client server model. This means that somewhere on the Internet is a server or group of servers to which the instant messenger software on your Mac connects, so it can tell other users who might want to talk to you that you are now available. These servers act much like a phone exchange—all the messages you send to a friend go through the server and are then directed out to the friend or the group of friends with whom you are chatting. This enables you to roam around like you do with a cell phone because the server is the one handling all the traffic direction and not your workstation.

Alas, while all four of these instant messenger systems uses the same basic technology, each one is incompatible with the others.

You may remember the headlines. When Microsoft first released Microsoft Network's Instant Messenger, it was capable of sharing messages with both AOL members and users of AOL's Instant Messenger service. But this feature is no longer available, the conclusion of that highly publicized battle in which AOL first blocked access, and Microsoft revised the program to get around AOL's attempts to restrict it. In the end, Microsoft threw in the towel, claiming the changes AOL made presented a potential security risk.

Because all these products are incapable of communicating with each other, if you want to chat with a user on one system, you need the client for that system.

Setting up and configuring each of the various instant messenger clients is a fairly simple procedure that you can complete in a few minutes. Each of the programs work differently, however, and as such, setting up all of them is reviewed, from installation to getting an account and finally, to using them to chat with other users.

ICQ

ICQ was the first and it is still one of the most popular tools users can use to communicate with each other across the Internet. Like all the other instant messenger systems, using ICQ is free. All you must do to register with them is provide an e-mail address and a name.

The guiding principle behind ICQ is the capability of others to seek you out and communicate with you. When you set up your ICQ account, you are given the chance to provide quite a bit of information about yourself, so others can find you and talk to you.

NOTE   *Given the current state of the Internet, you may not want to release too much information about yourself or to allow strangers to talk to you without first granting them permission to do so.*

Setting up ICQ is a relatively quick and painless procedure, which provides you with the option either to create a new ICQ account or, if one already exists, to configure the ICQ client you plan to install using your existing ICQ account.

You can download a copy of the program from the publisher's Web site at http://www.mirabilis.com.

To set up ICQ so you can communicate with your friends over the Internet, follow these steps:

1. Double-click the ICQ installer to start installing ICQ on your Mac. For this example, version 1.72 of ICQ for the Mac is installed, the version shipping at press time.

2. Once the installer has started, the first question you are asked is whether your Mac is connected to the Internet by a network connection, such as a cable modem or DSL, or if you use a modem to connect to the Internet. Click the radio button that best describes your connection to the Internet and then click the Next button.

Instant Messaging Clients
for the Mac

3. The installer next asks you if you want to participate in some market research surveys the ICQ folks put on occasionally. This is not mandatory and it's up to you if you want to participate.

4. Next, you need to select the password you want to use when creating your new ICQ account. Looking at the dialog box in Figure 36-1, enter the password you want to use for your ICQ account, and then click the check box labeled Remember my password if you want the ICQ program to store your password.

> **NOTE** *The best password to enter is a mixture of numbers and letters. Easy-to-remember passwords, such as a child's name or birth date, are simple to guess and you want the maximum amount of protection for your account.*

5. You now want to select the level of privacy projection you want while online. ICQ enables you to decide if just anyone should see when you are online and be allowed to contact you, or if you want only those people to whom you have given permission to see when you are online. Once you enter your password and set your security options, click Next to continue.

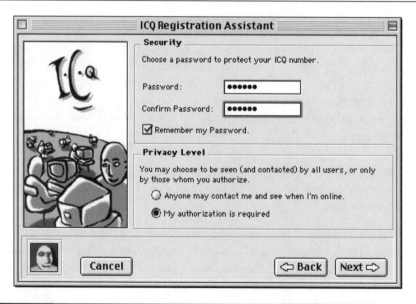

FIGURE 36-1   Set the password and security options for your ICQ account

6. Now ICQ asks you for some basic personal information so it can set up your ICQ account. In the dialog box shown in Figure 36-2, you are asked to enter your e-mail address, the user name you want to use on ICQ, and your first and last name. You needn't enter your primary e-mail address if you do not want to, but remember, other people are going to locate you on ICQ using this e-mail address and the other information you provide here. Once you enter this information, click Next to continue.

7. After you enter your primary personal information, ICQ asks you for some additional personal information. This data is completely optional. Think long and hard about how much information you want made available on ICQ. From this dialog box, you can enter the city, state, and country where you live, along with your age, gender, phone number, and, if you have one, your homepage. After you enter all the information you feel comfortable providing, click Next to continue.

8. The installer now contacts the ICQ servers and processes your request for an account on the ICQ system. You notice the little face in the lower-left corner rotating while the installer is talking with the ICQ servers. Once you are registered successfully, the installer displays a message that your registration has succeeded and the account number you are assigned. Click Next to continue to the final part of the installation process.

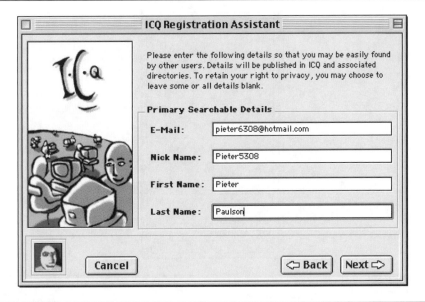

FIGURE 36-2   Enter the personal information you want to have made available online

Instant Messaging Clients
for the Mac

9. Finally, ICQ gives you a few tips about setting up ICQ with your list of friends, along with some other tips on how to use ICQ for the Mac. Once you finish reading these tips, click Done to finish the installation.

NOTE   *At any time during the installation process, you can click the Back button to go back to the previous dialog box. This is useful if you decide halfway through the installation process that you entered the wrong e-mail address or some other piece of information. Of course, as with most things in life, if you decide to change the information you provided to ICQ, you can do so after you have set up ICQ on your Mac. To change the information ICQ keeps in its database about you, simply select View/Change My Details from the File menu, and then go through all the tabs in the dialog box to make sure you are sharing only the information you want.*

Once ICQ client has been installed on your Mac, you are ready to use it to chat with your friends around the world. Looking at the ICQ floating window, as shown in Figure 36-3, you can see an empty window with two pop-up menus and a button located between it. To add ICQ users to the list of people who you want to know are online and available for chatting, click the Search/Add Users button.

FIGURE 36-3   The ICQ window enables you to see which of your friends is online, as well as your current ICQ status

After you click the Search/Add Users button, ICQ presents you with the dialog box you see in Figure 36-4. You can search for your friends by their e-mail addresses, their ICQ nicknames, their first and last names, or their ICQ registration numbers, and then click the Next button. Of these choices, the most reliable ways to search for your friends on ICQ are to use their e-mail addresses or, if you can get them, their ICQ registration numbers. ICQ then checks to see if a user (or users) matches the information you entered and, if so, ICQ displays all the users that match your search.

Looking at the list of matches, click the user you want to add to your list, and then click the Next button. If this user allows anyone to see when he is online and to chat with him, then you will see this user added to your list of ICQ users. If this user insists on approving you before being added to your list of ICQ users, you will see a dialog box asking you to send this user a message so he can decide if he wants to let you add him to your list. While you wait to get approval from this user, his name will be in your list, under the heading "Waiting for."

The ICQ dialog box, the menu located right below your list of friends online, has a list of hotlinks back to the ICQ Web site. These hotlinks include links back to the ICQ Home page, ICQ Message Boards, ICQ Network Status, and ICQ's help pages. The menu located at the bottom of the ICQ dialog box, under the

Instant Messaging Clients for the Mac

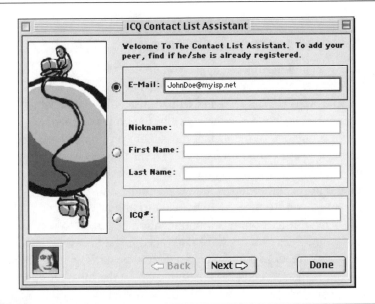

FIGURE 36-4   Enter the search criteria you want to find your friends on ICQ

Search/Add Users button, enables you to set your online status. Depending on your preference at the moment, you can choose to let folks on the ICQ network know you want to chat or that you are too busy and don't want to be bothered. To set your online status, click the status menu and select from one of the available options: Available, Away, Occupied, Privacy, and Offline.

NOTE   *If your network connection fails, you see your status change from what it was to Offline. Likewise, if you walk away from your computer for an extended period of time, you will notice your online status changes to Away.*

Using ICQ is exceedingly simple. All you must do to send a message to someone who is online is to double-click the person's name from the list of your friends. Then type the message you want to send in the Message dialog box displayed and click OK. Once you select a user from your list, you notice a new menu has appeared in the menu bar with her screen name. Using this menu, you can receive a chat request from her, send her a message, request a chat with her, send her a URL or send her a file. You can also send her an e-mail using your e-mail software, bring up her homepage, get her ICQ information, change the screen name you know her by, or even delete her from your list.

The World of Instant Messaging

Using *instant messaging software* opens you up to a new world on the Internet. Normally, your Net visits are done in isolation. You log on to your ISP or online service, browse the Web, and read and write e-mail. But you never actually talk with anyone, unless, of course, someone calls you on the telephone.

When you set up one of the instant messaging programs described in this chapter, suddenly your online life is less private. Your contacts know when you're online and they're ready to "talk" with you at a moment's notice. You hear a little chime, or the sound of a door opening, and suddenly, messages appear on your screen from people who want to talk to you.

A whole new world of online communication opens up to you. It's no wonder tens of millions of users have embraced instant messaging software.

With this new freedom comes some potential hazards. For example, you may not be in the mood to talk to someone, and yet the messages pop up on your screen. You don't want to appear rude by not answering the greetings.

Sometimes you might feel you want to go back to that private online world, without the intrusion of instant messaging, and then you get a message from a long-lost friend who has found you online or from someone offering you a cool business opportunity.

Suddenly, being in public doesn't feel so bad.

Besides, these programs all enable you to block access from strangers, so you can just as easily quit the program and return to your quiet online life.

America Online Instant Messenger

America Online's Instant Messenger software has tens of millions of users, making it the number one chatting program. It enables users on the Internet to chat with fellow surfers around the world as easily as with those on AOL's private network. The AOL Instant Messenger grew out of the instant messaging system AOL users have used for years to communicate on AOL. Over the next few pages, using AOL Instant Messenger to chat with your friends on AOL and around the Internet is discussed.

AOL Instant Messenger comes with Netscape Communicator and is part of the standard installation. If you don't intend to use Netscape as a browser, you can find the latest standalone version of Instant Messenger at AOL's Web site http://www.aol.com.

NOTE   *Apple Computer's default ISP, EarthLink, also has a special version of Instant Messenger, which is being offered to members from their Web site at http://www.earthlink.net.*

Installing *AOL Instant Messenger* (*AIM*) is extremely simple. To install the AIM software, double-click the installer program. You are asked to review the software license. When you OK it (you can't say no if you wish to continue), choose the location where you want to store the software. Upon finishing the installation process, the installer asks if you want to have AIM launch upon startup. Once you finish installing AIM, you have to restart your Mac, and then you're ready to configure the program.

1. The first time AIM launches, you see the startup screen, as shown in Figure 36-5. Make sure the Screen Name: says <new user>. Then click the Sign On button to connect to the AIM Web page, so you can create a new

Instant Messaging Clients for the Mac

screen name to use for yourself. If you don't already have an AOL account, AOL asks you to enter the screen name you want to use, the password you want to use with this screen name, and an e-mail address for you. Then click the Click Here button to register your screen name. If you already have an AOL account, you can click the AOL button. AOL asks you to enter the screen name you want to use with AIM, and then to verify it by entering your ZIP code.

NOTE *As with any instant messaging program, no duplication of user names can occur. If the name you enter is already taken, you are given a choice (perhaps with a few letters or numbers added) or asked to select a new name. This is common. With tens of millions of users, expect the most popular names to be taken already, so you may have to be creative and give yourself a name that reflects a personality trait instead (such as SpeedyReader or something similar).*

2. Once you register your screen name with AOL, close the Web browser, and then highlight <new user> and type in the user name you have registered.

FIGURE 36-5   This is AIM's startup menu

3. Then enter your password in the space provided and, if you want, click the check box that allows AIM to remember your password (remember the tip in the previous section about using random letters and numbers for a password?). Once you enter your screen name and password, click the Sign On button. AIM then connects to AOL and enables you to start chatting.

4. After you register with AOL, then you go through the various configuration settings you can change in AIM to customize it to your exact needs. Click the Setup button to display the Preferences dialog box.

5. Many different configuration screens are in the Preferences dialog box that you can customize, but you only want to focus on three or four. The first screen you want to look at is Connection. Click the entry for Connection in the Preferences dialog box. If you are a home user and do not use a firewall or a proxy, you can ignore this dialog box. If your connection to the Internet is by a corporate LAN or some other network, then you want to make sure you set up the options in this dialog box so they allow AIM to go through the firewall or proxy, and out to the Internet.

NOTE *If you have questions about how to set up AIM to use the firewall or proxy, contact your network administrators.*

6. The next screen to look at is Controls. Click Control in the list of options located on the left-hand side of the Preferences dialog box. This dialog box, as seen in Figure 36-6, displays a variety of options that enable you to control which users are allowed to contact you while you are using AIM. By default, AIM enables all users to contact you, but you may want to allow only those users you specify to contact you. You can specify the users you want to chat with by using either your AOL buddy list, provided you are an AOL member, or by listing their screen names in the space provided. Or, you may want to allow everyone but a few specific people to contact you. This feature is extremely important as it enables you to block users with whom you do not want to chat.

7. Once you determine who can chat with you and who cannot, then you want to click Chat to bring up the AIM preferences for chats. Chats are different from instant messages. They involve groups meeting in a central location, a *chat room,* where several people can talk (exchange messages). The Chat

Instant Messaging Clients for the Mac

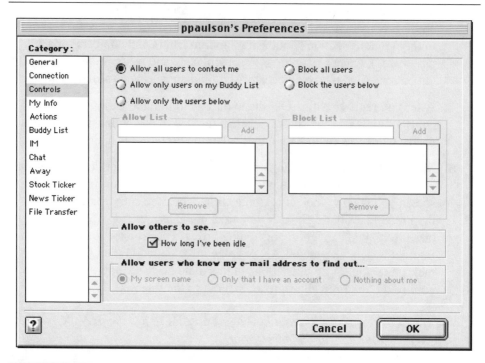

AIM enables you to limit those with whom you can send instant messages

Preferences dialog box you see in Figure 36-7 has several options. You can have a timestamp added to each user's message in the chat, make a note of when each user joined or left the chat and, if you want, block users from inviting you to chats. If you don't want to be invited to join chats, you should click the check box labeled Block all incoming Chat Invitations. You can also opt to change the font AIM uses to display the chat messages.

8. The last section you want to look at is the preferences for File Transfer. Click File Transfer from the list of preferences on the left-hand side of the Preferences dialog box to display the dialog box you see in Figure 36-8. Using the available options, you can choose to prevent file transfers between your Mac and some other user by clicking the check box labeled Block all incoming File Transfer invitations. Given the number of

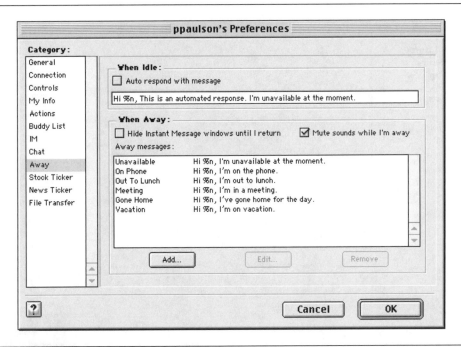

Instant Messaging Clients for the Mac

FIGURE 36-7   AIM enables you to limit those with whom you can chat

computer viruses currently being spread around, think twice before you allow AIM to accept files. Another nice feature in AIM is the capability to specify that all files being transferred to your Mac should be scanned by an antivirus program before they are saved. You can also configure AIM to store downloaded files in a specific folder on your hard drive and, if you want, to enable you to share a folder and its contents with other AIM users. Fortunately, AIM provides you with the ability to control access to this shared folder to only those users you want.

NOTE *Although computer viruses aren't as big an issue on the Mac as on the Windows platform, the growing popularity of the Mac has resulted in new virus strains being foisted on the public in recent years. The best protection is never to accept downloads from people you don't know and always to get up-to-date virus protection software. Chapter 30 covers the subject in more detail.*

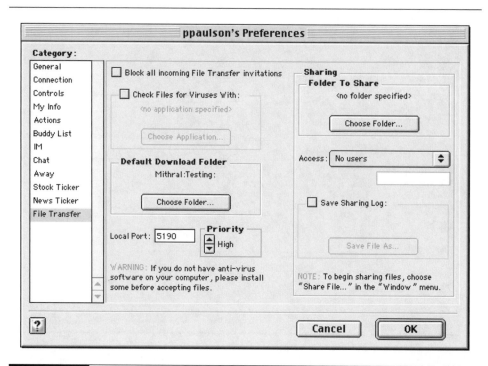

FIGURE 36-8 AIM enables you to control file transfers between AIM users

9. Like ICQ, adding users to your Buddy list in AIM is a simple process. You can search for users on AIM by their e-mail address, their names, or by common interests. Once your search is completed, you need to select the user you want to add to your Buddy list from the list of users, and then click the Add Buddy button.

10. One of the nicer AIM features is the capability to sort the members of your Buddy List into various groups, such as family, co-workers, or whatever you decide. To create a new group, simply click the List Setup tab in the AIM window, as seen in Figure 36-9, and then click the Add Group button and type in the name you want to identify the group to use.

FIGURE 36-9   Use this screen to set up users and groups for your Buddy List

NOTE   *If you are not certain this is the person you are looking for, you might want to click the IM button first to send him an instant message asking if he is the right person. Be sure you're using the right screen name, however, as it's easy to make a mistake and contact someone who might not appreciate receiving unsolicited messages from a stranger.*

11. Once you have added all of the people that you want to your Buddy list and sorted them into the appropriate groups, you can start using AIM to communicate with them. From the AIM window, click the Online tab (as shown in Figure 36-10) to see which of your friends are currently online.

12. To send an instant message to one of your friends who is online, simply click his name and then click the IM button. AIM then checks to see if the user is currently willing and able to accept an instant message from you. If he is, AIM displays the message to him and enables him to send messages back to you, if he wants to do so.

FIGURE 36-10   AIM shows you when your friends are online and ready to chat

13. If you want to invite some users to a chat, simply select them and then click the Chat button. You are then presented with a dialog box showing you all the users you are inviting to your chat, the text of the invitation you are sending out to all the users, and the name of the chat room you are creating to house this chat. After making all the changes you want to the user list, the message, or the name of the chat room, click OK to send the chat request.

TIP   *AIM also gives you the ability to join in on the big community chats AOL runs daily. These chats sometimes feature famous personalities in entertainment and politics. To see a list of these chats and join them if you want to, click the People menu and then select community chats.*

You can also use AIM to send a file or folder to a person on your buddy list, or to receive files and folders from that person. While this is a convenient feature when sharing files among friends, you should be careful about computer viruses. Use a good virus program to make sure you don't send or receive infected files using AIM. One other cool feature of AIM is the capability to create customized away messages. Unlike ICQ, which only enables you to leave one away message, AIM enables you to create a large list of away messages, each one customized to the message you want to convey.

To select an existing away message, click the People menu and then scroll down to I'm Away menu and select the message you want to use. If the message you want to leave does not exist, then select New Away Message from the I'm Away menu. Next, enter your new away message in the Away Info dialog box and save it for later use.

Chatting with AOL Instant Messenger is a little different from chatting with ICQ. Enter the message in your chat window and send it to the recipient. When your online contact responds, you see both the responses and your messages in separate panes on a chat window, so you can easily follow the drift of the conversation.

Basics of Online Chat Behavior

Over the years, some basic rules of behavior have been established for chatting and posting messages. For the most part, these rules are based on common sense. Treat others as you'd have them treat you, don't annoy strangers, and don't make personal attacks.

In addition, Internet providers from AOL to EarthLink have policies that govern the behavior of members. AOL calls it Terms of Service, EarthLink calls it Acceptable Use, but the fundamentals are no different. If you behave badly, you risk losing your membership.

Beyond being on your best behavior, little shortcuts exist to help you express yourself online, which help you better express your emotions. These are called *emoticons* or *smileys,* and they're designed to help you display your emotions far better than simple text (unless you're a novelist, of course).

Here's a quick list of common smileys you might encounter during your chats:

- :)   I am smiling.

- :D   I am laughing.

- ;)   I am winking.

- :*   I'm sending you a kiss online.

Instant Messaging Clients for the Mac

- ■ **:X** I'm sealing my lips.

- ■ **:(** I'm frowning.

- ■ **:'(** I'm crying.

- ■ **LOL** I'm laughing out loud.

- ■ **ROFL or ROFL** I'm rolling on the floor laughing.

- ■ **AFK** I'm away from the keyboard.

- ■ **BAK** I'm back at the keyboard.

- ■ **BRB** I'll be right back.

- ■ **OIC** Oh, I see what you're saying.

- ■ **IMO** In my opinion.

- ■ **IMHO** In my humble opinion (I'm not speaking for myself here because my opinions are never humble :).

- ■ **TTFN** Ta-ta for now (so long).

Yahoo! Messenger

The Yahoo! Messenger application is probably the simplest of the instant messenger applications widely used on the Mac. The reason for this simplicity is Yahoo! Messenger is designed only as an instant message tool and, as such, lacks such bells and whistles as file transfer or Internet group chats. As a result, Yahoo! Messenger is extremely easy to set up and use.

You can download a copy of the latest version from this Web site: http://messenger.yahoo.com. Here's what to do next:

1. Double-click the Yahoo! Messenger installer. The installer asks you to accept the user license and, once you accept it, the installer asks you where you want to install the application. Select the folder where you want to install Yahoo! Messenger, after which the installer copies all the files to your hard drive.

2. The final portion of the installation process occurs when the Installer asks you if you want Yahoo! Messenger to start each time you start up your Mac. Once you answer this question, the installer quits and Yahoo! Messenger starts up for the first time. Because this is the first time you have started Yahoo! Messenger, you are asked to enter your existing Yahoo! ID or, if you don't have one, to get one.

3. To get a Yahoo! ID, all you need to do is click the Get a Yahoo! ID button, and then wait until the Yahoo! ID Web page is loaded. Once there, you are asked for the Yahoo! ID you want to create and the password you want to use when logging in with it.

4. Once you enter the user name and password you want to use, you should select the question Yahoo! asks if you forget your password. You can choose between the city where you were born, the name of your pet, or your anniversary. After you select the question you want to answer, enter the answer, as well as your birthday and your e-mail address.

5. Next, Yahoo! asks for some more information about you, including your ZIP code, gender, occupation, and the type of industry in which you work. After you fill out this information, you are done. If you like, you can provide Yahoo! with some additional information about your personal interests.

6. After you enter all the information you want, click the Submit this Form button. Yahoo! then checks to see if your screen name is available and, if so, lets you know you have successfully registered. If that screen name is already in use, Yahoo! suggests a few available alternatives. Once you finish registering your Yahoo! ID, enter it in the space provided in the Sign In dialog box.

7. Now that you are signed in with your Yahoo! ID, Yahoo Messenger displays the list of friends you have set up in the various groups of friends with whom you chat. To add new users to your list of contacts, click the Add button located at the top of the window, which brings up the Add a Friend dialog box, as shown in Figure 36-11.

8. You can add a friend by simply typing in their Yahoo! ID, and then entering in a short message that will be sent to them to let them know that you have added them to your list. If you want to add the user to a group other than your default group, then you will want to click the pop-up menu and then select the appropriate group for the user.

Instant Messaging Clients for the Mac

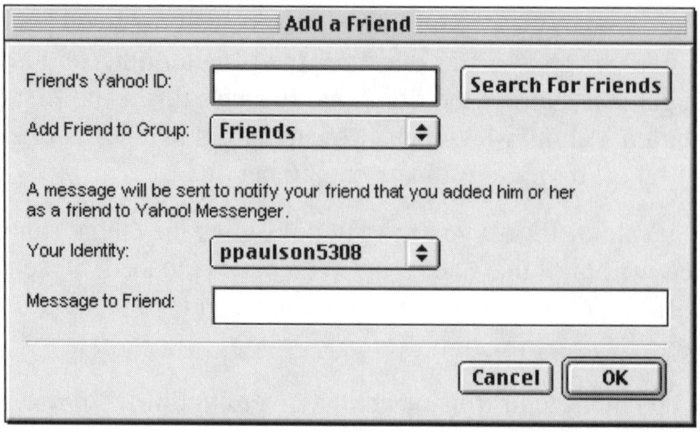

FIGURE 36-11   Adding friends to your user list is easy in Yahoo! Messenger

9. If you do not know the Yahoo! ID of the user you want to add, you can click the Search for Friends button to search for your friend's Yahoo! ID. Or, you can click the Friends button in the main Yahoo! Messenger window you see in Figure 36-12 to bring up the Yahoo! ID search page. Yahoo! enables you to search for users by their Yahoo! ID, their names, or by their personal interests.

10. Once you submit your search, Yahoo! displays all the users who match your search criteria. Then, from the list of users, select your friends and enter them in the Add a Friend dialog box.

To send a message to someone on your list, simply select the person to whom you want to send a message, and then click the Messages button located at the top of the Yahoo! Messenger window. An Instant Message dialog box is then displayed, where you type the message you want to send. Type your message and then click Send to transmit it to your friend.

Microsoft Network Messenger Service

The *Microsoft Network Messenger Service* (*MSNMS*) is the newest of the instant message clients available on the Mac. Like Yahoo! Messenger, MSNMS is a fairly simple chat program, designed only to send and receive messages between users. Although Microsoft made an effort to make the software compatible with AOL, it didn't work out that way.

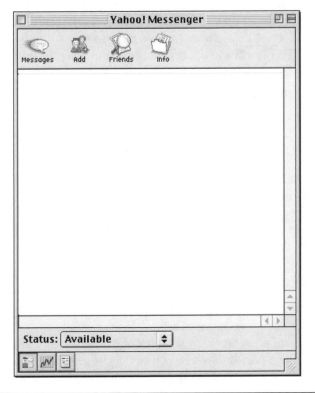

Instant Messaging Clients for the Mac

FIGURE 36-12   The Yahoo! Messenger Window displays all the friends you added

In the version shipping at press time MSN does not offer such options as sending files or enabling you to join into the large community chats on AOL or other services.

A copy of the latest version of MSNMS is available from this Web site: http://messenger.msn.com. Here's how to set up the program:

1. To install MSNMS on your Mac, double-click the installer program. Once the installer is running, you are asked to accept the license agreement, after which you specify where you want to store MSNMS on your hard drive. Select the folder where you want MSNMS located, and then click Install.

2. After MSNMS has installed, it starts up and asks you to log in for the first time (see Figure 36-13). MSNMS is based on Microsoft's Hotmail e-mail service. As a result, you need to have a Hotmail account before you can use MSNMS. To get a Hotmail account, go to the Hotmail Web site at www.hotmail.com.

3. Once you are at the Hotmail Web site, click the Sign Up Now link for new Hotmail users. Hotmail then presents you with the terms of service that govern your Hotmail account. After you accept them, you are presented with a request for information, so Hotmail can create your account.

4. To set up a Hotmail account, you need to provide them with your first and last name, the state, country, ZIP code, time zone, where you live, your gender, age, and occupation. Then you need to enter the screen name you want to use on Hotmail, along with the password you want to use. Hotmail also wants you to submit a secret question and its answer, so it can authenticate you in case you lose your password and need to reset it. When you finish, click the sign-up button to have Hotmail process your application.

5. If the screen name you picked isn't already taken, Hotmail comes back with a successful registration display. If your screen name is already being used, Hotmail presents you with a list of available alternative names. You can then select one of these, or you can create another name and check whether it's available. Once you successfully register your Hotmail screen name, then you can start using MSNMS.

FIGURE 36-13 Log in to MSNMS using your Hotmail user name and password

6. In the MSNMS Log On dialog box, enter your Hotmail screen name and its password. If you want MSNMS to save your password, click the Save this password so I don't have to enter it every time I log on check box.

7. Once you enter your Hotmail user name and password, click OK to log on.

8. After you log on, MSNMS displays a window (see Figure 36-14) showing all the users you have added to your list and if they are currently logged on. To add a user to your list, click the Add button located at the top of the Window.

9. Once you click the Add button, MSNMS displays the Add a Contact dialog box. You can search for a user using either her e-mail address or by her name. Select which method you want to use to locate the user online and then click the Next button.

10. Now, enter the e-mail address or the name, city, country, and state of the person you want to find, and then click Next.

Instant Messaging Clients for the Mac

FIGURE 36-14   The MSNMS window displays the online status of all your contacts

11. If you are searching by name, you are presented with a list of all the people whose names meet your search criteria. Select the person you want to add and click Next.

12. Once the user has been added to your list, you are asked if you want to search again. If you don't want to search for any other user, click Finish to stop adding new users to your list.

To send a message to another user using MSNMS, all you need to do is click the name of one of your friends who is currently online to select him. Then click the Send button to bring up the Message dialog box. Type in the message you want to send to your friend, and then click the Send button to speed your message on its way.

If you want to wander off during the day and let your friends know you are not receiving messages without the bother of logging off, you can change your online status. To change your online status, simply click the Status button, and then select the status setting you want to use. If you want to visit the MSN home site, click the Web button and select MSN Home. To check your Hotmail account, select Hotmail Inbox from the Web menu. To send mail from Hotmail, click Web and then select Send Mail.

Web-based Chats

As discussed briefly in the section on AOL Instant Messenger, chats are group conversations that take place in a single place, called a chat room.

Unlike instant messages, where you have two people talking only to each other, chats involve anywhere from two people to thousands of users all conversing together. Users can participate in chats on the Internet in two ways. One way a user can connect to and participate in an Internet-based chat is to use a client like AIM or an Internet Relay Chat program to connect to the chat. The other method is to use a Web-based chat client.

Web-based chat clients use a variety of methods to enable users who are using the Web site to connect to chat servers on the Internet. These Web pages can use scripting languages such as Perl or Active Server Pages that run on the Web servers themselves, or by using JavaScript or Java Applets that run on your Mac inside the browser. While Web-based chat clients, such as the ones you find at www.talkcity.com or at www.microsoft.com, are capable of giving you easy access to a chat, they are all slower than a dedicated chat client.

If you're only an occasional online chatter or you simply want to attend a special online event, you have no need for concern. Performance should be satisfactory for these purposes.

For you to use the Java and JavaScript-based clients, you need to make sure you are using a Web browser capable of supporting Java and JavaScript. Fortunately, the versions of Microsoft Internet Explorer and Netscape that come with Mac OS 9 support these standards, as do AOL 4.0 and 5.0.

If you are using an older browser, you should switch to one of the browsers that was placed in the Internet folder when you installed Mac OS 9.

You also need to make sure Java and JavaScript are both enabled. While Java is normally activated as a setting under Preferences when you install your Web browser, it is sometimes turned off as a protective measure. When you leave Java and JavaScript activated, you expose yourself to the risk of running a malicious Java applet or script, but this is not currently much of a problem. The future of Web-based chats probably lies in the dedicated chat plug-in, which will provide the performance of a dedicated chat client and the ease of use provided by the Web-based chat.

If you want to get involved in a Web-based chat, one of the best sources is TalkCity (http://www.talkcity.com). You don't need special software. Just log on and create a user name. You can find active chat rooms day or night, including an active list of special events (see Figure 36-15).

A TalkCity chat room also gives you the ability to send instant messages to people who are online and to keep a Buddy List of your regular contacts. If you want, you can even create a custom chat room for your friends or business contacts.

Although performance is somewhat slower than a dedicated instant messaging program, the advantage is you needn't install any extra software. All you have to do is call up the site, log in, and chat.

> **TIP** *A popular TalkCity chat room is called #Computer-MacSOS, hosted by Ilene Hoffman, which features weekly chats with noted figures in the computer industry. Check the TalkCity Events calendar for the schedule and guest list.*

AOL Chats

America Online built its reputation on having easy-to-use software and simple chat features, which can be accessed by most anyone. This has been both a blessing and

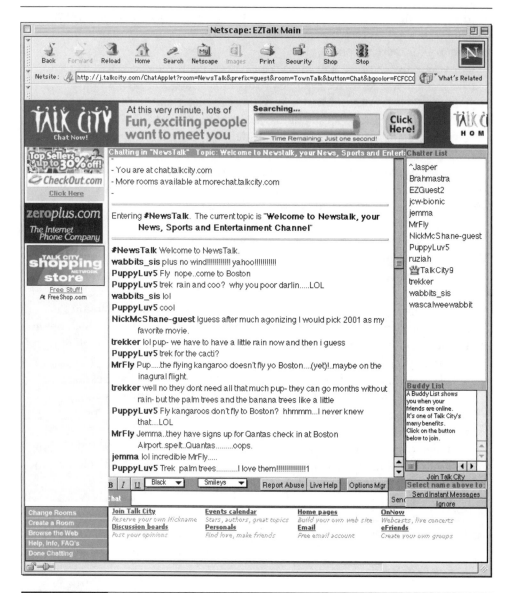

FIGURE 36-15   This is an early morning TalkCity chat devoted to news and lots of other stuff

a curse because the ease with which chat rooms are entered and used also attracts some unsavory elements.

However, AOL has also instituted a volunteer corps, called *community leaders,* who man the public chat rooms and the service's message boards to make sure chatters don't go beyond the bounds of good behavior.

AOL offers two types of chat rooms. One is the small chat room (see Figure 36-16) used for small groups. Such chat rooms can be public, meaning they are available by a directory on AOL and can be attended by any member. The other chat rooms are private. You create a custom name for your chat room, a name not listed on any directory, and only those who know this name (your online contacts, for example) can get into the private chat room.

The other type of AOL chat room is used in the fashion of an online auditorium, where thousands can gather in the audience to hear special guests on a variety of subjects. The auditorium is divided into smaller groups called *rows,* where you can chat with those in the same row. However, interacting with the guests, those on stage, is more difficult. All you can do is fill in an online form and send a question, which may or may not be answered by those conducting the session.

These online chats attract the famous from all walks of life, from best-selling authors to movie stars and politicians. A list of online events available at press time mentioned such personalities as actor Ewan McGregor (who appeared

FIGURE 36-16   AOL's intimate chat rooms are popular day and night

in *Star Wars: The Phantom Menace* and *Eye of the Beholder*) and actress Jane Seymour. AOL members can check out the latest schedules by the service's keyword *AOL Live*.

Internet Relay Chat

Internet Relay Chat (IRC) is a chat system that spans the Internet, linking thousands of different chat servers together into several huge chat networks. IRC is the oldest chat system on the Internet and has been around since the early 1990s. As such, IRC is the most widespread Internet chat system with thousands, if not millions, of users and thousands of servers participating in the various networks. Likewise, because of its age and huge size, IRC does not have all the bells and whistles you might find on some of the latest chat systems.

To chat with your friends on IRC, you need to decide which IRC network your friends will be using and the name of the chat room they are in. For example, some of your friends may have created a room called IlikeMacs on the Efnet IRC network. For you to join this chat, you need to use an IRC client on your Mac to connect to one of the many servers that make up Efnet. Once you are connected to Efnet, you simply need to join the IlikeMacs chat room to start talking with your friends.

Because chat rooms must be manned at all times to be available, almost all rooms that stay around for more than a day or so come equipped with resident robots (special software) that manage the room even when no one is around.

IRC Client Software

Two IRC clients stand out on the Mac: ircle 3.0.4 and Snak 3.1. Both of these clients are shareware and offer an extremely wide range of features designed to make your IRC experience as easy as possible. Using either of these two clients, you can connect to IRC servers around the globe and participate in chats. The main difference between these clients is the interface and the number of ancillary tools that come bundled with the application.

NOTE   *These two chat programs and others can be found in AOL's software libraries (if you're an AOL member) or by the popular VersionTracker Web site. Point your browser to http://www.versiontracker.com, and then enter the name of the program in the search box at the bottom of the site's home page.*

The latest version of the popular ircle IRC client is ircle 3.0.4. It is widely used on Macs around the Internet. This version of ircle offers many new features over the previous versions of ircle, along with a spiffy new interface. These capabilities include being able to connect to multiple IRC servers at the same time, along with improvements in ease of sharing files and logging your chats.

Snak 3.1 is another popular Mac IRC client. Snak 3.1 enables Mac users to connect to multiple IRC servers and networks as does ircle 3.0.4, as well as having a simple to use and intuitive user interface. The outstanding thing about Snak 3.1, however, is that the tools that come with it are a bit more comprehensive than those that come with ircle. Additionally, the interface for Snak is a bit simpler and cleaner, making it easier for a beginner to learn.

Setting Up Your IRC Client

The first key step you need to configure when setting up your IRC client is what server you want to connect to on any given IRC network. This is important because you want to find a server that accepts IRC connections from you, which is not too badly overloaded, causing you to wait endlessly for the server to respond. Because not all servers are up all the time, you need to make sure you have more than one server scoped out for each of the IRC networks to which you plan to connect.

Five major IRC networks exist, along with many smaller IRC networks and sites. The big five networks are Chatnet, Dalnet, EFNet, IRCNet, and Undernet. Each IRC network has a Web site you can visit to get the IP addresses and names of the various servers that make up its network.

The second key step you need to set up when configuring your IRC client is the nickname you want to use. As with the screen names or user names with instant messaging software, each nickname must be unique. If someone else is using your nickname, you can be forced to choose another to connect. Because you will be known by this nickname while online, think carefully about the nickname you choose. You probably will use the same nickname for a number of years. Nicknames in IRC can be up to nine characters long and can include any combination of letters and numbers.

Once you choose your IRC nickname, enter your IRC user name and password if you want to have one. You can also set up information listing your real name and e-mail address if you want. We don't recommend this, though, because many people scan the IRC servers to grab users' e-mail addresses so they can send out junk e-mail.

Internet Relay Chat

A Fast Look at IRC-Speak

As with other computing-related pursuits, the world of IRC has developed its own lingo to address common features and functions.

Here's a brief list of the terms you encounter when you begin to explore the world of IRC:

- **Channel**   An IRC meeting or chat room.

- **Chanop**   The moderator or host of an IRC chat room. You can usually identify a Chanop by an @ symbol before his nickname. A Chanop has unlimited powers to host a Channel, some of which can be quite arbitrary. For example, if he doesn't like what you're saying or feels you haven't been active enough, he can eject you from the room without advance warning.

- **IRCing**   The word, such as it is, is pronounced urk-ing and it simply means you're participating in a Channel.

- **Nickname**   This is the user name you select to use while present in a Channel.

Summing Up

Using the tools available to you on the Mac, you can communicate directly with your friends and others located across the globe. Instant Messenger software, such as IRC or AOL's Instant Messenger, gives you the ability to see when your friends are online and to have real-time, one-on-one conversations with them.

By enabling users to engage in real-time communication over the Internet, these tools are quietly revolutionizing the way we communicate with a computer. For users who want to hold conversations with more than one user at a time, it's possible to use the chat features in AOL Instant Messenger or participate in a chat through one of the many Web-based chat services cropping up all over the Internet. For the serious Internet chatter, Internet Relay Chat clients provide you with the tools needed to connect to the various chat networks present on the Internet.

Glossary

10BaseT   The standard form of Ethernet networking, using twisted-pair wires that resemble regular telephone wires. Ethernet capability has been offered in all Apple computers for several years. *See also* **Fast Ethernet.**

ADB (Apple Desktop Bus)   Apple's implementation of a bus standard for input devices, such as a keyboard, a mouse, or a trackball. *See also* **USB.**

access privileges   Used for file sharing, the act of allowing other users different levels of access to your shared drive.

active application   The application you are currently using, the one in which you are working.

active matrix screen   Typically used on a laptop computer, a form of LCD display, using a separate transistor for each pixel. By activating each pixel separately, it provides a clearer, faster display than the other type of LCD display, passive matrix. All current PowerBooks and the iBook have active matrix displays. *See also* **passive matrix.**

AirPort   Apple's wireless networking product line, based on IEEE standard 802.11, which provides networking services at approximately 10BaseT Ethernet speeds among devices for distances of up to 150 feet.

alias   A Mac OS feature (originated with UNIX), which creates a file that links or points to the original file, folder, or disk. You can activate an alias by double-clicking it; the original item is opened. You can use an alias to help organize your Mac desktop by keeping the original items in their original folders.

Altavec   The original name for the Velocity Engine used in the G4 CPU to provide noticeably speedier performance for programs designed to support the feature.

Anonymous FTP   A method to access files from an FTP resource by logging in as a guest. *See also* **FTP.**

AOL (America Online)   The world's largest online service with, as of press time, almost 21 million members around the world. AOL owns a number of other companies, including Netscape and the former number one online service, CompuServe.

AppleScript   A scripting language that is part of the Macintosh operating system. It enables a user to automate repetitive functions by writing little scripts that function as miniapplications.

application   Software that provides a specific productivity function, such as a word processor, an illustration program, or a Web browser. Examples of applications include Adobe PhotoDeluxe, AppleWorks, Microsoft Word, and QuarkXPress.

AppleShare   The server and client software that comes standard with the Mac operating system. You use AppleShare to exchange files with other networked Macs.

AppleTalk   The network standard protocol Apple Computer uses. Two types of AppleTalk exist: The original protocol, AppleTalk Phase 1, was introduced with the first Mac in 1984. A later version, AppleTalk Phase 2, is designed to address the networking limitations of the original version. All Macs (including the iMac and the iBook) use AppleTalk.

arrow keys   The keys used for navigation on a computer. The arrow keys are designed to move the cursor in all four directions.

ASCII (American Standard Code for Information Interchange)   The ASCII character set includes the basic 128 characters, including letters, numbers, and basic symbols.

ASCII text file   A file including ASCII characters, without the special formatting that identifies paragraph and text formats.

attach   A feature of e-mail that connects or links one or more files to your message. When you send your message, the file or files you attach go with it.

archive   The file you create when you compress a file to make it smaller. An archive may contain one or more compressed files. *See also* **self-extracting archive.**

backup   The process of making extra copies of your files, in case the originals are corrupted or destroyed. Backups may be made of individual files, folders, or an entire disk.

BBS (bulletin board system)   Essentially, the original online service. A BBS consists of one or more computers that store information, such as files, messages, news, and e-mail. Online services, providing a nationwide network of local access phone numbers, grew out of the concept of a BBS. *See also* **online service.**

beta   The common word for prerelease software. Beta software usually contains all or most of the features of the finished product, but it has bugs that may cause performance anomalies or system crashes. *See also* **preview software.**

BinHex   A file format commonly used for encoding Mac binary files. The process converts the files to text format, usually bearing the file suffix ".hqx." BinHex is designed to allow for transfer of files among multiple computer operating systems, yet retain the two elements of the Mac file format: the resource fork and the data fork.

bit   The smallest unit of computer data. Eight bits make a byte. *See also* **byte.**

bitmap   A standard for storing and generating computer-based images, which are made up of single dots (or pixels).

bitmap fonts   A font designed for display in a single point size. Compare with scalable fonts in PostScript and TrueType formats. Bitmap fonts designed to be used with scalable fonts are called "screen fonts."

bits per second (bps)   Typically the speed at which a modem transfers data. Normal speeds range from 28,000 bps to 56,000 bps. Higher speeds can be achieved by so-called "broadband" connection methods. *See also* **cable modem, DSL.**

boot   Refers to the process of starting your computer (this comes from the word "bootstrap"). On a Mac, the startup process includes a basic hardware check (including your RAM), and then the various components of the Mac OS load.

browser   A program designed to download Web pages. Reproduces the text, images, animations, and sound that comprise the original page.

byte   A byte represents a single piece of computer data. It contains 8 bits, which are represented by the binary numbers 1 and 0. *See also* **bit.**

cache   A portion of memory or storage space set aside to hold frequently used data. By using a cache, performance is boosted.

card   For personal computers, a printed circuit board installed inside a computer's case. It provides expanded capabilities, such as the capability to add an extra display, high-speed networking, and high-speed disk access.

cable modem   A technology that enables you to access the Internet through your regular cable TV connection. The cable modem is actually a router, which sends the signal to your Mac using its Ethernet port. Cable modem service may require rewiring by your cable provider and may not be available in all areas.

character set   The content of a font. It contains letters, numbers, and special symbols, such as a copyright symbol or a number sign. *See also* **ASCII.**

configuration   The term used to describe the settings you make for such things as your Internet and network setup.

CCD (charge-coupled display)   CCDs are typically used in camcorders and scanners to capture high-quality images for (in the case of camcorders) videos and (in the case of scanners) artwork.

CD-ROM (compact disc read-only memory)   A standard based on the audio CD, it enables you to store computer data on a CD. Commonly used today for games and as a carrier for software installers and backed-up files.

check box   A feature of the Mac operating system and other graphic computer interfaces. It consists of a small square box in a dialog box that is used to turn certain program features on or off. You click a check box and a check appears inside, which activates a specific program feature. When you click the check box again, the check mark is removed and the feature is turned off.

Chooser   A Mac program used to select AppleTalk network and printer connections.

click   The process of pressing and releasing the button on a mouse or other pointing device.

client   A computer that receives services from another computer, which is known as a server. Internet software, for example, is considered client software because it receives content from the Internet. *See also* **server.**

clip art   Boilerplate or canned images used for enhancing a document you create. Some firms and Web sites provide clip-art collections for you to install or download.

Clipboard   In the Mac operating system, a temporary location in which an item is stored so you can transfer it to another place in the document you are working on or into another document.

close box   A feature of the Mac operating system in which you click a small square in the upper left-hand side of a title bar to close that window.

collapse box   A box at the extreme right side of a window (in Mac OS 8 or later), which you click to reduce a window to only its title bar, and click again to restore to the previous size. A previous version of this feature was known as *WindowShade.*

ColorSync   A feature of the Mac OS that enables you to calibrate color on various devices, from displays to printers and scanners.

Command key   The main keyboard modifier key found on a Macintosh used, along with one or more keystrokes, to activate a specific function. Identified on a keyboard by an apple or cloverleaf symbol (usually both).

command line   An older style computer interface in which you type in commands rather than click an object to perform a specific function. The most popular command line interface was originally the MS-DOS operating system, but the various flavors of UNIX, including Linux, are the prominent sources of such an interface for the beginning of the twenty-first century.

commands   A set of instructions you give to your computer to tell it to carry out a specific function or set of functions.

compression   A technique used to make a file smaller by providing pointers to or removing redundant data. Compression protocols, such as StuffIt and Zip, are said to be "lossless" because the compressed files can be restored to their original form. Another compression type is called "lossy," which actually removes portions of a file that may not be audible or visible. The popular image formats GIF and JPEG are lossy in nature, as is the MPEG-based compression protocol used to pack a complete motion picture onto a 5.25-inch DVD.

CompuServe   Before AOL gained ascendancy as the world's largest online service, CompuServe was there first. Today, CompuServe is an affiliate of AOL and offers services to a more professional audience, with a rich resource of business information. *See also* **AOL, online services.**

control panel   A program used to direct system-related functions or the functions offered by a system extension. Examples of control panels include Mouse, which adjusts the speed and double-clicking performance of a pointing device, and Monitors, which sets up your display.

CRT (cathode ray tube)   The picture tube that is the main component of most computer displays and regular TVs. *See also* **active matrix, LCD, passive matrix.**

CPU (central processing unit)   The brain of a computer. Refers either to the principal microchip the computer is built around (such as the Pentium or PowerPC chip) or the box that houses the main components of the computer.

daisy chain   The way many computer devices are connected when using such topologies as ADB, LocalTalk, SCSI, and USB. You hook up one device, attach a second device to the first, and so on.

database   On a computer, a file that contains structured data that can be accessed and manipulated in a variety of ways. Databases are used for business records, address books, and so on.

DAVE   A program from Thursby Software Systems, Inc., which you use to network Macs and Windows computers. Especially useful in smaller networks because you needn't go through the fuss and bother of working with the complexities of setting up a Windows NT or a Windows 2000 network server.

debugger   A program or a component of a program used to locate and help fix programming errors. One example of a debugger is MacsBug, a program provided by Apple Computer to help programmers test software and identify potential problems.

default button   You can find this in many dialog boxes. The default button is the one surrounded by a bold border, which you activate automatically with the ENTER or RETURN key.

desktop   Also known as the Finder Desktop, the graphical background of the Mac operating system in which disk, file, and folder icons are displayed against a background pattern of one sort or another.

desktop publishing   A program designed to create and design completely formatted documents useful for printing or display. Word processing programs can be used for desktop publishing, but for professional caliber work, such programs as Adobe InDesign, Adobe PageMaker, or QuarkXPress are used.

device   A component that is part of a computer system. This may consist of a disk drive, keyboard, mouse, modem, printer, removable drive, or scanner.

device driver   The software that allows your Mac to communicate with a device, such as a printer or scanner. Examples of a device driver include the LaserWriter driver that comes with all Mac OS computers.

dialog box   A window in which you must OK an alert, check a box, or enter information to provide a result, such as naming and saving a file, or starting or canceling an operation.

DIMM (dual inline memory module)   A type of RAM module, typically used on many recent Macs. Compared to a SIMM (single inline memory module), a DIMM has a wider data path, which allows for speedier memory access.

dimmed   *See* **grayed out.**

DIP (dual inline package) switch   The small on/off switches you find on a hard drive, modem, or other device. Used to configure the product to support specific features or, in the case of a drive, to set SCSI ID or termination.

directory   A list of files or folders found on your Mac.

disk   The common storage medium for computer files. Such storage mediums come in the form of floppy disks for a floppy drive or media (such as Jaz or Zip disks) used for removable drives. A hard drive consists of one or more disks in a dust-tight enclosure.

disk cache   This sort of cache allocates part of RAM to store frequently used information from a disk. The end result is faster retrieval, which speeds performance.

disk drive   A device that contains one or more disks used to store computer data.

display   A device used to display the visual representation of a computer's output. Displays can use either CRT tubes or LCDs.

display adapter   Typically, a plug used to convert the signals from your Mac or graphic card so they can be seen on your display or the graphic card used to drive your display.

document   A file you create with an application. Documents may contain words, images, or animated matter. They are stored on a disk for later viewing, editing, or printing.

document window   A window that appears within an application in which a document you created in that application is displayed.

domain   A portion of an Internet address that identifies the name of the organization, network, or computer server being accessed; for example, apple.com, which is Apple Computer's domain, or rockoids.com, which is the author's site devoted to a science fiction adventure series.

double-click   The act of clicking a mouse button twice in fairly rapid succession. This is done to open an icon (which, in turn, opens a file, launches a program, or brings up a directory).

double-click speed   An adjustment you make in the Mouse or Trackpad Control Panel, which determines how fast you must click the mouse button to activate a function, such as opening an icon.

download The act of transferring a file from one computer to another. When you download something, you receive it. In contrast, you upload something to send it to another computer. *See also* **upload.**

downloadable font A scalable font sent to a printer to allow a document containing that font to be printed. Two downloadable font formats are PostScript fonts and TrueType fonts.

DPI (dots per inch) Measures the sharpness of a display or printed output.

drag An action done with a mouse or other pointing device. Done by clicking the mouse button, dragging the cursor (and whatever it selects) to another portion of the screen, and then releasing the button.

drag-and-drop The process of selecting an item and moving it to another location.

DVD-ROM (digital versatile disc read-only memory) Based on the popular DVD format used for video movies, DVD-ROM stores computer data, up to 5.2GB worth. A variation of the format, DVD-RAM, can be used to store data. The latter medium is suitable for backup purposes, but as of press time, a final standard hadn't been set.

DSL (digital subscriber line) A technology that uses your regular telephone line to offer fast Internet service, with speeds typically ranging from 256 Kbps to 1.5 Mbps. The capability to hook up to DSL depends on whether you are close to a phone company switch (usually three miles or less) and whether your ISP offers the service.

DHCP (Dynamic Host Configuration Protocol) This network protocol is used to automatically assign an IP address and other network information to a networked computer. The IP addresses are considered leased because they can be reused if they are not accessed for a period of time (usually specified by the network administrator).

e-mail The abbreviation for electronic mail. The method used to transfer messages from one computer or network to another.

emulation The method used to imitate another computer CPU or operating system. When Apple switched to PowerPC CPUs, it used an emulator to work with older software that supported the 680x0 CPU family. The programs that enable you to create a Windows environment on a Mac, such as Connectix Virtual PC and FWB's SoftWindows, are emulators.

Encryption   A technique that scrambles data in a form that cannot be read unless you use the proper password to reassemble the data back to its original form. Mac OS 9 includes Finder-level encryption capability.

Erase Disk   Available from the Mac OS Special menu and used to format a selected floppy drive or hard drive.

Ethernet   The standard for high-speed networking. Available on all currently produced Apple computers. The standard version offers performance of up to 10 Mbps. The high-speed version, called "Fast Ethernet," transfers speeds at up to 100 Mbps. The newest Ethernet variation, Gigabit Ethernet, is capable of up to one billion bps.

EtherTalk   Apple's method of supporting its AppleTalk networking protocol over Ethernet (though it hasn't been used since Apple introduced Open Transport).

extension   This word has two definitions. For Macs, it is a special program that adds or extends functions of the operating system. Such programs are placed in the Extensions folder within the System folder. The second use is file naming. DOS and Windows files, for example, have three-letter extensions that identify a specific type of file, such as .doc for Microsoft Word files.

Fast Ethernet   This variation of the Ethernet network standard offers speeds up to ten times faster than regular Ethernet, up to 100 Mbps (or up to 200 Mbps when networking is done in full-duplex mode).

Fax/data modem   The kind of modem that has taken over the market since the early 1990s. It functions as a modem to transmit and receive data, and can also support sending and receiving faxes, when used with software that supports the feature.

file   In the computer world, an item (such as a document or a program) stored on a disk or opened, using a computer's memory.

file extensions   The DOS and Windows operating systems identify a file's type by a three-letter extension or suffix. A typical example is using .jpg for a JPEG file or .doc for a Microsoft Word file.

file server   A computer that serves as a repository for files shared across a network (including the Internet). File servers may be dedicated, performing only file-handling tasks, or nondedicated, in which the computer may also function as a regular workstation.

file sharing　A feature of the Mac operating system in which users may share files across a network.

File Sharing Control Panel　A control panel used to configure and activate the file-sharing feature.

file system　The technology used on a storage medium that handles files stored on a disk.

Finder　The application that provides the unique look and feel of the Mac operating system. Used to provide both a desktop display and file handling features.

FireWire　Also known as IEEE 1394 or (by Sony) iLINK, a high-speed peripheral standard capable of speeds up to 400 Mbps. It's hot-pluggable and enables you to daisy-chain up to 63 devices, including digital camcorders, hard drives, removable devices, and scanners, without having to set special ID numbers or termination.

firmware　Software stored in a ROM chip, used by computer hardware to provide specific operating functions.

fixed disk　*See* **hard disk.**

fixed-width font　More often called a "monospaced" font, a font in which all characters have equal width spacing. Examples include Courier and Monaco. Fonts in which width values vary are called "proportional" fonts. *See also* **proportional fonts.**

floppy disk　Although this has been phased out of new Apple computer products, the floppy disk is one of the earliest storage mediums. "Floppy" refers to the flexible material inside the disks, used to store the data. *See also* **hard disk.**

flow control　The phrase generally applies to modems or networking functions. A method where one device communicates with another, indicating when information can be transferred. Also known as a "handshake."

folder　A directory on Mac and Windows computers (and other graphical operating systems). A container that may contain files or other folders.

font　A collection of letters, numbers, punctuation, and symbols, all fitting a specific design or size. Fonts of fixed size are typically bitmap fonts. Outline font formats, such as PostScript and TrueType fonts, are scalable fonts, meaning they can be specified in any size supported by the program in which they're used. *See also* **PostScript fonts, TrueType fonts.**

font family   A label for a group of fonts of similar style, such as the various forms of Helvetica or Times. Also refers to a class of fonts, such as serif or sans serif.

FontSync   A technology that's part of Mac OS 9, which enables you to match up the fonts in a document with those on your Mac or output device.

format   (1) Preparing a disk to receive files by clearing out all existing data and setting it up to support a specific computer operating system. A related process, initializing, wipes out a drive's directory. (2) The way in which the text in a document is set up, such as the type style, the size, paragraph indents, and so on. (3) The file type, such as an Adobe Photoshop document, or a Microsoft Word document.

fragmented   Usually a description of a condition in which the pieces of a file are spread around widely separated parts of a disk. Memory can also be fragmented when you quit and relaunch multiple programs on your Mac. *See also* **optimization.**

freeware   Software offered without charge, but the author or publisher retains rights to the product. Contrast with shareware.

FTP (File Transfer Protocol)   The Internet protocol for file transfers among Macintosh, Windows, and UNIX platforms. *See also* **Anonymous FTP.**

full backup   The process of making a complete copy of the disk you want to back up.

G3   The popular label for the PowerPC 750 CPU, developed by IBM and Motorola, and used in a number of Apple Computers.

G4   The newest family of PowerPC CPUs, also known by its design name, 7400. *See also* **Velocity Engine.**

Game Sprockets   These system extensions consist of system-related resources that games developers can use for their products. Enables them to work with various pointing devices and other products.

GIF (Graphic Interchange Format)   A popular file format for compressed graphic images developed by CompuServe. GIF files are commonly exchanged on the Internet and are used for images on Web sites because of their capability to provide animation and other effects.

GB (gigabyte)   The equivalent of 1,000 megabytes (MB).

Gopher   Developed by the University of Minnesota, a method of searching information on the Internet. A Gopher program typically locates text documents, but some of these programs can also deliver information about images and sounds.

grayed out   A phrase used to indicate that a specific command is not available or accessible, or has been disabled.

grow box   *See* **zoom box.**

handshake   *See* **flow control.**

hard disk   A type of disk drive that contains one or more rigid platters used for data storage, sealed in a dust-free enclosure. Hard drives can typically support as little as 10MB (obviously these are only the old hard drives) to capacities exceeding 73GB (based on capacities available at press time).

hardware   Various components of a computer system, which include the core component, consisting of CPU and disk drives, as well as displays, printers, and scanners. Contrast with software.

hardware handshaking   A special type of modem cable that supports automatic handshaking or flow control. All external high-speed modems require a hardware handshaking cable.

highlighted   When you select an object or text, it is shaded in a dark color or reverse video to indicate it has been chosen.

hierarchical menu   Also known as a submenu, identifies an extra menu that appears when you drag and hold the mouse cursor over an item.

home page   On a Web site, the opening page, typically used to offer a description or introduction of a site and to provide links to other content on the site and elsewhere.

HTML (Hypertext Markup Language)   The language of the Web, consisting of text documents with tags or formatting keys that describe how the text will look in a Web browser. A Web site contains one or more HTML documents.

HTTP (Hypertext Transfer Protocol)   The protocol used for the transfer of HTML and similar files, generally from sites on the Web.

hub A device that serves as a central connection point for connecting network or serial devices. Hubs are used for such things as Ethernet networking and expanding FireWire and USB ports.

hyperlink   A text or graphic that takes you to another page in a document or a Web site when you click it.

icon   A picture that provides a graphical representation of an item on a Mac or Windows computer (or a UNIX computer with graphical interface). Icons can represent such things as an application, a file, a folder, or a disk drive.

IDE (Integrated Drive Electronics)   A type of hard drive used on both Macs and PCs. Compare with FireWire and SCSI.

IEEE 802.11   *See* **AirPort.**

IEEE 1394   *See* **FireWire.**

infrared port   A feature on some Macs and other computers that allows for wireless networking. Replaced by Apple's AirPort wireless networking products.

i.LINK   *See* **FireWire.**

incremental backup   A backup that consists strictly of the files that have been added or changed since your last full backup.

initialization files   Also known as INITs, the original designation for system startup programs now known as extensions or system extensions.

initialize   Usually the process of resetting a hardware device or re-creating a disk directory. *See also* **format.**

insertion point   The flickering vertical bar you see in a text area indicating where text should be entered.

Intel   The world's largest manufacturer of CPUs, maker of the i86 and Pentium chips used in DOS and Windows-based computers.

interface   (1) The process of communicating with another component in a computer system (2) The face a program puts forth to the user. Also known as user interface.

Internet   The worldwide collection of computer networks that provides a variety of services, such as e-mail, FTP, and the World Wide Web.

intranet   A system of networking using Internet technologies within a single organization.

ISP (Internet service provider)   A company that offers a connection to the Internet. Such services include large national operations, including AT&T WorldNet and EarthLink, and smaller companies that offer connections in one or two cities. These include FastQ, which is affiliated with the Arizona Macintosh User Group, and Teleport.com. *See also* **AOL, CompuServe, online services.**

Java   Developed by Sun Microsystems, a platform-independent programming language often used to display special visual effects on the Web. When you access a Web site using Java, a small program, called an "applet," is downloaded to your browser (if it supports Java, and all recent browsers do) and run to display the appropriate content.

JPEG (Joint Photographic Experts Group)   A lossy format for compressed images, which makes files that are typically smaller than a GIF. Best for handling images rather than text and capable of extremely high quality, sometimes indistinguishable from the original.

Keychain   A Mac OS 9 feature that enables you to store all your passwords in a single location for quick access when they're needed.

kilobyte   Equivalent to 1,024 bytes. Usually abbreviated as KB and used to describe such things as file size, memory, and hard drive storage. *See also* **megabyte**.

L2 cache   A special type of cache memory that resides either next to the CPU, between the CPU and the main memory, or on the processor chip. Used to store frequently used instruction data, allowing the CPU to process those instructions faster. The primary memory cache, on the CPU chip, is called the "L1 cache."

LAN (local area network)   The common type of network that includes computers and printers, which is used to share data, programs, and messages.

laptop   A small personal computer, equipped with one or more batteries for power, and designed for convenient transportation.

laser printer   A printer that works in a fashion similar to a copy machine, using a laser beam to generate high-quality output.

LCD (liquid crystal display)   LCD is the display technology used in laptop computers and some high-priced computer displays. The most common types of LCD displays are active matrix and passive matrix.

LED (light-emitting diode)   LEDs are employed for display purposes in some electronic products.

link   *See* **hyperlink**.

list box   Typically found in a dialog box, it offers a listing of items, such as files and folders, you can select.

LocalTalk   The network hardware that, until recently, was built into all Macintosh computers. Uses the AppleTalk protocol to offer network services. Current Apple computers only support Ethernet as a network standard. LocalTalk is capable of speeds of 230,000 bits per second, compared with regular Ethernet, which is capable of up to ten megabits per second.

MacBinary   The file format used for transferring Macintosh files among different computer platforms. Places the data and resource folks of a Mac file in the datafork, so it can be easily transferred over the Internet and to other computing platforms. MacBinary files are usually saved in BinHex format.

Macintosh HD   The common name of a Mac's hard drive when it leaves the factory.

Mac OS   The popular abbreviation and Apple's official trademark for the Macintosh operating system, for example, Mac OS 9. Contrast to the former use of the word "System" to identify an operating system version, for example, System 7.

macro   An automated sequence of functions designed for simple repetition of complex tasks. The Microsoft Office program suite offers macro functions, as do other programs. Some programs, such as Adobe Photoshop, refer to macros as "actions."

math coprocessor   *See* **FPU.**

maximize   When you click a window's grow box to its largest size, you maximize it.

Mbps (megabits per second)   1,048,576 bits per second, the speed at which data is transferred. As modems and serial transmissions become faster, one hopes Mbps can be used to discuss their speed.

MB   *See* **megabyte.**

media   Typically, the name for items that carry data, such as floppy disks, hard drives, CD-ROMs, hard disks, removable drives, and tape drives. Can also refer to items that carry data for network transfer, such as cables and wireless technology.

megabyte   1,024 kilobytes of computer data. Abbreviated MB.

MegaFLOPS   Acronym for a Million Floating Point Operations Per Second, representing computer power.

MHz (megahertz)   The speed at which a computer's CPU runs, each hertz is one cycle. Because many factors govern CPU performance, the MHz rating isn't the only factor to use in comparing speeds of different CPU families.

memory   Temporary storage area for computer data. Memory products include RAM and ROM. Hard drives and other storage mediums are sometimes referred to incorrectly as "memory."

memory protection   The capability of a computer operating system to allocate a dedicated portion of memory to a program, which is designed to enhance stability. If an application crashes, it doesn't impact either the other programs or the operating system you are running. Mac OS X, for example, is designed to offer protected memory.

menu   In a graphical operating system, such as the Mac OS, a small screen in which a series of commands are available for the user to select.

menu bar   A single-line horizontal bar containing menus, which appears at the top of the screen on a Mac.

MIDI (Musical Instrument Digital Interface)   A protocol that allows for communication between musical instruments and computers.

MIME (Multipurpose Internet Mail Extension)   A method in which binary files (such as images, sounds, and word processing documents) can be transferred by e-mail.

MIPS (millions of instructions per second)   The speed at which a computer handles data. Supercomputers are said to handle billions of instructions per second. Because of its capability to achieve such levels of performance, the G4 CPU was promoted by Apple Computer as a "supercomputer on a chip."

modem   A device used to convert a computer's digital language to analog signals to allow data to be exchanged, typically over a telephone line.

monitor   *See* **display.**

motherboard   Also known as a logic board, the printed circuit board that stores the main components of a computer.

mouse   Invented in the 1960s, a small pointing device with a ball on the bottom and one or more switches at the top. As you move the mouse, the cursor on a computer's screen also moves. A so-called upside-down mouse, with the ball at the top, is known as a "trackball."

MPEG (Moving Pictures Experts Group)   The standard for compressed audio and video. It is "lossy," meaning data is lost as part of the compression process, but it is designed so the lost data has minimal impact on what you see and hear.

MS-DOS (Microsoft Disk Operating System)   A text-based computer operating system, also known as "DOS."

multimedia   A combination of various components of a computer experience, such as animation, audio, graphics, text, and video.

Multiple Users   A feature introduced in Mac OS 9 in which custom configurations and access levels can be created for each person who uses your Mac. *See also* **voice verification.**

multiprocessor   A computer with more than one CPU running at the same time for faster processing speeds.

multisync   A type of display that can run at different scan rates, providing a selection of different resolutions. All current displays are multisync.

multitasking   A technique that allows a computer to perform more than one task at a time. On a Mac, multitasking is cooperative, meaning the programs themselves do the task management, as opposed to preemptive, a part of Mac OS X in which the operating system does the task management. Preemptive multitasking helps reduce the speed hit when more than one program is performing a function on your Mac.

multithreading   The capability of a program to perform more than a single function at the same time. Compare to multitasking, in which more than a single program is being run.

Netscape   The company that made the original commercial Web browser for the Macintosh, Windows, and UNIX operating systems (based on the original program designed by NCSA), now part of AOL. Although the program is known by the name of the company, its full name is either Netscape Navigator or Netscape Communicator.

network   The process of linking two or more computers and other devices, such as printers, so they can exchange data.

Network Browser   An application used to access either local or Internet-based network services, such as another computer or Internet site.

newsgroup   An Internet-based discussion group, also known as "Usenet."

notebook   *See* **laptop.**

object-oriented graphics   Graphic objects represented by mathematical shapes rather than pixels. This allows for the objects to be scaled to any size without loss of quality.

open   An operation in which you display the contents of a file, folder, or disk, or launch an application.

OpenGL   A 3D graphics technology licensed from Silicon Graphics. This technology is used as the image-rendering engine for a number of games.

Open Transport   Apple's networking technology used for local networking and Internet networking.

Open Transport/PPP   *See* **Remote Access.**

operating system   The software that provides the core functionality of a computer, also known as "system software." Operating systems include the Mac OS, MS-DOS, Windows in its variations, UNIX, and others.

passive matrix display   A type of LCD display used on laptop computers. The display is accomplished with parallel wires running horizontally and vertically across the screen, which power the screen pixels. Current products do not use this type of display. Compare to active matrix.

password   A combination of letters, numbers, or both used to control access to a computer, the contents of a computer's drive, or a network or Internet service.

PC (personal computer)   Although the name usually applies to small IBM and compatible desktop and portable computers, Apple's computers are also, strictly speaking, personal computers.

PCI (peripheral component interconnect)   An expansion bus standard, developed by Intel, used on Macs, PCs, and Sun workstations. Allows for installation of printed circuit boards (cards) that provide enhanced graphic display, faster networking, faster SCSI, video capture, and other capabilities.

PCMCIA (Personal Computer Memory Card International Association)   A standard for hardware expansion cards, about the size of credit cards, used mostly on laptop computers. Commonly known as a "PC card" or in its current incarnation, "Card Bus."

PDF (portable document format)   A standard for creating and viewing electronic documents, created by Adobe Systems.

PC100   A high-speed RAM module that's used on a number of new Apple computers. Supports 100 megahertz logic board speeds.

peripheral   A device, added to a computer, that provides enhanced functions, such as a display, printer, or removable drive.

pixel   A single dot, the smallest graphic unit of display.

plug-and-play   Various hardware standards designed to enable you to hook up a device easily without having to go through special configuration steps. The ideal method of plug-and-play enables you to hook up a device without needing to turn off the device or the computer to which it's connected, and without having to do a special configuration to recognize the device (other than, perhaps, the installation of a software driver). Both FireWire and USB are plug-and-play standards. Also known as PnP.

plug-in   An add-on program that enhances an application's capabilities. For a Web browser, plug-ins are typically added to provide multimedia features (such as QuickTime and RealAudio). Some program plug-ins are also referred to as XTensions (for QuarkXPress add-ons) and XTras (used in some Macromedia products).

point   The act of placing the mouse cursor over a specific object on your screen.

pointing device   The name of an input device used to point to objects on a screen. A mouse and trackball are both common pointing devices.

POP (Post Office Protocol)   The standard that enables a user to receive e-mail from a mail server. Used by most ISPs.

pop-up window   A window that pops up on your screen when selected.

port   A jack into which you plug a cable from a device to make it work with your Mac.

post   The act of placing a message on a message board, either a newsgroup or a message board on an online service.

PostScript   Developed by Adobe Systems, a page description language that uses mathematics to describe the contents of a page. Device-independent, meaning output devices, such as laser printers, can reproduce the page at its maximum possible resolution.

PostScript fonts   A scalable font technology based on PostScript, which allows a font to be used in all available sizes with maximum quality. PostScript fonts are considered industry standards in the publishing and printing industries. Compare with TrueType, another scalable font format.

PowerPC   The generic name of a family of CPU chips designed by Apple, IBM, and Motorola. The current crop of PowerPC chips are the G3 and G4.

PPD (PostScript printer description) Usually consists of a text file that provides information to a printer about the device's unique features, such as extra paper trays or special paper size-handling capabilities.

PPP (Point to Point Protocol) Technically, PPP is a layer 2 network protocol, along with IPX, AppleTalk, IP and other protocols to be transferred. In general use, it's a TCP/IP standard that allows a modem to access the Internet or an online service.

PRAM (parameter RAM) A small amount of RAM on a Macintosh used to store basic system settings, such as display, networking, serial port, and startup disk. Zapping the PRAM is the act of clearing this portion of RAM to eliminate erratic system problems.

print queue A list of files sent to the printer and waiting to be printed.

print server A device, computer, or software designed to host and manage a print queue.

printer driver A program that works with a computer and printer, allowing the two devices to communicate with each other.

printer fonts Sometimes called outline fonts, the PostScript fonts downloaded to a printer and used to output your actual text. Sometimes also known as soft fonts. Compare with bitmap fonts.

program *See* **application.**

proportional font A font in which each character has a different space or width value, with a letter such as *i* having a narrow width and the letter *m* having a much wider width. Contrast with fixed-width or monospaced font.

pull-down menu When you click a menu bar, the pull-down menu provides the list of available commands. On the Windows platform, referred to as a drop-down menu.

preview software A version of software designed to promote interest in a new product. The software is usually in beta form, meaning it probably has bugs that may cause performance anomalies or system crashes.

queue A list of files destined for printing or processing of some sort.

QuickDraw 3D Apple's technology for creation and display of three-dimensional objects.

QuickTime   A multimedia technology from Apple Computer that provides support for dozens of audio and video standards. QuickTime technology is used for video editing, and to create online audio and video presentations. Available in both Mac and Windows versions.

QuickTime TV   A standard from Apple Computer designed to compete with RealAudio and RealVideo. Enables you to view streaming audio and video productions on the Internet. Apple has entered the competition with big guns by making the source code freely available and not charging a license fee for use of its server software (the software that sends the streaming productions).

radio button   A small circular button that appears in a dialog box. Clicking it activates a specific function.

RAM (random access memory)   The memory used as a temporary storage location for computer data.

RAM disk   A portion of RAM set aside to emulate the functions of a hard disk.

read-only file   The name for a file you can read, but you cannot change, either because the file is password-protected or on a storage medium you cannot write to (such as a CD-ROM).

RealAudio   The most popular protocol for streaming audio and video productions. RealAudio and its companion program, RealVideo, are available free, but users of the streaming software pay a license fee for its use.

reset switch   A button on a Mac that forces the computer to restart. Used to get the Mac working again when it crashes.

resolution   A measurement of the number of pixels in a document or display screen.

RISC (reduced instruction set computer)   A type of CPU, such as the PowerPC chip, which uses a smaller set of instructions to execute commands. The speed with which the instructions are processed accounts for the high performance of RISC-based CPUs.

ROM (read-only memory)   A computer chip onto which data is written that cannot be changed and does not disappear when the computer is switched off. A special type of ROM, called Flash ROM, allows the data to be changed with a special software program. Compare with RAM.

router   Software or a hardware device that directs data to different segments of a computer network.

scalable font   A font designed to work in all sizes available to an application. Scalable fonts usually are provided in PostScript and TrueType formats.

screen fonts   *See* **bitmap fonts.**

screen saver   A program that darkens the screen or provides a moving picture when your computer is idle for a specified period of design. With CRT-based monitors, this is designed to prevent a so-called burn-in effect, in which areas displayed for long periods of time are permanently etched onto the display. The jury is still out about whether screen savers really work with modern computer displays; they do nothing for an LCD display.

scroll   The act of moving through a display or document window.

scroll arrow   The arrow located at each end of a scroll bar used to navigate through the contents of a window or a list box.

scrollbar   The little bar that appears at the right and bottom of a window or list box when it's too small to show all its contents.

SCSI (Small Computer Systems Interface)   A standard used for storage devices. SCSI capability has been removed from Apple computers, in favor of FireWire and USB.

SDRAM   A type of memory used on first-generation iMacs and some Apple laptop computers. SDRAM chips are also found in PC100 RAM, the kind used in many of Apple's later desktop computers and the so-called slot loading iMac line.

select   The act of marking or choosing an item so you can perform an action on it. With a mouse or other pointing device, you select the item by clicking it.

serial port   A port provided on older Macs for use by modems and nonnetwork printers. *See also* **USB.**

shareware   Freely distributed software. After a brief trial, if you like using the software, the author or publisher requests payment.

Sherlock 2   A program used to search for content on your hard drive and the Internet. Can be custom configured with search modules and channels, which group your search requests by category.

SIMM (single inline memory module)   A type of computer memory module, mostly used on older model Macs and other personal computers.

SMTP (Simple Mail Transfer Protocol) A counterpart to POP, used for sending e-mail. SMTP transfers e-mail to server computers across the Internet using TCP/IP.

software A file containing instructions that tell a computer how to perform specific tasks. These include the Mac OS, the applications you run, device drivers, and so forth.

Software Update A Control Panel that enables you to check Apple's Web site on demand or by preset schedule in search of Mac OS software updates, which can then be retrieved automatically.

source code A text file that contains the information from which a computer program is compiled. Apple has released source code for some elements of Mac OS X and its QuickTime streaming software.

spool The act of transferring data to a device, usually a printer. A spool file is a file containing documents waiting to be printed. *See also* **print queue.**

startup disk The disk used to start your Mac, containing a usable System Folder. Startup disk settings can be made with the Startup Disk Control Panel.

spring-loaded folders A feature of the Mac OS (beginning with Mac OS 8) in which a folder expands to reveal its contents when you click-and-drag your input device over the folder.

StuffIt The industry-standard compression program for the Mac, published by Aladdin Systems. Uses a special algorithm to make files smaller by using pointers to redundant data. StuffIt archives (a file containing files compressed with StuffIt) are routinely transferred by disk, networks, or the Internet. This is the Mac counterpart of the Zip format, which dominates the DOS and Windows computing platforms. *See also* **compression, Zip.**

submenu A secondary menu that displays when you click a pointing device and hold it over the main menu's name. Also known as a hierarchical menu.

SuperDisk A removable disk standard that supports 1.4MB floppies and a special floppy-like high-capacity format. It's become popular since Apple removed floppy drives as standard issue on their computers. SuperDisk media can hold up to 120MB of data.

SuperDrive A floppy disk drive installed on many older Macintosh computers, which supports 400K, 800K, and 1.4MB floppies. With proper translation software, such as File Exchange, a SuperDrive can also read MS-DOS floppies.

surf   The act of exploring the Internet, typically the World Wide Web.

surge suppressor   A device designed to provide protection of electronics from power surges from a power line or because of a lightning strike. Surge suppressors typically have several outputs for connection of computer equipment and other electronic components (such as a TV or a VCR).

swap file   Used with virtual memory, a portion of your hard disk set aside to handle data that doesn't fit within the available amount of RAM.

system   The basic file that provides core functionality of the Mac OS, also known as a system file. Can also refer to the operating system itself, such as System 7, an older generation of the Mac OS.

system disk   *See* **startup disk.**

system software   *See* **operating system.**

TCP/IP (Transmission Control Protocol/Internet Protocol)   The networking standard used for Internet networking and connections.

text box   An enclosure on a document, icon, or dialog box window in which you insert text.

title bar   The top area of a window in which its name is displayed.

toolbar   A row of buttons in an application that you click to activate a specific function.

trackball   A pointing device resembling an upside-down mouse. You move the ball, rather than the device itself, to point to objects on your computer's screen.

tracking speed   An adjustment in the Mouse or Trackpad Control Panel that sets how fast a mouse pointer moves across the screen.

trackpad   Used on laptop computers, a pointing device consisting of a little square or rectangular pad on which you use your finger to move the cursor across the screen.

TrueType fonts   A scalable technology first released in 1990 by Apple Computer with Microsoft's help, in part as a way to avoid paying the then-high licensing fees for PostScript fonts. Beginning with Mac OS System 7, built-in support was provided for the display of TrueType fonts. Both Mac and Windows computers come with a small selection of TrueType fonts.

twisted-pair cable   The type of wiring used for both telephone and network connections. Twisted-pair cable is made up of two pairs of wires: one pair is used for receiving data, the other for transmitting data.

type style   An attribute of a type face, such as regular (or normal), bold, italic, shadow, strikeout, or underline.

typeface   A collection of characters, numbers, and symbols in a distinct form or design.

UNIX   A popular operating system first developed by AT&T in 1972. Provides all the features considered critical to a modern operating system, such as preemptive multitasking and protected memory. Many UNIX-based systems exist, including Linux and Mac OS X.

UPS (uninterruptible power supply)   A device that provides backup power in the event of a power failure. UPS devices available for personal computers commonly have a large battery used to provide power for a brief period. This gives the user time to shut down the computer safely without risk to the files or disk drives.

URL (uniform resource locator)   The address of a specific site on the Internet.

USB (universal serial bus)   A high-speed serial port standard developed by Intel and used on current Apple computers, beginning with the iMac. Used for input devices, digital cameras, storage devices, and other products.

Usenet   *See* **newsgroups.**

user interface   *See* **interface.**

utility   A program designed to help a computer function better. A utility may include a hard-disk diagnostic program or something that enhances computer performance, such as Adobe Type Manager, which offers a clear rendering of PostScript fonts.

virtual memory   A method of extending available memory on a computer by setting aside a portion of the hard drive to store and swap data that exceeds the size of available RAM.

Voiceprint password   An alternate way to store your password, using Mac OS 9's Multiple Users Control Panel. Repeating a word or phrase four times during setup allows the Mac to recognize your voice when you identify yourself.

Web *See* **World Wide Web.**

Web browser *See* **browser.**

window The rectangular screen in which the contents of a disk, folder, or document are displayed.

Windows 95 and 98 The consumer versions of Microsoft's 32-bit graphical operating system, which offer preemptive multitasking if the application is also 32-bit.

Windows NT and 2000 The so-called business version of Windows, used for content creation and for networked servers.

word processor A program that enables you to create, edit, and format text. Examples of word processors include one of the components of AppleWorks and Microsoft Word. Such programs also offer graphic-editing capabilities of one sort or another.

World Wide Web (WWW) A collection of Internet sites that offer a variety of content, ranging from text and pictures to animation and sound. You view a Web site with a browser, software designed to interpret Web documents, which are coded in HTML, ASP, or XTML. *See also* **browser, HTML.**

WYSIWYG (What You See Is What You Get) Pronounced "wizzywig," describes the ability to display a close representation of the look and feel of a document on your Mac's display.

Zip The DOS, Windows, and UNIX counterpart to StuffIt. A protocol that uses a special algorithm to reduce file size by using pointers for redundant data. Files compressed with Zip (which are said to be "zipped") are commonly used for file transfers. Mac versions of Zip are also available and are used to provide cross-platform compatibility. All current versions of StuffIt also can expand Zip files. *See also* **compression, StuffIt.**

Zip drive A storage device developed by Iomega Corporation using a small disk resembling a thick floppy disk. Zip drives store either 100MB or 250MB of data.

zoom box A box at the right of a window used to expand or reduce the window's size.

Index

N

U